THE ROCKY MOUNTAINS

THE ROCKY MOUNTAINS

A VISION FOR ARTISTS
IN THE NINETEENTH CENTURY

by

PATRICIA TRENTON

and

PETER H. HASSRICK

Published in association with the Buffalo Bill Historical Center, Cody, Wyoming

UNIVERSITY OF OKLAHOMA PRESS : NORMAN

By Patricia Trenton

American Art from the Denver Art Museum Collection (with Cile Bach) (Denver, Colo., 1969)
Colorado Collects Historic Western Art: The Nostalgia of the Vanishing West (Denver, Colo., 1973)
Picturesque Images from Taos and Santa Fe (with Richard Conn) (Denver, Colo., 1974)
Harvey Otis Young: The Lost Genius, 1840–1901 (Denver, Colo., 1975)

By Peter H. Hassrick

Frederic Remington: An Essay and Catalogue to Accompany a Retrospective Exhibition (Fort Worth, Texas, 1972)
Frederic Remington: Paintings, Drawings, and Sculpture in the Amon Carter Museum and the Sid E. Richardson Foundation Collections (New York, 1973)
The Way West (New York, 1977)
Frederic Remington: The Late Years (Denver, 1981)

By Patricia Trenton and Peter H. Hassrick

The Rocky Mountains: A Vision for Artists in the Nineteenth Century (Norman, 1983)

Library of Congress Cataloging in Publication Data

Trenton, Patricia.
  The Rocky Mountains.

  "Published in association with the Buffalo Bill Historical Center, Cody, Wyoming."
  Bibliography: p. 393
  Includes index.
  1. Rocky Mountains in art. 2. Art, American. 3. Art, Modern—19th century—United States. 4. Art, Modern—19th century. 5. Rocky Mountains—Description and travel. I. Hassrick, Peter H. II. Buffalo Bill Historical Center. III. Title.
  N8214.5.U6T73   1983   758'.1'0973   82-21879

This book is dedicated to two remarkable spouses,
Buzzy Hassrick and Norman Trenton,
and was completed with their untiring support, cooperation, and patience.

We would like to extend special thanks to the following for their generous assistance in helping to underwrite the costs of this publication:

Anschutz Corporation
D. Harold Byrd, Jr.
William Foxley
Geraldine Lawson

CONTENTS

ILLUSTRATIONS

ix

PREFACE

THE ROCKY MOUNTAINS, the grandest of the cordilleras in North America, span the breadth of our continent and, with a lacing of mighty rivers, tie its shores to a common backbone. This vast mountain range was known to early geographers by various descriptive names: Stoney Mountains, Mountains of Bright Stones, Shining Mountains.[1] The Rockies did not receive their current appellation until late in the eighteenth century, when they first appeared on American and European maps of the Far West (plate 1).[2] By the time of Lewis and Clark the name had come into popular usage.

Despite the general acceptance of the name Rocky Mountains, the great range continued to be described as two separate entities within one chain. The Stoney Mountains on the north served to drain the headwaters of the Missouri on the east and the Snake and Columbia on the west. Below this range, in southern Wyoming, central Colorado, and northern New Mexico, were the Park Mountains, distinguished by "a wilderness of crags" and separated by sweeping valleys known as "parks."[3] As late as the twentieth century these two ranges were spoken of independently, though the popular term "Rocky Mountains" prevailed and was eventually adopted officially.

The name, of course, conveys only a part of what men have felt about this mighty spine. Throughout the nineteenth century the Rockies inspired mixed emotions—a paradoxical combination of spiritual response and emotional resistance. The towering earth forms were at once awesome, beautiful, and forbidding.

Some considered the Rockies a physically and psychologically imposing barrier. Others regarded the great continental monolith as an impediment to national progress, a threat to the Union itself.

"So long as it remains a formidable undertaking to pass between New York and San Francisco," wrote Fitz Hugh Ludlow in 1870, "so long will there develop an independence of interest and feeling which, however gradual and imperceptible, cannot fail to result in two distinct nations."[4] One early visitor to Pikes Peak expressed his discomfiture with mountain prospects in near-Gothic strains: "The dreariness of the desolate peak itself scarcely dissipates the dismal spell for you stand in a confusion of dull stones piled upon each other in odious ugliness."[5]

An equal number of early recorded comments, however, praised the Rocky Mountain area in glowing terms. The artist Albert Bierstadt wrote to *The Crayon* in 1859:

> I am delighted with the scenery. The mountains are very fine; as seen from the plains, they resemble very much the Bernese Alps, one of the finest ranges of mountains in Europe, if not in the world. They are of a granite formation, the same as the Swiss mountains and their jagged summits, covered with snow and mingling with the clouds, present a scene which every lover of landscape would gaze upon with unqualified delight.[6]

It is understandable, then, that the chronicle of men's responses to the Rocky Mountains is a voluminous one. Every means of human expression, every form of poetry and prose, has gone into the account. In fact, from the very beginning, the breadth and variety of the subject decreed the necessity for more than mere verbal description. It was the artist's vision that revealed the full splendor, the commanding allure of the West.

Following the Louisiana Purchase of 1803, the vast new territories acquired by the United States became a lure for artists from the eastern seaboard and from European countries. They followed

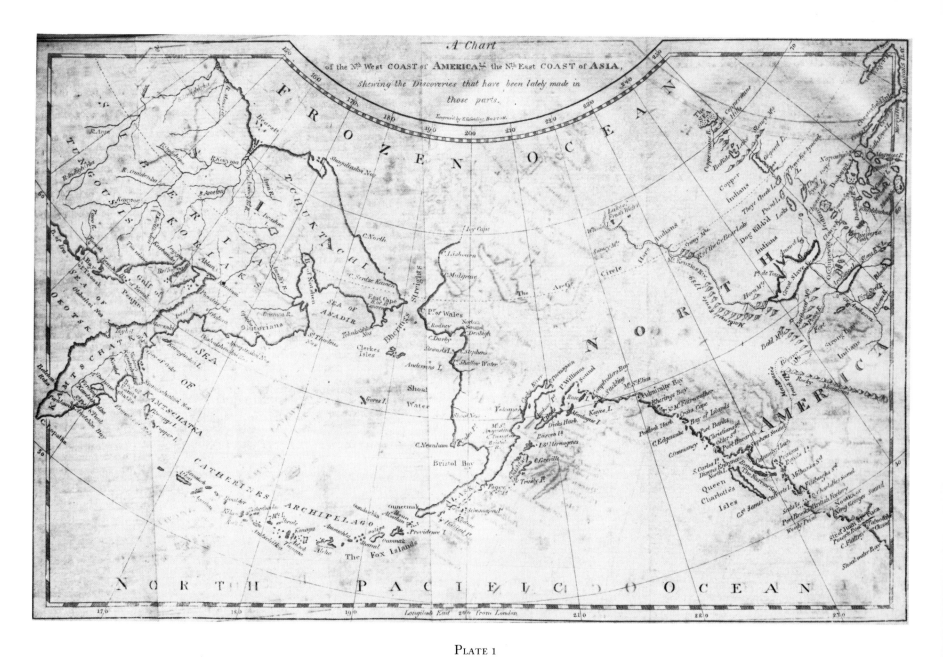

PLATE 1

E. G. Gridley, *A Chart of the Nth West Coast of America . . .* , ca. 1802, Engraving, 7¼″ × 11⅜″.
Courtesy American Antiquarian Society, Worcester, Mass.

government expeditions; they joined geological explorations; they participated in the excursions of sportsmen. They came to the Rockies with diverse backgrounds, different orientations, and varied painterly techniques.

This group of artists was referred to as "The Rocky Mountain school" by the early-twentieth-century American art historian Sadakichi Hartmann, who apparently coined the phrase merely as a convenient label. In his *History of American Art* (1901) he linked the western-school painters with the Hudson River School, which "had dealt wholly with externals" of nature, the subject alone, rather than "nature itself, the poetry and mystery of its simpler moods." According to Hartmann, "About 1860 the fame and the glory of the Barbizon school began to excite American artists, and under its rejuvenating influence the Rocky Mountain school soon paled into insignificance."[7] Albert Bierstadt, usually considered the leader of this school, made his first visit to the West in 1859, though the successful showpiece inspired by this journey, *The Rocky Mountains,* was not executed until 1863. The fame and fortune of his so-called school could not therefore have fallen from favor by 1860, as Hartmann indicates. One can only theorize that the serious use of the term "Rocky Mountain school" originated with Hartmann, since the critics of Bierstadt's day never used it to separate the latter-day mountain painters from those of the Hudson River School.[8]

The appellation has not reappeared until recently, and then primarily in the writing of James Thomas Flexner, author of several books on American art. In *That Wilder Image* (1962), Flexner, knowingly or not, uses Hartmann's label to classify certain nineteenth-century artists who painted in the Rocky Mountain region. In other writings he postulates that "every leading painter of the Far Western mountains" was foreign-born because the Hudson River School artists, whose style was developed for the eastern seaboard and for other continents, "seem to have felt that to depict another part of their own land would require as careful study as they gave the Catskills. And so the demand for renditions of the amazing scenery discovered in the Rocky Mountains was satisfied by foreigners with no such patriotic scruples."[9]

Flexner concurs with most other scholars in considering Albert

Bierstadt the founder of the Rocky Mountain school and includes as its members Thomas Hill, William Keith, and Thomas Moran. He points out that all these artists shared with Bierstadt not so much "particulars of technique" as "identities of attitude." He adds, "All believed that the more unusual and stupendous the scenery, the more exaggerated should be the image."[10] In accordance with this notion Flexner dismisses from the roster native artists T. Worthington Whittredge, John F. Kensett, and Sanford R. Gifford because their western scenes are less grand in format and more reminiscent of the eastern world as depicted by the Hudson River School artists.[11] Furthermore, he alludes to Bierstadt as the founder of the "school's style" but never develops that allusion, other than to mention the artist's own sources of inspiration and technique.[12] The author does not discuss developments in various regional centers after the middle of the nineteenth century but builds his case on a limited number of paintings of the Rockies (and the Sierra) executed in the panoramic manner. Such an interpretation excludes a host of important artists and memorable works.

This book focuses on those artists and those works—the product of a period of American history when the Rocky Mountains still embraced a vast, uncharted territory. Because we have chosen to use the definition of the area currently accepted by the Geological Survey of the United States Department of the Interior, our story of the American landscape artists is enacted within the boundaries of present-day Washington, Montana, Idaho, Wyoming, Utah, Colorado, and New Mexico.[13] Within this geographic framework the evolution of landscape painting in the Rocky Mountain West during the nineteenth century is examined, and the broad range of artistic interpretation in this scenic mecca is thus revealed, showing that no individual style or school of painting was exclusive to the Rocky Mountain region.

Paralleling the earliest developments of landscape art on the eastern seaboard, the pictorial history of the Rockies begins with the topographical artists who accompanied official government expeditions into the Trans-Mississippi West to record factually its remote and untamed regions. The true poetry of that ample geography was later recognized and portrayed by artist Alfred Jacob

Miller in the 1830s. Concentration on topographical detail became less important than form and mood in Miller's romantically inclined expression. Then, shortly after mid-century, Bierstadt's grandiloquent scenes of the Rockies heralded the westward extension of the professionally trained independent voyagers. Their paintings of the untrammeled wilderness complemented the efforts of successive waves of scientific artists bent on providing accurate geomorphic drawings for the Geological Survey. The cycle culminated in the late nineteenth century with the development of flourishing regional art colonies, especially in Colorado and Utah. It is hoped that this examination and reevaluation of early landscape artists in the Rocky Mountains may provide new insights into the overall development of landscape painting in America.

ACKNOWLEDGMENTS

This volume is the result of more than a dozen years of work which had their initial inspiration in two graduate studies, Patricia Trenton's doctoral dissertation, *The Evolution of Landscape Painting in Colorado, 1820–1900* (University of California at Los Angeles, 1980), and Peter Hassrick's master's thesis, *Artists Employed on United States Government Expeditions to the Trans-Mississippi West Before 1850* (University of Denver, 1969). In these two endeavors, and the subsequent collaboration, expansion, and elaboration, the assistance and cooperation of many individuals and institutions have been invaluable.

A special expression of gratitude must be extended to the following individuals: E. Maurice Bloch, Professor Emeritus, University of California at Los Angeles, for his enlightened scholarship and guidance; Otto Karl Bach, former director of the Denver Art Museum, and Cile Bach for their support and editorial assistance; Linda Taubenreuther for reviewing the manuscript and offering editorial suggestions; Edwin H. Carpenter, Huntington Library, for hours of proofreading; John Drayton, Julia Grossman, and Doris Radford Morris, of the University of Oklahoma Press, for their encouragement and constructive advice; David Fuller, of California State University, Northridge, for his assistance as a cartographer; the late Mitchell A. Wilder, former director of the Amon Carter Museum, for his inspiration; and Royal B. Hassrick for the same. Additional thanks must go to the Rockefeller Foundation for awarding Patricia Trenton a Rockefeller Fellowship in 1977, which provided funds for travel and research.

Two extraordinary sources of information must be mentioned here. First is William H. Goetzmann and his epic treatise on Western history, *Exploration and Empire*, which paved the way for our endeavor and set a standard for scholarship. Second is the rich font of materials on artists in the West found in the Robert Taft Papers, Kansas State Historical Society.

During the course of our research we found a number of institutions to be of special value both for their materials and their staff. Thus we extend our sincere thanks to the Huntington Library and their informed staff, including Faith Cornwall, Janet Hawkins, Barbara Quinn, Virginia Renner, Virginia Rust, Robert Wark, and Daniel Woodward; the Denver Public Library, Western History Department, and the gracious assistance of Eleanor Gehres, Bonnie Skell Hardwick, and Pam Rose, and, formerly of their staff, Alys Freeze and Opal Harber; the State Historical Society of Colorado and former librarian Enid Thompson, along with the current curator of Documentary Resources, Maxine Benson; Amon Carter Museum and the aid of our colleagues Carol Clark, Ron Tyler, Ann Adams, and Nancy Wynne, along with former library assistant, Kay Krochman; Kansas State Historical Society and staff members of that fine institution, including Robert W. Richmond, Mrs. George T. Hawley, Joseph Gambone, and James H. Nottage; National Archives and Records Service and the capable guidance of Richard C. Crawford, James Dillon, Elaine C. Everly, William H. Leary, and William F. Sherman; National Museum of American Art and the generous support of William H. Truettner, Judy Shimmel, and Roberta Mortimer; Buffalo Bill Historical Center and the hard work and welcome assistance of Kathy Heaton, Michael Kelly, Joyce Mayer, Tacie Merrill, and Sammi Reed. We offer an extra note of appreciation to Peg Coe and the board of trustees of the Buffalo Bill Memorial Association.

Many individuals made this work possible, lending help and

direction along the way. We extend a warm expression of thanks to the following: Alice S. Acheson, Washington, D.C.; Warren Adelson, Coe-Kerr Gallery, New York City; Paul A. Amelia, Peale Museum, Baltimore; Philip Anschutz, Anschutz Corporation, Denver; Marjorie Arkelian, Oakland, Calif.; Madeleine Barbin, Bibliothèque Nationale, Paris; William Bell; John E. Billmyer, Santa Fe; Ruth M. Blom; Sarah E. Boehan, Stark Museum of Art, Orange, Texas; Richard J. Boyle, Pennsylvania Academy of the Fine Arts, Philadelphia; John C. Broderick, Library of Congress, Washington, D.C.; Anna Jean Caffey, Stark Museum of Art, Orange, Texas; Marie T. Capps, U.S. Military Academy Library, West Point; Denny Carter, Cincinnati Art Museum; Cecilia Chin, Ryerson Library, Chicago; Judith Ciampoli, Missouri Historical Society, Saint Louis; JoAnn Clark, Altadena, California; J. D. Cleaver, Oregon Historical Society, Portland; the late Helen Coleman, New York City; Stiles T. Colwill, Maryland Historical Society, Baltimore; Everett L. Cooley, University of Utah, Salt Lake City; former librarian James Davis, Idaho Historical Society, Boise; Alan N. Degutis, American Antiquarian Society, Worcester, Massachusetts; the late Carl S. Dentzel, Southwest Museum, Los Angeles; Elizabeth G. de Veer, Englewood, New Jersey; William Dick, San Francisco; Bruce and Dorothy Dines, Denver; Ruth R. Draper, Utah State Division of Fine Arts, Salt Lake City; William D. Ebie, Roswell Museum and Art Center; Joyce Randall Edwards; Harrison Eiteljorg, Indianapolis; Charles C. Eldredge, National Museum of American Art, Washington, D.C.; former curator Elliot Evans, Society of California Pioneers, San Francisco; John C. Ewers, National Museum of Natural History, Smithsonian Institution, Washington, D.C.; Stuart Feld, Hirschl & Adler Galleries, New York City; James T. Forrest, University of Wyoming, Laramie; Frank H. Forrester, U.S. Geological Survey National Center, Reston, Va.; F. M. Fryxell, Rock Island, Illinois; Patrick W. Gabor, Buffalo and Erie Historical Society, Buffalo; Bernice George; Sanford Gifford, M.D.; Robert Goldstein, Museum of American Jewish History, Philadelphia; former curator Mildred Goosman, Joslyn Art Museum, Omaha; Gene M. Gressley, University of Wyoming, Laramie; J. D. Hale, University of Arizona, Tucson; former curator Archibald Hanna, Beinecke Rare Book and Manuscript Library, New Haven; Dorothy and William Harmsen, Denver; James Haseltine, Washington State Arts Commission, Olympia; Christoph Heilmann, Alte Pinakothek, Munich; Leda F. Hill; Robert V. Hine, University of California, Riverside; Jack Holliday, Jr., Indianapolis; John K. Howat, Metropolitan Museum of Art, New York City; Warren R. Howell, John Howell—Books, San Francisco; Hugh H. Hudson, U.S. Department of the Interior, Geological Survey, Denver; the late Hans Huth, Carmel; former editor Martha Y. Hutson, *American Art Review;* Janice R. Hynes, Boston Public Library; Kathe Jacoby; William R. Johnston, Walters Art Gallery, Baltimore; William Katzenbach; former librarian Mrs. H. H. Keene, Thomas Gilcrease Institute of American History and Art, Tulsa; James R. Kellogg; Jeanne Snodgrass King, Gilcrease Institute; Myron King, Denver; Kay Klepetko, Littleton; Phil Kovinick, Los Angeles; Jane R. Lane, Pittsburgh; Nancy E. Loe, Penrose Public Library, Colorado Springs; Richard Logan, University of California at Los Angeles; Laura C. Luckey, Museum of Fine Arts, Boston; Barbara B. McCorkle, Yale University Library, New Haven; Mike McCourt, Montana Historical Society, Helena; Garnett McCoy, Archives of American Art, Washington, D.C.; Charles H. McCurdy, Grand Teton National Park; the late John Francis McDermott, Saint Louis; John J. McDonough, Library of Congress, Washington, D.C.; Timothy R. Manns, Yellowstone National Park; Mr. and Mrs. Paul Mellon, Upperville, Virginia; Betsy R. Merrill, Vigo County Public Library, Terre Haute; Fred Meyer, Gilcrease Institute; Finis Mitchell, Rock Springs, Wyoming; Nancy Dustin Wall Moure, Los Angeles County Museum of Art; Francis Murphy, Smith College, Northampton, Massachusetts; David Nathan, Yale University Art Gallery, New Haven; Maria Naylor, Kennedy Galleries, Inc., New York City; Clifford M. Nelson, United States Geological Survey, Reston, Va.; Norman Neuerburg, Professor Emeritus, California State University, Dominguez Hills; Donald J. Orth, U.S. Board on Geographic Names, Reston, Va.; Wendell Ott, Roswell Museum, N.Mex.; Arthur J. Phelan, Chevy Chase, Maryland; Carol Pearson, San Marino; former curator Irene Rawlings, Anschutz Collection; Sue W. Reed, Museum of Fine Arts, Boston; Elinor Reichlin, Peabody Museum of Archaeology & Ethnology,

Cambridge, Mass.; former curator Lorne E. Render, Glenbow Museum, Calgary; Brenda Richardson, Baltimore Museum of Art; Robert Rockwell, Corning, New York; Anthony A. Roth, Historical Society of Pennsylvania, Philadelphia; Frank Sanguinetti, Utah Museum of Fine Arts, Salt Lake City; Christine Schelshorn, State Historical Society of Wisconsin, Madison; Philip A. Schlamp, Helena National Forest; Jean-Pierre Seguin, Bibliothèque Nationale, Paris; Delores Serode, New Bedford Free Public Library; Francis Silverman, Peabody Museum of Archaeology & Ethnology, Cambridge, Mass.; Gladys Smith, Livingston County Historical Society, Genesco; Elinor Solis-Cohen; Barbara M. Soper, Buffalo and Erie County Public Library, Buffalo; Lincoln Spiess, Saint Louis; Mildred Steinback, Frick Art Reference Library, New York City; Franz Stenzel, Portland; former photographer John Sullivan, Huntington Library, San Marino; Jackson Thode, Denver; former curator George Tomko, Joslyn Art Museum, Omaha; Owen Tweeto, U.S. Geological Survey, Denver; John A. Tyers, Yellowstone National Park; Larry A. Viskochil, Chicago Historical Society; W. von Kalnein, Kunstmuseum, Düsseldorf; Robert C. Vose, Jr., Vose Galleries, Boston; Robert Warner, University of Wyoming, Laramie; Joan Washburn, Washburn Gallery, New York City; Robert A. Weinstein, Los Angeles; Francis M. Wheat, Los Angeles; Thurman Wilkins, Queens College, New York City; James C. Wol, Newberry Library, Chicago; Gerold and Rudolf Wunderlich, Wunderlich & Company (formerly of Kennedy Galleries, Inc.), New York City; Harvey and Beverly Young.

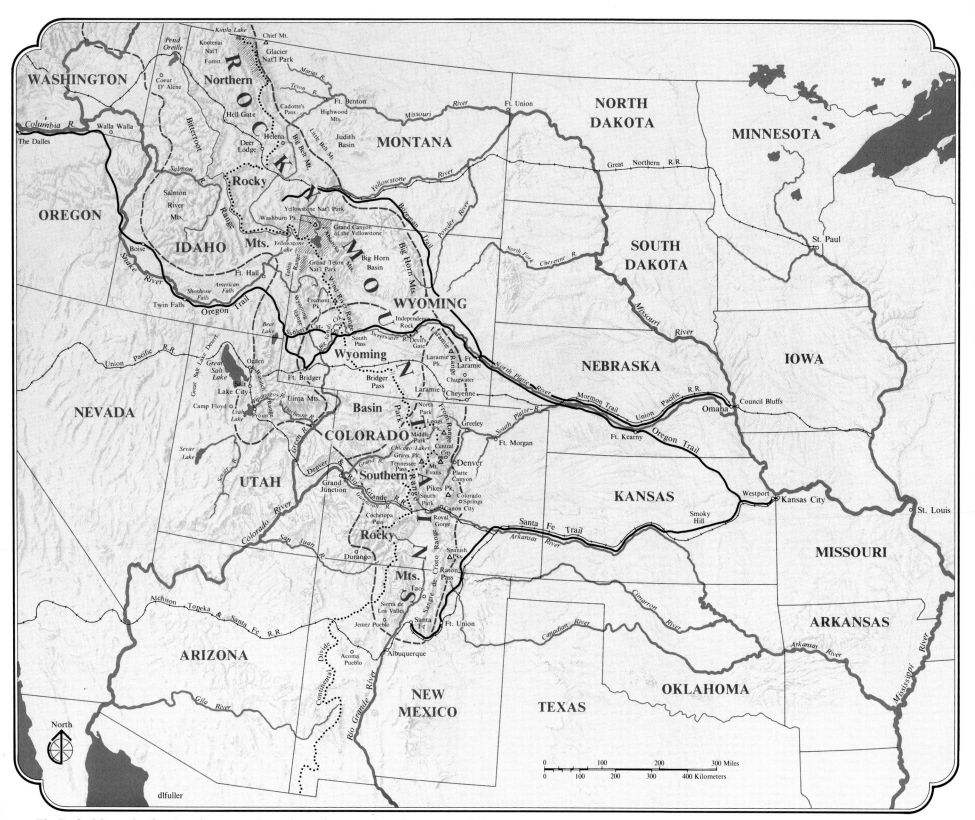

The Rocky Mountains showing the routes the early explorers took as they traversed the continent. Map courtesy of David Fuller, California State University, Northridge.

THE ROCKY MOUNTAINS

INTRODUCTION

CHANGING TIMES AND ATTITUDES TOWARD NATURE

This age, which fed its youthful imagination on "Thanatopsis" and its mature mind on Democratic Vistas, *has been called the age of Romanticism. That troublesome term has been applied narrowly to the revolt of European groups against the frozen formulas of their "classical" predecessors, and broadly to the timeless and endless war of Imagination against Reason. . . . If one's purpose is not to fit experience into categories but to understand one of the most complex periods in American art, one recognizes that life in both Europe and America in the late eighteenth and the early nineteenth centuries made necessary and possible a vigorous assertion of the individual and with it a changed attitude toward the world around him.* — Oliver W. Larkin[1]

WITH the rise of Romanticism and the change in the American intellectual climate, the American artist became involved with external nature in a new and personal way. To him "nature, as a projection of human states of mind . . . was a valid source of moral, emotional, and aesthetic truth, a manifestation of beauty and divinity in the visual world."[2] Because of this deeper significance of nature the painting of America's primeval landscape became a moral as well as an artistic act. The subjective views and feelings of the artist became important to the viewer for the spiritual truths and sense of beauty they conveyed. At this period America's religious heritage, with its moral concerns, was still too strong to allow the sheer appreciation of landscape for its own sake. By the midnineteenth century, however, the American landscapist was portraying nature in more realistic terms, no longer striving to synthesize its ideal and its real qualities to disseminate "the gospel of spiritualized landscape," as exemplified by the art of the early Hudson River School.[3]

Yet, as James Callow has aptly pointed out, the writers "were actually the cultural explorers who, by announcing their own discoveries of the American landscape in glowing terms, prepared the way for the future settlements by native painters and urged the public to accept these enterprises."[4] Many of the spiritual connotations and aesthetic values that dominated literary and artistic thought about America's landscape in the nineteenth century stemmed directly from aesthetic doctrines set forth in the works of British and Scottish aestheticians of the eighteenth century. The writings of Archibald Alison, Edmund Burke, Uvedale Price, and William Gilpin,[5] several of which were published in a number of American editions, provided the generally accepted presuppositions for describing and celebrating nature.

The spiritual values regarding American scenery certainly contributed to the emergence of America's native school of landscape painting, known as the Hudson River School; so too did the dynamic economic and social forces that were molding American society. The leisure time provided by industrialization and the optimism and economic expansion of the Jacksonian era were important factors in widening the narrow cultural order of the colonial period. The romantic view of nature was the privilege of the affluent, who were far enough away from the harshness of nature "to be able to see it as scenic backdrop and not, as in the case of the plain dirt farmer, in the relationship of daily antagonist."[6] Moreover, advances in scientific knowledge and the heightening of national and patriotic sentiment by the Revolution and the War of 1812 contributed to a growing interest and pride in the physical features of the country's landscape.

With this increased perception—undoubtedly stimulated by the camera and the many exploratory expeditions undertaken to chart the country—Americans began to observe nature with more honest eyes, less hindered by aesthetic classifications of natural phenomena and the association psychology of Archibald Alison.[7] As artists traveled westward in America and to other exotic places, wonderment and scientific curiosity supplanted the contemplation of nature for spiritual revelations and moral truths. Yet the very forces that were civilizing America were to be assailed by writers and artists as causing wanton destruction of primitive scenery.[8] To Thomas Cole, Americans were still in Eden, but "through their ignorance and folly" they were managing to build a wall that would eventually shut them out of the garden.[9] This dilemma made clear the immediacy of the artists' mission: to preserve on canvas those pristine features of America's unique scenery before they were doomed by the "axe of civilization."[10]

Landscape became a worthy subject for the painter's canvas late in the evolution of American art. During colonization the writings of early settlers tell more of the hardships of coping with the unruly countryside than of the aesthetic pleasures of nature's sensuous beauty. Nature was considered by some as the "Armed Enymie" or a "Ravenous devourer";[11] others considered it merely in terms of its usefulness to man's purpose. Nature as an artistic theme had to wait until Americans changed their attitude toward the land and became aware of their national identity. At this point in America's history the Puritans were reflecting seventeenth-century attitudes and the taste of a more mature mother culture.

With the growth of commerce and urban life came a gradual softening of the hard-line Calvinistic attitude toward life and nature and a shift toward Deism. More a philosophy of life than a religion, Deism was based on the Enlightenment's faith in reason and science: man was not controlled by predestination but could mold his own destiny. The tempering of the Christian ideals of the seventeenth century with popular Deistic teachings like those of the third earl of Shaftesbury, expanded the colonists' vision of the external world and their relationship to it.[12] Moreover, advances made in the various fields of science during the eighteenth century stimulated a genuine interest in knowledge about the geology of America and challenged the hold of supernaturalism. The imagination and passions of such men as Thomas Jefferson, John Bartram, and others were responsible for fostering an interest in natural history and disseminating a love of nature.

The growth of a secular spirit in the later decades of eighteenth-century America provided the proper atmosphere for the adoption of certain European literary trends that were shaping man's attitude toward nature. The pantheistic and romantic philosophy flowering in Europe eventually reached American writers and had a great effect on their "kindred spirits," the nineteenth-century Hudson River School artists. According to Hans Huth, the Lake poets, such as Samuel Coleridge and particularly William Wordsworth—whose works were well known through English and American literary magazines—exercised a steadily growing influence on American literature in the early part of the nineteenth century.[13] Typical of Wordsworth's influence is a passage from a *Rhapsody*, by an unknown poet, published in 1789:

> *There is a rude disorder in these wilds,*
> *A native grandeur, that, unaffected*
> *By the touch of art, transcends its graves,*
> *And strikes some finer sense within the soul.*[14]

How very different this sentiment of nature is from the Neoclassicist's appreciation of "purling rills" and "verdant lawns." One final obstacle stood in the way of acceptance of the native land on its own terms. America's delayed acceptance of its primeval scenery may have been caused by its sense of inferiority as a young nation and by the stigma of the European "Doctrine of Association":

Denigration of American landscape had practically become a tradition among the educated classes of Europe, and . . . some of the most sophisticated classes of the American population. European denigration was in part . . . [an] expression of the prevailing European commitment for formal doctrines of aesthetic appreciation that left little room for an unqualified approval of the American landscape.[15]

In his *Three Essays: On Picturesque Beauty* . . . , William Gilpin enlarged upon this idea with his "doctrine of romantic association,"[16] which seems to suggest that a scene is only beautiful and worth producing if it is associated with man's historical past.

Therefore, the defense of America's unique scenery—its uncivilized state—had to be sought through different channels. In promoting the "cult of the wilderness" and the sublime aspects of the uncultivated scenery, Washington Irving used the wilds of the Catskills as a scenic backdrop for his fanciful legends to enhance the romantic value of his native landscape. Thomas Cole's stirring message, delivered before the American Lyceum in 1835, attempted to cultivate America's appreciation for the beauties and virtues of its scenery.[17] In his rebuttal to those who acknowledge the "grand defect in American scenery—the want of associations," he said that the distinctive characteristic of American scenery was its very wildness—the primitive features that Europe had either destroyed or altered—which, according to Cole, "affect the mind with a more deep toned emotion than aught which the hand of man has touched." He added, "Amid them the consequent associations are of God the creator—they are his undefiled works, and the mind is cast into the contemplation of eternal things."[18]

In general, however, by the midnineteenth century, this dilemma of the inadequacy of America's landscape seems to have been somewhat remedied by the efforts of writers and artists. In view of the popularity of landscape gift books,[19] scenic prints, and paintings of the Hudson River School, it is evident that the public had finally recognized the grandeur and beauty of its own scenery. It is at this point that landscape painting became the dominant branch of the arts.

ARTISTIC MILESTONES: EVOLUTION OF LANDSCAPE PAINTING IN AMERICA

Before considering the emergence of the Hudson River School, it is necessary to trace the gradual evolution of landscape painting in America. The paintings that survive from the colonial and federal periods reflect the utilitarian nature of painting in these eras. The predominance of portraiture over all other branches of art at this time is understandable; in a growing society these likenesses confirmed the status of the newly arrived. Apart from the early reportorial drawings of America's land by the various draftsmen who accompanied foreign expeditions to this country in the sixteenth and seventeenth centuries, the meager legacy of landscape paintings left us from the eighteenth century proves beyond a doubt that only a marginal interest existed in such paintings. Enough evidence has accumulated to indicate, however, that "landskips" (as they were called then) were indeed painted in the colonial period. We have only to refer to the topographical prints of William Burgis (active from 1715 to 1731 in New York and Boston), the overmantel pieces and side-panel paintings of fanciful scenic views that decorated the Clark-Frankland house of Boston (1712–1714), and the many portraits featuring a conventional baroque or rococo landscape background primarily derived from foreign prints. Several portraits even include realistic details in the landscape settings, such as precise renderings of buildings and sites associated with the sitters. Eighteenth-century works by John Smibert, Charles W. Peale, and Ralph Earl provide visual documentation of this nascent activity.[20]

Occasionally landskips are mentioned in artists' advertisements, wills, and obituaries, as well as other documents of the colonial and federal periods.[21] Until the recent discovery of an early landscape, *View of Boston, 1738*, attributed to John Smibert,[22] it was impossible to ascertain whether any of the landskips mentioned were produced by resident artists; they could merely have been foreign prints or paintings imported by these painters. The Smibert oil hints at the possibility that some of the landskips may actually have been executed in America. Nonetheless, the paucity of extant early-eighteenth-century landscape paintings makes it difficult to arrive at any firm conclusions about the quality or style of landscape art of the period. Judging by the few surviving examples, one must conclude that it was rather simple and crude throughout most of the eighteenth century with the exception of the last few decades, when an emergent topographical view combined with the influx of European-trained artists into America.

Insofar as landscape painting had a limited patronage in the first half of the eighteenth century, it is reasonable to assume that this branch of art was practiced by the artist primarily for his own amusement. Smibert gained his reputation as an influential portraitist, if indeed he painted *View of Boston, 1738,* and it is likely that it was done for his own diversion alone. Unfortunately, the present whereabouts of his other recorded landskips are unknown, and we have no assurance that they were alike in style and motif.[23]

If it is by Smibert, *View of Boston, 1738* may well be the first academic landscape oil painted in America. It appears that the artist has relied on an engraving for the arrangement of his subject matter, as Smibert often did in painting backgrounds for his portraits. Atypically, he selected an early American topographical print for specificities of place. The artist may have referred to William Burgis's engraving of *Prospect of the Harbor and Town of Boston in 1723,*[24] which was undoubtedly familiar to him. Although interesting for its documentation of early Boston, the painting evinces an awkward handling of the subject and ineptness in the application of color. Nevertheless, it is interesting to note that this scene does prefigure the early direction of landscape painting in this country.

With the general political unrest throughout Europe in the last decade of the eighteenth century, America became a haven for a number of migrant artists, whose various skills broadened the country's taste in landscape painting and contributed to the popularization of the scenic print. Four Englishmen were among the many semi-professionals who descended upon America at this time; these men are usually considered the first professional landscapists in America because they devoted their careers exclusively to that particular genre.[25] George Beck, William Groombridge, William Winstanley, and Francis Guy arrived in America between 1790 and 1795 and, at various times, pursued their artistic careers in Philadelphia, Baltimore, Washington, and New York. Guy was self-taught; the others received academic training in England, where their work was exhibited on occasion. The simplified and symmetrical arrangement of their subject matter, typically framed with trees, reflects the influence of Claude Lorrain's pictorial formula; on the other hand, the addition of a few decorative and picturesque motifs harks back to provincial British topographical painting, the predominant influence in American art of the early nineteenth century. Groombridge's painting *Fairmont and the Schuylkill River, Philadelphia* (plate 2) leans heavily on classical precepts and Claude's ideas, while Francis Guy's *Brooklyn Snow Scene* demonstrates this artist's meticulous draftsmanship and strong topographical realism in a scene teeming with human activity.[26] As Frank Goodyear has noted, these "English-style landscapes of American scenes . . . varied from a meticulous, topographical realism in which architecture was prominent, to a more 'picturesque' treatment in which the qualities of William Gilpin's aesthetic prevailed, to classical compositions in the manner of Claude and Poussin."[27] At this point scenes of country estates or cities were more popular than the "wilder image" that would later preoccupy the Hudson River School. Yet the activities of Beck, Groombridge, and other artists of the time certainly left their mark on such artists as Thomas Doughty, Alvan Fisher, and even Cole, who first engaged in landscape painting while residing in Philadelphia from 1823 to 1825.[28]

The increased demand for scenic views of specific places, undoubtedly prompted by a growing nationalism, was also met by the engraved print. Less costly than most paintings, it appealed to a larger audience and later became a stereotypical ornamentation. The talent of those engravers and painters from Great Britain whose specialty lay in readying pictures for engravings made possible a large-scale production of scenic prints. To ensure the continuation

PLATE 2

William Groombridge, *Fairmont and the Schuylkill River, Philadelphia,* 1800, Oil, 25″ × 36″.
Courtesy Historical Society of Pennsylvania, Philadelphia, Pa.

of this trade in America, the art of printmaking was being passed on to the younger generation; for instance, William Birch engaged his son Thomas and friend Samuel Seymour as apprentices in his shop.[29] Because the standard of engraving had been improved in America by the efforts of trained foreigners, several elaborate albums and portfolios of printed views of American scenery were made available for public consumption (plate 3). These prints, as well as the engraved reproductions that appeared in periodicals, helped impart a growing "self-conscious nativism" during this period.

Along with the itinerant and the migrant artists, the professional American artist—the portraitist—was also to join the ranks of the landscapists in picturing America's scenery. As early as 1801, Charles Willson Peale hastily sketched the scenery along the Hudson River in watercolor. Although simple and somewhat crude, these representations reveal an interest in landscape painting by the professional artist.[30]

Just as the engraved scenic view began to emerge, another important event in the development of the aspiring young artist in early-nineteenth-century America was the advent of drawing books. First imported from England, they were manuals of instruction outlining the basic principles of drawing and painting. Once the rules were digested, the novitiate was advised to imitate nature, "to know her well," and then to copy the "Masters of the trade" for exposure to different manners of representation.[31] Thomas Doughty, a transitional figure who is often called one of the founders of the Hudson River School, was probably among those who turned to these basic sources for instruction, since the study of landscape art was omitted from the curriculum of the several American art academies then in existence.[32]

Like the eighteenth-century English landscapist Richard Wilson, Doughty elevated "the country house 'portrait' from topography to landscape art." In his *View of Baltimore from Beech Hill, the seat of Robert Gilmore, Jr.*, the landscape has become the artist's major concern; the house in the distance is simply an integral part of the pastoral setting. The painterly concerns of conveying light and atmospheric effects in nature are evident in this painting and in a number of Doughty's panoramic landscapes of the 1820s and 1830s,

revealing his debt to such artists as Richard Wilson and his follower George Barret.[33] Admittedly self-taught, the artist produced diluted versions of the wilder aspects of nature that seem to be derivative of English and Dutch art; yet with Doughty, and later Alvan Fisher, American landscape moved away from strictly topographical art to a real world of moods and natural effects.[34]

The artist responsible for transcending the vernacular—the topographical view—in painting was Thomas Cole, generally acknowledged as the originator of the Hudson River School. Cole first brought to public consciousness the identification of natural scenery with "godliness and superior virtue."[35] Employing nature's wilderness as a vehicle for his deep spiritual and moralistic concerns, he composed a series of pictures based on philosophical and historical themes to serve as illustrations of moral truths. Even though he was the first member of the Hudson River School to recognize and dramatize the peculiar wildness of America's scenery, Cole nevertheless felt that his paintings should be "more than [mere] imitations of nature," remarking that "the most lovely and perfect parts of nature may be brought together, and combined in a whole, that shall surpass in beauty and effect any picture painted from a single view."[36]

Yet, to judge from his writings, Cole was torn between the public's demand for the specific in nature and his own inclination to draw a "veil" over the real to present an imaginative composition. Although his sketchbooks abound with faithful portraits of nature, his heroic and noble ideas about life transcend the mere factual world. Cole's work demonstrates well his ability to synthesize the real and the ideal in his attempt to reproduce scenes of "truth and beauty," pictures that "impress the spirit of the entire scene on the mind of the beholder."[37]

Cole's renditions of local scenery include a welter of generic detail, a series of focal points, strong contrast of brooding darkness and eerie light, and devices borrowed from Salvator Rosa to produce heightened drama and sensations of the sublime. It hardly seems a coincidence that Cole's *Landscape with Tree Trunks* (1827, plate 4) and Salvator Rosa's *Mercury Deceiving Argus* (ca. 1670), bear a striking resemblance in elements and compositional order; Cole, who worked at the Pennsylvania Academy in 1824–25, would assuredly

have been familiar with the Rosa painting in the academy's collection.[38] As a general rule, however, it is more likely that Cole referred to prints for his solutions and thematic ideas.

Cole was much admired in his lifetime for his innovations and leadership in landscape art, but in their portrayals of nature the painters who followed him were not as caught up in his Burkean ideas of the sublime and moral expositories. Asher B. Durand, the senior member of the group, had been an engraver until 1836, when he decided to devote full time to painting. In contrast to Cole's sublime, dramatic, and didactic presentations of nature, Durand's landscapes are full of sentiment and seem to represent the more peaceful aspects of nature as a revelation of God's divine love and beneficence to man (plate 5).[39] A similar spirit is also represented in the poetry of William Cullen Bryant, and it has been mentioned that Durand translated into paint some of the poet's descriptive passages of nature.[40]

Durand's early paintings exhibit his meticulous rendering and careful regard for detail, as well as his hesitancy to use color, all of which reflect his training as an engraver. Following his discovery of the work of John Constable and Peter Paul Rubens on a trip to Europe in 1840, his oil studies from nature began to reflect a new interest in the tactile quality of paint and the spontaneous effects of broken brushwork. By painting directly out-of-doors, Durand became familiar with the "magical power" of atmospheric change. Although his formal studio compositions show an indebtedness to Claude's pictorial formula, Durand's intimate studies from nature reveal the spontaneous and natural way in which he composed his plein-air paintings. It is apparent that the artist's naturalistic bent led him in the same direction as his contemporaries, the French Barbizon painters, who were also inspired by Dutch seventeenth-century landscapists. Durand's poetry and his exploration of light effects in nature predated the popular luminist movement in American landscape painting.[41] His plein-air oil studies were innovative for their time and helped establish a trend toward realism in American native landscape art.

By 1860 artists like Kensett, John W. Casilear, Gifford, Whittredge, and James and William Hart were involved in a new and intense interest—the exploration of light.[42] Artists who shared this fascination for light effects have been grouped under the heading "luminists." Their style unqualifiedly evolved out of plein-air painting, no doubt inspired by the "simulated realism of the camera" and the revelations of contemporary scientific advancements.[43]

Yet one must not overlook the influence of seventeenth-century Dutch landscape and marine paintings on the early stages of the luminist movement,[44] suggested by the horizontal proportions, low horizons, mirrorlike water surfaces, and overall pervasive light found in early luminist paintings. On the other hand, the precise linear representation and subtle modulation of tones evident in the luminists' work strongly reflect the engraver's training of most of these artists.

Obviously, no single explanation exists for the luminist phenomenon. We can be certain, however, that these works are not *merely* manifestations of the "eternal spiritual light" but perhaps, as John Baur states, "a moment of poetic insight immaculately preserved."[45] A number of other artists discovered the limitless possibilities for personal expression and variety in style offered by light and atmospheric changes. Frederic Church, obviously inspired by the writings of the great German geographer and philosopher Alexander von Humboldt, made two journeys to South America, carefully recording with pigment, graphite, and camera his impressions of the exotic and mountainous scenery. Pencil studies such as *Composition with effect observed/June 5, 1857—Guaranda*[46] indicate that Church was not only a skilled topographer but also a naturalist at heart. Church's scientific expositions were, however, not mere imitations of nature but compositions full of artistic license. His splendid productions of nature seemed to express in visual terms Humboldt's ideas on the interrelationship of landscape painting, science, and nature. With Church, American landscape art was elevated to the rank of history painting, noble in feeling and grand in proportions.

Church's esteem and fortune rose considerably when his grand painting the *Heart of the Andes* (1859, plate 6) was exhibited in New York;[47] setting the stage for the transformation of native landscape art from the intimate pastorals of the Hudson River School

PLATE 5

Asher B. Durand, *Landscape, the Rescue*, ca. 1847, Oil, 45″ × 36″. Courtesy Anschutz Collection, Denver, Colo.

to pageants of illimitable space by artists like Church, Albert Bierstadt, and Thomas Moran, whose heightened effects evoked unique feelings of solitude and wild grandeur.

It is relatively certain that Church pioneered such oversized, theatrical renditions of nature. It was the "Düsseldorfians," however, who were responsible for providing the essential paradigms involved in this new trend of representation. The excitement engendered by the works of the legendary German romantics at the opening of New York's Düsseldorf Art Gallery in 1849[48] was sufficient to induce American artists to abandon the traditional European Grand Tour and pursue their formal studies in Düsseldorf—either at the academy or independently with German artists such as Andreas Achenbach, Karl Lessing, Johann Wilhelm Schirmer,[49] and German-American artist Emanuel Leutze. The role of Leutze as a befriender of fledglings can be compared with that of Benjamin West, whose studio was also available to his compatriots in an earlier period.

Among those who sought to emulate Church's success by producing pictures of equivalent size and magnitude was the German-American artist Albert Bierstadt, who was considered "a true representative of the Düsseldorf school in landscape."[50] His famous painting *The Rocky Mountains* (1863) launched a grand march to the Rockies by professional artists who—unlike the earlier, more scientific artist-reporter—were well equipped to capture the mystery and grandeur of the western wilderness.[51] One of the many independent voyagers on this arduous trek was Thomas Moran, whose paintings of sublime beauty and impressive expanse capture vividly the coloristic and atmospheric effects of the remote West.

Unlike Bierstadt, who was a product of Düsseldorf, Thomas Moran received his tutelage as an apprentice engraver and was influenced by the works of the English artist Joseph M. W. Turner.[52] Moran's bravura brushwork and romantic coloration have often been related to Turner's orchestration of color and light, but, unlike the English landscapist, Moran never dissolved his pictorial elements into pure color and light. Like most native artists, Moran's conservatism and fidelity to the specifics of nature never allowed him to infuse his works with the apocalyptic and highly imaginative

spirit of the master. It was the "character" of the region that he wished to preserve in his pictures, not a transcript of "a place as a place."[53] As he freely combined and arranged the components of nature for the desired pictorial effect, Moran was actually adopting the previously established ideal compositional formula of the Hudson River School—a set of classical principles that he learned through Claude, whose work he copied while in Italy. Even in those paintings obviously constructed on classical principles there is always an adherence to the integrity of form. Basically Moran was a realist with romantic sensibilities. That he sought to emulate Turner's color and aerial effects cannot be denied, but his paintings derived inspiration from other sources that will be analyzed in the course of this book.[54]

With the ascendancy of Munich and Paris as fashionable art centers in the 1860s and 1870s, the influence of Düsseldorf waned, and American taste shifted to the new European modes then in vogue. Artists such as George Inness, Homer D. Martin, and Alexander H. Wyant, whose art evolved from traditional pictorial conventions of the Native Landscape School, were early practitioners of the Barbizon mode.[55] Inspired by the paintings of the French artists Rousseau, Corot, and Díaz, their subject matter shifted from sweeping panoramas with infinite detail and polished surfaces to intimate pastorals broadly painted. In adapting to this new painterly mode, they simplified forms by massing color with highlights of opaque pigment to communicate a feeling for pure poetic nature. Their use of soft colors, close tonal values, and predominantly gray color schemes reflected the influence of their mentors. The linearism and slick finish typical of the Hudson River School salon paintings had been replaced by painterly effects. Some artists, including Martin, took the trend a step further and embraced a conservative form of Impressionism, but, though Americans fractured color and light, they were never to dissolve forms completely as the French did.[56] Others, like Inness, diluted the Barbizon mode, filling their pictures with vague and mystical overtones. Although the Barbizonesque style swept Europe and America, Impressionism was to remain a minor stream in American art, primarily attracting a well-known group of artists called "the Ten."[57] Americans came closest to a

true French Impressionism in the work of Childe Hassam, but even his palette was low-keyed in comparison with the blond tonalities of the French.

The growth of private fortunes during the post–Civil War years made the collecting of contemporary European art possible and fashionable. The consequent flooding of the United States with foreign art virtually destroyed patronage for American artists. The critics were scornful of this lack of appreciation toward American art:

> Our collectors of pictures, often utterly devoid of aesthetic cultivation or real judgment, and moved only by vanity and a love of display, garnish their galleries at enormous cost with works credited to famous artists, and think they are gaining a reputation for elegance and taste. . . . What they are getting are copies of inferior European paintings.[58]

Many artists found it difficult to acquire patronage. Others disguised their pictures with European picturesque motifs to compete with the foreign market. The struggle that ensued between older artists working in more conservative modes and the younger artists, the so-called Modernists, was not to find resolution until the following century.

As these developments unfolded along the eastern seaboard, other regions of the country were manifesting signs of artistic activity. With the expansion of America's frontiers new untouched areas of wilderness were revealed. At the beginning of the nineteenth century the Rockies, the geological backbone of North America, presented an ominous impediment to advancing civilization. By the end of that century those same magnificent mountains were beckoning artists westward. This dramatic change in America's image of the Rockies, and indeed of the West in general, through the gradual amelioration and popularization of their image by a group of pictorial artists, is the subject of this book. What follows is a broad overview of their artistic interpretations, a perspective on their cumulative efforts, and a discussion of the role they played in altering America's image of itself and its natural wonders.[59]

1

BEFORE THE GREAT SURVEYS: THE TRAILBLAZERS

It has frequently happened that the artists appointed to accompany expeditions fitted out at the national expense, have been chosen without due consideration, and almost by accident, and have been thus found less prepared than such appointments required; and the end of the voyage may *thus have drawn near before even the most talented amongst them, by a prolonged sojourn amongst grand scenes of nature, and by frequent attempts to imitate what they saw, had more than begun to acquire a certain technical mastery of their art.* — Alexander von Humboldt[1]

THE famous German scientist-explorer Alexander von Humboldt expressed a passionate desire to have artists with "breadth and vision" travel with expeditions to the remote interiors of the globe and capture their true image with "genuine freshness." Most depictions of the American landscape before the nineteenth century were left to amateurs like the explorer and Franciscan father Louis Hennepin, who first recorded Niagara, and Thomas Davies, a professional soldier who drew for his own amusement (a notable exception to this statement is the artist John Webber, who was appointed Captain James Cook's draftsman on his third and final voyage to the Pacific Ocean in 1776).[2] The early maritime expeditions of the English, French, and Dutch explorers furnished the first visual accounts of America, but they concerned themselves mainly with the configuration of the coastline.

Early on, reportorial impressions of things observed in newly discovered lands became an integral part of the report that most major expeditions were expected to compile.[3] As a general rule these documentary drawings or sketches were executed on the spot in pencil, ink, watercolor, or combinations of these media. Since they were to serve as the visual counterparts of a scientific and factual report, it was necessary to employ a skilled draftsman who could construct charts and plans as well as delineate topography

accurately. Often an official member of the expeditionary party doubled as artist—a fact borne out by Captain George Vancouver in his account entitled *Voyage of Discovery to the North Pacific Ocean:*

> It was with infinite satisfaction that I saw, amongst the officers and young gentlemen of the quarter-deck, some who, with little instruction, would soon be enabled to construct charts, take plans of bays and harbours, draw landscapes, and make faithful portraits of the several headlands, coasts, and countries, which we might discover; thus, by the united efforts of our little community, the whole of our proceedings, and the information we might obtain in the course of the voyage, would be rendered profitable to those who might succeed us in traversing the remote parts of the globe that we were destined to explore, without the assistance of professional persons, as astronomers or draftsmen.[4]

The visual record left us by one of these "young gentlemen," John Sykes, shows that he performed his task with the utmost competency.[5] Sykes's simple topographical drawings of California's coastal areas and other lands sighted along their journeys between 1790 and 1795 were later translated into engravings and published in Vancouver's report of the expedition. A comparison of Sykes's drawings with the engravings, however, reveals that the engraver took considerable artistic license, disregarding the integrity of the original sketches and adding discursive picturesque detail that loses the freshness of the originals and provides an inaccurate description of the country.

Early in the following century William Smyth, a British naval officer and one of the artists of the Beechey expedition,[6] painted California's coast. His wash drawings, far more sophisticated and daring than Sykes's, include familiar eighteenth-century pictorial conventions: small figures posed on an elevated knoll in the foreground and the depiction of the artist himself sketching the picturesque scene beyond.

The artist-explorer was part of a long-standing tradition whose roots can be traced back to the Renaissance, when man's horizons were widened by scientific and geographical discoveries (a tradition that was part of the rich and productive legacy of the classical world). The progress of exploration and the resulting renewal of interest in the temporal world created a growing demand for the topographical map, which had evolved out of a long tradition of mapmaking that originated with primitive man's maps of his own locality.[7] In the course of cartographic development geographical and pictorial descriptive elements were gradually combined. Although there are differences of opinion on whether or not cartography falls within the realm of topography, it seems apparent that mapmaking may be the purest and oldest form of topographical delineation, as J. G. Links suggests in his study of the antecedents of townscape painting and drawing. It might also be suggested that the early woodcut city views that illustrate books such as *The Nuremberg Chronicle,* published in 1493, and the popular *vedute* ("views") of the seventeenth and eighteenth centuries were outgrowths of the topographical map.[8]

As the demand for portraits of specific places increased during the fifteenth and sixteenth centuries, the popular bird's-eye view was employed for both maps and prints of city views. At this early period it is generally difficult to differentiate between maps and simple bird's-eye views. These early maps indicate the important role that the topographical draftsman played in the development of cartography.

During the eighteenth century topographical-view painting became diffused throughout the world, owing to the increased demand by travelers and connoisseurs for portraits of antiquarian and topographical interest.[9] Artists were commissioned to furnish drawings for prints and for the many scenic books then in vogue—books that mostly illustrated places admired on the Grand Tour or those known by reputation. The English collector became the principal patron of the view painter, demanding not only scenes of famous and picturesque places made memorable through his travels but also depictions of his own picturesque scenery.

Despite the growing popularity of topographical drawings and engravings from the late eighteenth century onward, this form of landscape art was still considered inferior to other branches of art. John Ruskin's uncompromising attitude, for example, was that the role of the topographer was analogous to that of the modern-day camera.[10] The reportorial nature of topography would concern artists until late in the second half of the nineteenth century, when the camera supplanted the artist as the recorder of fact. Until then the artist-reporter played a vital role in mapping the face of the land—especially in America.

America's insatiable curiosity about its own geography and natural history resulted in a zest for exploration into the vast unknown reaches of its country—the American West. This exploration was to provide a wellspring of new data, experiences, and perceptions for both European and American artist-explorers and scientists. Their approach to the various subjects was constantly molded by the philosophical concepts of the period. Although the artist-explorer who accompanied the official government expeditions had a bent for science, as his hyphenated title suggests, in most instances he saw the vast and spectacular scenery of the West through the eyes of a romantic. Consequently, what he viewed and recorded was somewhat colored by that vision and was inclined to be more pseudoscientific than factual.

Although the trans-Appalachian area of America had been ardently explored and recorded by artist-naturalists, the immense virgin wilderness west of the Mississippi remained inaccessible to men of science until one of them, Thomas Jefferson, made the Louisiana Territory a part of the United States in 1803.[11] Even before the formal transactions had taken place, the astute and foresighted Jefferson had secured appropriations from Congress to send a group of

American explorers in search of a transcontinental waterway. This expedition, led by Meriwether Lewis and William Clark, "demonstrated to the world at large the great width of western North America and its potential riches in . . . natural resources" and set a pattern and scientific tone for future explorations into the West.[12] Although it would be customary at a later date for government exploratory expeditions to require the services of an artist, the only visual recordings of this journey were the crude pencilings along the margins of the leaders' field notebooks.[13] The first five exploratory ventures into the Trans-Mississippi West undertaken during Jefferson's administration also failed to include a trained specialist in the sciences. Thus leaders like Captain Meriwether Lewis and Lieutenant Zebulon Pike were forced to perform the duties of astronomer, surveyor, commanding officer, guide, scribe, and naturalist. It was not until Major Stephen H. Long's expedition to the Rockies in 1820 that a trained specialist was included as a member of the official corps; this was also the first time that the heart of the western interior had been graphically recorded.[14]

Even though most expeditions into the West were under the aegis of the army or the navy, few were solely military in nature. Even when the chief objective was military, other aspects of investigation were pursued that demanded the skills of a scientific or reconnaissance force. Frequently the multiplicity of the expeditionary's role served as an advantage to the government: "Under the guise of a scientific expedition, a topographical survey could serve a series of political ends. At the same time, under the camouflage of military appropriations, internal improvements and various scientific subsidies could be attached."[15] Although each expedition had its specific orders, the chief objective of all of them "was to dramatize the West as the American destiny and to provide a vast range of scientific and economic information about the West that would . . . encourage overland emigration."[16]

Undoubtedly the key agent for disseminating information about the West was the official government report published after each expedition. These reports assiduously charted and cataloged all scientific data uncovered during the exploration, which unquestionably appealed to the Linnean curiosities of men like Humboldt, Benja-

min Silliman, Charles Willson Peale, and others with a propensity for science. At times this information had a far-reaching effect on the public; one example was Pike and Long's erroneous assessment of the plains as the "Great American Desert."[17]

The reports were often illustrated with various kinds of topographical charts and maps, painstakingly meticulous drawings of botanical and zoological specimens, carefully described and classified archaeological and ethnological information, and, of course, novel but simple and straightforward reportorial interpretations of the landscape, at times embellished with miniscule picturesque details to make the view more palatable. Most of the illustrations in the reports were based on original drawings by the artist-explorers. Some exaggerated and romanticized the landscape imagery to emphasize the sublime aspects of the grand and exotic scenery. Others constructed artful panoramas that were not only invaluable scientific documents but aesthetically pleasing landscape drawings as well. These trained topographers and geologists were to play a significant role in changing the face of science for future generations.

Many of the artist-explorers drawn to the West by the adventure of the unknown were less than competent craftsmen. A possible exception was Seth Eastman, whose professionalism was unique in the realm of topographical art (plate 7). Eastman, a graduate of West Point, studied drawing at the academy under artist-instructor Robert W. Weir and later served as his assistant from 1834 to 1840.[18] As a graduate military engineer he was trained in the technical skills of topographical survey work and was familiar with the scientific instruments and mathematical charts employed for measuring and recording scientific data.

As Robert Taft has pointed out in *Artists and Illustrators of the Old West*,[19] the problem of making a competent judgment about the artistic merits or documentary value of these pictorial records is further complicated in that many of the original drawings are preserved only as reproductions. Without the artists' drawings, it is impossible to determine faithfulness of the copies to the original works, since the reproductions were not done by the artists but by commercial craftsmen. In addition, the printing companies contracted by the government set patterns and color limitations that undoubtedly af-

fected the individuality of the original designs. To judge from the originals, most of the artists' designs seem to have been transformed in some way and embellished with discursive picturesque detail during their transfer to metal, wood, or stone. In all probability, engravers or lithographers invested these conventional scenes with a certain drama and grandeur to make them more exciting to the viewer. It should be kept in mind that it was the reproduction rather than the original sketch that gave the American public its idea of the nature of the country beyond the fringes of civilization.

In contrast to a professional artist like Moran, who "did not wish to realize the scene literally but to preserve and to convey its true impression,"[20] the artist-explorers were primarily concerned with providing a factual record of the western scenery. This is not to say that they totally disregarded the pictorial components of a scene, for many were able to combine successfully the factual and the picturesque to make a compelling statement without sacrificing the documentary value of their reportorial interpretations. Thus these artist-explorers should not be thought of as topographers in the strict sense of the word, though the landform maps, cross sections, and geographical charts they created belong to the realm of science and represent another phase of the artist-explorer's activity in the exploration of the West.

In a sense, the artist-explorer was an extension of a tradition that began in America at the turn of the nineteenth century. Like his eastern counterpart, he placed a greater emphasis on subject matter than on formalistic concerns, which may explain why his works are valued more for their historical significance than for their artistic merit. For the most part the artists employed by the government were fledglings with little or no formal training, willing to undergo the hardships and risks of travel into unknown lands at this early period. The rough conditions and meagerness of monetary compensation explain in part the government's failure to attract artists of merit for expeditionary work. It must also be remembered that, at the time of the government's greatest activity in examining the West, professional artists on the East Coast were enjoying a ready market for their work that made them reluctant to leave. Several independents did explore and sketch the western frontier, however; their pictures of America's scenery and native peoples reflect their European training and the romantic ideas of the time (see "Alfred Jacob Miller" below).

SAMUEL SEYMOUR: WEST WITH MAJOR STEPHEN H. LONG

On the 30th [of June] we left the encampment at our accustomed early hour, and at eight o'clock were cheered by a distant view of the Rocky Mountains. For some time we were unable to decide whether what we saw were mountains, or banks of cumulous clouds skirting the horizon, and glittering in the reflected rays of the sun. It was only by watching the bright parts, and observing that their form and position remained unaltered, that we were able to satisfy ourselves they were indeed mountains. —Edwin James[21]

At the encampment site on the bank of Bijeaus [Bijou] Creek, Samuel Seymour, the artist assigned to this government expedition, provided the earliest known depiction of the Colorado Rockies, reproduced as the frontispiece for the English edition of Edwin James's *Account of an Expedition from Pittsburgh to the Rocky Mountains . . . in the Years 1819 and '20* (plate 8).[22] Seymour, who was interested in making the view more palatable, included several picturesque motifs for effects. A single trail of buffalo and Indians traversing the plains, along with a bleached thighbone in the foreground, illustrated Long's wish that the region would "forever remain" the haunt of nomad and beast. The concept of vast, uninhabitable, and uncultivable tracts of land—the "Great American Desert"—was further strengthened by ensuing writers and cartographers who subscribed to Long's thesis.[23]

20

PLATE 8

Samuel Seymour, *Distant View of the Rocky Mountains*, 1820, Hand-colored aquatint, 4½″ × 7¼″.
Courtesy Huntington Library, San Marino, Calif.

Nearly three centuries had passed since artist-explorer John White and Jacques Le Moyne sketched the strange and alien New World. The Long expedition, however, was not the first to set foot in what is now Colorado; extensive tracks across the Rockies had been left by both early Spanish explorers and fur trappers, who penetrated this territory in the seventeenth and eighteenth centuries. None of these groups of men, however, took along an artist to record the splendors of America's western interior.[24] Major Stephen H. Long's party was not even the first official government expedition to traverse Colorado; Lieutenant Zebulon Pike and his force of twenty-three men had explored the Rockies as far north as the headwaters of the South Platte and as far south as the Sangre de Cristo range in 1806–1807 while reconnoitering the southwestern boundary of the Louisiana Territory.[25]

In the spring of 1819, Long's expeditionary force left Saint Louis on what was to become his so-called Yellowstone expedition "to establish military posts on the upper Missouri for the purposes of protecting the growing fur-trade, controlling the Indian tribes, and lessening the influence which British trading companies were believed to exert upon them."[26] In spite of the expedition's failure to realize its original objectives and Long's misconception of the plains area as land unsuitable for settlement, this government expeditionary force was the first to include trained scientists and artists who not only surveyed the vast southwestern plains and mountainous region with its complex river system but systematically recorded and illustrated the mass of scientific information they gathered along the way.

Most of Long's men were representative of a school of naturalists centered in Philadelphia, then the scientific capital of the country. There they could have made contact with leading scientific minds and visited institutions like the Academy of Natural Sciences, the American Philosophical Society, and the Peale Museum. Both Seymour and Titian Ramsay Peale, who was the artist-naturalist for the expedition, received their professional training there. Peale, the youngest son of the famous artist and naturalist Charles Willson Peale, had grown up among the great minds who frequented his father's museum. Of all Peale's children Titian shared most thoroughly his father's dedicated interest in the natural sciences, while showing, like the rest of the family, a youthful propensity for drawing and painting. Elected to the famed Academy of Natural Sciences at the age of eighteen,[27] he was appointed to serve as assistant naturalist to Thomas Say, the zoologist for the expedition, and was to be responsible for preserving and illustrating the specimens collected along the route.[28]

The actual appointment of Samuel Seymour to fill the role of painter for the expedition came just before the group's departure in March, 1819. According to Long's orders issued on March 31, the artist was to "furnish sketches of landscapes" and "paint . . . portraits . . . of distinguished Indians."[29] Despite the paucity of information on Seymour's appointment, there is documentation to support Long's interest in providing additional services for the exploration record. On March 2, Long requisitioned from Beck and Stewart's emporium in Philadelphia a wide selection of art supplies —assorted watercolors, sable "pencils," india ink, and sheets of royal drawing paper.[30]

For artists of limited experience and reputation appointment to a government expedition carried a certain distinction and glamor with possible rewards and fame, in spite of the risks involved and low pay ($1.70 a day).[31] Titian Peale, interested in the sciences and scientific illustration, was probably excited by the prospect of discovering new species, all specimens of which were to be deposited in the Peale Museum of Natural History.[32] For Samuel Seymour, who was nearly thirty-six and whose professional experience had been limited to engraving works of art, this was a golden opportunity to establish himself as a landscape painter.[33]

Since Seymour was the first artist to penetrate America's western interior and make sketches on the Upper Missouri and the plains and Rockies, as well as on the Red River of the North, it would seem that he should have a more prominent place in pictorial western art, as historian John Francis McDermott suggests. Little evidence is available, however, to reconstruct a biography of the artist beyond his two journeys with Long's western expeditions.[34] In his biography of Seymour, William Dunlap states that he was a "native of England" and a sketching companion of Thomas Birch.[35] A thorough search of various records, however, fails to reveal a documented date and place of birth. According to various biographical sources, Seymour was a practicing engraver of portraits in Philadelphia as early as 1796. Yet the one concrete piece of evidence, the *City of Philadelphia Census of 1810*, records the artist's age as between sixteen and twenty-six, indicating that Seymour probably arrived in America shortly before 1800, when he became an apprentice in engraving under the tutelage of the enamel painter and engraver William Birch.[36]

That Seymour was in Philadelphia before his departure with Long is confirmed by listings in city directories and by his many topographical prints that were published during those years. Through his friendship with the Birches this fledgling artist associated with leading professional artists like Thomas Sully, who was one of his companions on his sketching tours with Birch.[37] Apart from using the facilities of the Pennsylvania Academy, Seymour probably copied engravings, the usual drawing instruction for an untutored artist. Judging from his simple but factual views of Colorado's landforms, we can assume that he also referred to topographical scenic prints after the drawings of foreign artists who had recorded exotic places around the world. Inasmuch as the artists Thomas Doughty and Thomas Birch had exhibited landscapes after the colored aquatint plates of the English topographer William Daniell in *A Picturesque Voyage to India* . . . (London, 1810), it is likely that Seymour used the same set of prints as a learning device, since this book was available in Philadelphia.[38]

Like the younger Daniell, in his work Seymour shows a classical restraint and use of picturesque artifices, as well as a conventional approach to subject matter. It can be said to be close to the manner of English topographical art of the eighteenth and early nineteenth centuries. His drawings exhibit the familiar faint pencil outline visible through the restrained use of watercolor. Local color is applied in pale washes with some indication of light and shadow, but there is no attempt to convey painterly effects or aerial perspective. A simple horizontal format is employed, and, if recession is indicated, it is achieved by a progressive series of objects placed on planes. The familiar loop design for rendering foliage is seen, as well as the small picturesque figures that are placed in the foreground to enliven the drawing. They represent the members of Long's expedition engaged in various activities. Seymour's work seems to conform to a prescribed formula shared by most other topographical artists of that time; yet, despite their lack of originality, these drawings do reveal Seymour's own distinctive personality.

Sometime in early June, 1820, after the necessary arrangements had been made for the exploring party's departure from their winter encampment, near Council Bluffs, Iowa, Long's men proceeded westward from the Missouri country across the plains along the Platte River and up its southern fork. At this time the party consisted of scientists, two artists, two French trappers serving as guides and interpreters, attendants, and a detachment from the rifle regiment under the command of Major S. H. Long, United States topographical engineer, and his assistant, topographer W. H. Swift. The men had been outfitted with horses and mules, saddles and other rude equipage, provisions of clothing and food, instruments for topographical purposes, and rifles or muskets for the hunters, interpreters, attendants, and soldiers. James's report, however, fails to list the invaluable reference sources carried on the expedition, such as Humboldt's *Travels*, Lewis and Clark's *Journals*, Georges Cuvier's four volumes on animal species, John Melish's *Map of the United States*, and William Darby's *Map of Louisiana*.[39] The men probably referred to these sources frequently as they tracked over unfamiliar ground—even Peale, a skilled draftsman and naturalist, must have consulted a number of these scientific publications; but, as Jessie Poesch has pointed out, Peale probably was well enough informed to be able to know "what to look for and what to collect. . . . His associations with other scientific men had taught him to be accurate in making measurements and in immediately recording his observations.[40]

For Seymour there was no precedent for his activity in the Rockies. Unlike his fellow artist, he was totally unprepared to perform technical renderings of strange geological formations. Surprisingly, his pictorial recordings of the bizarre rock outcroppings observed at the base of the Rockies near the chasm of the headwaters of the Platte are accurate enough to enable one to pinpoint their specific area.[41]

Before obtaining his first view of the Rockies, Seymour had been sketching the neighboring Indian tribes of the Missouri country. In his views of Indian ceremonies and gatherings the landscape is merely a setting for the action, yet there is a hint of the compositional formula that Seymour was to employ in most of his simple drawings. For example, *Pawnee Indian Council* is symmetrically composed with two large trees serving as lateral enframements and a screen for the viewer.[42] Within the simple horizontal format Seymour has arranged the large number of figures seated or standing in a circular fashion. The drawing of the figures and scenery is rather crude. After constant sketching in the field, however, Seymour's handling of scenic views became more masterful, even though he never approximated the skill of Karl Bodmer or Alfred Jacob Miller or mastered the rules of anatomy and perspective.

In describing the company's march across the monotonous Great Plains, the expedition's botanist and geologist, Edwin James, spoke mainly of extensive tracts of desert land destitute of much vegetation or animal life. Apparently, Peale and Seymour were uninspired by the "dreary" country, for we have no record of their sketching until the group reached Colorado. On July 3, a few miles southwest of the present-day city of Greeley, Colorado, Samuel Seymour delineated his next work, *View of the Rocky Mountains on the Platte 50 miles from their Base*, which is preserved as a reproduction in the American edition of James's report.[43] Again the artist employed the strip horizontal format with the front range as a rampart in the distance. Long's Peak (on the viewer's extreme right) can be correctly identified as being viewed from south of Longmont, on the way to Denver, since it lacks its familiar notched shape. It is noteworthy to point out that this very scene was adopted by Titian Peale for an oil painting of the same subject executed in the 1870s[44] (plate 9). In it we see that, except for the prominent group of antelope in the foreground—lifted from one of Peale's watercolors—and the large

cactus plant on the extreme right, Peale has carefully followed Seymour's composition, thereby suggesting that the original drawing, now lost, may have been in Titian's possession.[45]

On the fifth the men left their encampment near Denver, crossed Vermilion Creek (Cherry Creek), and continued up the Platte to the western boundary of the Great Plains, where they first observed at a distance a spectacular range of "naked and almost perpendicular rocks" rising abruptly to a height of 150 to 200 feet. Seymour carefully documented this startling mass of red sandstone, resembling a "vast wall," which ran parallel to the base of the Rockies. At the foot of the first range of mountains the group set up camp "immediately in front of the chasm, through which the Platte issues from the mountain"; this "commanding eminence" was also recorded by the artist.[46] During the few days that the party camped in this sheltered valley south of Platte Canyon, Seymour hastily recorded his impressions of the colossal and fantastically shaped rocks, which, according to Long and his men, resembled ruins of some ancient civilization, standing "like pyramids and obelisks amid rolling mounds and hillocks."[47] The artist's views of the strange formations scattered over the area between the hogbacks and the foothills of the Rockies were the first to introduce Roxborough Park to the annals of recorded history.

In the artist's view of the headwaters of the Platte we have an example of a preserved drawing that has been illustrated in the report (plate 10), thus affording the opportunity to compare the original with the engraver's translation.[48] It is apparent here that the engraver has freely tightened up the sketchily composed pictorial elements in Seymour's drawing to convey an accurate descriptive understanding of the subject. In his attempt to present a straightforward view of the precipitous walls of the chasm, the printer has eliminated the small, picturesque Indian and hunter from the reproduction, thus directing the viewer's attention to the rugged and abrupt features of the mountainous country that the small exploring party had unsuccessfully attempted to penetrate.[49]

The drawing was obviously a favorite of the artist's, for he later presented it to his friend Titian Peale.[50] Thomas Doughty made a copy and an engraving after Seymour's drawing for use as an accom-

PLATE 9

Titian R. Peale, *Rocky Mountains . . . from a Sketch by S . . .*, n.d., Oil, 7¼″ × 13″.
Courtesy Joslyn Art Museum, Omaha, Nebr.

PLATE 10

Samuel Seymour, *View of the Chasm through which the Platte Issues from the Rocky Mountains*, 1820, Watercolor, 5″ × 8″.
Courtesy Collection of Mr. Paul Mellon, Upperville, Va.

panying illustration for "Letters from the West" in the March, 1822, issue of the *Port Folio and New York Monthly Magazine*, which seems to indicate that the American public was equally fascinated with the scene as a curiosity (plate 11).[51] Although Doughty's interpretation is far more dramatic and romantic than Seymour's, it retains the drawing's truthful rendering of topographical features.

Seymour's two existing watercolors of the sandstone district south of Platte Canyon attest to his topographical accuracy. In one drawing, *View near the base of the Rocky Mountains* (plate 12), the artist has added small figures to emphasize the immensity of the rocklike projections, the focal point of his composition. Seymour's other drawing, a *View parallel to the base of the Mountains at the head of the Platte*, shows a larger and more open view of the entire valley without the figural embellishments of the former.[52] It approximates the view captured by William H. Jackson in his photographs of the area in 1870.[53]

During July, as the small exploring party made its way south from the headwaters of the Platte to the headwaters of the Arkansas, Seymour managed to capture other views of spectacular scenery. In close proximity to their camp of July 8 and 9, the group observed some "insulated hills with perpendicular sides and level summits," which the artist hastily sketched.[54] One of those sketches, *Hills of the [Floetz] Trap Formation*, is among his most successful compositions.[55]

As the expeditionary force crossed "a small ridge dividing the waters of the Platte from those of the Arkansa[s]" on their way to the "high peak" (Pikes Peak)[56] the men observed a "singular" mass of sandstone, two to four hundred feet high, bearing a striking resemblance to an architectural monument in ruins.[57] Allowing his imagination a free rein, Seymour made a drawing suggesting the remaining massive walls, pillars, and arches of a ruined edifice. Even in this topographical work the artist shows an observant eye for the picturesque and an interest in antiquarian objects. Although there is an air of fantasy and artificiality about this view, Seymour's drawing nevertheless closely resembles the actual subject, known today as Elephant Rock.[58]

After traveling for a considerable distance, the men suddenly realized that they had passed the base of the "high peak" (Pikes Peak). On the following day they retraced their steps and camped "a short distance south of the site of Colorado Springs, where [Monument] stream flows into Fountain Creek."[59] There the men gained their first full view of Pike's "high peak." In describing that distant view, James noted: "At about one o'clock P.M. a dense black cloud was seen to collect in the south-west; and advancing towards the peak, it remained nearly stationary over that part of the mountains, pouring down torrents of rain."[60] Seymour's previously unknown drawing of a *View of James Peak in the Rain* (color plate 2), recently discovered,[61] serves as an illustration for this account. Why this drawing remained unpublished is a mystery, since it follows the report to the letter and is one of Seymour's most effective pictorial records.

One feature of the painting is typical of Seymour's work: the small rifleman with his back to the viewer, who appears in other drawings by the artist. The wavy line indicating grass and the innumerable small loops representing foliage are also characteristic of Seymour's drawing (the latter is a trait observed in English art of the eighteenth and early nineteenth centuries, including works by the English topographer Paul Sandby).[62] Unlike his other drawings, *James Peak* has been worked over in pen, making the viewer more aware of the many picturesque details that contrast sharply with the plain wash of the distant mountain range, its high, snowcapped peak outlined by stippling with a pen. This unusual technique for defining pictorial elements may represent a reversion to his former profession.[63]

Seymour's delineation of *James Peak [Pikes Peak]* is the first eyewitness pictorial record of a Colorado landmark that was to attract artist and traveler alike throughout the nineteenth century. Since James and his small band of men were the first to ascend the rugged and precipitous peak to its summit, Long named the landmark for him.[64] The appellation held until Frémont passed through the area in 1843 and discovered that the traders were calling the mountain after the explorer Pike; he thus adopted the name it bears today.[65]

From the time that Seymour visited the headwaters of the Arkansas (the mouth of the Royal Gorge) to his journey eastward along

PLATE 12

Samuel Seymour, *View near the base of the Rocky Mountains*, 1820, Watercolor, 5″ × 8″.
Courtesy Beinecke Rare Book and Manuscript Library, W. R. Coe Collection, Yale University, New Haven, Conn.

that river, he seems to have produced only three other drawings—a view of a Kiowa encampment, a portrait of three Indian chiefs (both extant as reproductions), and a *View on the Arkansa[s] near the Rocky Mountains,* a preserved drawing.[66] In making any judgments on Seymour's extant work, it is necessary to follow James's descriptive narrative closely, since these drawings were intended as accurate topographical records of events and scenes observed by the group during their journey west. In the past historians have referred to James's written account only to chart the movements of this expeditionary force with accuracy and not to use it as a basis on which to judge the artwork. In doing so, they may have missed the point of the pictorial record. As Taft has remarked, to judge an eyewitness pictorial record for its accuracy, it is necessary to establish some standard of reference.[67] In Seymour's drawings James's report must serve as this standard. It should be apparent by now that there is a close—almost exact—parallel between the two forms of description, which obviously infers some degree of competency by the artist. In addition, Seymour has given his small-scale and rather uniform drawings a certain charm.[68] His delicate watercolors reflect the earlier English topographical treatment of landscape and can be considered a continuation of a tradition launched in America at the turn of the century by the migrant artist.

Another common misconception is that Seymour worked in oil. Previous writers have been misled by Prince Maximilian's reference to the artist's "oil paintings of Indian villages and scenery" on display at the Peale Museum in Philadelphia at the time of his visit there on July 23, 1832.[69] What Maximilian—and perhaps his artist, Bodmer—saw were Charles Willson Peale's copies in oil after Seymour's drawings *Arkansas Village, Kanza Lodge,* and *Falls of the Ohio,* added to the museum's collection on February 16, 1822.[70] From the available evidence it appears that Seymour worked only in watercolor. Whether or not these finished drawings were prepared from preliminary field sketches is unknown, since none of the sketches has been found.[71]

KARL BODMER: THE ROCKIES OF THE UPPER MISSOURI

The vast tracts of the interior of North-western America are, in general, but little known, and the government of the United States may be justly reproached for not having done more to explore them. . . . Even Major Long's expeditions are but poorly furnished with respect to natural history, for a faithful and vivid picture of those countries, and their original inhabitants, can never be placed before the eye without the aid of a fine portfolio of plates by the hand of a skillful artist. —Prince Alexander Philip Maximilian zu Wied[72]

In the decade after Long's expedition many artists—both independent and government-employed—expanded America's pictorial knowledge to include many aspects of the frontier world. The Rockies, however, were not among them. Too formidable and inaccessible for all but the most intrepid mountain men, the Rockies submitted to initial recordings by Seymour and Peale, then withdrew once again into majestic solitude beyond the reach of the painter. It was not until 1833 that Prussian naturalist-explorer Prince Alexander Philip Maximilian zu Wied, recognizing the importance of a pictorial record of the range, added a painter to his expeditionary force: Karl Bodmer, a Swiss watercolorist and the most able of the early artist-explorers who viewed the Rockies. Unfortunately, Bodmer's first encounter with them was to be brief and tantalizing.

Born near Zurich, Switzerland, Bodmer came under the tutelage of his uncle, the noted Swiss engraver Johann Jacob Meier, at an early age. His training included sketching tours of the Rhine Valley and the Alps. When he was twenty-three, his precision as a draftsman and skill as a watercolorist attracted the notice of Prince Maximilian. In 1832, Bodmer became official artist on the prince's forthcoming expedition to the West,[73] an expedition which, owing to the pair's combined skills, remains one of the most thoroughly recounted adventures in the history of western exploration.

Bodmer and his patron arrived in Boston on Independence Day, 1832. They visited New York and Philadelphia and saw copies of Seymour's western watercolors in Peale's Museum, in Philadelphia. In March of the following year they were accorded a warm welcome to Saint Louis by General William Clark and given the opportunity to meet the artist Peter Rindisbacher and to study some of George Catlin's works owned by his nephew, Major Benjamin O'Fallon.[74]

While he was in Saint Louis, Maximilian discussed his desire to visit the Rocky Mountains. His plan was to join a cross-country caravan of the Rocky Mountain Fur Company and attend the annual rendezvous of traders and trappers on the Upper Green River. When he learned that those caravans avoided contact with Indians, Maximilian, deeply interested in scientific research and bent on capturing as many Indian likenesses as possible, elected instead to journey up the Missouri River and visit the American Fur Company posts.[75]

Long before he encountered the Rockies, the Prussian naturalist was intrigued by them. Although scheduled to spend the winter of 1833–34 within their boundaries,[76] he traveled no farther west than the vicinity of Fort McKenzie, for reasons to be discussed below. It was there that the party had a singular view of the Rocky Mountains. "On our right hand," Maximilian later recounted, was

> a fine prospect into the valley of the Teton River, which as a stripe of verdure, made an agreeable break in the yellow, scorched prairie. In the valley we saw three or four Indian tents under high poplar trees. . . . Before us, a little to the left, in a south-western direction, we saw, at some distance, the first chain of the Rocky Mountains.[77]

Bodmer's watercolor of this scene, *A View of the Rocky Mountains* (color plate 3), pictured the Highwood Mountains that rise south of present-day Fort Benton, Montana.[78] Precise and jewel-like in its execution, the painting represented an advance beyond the simple compositions of his predecessor Seymour, particularly in its reflection of his ability to express clarity of form, illusion of space, and precise color tonalities. Although, like Seymour, Bodmer utilized standard topographical techniques, his technical ability was far more developed. A comparison of Bodmer's watercolor with Seymour's *Distant View of the Rocky Mountains* (see plate 8), painted a dozen

years earlier, reveals only superficial similarities. In both works bleached bones in the foreground draw the viewer's eye into the landscape. Groups of Indians emphasize the vast scale of each landscape. Beyond these obvious similarities, however, the two artists' works are utterly different. Bodmer gave true density to his forms, attempting to model with paint, using light and shade to achieve effects far more dimensional than Seymour's linear descriptions.

It was fortunate that Bodmer was able to make this record, for his view of the Highwood Mountains was the first and only view of the Rockies enjoyed by the members of this expedition. A party of six hundred Assiniboins and Crees had attacked a Blackfoot camp at Fort McKenzie a few days before, and Maximilian knew that they "were our enemies, to whom our scalps would doubtless have been a very welcome acquisition."[79] Thus the journey was brought to a premature end, and the party escaped from the hostile region in a mackinaw boat.

Bodmer and Maximilian wintered at Fort Clark and started their homeward trek in April, 1834. Once on home ground in Paris, France, Bodmer began to fulfill his obligation to provide finished engraved illustrations for Maximilian's published journals, a task that was carried out over the next five years. The first edition of Maximilian's account, published in German in 1839–1841 under the title *Reise in das Innere Nord-America in den Jahren 1832 bis 1834* included eighty-one aquatints, which appeared later in French and English editions.

Bodmer grew to consider France his home, eventually becoming a French citizen. He married there and, in 1849, moved from Paris to Barbizon, where he spent the rest of his life in the company of other plein-air artists.

It was logical that Bodmer would find his true place in the forests of Fontainebleau. In fact, so consumed was Bodmer with his career as a landscape painter that, when approached by Jean François Millet to collaborate on a series of Indian paintings in 1850, he insisted that Millet provide the figures while he supplied the landscape background.[80] Although he worked primarily as an illustrator in his later years, Bodmer remained strongly devoted to the landscape discipline. He died in Barbizon in 1893.

ALFRED JACOB MILLER: TO "THE MOUNTAINS OF THE WIND"

To the west, rose the Wind river mountains, with their bleached and snowy summits towering into the clouds. These stretched far to the north-northwest, until they melted away into what appeared to be faint clouds, but which the experienced eyes of the veteran hunters of the party recog- *nised [sic] for the rugged mountains of the Yellowstone; at the feet of which, extended the wild Crow country: a perilous, though profitable region for the trapper.* —Washington Irving[81]

The American people were fascinated by the newly acquired western territories, but their visions and dreams of this vast dominion had been nurtured almost entirely by the printed word. Visual images were in demand. Alfred Jacob Miller was one of the first artist-explorers to meet this need. His sketches, gathered while he was on the trail, provided a rich heritage for his own and future generations.

Miller, born in Baltimore in 1810, early showed an artistic bent. He recorded that his schoolmaster, John D. Craig, made determined efforts to dissuade him from his youthful enthusiasm for art: "[I was forced] to destroy my drawings & caricatures that I scribbled on paper,—these without looking at he would roll up & put in the stove,—scold and dismiss me with a threat,—then I would hear a commentary from the boys . . . 'damn shame—no taste for art.'"[82]

Despite this obstacle, Miller's talents developed. At twenty-one he is thought to have studied portraiture under Thomas Sully; the following year he was sent by friends and family to Europe to improve his skills as a painter.[83] Miller enjoyed the Grand Tour, beginning in Paris and proceeding on to Lyons, Rome, and Florence, before returning home two years later. In Paris, according to Miller's own account, he was admitted as a student to the École des Beaux-Arts, where he found life drawing especially rewarding: "No doubt this drawing from nature improved me more than anything else,—for nature being reality, says to you 'thus it must be.'"[84]

Miller also profited from studying the old masters in the Louvre. Extant sketchbooks retained by the Maryland Historical Society and Miller's descendants give evidence of his preoccupation with copying scenes from the Old Testament by Rembrandt, landscapes by Jacob Ruysdael, and formal portraits by Sir Joshua Reynolds and Sir Peter Lely. It is apparent from his later works that he also gleaned much from his contemporaries, Eugène Delacroix and Turner.[85] Miller's debt to Delacroix is especially apparent in his treatment of horses; he also shared with his French contemporary a profound romantic fondness for faraway places. To Turner he owed much of his treatment of color and atmospheric perspective: "Turner, was lavish in his misty effects . . . but was reticent, and would tell no body [sic] how his marvelous mists were effected."[86]

In 1834, Miller continued his studies in Rome. He was admitted to the English Life School and enjoyed drawing from live models, who displayed, to his delight, a variation "in form from the Apollo to the Hercules."[87] His visits to artists' studios, however, especially that of the historical painter Horace Vernet, were the high points of Miller's instruction and experience. As he recounted in his "Notebook":

> To see him at work was the very thing I wanted & replete with instruction,—he was engaged in finishing a horse (the full size of life). I noticed that he used brushes from an inch to 1½ inches in breadth,— the paint was slapped on "Ad libitum" every touch telling in a masterly manner & producing powerful effects—a valuable lesson to me.[88]

When Miller returned to America in the mid-1830s, he established himself as a portrait painter in his native city Baltimore—but not for long. By the autumn of 1836 accumulated family troubles combined with what a fellow Baltimore artist termed a "restive disposition," precipitated his move to New Orleans to embark on a new career as a portrait painter.

The following spring Miller chanced to entertain in his studio a gentleman who was to change the course of his life. At that time Miller was working on a large view of Baltimore and experimenting with Turnersque coloristic effects and atmospheric perspective. Thus absorbed, Miller hardly noticed a tall Scotsman, Captain William Drummond Stewart, who wandered into the studio and admired the young artist's paintings. Miller later explained:

> . . . The size of the picture was about 5 ft. by 3½ ft, and the original sketch was drawn from what was then . . . the eastern confines of the City of Baltimore;—at about 5 o'clock, the sun would be (as it were) behind the city, throwing a mysterious haze over every object producing a truly charming effect. Now, the thing for me to do was to reach this glorious brilliant appearance. After getting in the Sky, I then commenced the detail of the buildings,—churches, Town (clock?) Monument, Cathedral, & ect [sic]—these "I kept down" to use a professional phrase, and approached the tint as nearly as I could, but I found after finishing my foreground that a great heaviness hung ore [sic] the City, with too much detail in the buildings, considering that they were over two miles distant. In going out on the hill several times, I saw that there was no detail that a general mist rested over everything & gave the imagination full swing. Now I had read of "dry scumbling" but had never tried it practically, & here was the subject to try it on, so mixing up on my palette portions of white, blue, vermilion & black until I had achieved what I conceived ought to be the color,—I then took a large brush & with this mixture covered all the buildings in the distance;—the effect was like magic,—it *destroyed* the detail, massed all of a general tint, & made it appear as if you were looking through a hazy atmosphere,—no amount of labour with solid colors would have produced this.[89]

Stewart was impressed, and, when he returned a few days later, he presented Miller with an important invitation. He told him that

> he was making preparation for another journey to the Rocky Mountains,—(he had already made 2 or 3) and wished to have a competent artist to sketch the remarkable scenery & incidents of the journey,—now (he said) I am very well satisfied with your work. I should like you to accompany me.[90]

Miller soon began an odyssey destined to make him the first artist to penetrate deep into the Rockies.

The itinerary of Miller's western travels has been set down in many accounts.[91] Miller and Stewart journeyed overland with American Fur Company men who were on their way to the Wind River Mountains in the Oregon country for the eleventh annual rendez-

vous of trappers and traders. As they traversed the prairies along what would later be known as the Oregon Trail, Miller's deft pen and brush recorded landmarks such as Independence Rock and Devil's Gate, soon to become beacons in westward migration.

Unlike Seymour and Bodmer, Miller had little interest in the reportorial approach. He found his reward in rendering romantic scenes that became souvenirs of the journey for his patron. Neither artist nor client was much concerned with the documentation of fact; their interest lay rather in preserving the spirit of far-western life and its spectacular wild scenery.

Miller's romantic proclivities are seen as dramatically in his landscapes as in his human studies. Although he focused on the trappers and Indians who passed before him that summer, it was apparent that he often employed the human element simply because it lent a historic air to his scenes. The untrammeled wilderness and expansive vistas he saw in the West convinced him that the subject as well as the painter made the picture, and here were magnificent landscape subjects that had never before been recorded. The artist described the exhilaration of capturing these fresh vistas by comparing scenic wonders of the Old World with those of the New:

> The tourist who journeys to Europe in search of a new sensation, must by this time find that his vocation is nearly gone. Italy and its wonders have been described so often that they begin to pale. Egypt, the River Nile, Cairo, and the pyramids have been "done" to death. Greece and her antiquities are as familiar as household words. What will the enterprising traveller do under these untoward circumstances? Well, here is a new field for him. These mountain Lakes have been waiting for him thousands of years, and could afford to wait thousands of years longer, for they are now as fresh and beautiful as if just from the hands of the Creator.[92]

Miller's own remembrance of the Wind River country was reinforced by the drawings and watercolors he brought back with him. Unlike later Hudson River School artists, who typically made their plein-air studies in oil, Miller apparently initially rendered most scenes in pencil in a pocket notebook; then he embellished the drawings with ink washes and highlights of chinese white. Some of these were further elaborated into watercolor, probably after the artist returned to camp.[93] So successful was his spontaneous response to these scenes that, even when he copied them in watercolor years later, the resulting paintings have the same brilliance and spirit of his on-the-spot depictions.

One opportunity for such comparison is offered by his watercolor *The Wind River Chain* (plate 13) and the oil version of the same subject, *Trappers Saluting the Rocky Mountains* (color plate 4).[94] Compositionally they mirror one another, details altered slightly but major elements essentially the same. The water appears more fluid in the oil, and the scale is also more carefully considered, resulting in the elimination of the imposing *repoussoir* of the dramatic, defoliated tree. The trappers saluting the mountains express a special tribute to man's respect for this wilderness and his natural place in it.

A small oil study of a similar scene, *Indian Encampment—Wind River Country*, may provide additional insight into Miller's fieldwork. Although most scholars assume that the artist sketched exclusively in pen and ink and watercolor,[95] no documented evidence exists that he did not also make oil studies in the field, as Albert Bierstadt and others are known to have done in later years. This oil, which could easily be a plein-air study of the wild country, explores the full spectrum of the romantic idiom—reflecting the influence of the French Romantics and Turner.

One of Miller's largest and most important finished landscapes, *Stewart's Camp, Wind River Range, Western Wyoming* (plate 14),[96] captures the full measure of his romanticism. Preliminary studies for the work were painted far from the Saint Louis fur-trade emporiums and his own Baltimore. After the rendezvous Stewart led his party to the headwaters of the Green River and into the vicinity of the present New Fork Lakes, on the western slopes of the Wind River Mountains. Stewart and his companions, including the illustrious half-blooded hunter Antoine Clemente, are seen here as explorers at the farthest reaches of conquest. The Noble Savage, the heroic landscape, and the aura of nature's timeless simplicity—all are included. Miller later wrote about such scenes:

> The most favorable time to view these Lakes (to an artist especially) was early in the morning or towards sunset;—at these times one side or the other would be thrown into deep purple masses, throwing great

broad shadows, with sharp light glittering on the extreme tops,—while the opposite mountains received its full complement of warm, mellow & subdued light;—thus forming a *chiaro obscuro* [sic] and contrast most essential to the picturesque in color.[97]

Upon his return to New Orleans in the autumn of 1837, Miller began at once to work up some of his field sketches into finished compositions, though he did not begin his large oil of *Stewart's Camp . . .* until many years later.

By the following summer Miller had produced enough paintings to mount an exhibition in Baltimore. One critic praised the showing, saying that Miller, with the benefit of European study and "a matured judgment, . . . has travelled through remote sections of the 'Far West' where he has succeeded in giving views of the Rocky Mountains and other scenery that do him much honor."[98]

A set of eighteen paintings that Miller prepared for Stewart's Murthly Castle was exhibited in the spring of 1839 at New York's Apollo Gallery. Three of the paintings were landscapes depicting scenes in and around the Wind River Mountains. A fourth, *Camp of the Indians at the Rendezvous of the Whites, near the Mountains of the Wind*, elicited a favorable comment from the *New York Weekly Herald:* "The waving blue mountains in the back-ground, and the bustle and animation in the fore-ground, are beautiful. The Alps are nothing to these cold, blue Mountains of the Wind."[99] Soon thereafter the paintings were shipped to Scotland. The artist followed them in the fall of 1840 and remained in the British Isles for the next two years.

Miller spent the winter of 1841 in London. In February he visited with Catlin, who had recently "had the honour of exhibiting his model of Niagara to the Queen." In a letter to his brother Decatur, Miller voiced disapproval of his fellow artist: "There is in truth . . . a great deal of humbug about Mr. George Catlin. He has published a book containing some extraordinary stories and luckily for him there are but few persons who have travelled over the same ground."[100] This meeting must have been especially frustrating for Miller, who, owing to ill health, was unable to accompany Stewart on a subsequent expedition to the Rockies.[101]

Miller returned to Baltimore that spring and settled into a suc-

cessful career as a portrait painter. He also made a lucrative business reproducing images from his western journey throughout his life.[102] That they continued to sell gives further evidence of the enthusiasm for the West felt by so many Americans at this time. In 1858–59, Miller received his largest single commission from his Baltimore patron, William T. Walters, for whom he created two hundred watercolors. Over twenty of these works were landscape studies.

The artist spent the rest of his life in Baltimore, and, despite his continuous production of salable paintings, his style of life was modest.

Miller's love for the West and for painting he passed on to many students who came to his studio for instruction and inspiration. Among them was "Colonel" John R. Johnston, who was later recognized for his landscapes of rural Pennsylvania and Maryland. Frank B. Mayer, who studied in Paris after working with Miller, wrote his mentor from France in 1865: "I have no higher ambition than to place my name near yours as a painter of Indians for I think that your Indian pictures are the best things of the kind yet produced. Bodmer's I would place next tho' they do not embrace so wide a field nor do they sieze [*sic*] so truly the spirit of Indian life."[103] Although Mayer never devoted himself primarily to landscape, he was the only known pupil of Miller's to follow his master's footsteps into the West, where in 1851 he practiced his art among the Sioux of Minnesota Territory.

For a romantic like Miller the colorful and exotic actors of the American frontier generally took precedence over the wild and grand scenery that he usually treated in a decorative fashion to serve as a backdrop for the dramatic content of his pictures. Like several other artists of his day, he was romanticizing, in the illustrative sense of the word, and his work rightfully belongs to the realm of narrative art. Miller's art epitomizes that of the romantic who saw the West through rosy filters and idealized its features to create picturesque scenes.

2

MILITARY ROADS WEST: THE PATHFINDERS

Here [before the Wind River Mountains] a view of the utmost magnificence and grandeur burst upon our eyes. With nothing between us and their feet to lessen the effect of the whole height, a grand bed of snow-capped mountains rose before us, pile upon pile, glowing in the bright light of an August day. Immediately below them lay the lake, between two ridges, covered with dark pines which swept down from the main chain to the spot where we stood. Here, where the lake glittered in the open sunlight, its banks of yellow sand and the light foliage of aspen-groves, contrasted well with the gloomy pines. —John C. Frémont[1]

THIS colorful, literary description was composed by one of the preeminent and most controversial explorers of the nineteenth-century American West—John C. Frémont. Recognized as a national hero in his lifetime, he was nevertheless "a romantic, stormy figure, . . . a man of many moods and differing fortunes and attitudes." Having carved out his destiny while pursuing a military career, Frémont became the most famous member of a small but influential cadre of explorers known as the Corps of Topographical Engineers, a branch of the United States Army. Although this unit

> followed in the shadow of those larger-than-life heroes, the mountain men, no other group of comparable size contributed so much to the exploration and development of the American West. . . . [The] Corps of Topographical Engineers was a central institution of Manifest Destiny, and in the years before the Civil War its officers made explorations which resulted in the first scientific mapping of the West.[2]

Apart from their geographic discoveries, they established national boundaries, located and constructed wagon roads, improved rivers and harbors, assembled and recorded scientific data, and performed as a military unit in the fighting forces.

The origin of the corps goes back to the time of the American Revolution, when General George Washington appointed the first geographer and surveyor in the Continental Army. Later, during the War of 1812, a fully developed topographical engineering unit was formed, though the corps itself did not receive formal recognition as an independent unit until an official government act of July 5, 1838. During the era of Manifest Destiny the corps played the most active and effective role in "carrying the burden of civilization to the wilderness and the lessons of the wilderness back into civilization."

Another characteristic of the corps was its fostering of a "kinship between science and art. Many of the topographical reports, like those of Frémont and Joseph C. Ives and William F. Raynolds, read like self-conscious literary compositions. Incidents were selected, episodes heightened, characters drawn, and exotic background sketched in, so that often the scientific report read like a draft of Walter Scott or Francis Parkman." Like the artists' drawings, however crude, they blended emotion with scientific fact.

Not all the members of the corps were as colorful or adventuresome as Frémont; however, expeditionary leaders like Stephen H. Long, Howard Stansbury, William H. Emory, and James H. Simpson, all of whom had distinguished careers in the West, made notable contributions to scientific knowledge through their exploratory achievements. The role of the topographical-engineer corps unfolds as the explorer and his staff artist chart and record America's vast wilderness.

GEORGE CARL LUDWIG (CHARLES) PREUSS: MILITARY ROADS WEST WITH JOHN C. FRÉMONT

August 4 (Thursday) [*1842*]

Today we had the [Wind River] mountains before us all day. Even yesterday afternoon we had a glimpse of them. Whoever has seen Switzerland and expects something similar here is bound for a great disappointment. An American has measured them to be as high as 25,000 feet. I'll be hanged if they are half as high, yea, if they are 8,000 feet high. A little snow on their peaks; that is all, as far as I can see now, that distinguishes them from other high mountains. —Charles Preuss[3]

Preuss, who served as Frémont's assistant topographer on three of his five expeditions to the West, was a German-born and -trained cartographer whose reputation had already been secured by his cartographic achievements: "His maps were the first of the territory between the Mississippi and the Pacific Ocean based on modern principles of geodesy and cartography."[4] He was born in Höhscheid, Germany, on April 30, 1803. Trained in the science of geodesy in his native land, he served as a surveyor for the Prussian Government before immigrating to America in 1834. There he obtained immediate employment with the United States Coast Survey under Ferdinand Hassler, who recommended him to Frémont as a draftsman for his first expedition. In his *Memoirs*, Frémont describes their meeting in December of 1841:

> One stormy evening near Christmas, when we were quietly enjoying the warm glow of firelight, a note was brought in to me from Mr. Hassler. The bearer was a strange figure—a shock of light curly hair standing up thick about his head, and a face so red that we attributed it to a wrong cause instead of to the cold. . . . I found that he was a German, a skilled topographer, who came to me with this letter from Mr. Hassler requesting employment for him if we had any to give. . . .
>
> There were astronomical observations remaining unreduced. That work, I told him, I could get for him. This he said he was not able to do. His profession was topography—in this he excelled, but that was all. The only thing I could devise was to get him this astronomical work and do it myself. . . . The little service which I was able to render him he amply repaid by years of faithful and valuable service as topographer on my journeys. . . .[5]

On May 2, 1842, Preuss set out with Frémont on his first expedition to the Wind River country to assist him as topographer and cartographer. The young lieutenant had been ordered by Colonel J. J. Abert, chief of the Corps of Topographical Engineers, to "explore the country between the Missouri River and the Rocky Mountains"; the implied purpose of this reconnaissance, however, was to open a road for immigration to the Oregon Territory.[6] Thus, in the guise of a scientific expedition, this topographical survey was to serve both military and political ends, abetting future expansion into Oregon, then a national aim. With his small party of experienced men, Frémont embarked across the prairies along the Oregon Trail, ending at the Wind River Mountains.

Apart from his cartographical work, Preuss made a number of sketches of the scenery during his travels with Frémont. Unfortunately, these are available today only in the form of lithographs, illustrating Frémont's report of his first and second expeditions. This makes it difficult to form an honest judgment about the artist's ability. A comparison of these illustrations with the few simple profiles of Mount Hood and adjacent peaks sketched in the artist's diaries[7] seems to indicate that the lithographer has taken certain liberties and filled in the outline drawings with details and embellishments to make a more pleasing and effective composition. That could well have been the case, since Preuss was basically a cartographer and was unprepared to meet the challenges of the novel scenery. His drawings are stiff, awkward, and almost primitive.

Like so many other untrained professionals, he visualized his subjects in terms of outlines rather than solid or naturalistic forms.

Preuss's *Central Chain of the Wind River Mountains* (plate 15; cf. 16), for example, with exaggerated peaks like sawtoothed "minarets," is diverting in its naïveté. Despite its fanciful appearance, the drawing is a perfect accompaniment to Frémont's description of the lofty range: "Around us the whole scene had one main striking feature, which was that of terrible convulsion. Parallel to its length, the ridge was split into chasms and fissures; between which rose the thin lofty walls, terminated with slender minarets and columns, which is correctly represented in the view from the camp on Island Lake."[8] In a distant view of the same chain of mountains, however, Preuss presents a more naturalistic rendering, indicating that at times he could be a careful observer of nature.[9] To him the lofty mountains could be pleasant yet equally awesome.

Despite his rude means, Preuss could at times present a fairly accurate topographical pictorial record. In his *The American Falls of Lewis Fork* [*Idaho*] (plate 17),[10] he gives visual form to Frémont's factual description of this scenic landmark:

> . . . at a great distance to the north is seen the high, snowy line of the Salmon River Mountains, in front of which stands out prominently in the plain the three isolated rugged-looking little mountains commonly known as the Three Buttes. . . . By measurement, the river above is eight hundred and seventy feet wide, immediately contracted at the fall in the form of a lock, by jutting piles of scoriaceous basalt, over which the foaming river must present a grand appearance at the time of high water.[11]

It is almost certain that Preuss carried a pocket sketchbook during his travels with Frémont, for we learn from his diaries that he made a point of sketching whenever he observed an important topographical feature in the landscape. His diaries, however, fail to mention the manner in which he took his sketches. Judging from the two simple profiles in these diaries, we might assume that his fieldbook sketches were in pencil on paper of similar type and size.[12]

These diaries also recount two unsuccessful attempts by Frémont to use a daguerreotype camera. In his rather perverse fashion, the artist blamed the failure on American ineptitude: "That's the way it often is with these Americans," he wrote. "They know everything, they can do everything, and when they are put to a test, they fail miserably."[13] Frémont's journal does not include these ill-fated photographic attempts, but, if Preuss's report is true, it documents the first known use of the daguerreotype in the West.[14]

From a scientific standpoint the expedition of 1842 had little value, but it did achieve two significant results. It made Frémont an instant hero and inspired him to attempt two even more enterprising ventures, in these instances to the Pacific Coast, one in 1843–44, and another in 1845.

For the trip of 1843, Frémont again chose Preuss as topographer. They left Fort Leavenworth in late May with a party of twenty-nine mounted men, twelve carts, and a mountain howitzer—the howitzer used, among other things, in the not-so-sporting amusement of shooting buffalo. They first headed west toward the central Rockies; then, at Fort St. Vrain, Preuss and Frémont began a reconnaissance of the area just east of the Front Range, traveling as far south as Pueblo. Along the way Preuss made a sketch of Pikes Peak which, since Seymour's study of the same mountain was never published, was the first view to receive public attention. *Pikes Peak* (1843), like Preuss's other drawings, is visually unexciting, merely an accurate rendering of the "luminous and grand" mountain barrier.[15] Yet this view, too, is a perfect accompaniment to Frémont's graphic verbal sketch of the "valley of the Bijou":

> The annexed view of Pike's Peak from this camp . . . represents very correctly the manner in which this mountain . . . presents itself to travellers on the plains, which sweep almost directly to its bases; an immense and comparatively smooth and grassy prairie, in very strong contrast with the black masses of timber, and the glittering snow above them. This is the picture which has been left upon my mind, and its general features are given in the accompanying view.[16]

After returning to St. Vrain in July, the group continued north to the Sweetwater River, then west through South Pass along the newly worn ruts of the Oregon Trail, and south to Salt Lake. They surveyed the area, but the job was incomplete, and Howard Stansbury was ordered to survey it again in 1850.[17] A year after its departure, Frémont's expedition, having trekked through Oregon and

PLATE 15

Charles Preuss, *Central Chain of the Wind River Mountains*, 1843, Lithograph, 4⅛″ × 7⅜″.
Courtesy Huntington Library, San Marino.

PLATE 16

Finis Mitchell, *Cirque of the Towers, Wind River Range,* 1979, Photograph, 5″ × 7″.
Courtesy of the authors.

PLATE 17

Charles Preuss, *The American Falls of Lewis Fork* [*Idaho*], 1845, Lithograph. 4¼″ × 7″.
Courtesy Hunting Library, San Marino.

California, recrossed the Rockies to Pueblo, Bent's Fort, Independence, and then homeward. Although Preuss must have continued sketching, no illustrations remain from the last half of this trip.

Recognizing that this exploit represented the most spectacular overland reconnaissance since that of Lewis and Clark, Frémont went straight to work recording the results of his survey. He must have considered Preuss's role a relatively minor one, for he mentioned the artist only in connection with completion of the maps and makes no allusions to his drawings.[18]

The report was finished in 1845 and was published by the government in an edition of ten thousand. It also went through private English and American editions, some running into thousands of copies.[19] Frémont was a national hero, and, to a more limited audience, so was Preuss. Although his depictions were somewhat naïve, his sense of perspective inaccurate, and his landforms at times exaggerated and fanciful, his adventures probably inspired many more artists than did those of his less well-publicized predecessors. Preuss should be recognized both for his pioneer efforts to record, however rudely, the Wind River range—and for his role as the first scientific mapmaker of America's western interior.[20]

JAMES W. ABERT (1820–1897): THE RECONNAISSANCE OF SOUTHERN COLORADO AND NEW MEXICO

On the second of August [1845] we reached Bent's Fort, on the Arkansas River. This was our real point of departure. It was desirable to make a survey of the prairie region to the southward, embracing the Canadian and other rivers. I accordingly formed a detached party, in charge of which I placed Lieutenants Abert and Peck, Lieutenant Abert being in chief command. —John Charles Frémont[21]

When Frémont left Fort Leavenworth in June, 1845, to begin his third and final government expedition, he had instructions to survey the Arkansas and Red rivers. At Bent's Fort, in direct violation of official orders, he divided his command and instructed his assistant, Lieutenant James W. Abert, to make a reconnaissance of "the Canadian from its source to its junction with the Arkansas, taking in his way the Purgatory River, and the heads of the Washita," the expedition's original objective.[22] As Abert and Peck's group began its journey, Frémont and the rest of the party set out on a transcontinental expedition to California.[23]

Abert was a member of the distinguished Corps of Topographical Engineers and a graduate of West Point. He was born in Mount Holly, New Jersey, on November 18, 1820. Maintaining a family tradition, he entered the United States Military Academy on graduation from Princeton in 1838. There he received both his technical training in engineering and his instruction in the principles and skills of drawing under the esteemed American artist Robert W. Weir, whose acute observation and deep feeling for the beauty of nature were undoubtedly passed on to his students. Except for his excellence in drawing, Abert's scholastic record at West Point was not a particularly outstanding one. After graduation he was assigned to the infantry, but—both because of his artistic skills and because his father was chief of the corps—Abert was soon transferred to the Topographical Engineers, a much-sought-after and highly significant branch of service. After several years of surveying in the West, the lieutenant returned to the academy, where he served as an assistant instructor in drawing from 1848 to 1850. At the close of the Civil War he retired from active service with the rank of colonel and became professor of mathematics and drawing in the University of Missouri.[24]

In spite of his instruction and rank in drawing at West Point, Abert's drawings seldom attain the level of professionalism. The intimate, quiet scenes along the Hudson that he had dutifully sketched under Weir's direction had hardly prepared him for the challenges of this strange land with its ever-changing light and color. Like other artist-explorers who preceded him to the West, he was hesitant to

44

PLATE 18

James Abert, *"Wah-to-yah"* [*Spanish Peaks, Colo.*], 1846, Hand-colored lithograph, 4″ × 7″.
Courtesy Huntington Library, San Marino.

EDWARD AND RICHARD KERN: EXPLORING WITH JOHN C. FRÉMONT AND JAMES H. SIMPSON

. . . Mr. Preuss was not with me this time; but . . . in his place Mr. Edward M. Kern, of Philadelphia, went with me as topographer. He was besides an accomplished artist; his skill in sketching from nature and in accurately drawing and coloring birds and plants made him a valuable accession to the expedition. —John Charles Frémont[38]

In the summer of 1844, soon after Frémont's return from his second expedition, he became involved in preparations for a third journey—a projected transcontinental expedition to California, which departed in late June of the following year.[39] This time Frémont and his men were to be mainly in Mexican territory, despite the rumors of war. During this reconnaissance they were to locate the sources of the Arkansas, the Rio Grande, and the Colorado; examine the Great Salt Lake and surrounding territory; and then proceed across the Great Basin to survey the Sierra in California and the Cascade Range in Oregon—in hope of discovering passes through them to the Pacific for a new overland route. Once again Frémont was in direct violation of his official orders, which included only a survey "of the localities within reasonable distance of Bent's Fort, and of the streams which run east from the Rocky Mountains."[40]

It will be remembered from the section devoted to the topographer-artist Abert and his participation in this third expedition that Frémont had divided his force, placing Abert in command to explore "the Canadian from its source to its junction with the Arkansas." Frémont and the rest of the party continued the unofficially recognized goal of the expedition, namely, a transcontinental reconnaissance trip to California. Edward Meyer Kern (1826–1863) was included in this official exploratory party. His brother Richard was to follow the same path a few years later.

The arrangements for Edward to accompany Frémont's third and final government expedition were worked out by his friend and fellow artist Joseph Drayton, who was then in Washington working with Arthur Agate on the illustrations for the official report of the Wilkes Pacific expedition (1838–42). He recommended the young Philadelphian to Frémont[41] and when, at Drayton's suggestion, Edward sent the captain a sample of his work, he was rewarded with a positive response: "I like the specimens you sent & judge from them that you sketch rapidly & correctly. I will send you your appointment in a few days, & should like to see you before you go to the West."[42]

Edward, or Ned, as he was known by his family and close friends, had been one of forty-two applicants for this special assignment with the famous Frémont, who was by now "a symbol of the trans-Mississippi West, a Galahad on horse or in rubber boat, jousting with the unknown."[43] The youngest of eight well-educated children from comfortable circumstances, Kern was properly prepared for this appointment. He and two of his brothers—John, Jr., and Richard—were established Philadelphia artists and teachers of drawing whose works had been exhibited publicly.[44]

Judging by several of his early watercolor drawings of eastern scenery, preserved in a private collection, Kern employed conventional methods of topographical artists of his day. Like Doughty and Thomas Birch, he was also fond of representing prospects that included all the picturesque effects necessary to appeal to public taste. For example, though the artist intended *Leheigh near the Delaware Gap* (ca. 1844),[45] to be an accurate record of a specific place, he included a few familiar artifices to make the view more palatable. It is apparent at this stage in Kern's artistic career that he was skillful in handling watercolor.

These large watercolors demonstrate his competent knowledge of color, light and shadow, and pencil-and-brush technique. He was obviously ready to meet the challenges of reportorial work, in which he would have to capture his subject on the spot, carefully taking note of colors and details so that he could apply the finishing touches at a later date. Most of his western drawings known today are of Indian and archaeological subjects which, unfortunately, are of no concern here.

Little information is available on the Kerns' early formal training, but they no doubt studied the many art objects in the Pennsylvania Academy's collection and sought the advice offered by the countless instruction manuals of the day. As Edward Kern's biographer Robert V. Hine has remarked, "The Kerns knew personally many of the younger artists [of the city], and tramping through the galleries could substitute for considerable institutional training."[46] A shred of evidence leads us to believe that Edward might briefly have known or even worked under the German landscapist Paul Weber. Among Edward's preserved effects is a "recipe" for painting landscapes by Weber, who had left his native country and relocated in Philadelphia during the mid-1840s.[47] The fanciful bare-limbed trees with forked branches in Kern's watercolor *Saturday Evening Camp, November 4, 1848* [*Walnut Creek, Kansas*] recall "the enchanted forests in German fairytales,"[48] which may or may not hint at Weber's influence. It is more likely that the brothers gained their experience in the field, as demonstrated by Edward's early watercolors. It is known that Richard (and probably Edward) made scientific drawings on request before engaging in expeditionary work.[49]

Hine believes that one of the factors that prompted Edward to journey west with Frémont was that all three brothers shared the same studio and income from their teachings. Being the youngest of the three, Edward certainly would not have received the lion's share, and the prospect of a western journey with its associated adventure and remunerative rewards must have been appealing. His curiosity about the West was probably also stimulated by Drayton's stories. In fact, after the confirmation of his appointment Edward wrote his friend to seek advice on clothing and supplies.[50] Drayton's reply is revealing:

> You will want 100 pieces of thick drawing paper medium folio, protected by 2 pieces of binder board the same size, . . . all of which get squared up boards and all by a book binder to make it compact get . . . block paper Royal 8. vo size 3 of these blocks will contain 70 pieces of paper, you will want 60 or 70 pieces of quarto size pieces of thick Drawing paper, done up like the folio size—you can judge of lead pencils & brushes yourself get by all means 2 of the French flat tin boxes of wafer colours, . . . get allso a lot of the coloured pencils. . . . Take with you if you can use it a camera lucida . . . [and] a good pocket compas[s] get a [?] napsack or bag . . . in which you can allwase keep 40 or 50 pieces of drawing paper, one of the french boxes of colours 5 or 6 pencils, your coloured pencils if you like, your camera lucida, brushes &c, get a flat metal flask small, for water incase you get where there is no water, & you want to make a coloured drawing— Make full notes of colours & everything els on the back of the drawings, and interview with Capt Fremont, what sizes you shall addopt for paintings &c, always finish your drawings on the spot, as much as possible & leave little for notes, be guided by Capt. F. in your department as to how, and what he wishes drawn, and take advantage of every opportunity to produce other drawings your own judgement will dictate for usefullness to the Capt. . . .[51]

Edward departed for Saint Louis (the designated meeting place for the Frémont party) in the first week in May, 1845. There he met the other men who had joined Frémont's force, which had been increased to deal with the contingencies of war with Mexico—a dispute whose "chief subject" was California.[52] During their trip across the prairie country of Kansas, Edward took full advantage of all opportunities to practice his sketching technique. The small pen-and-ink sketch of *Bent's Fort* contained in his journal of 1845 attests to the familiar adage that practice makes perfect. The group arrived at the fort on the second of August and spent considerable time there,[53] taking care of last-minute arrangements probably necessitated by the aforementioned change of plans and strategy.[54] Since Edward was now to assume the role of topographer as well, Abert and Peck were expected to acquaint him fully with the tools of topography before they departed on their own mission. According to Hine, "Kern must have brought some mathematical knowledge with him," for he learned rapidly how "to correct chronometers by astronomical observations for time, manage a telescope and the printed tables of an *Ephemerides* to determine latitude, and read the sextant, adding its triangulations to those of the stars and tables to calculate the longitude" while familiarizing himself with other instruments that would aid him in recording scientific data.[55]

On August 16 (or 17, according to Edward's journal entry), the party of sixty broke camp and proceeded upstream along the Arkansas on their journey beyond the Rocky Mountains.[56] Twenty-five miles out, the group obtained its first view of the mountains and the "grand peak." On the nineteenth, Edward was afforded a sweeping panorama of the mountains, taking in both Pikes Peak and, farther south, the Spanish Peaks; he was to record this same view on his next tour with Frémont, in 1848.[57] Passing an old, abandoned adobe trading post known as Gant's, they camped on the Arkansas, near the present city of Pueblo, for three days to take the first important calculations. Joined by their guide, Bill Williams, who was from a settlement near the mountains, they continued through the hilly, rocky country to the base of the mountains and the Royal Gorge of the Arkansas, which Frémont described as the "Great Canyon." There, on the twenty-sixth, the party set up camp, and Edward recorded his view of this bold spectacle of nature. The small watercolor sketch *Cañon of the Arkansas [Royal Gorge]* (color plate 5) in his journal complements his written description: "At the foot of the mountains on the Arkansas; . . . on the right of where the river breaks through the mountains are high bold red rocks standing in fine relief against the glowing tints of a beautiful sunset. Making on the whole quite a pretty picture."[58]

Leaving the river, the group continued northwest to the upper valley of the Arkansas, which, as his journal reveals, immediately impressed Edward as extremely beautiful country, abounding with a number of "pretty prospects." On September 2 the party camped for the night at the headwaters of the Arkansas, where they crossed the divide and descended the western slope. While traveling westward across the mountain slopes, the group was afforded a fine, extensive view of the "Colorado Valley," which, according to Frémont, Edward sketched.[59] *West Rocky Mountains Bordering Great Colorado Valley*, one of the many unattributed illustrations in Frémont's *Memoirs*, could well be this view.[60]

After traveling over rough, mountainous country for several days, the party crossed over to the Grand River, where they set up camp.

On the ninth the men climbed the mountains to gain a panoramic view of the adjacent country, which Edward described in glowing terms: "The Elk Mountains and the head of the Eagle Trail, redden[ed] by the very tints of the setting sun, the broken country in the middle distance . . . the foreground [with] . . . our camp make a pretty picture [that] one would wish to look on."[61] Nevertheless, he apparently failed to make a sketch of it.[62]

From Kern's journal we learn that the group reached the headwaters of the White River and then proceeded westward along its course, across the Green River, and down the Duchesne River.[63] At this juncture in the journey there is a gap in both Kern's and Frémont's accounts until October 2, when we rejoin the party encamped on a branch of the Timpanogos River. As assistant to Frémont in charge of topography, Edward probably had little time left for sketching the surrounding scenery. Although the artist does mention taking sketches at the "valley of Utah Lake," only one pictorial record remains of the party's trip through the present state of Utah. Once when the artist and another staff member, Theodore Talbot, became separated from the rest and had to spend a night in the woods, Edward amused himself by making a small watercolor sketch of himself and Talbot huddled together under a clump of pines before a glowing fire, which he appropriately titled *The Babes in the Woods*.[64] The following morning they met up with the group and continued their march across Utah, visiting Salt Lake before crossing the Great Basin on their way to California.

Despite the omission here of reportorial efforts and military exploits in California, one may obtain some idea of his contributions to the field of science and the nature of his artwork through a study of the few preserved sketches from his first trip to the Rockies. They evince not only his concern for topographical accuracy but also his facility with watercolor. Unlike Seymour, who employed thin, delicate washes of mixed colors, one over the other, to achieve the desired depth and color effect, Edward generally applied his colors boldly, directly, and with greater fidelity to nature, moving away from the early, traditional English watercolor method. To capture the luminous and colorful sunset skies that appealed to his eye for the picturesque, Kern applied his intense color tones to paper that had been thoroughly saturated with water, using a wet water-color technique.[65] The Kern brothers' scientific orientation was more evident in their pen-and-pencil sketches, in which the subject was captured on the spot by the simplest and most economical means and further elaborated by the printmaker. They merely attempted to reproduce their subjects as accurately as the "eye" of a camera.

When Edward finally rejoined his brothers in Philadelphia after two exciting and eventful years in the West, he had many adventuresome tales to relate. His enthusiasm for expeditionary work must have been contagious, for when it came time to sign up for Frémont's fourth expedition, two of his brothers, Richard and Benjamin (a medical doctor), were there to join him. It was obviously Edward's persuasiveness, not financial considerations, that prompted the brothers to join forces: in a letter to Edward, Richard had indicated that between their commissions and their art classes he and John had been able to maintain themselves comfortably.[66] Obviously, the veritably unknown and untapped West simply offered Richard more excitement and artistic challenge than did the familiar natural wonders of the eastern wilderness.

Richard Hovenden Kern (1821–1853), two years Edward's senior, was also a practicing artist.[67] Like Edward, he was largely self-tutored, having learned by studying drawing manuals and the work of professional artists. Richard's artistic career closely paralleled Edward's. Apart from their teaching duties both spent considerable time studying natural history and making meticulous scientific drawings. As Hine points out, "Without some knowledge of botany they could not have drawn plates of flowers and trees which would have any value for eastern scientists; without zoology, they could not have intelligently sketched creatures from mice to bison."[68] Like his younger brother, Richard carefully sketched the native scenery and made a number of large watercolors, some probably on commission and others for his own amusement.[69] Although he had experimented with oils early in his career and found that they were easy to manipulate, Richard, like Edward, worked mainly in watercolor;[70] the practical aspect of the lighter medium, its portable nature, and its quick-drying capability lent itself better to expeditionary work. The brothers' styles were also alike, and it is difficult at times to separate the work of the two. This fact is most apparent in their drawings and sketches of Indians, in which the figures are drawn "in flat profile or puppet-like activity."[71] Amusingly enough, the same color "recipe" for painting flesh and hair was found in the effects of each brother.[72]

Yet these drawings and their few preserved scenic views allow us to separate stylistically the two brothers' work, most of which is unsigned.[73] It is evident that Edward was the more finicky of the two; his drawings appear to be more tightly constructed than Richard's. Perhaps the demands of mapmaking enabled him to portray his subjects with greater precision; on the brothers' joint ventures into the West, Edward was to serve both as topographer and as artist.

By way of explanation, the distinction between artist and topographer in these early exploratory expeditions was usually clear. The artist was instructed to capture the romantic realism of a vast new country. The topographer, on the other hand, was required to record with factual precision the enormous variety of flora and fauna, the exact geological formations, and other topographical aspects of the terrain. Both Edward and Richard Kern served in these dual capacities. Edward, however, was the first to be lured west with Frémont—and it is perhaps this early experience as a precise scientific recorder of astronomical calculations and careful delineator of maps that separates the work of one brother from the other.

By the time of Frémont's fourth expedition, in 1848, Edward and Richard were already recognized for their artistic and scientific accomplishments and, along with their brother Benjamin, had been elected members of the prestigious Academy of Natural Sciences of Philadelphia.[74] Although the Kerns were well prepared to meet the normal requirements of expeditionary work, they were hardly ready for the hardships they were to suffer during Frémont's ruinous misadventure.

Frémont's transcontinental expedition of 1845 to California had caught him in a web of conflict between naval officers and the government-approved army expedition—a conflict that eventually led to his court-martial. Consequently, he was forced to seek private financial support for his reconnaissance of 1848. Fortunately, on one of his visits to Washington, D.C., he had met and married Jessie Benton, the daughter of United States Senator Thomas Hart Benton. An enthusiastic expansionist, Benton became not only Frémont's father-in-law but also his adviser and sponsor. This sponsorship enabled Frémont to accomplish the mapping of much of the territory between the Mississippi Valley and the Pacific Ocean within the next several years. The project of 1848 was conceived with daring expectations, partly rooted in Frémont's determination to regain his reputation and honor. He hoped to lead the expedition in midwinter across the Central Rockies (near the 38th parallel) to prove the practicability of the route for a transcontinental railroad. According to Robert V. Hine, "He and Benton had long shared the hope of proving the central route for a transcontinental railroad, not only to keep the future road away from the slave-ridden South, but to make Saint Louis the eastern terminus of the western cornucopia."[75] To determine whether snow would hamper the accessibility of this route in the middle of winter, they were to chart passes, measure snowfall and snowpack, and record temperatures and gradients.[76] Frémont had therefore set a late-autumn departure date.

Since army funds were no longer available, Frémont turned to Benton and the businessmen of Saint Louis for financial support. Salaries and expenses were to be kept to a minimum. Several members of the expeditionary party, among them the three Kerns, had agreed to serve without pay, while others trusted Frémont to reimburse them after the journey. Frémont was fortunate to obtain thirty-three men for his party, most of whom were experienced western travelers, some of them veterans of Frémont's previous expeditions. Preuss was to serve once again as topographer and mapmaker, while Edward was to handle the artistic duties, Richard was to assist Edward while training in the field, and Ben was to pitch in wherever Frémont felt an extra hand was needed—an arrangement that was eventually to cause dissension between Ben and the commander.

On October 20, 1848, Frémont's party left Westport, traveling westward first along the Kansas River and then on its Smoky Hill Fork.[77] By mid-November they had reached Bent's Fort, where Frémont first learned of the extraordinary depth of the snow in the passes and the probability of a severe winter.[78] Undaunted by this information, which was repeated at Pueblo by the traders and Indians, Frémont was determined to carry out his original objective. Until this point all had proceeded reasonably well, and the trip had been tolerably pleasant; why not trust his luck further? During the few days they camped along the Arkansas opposite Bent's Fort, Edward and Richard spent their time working on sketches. On the seventeenth the two climbed a bluff to gain a clear view of the surrounding country. Before their eyes was a sweeping panorama of the snow-covered plains encircled by the distant, snow-crowned Rockies. Since the day was cold and clear with very little wind to disturb atmospheric conditions, they were able to take in the Spanish Peaks on the south, covered with snow, mountains that were dark blue and tipped with snow to the north, and, much farther north, Pikes Peak.[79] Before raising camp on the eighteenth, a delicate watercolor was made of this spectacular view (plate 19).[80] Its strong topographical realism, subtle coloring (mainly washes), and meticulous draftsmanship (seen in the visible pencil outline) indicate that the hand is probably Edward's; it bears little similarity to Richard's known watercolors from the same trip.[81] Since Richard made a sketch of the same view, however, the drawing may be a product of their combined efforts.[82]

Because the account of this calamitous journey is well known through the journals and letters of its members,[83] only the events and places that relate to extant drawings will be discussed here. Although their diaries are sketchy, both Richard and Benjamin provide us with enough information to follow their march across mountains and through valleys to the San Juan Mountains, where they encountered insuperable obstacles while struggling to stay alive. We learn also of their admitted defeat and return to the valley of the Rio Grande, where they were finally rescued and taken to Taos, New Mexico. Considering the hazardous conditions they had to overcome—deep snow, bitter cold, and famine—it is amazing that the Kerns were able to sketch at all. Richard's diary includes a number of small pencil sketches of interesting topographical features he sighted along the way. Of particular interest is Richard's sketchbook, a series of scenic views in watercolor, which has recently come to light.[84] His sketches of southern Colorado effectively convey the

bleakness and desolation of the difficult climb over the snow-packed, mountainous terrain. True to nature, the artist appropriately employed a predominantly gray color scheme with strong accents of white and black. Although he never allowed aesthetic considerations to take precedence over factual content, Richard still managed to arrange his compositions artfully. It seems a pity that Frémont did not choose to reproduce these views in his *Memoirs;* they are far less contrived than those illustrating the book.

At the beginning of the sketchbook is a view, *Pike's Peak,*[85] which complements the entry in Benjamin's journal on November 20: "raised camp at 8 o clock Clear & cool on starting . . . cold bitter west wind—bands of Antelope plenty—yucca as for several days past plenty also, two varieties of cacti, fine view of Pikes peak campd in a nice warm bottom."[86] We can assume that on this particular day Richard hastily made his watercolor sketch of the familiar hump-shaped peak while the party was camped along the Arkansas, a short distance below Pueblo. Unlike the brothers' sweeping panorama of the Rockies, executed earlier on the trip, this scenic view illustrates the use of a prescribed formula of receding planes with the inclusion of small figures to provide scale and interest in the middle distance, a technique recommended by the standard instruction manuals. Although the picture is not altogether true to nature, its topographical value as a pictorial document cannot be discounted.

By the time Richard produced his next watercolor sketch, *Robidoux Pass [Mosca], White Mts., N.M. [Sangre de Cristos, Colo.],*[87] the men had already made their way to the Sangre de Cristo Mountains. On December 2, just before they ascended into Robidoux Pass [Mosca], the artist made a small pencil sketch in his diary, *Cañon of Wafeneau [Huerfano].* Following the party's retreat after a futile attempt to cross the snow-covered San Juans at their highest point, Richard made another watercolor, *Chowatch [Sawatch] Mts.,* on December 31, during the tortuous journey back to the Rio Grande.[88] On January 29, at the time of their rescue by the relief expedition from Taos, the artist captured a view of the small party huddled together near a grove of pines with the towering Sangre de Cristos in the background (see color plate 6).

Apart from the Colorado scenes, most of the remaining sketches in Richard's sketchbook are of New Mexico; *Acapulco, Mexico* (1852) and several sketches of architectural monuments in Washington, D.C. (1853) are also included.[89] One other view of Colorado, titled *On the "Proutx" Creek, Chowatch Mts., N.M. [Sawatch Mts., Colo.],* stands as an ugly reminder of the disastrous expedition.[90] In this view Richard has recorded without embellishment the rugged canyon site where the Kerns hurriedly cached their possessions during their retreat from the mountains. Aside from these watercolors and the pencil sketches included in Richard's diary, no original work from this journey has been located. Yet three illustrations in a salesman's dummy for Frémont's *Memoirs,* portraying the small party in the midst of the wintry waste of the San Juans, hint that other sketches were made during the trip. Although these plates are not credited, certain characteristic features—the forked limbs of the trees, the massing of landforms, and the postures of the small, gesticulating figures—indicate that the artist may well have been one of the Kerns.[91] Since Frémont employed several artists and engravers to redesign the original sketches and daguerreotype views, however, it is impossible to determine how much of the original hand or hands has been preserved in the reproductions.[92]

After the party's disastrous attempt to cross the San Juans, the Kern brothers refused to continue west with Frémont and decided to remain in Taos until spring and then return to Philadelphia. Later Benjamin and the guide, who became famous as Old Bill Williams, left to retrieve their belongings that had been abandoned in the mountains. Both died in the attempt at the hands of the Utes.[93] Discouraged by this tragic news and seeing no future for them in Taos, the two surviving brothers moved on to Santa Fe in the early summer of 1849.

At approximately the same time a young lieutenant, James Hervey Simpson, of the Topographical Engineers, marched in with Captain Randolph B. Marcy from Fort Smith, on the Arkansas.[94] Simpson had planned to follow Marcy to California, but on his arrival in Santa Fe he found counterinstructions ordering him to remain there and to submit to Washington immediately a report of the route he had just taken. Simpson promptly recruited the Kern brothers to assist him in this task by making illustrations and finishing a map for the report[95] (the lieutenant quickly ransacked every store in Santa Fe for available supplies). Although poorly equipped, the Kerns must have performed their task satisfactorily, for they formed a close association with Simpson in the course of their work together.

When Colonel John Macrae Washington, military and civil governor of New Mexico, decided to make a punitive advance against the Navahos, he needed a "scientific" guise with which to mask the expedition's military purpose. The Kerns and Simpson were thus commandeered, and, in mid-August, a force of 175 men left Santa Fe for Jémez Pueblo and beyond.[96] When the party halted at Jémez to reorganize, the Kerns had an opportunity to observe Indian life, pueblo architecture, and the southern spur of the Rockies. Edward and Richard, whose interests were largely ethnological, took sketches of the green-corn dances *(you-pel-lay)* they observed there. Richard also made sketches of this picturesque pueblo and surrounding countryside, which were later adapted for an illustration in Simpson's report.

The preliminary pencil sketch, inscribed *Pecos village of Jémez from the east* (plate 20), reveals Richard's manner of working in the field. Although summarily treated, mainly in outline, the sketches still convey Kern's feeling for textures, shade, and bright light. As with most other field sketches, Kern noted the various materials to be used and objects to be included in a more detailed work. Kern later adapted this pencil sketch as a more finished ink-wash drawing (plates 21 and 22), used by the lithographer as a model for the illustration in Simpson's report. The lithographer has taken the liberty of tightening up and clarifying the sketch by adding definition and filling in with shading. Although much of the sketchy quality of the preliminary studies is missing, the original composition has essentially been followed, except for the cropping of the blank foreground, which provides us a closer view of the small village. The printmaker has even followed Kern's instructions by filling in the corral indicated by the artist with a few strokes and a penciled notation.

From Jémez the expedition proceeded northwest toward Canyon de Chelly, then south to Zuñi, across to Albuquerque, and back to Santa Fe, the point of departure—a circle of almost six hundred miles. That the Kerns had performed their assignment admirably is attested by Simpson's letter to Colonel Abert:

> I also submit a number of sketches illustrative of the personal, natural, and artificial objects met with on the route, including portraits of distinguished chiefs, costume, scenery, singular geographical formations, petrifications, ruins, and facsimiles of ancient inscriptions found engraven on the side walls of a rock of stupendous proportions. For these truthful delineations, and the topographical sketches, I am indebted to my two assistants, Messrs. R. H. Kern, and E. M. Kern . . . the former having furnished with few exceptions, all the sketches of scenery, &c., and the latter the topography and other artistical work displayed upon the map. To both of these gentlemen I tender my grateful acknowledgements for the kind, zealous, and effective manner in which they were found ready to cooperate with me in the discharge of my duties.[97]

The two Kern brothers remained in Santa Fe for another year, working at various odd jobs and finishing their sketches for the lithographer. Then, in August, 1851, they left Santa Fe, in different directions. Edward, turning his back on the Rockies, set out eastward with Captain John Pope.[98] Richard headed west with Lieutenant Lorenzo Sitgreaves and was later to play an important role in the struggle to establish a transcontinental-railroad route.[99]

Although their contributions to the knowledge of Colorado's natural history are considerable, the Kerns are best known for their many descriptive drawings of New Mexico.[100] In evaluating the artistic merits of the Kerns' work, it must be remembered that they were hired specifically to record, collect, and amass scientific data. Thus their work, unlike the more narrative illustrations of Bodmer and Miller, possesses little imaginative flair or verve. Although outranked by the later professionals who painted the grand showpieces of the West, the Kerns' western images nonetheless provide us with an intimate knowledge of the southwestern land and its native people.

PLATE 20
Richard Kern, *Pecos village of Jémez from the east*, 1849, Pencil, 7½″ × 9½″.
Courtesy private collection.

PLATE 22

Richard Kern, *Pueblo of Jémez from the East, Aug. 20, 1850*, Lithograph, 4¼″ × 7¼″.
Courtesy Denver Public Library, Western History Department, Denver, Colo.

Color Plate 1

James Madison Alden, *A Rocky Mountain Reconnoissance*, 1860, Watercolor, 11¼″ × 17¾″.
Courtesy Washington State Historical Society, Tacoma, Wash.

COLOR PLATE 2

Samuel Seymour, *View of James Peak in the Rain*, 1820, Pen and watercolor, 4⅝″ × 10¼″.
Courtesy M. and M. Karolik Collection, Museum of Fine Arts, Boston, Mass.

Color Plate 3

Karl Bodmer, *A View of the Rocky Mountains*, 1833, Watercolor, 11½″ × 16¾″.
Courtesy Northern Natural Gas Company Collection, Joslyn Art Museum, Omaha, Nebr.

Color Plate 5

Edward Kern, *Cañon of the Arkansas* [*Royal Gorge*],
1845, Watercolor, 8″ × 6¼″.
Courtesy private collection.

Color Plate 6

Richard H. Kern, *Relief Camp on the Rio
Grande Del Norte, N.M.*, 1849, Watercolor, 4⅜″ × 5⅞″.
Courtesy Amon Carter Museum, Fort Worth, Texas.

COLOR PLATE 7

John Mix Stanley, *Butte on the Del Norte*, 1846, Oil, 9⅞″ × 12⁹⁄₁₆″.
Courtesy Harrison Eiteljorg Collection, Indianapolis, Ind.

Color Plate 9

Solomon Nunes Carvalho, *Grand [Colorado] River,* 1875, Oil, 20″ × 30″.
Courtesy Kahn Collection, Oakland Museum, Oakland, Calif.

3

TRACKS THROUGH THE ROCKIES: THE PACIFIC RAILROAD SURVEYS

There would be no difficulty in the way of constructing a railroad from the Atlantic to the Pacific ocean; and probably the time may not be very far distant, when trips will be made across the continent, as *they have been made to the Niagara Falls, to see nature's wonders.* — Rev. Samuel Parker[1]

MANY years before rumor spread of an Eldorado in California, men linked the shores of America's two great oceans in their minds: men like Samuel Parker who had traversed the continent themselves viewed the idea not only with a general sense of patriotic mission but with firsthand knowledge that such an aspiration was not beyond practical realization. Upon crossing the Rockies in the late 1830s, Parker had noted that

> the passage through these mountains [at South Pass] is in a valley, so gradual in the ascent and descent, that I should not have known that we were passing them, had it not been that as we advanced the atmosphere gradually became cooler, and at length we saw the perpetual snows upon our right hand and upon our left, elevated many thousand feet above us.[2]

Observations like these convinced people that, although the Rockies were a physical and psychological barrier, they were not impenetrable—tracks could be laid, allowing the enterprises of commerce and communication to be accomplished.

By the midnineteenth century the need for a transcontinental transportation system seemed clear. Discoveries of gold in California brought the nation's—in fact, the world's—attention to the Pacific Coast. The gold-washed sluiceboxes of Sutter's Creek became a popular metaphor for America's hopes, and the West became a common focus for the subject of manifest destiny. One demand was soon heard from every quarter: get people west and get them there as quickly and directly as possible.

On December 4, 1849, President Zachary Taylor presented his Annual Message to Congress:

> The great mineral wealth of California, and the advantages which its ports and harbors, and those of Oregon, afford to commerce, especially with the islands of the Pacific and Indian Oceans, and the populous regions of Eastern Asia, make it certain that there will arise in a few years large and prosperous communities on our western coast. It, therefore, becomes important that a line of communication, the best and most expeditious which the nature of the country will admit, should be opened within the territory of the United States, from the navigable waters of the Atlantic on the Gulf of Mexico to the Pacific.[3]

Asa Whitney, a China trader and New York businessman, had been encouraging Congress to consider such a plan for several years. Sectional differences complicated matters, however, making the logical route—one already tested, the Oregon Trail—a controversial one. Southerners urged exploration through the territories recently acquired from Mexico; northern interests, not to be outdone, insisted with equal ardor that attention be paid to alternate routes through the northern Rockies. In the spring of 1853, Congress mandated Secretary of War Jefferson Davis to survey four possible courses with the hope that one would prove sufficiently suitable to meet all demands.

F. R. GRIST AND JOHN HUDSON: EXPLORING THE GREAT SALT LAKE

The route pursued by the expedition . . . will, perhaps, lead to further investigation of that remarkable depression lying between the Park Mountains and the South Pass. That a feasible route may be traced through this depression has been satisfactorily demonstrated; and the saving in distance cannot but prove an object of importance, either in the establishment of a post route, or in the construction of a railway communication across the continent. —Howard Stansbury[4]

Although Frémont's search of 1848 for a rail path through the Rockies had faltered for lack of government sanction and support, federal interest had followed close on his heels. In the spring of 1849, Captain Howard Stansbury, of the Topographical Engineers, received orders to pursue a route from Independence, Missouri, to the Great Salt Lake, survey the Mormon empire, and return by a southeastern course through Santa Fe. Although nominally the object of the expedition was a survey of the Utah valley, Stansbury's secondary motivation seems to have been to discover a suitable route for a transcontinental railroad—a deduction implied by the title of his official report, *Exploration and Survey of the Valley of the Great Salt Lake of Utah, Including a Reconnaissance of a New Route Through the Rocky Mountains.*[5]

Stansbury and his assistant, Lieutenant J. W. Gunnison, also of the Topographical Engineers, had intended to accompany a troop of mounted rifles as far as the Salt Lake. Unfortunately, they reached Independence too late and were obliged to form their own retinue,[6] which left the Missouri River on June 1. Stansbury's group consisted of eighteen men, "principally . . . experienced *voyageurs,* who had spent the best part of their lives among the wilds of the Rocky Mountains, and to whom this manner of life had become endeared by old associations."[7]

One of the less "experienced *voyageurs*" in the entourage was an artist, F. R. Grist. He is assumed to have been Franklin R. Grist, a genre painter from New Haven, Connecticut.[8] It is not known whether he was hired as an official artist or was merely an enlisted man with talent as a draftsman, and none of his original drawings is known to have survived. Lithographs published in Stansbury's report are the only available visual record of the expedition; al-though they are unsigned, several sources attributed at least some of those illustrations to Grist and his replacement, John Hudson.[9]

The party's route followed the Oregon Trail, which by this time was a well-marked highway for the myriad gold seekers who pushed west from Independence in the spring and summer of 1849. Grist's first visual record of the trip is a view of Fort Laramie, which the party first glimpsed on July 12. It was a far more bustling place than the one visited by Preuss and Frémont seven years earlier. As the group continued along the trail, they passed discarded belongings—harbingers of the hardships ahead. Almost daily they had news of calamities from parties that had preceded them, as cholera, fatigue, and demoralization ravaged the ranks of the forty-niners.

The group finally reached Fort Bridger, an Indian trading post, on August 11. Stansbury, intent on examining a possible alternate, or cut off, route for travelers destined for Oregon or California, secured the services of Major Jim Bridger, who was stationed there. While Stansbury and Bridger pursued a direct course to the head of Salt Lake, Lieutenant Gunnison led the rest of the group along the established Mormon immigrant trail toward the southern part of Salt Lake valley, where they were to make a reconnaissance of the Great Salt Lake and the valley in Stansbury's absence.

While traveling along the alternate, or cut off, route, Stansbury continued a detailed account of his own journey with Bridger; he did, however, include a synopsis of Gunnison's operation during his absence. This summary and several extant letters from Gunnison to his wife during the two-month period provide a glimpse into the group's activities. Two of Gunnison's letters written from their Utah-based camp, dated October 7 and 9, 1849, actually document Grist's presence in the group: "Our Artist, for whom I have named our camp near the mouth of the river Jordan, connecting Utah and Salt Lakes, having finished a lunch with me . . . [has] taken his portfolio off with him to a lodge beside my tent . . . ." In the following letter he mentioned that the artist had just sketched him in his "present toggery" on a mule, a pose Grist suggested for the portrait.[10]

In his summary Gunnison reported that "a thorough exploration was made, with the view of ascertaining the points for such a base line as would best develop a system of triangles embracing both the Salt Lake and Utah valleys." For this purpose fourteen principal triangulation stations were erected, consisting of "large pyramidal timber tripods, strongly framed, . . . covered, when required for use, by cotton cloth of different colours, according to the background. The triangles extended to the south shore of Utah Lake, and embraced an area of about eighty by twenty-five miles." Grist recorded a detailed view of triangulation entitled *Station East End of the Base Line* (plate 23).[11] Here the artist relies on the triangular form to group his figures; however, he has made no attempt to integrate the figures with the landscape setting. Like most of the other views that can tentatively be assigned to Grist, this scene includes a screen of tall, waving, enlarged prairie grass in the foreground—seemingly the artist's trademark.

After Stansbury was reunited with his party around November 7, winter set in so severely that work had to be discontinued. When they reassembled in the spring of 1850 to continue the survey of the Great Salt Lake, Grist had gone north with Lieutenant George M. Howland on another expedition.[12] In his absence another artist, John Hudson, was placed on the payroll as draftsman, and several of his lively views of the lake scenery are included in Stansbury's report. Little information on Hudson is available. The late historian Dale Morgan suggested that he may have been the J. Hudson from New York who traveled west with the Colony Guard, a group of forty-niners who split up somewhere along the trail.[13] It is possible that a few of these travelers spent the winter of 1849-50 in Salt Lake; John Hudson may have been among them.

On the other hand, Grist's replacement may have been the ornamental and landscape painter John Bradley Hudson (1832-1903),

who worked in Portland, Maine, from the late 1850s to the 1890s and contributed paintings to exhibitions in the Boston Athenaeum; he moved to Weston, Massachusetts, in his later years.[14] This artist's picturesque and romantic landscape entitled *A View in Maine* (1859) in the Karolik Collection[15] shares a similar mood and style with several illustrated views of Salt Lake that may be by Stansbury's Hudson. Since, however, there is no record that the John B. Hudson from Maine traveled to the Far West—an experience that would seem to be a high point in a seventeen-year-old artist's life—it is doubtful that the Maine landscapist and Stansbury's draftsman were the same man.

On the contrary, in fact, Hudson's journal, which is preserved in the National Archives, suggests that he was an Englishman.[16] Certainly it reveals that he was literate and appreciative of nature's wonders, in addition to having a keen eye and skilled hand. The illustrations that might be attributed to him indicate that he had a strong imagination and a bent for the romantic and bizarre. One of them, *Cave on Fremont's Island* (plate 24), is based, in spite of its romantic aura, on an actual incident during the party's survey by boat of the Great Salt Lake. Because of extraordinarily high gales the men were obliged to leave their boats and take refuge for the night inside a cave under a high cliff that had been used by Indians as a shelter; they built a fire there to keep warm. From this illustration and others that may be assigned to Hudson's hand, it is apparent that he was far more interested in producing romantic and imaginative interpretations of the group's experiences than in making straightforward topographical recordings like those of his predecessor, Grist.

On the other hand, when necessary, Hudson could be simply a topographer. For example, the literal *Panoramic view from Rock Gate Camp—Looking N. E. Across Bear River Bay—Great Salt Lake* (plate 25) seems to be Hudson's, in light of his journal entry for April 16, 1850:

> The early part of the morning I spent in writing for Lieut Gunnison; this finished I rambled . . . along the little valley formed by Rocky Gate on the E & Promontory range on the W.; after walking about 3 miles upon an Indian trail, upon which signs of travel were

PLATE 23

Franklin R. Grist, *Station East End of the Base Line*, 1849, Toned lithograph, 4½″ × 7¾″.
Courtesy Denver Public Library, Western History Department, Denver.

PLATE 24

John Hudson, *Cave on Fremont's Island*, 1852, Color lithograph, 4½″ × 7¾″.
Courtesy Harold McCracken Research Library, Buffalo Bill Historical Center, Cody, Wyo.

PLATE 25. John Hudson, *Panoramic View from Rock Gate Camp—Looking N.E. Across Bear River Bay—*

recent—I came to a ridge where a steep descent led to the plains on a level with the lake; from the point upon which I stood I beheld a noble [amphitheater], on either hand bold rocks sloping to the verdant plains with the lake lying like a mirror on its bosom . . . the background, composed of precipitous mountains "The Palaces of nature," whose vast walls have pinnacled in clouds their snowy scalps. I sketched this panorama continuously upon three peices [*sic*] of paper, & then observing the threatening appearance of the sky, I rose from the damp ground & returned to camp.

Here Hudson has fallen back on a typical topographical artist's formula to construct his panoramic view, which appears as a threefold illustration in the report; yet the picture does convey Stansbury's negative reaction to the desolate scene spread out before him: ". . . the bleak and naked shores, without a single tree to relieve the eye, presented a scene so different from what I had pictured

in my imagination of the beauties of this far-famed spot, that my disappointment was extreme."

In their own ways Stansbury and his artist helped close the tremendous gap in Americans' knowledge of the land west of the Rockies, thereby increasing their awareness and appreciation of their country's western wilderness. Many particulars that had eluded Frémont's scrutiny in his survey of 1843 were accounted for and described in Stansbury's official report. On his return home in the fall of 1850, Stansbury again explored possible routes for a railroad. Although not officially a railroad survey, his trek covered most of the same territory as the later Union Pacific venture. The first recognized government railroad survey was to follow three years later—led by Captain John W. Gunnison,[17] who had served as one of Stansbury's lieutenants on the Great Salt Lake Expedition.

Great Salt Lake, 1852, Toned lithograph, 5¼″ × 25¾″. Courtesy Huntington Library, San Marino.

RICHARD KERN: TRACKS THROUGH THE CENTRAL ROCKIES—PACIFIC RAILROAD SURVEYS

Under the 10th and 11th sections of the military appropriation act of March 3, 1853, directing such explorations and surveys as to ascertain the most practicable and economical route for the railroad from the Mississippi river to the Pacific ocean, the War Department directs a survey of the pass through the Rocky mountains, in the vicinity of the headwaters of the Rio del Norte, by way of the Huerfano river and Coo-che-to-pa, or some other eligible pass, into the region of Grand and Green rivers, and westwardly to the Vegas de Santa Clara and Nicollet river of the Great Basin, and thence northward to the vicinity of Lake Utah on a return route, to explore the most available passes and cañones of the Wahsatch range and South Pass to Fort Laramie.—Lieutenant Edwin Griffin Beckwith[18]

In the spring of 1853 the Kern brothers departed on separate missions. Edward, determined to widen his horizons, became a member of Commander Cadwalader Ringgold's North Exploring Expedition of 1853.[19] Richard Kern, who had established a considerable reputation as an authority on the Southwest, was once again tapped to serve on a western expedition—this time as artist and topographer of the official exploration party commanded by Captain John W. Gunnison, whose task it was to survey and map the regions near the 38th and 39th parallels from the mouth of the Kansas River to the Sevier River in the Great Basin. The results were of vital interest to the government: a "dearth of accurate information on the nature, character, and aspect of most of the trans-Mississippi country, and especially in reference to the facilities presented by it for railroad communication" had finally prompted congressional approval of an appropriation of $150,000 for this first official survey of several proposed routes for a transcontinental railroad.[20] Ironically, Richard had strongly advocated the 35th parallel as "the shortest and most practicable route" for the Pacific railroad in a twenty-four-page report to Senator William M. Gwin of California, written before his appointment.[21] Despite his own personal views, Richard's real concern over the Pacific railroad led to his decision to join Gunnison on the central route. For him, as for Gunnison and for the party's botanist, Frederick Creutzfeldt, this assignment to explore the country near the 38th was by no means new; all three men had tracked over the same ground on previous exploratory missions.

Although preliminary reports had been published from time to time, the complete reports of all the surveys with additions and revisions were published by the government in a comprehensive and magnificently illustrated twelve-volume work authoritatively titled *Reports of Explorations and Surveys to Ascertain the Most Practicable and Economic Route for a Railroad from the Mississippi River to the Pacific Ocean.*[22] As Taft has pointed out, "These volumes . . . constitute probably the most important single contemporary source of knowledge on Western geography and history and their value is greatly enhanced by the inclusion of many beautiful plates in color of scenery, native inhabitants, fauna and flora of the Western country."[23] Of the many plates contained in these reports, the scenic views probably attracted the greatest interest. Most are full-page lithographs printed in two or three colors on heavy paper. Twelve landscape views by Richard Kern, one of eleven illustrators employed by the various surveys, are included in the Gunnison report. Kern's sketches not only reinforce the written descriptions but indicate the party's route. With the exception of one field sketch by Richard, *Grand [Gunnison] River*, these plates are the only available pictorial record of this expedition.

According to the official report, Captain Gunnison launched his expedition westward from a point about five miles from Westport, Kansas, on June 23, generally following the Santa Fe Trail through modern Kansas and occasionally branching off on side trails to ascertain alternate railroad routes.[24] Until the party reached Bent's Fort on July 29, the journey was fairly routine. From this landmark they continued northward along the Arkansas to the Apishpa River, which they mistook for the Huerfano, their intended route to the mountains. After traveling several miles southward on the Apishpa

toward the Spanish Peaks, the group forded the river and proceeded westward toward the Cuchara. Here the men had their first full view of the Spanish Peaks; and Richard's *Wah-Ha-Ta-Gas or Spanish Peaks* is the first illustration in the Gunnison report.[25] This highly romanticized work with its lone Indian rider in the foreground is surely a much-enlarged and redesigned version of a lost field sketch or drawing, since the artist-explorer John Mix Stanley redrew all of Kern's sketches after Kern's premature death.[26] To judge from a recently discovered field sketch by Richard, Stanley and the various lithographers who produced the plates took considerable artistic license in creating picturesque scenes of the wild, mountainous country—illustrations no doubt intended to indicate the difficulties of building a railroad over the exceedingly rugged terrain, a task that would require special engineering and considerable financial outlay. Nevertheless, Gunnison found the route favorable for a transcontinental railroad.

After ascending the Huerfano for some distance, the group crossed the first range of mountains by way of Sangre de Cristo Pass. At the point nearest its summit Richard captured three different views of the pass and the surrounding country, looking "northeast from camp," "down Gunnison's Creek," and "towards San Luis Valley with Bald Peak and Sierra Blanca in the distance."[27] Most of these views are similar and have a limited color range of yellow ocher or rust, brown, blue, and gray. Plate two in the report shows, in a rather amusing way, the party and their animals ascending the dividing ridge on the narrow, winding trail. To call our attention to this comical procession, Kern (or Stanley) has placed two small figures on the elevated mountain slope in the foreground. One is on horseback; the other, dressed in a toga, carries a staff in one hand and extends the other in the direction of the diminutive figures winding their way up the crooked trail. Unlike the scientific depictions of later practitioners, none of these illustrations attempts to record accurately the geological structure of this mountainous terrain.

After crossing the first range, the party descended into the San Luis Valley, where they camped for several days. At this time Kern made sketches of the fort and Mount Blanca that appear as illustrations in the report.[28] Since these views also reflect a fusion of romanticism and realism, it is obvious that the lithographer added his own concepts and details to Richard's simple topographical renderings. Continuing north through the San Luis Valley, Gunnison selected Cochetopa Pass for their crossing to the valley of the Grand (Gunnison) River. On the first of September, Richard recorded a view of the eastern entrance to the pass, *Coo-Che-To-Pa Pass*, "looking up Sahwatch Creek,"[29] depicting the narrow valley of the Sahwatch and the large cliff portals of the pass beyond. As the party moved down the valley of the Grand (Gunnison) River, the artist made several views of the canyon country from different vantage points along the route.[30] The versions of these views in the report are simply constructed and probably follow Richard's sketches closely, since they reflect more of the true topography and physical geology than do the preceding plates. It was probably while the expeditionary party was ascending the hills to skirt the deep ravines of the Grand (Gunnison) that Richard made his single extant field sketch of the *Grand [Gunnison] River Mesa* and surrounding country (plate 26),[31] working in pencil and sepia wash and adding color suggestions and notations on the different geological structures. In describing the view from the hills, Gunnison tells of the character of the country that Kern so carefully documented in his field sketch:

> The Elk mountains tower high above us to the west, the hills immediately along the valley being high and more or less of a table character, or what the mountain men, of Spanish descent, term mesas— elevated level spaces of land, terminated on one or more sides by precipices and lower levels. Grand [Gunnison] river is at present a fine, clear stream of cold water, one hundred feet wide and three feet deep, flowing rapidly over a paving-stone bed.[32]

In his sketch Kern adds to Gunnison's description by locating the "Black Mesa" with a dark wash and a pencil notation indicating that the party was still several miles east of this distinctive landform.[33]

Before the men crossed over into Utah, Kern made a sketch titled *View of the Roan or Book Mountains, Oct. 1st [1853]* (plate 27), which has a certain stylized charm and picturesqueness reminiscent of a view from the *Hudson River Portfolio*. While he was in Utah,

he produced a second view, *Rock Hills between Green and White Rivers*,[34] which indicates that the party was traveling northward and westward through Utah toward the great Sevier Valley (central Utah).

On October 25, Captain Gunnison, Richard Kern, Creutzfeldt, their guide William Potter, and an escort of eight men separated from the main party to explore in the vicinity of Sevier Lake, in west-central Utah. The next day, Gunnison and his small detachment were ambushed by a band of Pah-Utah Indians. Only four of the men escaped death. News of the tragedy reached the main camp late in the afternoon. Brevet-Captain Robert M. Morris and Lieutenant Beckwith departed immediately for the scene of the massacre, where they found the disfigured bodies of Captain Gunnison, Kern, Creutzfeldt, and Potter.[35] Lieutenant Beckwith assumed leadership of the survey and continued northward to Salt Lake City, where he eventually recovered Kern's sketchbooks, most of the instruments, and all of the field notes captured by the Indians. Unfortunately, the whereabouts of these invaluable pictorial records, apart from one field sketch by Richard, are unknown today.[36]

Since Richard's life had been snuffed out midway in his career, one can only assume that his skills would have continued to sharpen as he gained exposure to and knowledge of the natural topography. That Richard Kern achieved a certain renown for his achievements in exploring and recording the expanding western frontier during his brief lifetime is reflected in an article in the *St. Louis Evening News*, dated December 18, 1853:

> One of the victims of the Gunnison Massacre was Mr. Richard H. Kern, of Philadelphia, one of the most valued and promising officers of the country. . . .
> Mr. Kern was one of the most daring, intelligent, experienced, and cultivated pioneers of our vast western wilds. He had several times crossed the continent, and was on Fremont's last ill-fated expedition. . . . Richard, whose sad fate is now mourned by his friends, was a very superior draughtsman, a thorough scholar, an accomplished linguist, and gifted with that sagacity and energy which are so invaluable to those who lead a mountain and frontier life. Had he lived, he would doubtless have rendered good service to the country.[37]

PLATE 26
Richard Kern, *Grand [Gunnison] River Mesa*, 1853, Pencil and sepia wash, 8″ × 12½″.
Courtesy private collection.

JOHN MIX STANLEY: THE PATHFINDER'S ARTIST

. . . Whatever he undertakes—whether a wild Western prairie or mountain scene, an Indian dance, a buffalo hunt, or a portrait, his drawing seems *equally strong, his perception of form equally accurate, and his treatment of color equally judicious and effective.*—"Art Gossip," ca. 1865?[38]

Of the eleven artists who traveled in an official capacity with the Pacific Railroad Surveys through the West, John Mix Stanley was by far the most celebrated. By 1853, when he signed on with the Isaac Stevens Expedition to survey a northern route from Saint Paul to Puget Sound, Stanley had already logged over a decade of adventure in painting the West and its inhabitants. He was recognized as one of America's most knowledgeable and perceptive interpreters of the western scene, standing in the forefront of American art of his day. His humble beginnings would not have foretold such an illustrious career.

Stanley was born in Canandaigua, New York, on January 17, 1814.[39] At fourteen he was apprenticed to a wagonmaster in Naples, New York, where he may have begun his career as a painter of sideboard designs. In 1832, Stanley moved to Buffalo and established himself briefly as a house and sign painter. Then in 1834, he went to Detroit where, according to later accounts, he was taken under the wing of a portrait painter named James Bowman, who, impressed by the young artist's potential, sought him out and offered him free instruction.[40]

It is known that, in 1839, Stanley traveled into the frontier as far as Fort Snelling with the probable intention of painting likenesses of Indians; during the next few years he was recorded as a portrait painter in Detroit, Chicago, and Galena, Illinois.[41] Perhaps to sell Indian paintings and possibly to garner more commissions for his portrait work, he then turned eastward and between 1839 and 1843 tendered his services in Philadelphia, Baltimore, New York, and Troy. These were cities in which Catlin and Miller had made reputations for their Indian and western scenes only a few years earlier. Their successes no doubt encouraged Stanley to direct his attention again toward the frontier—to what Catlin called "the vast and pathless wilds which are the great 'Far West.'"[42]

In Troy, Stanley formed a close association with Sumner Dickerman, who became his traveling companion and part owner of an "Indian Gallery" modeled closely on Catlin's. Their adventures took them deep into the southwestern frontier; between 1842 and 1846 they visited Arkansas, Texas, Oklahoma, and New Mexico. Stanley's paintings made such an impression in Arkansas that the *Arkansas Intelligencer* twice reported on the progress and merit of his labors. After a second visit to the artist's temporary studio, the paper reported:

We all have heard of, and many have seen, "Catlin's Gallery," how he spent time and money, and meanderings among our aboriginal specimens, collecting subjects, traditions and sketches. But he has a fair rival in the field, who in the opinion of connoisseurs will bear the palm away from the Catlin, although the latter is the originator of the scheme. We allude to Messrs. Stanley and Dickerman, artists from Troy, N.Y., who are now in the Indian country, assiduously engaged in talking [taking] portraitures, sketches and designs of and among the principal Indians. . . . Mr. Stanley is an artitse [artist] of fine talents, and the specimens of his own labor which are exhibited in his studio, are well worthy a genius ranking of the first order: and why not? Why not a great American, as well as an Italian artist? Why not Stanley as well as Ruben[s]?[43]

One newspaper report suggests that Stanley and Dickerman may have reached the Rockies in those early years, stating that they had "traversed the country between the Missouri and Colorado Rivers," yet other evidence points to the conclusion that their focus remained on the southwestern plains.[44] Despite this brief western experience, Stanley by early 1846 had accumulated eighty-three oil portraits and scenes of Indian life; in that year he initiated a tour of these works that began in Cincinnati[45] and moved to Louisville. At this point, unwilling to commit himself to the confining schedule of a traveling show, he left Dickerman in charge of the gallery and turned once again to the West.

That August he joined Colonel Stephen Watts Kearny's "Army of the West" on its march to California—an opportunity occasioned in part by the illness of the two artists assigned to William H. Emory's topographical unit, Lieutenants James W. Abert and G. W. Peck.[46]

The expedition moved south along the Rio Grande, soon passing beyond the southern extent of the Rockies. Stanley's *San Felipe, New Mexico* (plate 28), one of thirteen extant landscape paintings in oil resulting from the Kearny Expedition, is the only one known to illustrate a scene within the parameters of the Rocky Mountains.[47] The scene portrays Kearny's forces proceeding south toward the headwaters of the Gila River, where they were to turn westward toward California. On the left, Emory recounted, was the "pretty village of San Felippe, overhung by a steep craggy precipice, upon the summit of which are the ruins of a Roman Catholic church, presenting in the landscape sketch the appearance of the pictures we see of castles on the Rhine."[48]

Such associations were refreshing for Emory and other men experienced on the trail, who satisfied themselves as much with the surroundings and their history as with the promise of conquest ahead. The crumbling ruins in the foreground of Stanley's small field sketch provide a pictorial metaphor on the passing of ancient civilizations, while the disappearing column of troopers suggests the infinite breadth of the western landscape; the crows which flock ominously above them are perhaps omens of the encounters to be faced.[49] Another oil study, *Butte on the Del Norte* (color plate 7), was captured in the early stages of the journey; it depicts a scene just south of the Rockies. In its bold yet simple articulation of form, its grand, silhouetted geomorphic masses, and its muted tones highlighted with variegated sunlit foliage, the small study is typical of Stanley's field work of 1846.

Stanley, who was listed in the Emory report as "draughtsman,"[50] provided continuous visual documentation as the troop proceeded westward. That Emory relied on the artist's abilities is evident in his description of the Gila Valley, which they reached in November:

About two miles from camp, our course was traversed by a seam of yellowish colored igneous rock, shooting up into irregular spires and turrets, one or two thousand feet in height. It ran at right angles to the river, and extended to the north, and to the south, in a chain of mountains as far as the eye could reach. One of these towers was capped with a substance, many hundred feet thick, disposed in horizontal strata of different colors, from deep red to light yellow. Partially disintegrated, and laying out the foot of the chain of spires, was a yellowish calcareous sandstone, altered by fire, in large amorphous masses.

For a better description of this landscape, see the sketch by Mr. Stanly [*sic*].[51]

By the time Kearny's troop reached the Pacific Coast, Stanley had enlarged America's vision of the pictorial western panorama by recording a large part of what is now southern New Mexico, Arizona, and California. His subjects had ranged from his favorites, Indian portraits, to skillful botanical sketches, landscapes, views of the major points of travel, and even petroglyphs inscribed on several canyon walls.

Before arriving at San Diego, the group had two major encounters with the Mexican army, one of which was the battle of San Pascual. Stanley, left with a small group to guard the baggage, did not witness the battle.[52] In a subsequent engagement between the two forces Stanley lost all his personal belongings but was able to save his most precious possessions—his sketches of the trip and his painting materials.[53] In late December the American forces ascended a small hill and looked for the first time on San Diego and the Pacific.

The long trip had come to an end. Stanley was allowed to go aboard the sloop *Cyane*, then anchored in San Diego harbor, to convert his sketches into finished paintings.[54] Although they are generally considered in situ studies, it is difficult to determine whether small oils such as *San Felipe, New Mexico*, represent fieldwork, paintings worked up from field sketches, or both. In a letter to Sumner Dickerman written from San Diego in late January, 1847, Stanley indicates at least some of his work was in watercolor: "Captain Emory takes a part of my sketches with him; as yet they have been

John Mix Stanley, *San Felipe, New Mexico*, 1846, Oil on board, 10″ × 12¾″.
Courtesy Stark Museum of Art, Orange, Texas.

confined to plants and are in water color. I have become a proficient in this branch of the art."[55]

Stanley remained with the *Cyane* when it sailed to San Francisco in the spring of that year. There he delivered a number of small oils to Emory, and it was from these that the lithographs for the finished report were made. Edwin Bryant, an American visiting California, saw the oils and remarked:

> Mr. Stanley, the artist of the expedition, completed his sketches in oil, at San Francisco; and a more truthful, interesting, and valuable series of paintings, delineating mountain scenery, the floral exhibitions on the route, the savage tribes between Santa Fe and California—combined with camp-life and marches through the desert and wilderness—has never been, and probably never will be exhibited.[56]

From San Francisco, Stanley turned north. Traveling deep into Oregon, he painted many landscapes, as well as portraits of settlers and Indians. In the spring of 1848 he set sail for Hawaii, where Kamehameha III and his queen sat for him for their portraits.[57]

Stanley was back in New York by the end of November, 1850, when an advertisement in the *New York Tribune* announced the exhibition of 134 oil paintings in "Stanley's North American Indian Gallery." The exhibition comprised portraits, Indian scenes, and landscapes, "all of which have been painted in their own country during eight years travel, . . . the whole forming one of the most interesting and instructive exhibitions illustrative of Indian life and customs ever before presented to the public."[58]

In early 1852, Stanley moved the collection to Washington, D.C., where the Indian portraits and "several exquisite pieces of landscape of different character" were received enthusiastically. As the *National Intelligencer* observed, Stanley's move was overtly political:

> Learning that it was agitated by some judicious and patriotic members of Congress to purchase Catlin's collection, which is now in Europe, and perhaps will always remain there, Mr. Stanley brought his to the metropolis that members might see for themselves and judge of its fitness to become the foundation of a great national gallery.[59]

Stanley's paintings soon found their way into the Smithsonian Institution, where they remained for more than a dozen years.

In December, 1852, the Smithsonian issued a seventy-six-page catalog of his works, *Portraits of North American Indians, with Sketches of Scenery, Etc., Painted by J. M. Stanley*. Said the artist, "The collection embraced in this Catalogue comprises accurate portraits painted from life of forty-three different tribes of Indians, obtained at the cost, hazard, and inconvenience of a ten years' tour through the South-western Prairies, New Mexico, California, and Oregon."[60] Such claims could not have been made by any of Stanley's colleagues, including George Catlin, who had long shared similar ambitions and national attention.

Evidencing the same restlessness that had taken him west in the 1840s, Stanley soon turned his back on his newfound success on the eastern seaboard. From the Pacific shore the *Oregonian* advised its readers in June, 1853, that Stanley was once again on his way to the Far West: "It is said that J. M. Stanley, Esq., the artist, is to accompany Governor Stevens to the new Territory of Washington, to assist in the necessary surveys of that comparatively unexplored region."[61]

By the date of this account the Stevens Expedition had already left Saint Paul and was working across the prairie in search of the most practical route west between the 47th and 49th parallels. A report from Saint Paul noted that Stevens had employed two artists, John Mix Stanley and Max Strobel. "I have already seen some of the Artists' work," the account related, "and can promise the public when Gov. Stevens's Report is made up and given to the world, there will be something as pleasing to the eye as to the mind."[62] Unfortunately, Stanley was not to have the assistance of a fellow artist for very long. A little over a month after the journey had begun, Strobel was back in Saint Paul, leaving Stanley alone with the task of recording the vast tract of plains, mountains, and rivers to be traversed in the months ahead.[63] It was a challenge that he was fully able to meet. By mid-September, Isaac Stevens could write from Fort Benton on the Upper Missouri that "J. M. Stanley, Esq., the artist of the expedition, has taken a great many sketches, . . . besides taking at various points on the way numerous daguerreotypes of Indians."[64]

It was in the vicinity of Fort Benton, while the Stevens party surveyed the broad valley of the Teton River, that Stanley made the sketch that was to inspire his later masterpiece *Encampment in the Teton Country* (color plate 8).[65] The original sketch was probably made in watercolor, for extant fieldwork from the expedition is in that medium.[66] Unfortunately, its whereabouts is not known today. The view of the Teton Valley that appeared as an illustration in the Stevens report was without figures and was taken from near the valley floor.[67] Its intimate interpretation is in opposition to the expansive, almost grandiose vista portrayed in *Encampment.*

Despite the imposing nature of the central figures in the foreground of the composition, Stanley's painting is very much a part of the panoramic landscape tradition. The scenic view stretches across the width of the picture plane, devoid of any artifice that might divert or direct the viewer. As a consequence, a truly panoramic vista is achieved wherein the eye moves casually from place to place in no predetermined pattern. It is a natural solution to the problem of representing the illimitable distance observed in the western country, and it also reproduces the very randomness with which one might observe the topography from an elevated position, such as the summit of a mountain. Stanley was to record many views of the Rocky Mountains in the weeks that followed this initial look at the front range.

As the party crossed the Rockies at Lewis and Clark Pass and proceeded westward to Vancouver, Washington, its final destination, Stanley added to his sketchbook a charming depiction of civilization's early encroachment on the western wilderness, *The Coeur d'Alene Mission, St. Ignatius River* (plate 29). Like his other fieldworks, the watercolor is broadly painted, conveying, along with its spontaneity, a certain charm and casualness. Unlike his studio painting *Encampment,* this view is not a panorama but a more intimate scene. Sketches such as this were later used to illustrate the official government reports (plate 30). Although somewhat tighter and more descriptive in their execution, the corresponding lithographs produced by the firm Sarony, Major, and Knapp of New York retain much of the charm and immediacy of the originals. The twelfth volume of the *Reports,* which contained Stevens's account and Stanley's illustrations, is recognized as one of the most beautiful and imposing books produced in midnineteenth-century America.

That Stevens was pleased with "the various labors of Mr. Stanley"

is attested to in the first volume of the *Reports,* where the expedition's leader boasts of Stanley and his many assets:

> Besides occupying his professional field with an ability above any commendation which we can bestow, Mr. Stanley has surveyed two routes —from Fort Benton to the Cypress mountain, and from the St. Mary's valley to Fort Colveille over the Bitter Root range of mountains— to the furtherance of our geographic information, and the ascertaining of important points in the question of a railroad; and he has also rendered effectual services in both cases, and throughout his services with the exploration, in intercourse with the Indians.[68]

By early January, 1854, Stanley was back on the East Coast,[69] and by September he was preparing his sketches for publication.[70] Between January and September, 1854, he was actively involved in working up his sketches into finished oils for his collection at the Smithsonian, but his considerable energies were also being expended on the production of a great moving panorama, *"Stanley's Western Wilds, or, the Indian and His Country, . . .* showing the Northern Pacific Railroad Route, as recently surveyed by Governor Stevens."[71] This ambitious enterprise, consisting of forty-two episodes and requiring two hours to view, was completed in late summer and began its tour in Washington, D.C. That autumn it was shown in Baltimore, where the press "proclaimed it the most beautiful and instructive work of art ever seen there."[72] In Washington members of Congress were encouraged to view the massive panorama of western images to acquaint themselves with the type of country "through which the Northern Railroad route to the Pacific . . . [was] destined to pass."[73] Thus Stanley, beyond his achievements as a painter and explorer, was to serve as a protagonist in a cause of national significance, one for which he had committed at least ten months of his time in on-site documentation.

Other elements of success for Stanley's panorama included the novelty of its theme and the true-to-life quality of its images. Visitors to *The Western Wilds* were sold a ten-cent booklet by the poet Thomas S. Donaho titled *Scenes and Incidents of Stanley's Western Wilds;* on every page the reader was reminded of Stanley's direct observation. As with other popular panoramas of the period, the work successfully interspersed landscapes with narrative scenes; works like *The*

PLATE 29

John Mix Stanley, *The Coeur d'Alene Mission, St. Ignatius River,* 1853, Watercolor, 8⅝″ × 10⅞″.
Courtesy the Collection of Mr. Paul Mellon, Upperville, Va.

PLATE 30

John Mix Stanley, *Couer d'Alene Mission, St. Ignatius River*, 1855, Color lithograph, 5¾″ × 8⅞″.
Courtesy Denver Public Library, Western History Department, Denver.

Coeur de Laine [sic] *Mission* and *Valley of the Teton* were comfortably mixed with scenes of buffalo hunts, Indian councils, and preying wolves. Unfortunately the great panorama was eventually lost. The last reports note its departure for Boston and London; no further traces of it have been found.[74]

After 1853, Stanley never went west again, though he continued throughout his career to produce work inspired by his journey to America's frontier. In 1863 he moved to Buffalo. A year later he settled in Detroit, the site of his sign-painter beginnings; there he began what biographers have called "his most important single work,"[75] *The Trial of Red Jacket.* It was not long after his return to Detroit that Stanley received devastating news: his "Indian Gallery," still housed at the Smithsonian, had been destroyed by fire. Of the collection, which by then numbered over one hundred and fifty paintings, only five were reported to have survived. In the Smithsonian's "Proceedings of the Board of Regents" for 1865 it was recorded that the loss amounted to $20,000—small compensation, which he incidentally never received, for all his years of labor.[76]

In the nearly two decades between Stanley's return from the West and his death in 1872, his interest in the Rocky Mountains continued. One example is a landscape, completed in Detroit several months before the fire, titled *Black Foot Pass in the Rocky Mountains.* The painting, whose whereabouts today is unknown, was celebrated for its affinity with American sentiments. One Detroit paper explained, "It is no such a daub as Ruskin describes some of the productions of our English cousins to be, but a faithful representation of nature in this grandest of all mountain chains."[77]

From a vantage point over a century after his time, one might conclude that John Mix Stanley's position as a leader in interpreting the western scene lies in his versatility: he worked as effectively within the confines of topographical documentation as he did in the imaginative, romantic idiom of his artist contemporaries.

GUSTAVUS SOHON: GERMAN TOPOGRAPHER WITH THE FOURTH INFANTRY IN THE ROCKIES

Mr. Sohon's early connexion with my explorations in 1853 and 1854, his knowledge of the Indian language, his familiarity with the general scope of country to be traversed, and the influence he had always so beneficially exerted over the Indians, all pointed him out as the proper person to explore the new and dangerous region. —Captain John Mullan[78]

Another artist who served in the employ of Governor Isaac Stevens (though not necessarily in Stanley's party) and then remained in the Rocky Mountain West for almost a decade was Gustavus Sohon. Born in Tilsit, Germany, on December 10, 1825, he came to America in 1842.[79] Ten years later he enlisted in the United States Army; in the summer of 1853 he was with Company K of the Fourth Infantry Regiment under Captain George B. McClellan. His party had been ordered to work eastward from the Pacific to Fort Dalles on the Columbia River while Stevens and his party moved westward. In mid-July, continuing the eastward thrust, Sohon's company left Fort Dalles and headed for the Bitterroot Mountains, just west of the main chain of the Rockies. There he was assigned as "artist, barometer-carrier, and observer"[80] to a surveying team under the command of Lieutenant John Mullan. The initial job confronting this auxiliary group was a critical one, summarized in Mullan's *Report:*

> The problem of a railroad connexion from St. Paul across the prairies to the eastern water-shed of the Rocky Mountains, in latitude 46 and 47 degrees, was one of easy solution, and the country was therefore accurately and rapidly explored; but the late autumn of 1853 found our labors of exploration truly only begun; for we now entered the more difficult section of the Bitter Root range of the Rocky Mountains, where the lateness of the season, the difficulty of the country, the importance of our mission, the scarcity of our supplies, the meagerness of the information we then possessed, and the necessity felt for a

PLATE 31
Gustavus Sohon, *Hot Spring Mound in the Deer Lodge Prairie of the Rocky Mountains,* 1853, Pencil, 8″ × 12⅛″.
Courtesy the Collection of Paul Mellon, Upperville.

more detailed and thorough exploration of the Rocky Mountain section, since proved to be the key of the work, together with other equally cogent reasons existing at the time, all conspired to influence Governor Stevens to leave in the mountains a small party for the winter in 1853, for further explorations, and thus supply that information which a lack of time did not allow to collect at an earlier period.[81]

During the winter of 1853–54, Sohon assisted Mullan in the search for viable railroad routes through the northern ranges of the Rockies. He was described as "an intelligent German, a clever sketcher and competent to take instrumental observations."[82] An accomplished linguist, he was also involved in interpreting and assisting in negotiations between Mullan and the Flathead and Pend d'Oreille Indians. His most enduring contributions, however, were the watercolors and pencil drawings he produced as a result of that winter's tour (plate 31). So impressed was Stevens by Sohon's abilities that he had the artist transferred to his own command in 1855.

Sohon had crossed the Rockies many times during his winter with Mullan. Now he recrossed them with Stevens en route from Fort Walla Walla to Fort Benton. The main purpose of this trip was to establish treaties with the Indians that would result in cession of certain of their lands. Sohon served as interpreter and liaison on most of these occasions. In connection with the railroad surveys he also assisted Stevens in determining acceptable approaches to Cadotte's Pass over the Rockies. His panoramic view, *Main Chain of the Rocky Mountains from the East* . . . (plate 32), was one of twelve of Sohon's illustrations in the official survey reports.[83]

The drawing appears as an illustration in editions of both 1859 and 1860 of the report. In the edition of 1859 it is credited to Stanley, while in the edition of 1860 the caption reads "Stanley, Del. after Sohon."[84] The original work, however, is decidedly that of Sohon. The contour outline of the distant range and the painstakingly precise delineation of topographical features, particularly in the shaded areas of the valley wall in the middle distance, are typical of Sohon's tightly controlled style and in direct contrast to Stanley's broadly washed watercolor field studies. In the published version the view is treated somewhat more broadly, and many embellishments have been added.[85]

Sohon was very much a part of the topographic tradition. Although nothing is known of his artistic training, he was obviously a qualified technician and a careful recorder with an eye for the topographic details of nature. Before joining the army, he was variously reported to have been a wood-carver, a photographer, and a bookbinder; his precise drawings are perhaps an outgrowth of skills learned in those trades.

After completing his services for Stevens, Sohon spent several years in Washington Territory and California. In 1859, as a result of major appropriations from Congress for a wagon road from Fort Benton to Fort Walla Walla, Lieutenant Mullan was called back into the Rockies. Because of Indian unrest Sohon's talents as a diplomat were especially sought for the mission.

Throughout the summer of 1860, Mullan and Sohon surveyed and made initial plans for a road over the northern Rockies. In the autumn Sohon guided a force of three hundred military recruits and civilians from Fort Benton to Fort Walla Walla, following, and thus proving, the newly established route. He later assisted in construction of the road, working in the field with Mullan until 1862, when they both went to Washington, D.C., to prepare the published report.[86]

Sohon never returned to the Rockies. He worked for a few years as a photographer in San Francisco and then moved back to Washington, D.C., where he spent the rest of his life in the shoe business. It is not known whether he pursued his art further; no examples appear to have survived. The work he produced throughout nearly a decade in the Rockies, however, had established his contribution as an artist and topographer.

PLATE 32. Gustavus Sohon, *Main Chain of the Rocky Mountains from the East . . .* , 1853, Watercolor in three parts,

GWINN HARRIS HEAP: WEST THROUGH THE CENTRAL ROCKIES WITH EDWARD F. BEALE

In the journal now offered to the public, I have endeavored to give a correct representation of the country which we traversed; and, although I do not pretend to do justice to the subject, I trust that these notes will *not be altogether without value, particularly at a time when the public mind is engrossed with a subject of such stupendous magnitude as the establishment of a trans-continental railway.* —Gwinn Harris Heap[87]

In the same year that Gunnison received an official command to survey the lands between the 38th and 39th parallels for a trans-continental railroad, Thomas Hart Benton—dissatisfied with the government's choice—instigated and promoted the launching of two independent ventures to explore the central route "in an attempt to offset any possible negative opinions by Gunnison's official party."

8 5/16″ × 12 5/16″, 8 3/8″ × 12 3/16″, 8 5/16″ × 8 3/4″. Courtesy the Collection of Paul Mellon, Upperville.

Edward F. Beale was leader of one party, while Frémont, on his fifth expedition (another midwinter reconnaissance), commanded the other.[88] In his book *Central Route to the Pacific* (1854), the artist Gwinn Harris Heap, Beale's chronicler and kinsman, gives an interesting account of the trip.

As Heap informs us, the route Beale followed was in accordance with his instructions to find the "shortest and most direct" path to California, while leaving sufficient time to explore possible new locations for the Indians of California.[89] According to Heap, the small party left Washington, D.C., on April 20 for Westport, Missouri, the jumping-off point for their westward journey, and then followed the routine course of travel up the Kansas River to the Arkansas River. Following the Arkansas as far as the Huerfano, they ascended this river to the Sangre de Cristo Mountains and crossed over to the San Luis Valley. Reaching the western slope of the Rockies by Cochetopa Pass, they continued their journey westward along the Gunnison and the Grand into Utah (a route that Gunnison and Frémont were later to travel), proceeding from there into California.[90]

Information about the life and artwork of Gwinn Heap is not as extensive as that about other reportorial artists who traveled westward.[91] Heap, whose "great-grandfather George had been sent by the British government to serve as surveyor general of Pennsylvania," was born in Chester, Pennsylvania, on March 23, 1817.[92] Most of his early life was spent in Europe and North Africa, where his father served as United States Consul. Sometime in 1846, after his family returned to America, Heap obtained a position as a government clerk in Washington, D.C. In March, 1853, he joined his cousin's expedition to California to serve as topographer and chronicler. During the journey (as Beale says in a letter to the editor of the *National Intelligencer,* written on September 5, 1853) Heap took detailed daily notes on the operation and "sketches of all camping places of note."[93] In 1854, after the publication of his journal, Heap returned to government work, following closely in his father's footsteps. He died on March 3, 1887, while serving as consul general in Constantinople.[94]

In spite of Heap's limited artistic skills, his designs for the thirteen illustrations represent fairly accurately the character of the country traversed by the expeditionary party. It is nevertheless obvious from the lithographs, which must serve in place of the lost originals, that the artist-chronicler's sense of perspective and proportion was far from correct. Despite a certain awkwardness in his drawing, Heap's scenic views do have a certain charm. Several of his views were also pictorial firsts for Colorado, among them *Coochatope Pass* and *Huerfano Butte,* scenes of topographical features that were recorded by Richard Kern and S. N. Carvalho in the same year.[95]

It is doubtful that Heap received any formal instruction in art during his early years. It is more likely that he was self-tutored, to judge from the simple views in his published journal—the only examples of his artwork available today. Here again, the task of making an artistic judgment of Heap's only known artistic endeavor is complicated because his scenic views exist only as reproductions. Typical of other artist-explorers who traveled through southern Colorado, Heap was attracted to the pyramid-shaped Spanish Peaks,[96] standing like sentinels on the edge of the great sandy plains. Like Seymour, he followed a prescribed formula for picture making that was a provincial reflection of eighteenth-century English topographical art, which indicates that he may have been among the many artists who referred to prints as a method of learning. Although this picture includes quaint and picturesque motifs, the artist has not sacrificed topographical accuracy in his representation of a familiar southern Colorado landmark. Another prominent landmark for itinerants, *Huerfano Butte* (plate 33), also attracted Heap's attention, reminding him of "a huge artificial mound of stones."

Heap's two depictions of *Coochatope Pass* were the first recordings of this accessible gateway to the western slope. In his first view[97] the weary travelers are shown resting in front of the huge portals that flank the opening to the pass. In the second view[98] we observe a small party on mules winding their way up the pass. The quaintness of the small, comical figures and the artist's lack of sophistication in handling perspective lend a certain naïve charm to the picture.

Unlike the more experienced topographers of the period, such as the Kern brothers, Heap presumably had little opportunity to prepare for his artistic assignment; as a result his sketches lack evidence of discipline and academic training. His contribution to the visual documentation of western expansion in the nineteenth century is thus important from a historic rather than an artistic point of view.[99]

PLATE 33

Gwinn Heap, *Huerfano Butte*, Lithograph, 4″ × 7″.
Courtesy Huntington Library, San Marino.

SOLOMON NUNES CARVALHO: TRACKS THROUGH THE CENTRAL ROCKIES WITH JOHN C. FRÉMONT

We then started for the Rio Virgin, the approach to which, was through the most beautiful and romantic pass I ever saw: it is a natural gorge, in a very high range of mountains of red sandstone, which assume, on either side, the most fantastic and fearful forms; many look as if they were in the very act of falling on the road below them. . . . I have travelled through the beautiful passes in the Rocky and Warsatch [sic] Mountains, but I have seen nothing that could excel this, either for the facilities of a railroad, which could be constructed through it without grading, or for the magnificence of the combinations which are requisite to produce effect in a grand landscape. —S. N. Carvalho[100]

Frémont had fervently desired to be chosen to lead the government's railroad exploratory expedition of 1853, but he was overlooked in favor of John W. Gunnison. Determined not to be denied this opportunity, Frémont organized a private expedition with the support of his friends and his influential father-in-law, Senator Thomas Hart Benton. The party essentially followed the trail Gunnison had traversed some months earlier, over Cochetopa Pass and across south-central Colorado into Utah. Solomon Nunes Carvalho, the artist and daguerreotypist for the expedition, has left a vivid account of the journey in his *Incidents of Travel and Adventure in the Far West*.

Carvalho's background until this time had been totally urban. He was born on April 27, 1815, in Charleston, South Carolina, where his father was a successful merchant and watchmaker. In 1828 the family moved to Baltimore, where the senior Carvalho established a marble-paper factory. When Solomon was twenty, the family moved to Philadelphia, and it was there that he began his career as an artist and daguerreotypist. In 1853–54 he joined Frémont's fifth expedition to the West. In 1860, soon after his father's death, he and his wife and four sons moved to New York City, where he worked as an artist and daguerreotypist until 1880, when he established the Carvalho Heating and Super-Heating Company. He died in New York on May 21, 1897, after a successful career as an artist, daguerreotypist, and inventor.[101]

As with so many other obscure western artists, no evidence exists to document Carvalho's first propensity for art or "with whom he studied, other than a vague family tradition that he did some work with Thomas Sully in Philadelphia."[102] It seems probable that he began dabbling in art after the family moved to Philadelphia, where he could have availed himself of the best professional talent. It is certain that by 1838 he had launched his career as a part-time artist while working intermittently as a salesman in the West Indies —a fact documented by his painting of the *Interior of Beth Elohim Synagogue* (Charleston), executed after the destruction of the synagogue by fire in 1838. The hard linear construction and one-point perspective that characterize this work indicate that the artist was an amateur following the advice of a simple drawing and painting instruction book.[103] Extant portraits of Carvalho's kinsmen in the Barbados, which he executed between 1840 and 1844, indicate that the artist had embarked on a career as a portraitist[104]—a deduction substantiated by an advertisement in the Charleston *Courier* dated June 10, 1841, announcing that Carvalho was accepting portrait commissions.[105] After his marriage in 1845, Carvalho listed himself in the city directories of Philadelphia, Baltimore, and Charleston as a professional daguerreotypist and portraitist.[106] This is the earliest concrete evidence we have that Carvalho was engaged in the popular new process of daguerreotypy, which would make him a likely candidate for the position of photographer and artist on Frémont's fifth expedition.

Just what a dramatic, uncharacteristic activity the Frémont expedition was in Carvalho's life is expressed in the preface to his published journal:

On the 22d August, 1853, after a short interview with Col. J. C. Fremont, I accepted his invitation to accompany him as artist of an Exploring Expedition across the Rocky Mountains. A half hour previously, if anybody had suggested to me, the probability of my undertaking an overland journey to California . . . I should have replied there were no inducements sufficiently powerful to have tempted me. Yet, in this instance, I impulsively, without even a consultation with my family, passed my word to join an exploring party, under command of Col. Fremont, over a hitherto untrodden country, in an elevated region, with the full expectation of being exposed to all the inclemencies of an artic [*sic*] winter.

Col. Fremont's former extraordinary explorations, his astronomical and geographical contributions to the useful sciences, and his successful pursuit of them under difficulties, had deeply interested me, and aided in forming for him, in my mind, the beau ideal of all that was chivalrous and noble.[107]

The journal also reveals that it took Carvalho ten days to assemble the various materials needed for his special assignment on the mission. That he anticipated the problems involved in making daguerreotypes en route is borne out by the following paragraph:

> Buffing and coating plates, and mercurializing them, on the summit of the Rocky Mountains, standing at times up to one's middle in snow, with no covering above save the arched vault of heaven, seemed to our city friends one of the impossibilities. . . . I shall not appear egotistical if I say that I encountered many difficulties, but I was well prepared to meet them by having previously acquired a scientific and practical knowledge of the chemicals I used, as well as of the theory of light: a firm determination to succeed also, aided me in producing results which, to my knowledge, have never been accomplished under similar circumstances.[108]

Carvalho left New York for Saint Louis by stagecoach on September 5, 1853, burdened not only with cumbersome daguerreotype equipment but with paintings and "other such provisions as food stuffs." From Saint Louis he and Frémont embarked for Kansas on the steamer *F. X. Aubrey.* This portion of the journey was somewhat delayed because the river was low; they did not reach the Kansas dock until the fourteenth. Ten days later the party set out for the West from the Shawnee Mission.

Early in the trip Carvalho described in his journal night light effects he had observed near one encampment. The description reflects his extensive knowledge of traditional schools of art in the romantic vein: "The full moon was shining brightly, and the piles of clouds which surrounded her, presented magnificent studies of light and shadow which Claude Lorraine so loved to paint."[109]

Before starting on the long journey, Carvalho sent his painting materials back to Saint Louis because, as he wrote in his journal, "the weather continuing so cold, I found it inconvenient to use my oil colors and brushes."[110] This entry is important in the documentation of his artistic production on this expedition, for it indicates that his work consisted largely of daguerreotypes.

Of all the journals produced by itinerant artists and topographers, Carvalho's is one of the most personal, revealing his romantic sensibilities and deep religious convictions. This aspect of his personality was counterbalanced by an inventive, scientific mind and the ability to capture with anatomical precision the bison and other animals of the great prairies. In his account of the long, toiling ascent to the summit of the Cochetopa Pass, the artist describes his reaction to this challenging vista in poetic, almost lyrical terms:

> . . . [We] beheld a panorama of unspeakable sublimity spread out before us; continuous chains of mountains reared their snowy peaks far away in the distance, while the Grand River plunging along in awful sublimity through its rocky bed, was seen for the first time. Above us the cerulean heaven, without a single cloud to mar its beauty, was sublime in its calmness.
>
> Standing as it were in this vestibule of God's holy Temple, I forgot I was of this mundane sphere; the divine part of man elevated itself, undisturbed by the influences of the world. I looked from nature, up to nature's God, more chastened and purified than I ever felt before.[111]

At this point, high on a lofty peak and plunged to his waist in snow, Carvalho "made a panorama of the continuous range of mountains" around them.

In Utah the exploring party encountered great difficulties, deep snows, dwindling supplies, and exhaustion caused by the rigors of their travels through an uncharted country of "almost impassable" mountains and canyons. At this point all excess baggage, including Carvalho's daguerreotype equipment, was abandoned, "but the plates, prepared with great toil, were carried with the party, which finally reached the Mormon settlement of Parowan."[112] Apparently the many views that Carvalho took were to have illustrated a scientific report planned by Frémont;[113] in 1856, however, after being nominated for the presidency by the national Republican party,

Frémont abandoned the project. He did, however, take the plates to New York, where they were copied into photographs by the well-known photographer Mathew B. Brady. These same paper prints were later employed for Frémont's *Memoirs*. The reason for the difficulty in attributing most of the illustrations in this book becomes clear in light of Jessie Frémont's explanation of the work on Carvalho's plates:

> . . . Mr. Frémont worked constantly at Mr. Brady's studio aiding to fix these daguerre pictures in their more permanent form of photographs. Then at our . . . house I made a studio of the north drawing-room. . . . Here for some months [James] Hamilton worked on these views, reproducing many in oil; he was a pupil of Turner and had great joy in the true cloud effects as well as in the stern mountains and castellated rock formations. The engravings on wood were also made under our home and supervision; by an artist young then, a namesake and grandson of Frank Key, the author of "The Star-Spangled Banner." From these artists their work was passed to artist-engravers of the best school of their art. Darley also contributed his talent. Some pictures he enlarged into india ink sketches, and from his hand came the figures in many of the plates.[114]

It is possible, however, that some of the illustrations in Frémont's *Memoirs* were directly based on Carvalho's original "views" as recounted in the narrative. Although Frémont never specifically states which ones are Carvalho's, several plates seem closer to actual views of nature than purely illustrative copies.[115]

When the artist-photographer finally arrived in Salt Lake City on March 1, 1854, he was fortunate enough to meet Lieutenant Beckwith, who supplied him with painting materials, enabling him to make a number of drawings of the surrounding country. Regrettably, none of them have been found. Several of these western landscapes, including *View in the Cochotope pass Rocky Mountains, discovered by Col. Fremont, Painted from Nature*, were exhibited at the Maryland Historical Society (Baltimore) in 1856.[116] In 1875, Carvalho painted another version of the same pass, which he titled *Entrance to the Cochotoopie Pass, Rocky Mountains from Nature*.[117] Since Carvalho mentions leaving his paints and drawing materials behind, these Colorado landscapes could not have been painted directly from nature as their titles imply; it is more likely that they

were taken from his daguerre views. In 1875, Carvalho also painted *Grand [Colorado] River* at a point somewhat west of present Grand Junction where the river winds through high cliffs in Ruby Canyon and Horsethief Canyon.[118] Both paintings are signed and dated in the artist's own hand, negating Sturhahn's statement in her biography of Carvalho that he ceased painting sometime in the late 1860s when his eyesight began to fail.[119] Carvalho listed himself as an artist and photographer in the New York City directory until 1880, which resubstantiates that he was still professionally active in the 1870s.

Although well educated and cultivated, Carvalho was deficient in artistic skills. His two extant Colorado landscapes bear witness to his lack of facility with brush and paint and his inability to deal with the problems of color, light, and shade to create a sense of three-dimensionality. In *Grand [Colorado] River* (color plate 9), the pinkish-colored, castellated cliffs are modeled far too rigidly to be convincing as natural landforms; they seem more like scenic backdrops for a stage setting. While the artist does convey a sense of breadth, the painting has a picture-postcard quality. Although the picture demonstrates Carvalho's lack of technical proficiency, its relationship to an actual place is obvious, suggesting that a daguerreotype may have been employed as an aid. The artist's small oil study *Entrance to Cochotoopie Pass* is less successful as a composition and rather crudely handled. It affords us no opportunity to gain an insight into the artist's method of working, except to reinforce the idea that he probably referred again to a daguerreotype to jog his memory —suggested in both landscapes by the distribution of light and dark.

Two important landscapes recorded for Carvalho have still not come to light. *Rio Virgin* was shown at the National Academy of Design in 1862 and listed for sale.[120] We are first informed about the other picture in a letter Carvalho wrote to Dr. J. Solis-Cohen on May 13, 1865 [?]:

> . . . I have just completed a very large painting. Representing the Grand Cañon of the Colorado River where the party of Major [John Wesley] Powell was supposed to have been lost.
> I consider it my best picture, dimensions 50 × 60 inches.
> I have not decided what to do with it.[121]

The date of the letter is puzzling, and, since it is a copy of the original (apparently lost) and is "almost illegible," it may have been misread. Powell did not make his first trip down the river canyon until 1869, and on that trip he was not accompanied by an artist. Therefore, Carvalho could not have painted this picture until sometime in the 1870s. It seems likely that his view of the great canyon was a copy after a reproduction in Powell's official report, which was published in 1875 and liberally illustrated by Thomas Moran. Perhaps the artist was inspired by Moran's famous painting *The Chasm of the Colorado*, which was completed in 1873 and purchased by Congress for $10,000 as a companion piece for the artist's *The Grand Canyon of the Yellowstone* (color plate 25), displayed in the Senate lobby.[122]

The scant pictorial evidence available makes it impossible to obtain a complete picture of Carvalho's development as a painter. Extant paintings (including portraits) give the impression that he had only limited ability to handle color, model forms, and cope with compositional problems. Because he was unaware of the possibilities of his medium, his work reveals the crudities associated with itinerant painters. Perhaps if Carvalho had been less deeply involved in other pursuits, he might have developed a greater awareness of the elements that make up good craftsmanship and produced better pictures. On the other hand, it is possible that he was a better daguerreotypist than artist, though evidence for this theory is equally scant since the plates and prints from the Frémont expedition are still unlocated. Although Carvalho was not the first daguerreotypist to venture west with an expedition, he will nonetheless be remembered as a pioneer in the photographic field of pictorial recording. It is unfortunate for the annals of western art that he was unable to capture on canvas those glowing impressions he expressed so eloquently in words throughout his journal.

ACROSS THE CONTINENT: ARTISTS ON THE ROAD WEST

Nothing added more to the cheerfulness, comfort, and romance of our journey than good campfires on cool nights, and wherever fuel was found plentiful we used it without stint; though, on dark nights bright fires in deep, narrow valleys, surrounded by mammoth rocks and steep hillsides, formed a weird scene, giving us a realizing sense of our complete isolation from the civilized world and reminding us of the fact of our being in the heart of a vast mountain wilderness, surrounded by wild beasts and wilder Indians. It often produced a sense of loneliness, thoughts of home and friends, and the comforts of civilization. —Reuben Cole Shaw[1]

No one felt more acutely the awesome size of the American continent and the vast distances required to traverse it than the thousands of adventurers who were beckoned by the aureate call of California's wealth in 1849. They were not the first, to be sure—the Oregon and Mormon pioneers had preceded them earlier in the same decade—but the forty-niners far outnumbered their predecessors. Great hordes of people took to the roads, and countless newspaper accounts describe the immensity of this mass migration. A September, 1848, issue of the Washington, D.C., *Daily Union* exalted:

. . . the golden chicken [has] burst its shell; and is now a full-grown cock, whose crowing has woke up all California and will yet disturb the slumbers of other lands. The El Dorado of fiction never prompted dreams that revelled in gold like the streams which shout their way from the mountains of California. They roll with an exulting bound, as if conscious that their pathway was paved with gold.[2]

A great variety of artists responded to the call for many different reasons. Some went to seek new patrons, some to gather new visual material, and some simply to try their luck as prospectors. As the era of road building and exploration expanded through mid-century, many artists, both under government sponsorship and as lone independents, fanned out across the West, crossing and recrossing the Rockies, recording again and again the image of the Oregon Trail.

WILLIAM HENRY TAPPAN AND JAMES F. WILKINS: ARTISTS ON THE OREGON TRAIL

Since leaving Fort Laramie, we had passed over a fine range of country. . . .
The scenery from the top of the ridge was very picturesque. Laramie's peak and the range of Black Hills could be very distinctly seen, and frequently reminded me of some of the mountain scenery I had met with in Mexico. I ascended several high hills, and had a fine view of the country, . . . but there is nothing to recommend it except the beauty of the scenery, as the land is very poor and barren, being of very light soil, and covered principally with wild sage. —Osborne Cross[3]

In the spring of 1849 several detachments of the Regiment of Mounted Riflemen set out along the Oregon Trail under the command of Colonel William W. Loring. Their assignment was to organize posts for the establishment of order along the road. An army quartermaster, Major Osborne Cross, maintained the records of the trip, and his report of 1850 became a vital source of information for subsequent travelers.[4] Published in three editions because of its popularity, the report was illustrated with thirty-seven lithographed plates that represented the first official and extensive pictorial record of the Oregon route.

Unfortunately, none of the sketches reproduced in the final publication was signed—foiling all attempts at attribution, since several artists were in the retinue that followed Osborne and Loring across the continent in the summer of 1849. They included two civilians—William Henry Tappan, who had been hired as the artist-recorder for the trip, and George Gibbs, a voyager whose avocation was art.[5] Two of the military leaders, Lieutenant Andrew Jackson Lindsay and Major Cross, were trained in topographical drawing and were capable of adding to the pictorial documentation. To compound the mystery, a series of sketches by James F. Wilkins, who made the same trip in the same period, has been discovered in this century.

Of the four artists who were recorded on the roster of the riflemen expedition, Tappan, as the illustrator of the final report, was most likely the artist on whose works the lithographs were based. Tappan's background would indicate that he was well qualified for the position. He was born in Manchester, Massachusetts, in 1821. Although nothing is known of his early training, he is recorded as a producer of mezzotints and line engravings in Boston in 1840, where he apparently worked in association with a portrait engraver named Joseph Andrews.[6] He also worked with George C. Smith in the business of reproducing daguerreotypes in mezzotint and served as a draftsman for the United States Mint in Philadelphia.[7] While he was in Boston, Tappan became acquainted with some of the distinguished scientists at Harvard University and through these associations was invited to join Louis Agassiz's first scientific expedition to the shores of Lake Superior in 1848. The results were published in a volume entitled *Lake Superior*, a copy of which was later sent to Charles Darwin, who received it with great enthusiasm.[8] Although Tappan did not illustrate the book, he undoubtedly gained much valuable experience in the methods of scientific observation during that expedition.

Because there were several different detachments in the large force of mounted riflemen, it is not known exactly when or with whom Tappan started his journey across the plains[9]—only that sometime in the middle of May he departed for Fort Kearny on the Platte River. Cholera epidemics made health perilous, while downpours converted the dirt road into a quagmire and the streams into rushing torrents. In addition to these obstacles the progress of the train was constantly hindered by inexperienced teamsters and deserting soldiers. As Cross later wrote:

> My outfit was as indifferent a one as ever left for any station, much less the Rocky Mountains. The mules were poor, unbroken, and by no means calculated for such a march. . . . The drivers were not only stupid but totally ignorant of the duty, as they had never been employed in the capacity before, and seemed to have no other object in view than to reach the gold region with the least possible expense or trouble to themselves.[10]

Despite these typical hardships of western travel, the troop reached Fort Kearny by the first week in June, where Tappan joined the expedition and met George Gibbs, an amateur artist and lawyer in search of adventure and fortune. On June 22 the party arrived at Fort Laramie. Tappan made a sketch of the fort that appeared as the first plate of the Cross report.[11]

As they moved onward, Tappan produced sketches in almost abandoned profusion. Despite being highly recommended and having had previous experience as an engraver, Tappan showed a lack of ability as an accurate draftsman throughout. This is nowhere more evident than in his sketch of the wagon train as it passed between the Sweetwater River and Independence Rock.[12] Were the foreground figure not an Indian in pursuit of what must be a buffalo, the animal might well be mistaken for the king of beasts. At best, Tappan's renderings have the charm of naïveté. As the Loring-Cross party approached South Pass, the Wind River Mountains loomed into sight—a dramatic backdrop that had already inspired western artists ranging from Charles Preuss to Alfred Jacob Miller. Tappan's rendition of the scene (plate 34) is much closer to the work of Preuss than to Miller's.

The itinerary of the expedition continued directly west across South Pass to the Bear River through what was called Sublette's Cut-Off and then from Fort Hall to Fort Boise, almost the breadth of present-day Idaho. Tappan produced sketches of the two forts that once again revealed his limited knowledge of perspective; they are, nevertheless, valuable historic documents.

One incident that occurred on the trip through Idaho helps substantiate the hypothesis that Tappan was responsible for the sketches illustrating the Cross report. On August 15, Cross's guide made a side excursion accompanied by George Gibbs and Lieutenant Lindsay. The three journeyed to the Shoshone Falls, which the two artists pronounced "one of nature's greatest wonders." Gibbs—and possibly Lindsay as well—took time to record its image in their sketchbooks (plate 35).[13] Cross devoted almost two pages of his report to a description of this spectacular natural phenomenon,[14] but no illustration of the falls appears in the final report—from which one might theorize that no sketch by Tappan was available, possibly because he was not a member of this particular excursion. The very next day Tappan did sketch the far less spectacular Salmon Falls, which was illustrated in the report.

From Fort Boise the expeditionary force moved north and west across the northeast corner of Oregon until it reached the Columbia River, where it turned west downriver. The men spent some time at the Dalles, the subject of nine of the illustrations in Cross's report. One of the sketches is *Mission Near the Dalls* [*sic*],[15] to which Tappan returned to make an oil painting, one of the two extant works by the four artists involved in the expedition of 1849. The painting provides yet another piece of evidence substantiating Tappan as the illustrator of the Cross report. Although the sketch and the painting are not the same—the sketch is an exterior view of the mission and the painting an interior view—the rendering of the perspective in the buildings and the almost primitive handling of distance and landscape suggest the same hand.

When the party reached Oregon City just south of Fort Van-

couver on the ninth of October, Tappan's job as official artist ended. Yet the attraction of the Northwest Coast lured him into remaining, and he settled in Clark County, in the present state of Washington. In 1854 he served on the first territorial council of Washington Territory and was connected with the Indian Department.[16] How faithfully he continued his artwork is not known, but, in addition to his two surviving paintings, he is credited with designing and engraving the seal of Washington Territory. In 1876, Tappan returned to his hometown, Manchester, Massachusetts. He served in both the state House and the state Senate and later became a local historian of note with the publication of his *History of Manchester*.[17]

Contemporary scholars attempting to establish attribution for the illustrations of the Cross report were further confused when a collection of fifty monochrome wash drawings came to light.[18] They showed marked similarities to the plates in Cross's report, though none is a replica of the published illustrations. This dilemma was resolved with the discovery of the diary of James F. Wilkins, who had previously been considered a possible artist of the unsigned illustrations, since he followed the same route at approximately the same time. His diary revealed, however, that he was always behind or ahead of the Loring-Cross entourage.[19]

Wilkins was an independent on the trail for his own purpose: to secure material for a moving panorama, a kind of entertainment that had become most popular both in the States and abroad. Wilkins, an Englishman, was a fairly successful miniature-portrait painter who had exhibited at the Royal Academy in London in 1835 and 1836. Records next show him in Peoria, Illinois, and then in New Orleans, where he taught painting, drawing, and perspective. He later moved to Saint Louis, the Gateway to the West. It was there that he first envisioned a journey into the gold country to gather material for a panorama.[20]

In the spring of 1849, Wilkins signed on with a small ox-drawn wagon train scheduled to depart from Saint Louis on April 25 and to cover about fifteen miles a day.[21] This leisurely pace delighted Wilkins, since it would afford him time for painting and sketching along the way. The journey was beset with all kinds of delays, and finally the wagoner offered a three-yoke oxen team to any six men

PLATE 34

William Tappan, *View of the Wind River Mountains*, 1849, Lithograph, 4⁵⁄₁₆″ × 7⅞″.
Courtesy Denver Public Library, Western History Department, Denver.

Shoshonee Falls of Snake River, August 15. from below.   Height 180 feet

PLATE 35

George Gibbs, *Shoshonee Falls of Snake River, August 15, from below,* 1849, Pencil, 5½″ × 8⅜″.
Courtesy Peabody Museum, Harvard University, Cambridge, Mass.

PLATE 36

James Wilkins, *First View of the Rocky Mountains*, 1849, Ink-wash drawing, 8½″ × 10″.
Courtesy State Historical Society of Wisconsin, Madison, Wis.

who would care to go on alone. Wilkins was one of those who accepted, setting out on an arduous journey of 151 days. In his diary of his experiences along the trail, he wrote that on July 12 "We came in sight this morning for the first time of snow capped mountains, being the great wind river chain of the Rocky Mountains, the craggy peaks and white dazzling snow had a very picturesque effect."

Wilkins's *First View of the Rocky Mountains* (plate 36) is a typical example of his fieldwork. This and his other spontaneous impressions were to provide the inspiration for the monumental panorama, which he began shortly after his return home. *The Moving Mirror of the Overland Trail* first opened in the autumn of 1850 in Peoria, Illinois, and was a grand success. One of the most interesting scenes was Wilkins's view of the Rocky Mountains, about which the *Peoria*

Democratic Press commented, "Mountains with their snowy tops and ragged sides, seen in the distance, gilded by the last rays of the setting sun, remind us all that Byron or Colridge [*sic*] have written or sung of the far famed Alpine scenery."[22]

After his western journey Wilkins reestablished himself in Saint Louis, where he painted several imaginary views of the Rocky Mountains. Probably inspired by his fieldwork of 1849, the artist enlarged upon his simple repertory to produce his studio oils. *Immigrants in the Rockies* (color plate 10), for example, is typical of this romantic visionary's later work.[23]

Together Wilkins and his fellow artists on the Oregon Trail left an alluring pictorial record of the road to California. Their paintings celebrated one of the truly epochal sagas of the westward movement.

H. V. A. VON BECKH AND JOHN J. YOUNG: FROM THE WASATCH TO THE PACIFIC

To California Emigrants and the Citizens of Utah Territory.

The undersigned is informed that there are many persons at Salt Lake City destined for California, who are in doubt as to the route they should take. He would inform all such, that by direction of General [Albert Sidney] Johnston, he has within the past three months, explored and sur-veyed two new routes to California, either of which is about 300 miles shorter than the old Humboldt or St. Mary's river route; and, from all he can hear and has read, incomparably better in respect to wood, water and grass. —Indeed, by this route, the Great Salt Lake desert is entirely avoided, except at a few points. —James H. Simpson[24]

Ten years after Loring's reconnaissance along the Oregon Trail, government-supported expeditions in search of suitable routes to California were still being commissioned. The Oregon Trail lay too far north to be useful beyond Fort Hall, and the California Trail across the Great Basin and Donner Pass was sorely depleted of the forage necessary to support the flow of traffic. As a consequence, when General Albert Sidney Johnston[25] went west in 1857 to help settle the "Mormon war," he also found a pressing need for more and better roads into the heart of the newly admitted Utah Territory. With a proper road from Fort Bridger to his headquarters at Camp Floyd, south of Salt Lake City, Johnston considered that he could bring people and supplies into the valley through the south-ern Wasatch Mountains and that subsequent explorations west from Camp Floyd might uncover a new route to California across the Great Basin. The two roads combined would shorten the trek to San Francisco by several hundred miles.

Johnston assigned the task of exploring these new routes to Captain James Hervey Simpson, a western veteran of the Topographical Corps of Engineers with a broad knowledge of western travel[25] and an ardent proponent of serviceable wagon roads. Simpson's first job was to survey a road through the Timpanogos (Provo) River Canyon between Camp Floyd and Fort Bridger. Nine days and 155 miles after he left Camp Floyd on August 25, he and his party had traversed some remarkable country and established a route that he would modestly refer to as "very fair for a mountain road."[26]

In October, Simpson ventured southwest across the Great Salt Lake desert, investigating a new supply route into the Rush and Skull valleys. In the spring of 1859 he selected a more northerly route and proceeded west toward Genoa, at the foot of the Sierra Nevada. In his entourage was an artist, H. V. A. Von Beckh, an enlisted man. Unlike the Kern brothers, who had accompanied Simpson on his earlier expedition through New Mexico and Arizona, Von Beckh was not listed as official artist, but his sketches were adopted as illustrations for Simpson's final report on the first and two subsequent forays into the Great Basin. Reworked into finished watercolor drawings by John J. Young, the War Department's topographical draftsman, the Von Beckh views are much grander in their presentation of western scenery than the standard topographical work of the day. In his *Beautiful Cascade, Timpanogos River Canon* (color plate 11) Young dramatizes the verticality of the towering cliffs and precipitous falls,[27] employing an exaggerated perspective with strong contrasts of light and dark similar to that of his Gustave Doré-like view of the Grand Canyon, redrawn from a sketch by F. W. von Egloffstein and reproduced in the J. C. Ives report. In his skillful drawing *Crossing the Great Salt Lake Desert*,[28] he creates aerial perspective through graduated tones of color, emphasizing the illimitable distances of the western landscape. The long train of wagons and riders winding their way across the picture plane further emphasizes the flatness and expansiveness of this desolate country.

Simpson's reconnaissance of the Wasatch Mountains and the Great Basin was, as he had hoped, one of pivotal importance. The routes west to California and north to Fort Bridger became well-traveled avenues bridging the vast domain of the Southwest. The pony express traced one of his trails across the Great Basin that telegraph lines were soon to follow. The Civil War postponed the publication of Simpson's final report until 1876,[29] when Von Beckh's sketches as redrawn by J. J. Young opened the eyes of many travelers to the beauties of Utah and the expansive terrain between it and the Pacific.

JOHN STRONG NEWBERRY: WEST WITH JOHN N. MACOMB—"THE GREAT RECONNAISSANCE"

United States Engineer's Office,
Rock Island, Ill., June 18, 1875

GENERAL: I have this day forwarded to you the Geological Report of Dr. J. S. Newberry, geologist of the San Juan exploration party, which went from Santa Fé, New Mexico, to the vicinity of the junction of Grand and Green Rivers, in Utah, and back to Santa Fé, in the summer of 1859, and which party was in my charge.

This is the report to which I alluded in my report to you of November 1, 1860, as setting forth whatever the route above mentioned afforded of interest to the public at large or to the man of science. I trust it may be found possible to publish it.

The report is arranged in seven chapters, with a prefatory note, and is accompanied by the following sketches and drawings, viz:

Eleven water-color sketches, showing characteristic scenery of the region in Northwestern New Mexico, Southwestern Colorado, and Southeastern Utah. Also, eleven drawings (eight of fossils and three of scenery), all of which are interesting and important in connection with the report.

My map of the route was engraved on a steel plate, and is on the files of the Engineer Department.

I remain, very respectfully, your most obedient servant,

J. N. Macomb.[30]

In the summer of 1859, Captain John N. Macomb, of the Corps of Topographical Engineers, led his men across the rugged country of the San Juan Mountains to the junction of the Green and Grand rivers and back to Santa Fe, the expedition's point of departure. Owing to the outbreak of the Civil War, the official report of the expedition remained unpublished for nearly seventeen years.[31] Later, as attention was again drawn to the region bordering the San Juans and upper Colorado, the results of the San Juan Exploring Expedition acquired a timely significance, rendering such a publication invaluable.[32] Dr. John Strong Newberry (1822–92), the geologist for the expedition, had carefully and zealously examined the country traversed by the Macomb party and was responsible for narrating and illustrating his important geological report. His assignment, "which linked up with his [previous] work in the Grand Canyon country" under Lieutenant Joseph Ives, made clear "the whole complex drainage of the Colorado Rivers system." Even though Newberry was considered a scientist of "the old school, a general naturalist rather than a specialist," his geological report reflected the historical changes that were taking place in American scientific endeavor—among them the shift toward specialization and the rise of the "new scientific explorer," who had been trained as a specialist in Europe or America.[33] This change in trend is somewhat evident in Newberry's illustrations as well, particularly in his sweeping panoramic views of the mountain-and-canyon country. Here the geologist-illustrator has moved closer to the area of the panoramist and the later practitioners of topography, who attempted to portray endless miles of geography. Although Newberry was aware of earth-shaping processes like erosion and mountain making, his scenic views fail to reflect this scientific knowledge. Nowhere in these illustrations do we find visual reinforcements for the scientific explanations that make up Newberry's report; the shaping of landforms that he so carefully formulated in his mind—the true physical geology of the area—is missing from his pictures.

Unlike the men who had accompanied earlier exploring expeditions to record the western scene, Newberry was a practicing physician as well as a trained geologist. As a boy he had been attracted to the plant remains in the coal mines near his home in Cuyahoga

Falls, Ohio—an early indication of his scientific propensities. He also enjoyed assembling collections of fossil remains. There is nothing in his biographical data that alludes to his artistic training. One can only assume that his medical instruction included sketching various parts of the anatomy, which provided opportunities to develop the skill and interest he would need in his later assignment with Macomb. The period with Macomb marked the culmination of his expeditionary work and the beginning of his career as a professor of geology and paleontology in the School of Mines in Columbia University, a position he held for the rest of his life.[34]

By the time Newberry joined Macomb's expedition, he had tracked a considerable portion of the West and was adequately prepared to meet the challenges of his new assignment. The exploratory party traveled northward from Santa Fe along the Old Spanish Trail, across the headwaters of the San Juan River, and west past the southern edge of the Sierra de la Plata onto the Colorado plateau to the junction of the Green and Grand rivers.[35] Newberry made a number of sketches of the scenery along the way as viewed from the various campsites. John J. Young later made eleven of these views into watercolors for reproduction. To judge by the three linear black-and-white illustrations credited solely to Newberry, it seems that Young, a draftsman-engraver for the War Department, followed the geologist's original designs closely but brought to them a greater facility for expression. Young's preserved drawings from other expeditionary reports exhibit his understanding of the possibilities of this medium.

Newberry's report, unlike Carvalho's narrative of his personal experiences, provides a more accurate and scientific account of the land. The contrast between the two chronicles can best be realized by quoting Newberry, as he describes an objective of this scientific mission: "It is to be hoped that one result of our expedition will be to bring something like order out of the confusion of ideas which has prevailed in regard to the intricate mountain ranges of this region."[36]

The geologist-illustrator made his first scenic view of Colorado as the group approached a narrow valley on the upper streams of the San Juan. Newberry described this amphitheater as being "three miles long by one broad; a verdant meadow of the finest grass, thickly strewed with flowers, through which winds the bright and rapid river, margined by clumps of willows, and most graceful groups of cotton-wood."[37] In his *The Pagosa and San Juan River, Looking Easterly (Camp 12) [1859]* (plate 37), the geologist-illustrator has presented an extensive panorama of this high country, plotting his composition along a series of receding horizontal planes. The focal point of the work is the Pagosa, "one of the most remarkable hot springs on the continent, well known . . . among the Indian tribes" but never before seen by a white man.[38]

Although the commercial lithographer has produced an attractive color scheme,[39] his means of reproducing the rich tints in nature and the crystalline sky typically manifested in that region of the country were obviously limited.

As the group moved in a westerly direction, along the southern edge of the Sierra de la Plata, Newberry captured another sweeping view of the high country.[40] On August 10 from a summit of a hill he reproduced the "Rio Delores" winding its way through a fertile valley surrounded by perpendicular bluffs. In the east he portrayed the Sierra de la Plata as one continuous high wall below a canopy of billowy clouds.

Newberry's illustrations of the vast virgin country seem to form the connecting link between the work of the early artist-reporters and the later practitioners of topographical art. Newberry's contribution to this later phase—a viewpoint less highly colored by romantic sentiment and more reflective of new scientific changes occurring in America—makes him worthy of inclusion among the many illustrators who furnished invaluable firsthand pictorial records of the West.[41]

JOSEPH HEGER: DRAFTSMAN PRIVATE WITH COMPANY K

At midday we reached Fort Union [New Mexico] again. Everybody was delighted to see us. All were well and I was very happy. The distance from Salt Lake City . . . by the road upon which we returned is 821.6 miles and from Fort Union back again 1704.6 miles—a long road to spend

an entire six months on. I have enjoyed my summer very much. I have seen the saints and passed over a section of country worthy of examination.
—Second Lieutenant John van Deusen Du Bois[42]

One of the most interesting narratives of the "Mormon war" period is provided by this young lieutenant, a graduate of West Point who served with Company K of the First Regiment of Mounted Riflemen. He and twenty-five fellow soldiers spent six months in 1858 escorting Captain Randolph B. Marcy from Fort Union, in northwestern New Mexico, to Camp Floyd, in Utah. Having delivered Marcy, the troop then marched back to Fort Union. Captain Marcy had been sent to New Mexico in 1857 to secure provisions for the Army of Utah—United States forces that had come west to deal with the Mormon crisis, "that abortive clash between Deseret and the United States that took place in 1857."[43]

One of the twenty-five soldiers under Du Bois's command was an artist of unusual ability. German-born Joseph Heger,[44] a lithographer by profession, was one of a number of military men who made sketches of their experiences in the field—some of them made for their own diversion and others undertaken as specific projects. Heger had served under Du Bois from the time he enlisted in the army in 1855. His pencil sketches of towns and sites along the trail, historic forts and encampments, and natural scenery correspond to his superior's journal, a log of three major western episodes in which the company took part: the Gila-Apache campaign of 1857, the so-called Utah War of 1858, and the later Navaho campaigns of 1859. One historian has suggested that Heger's drawings and Du Bois's journals belong together;[45] perhaps that was the intended purpose of

PLATE 37

John Strong Newberry, *The Pagosa and San Juan River, Looking Easterly (Camp 12 [1859])*, 1876, Color lithograph, 6″ × 9″.
Courtesy Huntington Library, San Marino.

the lithographer's work, since they parallel each other so closely.

A group of twenty-four pencil drawings by Heger made during their return march to Fort Union, New Mexico,[46] provide a pictorial record of the troop's movements from the northern Wasatch Mountains south and then east through Utah, the Colorado Rockies, and finally the San Luis Valley toward their Fort Union base. One of Heger's pencil drawings, *Near the Summit of Wahsatch Mts., July 30th/58* (plate 38), was captured while the troop was making its way across the mountains toward the broad valley with the Green River beyond. The artist's soft, remarkably fluid pencil-line technique seems to approximate a lithographer's crayon method. Long, closely parallel pencil lines move quickly back and forth, providing shadings while leaving areas of paper untouched for highlighting. This free technique is well suited to recording spontaneous impressions of the terrain, producing a sort of animated factual report. Whereas Heger's landscapes are rapid notations, his drawings of military installations are more precisely articulated with controlled, short strokes of the pencil. Art historian James Ballinger suggests that Heger may have used a mechanical device to record accurately and precisely such detailed subjects as buildings, pointing out the crudity of his foreground features as opposed to his more carefully controlled handling of the background.[47]

Another drawing, *In Sahwatch Pass/Sep. 1st/58* (plate 39), made on September 1 near the end of their march, illustrates the site at which Captain Marcy had encountered his most difficult hardships during his trip to Fort Union the previous year. After winding through the canyons that make up Sawatch Pass and following Sawatch Creek, they came to a peculiar hill that rises in the very center of the pass. There, they "found the remains of an old camp of Capt. Marcy, who, when at this place, was waiting with intense anxiety to see the longed for return of his expressmen, who had gone on to Fort Massachusetts. A few miles beyond he met them returning with two wagons full of provisions."[48]

Heger and Du Bois shared a number of other adventures in the West. In 1859 they undertook an engagement against the Navahos that took them from Abiquiú across the New Mexico Rockies as far west as Cañon de Chelly under the command of Major John S. Simonson. Heger's drawings of the natural wonders encountered in this fabulous section of country celebrate the awesome splendors of some of the Southwest's most spectacular scenery.[49]

This soldier-artist's five years of service were spent on the frontier. After his discharge at Fort Union, in 1860, he disappears from the records until 1896, when he filed an application for his pension from Tennessee; in 1897 he was refused and never heard from again. Today Heger is known only through his portfolio of drawings.

ANTON SCHONBORN AND JAMES D. HUTTON: EXPLORING THE BIG HORNS AND BEYOND

Sir: *Under clauses of the military appropriation acts, providing for "surveys for military defences, geographical explorations and reconnoissances for military purposes," I am directed by the Secretary of War to instruct you to organize an expedition for the exploration of the region of country through which flow the principal tributaries of the Yellowstone river, and of the mountains in which they, and the Gallatin and Madison forks of the Missouri, have their source.* —A. A. Humphreys[50]

Anton Schonborn was another German-born soldier-artist who served in a dual capacity. He made his first known trip to the Rocky Mountain region in 1859 as a member of Captain William Franklin Raynolds's expeditionary party, whose mission was to explore the Yellowstone River and the headwaters of the Missouri River. Unlike his fellow soldier-artist Joseph Heger, nothing is known about Schonborn's life before his enlistment in the army.[51]

The journey of 1859, the last major western expedition per-

PLATE 38

Joseph Heger, *Near the Summit of Wahsatch Mts., July 30th/58*, Pencil, 5⅞″ × 10½″.
Courtesy Beinecke Rare Book and Manuscript Library, W. R. Coe Collection, Yale University, New Haven.

PLATE 39

Joseph Heger, *In Sahwatch Pass/Sep. 1ˢᵗ/58*, Pencil, 6¼″ × 10⅞″.
Courtesy Beinecke Rare Book and Manuscript Library, W. R. Coe Collection, Yale University, New Haven.

formed by the Corps of Topographical Engineers, departed from Saint Louis on May 28, 1859, proceeding overland from Fort Pierre, South Dakota, on a general reconnaissance to ascertain

> everything relating to the numbers, habits, and disposition of the Indians, . . . its agricultural and mineralogical resources, its climate and the influences that govern it, the navigability of its streams, its topographical features, and the facilities or obstacles which the latter presented to the construction of rail or common roads.[52]

Raynolds was ordered to employ a cadre of professional assistants at a salary not to exceed $125 a month. His impressive roster included the services of naturalists, meteorologists, astronomers, surgeons, and artists, among them Dr. F. V. Hayden, naturalist and surgeon; J. D. Hutton, topographer and assistant artist; and Anton Schonborn, meteorologist and official artist.[53]

The party proceeded west from Fort Pierre along the north fork of the Cheyenne River (north of the Black Hills) to the Powder River, made its way up the Powder to the Yellowstone River, then looped south again along the far side of the Big Horn Mountains to the Oregon Trail. The Big Horns proved to be an excellent subject for the varied interests of the exploring party. On September 27, Raynolds reported that an adjunct group had returned from a foray into this vast range: "Mr. Snowden [J. H. Snowden, the topographer] claims to have decidedly improved his acquaintance with the mountain ranges. Dr. Hayden found several new plants and many fossils, and Mr. Schonborn obtained a number of admirable sketches."[54]

Only six sketches by Schonborn are known to remain from this trip of 1859, all of them depicting scenes east of the Rockies.[55] A few sketches of the Tetons, captured the following summer by his colleague James D. Hutton, do exist. The Captain described his first impressions of these grand monarchs:

> Far off, a barrier apparently stretched across the valley in the form of a ragged cliff of brilliant red, above whose centre shone with even greater brilliancy the snow-covered peaks of the Great Téton, dazzling in the clear atmosphere, with the reflected rays of the newly-risen sun. The magnificence of this view elicited universal admiration, and the accompanying sketch fails to do justice to the theme, the artist confessing his inability to represent the gorgeous coloring.[56]

Since Raynolds fails to mention the artist's name, it is impossible to know to which of the two men he was referring. Both Schonborn and Hutton were at his side when, on June 9, he stood before the Tetons on the banks of the Gros Ventre River. Hutton's pencil sketch *Great Teton & Pass no Pass From S. K.* (plate 40)[57] is the only surviving pictorial record of this encounter; it is a straightforward topographical rendering that reflects its author's orientation and training.

In October, 1860, the Raynolds party completed its survey and returned to Omaha, where the expedition was disbanded. What happened to Hutton after this trip is not known. There is little information on Schonborn's whereabouts until the summer of 1871, when he joined Hayden on an exploration of Yellowstone Park (see chapter 6). One historian suggests that he "traveled along the Bozeman Trail between November, 1867, and June, 1868,"[58] evidenced by a small group of pen-and-ink drawings he made of Wyoming forts along this trail in 1867.[59] He further notes that Schonborn "reportedly was stationed at Fort C. F. Smith, in Montana" during 1868[60] but gives no evidence for this statement. A set of eleven small, finished watercolor drawings by Schonborn depicting frontier outposts in the Wyoming, Utah, and Colorado Territories, and Nebraska was commissioned by Brevet Brigadier General Alexander James Perry, of the Quartermaster Department, in 1870,[61] indicating that the artist might have been attached to that department during the late 1860s. The position would have required him to travel to various forts to deliver supplies, giving him an opportunity to sketch them.

Schonborn's panoramic bird's-eye view *Fort Laramie, Wy. T. View from the East* (color plate 12) is a typical example of his work. The carefully articulated buildings and correctly rendered topography of the surrounding country not only indicate Schonborn's orientation toward draftsmanship but even suggest that he might have been professionally schooled in cartography in Germany: his views are simple, straightforward, and without artistic artifices. Schonborn can be counted among a handful of army men such as Joseph Eaton, Charles Frederick Moellman, Caspar Wever Collins, and Heger

Great Teton & Pass no Pass – from S. K.

PLATE 40

J. D. Hutton, *Great Teton & Pass no Pass From S. K.*, 1860, Pencil, 12½″ × 17″.
Courtesy Beinecke Rare Book and Manuscript Library, W. R. Coe Collection, Yale University, New Haven.

who left invaluable pictorial and social-historic documents of military posts.[62]

In June, 1871, Schonborn joined F. V. Hayden as chief topographer on a historic exploration of Yellowstone Park. Twelve years before, as a member of Raynolds's party, he had approached the boundaries of the present-day park, but, because of an inadequate map, the troop's progress was blocked by the Absaroka Mountains near the Great Divide, and they failed to gain entrance to the scenic wonders of upper Yellowstone Valley.[63] This time, under Hayden's guidance, Schonborn and the party successfully penetrated the valley. The story of their journey through Yellowstone will be told in full later (see chapter 6, "The Great Surveys").

Although a complete pictorial record of this journey by artists Thomas Moran and Henry Wood Elliott and photographer William Jackson remains, Schonborn's artistic records unfortunately do not—possibly because Schonborn committed suicide on October 14, 1871, soon after this trip. Hayden later lamented that "the loss of . . . [his] chief topographer, . . . whose death occurred at Omaha after he had returned from the trip, with the notes which he had taken with zeal and ability, seemed almost irreparable."[64] Schonborn's maps and charts were ultimately compiled and redrawn by E. Hergesheimer, head of the engraving division for the United States Coast Survey. In the end Schonborn's reputation rests more on his pictorial representations of historic western outposts than on his contributions to survey work.

JAMES MADISON ALDEN AND WILLIAM MCMURTRIE: TO THE CREST OF THE CONTINENT WITH THE NORTHWEST BOUNDARY SURVEY

Our work during the next season will extend from the Columbia River to the Rocky Mountains. From careful inquiry, the entire distance is represented as mountainous and timbered, excepting perhaps a short stretch in the valley of the Kootenay, near the base of the Rocky Mountains. — John G. Parke[65]

In early August, 1856, Congress passed an act authorizing the official survey and marking of the United States and Canadian boundary from the Pacific Ocean to the Continental Divide. Ten years earlier the Oregon Treaty had established the 49th parallel as the "line of boundary between the territories of the United States and those of her Britannic Majesty,"[66] yet a formal reconnaissance of the area and a demarcation of the border had never taken place.

The survey was to be undertaken jointly by British and American crews. In February, 1857, President James Buchanan appointed Archibald Campbell as United States commissioner and Lieutenant John G. Parke, of the Corps of Topographical Engineers, next in charge, as chief astronomer and surveyor.[67] Campbell's party went directly to Oregon and were in the field by the summer of 1857. Their British counterparts, under Colonel J. S. Hawkins, of the Royal Engineers, did not begin work until the following spring. Together they defined the area of their interest as the international line stretching "from the summit of the Rocky Mountains westward along the forty-ninth parallel to the sea coast at Point Roberts and thence through the waters of Georgia, Haro, and Juan de Fuca straits to the Pacific."[68]

The United States team spent four years in the field, gradually working its way eastward over the difficult, forested terrain. The ranks included an astronomer, a surgeon-naturalist, and a topographer, as well as technicians and laborers. In fact, all the party members served several functions. George Gibbs, one of the amateur artists on the Oregon Trail in 1849[69] was employed as "geologist, ethnologist, guide, interpreter, and naturalist."[70] James Madison Alden, who in the summer of 1857 acted as purser's steward, was eventually recognized for his talents as a painter and was designated official artist from 1858 to 1860, when the field work was completed.[71]

Alden was the nephew of James Alden, Jr., a veteran of two United States naval expeditions that had significant impact on the Far West—the United States Exploring Expedition and the United States Coast Survey.[72] When young Alden's father died in 1853, his uncle encouraged the eighteen-year old to embark on a naval career. This he did, joining the United States Coast Survey in which his uncle served as a lieutenant. Recognizing Alden's bent toward art, the lieutenant advised him to seek training in cartographic drawing. James followed this advice as well, studying both at the survey headquarters' printing office in Washington and under the tutelage of Thomas Cummings in New York City.[73] In early 1854, Alden sailed for San Francisco to join his uncle. He was to serve as assistant to the official survey artist, William Birch McMurtrie, who had been with the Pacific Coast Survey since 1849. Three years later, again through the influence of his uncle, Alden received an appointment to the Northwest Boundary Survey.

Both Alden and McMurtrie apparently joined the boundary expedition at the same time, in early June, 1857. Alden is listed as "Purser's steward," and McMurtrie as "Captain's clerk."[74] The following year, owing to his uncle's recommendation and his own developing artistic skill, young Alden was advanced to the position of official artist. His colleague McMurtrie seems to have preferred a less active role, serving mainly as a draftsman in later years.[75]

It was not until 1860, the fourth year of the boundary survey, that the American party reached the Rockies (color plate 1). George Gibbs had led the initial reconnaissance the previous autumn, enabling the main troop to "commence in the early spring with a working party on this route."[76] He and his followers had found the country most impressive and challenging as they moved eastward into the boundaries of present-day Glacier National Park. Charles Wilson, a member of the British team, perhaps summarized best their impression when he wrote:

> They are well called Rocky mountains, the range as far as we saw them being rugged peaks of bare rock of all shapes and sizes and many of them seemingly inaccessible; I went up to the top of one of the peaks about 8200 feet high with some of our party and we had a glorious view, a perfect sea of peaks all around us and running off to the north and south, whilst on the west we looked into the valley of the Flathead, small lakes of the most brilliant blue, with their borders of bright green herbage lay scattered in all directions in the hollows, hundreds of feet beneath us and (where it could still cling) some patches of snow and small glaciers heightened the beauty of the scene.[77]

Alden's perceptions of this vast mountain terrain were both practical and aesthetic. His accounts provided Gibbs with important geological information,[78] while his drawings carefully delineated the impressive sweep of variegated landforms heretofore undocumented by any artist. His watercolor *Kintla Mountains from the Summit of Kishnehnehna* (color plate 13)[79] anticipates John Muir's later sentiment that the effects of sun, glacier, and stone were "indescribably glorious."[80]

Alden and his colleagues remained in the field until late November, 1860, when he and the party leaders, having completed their task, departed for Washington, D.C., to begin work on an official report.[81] Alden is reported to have served out the year 1861 with the Boundary Commission, working up field sketches into finished watercolors.[82] His friend McMurtrie was also employed by the same office to provide "Drawings for Geol. Rep."[83] Both men labored in vain. The report and its many appendices, maps, and charts were never published; moreover, the preliminary draft was lost.[84] Alden's paintings never reached the public, and the splendors of present-day Glacier National Park were not publicized until the 1870s, when Archibald Campbell undertook the formal survey of the northwest boundary west from the Lake of the Woods to the Continental Divide.[85] In 1900, Marcus Baker was assigned the futile task of reconstructing the report of the initial survey. He mentions the importance of Alden's contribution:

> The artist, Mr. James M. Alden, Produced a fine series of colored sketches of scenery along the boundary line. These sketches, obviously intended to illustrate the final report, are in the State Department. There are 65 of these, all but two (large ones) included in three portfolios. These sketches and the constantly recurring allusions to the final report, and the conclusive proof that such report was prepared, sharpen the desire and emphasize the need of recovering it.[86]

Shoshonee Falls Snake River

PLATE 41

William McMurtrie, *Shoshonee Falls, Snake River* [*Idaho*], ca. 1850, Pencil and watercolor, 7⅛″ × 10⅞″.
Courtesy M. and M. Karolik Collection, Museum of Fine Arts, Boston, Mass.

After 1863, Alden served in the Union Navy and later became secretary to Admiral David Dixon Porter. His greatest contribution to the art of the American West, however, had been made during his service in the Northwest during the decade of the 1850s. He died in Orlando, Florida, in 1922, but until 1975, when his drawings were placed on exhibit at the Amon Carter Museum, he was virtually unknown to students of American art.[87]

Alden's colleague William McMurtrie, another obscure artist, was born in Philadelphia in 1816. He was named for a family friend, the painter and engraver William Russell Birch. Perhaps best known for his *San Francisco Bay,* published as a lithograph by Nathaniel Currier in 1851, McMurtrie served with the Pacific Coast Survey between 1849 and 1853.

It is doubtful that McMurtrie penetrated as far into the Rockies as Alden when he served in the Northwest Boundary Survey. A watercolor, *Shoshonee Falls, Snake River* [*Idaho*] (plate 41), is his only known scene in the Rocky Mountain region.[88] In contrast to John Henry Hill's more skillful and painterly version (see color plate 20), McMurtrie's interpretation is a typical outline topographical drawing with filled-in pale washes of watercolor. Coincidentally, McMurtrie included a rainbow before the falls like that in O'Sullivan's photograph of 1868 of the same view, which was captured from a similar vantage point and reproduced in the King report (see chapter 6).

5

ALBERT BIERSTADT: THE GRAND PANORAMIC VISION

Ever since my arrival I have been studying the mountains. Their beauty and grandeur grow upon me with every hour of my stay. None of the illustrations accompanying the reports of exploration, and other Government documents, give any distinct idea of their variety and harmony of forms.

. . . You cannot cram this scenery into the compass of a block-book; it requires a large canvas, and the boldest and broadest handling. The eye *is continually cheated, the actual being so much more than the apparent dimensions of all objects. Though so familiar with the effect of extraordinarily pure, thin air, and great clearness of outline, I am still frequently at fault. What one sees small, is always small in the drawing. Even photographs here have the same dwarfed, diminished expression. I can now see how naturally Bierstadt was led to a large canvas.* —Bayard Taylor[1]

ALBERT BIERSTADT's grand and impressive interpretations of Rocky Mountain scenery, along with his other western scenes, were alternately praised and faulted by the critics of his day. Although condemned for his excessive use of artifices and conventions, as well as for his oversized canvases, he was also recognized as "not a mere copyist of Nature" but an artist who had "definite artistic intentions" and knew how to carry them out "with care and resolution."[2] His mode of representation was often compared with scene painting, but his use of this approach was considered justified because it best portrayed the overwhelming natural grandeur of the wild scenery. At times Bierstadt was criticized for using techniques reminiscent of those he learned in his native Düsseldorf (snowcapped, pink-tinged mountain peaks elevated and sharpened; highly polished lake surfaces that mirrored foliage; plunging declivities; and most important, theatrical lighting) to emphasize the sublimity and magnitude of this scenic wilderness. Despite the mixed attitudes of foreign and American critics toward Bierstadt's dramatic showpieces, they were still the first paintings to capture successfully the wonder and excitement that the artist and other early trailblazers

felt when they confronted the spectacular western scenery. His panoramic scenes of the Rockies therefore attracted universal attention in the 1860s and, according to one artist, induced thousands to discover for themselves what Samuel Bowles in 1869 christened the "future Switzerland of America."[3]

As an internationally celebrated artist in the 1860s and 1870s, Bierstadt had no rival save Frederic Edwin Church in the execution of "the full-length landscape," as one artist dubbed it. Bierstadt was appreciated more by sophisticates abroad than by his fellow American critics, who seemed to prefer Church's naturalism over his exaggerated and sensational effects.[4] Unlike his competitor, however, Bierstadt was a self-made man who cleverly managed to become a member of fashionable society, hobnobbing with railroad magnates, English nobility, and royalty. He soon became a familiar figure in the drawing rooms of the wealthy, and this exposure afforded him the opportunity to promote his works and expand his following. At that time it was "fashionable for gentlemen of means, who were founding or enlarging their private galleries, to give [the artist] an order for a Rocky Mountain landscape," even though these popular

116

showpieces were then commanding anywhere from $5,000 to $35,000 each.[5]

In the mid-1870s, Bierstadt's popularity began to wane; several decades later he was almost forgotten. His meteoric rise and rapid decline have been attributed to a change in the tastes and values of American society. A case could be made that Bierstadt's grandiloquent transcriptions of nature were in perfect keeping with the gargantuan vulgarity of the new business class that arose during the post–Civil War years, with "its tawdry and grandiose buildings, its conspicuous waste and display, [and] its generally meretricious splendor."[6] As one historian has remarked, Bierstadt became "for . . . a moment, the right man, at the right place, at the right time."[7] With the shift in aesthetic taste and the adoption of the new European painterly mode in the late 1870s, the influence of Düsseldorf began to decline—and so did Bierstadt's popularity.

Interest has recently been rekindled in Bierstadt's stagy, over-sized masterpieces, as well as in his small, sketchily impressionistic plein-air studies, which appeal to contemporary tastes. Although recently some critical treatments have been done of his style and artistic influences, most of them have dealt chiefly with the historical and biographical aspects of his life and career.[8] What is now needed, in the light of twentieth-century art criticism, is an examination of Bierstadt's perception of his subject matter—the spectacular mountain-and-plains scenery of the West—and its influence on his style at a time when growth and bigness were bywords. Since the whereabouts of much of Bierstadt's correspondence, papers, and other documentary material is presently unknown, it is necessary to rely primarily on pictorial evidence for an interpretation and evaluation of his artistic accomplishments.[9]

Bierstadt's romantic and theatrical showpieces scarcely reflect his humble beginnings. He was born in Solingen, near Düsseldorf, Germany, on January 7, 1830, and emigrated to the United States with his family in 1832.[10] In New Bedford, Massachusetts, his father provided a modest income for his family as a cooper. Unlike his brothers Charles and Edward, who followed their father into woodworking and later became photographers, Bierstadt is said to have worked for a local cake decorator, a framer, and a glass manufacturer. Gor-

don Hendricks, Bierstadt's current biographer, believes that the artist's work in the frame shop brought him in contact with paintings, which led to his involvement in art.[11] Bierstadt's career as an artist is first documented in the *New Bedford Evening Standard* on May 13, 1850, in an announcement that he was offering classes in "Monochromatic Painting."[12]

Exactly when or where Bierstadt began his art career is not known, but it can be assumed that he had several years of local art training and exposure before establishing himself as an art teacher. The absence of recorded information about his training suggests that he was primarily a self-made artist who leaned by referring to art manuals and copying the works of others. It is possible that he sought the advice of the local portrait-and-landscape painter William Allen Wall; he may also have traveled to Boston, an active art community, for additional instruction in painting.[13] We can, in any case, be certain that Bierstadt was well versed in academic and technical methods by the time he established his classes in monochromatic painting.[14] As Donald Strong has pointed out, this technique, which depended on light and shade for its effects, probably helped the artist develop a "sensitivity to tone and its modulation" in the representation of light. Luminous backgrounds and the dramatic interplay of light and dark indeed play an important role in Bierstadt's paintings, leading one to speculate that the artist's interest in light effects might have evolved out of an earlier American art phenomenon, the luminist movement.[15] The dramatic and theatrical quality of Bierstadt's light, however, is far removed from the glowing and mellow lumination found in the paintings of John Frederick Kensett and Fitz Hugh Lane. It would perhaps be more appropriate to link Bierstadt's concern with light to that of his rival Frederic Church, whose large panoramas of tropical scenery were flooded with a blaze of fiery light. In the end Bierstadt's treatment of light is uniquely his own. During his lifetime some critics viewed it as indicating spiritual reverence, others felt that it was used for sheer drama, and still others saw it as arising out of his entrepreneurial desire to further his artistic career. All were probably correct to some degree.

Exhibition listings and newspaper accounts document Bierstadt's early artistic activities during these formative years before his departure for Düsseldorf in 1853. The artist conducted painting classes and exhibited works in several shows in New Bedford and Boston, securing for himself a local reputation and patronage.[16] We know that Bierstadt was experimenting in watercolor, crayon, and oil at this time, since several of these early works were included among a group of forty-one paintings auctioned off in the estate sale of 1870 of art-patron Thomas Thompson. These early efforts were apparently rather crude and academically unsophisticated, for they were singled out by a New York critic as the "very worst" of the collection. Bierstadt responded by fervently denying they were his.[17] None of them has surfaced to date to refute this denial.

In 1851, Bierstadt produced several light shows using painted views of American scenery by the English artist George Harvey. In these shows a "dissolving lantern" was used to blend one scene into another, creating an animated travelogue. Most of the shows were produced in collaboration with a local daguerreotypist, Peter Fales.[18] Bierstadt's involvement in this kind of activity seems to indicate that he was well aware of America's insatiable curiosity and its taste for mechanical devices and armchair travel, which had reached a climax with the creation of moving panoramas of the Mississippi River in the late 1840s.[19] It also reflects both his proclivity for showmanship and his interest in the panoramic format, which he was to adopt for his large masterpieces. His early association with a daguerreotypist no doubt also made him aware of the possibilities offered by the photographic image; the illusion of space and the wealth of realistic detail in his pictures reflect the influence of photographs, particularly stereograph views taken on a journey west in 1859.[20]

Bierstadt probably realized early in his career that his artistic skills were limited and that schooling in one of the European art centers could offer many advantages. Düsseldorf was an obvious choice, since his mother's cousin Johann Hasenclever, a distinguished genre painter, was associated with the academy there.[21] Moreover, the Düsseldorf academy was well recognized in America, touted by such eminent midnineteenth-century critics as Henry Tuckerman.[22] Bierstadt probably first became acquainted with the works of the German masters in New York in 1849 at the opening of the Düsseldorf Gallery, which had received much attention and

praise from the local press. The scope of the collection, which had been assembled by John G. Boker, the German consul, included genre, history, and landscape paintings by the Düsseldorf masters.[23] There the artist could have become familiar with works by Karl Lessing, Andreas Achenbach, Hans Gude, and others, noting in particular the German technical facility for minute detail, hard coloring, and meticulous finish that would eventually influence his own development. Although Bierstadt drew from several artistic sources during his formative years, he eventually evolved a distinctive style of painting.

The exact date of Bierstadt's arrival in Düsseldorf is uncertain; he had certainly left before Hasenclever's death, late in 1853.[24] Apart from pictorial evidence, most of the information pertaining to his stay at Düsseldorf and his later sketching tours through Switzerland and Italy is drawn from the journals and works of fellow American artists, particularly T. Worthington Whittredge's autobiography.[25] Arriving at the German art center with very little money, Bierstadt struck up a friendship with Whittredge, who offered to share his studio with him. The author-painter vividly recalled the circumstances:

. . . for a time [Bierstadt] worked in my studio which was in the same building with Leutze. While I did not give lessons, he called himself my pupil during the time that he was with me. He brought with him a few studies which he had made in America, in the hope that by showing them to us, he could induce us to intercede for him and persuade Achenbach to give him lessons. The studies had nothing in them to recommend Bierstadt as a painter. They were in fact absolutely bad and we felt compelled to tell him very decidedly that Achenbach never took pupils. . . .

. . . After working in my studio for a few months, copying some of my studies and a few others which he borrowed, he fitted up a paint box, stool and umbrella which he put with a few pieces of clothing into a large knapsack, and shouldering it one cold April morning, he started off to try his luck among the Westphalian peasants where he expected to work. He remained away without a word to us until late autumn when he returned loaded down with innumerable studies of all sorts, oaks, roadsides, meadows, glimpses of water, exteriors of Westphalian cottages, and one very remarkable study of sunlight on the steps of an old church. . . . It was a remarkable summer's work for anybody to do, and for one who had had little or no instruction, it was simply marvelous. He set to work in my studio immediately on large canvases composing and putting together parts of studies he had made, and worked with an industry which left no daylight to go to waste.[26]

At this early stage in his career Bierstadt was already establishing his manner of working; later he would continue to draw upon his plein-air studies for a wealth of realistic detail, freely rearranging them into an artful finished composition. Whittredge notes that most of these pictures were quickly dispatched back to New Bedford to be sold so that the artist could recoup his expenses.[27]

Several of the paintings that resulted from Bierstadt's Westphalian sketching tours clearly evince the influence of the seventeenth-century Dutch painter Meyndert Hobbema, whose work may have been brought to his attention by Achenbach, himself inspired by the Dutch master.[28] The influence of Hobbema on both artists seems to indicate that, although Bierstadt may not have been a pupil of Achenbach, some kind of arrangement or relationship existed between the two. Perhaps when the young Americans met with the German masters at their meeting place, the Malkasten (Paint Box), an exchange of ideas took place, as Sanford Gifford indicated in his letters.[29] In any case, Bierstadt's rustic scenes with farmhouses nestled in the woods stylistically and thematically resemble pictures by Hobbema of similar subjects.[30]

On the other hand, Bierstadt's view of a river winding its way through the Westphalian countryside with scattered clouds and luminous skies closely favors Lessing's naturalistic *Waldlichtung*, also executed in 1855.[31] A mingling of influences seems to exist here, a blending of the Hudson River School's luminous effects and the German school's hard coloring and meticulous finish. Whittredge remarks that Bierstadt was ever watchful of transient effects in nature, making chalk studies of the clouds and skies from his studio window at various hours of the day.[32] These elements of nature were to figure prominently in his romantic and theatrical representations of the Rocky Mountains—a predisposition that reaches a climax in his oversized melodramatic painting *The Last of the Buffalo*. In his naturalistic treatment of the Westphalian landscape Bierstadt was reflecting the change in direction taking place at Düsseldorf—

from the former "idealized romantic vision" of German artists Caspar Scheuren and Johann Schirmer to a "greater feeling for objective reality" evidenced in landscape painting by Achenbach and Lessing in the 1850s.[33]

During his three and a half years abroad Bierstadt spent much time sketching directly from nature. His reluctance to enroll in the academy's landscape-painting class was probably because of his meager finances.[34] In lieu of formal training, he undoubtedly sought the counsel of a German master—like many other students of his day—or joined a group on a scenic jaunt led by one of the German painters.

In the summer of 1856, Bierstadt, Whittredge, and several other American artists traveled through Germany, Switzerland, and Italy, filling their portfolios with fresh studies of the mountain scenery.[35] While he was in Rome, Bierstadt took a number of side excursions, making hastily recorded studies of the hilly countryside to be transformed later into finished works. One such painting of the village *Olevano* seems to be a conscious emulation of Claude Lorrain, whose pictures Bierstadt undoubtedly viewed in Rome.[36] This hilly landscape is composed along a succession of planes leading back into a veiled distance. Small pastoral figures grace the foreground, where an imposing foliated tree silhouetted against the light serves as a pictorial framework. The work shares stylistic affinities with similar bucolic scenes by the French painter.[37] The alternation of light and dark areas and the classical spatial organization that Bierstadt employs here demonstrate that the artist had already established a compositional formula. They also indicate that at this early date Bierstadt had a good sense of spatial values and the ability to convey breadth and atmospheric perspective. He continued to employ this basic formula in constructing his pictures, varying it only in the arbitrary placement of dark and light and the occasional use of strong diagonal thrusts, often achieved by swirling cloud masses. His predilection for the panoramic format is more apparent in a later, larger version of the same scene, in which the distance has been extended and the vista opened to include the rolling, hilly countryside beyond.

By late August, 1857, Bierstadt had returned to the United States.

He immediately reestablished himself in his adopted city, New Bedford, setting up classes in oil painting and arranging shows for new pictures based on studies made in Europe.[38] The local newspapers were once again effective sales agents. In July of the following year, in association with John Hopkins, Bierstadt set up a large exhibition of paintings in the former's offices in the Ricketson Block, causing quite a stir in the community. In addition to a large number of American paintings the exhibit included works by several foreign artists, including Achenbach and Alexandre Calame.[39] Fifteen paintings of foreign subjects by Bierstadt were also shown. Although the American contingent was mostly made up of well-known names, several local artists were represented, among them Francis S. Frost, who was later to join Bierstadt on his first trip west.[40]

With his new skills and a "relish for, and understanding of, landscape painting," Bierstadt set out to make fresh studies of the New World "full of character and masterly effect."[41] It is easy to imagine that he found himself less than inspired with the scenery along the eastern coast and "encountered the same difficulties in tackling home subjects" that faced other American artists who had spent some time abroad.[42] Like Whittredge, he probably vividly recalled the impressive sights of grandeur and sublimity they encountered while traveling across the Alps. It is most likely that he was lured westward in search of subjects comparable to the rugged, perpendicular mountains of Europe, "capped with everlasting snow, shining like silver."[43]

Exactly when and why he decided to join Colonel Frederick Lander and his wagon-train expedition to the Wind River country is uncertain. It has been suggested that Bierstadt first conceived of the idea to travel west "on the fourth day of the new Year, 1859, when Bayard Taylor, famous traveler, lecturer, and author of *Eldorado*, came to town and talked of his travels in the American West,"[44] but the association is rather tenuous. It is reasonable to assume that his usual resourcefulness and his determination to travel west enabled the artist to establish the proper contacts to make the trip a reality.

On January 17, 1859, the *New Bedford Daily Mercury* announced that Bierstadt was "about to start for the Rocky Mountains, to study the scenery of that wild region, and the picturesque facts of Indian life, with reference to a series of large pictures." He expected to remain there "more than one year, and ha[d] engaged companions, among them a photographer."[45] Whether this was a prediction or a report of a consummated arrangement, this newspaper announcement preceded by two months the official designation of Lander's expedition. Colonel Lander, chief engineer and superintendent of the Fort Kearny, South Pass, and Honey Lake wagon roads, received government orders on March 25, 1859, to proceed westward to South Pass and then over the newly opened road to make any improvements he might deem necessary.[46]

It was not until shortly before April 15, however, that Bierstadt and his companion Francis S. Frost, a Boston artist, set out to join Lander's wagon-train party at Saint Louis.[47] According to Lander's official account, a "full corps of artists, bearing their own expenses," accompanied Bierstadt. This seems to be a hyperbole, for available evidence substantiates only Frost's participation in the journey.[48] Recently, however, small watercolor drawings by another Massachusetts artist, Henry Hitchings, have turned up, indicating that a third participant may have been associated with Bierstadt's artistic venture. Like Francis Frost, Hitchings painted scenes in the Wind River country in June, 1859—sights that were also observed by Lander's party.[49] His watercolor *Near Rock Creek, Nebraska Territory*/ *Distant View of the Wind River Mts.*, observed from the Sweetwater River about six miles due south of Old South Pass, was captured on June 24, 1859, the very date Lander's party reached the pass.[50] The connection between Hitchings and Lander's group is still tenuous— the matching dates are perhaps purely a coincidence.

Extant stereographs of "emigrant trains, Indians, camp scenes, &c.," taken by Bierstadt (or a photographer) along the route, together with a few letters and newspaper reports, afford us a glimpse of the country they traversed and a fairly clear idea of their itinerary.[51] Lander and his party appear to have left Troy/Saint Joseph the first week of May and headed toward Fort Kearny, continuing along the Platte River to Fort Laramie, finally reaching South Pass, the southern edge of the Wind River Mountains, on June 24.[52]

While skirting the Wind River chain about fifteen to forty miles out, along Old Lander Trail, Bierstadt continued to take stereoscopic views—though not as many of the mountain scenery as he wished—

and to add color studies to an already bulging portfolio.[53] On July 10, about ten days before he, Frost, and an orderly left Lander's party a short distance from the Wyoming Range (eighty miles west of the Wind River Mountains), Bierstadt drafted a letter to the editor of the *Crayon* about his experiences and impressions of the spectacular country:

> If you can form any idea of the scenery of the Rocky Mountains and of our life in this region, from what I have to write, I shall be very glad; there is indeed enough to write about. . . . The mountains are very fine; as seen from the plains, they resemble very much the Bernese Alps. . . . They are of a granite formation, the same as the Swiss mountains and their jagged summits, covered with snow and mingling with the clouds, present a scene which every lover of landscape would gaze upon with unqualified delight. As you approach them, the lower hills present themselves more or less clothed with a great variety of trees, among which may be found the cotton-wood, lining the river banks, the aspen, and several species of the fir and the pine. . . . And such a charming grouping of rocks, so fine in color. . . . Artists would be delighted with them. . . . In the valleys, silvery streams abound, with mossy rocks. . . . We see many spots in the scenery that remind us of our New Hampshire and Catskill hills, but when we look up and measure the mighty perpendicular cliffs that rise hundreds of feet aloft, all capped with snow, we then realize that we are among a different class of mountains; and especially when we see the antelope stop to look at us, and still more the Indian, his pursuer, who often stands dismayed to see a white man sketching alone in the midst of his hunting grounds. . . .
>
> I have above told you a little of the Wind River chain of mountains, as it is called. Some seventy miles west from them, across a rolling prairie covered with wild sage, . . . and different kinds of shrubs, we come to the Wahsatch [Wyoming Range], a range resembling the White Mountains. At a distance, you imagine you see cleared land and the assurances of civilization, but you soon find that nature had done all the clearing. . . . The mountains here are much higher than those at home, snow remaining on portions of them the whole season. The color of the mountains and of the plains, and, indeed, that of the entire country, reminds one of the color of Italy; in fact, we have here the Italy of America in a primitive condition.[54]

By September 3 he and Frost had reached Wolf River, Kansas (near Saint Joseph, Missouri). The date and place are corroborated by the artist in a later letter, in which he recounts their experiences with the Indians at Fort Laramie and during their travels along the Platte, as they continuously gathered more sketches and stereo views of the scenery and Indians.[55] An extant stereograph of arched trees over Wolf River, flooded with bright sunlight, is similar in imagery to a painting by Bierstadt of the same subject,[56] also full of luminosity but observed from a slightly different vantage point. The similarities indicate that the artist occasionally relied on photographs in working up his large paintings.

Although he unabashedly admitted that his own country had "the best material for the artist in the world"—"beautiful cloud formations," "fine effects of light and shade," and "glorious golden sunsets"—Bierstadt's fertile imagination nevertheless allowed him to conjure up images recalling distinctive features of the Old World.[57] In Bierstadt's day only the hardiest of men—a few trappers and the explorer Frémont—had ventured into the interior depths of these giants. To judge by his extant field studies and his finished paintings of Wyoming scenery, Bierstadt seems to be among the majority of artists who never penetrated the rugged, massive mountains but instead gathered their material, both for closeup studies of nature and for extended views of the mountains, on the plains. Thus it is reasonable to assume that Bierstadt referred to his alpine studies for imagery in composing some of his exaggerated and theatrical pictures of western mountain scenery.[58] Occasionally these pictures include some topographical details of the area to suggest a specific place, but Bierstadt—and later Thomas Moran—was more interested in conveying the impression or character of a place than a literal or photographic transcription. Even those works that can be ascribed to a specific geographical location are often erroneously titled, owing to the artist's confusion regarding western geography.[59]

Although it was chiefly the scenery that drew his attention, Bierstadt managed to obtain a number of plein-air oil studies of the local Indians and the animals he observed during his travels.[60] Hesitant to venture too far from the campsite, the artist viewed from a distance the "charming" figures of the Indians, "travelling about with their long poles trailing along on the ground, and their picturesque dress" that "renders them such appropriate adjuncts to the scenery."[61] Small, colorful Indian encampments frequently enliven his

121

large scenic western pictures of the 1860s. Bierstadt believed that the rapidly vanishing customs and manners of the Indians ought to be recorded by the painter as well as by the writer; "a combination of both will assuredly render . . . [their history] more complete." At this point Bierstadt appeared to be expressing a prevailing romantic philosophy concerning the plight of the Indian, doomed to extinction by the onrush of civilization.[62]

Soon after returning from his first western venture, Bierstadt moved to New York City, where he opened a studio in the famous Tenth Street Building—possibly following the lead of his friend and fellow-artist Whittredge.[63] There he spread out before him the prolific results of his artistic endeavors—portfolios of studies and sketches, stereographs, horned-animal specimens, and Indian trophies[64]—and began drawing from them particular verities of nature to create his idealized compositions that reflected the character or spirit of the localities portrayed. Although his first large western painting, *The Base of the Rocky Mountains, Laramie Peak*—exhibited at the National Academy of Design in 1860—is now lost, a number of the Wind River Mountain landscapes remain to give us an idea of the artist's early visual perception of the West.[65] For example, his famous showpiece *The Rocky Mountains—Lander's Peak* is a formulated studio composition, exemplifying "the hybrid aesthetic of the real-ideal." Other paintings, however, clearly reveal Bierstadt's close observation of mountain configurations and the native flora and fauna and can be conclusively identified with actual views taken on the spot in 1859. Several of these plein-air sketches depicting the Wind River Range, identifiable by its peculiarly jagged profile, attest to the accuracy of his eye and hand. One view captures the Continental Divide as observed by the artist from the Old Lander Trail, about forty-five to fifty-five miles west of the peaks, looking north, halfway between the Wyoming Range and the Wind River chain (plate 42). Glancing from left to right, "we can easily recognize Mt. Helen, Mt. Sacajawea, . . . Fremont Peak, . . . Jackson Peak, and Knifepoint."[66]

Many of the remaining studies of Indians engaged in various activities, native wildlife, and mountain peaks swathed in clouds and mist (plate 43), freely executed in thinly applied oil colors, are hastily recorded impressions intended merely to jog the memory later.[67] They contrast sharply with his composed studio versions, which have lost the artist's spontaneity in their transformation into dramatic and sensational pictures. As is apparent in many of his early finished paintings, Bierstadt had developed a distinctive formula that he used throughout his career. Such examples include *On The Sweetwater River near Devil's Gate, Nebraska* [sic], *Thunderstorm in the Rocky Mountains* (plate 44), and *Wind River County*, all basically laid out on the same pattern—a series of overlapping recessional planes with strong framing elements in the foreground. In all three paintings abrupt contrasts of light and dark areas help lead the eye back to the distant mountains veiled in suffused light. Dramatic skies with swirling clouds, surreal light effects, and an occasional blasted tree in the foreground seem to enhance the theatricality of the presentation. Although the artist has synthesized various pictorial components into a unified, ideal whole, these paintings can still be identified with particular sites. Executed shortly after his return in 1859, they can be considered preludes to his later and more celebrated monumental pictures.[68] As Gordon Hendricks has noted, little enthusiasm was generated over his early western efforts until the exhibition of *The Rocky Mountains* in 1864.

Nonetheless, contemporary criticism praised Bierstadt's maiden efforts, announcing the completion of two paintings "which worthily present his great talents as a landscapist." The reporter singled out his *Scene among the Rocky Mountains* (retitled by a modern gallery *Wind River Country*) as "a magnificent study from nature, grand in its perspective, rich in coloring, and truthful and harmonious in detail." A detailed description of the picture followed, ending with a warning that "the painting as a whole will warrant an hour's careful study."[69] Here is an instance in which Bierstadt willingly sacrificed the integrity of a place to artistic invention and combined two separate views of the Wind River country. Because of the placement of Fremont Peak, skirted by mountains on its left and with a butte closer in on the right, the artist's vantage point should have been from the East Fork River as he traveled along the Old Lander Trail. Instead, however, Bierstadt chose to represent the rocky, hilly terrain along the Sweetwater River southwest of the Narrows. In this

PLATE 42

Albert Bierstadt, *Wind River Range*, 1859, Oil on paper, 4¾″ × 9″.
Courtesy Carl S. and Elisabeth Waldo Dentzel Collection, Northridge, Calif.

PLATE 43

Albert Bierstadt, *Wind River Range*, 1859, Oil on paper, 6¼″ × 8″.
Courtesy Carl S. and Elisabeth Waldo Dentzel Collection, Northridge.

PLATE 44

Albert Bierstadt, *Thunderstorm in the Rocky Mountains*, 1859, Oil, 19″ × 29″.
Courtesy Museum of Fine Arts, Boston. Given in memory of Elias T. Milliken by his daughters.

panoramic view the winding river cuts its way diagonally across the valley floor, directing attention to the prominent snowy peak on the horizon.

From elevated vantage points such as rocky outcroppings, Bierstadt, while looking northwest or due west, captured several other sweeping views of the valley with snowy mountains dimly visible on the horizon. The artist identified them as the "Wahsatch," but since he and his companion Frost sketched mainly in the vicinity of South Pass along the Old Lander Trail, it would have been virtually impossible for them to have seen the Wasatch Mountains from their geographical position.[70] What the artist really saw "some seventy miles west from them, across a rolling prairie covered with wild sage," was the Wyoming Range.[71] Bierstadt recorded the scene he described in an oil entitled *Wind River Country* (plate 45). A similarly composed picture, incorrectly identified by the artist as "looking Northwest from the Wind River Mountains, the Wahsatch Mountains seen in the distance," is actually a view looking up the Pacific slope of the Wind River Mountains from the west end of Prospect Mountain, where the Old Lander Trail heads off for Snyder Basin on the southern end of the Wyoming Range.[72] Both paintings share the familiar stacked-rock formations in the foreground and middle distance, substantiating the artist's vantage point. In these small panoramas the impression of vast space stretching to infinity has been skillfully achieved through subtle gradations of light.

Another painting misidentified as the "Wahsatch Mountains" (unmistakably Island Lake) demonstrates Bierstadt's ability to develop and expand his small studies into highly finished, detailed compositions while retaining the initial impact of his vision. The bend in the shoreline indicates that the distant range veiled in hazy light is none other than the Wind River Range in the vicinity of South Pass (color plate 14). Unlike the small, more freely brushed study,[73] the larger work is executed with minute brushstrokes, delicately and meticulously applied to produce a highly polished surface—exemplifying what has been called his Düsseldorfian mode.[74]

That Bierstadt freely manipulated light effects in his pictures to increase dramatic impact is particularly apparent in his oversized theatrical canvases of mountain scenery. Like a photographer, the artist was aware of the wide range of light effects and took special care to study light and atmospheric conditions. He judiciously used back-, cross-, and sidelighting to create the highlights and shadows that resulted in a separation of planes and a three-dimensional effect. These alternating light and dark areas created a balance for his forms and shapes. Like the photographer, he recognized that the negative space around a highlighted object was as important to the total pictorial effect as the focal object itself and that shafts of light streaming through trees and rents in clouds were an effective means of heightening dramatic impact. Like the lens of a camera, Bierstadt's eye selectively focused on small flowers, leaves, and grasses in the frontal plane of the picture, magnifying them a hundredfold to show details, shapes, and delicate textures.

Many of these pictorial artifices, with their dramatic overtones, are fully realized in the sensational full-length landscapes—often described as his "Wagnerian exultations"[75]—that became Bierstadt's trademark from the 1860s. Perhaps the earliest manifestation of this heroic type of artistic expression is *Sunset Light, Wind River Range of the Rocky Mountains* (color plate 15, 1861),[76] an earlier version of his critically acclaimed larger picture *The Rocky Mountains—Lander's Peak* and probably his first attempt at matching Church's grand-scale productions. *Sunset Light* bears a remarkable resemblance to the larger version executed two years later, suggesting that they are views of the same subject. Basic differences, however, exist between the two. *Sunset Light* shifts the viewpoint from head on to a slightly oblique angle while retaining the lateral frames—then zooms in on the Indian encampment spotlighted on the banks of the river, cropping off some of the broad green amphitheater stage of the larger work. The later and larger version gives a more expansive vista of the landscape. Apart from these dissimilarities, both paintings are typically built up on a series of successive planes, reaching a climax with the soaring, jagged, snowcapped peak. All design elements, horizontal and vertical, are properly balanced, producing a somewhat static, symmetrical composition relieved only by the dramatic interplay of light and dark at the approach of evening.

Like the more monumental version, *Sunset Light* is a formulated studio production, undoubtedly also worked up from objective topo-

PLATE 45

Albert Bierstadt, *Wind River Country*, ca. 1860, Oil, 14½″ × 23½″.
Courtesy private collection.

graphical field studies.[77] The artist has freely and skillfully combined his materials into a novel artistic arrangement. In spite of this artistic license, topographical features are still recognizable. In both pictures the prominent snowcapped peak has been described as Fremont or Lander's Peak, but, because of its distinctive configuration, it can be none other than Temple Peak with its "big step" as observed from the west. Furthermore, the foreground area is an exact duplicate of the site where the East Fork River emerges from the Wind River Range, indicating that the artist was on the Old Lander Trail looking back (east) across the Big Sandy River (following the contour of the Wind River Range where the trail heads west toward the Wyoming Range). As the river leaves the range, it emerges from a split-walled gorge, exactly as depicted here, beyond the Indian encampment. The artist has perhaps intentionally opened up the center field to place more emphasis on the prominent peak (more apparent in the larger, straightforward view, where the waterfall takes a central position). The position of the "big step" (plate 46) in the picture establishes with certainty that the view was taken from the west looking east, making it impossible for Bierstadt to have seen the setting sun shown in the painting.[78] In all probability the artist arbitrarily arranged his lighting for maximum effect, vividly recalling the gorgeous sunsets he had observed on the plains during his travels with Lander.

This initial version obviously paved the way for its colossal successor *The Rocky Mountains* (plate 47),[79] which became an immediate sensation, catapulting its author into national fame and making him a serious contender for Church's crown. Its popular acclaim caused one critic to remark extravagantly that his picture deserved "to take rank among the highest existing productions of American landscape art,"[80] while another dared to suggest that Bierstadt might now be considered "superior even to Church."[81] Prophetically, Bierstadt's chef d'oeuvre was displayed directly facing Church's *Heart of the Andes* at the New York Sanitary Fair's Art Gallery in April, 1864. The following year, after being exhibited at Chicago's Sanitary Fair and at Seitz and Noelle Gallery in New York City, the painting was purchased by James McHenry, an American railroad tycoon living in London, for the unprecedented sum of $25,000. From New York

the picture was sent to Europe, where it was exhibited at the Paris Universal Exposition and later at the Haymarket in London. It continued to generate public and critical enthusiasm, while establishing for the artist a permanent place in the world's art market, until its eventual removal to McHenry's large London house, Oak Lodge.[82]

Long before the painting left the United States, Bierstadt had set about having an engraved reproduction of it made to reap additional profits. The flyer that accompanied the engraved print, published by Bierstadt, was carefully worded to assure its purchaser that the picture possessed "a geographical and historical value, such as few works by modern artists have obtained." It elaborated on this bit of puffery by adding:

> Nor will time destroy its worth, but rather add to it. It is not only a correct representation of a portion of our country of which we as yet know comparatively little; but it introduces into it the every-day life of that race which, before the advance of civilization, fades away like the mists of morning before the rays of the rising sun. Their customs and habits through it will be preserved when, perhaps, the scene which it depicts, will no longer echo to the ring of their war-cry, or mark their stealthy step following in the chase. Upon that very plain where now an Indian village stands, a city, populated by our descendants, may rise.[83]

The reader was also told that the picture represented a particular portion of the scenery on the western slope of the Wind River Range and that the streams seen "leaping down their sides—the waters of which form a lake in the basin of the valley—[were] the head waters of the Rio Colorado." The artist identified the principal peak in the group as Mount Lander and described the scene as lying about seven hundred miles northeast of San Francisco,[84] leaving no doubt in the beholder's mind that the exaggerated and idealized scene with its soaring peak, glistening white glaciers, and fanciful plunging waterfall was representative of a well-documented geographic site—which could hardly be disputed by the average reader of the time.

The reputation of the painting was further enlarged by the glowing rhetoric of the contemporary art critic Tuckerman:

> No more genuine and grand American work has been produced in landscape art than Bierstadt's "Rocky Mountains." Representing the

PLATE 46

Finis Mitchell, *Temple Peak, Wind River Range,* 1979, Photograph, 5″ × 7″.
Courtesy of the authors.

COLOR PLATE 10

James Wilkins, *Immigrants in the Rockies,* ca. 1855, Oil, 22¼″ × 30¼″.
Courtesy Missouri Historical Society, Saint Louis, Mo.

COLOR PLATE 11

John J. Young after H. V. A. Von Beckh,
Beautiful Cascade, Timpanogos River Canon, ca. 1859,
Watercolor, 9″ × 6″. Courtesy Center for
Cartographic and Architectural
Archives, National Archives, Washington, D.C.

COLOR PLATE 12

Anton Schonborn, *Fort Laramie, Wy. T. View from the East*, 1870, Watercolor, 5¼″ × 12¾″. Courtesy Amon Carter Museum, Fort Worth.

COLOR PLATE 13

James Madison Alden, *Kintla Mountains from the Summit of Kishnehnehna*, 1860, Watercolor, 16″ × 22″. Courtesy National Archives and Records Service, Washington, D.C.

COLOR PLATE 14

Albert Bierstadt, *Island Lake, Wind River Range, Wyoming*, 1861, Oil, 26½″ × 40½″.
Courtesy Buffalo Bill Historical Center, Cody.

134

COLOR PLATE 15

Albert Bierstadt, *Sunset Light, Wind River Range of the Rocky Mountains*, 1861, Oil, 38½″ × 59½″.
Courtesy Free Public Library, New Bedford, Mass.

135

COLOR PLATE 16

Albert Bierstadt, *A Storm in the Rocky Mountains—Mt. Rosalie,* 1866, Oil, 84⅜″ × 144⅛″.
Courtesy Brooklyn Museum, Brooklyn, N.Y.

136

Color Plate 17

Albert Bierstadt, *A Storm in the Rocky Mountains—Mt. Rosalie* (detail), 1866, Oil, 84⅜″ × 144⅛″.
Courtesy Brooklyn Museum, Brooklyn.

137

COLOR PLATE 18

Albert Bierstadt, *The Fountain Geyser, Yellowstone Park*,
1881, Oil on panel, 13⅞″ × 19″. Courtesy
Collection of the Honorable Robert D. Coe, Cody, Wyo.

COLOR PLATE 19

Ransom G. Holdredge, *A Sioux Camp
in the Rocky Mountains*, ca. 1882,
Oil, 42″ × 69″. Courtesy
Arthur J. Phelan, Jr., Collection,
Chevy Chase, Md.

sublime range which guards the remote West, its subject is eminently national; and the spirit in which it is executed is at once patient and comprehensive—patient in the careful reproduction of the tints and traits which make up and identify its local character, and comprehensive in the breadth, elevation, and grandeur of the composition. Almost a virgin theme, the novelty of the subject alone would attract the student of nature and the lover of art; both of whom must feel a thrill of surprise and delight to find a scene so magnificent rendered with such power and truth. . . . the whole picture . . . is a grand and gracious epitome and reflection of nature on this Continent—of that majestic barrier of the West where the heavens and the earth meet in brilliant and barren proximity, where snow and verdure, gushing fountains and vivid herbage, noble trees and azure sky-depths, primeval solitudes, the loftiest summits, and the boundless plains, combine all that is most vast, characteristic, and beautiful in North American scenery.[85]

Bierstadt's novel, majestic interpretation of the Rocky Mountains unquestionably shaped the way Americans and Europeans saw the western wilderness throughout the greater part of the nineteenth century. The only possible fault that could be found with the picture at the time was the controversial intrusion of the Indian encampment (the apocryphal "Shoshone Village") with its scattered implements of the chase, warfare, and domestic use in the foreground. Its presence in the landscape was defended philosophically by one vocal critic, who maintained that "the scene would have been comparatively voiceless, meaningless, and dead, but for the addition of the wild men of the mountains in their own life and manners."[86] Another insisted that the small accessories were certainly within the accepted canon of landscape art and were strictly there "to minister to the subject": "To the beholder who enters into the spirit of the Rocky Mountains, the human life in Bierstadt's foreground is a help at comprehension of the peak."[87] Yet to the famous art critic James Jackson Jarves, Bierstadt's picturesquely grouped figures ("prosaically true to actual life"), though "giving additional interest to most observers," in fact rendered "his great work, the Rocky Mountains, confused, and detracting from its principal features, beside making it liable to the artistic objection of two pictures in one, from different points of view."[88]

Jarves's critical judgment discloses what are probably the principal artistic flaws in Bierstadt's first major work: its two obviously different points of view and its lack of unity. Since Indians held a special attraction for the artist at the time, it was inevitable that they should figure prominently in his first panoramic landscape, competing openly with the scenery for attention. It is tempting to speculate that the Indian encampment was introduced into the landscape as an afterthought to make it more palatable and marketable—the idea perhaps occurring to Bierstadt late in the development of the picture. The awkward handling of the figures, which are wanting in proportion, could support the idea that they were hastily added as a last-minute thought, in spite of the detailing of their costumes and accoutrements. Since, however, Bierstadt was not essentially a draftsman, particularly of the human form, a case cannot be built on this deficiency alone. Working within his limitations, the artist cleverly left his foreground in deep shadows cast by the waning sun, obscuring for the most part the small, awkward figures and the encampment. The distribution of light—highlighted in the upper regions, attenuated and graduated as it spreads downward and across to the middle distance, then gradually disappearing in the palpable nearness of the foreground—leaves no doubt that the primary attraction of the picture is the glorious, sublime spectacle of nature, the manifestation of Bierstadt's discovery. The Indian encampment here merely provides the proper time frame and specificity of place; thereafter it would be reduced to a lesser role in his landscapes, used merely as a pictorial accent to heighten romantic sensibilities.

Although parts of the picture are well articulated, the necessary formal relationships are not resolved completely to produce a unified composition. In this first major work Bierstadt demonstrates a lack of surety in handling formal considerations on a monumental scale. The desired harmonious relationships and subtle modulation of light and color tones would be fully realized in his second dramatic, monumental picture *A Storm in the Rocky Mountains—Mt. Rosalie* (1866), inspired by his visit to Colorado in 1863. In spite of its weaknesses Bierstadt's first panoramic landscape nevertheless launched his career, establishing his reputation and creating a ready market for his work.

Once the artist had established his panoramic format as a viable means of conveying his impressions of the western wilderness, he was prompted to seek sites whose grandeur and amplitude were suited to it. Bierstadt's persistent fascination with the Far West was perhaps augmented when he saw Carleton E. Watkins's remarkable photographs of Yosemite Valley at Goupil's Gallery in New York.[89] Although he expressed interest in another painting expedition as early as March, 1862, he failed to secure government funding because the national focus was directed to the exigencies of the Civil War.[90] In the spring of 1863, however, his hopes for a western expedition were realized when he and his friend Fitz Hugh Ludlow, the *New York Post* critic, headed across the plains toward Colorado and then on to California, the final leg of their journey.[91]

The principal account of their journey is provided by Ludlow in a descriptive and anecdotal narrative that was first published as a series of articles in the *Atlantic Monthly* and later expanded into book form.[92] Ludlow recounts with verve and occasional scientific exactitude their experiences and impressions of the scenery as they traveled across the varied, rugged frontiers of civilization. He often allows his romantic sensibilities to come into full play while observing nature's evanescent moods, vividly describing his impressions in language that showed once again that literature and art had joined forces to reveal kindred spirits.[93] He and Bierstadt were equally attracted to nature's profound and colorful effects and readily transported by its theatrical displays.

They caught their first sight of the Rocky Mountains about one hundred miles out of Denver. As Ludlow recalled, "Out against the bright sky dawned slowly the undefined shimmering trace of something a little bluer. . . . It might have passed for a vapor effect on the horizon, had not the driver called it otherwise."[94] Although Bierstadt made a number of pencil sketches and rapid color studies, several of which were used to illustrate Ludlow's narrative, none exist to complement the author's emotional response to their first view of the Rockies.

About June 6, Bierstadt and Ludlow reached Denver, which they found larger and more settled than they had expected. The town lay at the bottom of a basin formed by the lowest foothills; "its white dots, relieved against the rich brown of the hills, made a very cheerful contrast."[95] During the several days they remained in Denver, Bierstadt busily occupied himself making sketches of the scenes surrounding immigrant wagons, which were replenishing supplies before heading west.[96]

Thoroughly rested from their arduous trek across the plains, Bierstadt and Ludlow set out on June 10 with a few friends for a "seventy miles' journey to the base of Pike's Peak," the first of two side excursions out of Denver. Their intention was to make notes and sketches of the "remarkable scenery and geological formations" between Denver and Colorado City. Ludlow acknowledged the generosity of the territorial governor, John Evans, who furnished them with a comfortable vehicle plus a buckboard and horse to carry the artist and his color box.[97] After six miles of level traveling, they ascended a small divide and got a full view of the plains stretching for hundreds of miles eastward, which Ludlow likened to "the sea of the Ancient Mariner."

As they descended into a valley of the divide, they encountered for the first time the remarkable "sculpturesque freaks of geology" that are a distinctive feature in the Rocky Mountain region. Captivated by these curiosities of nature, Bierstadt stopped to sketch some of the odd, mimetic shapes they encountered along the way. Farther south on one of the rolling hills of the divide, the artist captured a color study of Pikes Peak that Ludlow called the "finest" view of it obtained during their trip.

Ludlow continues the narrative of their travels with no further mention of the artist until their arrival at the Garden of the Gods, a site with similarly curious geological formations about two miles north of Colorado City. It was a great disappointment to Ludlow and the other party members that Bierstadt "did not choose the Garden of the Gods for a 'big picture.'" As Ludlow recounted rather regretfully:

It was such an interesting place in nature that they could not understand its unavailability for art. Everywhere we went during our journey, we found the same ideas prevailing, and had to be on our guard against enthusiasms, lest we should waste time in getting at the "most magnificent scenery in the world" to find some solitary castle-rock or weird simulation of another kind, which, however impressive it might be outdoors, was absolutely incommunicable by paint and canvas, when the attempt to convey it, being simply the imitation of an imitation, must have looked either like a very poor castle, or a mountain put up by an association of stone masons. But the artist's selective faculty is not to be looked for among practical men.[98]

It was on Bierstadt's second excursion "to the summit of the snowy mountain cluster directly west of Denver" that the idea for his next large painting began to germinate. On June 17, Bierstadt and his guide, William Newton Byers, the editor and publisher of the *Rocky Mountain News,* left on a four-day expedition to Chicago Lakes and vicinity. The *News* announced that the artist would "take likenesses, true to life, of mountain and cañon views on the trip" and that Byers would "make a pretty good pilot to tow him through the channels of choicest scenery."[99] As Byers reported later, the object was to secure "sublime and grand" views of mountain scenery to be incorporated into Bierstadt's forthcoming picture of Colorado.[100] The first day's journey along the Apex road to Idaho Springs was "devoid of special interest," according to the editor—but the artist did manage to make two "fine drawings," one of the *Snowy Range and Clear Creek Basin* from the summit at the head of Mount Vernon Gulch, and another of *Pleasant, or Elk Park*[101] with its surroundings, including Squaw Mountain. The second day, the eighteenth, proved more rewarding for them. They set out on mules, traveling up Chicago Creek, which Byers described as a "difficult and tedious" route, one that "alternately [went] through swamps, over rocky points, winding among fallen timber and tangled underbrush"—definitely "no place for broadcloth or fancy outfits." Byers recorded Bierstadt's reaction upon entering the amphitheater below Chicago Lakes:

> Mr. Bierstadt was in raptures with the scenery, but restrained his inclination to try his pencils until within two or three miles of the upper limit of tree growth—There upon suddenly turning the point of a mountain and entering a beautiful little grassy park, a vast amphitheatre of snowy peaks, lofty cliffs and timbered mountain sides burst suddenly upon the view. Patience vanished, and in nervous haste, canvass, paints and brushes were unpacked and a couple of hours saw, under his skillful hands, some miles of mountains, hills, forests and valley reproduced with all its vivid coloring, and the cloud shadows that were sweeping over it.

After securing his color studies, Bierstadt rejoined Byers and they hurriedly repacked their belongings and remounted for a short ride up the creek to the margins of Trout Lake (present Lower Chicago Lake), "in the extreme upper verge of the timber." There they set up camp on the grassy shores of its head, at the base of an immense rock cliff over which streamed a "great waterfall." In a state of exalted delight Byers noted in his journal that "a more beautiful or romantic spot . . . [could not] be pictured even in imagination." In the few remaining hours of daylight Bierstadt made his way to "the lower extremity of the lake" and produced a color study that prompted Byers to exclaim that "pleasure hunters who travel thousands of miles to view the Alps [would] be justly surprised" at the equally glorious scenery of home.

The following morning they got up shortly before daybreak to reach the mountain top before the sun rose. Leaving their animals behind, they began the circuitous, perpendicular climb of about 500 feet to the upper lake (present Upper Chicago Lake), the smaller of the two on Chicago Creek. It was also "enclosed in an amphitheatre of mountains," but lacked the fresh, vibrant greenness of flourishing vegetation surrounding the lower lake. Continuing south, they made another climb of about 1,500 feet up a "weather worn gorge, enclosed between lofty vertical masses," to a third and separately fed lake, the loftiest and largest. Since it was on a summit of about 12,500 feet, they named it Summit Lake. The "three-pointed star"–shaped lake, partly covered with ice, was "the centre of an amphitheatre, more vast and lofty than those [below], and its rim . . . the loftiest mountain [Mount Evans] seen from Denver."[102] The mountain and its neighboring peak, now called Mount Bierstadt, were recorded by the artist and later incorporated into his large, dramatic Colorado picture *A Storm in the Rocky Mountains—Mt. Rosalie* (color plates 16 and 17), considered lost until its rediscovery in 1974.[103] Bierstadt named the principal peak Mount Rosalie for his friend Ludlow's wife. The choice of name implies the existence of a triangle—and perhaps not so coincidentally: Rosalie became Bierstadt's wife on November 21, 1866.[104]

Once the artist had completed a sketch of the scene spread before them, he and Byers turned their faces toward the summit and climbed the mountain that towered more than two thousand feet above them. As they stood upon one of the "loftiest [summits] in the world, A vast panorama of mountains, valleys and plains was spread out before and around [them]." Byers reported that the artist hastily captured in pencil an outline sketch of the 360-degree panorama, putting in all the major geographic landmarks visible in all directions. With the naked eye, he continued, they could even distinguish houses far off in the distance; with the aid of a powerful glass they traced the meanderings of the Platte and its tributaries for a hundred miles outside the mountains.

On June 21 they headed back toward Denver, halting three times to allow Bierstadt to make sketches. One of them, depicting a storm brewing over the "small crystal lake and grassy beach," was undoubtedly the inspiration for the theme of his major Colorado picture. After half a day of treacherous climbing and winding their way through fallen timber and tangled underbrush, they reached Idaho Springs, crossed over to Central City, and finally arrived at their home base two days later. Concluding his account of their journey to Chicago Lakes, Byers proudly announced to his readers that the artist was in "ekstasy" over the scenery, "pronouncing it the finest he [had] ever found." Coloradans could consider this a particularly "high encomium," he noted, since Bierstadt was "familiar with the Alps throughout their length, and also with all the mountains of the eastern states."

Byers's chronicle offers a glimpse into the artist's working methods. It also documents that Bierstadt obtained a great number of valuable color studies and pencil sketches in preparation for his large painting. With the exception of one rough pencil sketch, depicting the rugged cliffs surrounding the glacial valley, none of this field-work has come to light. To judge from the one extant sketch, which clearly demonstrates how the artist obtained his sightline—the slope of the rugged cliff on the right (partly incorporated into the finished work)[105]—his other studies must have been equally useful in developing his first large Colorado picture. Despite the sensational effects of *A Storm in the Rocky Mountains*—the spiraling gray thunderheads, the high-pitched light, and the exaggerated height of the mountain peaks—the picture is still based in reality. This dramatic interpretation is unquestionably of the Chicago Lakes district[106]—a visual testimony to the glorious discovery Bierstadt made in the heart of the Colorado Rockies.

On June 23, Ludlow and Bierstadt rejoined forces and resumed their overland journey toward California with a second brief stop-over in Salt Lake City.[107] In his account Ludlow again acknowledges the courtesies extended to them by the stagecoach operators, who instructed their drivers to halt whenever the two travelers wished to take scientific notes, specimens, and sketches. Bierstadt's studies of this portion of the trip are also unlocated. Available pictorial evidence indicates that Bierstadt revisited the area in 1881, taking in a number of the same scenic spots described by the author.[108] Ludlow continues his descriptive narrative by chronicling their ventures into northern California and Oregon, particularly Bierstadt's sketching tour of Yosemite Valley—the inspiration for a great number of his paintings in the 1860s and 1870s.

In late December, after spending eight months in the West, Bierstadt and his traveling companion returned to New York City, where the artist began developing themes for new paintings based on fresh material gathered in the field.[109] Although he was to devote much of his creative energy to California subjects for the next two years, he managed to set aside some time early in 1865 to begin his monumental painting *A Storm in the Rocky Mountains*.[110] Reacting to popular taste and the temper of the times, Bierstadt chose to make *A Storm in the Rocky Mountains* the first work to combine his heroic landscapes of mountain grandeur with dramatic sky effects.[111] Falling back on the aesthetics of his Düsseldorfian legacy,[112] he captured on canvas the dramatic impact of a tempest in the high country. The tumultuous, spiraling gray thunderheads hover over endless miles of rugged mountains. The U-shaped glacial valley below is a giant amphitheater, with two small lakes and a winding creek in the center. On this stagelike setting the picture's story unfolds:

> There has just been a tremendous clap of thunder. . . . It shook a black bear out of its snooze to send it bouncing into the lower right-hand corner of the painting. It frightened some ducks, who fly off just below, and also scared two ponies, one already unsaddled, who scoot down the

valley toward an Indian village by the river [Chicago Creek]. They're bolting for home. Two Indians chase them on foot, another on horseback. At the lower-right edge of the painting is . . . [a] hunting camp. . . . A campfire, the empty saddle of the pale horse that runs to the center of the picture, and the carcass of a deer the Indians recently killed [are all that remain after the thundrous clap which drove human beings and animals into action].[113]

The narrative begins on the elevated, sloping pasturelands in the right foreground, an area that technically becomes a *repoussoir*—a stage or platform for the action. The stage here is the western slope of the rugged amphitheater's cliff wall, from which Bierstadt first viewed the sweeping panorama spread out before and around him, about two hundred feet above the floor of the valley and its small "crystal" lake (Lower Chicago Lake).[114] The abrupt alternation of light and dark areas reinforces this progression of the eye into space, while diagonal thrusts accentuate the picture's somewhat agitated movement. The result is in total opposition to the static quality of *The Rocky Mountains.* The classical restraint of the latter has given way to an unnatural turmoil and dramatic impact achieved mainly by strong contrasts in light and dark and the animated forces of the swirling cloud masses. In this huge amphitheater of mountains the miniscule figures are barely visible, suggesting that they are to be thought of as part of the larger scene—the spectacular mountain scenery.[115] Here Bierstadt has forgone his concern for historical associations to share his wonderment of the glories of nature with mankind.

Although the repetitive sections and the carefully worked out spatial progression suggest that this is "a synthesis of sketches and memories" from his second journey rather than a naturalistic scene,[116] Bierstadt could easily have seen the entire landscape from his elevated vantage point on the western slope. He undoubtedly referred to the great number of sketches he gathered to jog his memory and reconfirm topographical details, but the disposition of the entire scene was established on the site and was the true inspiration for the painting. The scene can be identified with certainty as the Chicago Lakes district,[117] though its scenic features have been drama-

tized and exaggerated to produce theatrical effects and lend visual impact. As one writer noted, "Geology was never quite so melodramatic."[118] For a viewer standing on the floor of the valley looking up at the enormous, awesome mountain beyond and above, the impact is overwhelming—and that is the effect Bierstadt undoubtedly wished to convey. Unlike those of his first hesitant production, all pictorial elements here are harmoniously unified by meticulously detailed brushwork and the force of lurid light, including theatrical sidelighting that suffuses the middle distance. Even the work's objectionable hard coloring, dark glazes, and highly polished surface contribute to this pictorial unity, producing an appropriately cold and somber effect. Although condemned as "scene-painting," the picture effectively achieves the artist's "object . . . to produce a powerful impression of overwhelming natural grandeur." This is, as one journalist put it, "magnificent scene-painting"[119]—of a more elevated and novel kind, reflecting greater skill, than that of the German school of late Romantic painters or the Swiss alpine painter Alexandre Calame.

The picture that was to earn the epithet "sublime" from one critic was completed in January, 1866—just in time to make its debut at Somerville and Minor's Gallery in a benefit exhibition for the Nursery and Child's Hospital.[120] Like Bierstadt's first major work, *A Storm in the Rocky Mountains* created a stir in critical circles. There were those, among them the *Rocky Mountains News* correspondent, who pronounced it "the best production of an American genius" and staunchly defended its truthful effects:

> The art critic of the *Tribune* [has] seen fit in his wisdom—or rather want of it—to say some unfavorable things, but in doing so he only displayed his own ignorance. Many people who see it are puzzled at its—to them—peculiarities. They never have seen such a combination of scenery; such clouds and storm, such lights and shadows; hence they are in doubt if such can be, and "that's what's the matter" with the *Tribune* man, only he didn't stop to doubt but decided that they couldn't. Poor fellow. He had better travel and learn, or else dry up.[121]

Others railed against the picture's "bigness," hard coloring, and dry, mechanical, Düsseldorfian finish. The critic of *Watson's Weekly Art*

Journal went so far as to question, in a tongue-in-cheek manner, the artist's understanding of the "laws of gravitation":

> The whole science of geology cries out against him. . . . The law of gravitation leagues itself with geological law against the artist. Away up, above the clouds, near the top of the picture, the observer will perceive two pyramidal shapes. By further consultation of the index-sheet, the observer will ascertain that these things are the two "spurs" of Mount Rosalie. Now, let him work out a problem in arithmetic: The hills over which he looks, as we are told, are three thousand feet high; right over the hills tower huge masses of cloud which certainly carry the eye up to ten or twelve thousand feet higher; above these . . . the two "spurs"; what is the height of Mount Rosalie: Answer: approximately, ten thousand miles or so. Impossible.[122]

Some time before Bierstadt sent his painting to the International Exposition in Paris, in April, 1867, a journalist announced that it had already been purchased "by a gentleman in Europe."[123] It is conceivable that the buyer, Bierstadt's English friend Sir Samuel Morton Peto, saw the work in progress during his visit to the United States in the fall of 1865 and purchased it then.[124] It is generally believed, however, that the work was sold to Peto in 1867 after the close of the Paris exposition. Undoubtedly because of financial reverses Peto sold the picture a year later to his friend and associate Thomas William Kennard, who, coincidentally, was also associated with the owner of Bierstadt's first major Rocky Mountain picture.[125] This transaction probably took place after the painting had been on exhibit on the Isle of Wight at a benefit honoring Queen Victoria. Its appearance there followed a successful showing at McLean's Gallery, in London's Haymarket, in June, 1867. The favorable reviews of the picture in the London press probably caught Kennard's attention; the *Illustrated London News* went so far as to state boldly that it "surpassed in interest and artistic merit" Bierstadt's first Rocky Mountain picture, deserving to be considered "an epic of landscape art."[126] The most accurate and incisive description of all was provided by a critic of the *London Saturday Review*, whose complimentary comments defended the artist's use of artifices to achieve his artistic ends:

> The qualities which strike us in Mr. Bierstadt, as an artist, are first, a great audacity, justified by perfect ability to accomplish all that he intends. He is not a mere copyist of nature, but an artist having definite artistic intentions, and carrying them out with care and resolution. Observe, for instance, how strictly in this work everything is arranged to enhance effect. It strikes you at once as a work of art, not a literal production of nature; indeed, the artifices used are sometimes even too evident. But in an age when some hold the theory that art may be dispensed with, and that mere copyism is enough, we welcome a man like Bierstadt, who, though as devoted a lover of the grandest scenes in nature as any painter who ever lived, is, at the same time, given to plotting and planning for purely artistic ends. He is always trying for luminous gradations and useful oppositions, and reaches what he tries for. The excess of his effort after these things may be repugnant to some critics, because it is so obvious, and seems incompatible with the simplicity and self-oblivion of the highest artist[ic] natures. We believe, however, that in art of this kind, where the object is to produce a powerful impression of overwhelming natural grandeur, a painter must employ all the resources possible to him. This may be condemned as scene-painting, but it is very magnificent scene-painting, and we should only be too happy to see more of the same kind.[127]

A Storm in the Rocky Mountains is the only known major visual evidence of Bierstadt's excursion of 1863 to the Chicago Lakes district. Apart from this monumental picture and another smaller work, *Summit Lake, Colorado*, shown at the National Academy in 1888,[128] most of the works he produced immediately following this second trip west were based on his California sketches and color studies. In fact, he later set up a temporary studio in San Francisco in 1871 and spent the greater part of the early 1870s successfully engaged in painting California subjects. Why he was prompted to execute a picture of the "three-pointed star"–shaped lake nestled at the base of Mount Evans some twenty-five years after he viewed it is a perplexing question. Perhaps he had run across Jackson's photograph of the same subject, taken sometime in the 1880s,[129] which could have jogged his memory and inspired him to paint another Colorado picture, referring to the first as a model. The present whereabouts of *Summit Lake* is unknown.

On the way home from California in late October, 1873, Bierstadt and his wife stopped briefly in Denver and were then reported to be heading for Chicago.[130] It is unlikely that the artist engaged in sketching during his brief stopover in the city, yet several small Colorado studies have come to light bearing the seemingly spurious date 1873.[131] They should probably be reassigned to his second sketching tour in Colorado, which occurred in the winter of 1876–77, when he was gathering fresh material for a commissioned painting of Estes Park. He and his new patron, the Irish hunter-sportsman-author Windham Thomas Wyndham-Quin, the fourth earl of Dun-raven, arrived in Denver and registered at the Charpiot Hotel on December 22, 1876. On the twenty-third they departed for Estes Park, remaining there two weeks while the artist secured "sketches of winter scenery and effects in the high mountains"[132]—a comment that allows us to assign to this first trip a number of his undated studies of Estes Park under a mantel of snow.[133] It was probably on the high road, just before the two made their descent into the park, that Bierstadt gained his first impression of the subject. Suddenly, bursting into view below and beyond him was

> the park, with all its marvelous natural beauties. . . . Every variety of scenery [came] into view at once. An imperial panorama, great alike in extent and grandeur, transfixe[d] . . . the attention; . . . the park appear[ed] like a lovely amphitheatre, shut in on all sides by lofty mountains, whose partly timbered and partly sterile slopes, and whose snow crowned and storm swept summits afford[ed] infinite variety of form and color. The floor of the amphitheatre itself seem[ed] smooth and inviting as a lawn, and to complete the landscape, the broad and shining surface of the river [was] seen winding for miles through the smiling meadow.[134]

The one novel bit of scenery missing from this picturesque description was the double-crested, snowcapped Long's Peak, which was to become the focal object of the painting *Long's Peak, Estes Park, Colorado* (plate 48).[135]

Bierstadt's patron had first come to Estes Park in 1872 to hunt game; in fact, with the intention of establishing a private hunting preserve, he arranged through his agent, Theodore Whyte, to purchase a large tract of land in the park. His plans were later to be foiled by opposition from homesteaders, who filed counterclaims, but at the time of his visit of 1876 with Bierstadt, who had recently been Dunraven's guest at a moose hunt in Canada, preparations were already under way to build a large English tourist hotel.[136] "The artist himself is said to have selected [the site] on Whyte's Lake, . . . which was yet to be created by damming [Fish Creek]."[137]

The artist spent the rest of 1877 working in his studio on the large commissioned painting, stopping only to make a brief return visit to Estes Park in August for the hotel's grand opening. When he was not involved in the social festivities, Bierstadt took advantage of the change in seasons to gather studies of Estes Park. At that time the *Rocky Mountain News* correspondent reported that the artist was "putting the finishing touches" on his new painting.[138] The work was not pronounced completed, however, until late December, 1877, when it was sent to Boston for a brief showing before being shipped overseas.[139] It is likely that Bierstadt, inspired by his summer jaunt, decided to alter his picture to include more of the native flora and fauna.

Before the painting was placed in its permanent home, Glin Castle, in Limerick, Ireland, it was exhibited at the Royal Academy in London from May to August, 1878. It was judged by one journalist as falling "far below" other Bierstadt works he had seen; its prominent place in the gallery, he believed, was attributable more to "the grandeur of the subject than [to] the power of the picture."[140]

In a modern restoration *Estes Park* was skinned badly, and much of the artist's original brushwork was lost under inpainting—making it difficult to assess the work fairly.[141] In its present altered state the work lacks the dynamic impact of Bierstadt's first large Colorado picture. Spatial progression is not counterbalanced by tensions, as in *A Storm in the Rocky Mountains;* the effect is heavy and labored, lacking the excitement and drama of the earlier piece. Bierstadt not only has relied on a familiar academic formula in constructing his composition but has even taken a cue from W. G. Chamberlain's stereoscopic view of the same subject *Long's Peak, Estes Park,* produced in the early 1870s (plate 49). Like the photographer, the artist has captured his scene from the vantage point of Dunraven's Fish

PLATE 49

W. G. Chamberlain,
Long's Peak, Estes Park, ca. 1875,
Stereoscopic photograph, 3⅞″ × 6⅜″.
Courtesy Denver Public Library,
Western History Department, Denver.

Creek cottage, showing the narrow stream winding its way through the valley dotted with evergreens. Beyond are the snow-crowned mountains: Long's Peak flanked by Twin Sisters and Mount Meeker. Yet another cliché is the fallen tree trunk Bierstadt has employed as an obvious directional device to lead the eye back to the body of water in the middle distance and up and beyond to the snow-crowned mountains. *Estes Park* might be classified as scene painting that exemplifies the artist's declining technical virtuosity.

A more spontaneous vision of the picturesque valley, however, is readily observed in the remaining sketches and studies that resulted from his trips. Many are impressionistically handled, reproducing only the essential characteristics in an abstract, simplified manner.[142] In contrast to his painstakingly detailed renderings, Bierstadt has recorded his immediate impressions in facile, simple broad brushstrokes, making color notes purely for his own enjoyment and information.

Although scarcely sharing the startlingly modern approach of his impressionistic studies, some of Bierstadt's small, skillfully crafted pictures of Estes Park (obviously produced for the market) recreate the same forceful physical presence of nature. *Snow Scene, Long's Peak, Estes Park, Colorado* (plate 50) is such a picture, in spite of its close reference to a photograph of the same scene by Jackson.[143]

147

PLATE 50

Albert Bierstadt, *Snow Scene, Long's Peak, Estes Park, Colorado,* ca. 1876, Oil on paper, 13⅞″ × 19⅜″.
Courtesy Hirschl and Adler Galleries, New York City, N.Y.

Although the artist had spent several seasons in the Rocky Mountain region gathering material for his portfolio, it was not until late July, 1881, that he actually got around to visiting its principal scenic attraction, Yellowstone National Park.[144] Sometime in the middle of July, Bierstadt left for Chicago, where he met the other members of his small expeditionary party: Senator John Sherman of Ohio, Sherman's cousin Alfred M. Hoyt of New York, and their friend Justice William Strong. At Virginia City, Montana, the group was joined by Lieutenant Samuel M. Swigert and a dozen troopers, who escorted them into the park. Bierstadt's own statement provides the reason for this unexpected visit:

> I went West with the fixed intention of spending the greater part of my time about the geysers, and also to study them as thoroughly as I could in the protracted period I had allotted to myself. I have always had an inclination towards geological studies, and here I had a whole world of geological phenomena spread before me.[145]

Pictures of geysers remain to corroborate this curiosity and interest. It seems that little else occupied the group's attention, save for the large inland body of water and the celebrated Yellowstone Falls, which Bierstadt elaborated into a finished painting. At their campsite near Old Faithful the men were within walking distance of nearly all the important geysers in the upper basin. The artist took advantage of their close proximity to make sketches and studies of them to jog his memory.[146] His *The Fountain Geyser, Yellowstone Park* (color plate 18), showing Sherman and Hoyt in the foreground with the geyser in full action, is probably one of the sketches he later expanded into an oil painting. Unfortunately the sketchbooks containing these quick pencil sketches and notes drawn from the trip through Wyoming, Montana, and Yellowstone National Park are now missing. Most of the remaining pictorial recordings are small oil studies broadly brushed in on paper of similar size.[147]

As the foremost midnineteenth-century American painter of mountain grandeur, Bierstadt became a model of success. His celebrated pictures of the Rocky Mountains and California attracted a number of disciples, who took their cues and inspiration from his works,[148] not only adopting his grand, panoramic format but employing similar conventions for producing dramatic effects. Although many of these works were large and somewhat imaginative, they never quite exhibited the technical virtuosity, unique qualities, or dynamic impact of Bierstadt's major western showpieces. The disciples who created them, however, should be counted among the multitude of artists who left a viable pictorial record of America's untrammeled western wilderness.

BIERSTADT'S DISCIPLES: HENRY ARTHUR ELKINS AND OTHERS

Three years after Bierstadt made his first visit to Colorado, the Chicago artist Henry Arthur Elkins, then only nineteen, traveled across the open plains in an overland wagon toward the same mountain-and-plains territory. His party of eight, which included two other Chicago artists, James F. Gookins and Henry C. Ford, presumably started out from the Missouri River, probably Omaha, in late May, joining an immigrant train on its way west.[149] Gookins, a free-lance artist-correspondent for *Harper's Weekly*, recorded their adventurous journey across the plains and into Colorado. Several of Gookins's sketches, along with his letter to the editor of the *Weekly*, were published in the October 13, 1866, issue. The *Rocky Mountain News* also noted the party's movements but failed to mention Elkins in their reports.[150]

In the latter part of June the travelers arrived in Denver, then made their way up the Platte Canyon toward South Park and the Arkansas Valley, the first location on their sketching tour. While camped in the valley during their approach to South Park, they encountered the author-lecturer Bayard Taylor and the Cincinnati artist William Beard, who were winding up their summer tour in the mountains and heading for Denver. Taylor recorded this encounter:

> We had not gone a mile down the Valley next morning before we came upon another camp, much more luxurious than our own. There was a powerful two-horse wagon, a tent, trunks, and provision boxes. The party which had thus preëmpted one of the prettiest spots in the Valley consisted of Mr. Ford, the artist, of Chicago, with his wife, and Messrs. Gookins and Elkins, also Chicago artists. . . . Mrs. Ford, I was glad to notice, was not the least satisfied member of the party, though the artists were delighted with what they had found.[151]

Small pencil sketches from Elkins's sketchbook of 1866 illustrate their campsite on the approach to South Park; one featuring "Mrs. Ford at work" indicates that the artist's wife was apparently in charge of kitchen detail.[152]

After spending about two months in the mountains, Elkins's party returned to Denver. Owing to inclement weather, the artists failed to take as many sketches as they had planned. The local press, however, praised their views of the Arkansas Valley and reported the group's return to the mountains to sketch in the vicinity of Middle Park.[153] Weather permitting, the artists were to remain in the mountains until October, but the *Rocky Mountain News,* which had been charting their movements, reported them back in Denver on September 22, finishing up their pictures to send off to the local fair. By September 27 the small party was headed home to Chicago, where they planned to work up their sketches into finished paintings during the fall and winter seasons.

Destined to become a noted specialist on Rocky Mountain scenery, Elkins was born in Vershire, Vermont, on May 30, 1847.[154] His education was rudimentary: he attended common school in Vershire and in Chicago, where the family moved in 1856. At an early age he was already neglecting his studies, spending most of his time drawing. Before his first trip west he was obliged to clerk in retail stores, leaving only his leisure hours free for artistic pursuits. In 1866, however, local publicity generated by the sale of his first large Colorado oil, *Morning in the Valley,* to the Honorable Schuyler Colfax, a future vice-president of the United States, launched Elkins's career and established his reputation.[155] In 1873 he was again honored when his monumental painting *Mount Shasta* won first premium at the International Exposition in Vienna.[156] In the same year Elkins traveled to Colorado to gather sketches for his next large painting, *The Crown of the Continent,* intended as an equally large and grand companion piece to his *Mount Shasta.*[157] During his stay in the mountains, a *Rocky Mountain News* reporter noted, the artist took more than seventy-five sketches of mountain scenery and cloud effects. Most of them were captured from Russell Gulch above Central City and focused on Gray's Peak; the grand bit of scenery around Virginia Canyon and beyond to the soaring peak were to figure prominently in Elkins's second major showpiece. The artist also painted six small literal pictures of the same scenery for the Industrial Exhibition in Chicago.[158]

Elkins's "chef d'oeuvre" was unveiled in his Chicago studio at a special press preview in March, 1875. Sharing Bierstadt's entrepreneurial spirit, Elkins had a built-in press to promote his pictures. Reporters showered the work with glowing remarks. The *Chicago Times* announced that Chicago could take "special pride in the artist whose fame [would] be greatly increased by this crowning work of his life."[159] Unfortunately, all that remains of that grand panorama is a faded reproduction on a souvenir postcard,[160] which has little definition left for reading, but an elaborate and critical review by the *Times* on March 9, 1875, affords us a glimpse of Elkins's first monumental Colorado painting:

> From vast table-lands, enshrouded in mist, "The Crown of the Continent" rises high above the whole range, with those distinct markings for which our western mountains are noted. The highest point is a solid body of great extent, on whose side lies a lengthened field of snow, suggesting the presence of a deeply carved cañon. Back of the summit is a succession of turrets, thus giving a suggestion of a crown to the traveller. . . .
>
> The only descent from the mountain is by retracing the steps and following the serpentine arrangement of the sunlight in the form of a great S. . . . By the line of light the eye is guided from the sunny cloud masses to the central mountain summit, over the great snow fields to the forest-clad foothill, into the quiet valley, at whose head a waterfall can just be seen. . . .
>
> The whole picture has been faithfully, solidly painted, and no part has been neglected in order by the contrast to give greater prominence to the rest. The foreground consists of stony table-land, but its surface

is broken by loose bits of rock, some of which are coated by bright lichens. The great body of dense shadow covering nearly the whole of the range in the middle distance is as carefully painted as the brilliant foliage of the forest. . . . It would be hard anywhere to find a scene which brings the beholder more fully into the heart of the mountains—mountains in front, on every side, and even rising behind, with the majestic monarch, crowned by turreted peaks, towering above them all.

Following this major triumph, Elkins continued producing Colorado scenes. Particularly notable among them were *The Thirty-Eighth Star* (1877); another monumental showpiece, *The Valley of the Tomichi* (1881), probably based on a sketch taken that summer; and *Elk Park, Colorado* (1878, plate 51), occasionally referred to as *Indian Camp in the Rocky Mountains*. The last, reported slightly damaged in a fire at Findlay's Gallery, in Kansas City, Missouri, in 1884, is currently in a private collection; the others have evidently been lost or destroyed.[161] *Elk Park* is an excellent example of the artist's mature style, including the typical Elkins trademarks. In this picture the artist employs artistic devices similar to those found in Bierstadt's paintings, but he never handles them as skillfully and convincingly as his mentor did. Much of Elkins's coloring is dark—a result of umber-and-white underpainting (the artist could have learned this method from the works of the late Romantic German painters, whose coloring was also dark and hard).[162] In *Elk Park*, however, Elkins has lightened his scene somewhat by veiling his distant snowcapped mountains in suffused-light effects, tinged with rosey hues, providing a fine contrast with the dark foreground. As in a number of Elkins's other works, the spectator is barred from entering the landscape by its stagelike arrangement.

To judge from the great number of extant sketches in his family's possession,[163] Elkins was a prolific recorder of America's western and eastern scenery. His sketchbooks abound with scenic views of Colorado, New Hampshire, Illinois, California, New Mexico, Maryland, and other locations in the United States. He set out routinely each summer to sketch mountain scenery, filling his portfolio and sketchbook with inspirations for his winter's work. In his Chicago studio and later in Bloomington, Illinois, and Kansas City, Missouri,[164] he would spread his fresh material before him—both simple linear notations and more elaborate works in pen or pencil, highlighted with chinese white and executed on tinted papers of various sizes. Then, keeping pace with the demand for Rocky Mountain pictures in the 1860s and 1870s, Elkins transformed these spontaneous recordings into fanciful, theatrical mountainscapes, both small and large.[165]

Although based in reality, Elkins's Rocky Mountain paintings seem to be fanciful interpretations drawn largely from the artist's imagination. That many of them are inscribed with Elkins's own lyrical titles not only reinforces this assumption but makes it difficult to determine the geographic locations of the works. Like his mentor, Bierstadt, Elkins employed a basic formula for composing his landscapes: he laid them out symmetrically on receding planes, using graduated-light effects to create aerial perspective. Pictorial frameworks made up of trees and boulders were often used to direct the eye back into space. To judge from his extant landscapes, Elkins appears to have relied on two types of composition. One features a parklike amphitheater with a body of water in the middle ground, surrounded by jagged, snow-crowned peaks, shrouded in clouds and mist, turned pink and gold by the setting sun. In the other a large body of water (cascade or lake) dominates the foreground, hemmed in by lofty, snow-covered mountains. Invariably the central snow-capped peaks and the reflective waters are highlighted by a shaft of eerie white light, making the picture all the more fanciful. Elkins undoubtedly used chiaroscuro to heighten his works' romantic qualities and dramatize the wild aspect of the primitive scenery. Small incidental figures are occasionally included in these stagelike settings, but purely for picturesque effect, never to act out a story. Elkins's techniques can hardly be termed sophisticated; they lack the subtle tonal modulations and light effects of Bierstadt's grand productions. Instead of painterly effects, Elkins's work, like that of most other scene painters, has a strong linear definition. Although a student as well as a collector of the European masters, Elkins was limited in his ability to carry out the technical lessons he might have learned from those works.[166]

Since most of Elkins's landscapes are undated, it is difficult to trace his stylistic evolution. Those paintings that can be placed in an approximate time frame by matching them with corresponding news releases however, show that Elkins established his manner of

PLATE 51

Henry A. Elkins, *Elk Park, Colorado*, 1878, Oil, 36″ × 60″.
Courtesy Anschutz Collection, Denver.

picture making early in his career, making few stylistic changes in his later works. Elkins's pictures appear to vary only in technical execution: some seem to exhibit a hasty production, perhaps owing to financial exigencies (his extravagant ways were occasionally alluded to in the Chicago papers; in 1877 he was forced to sell his entire collection of European and American paintings).[167]

It has been said that Elkins considered himself a pupil of Bierstadt and that his first monumental painting, *Mount Shasta*, was inspired by his mentor's showpiece *Yosemite;* but, although he made western scenery his specialty, Elkins was certainly no competitor of Bierstadt's.

In the next several decades a great number of artists continued to follow in Bierstadt's footsteps. Although none of them achieved great status as artists, several received regional notoriety and should be mentioned here. Two members of the California contingent, Ransom Gillette Holdredge and Frederick Schafer, painted pictures reminiscent of Bierstadt's Rocky Mountain showpieces. With sketch pads in hand both men crisscrossed the Rocky Mountain region on their way to and from Europe. The large, dramatic paintings that resulted from their trips seem to have all the characteristic heightened effects necessary to appeal to their public's romantic sensibilities.

Holdredge, the older of the two, was born in New York in 1836.[168] He arrived in San Francisco around 1864, where he was listed as a "draughtsman." From 1867 he was an active member of the California contingent of artists, often engaging in sketching tours in the northern part of the state and the Northwest and exhibiting in various local shows. In fact, Holdredge is listed as one of the founders in 1868 of the Art Union, an early artists' society in San Francisco.[169]

According to the *San Francisco News Letter* of November, 1873, Holdredge and Arthur Lemon, a former resident of California, spent the summer of that year sketching along the overland route (Union Pacific Railroad line) on their return home from the East Coast. The same paper reported that Holdredge had made a number of sketches of Utah canyons. His large mountainscapes with small Indian encampments resulted from a subsequent trip through the Rocky Mountain region on his way home from Europe in the sum-

mer of 1879. Soon after this trip he produced several important landscapes of Utah, Wyoming, Colorado, and Montana that exhibited a European-influenced shift in style from his tight delineations of the 1860s and 1870s to a more vigorous handling. Although these pictures reflect the inspiration of the French Barbizon painters and the Munich School of artists, their dramatic impact and theatrical staging seem to indicate the influence of Bierstadt's western showpiece, which the artist could have seen in San Francisco. Several of Holdredge's large mountain landscapes were listed in a sale of 1882.[170] Although they display the characteristic gray-green tonalities reminiscent of the Barbizon painters, these pictures are large and formidable, lacking the intimate and poetic passages of the French works. Like Bierstadt's paintings, they are loaded with atmospheric effects. The body of water in the middle distance of each suggests that Holdredge may have adopted Bierstadt's established formula for his picture making. In one painting, *A Sioux Camp in the Rocky Mountains* (color plate 19), Holdredge goes so far as to include an Indian amulet prominently in the foreground, aping his predecessor's famous showpiece *The Rocky Mountains*. Even though the San Francisco artist's large mountainscapes had their basis in reality, they are obviously imaginative interpretations of the western wilderness.

While Holdredge was a product of his American environment, his counterpart, Frederick Ferdinand Schafer, was obviously influenced by his German background. Schafer was born in Braunschweig, Germany, on August 16, 1839. He apparently left his native land for the United States sometime in late 1876;[171] the first mention of his name occurs in a San Francisco newspaper in October of that year in a sales announcement of his German work at a local emporium.[172] Whether Schafer was settled in San Francisco at the time of the sale is unknown; there is evidence, however, that he returned to the East Coast (and perhaps Europe) in 1879 to bring his wife and son to California.[173]

It appears that Schafer had established a professional reputation in San Francisco by the mid-1880s. His works, recorded in a number of exhibitions, included views of California, the Northwest, and the Rocky Mountain region. Two of the last, *Morning in the Rocky Mountains* and *Valley of the Rocky Mountains* (currently unlocated), were

PLATE 52

Frederick Schafer, *After a Storm in the Rocky Mountains*, ca. 1880, Oil, 20″ × 34″.
Courtesy William Dick Collection, San Francisco, Calif.

listed in an auction sale in September, 1884. The titles are somewhat reminiscent of those used by Bierstadt. Additional scenes of the Rocky Mountains by Schafer were recorded in a sale of "214 Paintings and Sketches" held at Irving Hall, in San Francisco, on November 17, 1885. In the collection (which the sales catalog describes as "the best works of six years") were "views of Colorado along the Overland R. R., including Salt Lake City, San Francisco, Maine and Russian River." It is likely that these Rocky Mountain pictures were developed from field sketches taken on the overland trip of 1879. In fact, some of the sketches themselves could have been included in the sale. Unfortunately the present whereabouts of the catalog with the listed works is unknown.[174]

Like Holdredge, Schafer adopted several of Bierstadt's characteristic trademarks. Remembering Bierstadt's paintings of similar subjects, Schafer frequently composed imaginary mountainscapes. *After a Storm in the Rocky Mountains* (plate 52) is typical of this kind of composition, bearing no resemblance to an actual site. As he often did, Schafer identifies this view in an inscription penciled on the back of the canvas. Like the pictures of many regional artists, Schafer's works are often uneven in appearance—varying in technique from meticulous brushwork to a more vigorous handling that sometimes borders on a slapdash treatment.

It appears that for his models Schafer relied more on chromolithographs and engraved illustrations in books and magazines than on actual paintings. His painting *Mount of the Holy Cross*,[175] a composite view of Jackson's photograph and Moran's picture of the famous landmark, seems to reinforce this idea. This method of composing became even more popular with artists outside the mainstream late in the nineteenth century. It is possible that Bierstadt's chromolithographs could have been the impetus that encouraged another of Bierstadt's disciples, Chicago scene painter William R. Eaton, to travel to Estes Park. His large, dramatic showpiece *Long's Peak*, executed in 1884,[176] seems to take its cue from Bierstadt's theatrical renditions, though it lacks the true mastery of its model and is a typical scene painting.

In some ways Bierstadt's art could be considered symptomatic of an international mode that had its inception in the Düsseldorf School and was carried forward to America. Bierstadt's work, however, had its own individual personality and unique quality, mirrored, however falteringly, by the art of the provincials who attempted to emulate his success. In the light of history Bierstadt takes his place as a celebrated American master who left an indelible mark on the nineteenth century and beyond.

6

THE GREAT SURVEYS

One clear and pleasant day in the late summer of 1866, King and Gardner found themselves in the region east of Yosemite, perched on the summit of one of the high peaks of the Sierras. Eastward as far as their eyes could see were the deserts and ranges of Nevada. Their conversation wandered: they talked of problems of geology and about their future careers. Their previous activities in Arizona and California had made it clear that a true comprehension of the geology of the West could be mastered only through studying "the structure, topographical and geological, of the whole mountain system of western America from the Plains to the Pacific." And as the cool west wind tore at their clothing and the sun beat down its ultra-violet rays upon them in that rarefied atmosphere, the two young scientists developed an exhilarating idea: why not make a scientific continental cross section of the fortieth parallel?—Richard A. Bartlett[1]

FOLLOWING the Civil War a renewed and intensified exploration of the vast western territories began. Between 1867 and 1879 four far-reaching geological and geographical surveys were conducted under the leadership of remarkable men: Clarence King, George Montague Wheeler, Ferdinand Vandeveer Hayden, and John Wesley Powell.[2] The four expeditions are frequently referred to as the "Great Surveys." King, the first to assume leadership of one of these reconnaissance parties, was only twenty-five when he went to Washington, D.C., to secure government patronage for the project. Despite his age he had much in his favor: he was a trained scientist with the enthusiasm of youth and compelling ability as a salesman. He argued that the uninformed frequently described the region newly traversed by the continental railroad as barren—filled only with "sagebrush and greasewood, rattlers, kangaroo rats, and jackrabbits." To the eyes of a trained geologist, he declared, a survey might reveal valuable natural resources—coal, iron, and precious metals. His vision, captured on a mountain peak, was to conduct a survey across the West from the crest of the Sierra Nevada to the western slope of the Rockies. It was a daring proposal. King's vigorous presentation and his obvious dedication to the project won the approval of Congress for the survey, and he was appointed head geologist.

So all encompassing was the plan for this survey of 1867 that King actually wrote his own orders, decreeing that it was to extend from the 120th meridian eastward to the 105th meridian, running along the 40th parallel. King actually realized this ambitious project and eventually produced an atlas and seven volumes of detailed geological descriptions, topographical maps, and extensive illustrations.[3]

In preparing for the reconnaissance of 1867, King selected a distinguished group of advanced scientists, many of them young; photographer Timothy O'Sullivan was also included. Many in this nucleus of experts were to continue to serve under King during the years of the Fortieth Parallel Survey.

On July 15, King joined his party at Glendale near the site of present-day Reno, Nevada; there they established their first base camp. His parties were to work on a block of land "between California's Sierras and the Shoshone Mountains to the east, an area of some 15,000 square miles."[4] King's objective, the Shoshone Range almost halfway across Nevada, was never reached; yet he felt they had made enough progress. Since there was no artist among the party members, the only visual record of this expedition is O'Sullivan's photographs.

After wintering in the East, the King company regathered in May, joined by guest-artist John Henry Hill. That year's survey focused on central and eastern Nevada and western Utah, whose awesome sights were vividly described by King and visually captured by Hill and photographer O'Sullivan.[5] Hill was the logical choice for graphic recorder on King's second expedition. Both men had been founders of the Society for the Advancement of Truth in Art—America's Pre-Raphaelite brotherhood—whose Ruskinian doctrine was disseminated through their journal, the *New Path*. The group believed that

> all nature being the perfected work of the Creator should be treated with the reverence due to its Author, and by nature they do not mean only the great mountains and wonderful land effects, but also every dear weed that daily gives forth its life unheeded, to the skies; every blade of grass that waves and shivers in the wind; every beautiful pebble that rolls and rattles on the sea sand.[6]

Hill's pictorial representation of *Shoshone Falls* (color plate 20) carried out the group's dictum: to present a precise and truthful appearance of nature without disguising or altering any of its parts. This version of *Shoshone Falls* was executed in 1871, several years after Hill viewed the falls with King, who described in his journal how the river plunged "into a labyrinth of rocks, tumbling over a precipice two hundred feet high, . . . a strange, savage scene." The work is almost a replica of the picture he had captured on the spot on September 30, 1868. Hill had also made a rough watercolor study of the same view that day. All three relate closely to O'Sullivan's photographic view; however, Hill, like his fellow artist Gifford, chose to eliminate the small figure embellishments in an effort to reinforce the barrenness and sublimity of this desolate region.[7]

Like several other Pre-Raphaelite followers, Hill worked as an aquatintist and etcher as well as a watercolorist. His involvement with graphic techniques is apparent in his use of fine parallel lines of color to create textures and shading. Here the earlier semitransparent washes of color seen in Seymour's work have been replaced by overall minute touches of opaque color to build up forms, a technique approximating the effect of oil.[8] A luminous quality envelops the entire composition with particular focus on the foaming white of the falls. The rugged, barren brown canyon country has been truthfully portrayed with a Ruskinian reverence that must surely have met with King's approval; yet, surprisingly enough, he did not reproduce any of Hill's work in his publication. King continued to invite guest artists to accompany him on his expeditions; the following year he was joined by the engraver and landscape painter Gilbert Munger.[9]

The second expedition was a triumph of accomplishment: King and his men completed the topography and geology of a huge tract of land stretching from the Great Basin to the Salt Lake, encompassing a territory one hundred miles wide and five hundred miles long. The resulting collection of specimens, maps, and geological reports filled fifty large boxes, which were shipped to Washington— a source of amazement for eastern scientists and an encouragement to members of Congress, who appropriated funds for a third expedition. King's master plan for the summer of 1869 was to follow an eastern trail to the Wasatch Mountains, on to the Uinta Mountain range and Green River country, and finally to the Green River divide.

In mid-July the field parties reconvened. Munger marched with King's own division through Echo Canyon along the Union Pacific and then to the Bear River valley. Beneath the towering, rocky Uinta Mountains he made sketches of the surrounding scenery and various geological formations. The wild alpine scenery of the Bear River valley, fascinating to King, was recorded by both O'Sullivan and Munger. Two of Munger's Bear River valley views were later reproduced in King's sumptuous scientific report.[10] One of them, *Upper Valley of Bear River—Uinta Range—Utah*, depicts the lower valley of the middle fork of Bear River, a broad glacier canyon surrounded by high mountains with a river winding through its center. The controlled, linear quality of Munger's picture betrays his engraver's technique. The subtle gradations of color, atmosphere,

PLATE 53

Gilbert Munger, *Lake Lal and Mt. Agassiz—Uinta Range—Utah*, 1871, Oil, 26″ × 44″.
Courtesy Merrill Gross, Wyoming, Ohio.

and light so apparent in Bierstadt's mountain paintings are missing from Munger's tightly constructed pictures. Like many other self-tutored artists, he has fallen back on a simple academic formula for composing his picture.

The other scene depicts Lake Lal, lying at the foot of Mount Agassiz, which the artist also worked up into a large oil painting (plate 53) executed from a slightly different vantage point and at a different hour of the day.[11] It is likely that Munger also relied on O'Sullivan's photographs taken in the same area in translating his small field sketches into finished works.[12]

To judge by the number of scenic views reproduced in King's "Systematic Geology," Munger must have been a prodigious recorder. Among his more interesting views are *Wahsatch Range—from Salt Lake City—Utah* (color plate 21),[13] *Badlands of Wyoming, Cañon of Lodore* (in Dinosaur National Monument, Colorado), and *Eocene Bluffs—Green River—Wyoming.* King described the last view:

> . . . in the immediate vicinity of the [Union Pacific] Railroad rise isolated, tower-like rocks, which possess all the abruptness and hardness of outline of artificial fortifications. The sculpture of the shales along the river banks is also extremely interesting displaying vertical cuts 300 or 400 feet high, capped by rounded hill-tops, and these in turn by towers.[14]

The same sight was to capture the imagination of later traveling artists like Thomas Moran, and Samuel Colman.[15] King was apparently pleased with Munger's sketches, for he invited the artist to join him again on his expedition of 1870.

Munger spent three years traveling and sketching in the Rocky Mountains, California, and Canada. Some twenty years later he commented on how his experiences at home and abroad had influenced his style:

> There is a crystallization of style in painting, as in literature. It is, of course, a slow process, and, in my own case, is the fruit of long seasons of painting in the foothills of my own Rocky Mountains, in the shadow of El Capitan in the Yosemite; . . . of solitary toil in the lagoons of Venice, and finally, of the long and thoughtful season of severe effort in Fountainebleau Forest in the track of the masters.[16]

Another dynamic figure in the history of the "Great Surveys"

is Ferdinand Vandeveer Hayden.[17] A self-made man, Hayden carved a brilliant, ambitious career to match that of Clarence King; however, the two men had quite different personalities and techniques. In contrast to the systematic precision of King, Hayden's approach to his explorations and field reports was impetuous, almost offhand. Furthermore, he was a born entrepreneur and promoter, as interested in the pragmatic implications of his explorations as in the more scientific minutiae.

Although Hayden, working out his tuition, earned a degree from Oberlin College and went on to achieve a medical degree from Albany College in 1853, he had always dreamed of the West—fascinated by the work of geologist John Strong Newberry and the eminent James Hall, author of the monumental work *Paleontology of New York.* It was, in fact, Hall who was instrumental in securing for Hayden his first job as a scientific investigator.

In 1867, Hayden was awarded his first government-survey job. The immensity of his pyramiding reconnaissance journeys is well covered in his summary report of 1878 to the government office of the United States Geological and Geographical Survey of the Territories, covering the years 1867 to 1877. His ballooning success and the expansion of his retinue are reflected in numerical statistics: from a small group of eight or ten men, two wagons, and pack mules, Hayden's field groups grew until they often numbered in the sixties, with many wagonloads of equipment. The territory they covered in a single season topped the 20,000-square-mile figure several times. Appropriations beginning in 1867 and 1868 at only $5,000 were augmented each year until in the years 1873–75 and 1877 the annual grants were $75,000.

Although Hayden frequently resorted to expedient techniques, he left an extensive document of his journeys in his annual reports, which might be considered a popular extension of King's seven volumes. Hayden's *Atlas,* published in 1877,[18] is as important a contribution to scientific knowledge as the King publication; it includes various kinds of maps as well as panoramic views of Colorado and adjacent territories.

Perhaps Hayden's ultimate achievement was his role in persuading the United States Congress to establish the Yellowstone area as a national park—an action made official in a bill passed unanimously and signed on March 1, 1872, by President Ulysses S. Grant. As early as 1869 a proposal to convert the Yellowstone area into a national park had been made by David E. Folsom, a local rancher, but in the summer of 1871, Hayden became the first to receive congressional funds to conduct an official survey into the Yellowstone area. Upon his return from this reconnaissance Hayden appeared at many committee meetings with Jackson's photographs and Moran's watercolors as "visible truth of Yellowstone's wonders"; his eloquent presentation, coupled with this visual evidence, undoubtedly helped persuade Congress to give unanimous assent to the park bill.

In 1869, Hayden undertook his first extensive survey of Colorado and New Mexico. Henry W. Elliott joined his party as staff artist, a paid and official member of the field force. This was a departure from King's policy of merely receiving guest artists who wished to accompany his reconnaissance trips. Because of time and budget limitations, as Hayden stated in his annual report,

> I arranged my plans so as to cover as much ground as possible and secure the greatest amount of geological information. . . . It seemed best, therefore, to make my examinations southward along the eastern base of the Rocky Mountains for the purpose of studying the upheaved ridges, or "hog backs," as they are called in this country. These ridges afford peculiar facilities for working out the geological structure of the country.[19]

The party proceeded, said Hayden, from "Cheyenne, Wyoming, along the eastern foot of the Rocky Mountains to Santa Fe, New Mexico, returning through the parks of Colorado." The explorer concluded his report with a note of special praise for his artist: "Mr. Elliott . . . has labored with untiring zeal, and has made more than four hundred outlines of sketches, and about seventy finished ones for the final reports. Each one of these sketches illustrates some thought or principle in geology, and, if properly engraved, will be invaluable." Elliott's profiles, sections, and individual field sketches were executed to show "clearly the lines of travel across the country along which the sections were taken." Apparently because of budget limitations Hayden was unable to illustrate his first annual report; Elliott's accumulated efforts thus remained unpublished until 1872, when they were printed separately in a volume lithographed by Julius Bien under Hayden's direction.[20]

Hayden's appointee was well qualified to carry out his assignment, having served as private secretary to Joseph Henry, of the Smithsonian Institution.[21] To judge by his somewhat naïve field drawings, it is reasonable to assume that Elliott was self-trained, perhaps accumulating knowledge of the principles of mapmaking and scientific rendering by studying the many illustrated reports that had been amassed at the Smithsonian since Long's expedition of 1820. It is also evident that he understood enough scientific jargon to be able to produce detailed visual aids for Hayden's descriptive text.

Elliott's field sketches and finished drawings for the expedition document of 1869 reflect the geologist's observations. Contours and geological formations are carefully illustrated and identified; basic resources essential for development and settlement, like mineral veins, rivers, coal and lignite beds, and iron deposits, are recorded; and picturesque scenic areas chosen to attract the tourist and sportsman are singled out. Hayden was more concerned at this point with inventorying the new country than with providing scenic views to lure the settler westward. Only in subsequent years did he fully realize the advantage of including a photographer and a professional landscapist in his group.

The reconnaissance of 1869 of Colorado Territory drew a mention in the press; on June 7 it was announced that Hayden and his party were "en route west, to make a geological survey of Colorado and New Mexico."[22] They were to commence their field labors on June 29 from Cheyenne, heading south toward Denver on the first leg of their journey. Elliott's profile sections illustrate successive stages of their route as they traveled along the base of the foothills past the distinctive "upheaved ridges," or hogbacks, which he rendered in outline and filled in with fine parallel lines and crosshatching to indicate sedimentary layers and folds. In most of these drawings the artist has assigned key letters to identify geological and topographical features. Like his rough field sketches of isolated landforms, the profiles were first worked up in pencil on brown-tinted onionskin paper and then transferred to heavy white construction paper and elaborated in pen and ink—no doubt to aid the engraver in reproducing them. A series of these strip sections, each one representing a leg of the reconnaissance of 1869 and based on a scale of eight miles to the inch, were reproduced in the illustrated volume of 1872 along with profiles showing the routes of the surveys of 1870 and 1871. Elliott deviated from this practice only when the party made its return trip through the Colorado parks. At that time the artist made a panoramic view of South Park from a point one mile south of the Salt Works (Hayden remarked that they could give only "a glance at the salt springs and gold mines" in this park). It is evident from the many sections and individual topographical features illustrated in the same publication that for the geologist Colorado was "almost encyclopedic in its character, containing within its borders nearly every variety of geological formation."

Elliott's field sketchbooks of 1869 are filled with scenes from the summer's journey across "a belt about five hundred and fifty miles in length from north to south, and almost two hundred in width from east to west." One of his pen-and-ink sketches, also reproduced in the volume of drawings, shows the distinctive hogbacks at the base of the Rocky Mountain foothills near Cache la Poudre.[23] The sketch was made on July 2 while Hayden "visited the supposed gold and copper mines at or near the Cache à la Poudre River." Many of the sketches in the same notebook include quaint figures of men and animals, in most instances totally out of scale with the rest of the picture. In fact, most of Elliott's sketches and drawings show little knowledge of correct perspective. Apart from his detailed scientific notations of physical geology, Elliott's renderings are generally playful and even slightly comical. A drawing depicting some buttes on the plains north of Trinidad includes a mounted Indian chasing a small rider who is having a difficult time keeping ahead of his charging assailant.[24] Another scene near present-day Cañon City, where the Arkansas issues from the mountains, shows the familiar hogbacks and features two small riders who look like cowboys getting ready for the roundup. The drawing incongruously accompanies a section in the text that describes the area in stilted scientific prose. In the same sketchbook the artist also recorded Golden City with its small, cubical houses nestled at the foot of Table Mountain (plate 54).

Like all of Hayden's other survey reports, these were sent off with incredible dispatch to the secretary of the interior, and the annual report of the 1869 survey was so well received that all eight thousand copies were distributed in three weeks.[25] Congress responded with another increase in funding—$25,000 for the expedition of 1870.[26] Consequently, Hayden was once again able to augment the roster of his topflight specialists, scoring a coup with the hiring of the photographer William H. Jackson. Elliott continued as the official artist. The group included an agriculturalist, a secretary, a mineralogist, a zoologist, a naturalist, a general assistant, a wagon master, four teamsters, three cooks, and a laborer. S. R. Gifford, a landscape artist from New York, accompanied the party as a guest from the point of departure in Cheyenne to Fort Bridger.[27]

The scope of this third survey was limited to Wyoming and "portions of contiguous territories." Hayden's report of the party's progression is again a detailed one. He notes that when the party arrived at Fort Bridger they set up camp for about twenty days, "exploring, with considerable care, the northern slope of the Uinta Mountains [plate 55]. This range is one of wonderful beauty, a unique creation, without a parallel in the West."

Winding their way through Wyoming Territory, Hayden and his men returned to Cheyenne about November 1. Most of the group headed homeward, but Hayden, Elliott, and a few others stayed on to study further the "interesting geological features along the line of the Union Pacific Railroad from Cheyenne to Salt Lake Valley." Hayden continues his report with special reference to the artist's contribution:

> Mr. Elliott constructed an excellent pictorial section of the entire road, bringing out all the surface features with remarkable clearness and beauty. In addition to hundreds of local sketches and sections, Mr. Elliott has delineated three continuous pictorial sections across the territory of Wyoming which, if properly engraved, will form a new era in the exhibition of structural geology. . . . the artist, Elliott, worked with untiring zeal, and his sketches and sections have never been surpassed for beauty or clearness.

PLATE 54

Henry Wood Elliott, *"Table Rock" Golden City, July 28, 1869*, Pencil, 7″ × 9½″.
Courtesy United States Geological Survey Library, Reston, Va.

PLATE 55

William H. Jackson, *Henry Wood Elliott sketching a view from the foothills, bordering Bear River, of the Uintah Mountains*, 1870, Photograph, 5″ × 7″.
Courtesy Western History Research Center, University of Wyoming, Laramie, Wyo.

Once again Elliott made profile sections of their route, this time along the line of the Union Pacific Railroad as they made their way westward through Wyoming. One of the profile series shows a sweeping panoramic view of 128 miles of varied topography near Green River.[28]

Elliott frequently joined Jackson and Gifford on side excursions, departing from the high road to travel up a mountainside or down a stream bed "to gather rock specimens, to survey and map, and to paint and photograph."[29] It is interesting to compare Elliott's rather stiff linear drawings with Gifford's painterly versions and Jackson's straightforward photographic views of the same landforms.[30]

One of Elliott's more elaborated pen-and-ink drawings depicts an extensive vista, Sweetwater Valley, from near their camp at Big Bend, looking east at Devil's Gate (plate 56). The physical geology of this area is identified as usual by his key letters.

The expedition of 1871 focused on Montana and portions of adjacent territories and included the wilderness area of Yellowstone. The government appropriation for this survey was larger than previous ones, enabling Hayden to assemble an "unusually large" party.[31] Elliott signed on again as official artist, assisted this season by Campbell Carrington, who was also in charge of zoological collections. Photographer Jackson was a member of the party for the second time and continued to serve with Hayden until the completion of the surveys. Anton Schonborn was selected as chief topographer.

Thomas Moran, a distinguished artist from Philadelphia, accompanied the group as a guest, "to secure studies of the remarkable scenery of the Yellowstone."[32] Moran had developed the illustrations for an article in *Scribner's Monthly* on the Washburn-Doane venture in the preceding year[33] from sketches taken en route by expeditionary members Charles Moore and Walter Trumbull.[34] Consequently, he was eager to see this fascinating territory with his own eyes.

The men left Ogden early in June, marking each stage of the journey with careful scientific observations until they reached Bottler's Ranch, between the drainage of the Missouri and the Yellowstone, where Hayden established a permanent camp. From the ranch the group "proceeded up the valley of the Yellowstone, surveyed the remarkable hot springs on Gardiner's River, the Grand Cañon, Tower Falls, Upper and Lower Falls of the Yellowstone, thence into the basin proper, prepared charts of all the Hot Spring groups, which were very numerous, and continued up the river to the Lake."

At the culmination of the season's work in October, a small group once again stayed on with Hayden for another few weeks to review "points of geological interest along the railroad." Hayden concludes his report with special commendations for both Elliott and Jackson, noting that the photographer had obtained "nearly 400 negatives of the remarkable scenery of the routes, as well as the cañon, falls, lakes, geysers, and hot springs of the Yellowstone Basin, and they have proved, since our return, of very great value in the preparation of the maps and report." They were also an invaluable aid to Moran in working up his finished watercolors and large oils, as will be seen in the following chapter.

Hayden's fifth annual report is profusely illustrated with Moran's watercolors, Jackson's photographs, and Elliott's sketches of geological landforms with their occasional small, amusing figures. One of the last, a rock study described as being like "a picturesque ruin," includes a seated figure sketching before the weathered object. Many of Elliott's sketches and pictorial sections, like those of 1869, were reproduced to document the physical geology of the country the men viewed as they marched through Idaho and Montana to Yellowstone (plate 57). Moran's watercolors, on the other hand, illustrated the most spectacular scenic views of the Yellowstone area.

Yellowstone, of course, provided endless scenic wonders for both artists and the photographer. To judge by the illustrations included in the report for this area, Elliott seems to have directed his attention mainly to the bubbling, steaming, multicolored caldrons scattered over Yellowstone's wilderness. All the men were "filled with enthusiasm" when they arrived at Yellowstone Lake, as Hayden noted: "The lake lay before us, a vast sheet of quiet water, of a most delicate ultramarine hue, one of the most beautiful scenes I have ever beheld. . . . Such a vision is worth a lifetime, and only one of such marvelous beauty will ever greet human eyes." Hayden compared the "great object" to a human hand: ". . . the northern portion would constitute the palm, while the southern prolongations

a granite domes on Sweet Water River
b Sandstones upturned by
d lava & reddish basalt
c Sweetwater Mts —
e great plateau of Tertiary beds & marls

Sweetwater Valley from
Camp at Big Bend, Looking

PLATE 56
Henry Wood Elliott, *Sweetwater Valley from near Camp at Big Bend,* 1870, Pencil, 8″ × 22″.
Courtesy National Archives, Washington, D.C.

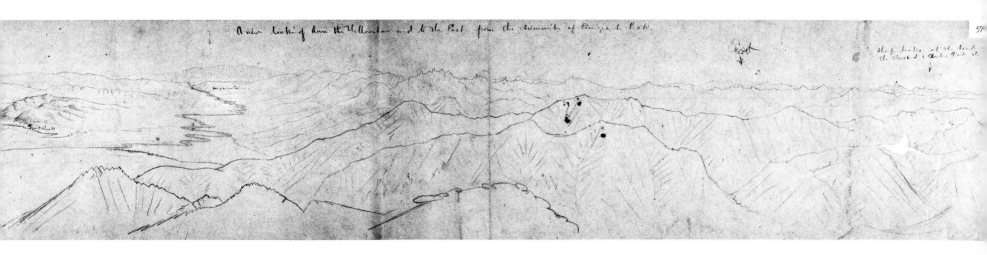

PLATE 57
Henry Wood Elliott, *A view looking down the Yellowstone and to the East from the summit of Emigrant Peak,* 1871, Pencil drawing in three parts, 8″ × 36″.
Courtesy National Archives, Washington, D.C.

or arms might represent the fingers." Elliott and Stevenson were directed to survey and explore its shorelines from a boat, which they christened Anna after the daughter of Senator Henry L. Dawes, who had been responsible for securing the congressional appropriation enabling them to explore the marvelous region.

Moran and Elliott apparently shared Hayden's enthusiasm for the large freshwater basin, for both artists made watercolors on the spot (color plate 22).[35] Moran's version was later reproduced in the report of 1871. It seems evident that Elliott hoped that his quaint picture, which is similar in technique to Seymour's simple topographical views, might be considered for reproduction. The small picture was later presented to his friend and coworker James Stevenson.

For three successive surveys Elliott accompanied Hayden, sketching the geological formations and producing continuous profile sections of their route. After this trip to Yellowstone the artist resigned to pursue a different career, eventually becoming a leading authority on the seal-fur industry.

In 1872 when the Forty-second Congress met to consider the appropriations necessary for further explorations of the western territories, they were so deeply impressed by Hayden's record of achievement that they granted the unprecedented sum of $75,000 for his sixth government-sponsored survey. This figure was further augmented by a sum of $10,000 allocated for engraving,[36] undoubtedly granted because of Hayden's glowing accounts of the illustrative material provided by his official artist and photographer. This ample funding allowed Hayden to organize two major divisions, both including specialists in geology, topography, astronomy, and meteorology, plus assistants and helpers.

One of the divisions, under the direction of James Stevenson, departed for the unknown region of the upper Snake Valley and the Teton Basin. The highest peak, according to the famous mountain man Jim Bridger, was impossible to ascend, and it became a challenge to the party to climb to the top. Eleven of the group made the attempt; only Stevenson and Langford succeeded. Jackson, a member of the party, returned with photographic evidence of the achievement.

The other division, headed by the geologist, included the usual coterie of specialists and the newly appointed official artist, William Henry Holmes, who was to continue as a staff member throughout the remaining Hayden surveys. Their goal was a second trip into the Yellowstone area to reaffirm and expand the discoveries of the previous season.

As a prelude to his seven-year association with Hayden, Holmes had taught several years at various levels of instruction.[37] He also attended several art academies, finally entering the Washington, D.C., studio of Theodore Kauffman, where Mary Henry, daughter of the secretary of the Smithsonian Institution, was also studying. She introduced Holmes to her father, and the artist at once found an outlet for his artistic bent in the recording of scientific specimens. It was through this association that Holmes secured his appointment with Hayden's expedition.

After his service with Hayden, Holmes went on to enviable positions as artist, topographer, geologist, anthropologist, and finally director of the National Collection of Fine Arts. He was also recognized as one of the first to develop an acceptable formula for museum classification. His notes in twenty bound volumes—a summation of a life's endeavors—are now in the National Museum of American Art Library, Smithsonian Institution.[38]

In his "Random Records" for 1872, Holmes covers the highlights of his first expedition, beginning with his appointment in May as official artist at a salary of $1,800. This account is full of anecdotal situations and glowing remarks about the scenery, but a considerable portion of his narrative is devoted to Yellowstone and its scenic wonders. It was in this awe-inspiring area, at a 10,000-foot elevation, that Holmes made his first huge panoramic view. Over the years he sketched countless such panoramic scenes, and was eventually recognized as the supreme expert in his field.

In 1873, Hayden initiated a systematic survey of Colorado; the point of departure was Denver, where the organization was set up (plate 58). He stated in the initial paragraphs of his annual report:

> For the past two years the survey has operated about the sources of the Missouri and Yellowstone Rivers; but the expenses of transportation, subsistence, and labor are so great that it seems desirable

Plate 58

William H. Jackson, *Camp on Clear Creek near Denver*, 1873, Photograph, 5″ × 7″.
Courtesy Western History Research Center, University of Wyoming, Laramie.

to delay the further prosecution of the work in the Northwest until railroad-communication shall be established. The Indians, also, are in a state of hostility over the greater portion of the country which remains to be explored. It seems desirable, therefore, to transfer the field of labor for the coming season, to the eastern portion of the Rocky Mountain range, in Colorado and New Mexico . . . .

. . . the prospect of its rapid development within the next five years, by some of the most important railroads in the West, renders it very desirable that its resources be made known to the world at as early a date as possible.[39]

In this annual report Hayden also summarized the vast amount of publication his efforts had already generated—including the report on each seasonal survey, many maps, and the specialized quarto publications by some of the field experts. He also defended his conviction that speedy publication was important "to bring our results before the public at as early a date as possible. Should mistakes occur, (and they cannot be reasonably avoided,) we hope to correct them in future publications."

The high point of the summer expedition was the "discovery" of the Mount of the Holy Cross (Santa Cruz). Its existence had been known for some time, but its exact position had never been determined, and no one had recorded the mysterious marking of the peak in sketch, painting, or photograph. In fact, very few people had seen it, since its view from the east was blocked by Notch Mountain. The complete revelation of the peak was the determined goal of the entire survey group, but for photographer Jackson and artist-geologist Holmes, who would be able to furnish concrete visual evidence of the natural wonder, it was a challenging dream. The dream came true at the summit of Gray's Peak, where the coveted Santa Cruz was first observed from a distance of nearly forty miles across the valleys of the Blue and Eagle rivers. It was at this point that Holmes recorded in pencil their first "glimpse" of the fabled peak.[40]

In August the exploring party set out north from Twin Lakes, across Tennessee Pass to Eagle River. After several days of rugged climbing, they finally reached their destination.[41] In an article published on May 1, 1875, in the *Illustrated Christian Weekly,* Holmes reminisces about the remarkable journey of 1873 and the eager an-

ticipation of the party as they made their plans to pinpoint the mysterious Holy Cross:

. . . [we] steadily advanced up the valleys, into dense timber, up long, steep slopes, through swamps and torrents and treacherous snowbanks; and long before the grass and flowers of those upper regions had felt the touch of spring, we were there. And many days before winter had finally surrendered the lofty summits, from a peak more than 14,000 feet above the sea we looked around upon one of the grandest panoramas that the world affords. To the east the great plain gave a horizon entirely unbroken, to the west innumerable mountains notched the sky like saw teeth. . . .

. . . But one among all these summits caught the eye and fixed the attention. Far away to the westward, we discovered a peak, a very giant among its fellows, a king amidst a forest of mountains, that bore aloft on its dark face a great white cross, so perfect, so grand in proportions that at a distance of sixty [?] miles, we felt outselves [*sic*] in its very presence.

Upon reaching their destination, the group divided into two parties. The larger of the two, which included Holmes, ascended the Mount of the Holy Cross with the object of establishing a triangulation station on its summit. The other party, with Jackson and his helpers, who carried the burdensome photographic equipment, set off to climb Notch Mountain in the hope of obtaining photographs of the snowy peak from across the ravine. Holmes described the photographer's first glimpse of the cross:

Suddenly . . . [he] glances upward, and beholds a vision exceedingly dramatic and beautiful. He is amazed, he is transfixed. There, set in the dark rock, held high among the floating clouds, he beholds the long-sought cross, perfect, spotless white, grand in dimensions, at once the sublimest thing in nature and the emblem of heaven.

Unfortunately, the weather closed in on him, and Jackson had to wait until the following morning to capture his famous view, which not only thrilled the public but also inspired Moran, Holmes, and other artists to create pictures of the peak.

Holmes's watercolor of 1873 (plate 59), reproduced in the story of Jackson's *Quest of the Snowy Cross,* has recently been rediscovered.[42] It is derived from Jackson's photograph (plate 60), though the artist has added the intervening ravine and the rocky terrain in the fore-

PLATE 59

William H. Holmes, *Mountain of the Holy Cross*, 1873,
Watercolor, 18½″ × 12″. Courtesy Dr. Carl F. Rainone,
Arlington, Texas.

PLATE 60

William H. Jackson, *Mountain of the Holy Cross*, 1873, Photograph, 7″ × 5″.
Courtesy United States Geological Survey Library, Reston.

ground. The work is far less elaborate than Moran's famous oil painting, executed at a later date.[43] Holmes chose to represent the subject in realistic terms; Moran's interpretation is a composite view, including the cascading Holy Cross Creek seen from below as one approaches the peak. The entire scene is rendered in a sure, deft hand, revealing Holmes's ability to master the watercolor medium and to create the proper light and atmospheric effects. Holmes made several later watercolor views of the famous peak, but they lack the poetry and sensitivity of his initial effort.[44]

As Holmes and his group were descending from "the crest of the northern spur," they stopped near the edge to watch the storm clouds below and witnessed the most "unusual phenomenon display." Holmes made a pencil sketch of the image[45] and recorded the spectacle in his reminiscent article of 1875: "The sun at our backs broke through the clouds, and there was immediately projected on the mists that filled the dark gulf a brilliant rainbow; not the arch, as usually seen, but an entire circle, a spectral ring, which, as we still gazed, faded away, and in a minute was gone." During the survey of 1873, Holmes, who now performed the duties of geologist and artist, "took an active part not only in sketching the ranges and making drawings of all kinds of geological and other subjects, but in observing and recording the diversified geological phenomenon."[46] At the end of that season Holmes claimed to have "climbed eleven mountain peaks, most of which were between 13,000 and 14,000 feet in height."[47] In the course of this extensive survey of Colorado the artist made a number of deft field sketches. Included among them are panoramas from above Golden looking out toward Denver; geomorphic renderings of the granite dome structures found in Estes Park; and illustrations of the turret outcroppings of Silurian limestone and red feldspathic granite near the residence of General William J. Palmer in Glen Eyrie.[48] In his typical draftsmanlike manner the artist-scientist has precisely sketched the physical configuration and underlying structure of the formation. Employing an inverted type of perspective, he creates a foreground that is vague and indistinct in comparison with the landform beyond, which he intensifies with sharp, clean lines and skillful shading. As is evident in his less scientific sketches, Holmes's pictorial "sense is highly

developed and yet occasionally he satisfies not only himself but his observers by rendering with infinite skill a detached fragment of nature."[49]

Early in his association with the Hayden surveys, Holmes began executing extensive panoramic views that stretched across the horizon for miles. These views became his forte and gained him richly deserved recognition and fame. His panoramas were far more technical and scientific than those produced by early pathfinders like the Kerns and Gustavus Sohon. His vantage points were the high mountain triangulation stations established by the topographers, where he could command immense vistas over countless miles of rugged, wild terrain. His pencil recorded with meticulous, sharp line an enormous variety of landforms—peaks, craters, cones, knolls, dunes, plateaus, and promontories—detailing essential features like "angles, bends, spurs, saddles, and changes in the slope of the land."[50] He filled in the intervening landscape with additional features, such as rivers, creeks, trees, ranches, towns, and other points of interest. To aid the mapmaker, he noted the horizontal angular distances (azimuths) of certain faraway peaks sighted from his fixed positions on the summits. It is obvious that Holmes's artistic and geomorphic panoramic sketches and sections were an integral part of mapmaking.[51]

The survey of 1874 continued as in the previous season with the same meticulously systematic triangulation and scientific tabulation initiated by James Gardner.[52] The party separated into seven divisions and fanned out across the vast territory of Colorado and New Mexico. The group under the immediate direction of Hayden, which included Holmes and the topographer G. B. Crittenden, began its exploration from Colorado Springs, where Crittenden established forty-five topographical stations on the sedimentary rocks "within ten miles of the springs, embracing the Garden of the Gods and Monument Park, so curious on account of their geological structure." From there they crossed the South Park to the Arkansas Valley, where they studied the masses of morainal deposits, then headed northwest toward the Elk Mountains.

During the summer Holmes (serving now as artist and geologist) and the topographer worked side by side. Holmes made a number of panoramic sketches from the high mountain stations he and Crittenden had established, illustrating in bird's-eye views the geology and topography of the entire mountain system. These views were intended to be "instructive" as well as "pleasing to the eye"; they were to aid the topographer in working up his notes by expressing the peculiarities of mountain forms and the geologist by calling to mind "the surface-features, inclination of strata, proportion of valley to mountain land and of timber to the rocky summits lying above it." Several of these panoramic views were made on grid paper usually reserved for geological sections,[53] perhaps to secure proper scale and relationship among forms. Holmes's "usual zeal and skill" were once again recognized by Hayden, who claimed that "much of the accuracy and value of the [season's] work" was due to the artist-geologist's efforts.

One such view sketched that summer is a section from the *Maroon Bells* panorama with Castle Peak notated (plate 61), an elaboration not only scientifically instructive but rather amusing. Evidently by stretching his imagination, Holmes conjured a human face out of the twisting, folding sedimentary layers below Castle Peak, which he outlined sharply in pencil and then neatly circled. The view, sketched on grid paper, is included in one of his sketchbooks. His panoramic views *Elk Mountains*, *Twin Lakes*, and *The Pike's Peak Group from Bluffs East of Monument Creek* (plate 62)—also taken during the season of 1874—were reproduced in Hayden's monumental *Atlas of Colorado and Portions of Adjacent Territory*. The latter view was also produced in watercolor.[54]

In addition to his panoramic sketches Holmes made several watercolor studies of singular landforms. Among the more interesting ones are *Long's Peak* and *A Great Geological Arch*,[55] studies of the forms observed in Middle Park and hastily captured in pink-and-brown washes heightened with white, and the fantastically shaped wonders shown in *Monument Park, Colorado* (color plate 23).[56] The latter, a finished watercolor delicately rendered and sensitively perceived, focuses on an irregular sandstone formation known as the "Quakers," standing a few miles north of Colorado Springs in the Garden of the Gods. Here the monument, a solid curiosity of nature, seems to share the rhythm and movement of the branches and trees. To indicate the hugeness of these geological forms, Holmes has whimsically placed a small rabbit in the foreground.

Holmes spent the summers of 1875 and 1876 in the division of Hayden's survey that concentrated on the ruins of Mesa Verde, and his account of this exploration was submitted as the official letter of transmittal addressed to the secretary of the interior.[57] He covers the area in minute detail, noting the geological, geographical, and even sociological implications that could be determined from the ruins. Holmes also describes the various kinds of dwellings, including the remarkable cliff houses, the towers, and the circular underground chambers. He concentrates on the dwellings found along the Rio Mancos:

> The walls were in many places quite well preserved and new looking, while all about, high and low, were others in all stages of decay. In one place in particular, a picturesque outstanding promontory has been full of dwellings, literally honey-combed by this earth-burrowing race, and as one from below views the ragged, window-pierced crags, . . . he is unconsciously led to wonder if they are not the ruins of some ancient castle.

Climbing onto the rocky ledge of one of these escarpments, Holmes recorded a view of the cave dwellings, carefully describing their picturesque "mouldering" walls with the precision required of a scientific report.[58] Simple pale washes of blues, grays, and pinks make up the color orchestration, while topographical detailing is filled in with fine brush lines. Sketching from an oblique angle, Holmes provides the viewer with a glimpse of the adjacent canyon formations and distant plateau country veiled in hazy sunlight. Like most of his other artistic creations this work shows the incredible detail Holmes was capable of recording: "Holmes demanded that his viewers appreciate the immense amount of time it took to shape the plateaus and canyons. Thus, more than being merely picturesque, his drawings evoke the infinitude of time itself."[59]

Holmes also captured in an oil a view of the nearby ruins, *Cliff-Houses of the Rio Mancos*,[60] revealing his unsure hand when employing the heavier medium. Here the modeling of the massive cliffs lacks the clear understanding of their underlying structure, and the delicate palette of the former has been transformed into

PLATE 61

William H. Holmes, *"Castle" Group from the West, Maroon Bells, Colorado,* 1874, Pencil, 7″ × 12″.
Courtesy National Archives, Washington, D.C.

PLATE 62. William H. Holmes, *The Pike's Peak Group from Bluffs East of Monument Creek*, 1874,

heavy, muddy colors. The small oil only confirms that Holmes was far more competent as a watercolorist.

Up to the time of Jackson's visit in 1874,[61] these strange and interesting ruins had been known only through rumors, mostly interwoven with romance; few people took them seriously. Earlier exploratory reports threw very little light on these incredible cliff dwellings and towns north of the San Juan; however, Jackson's photographs and Holmes's geologic narrative and accompanying illustrations eventually awakened the public's interest. On the occasion of the Centennial Exhibition at Philadelphia, models of them were prepared to give a more tangible illustration of their "peculiarities"; four were completed in time for the opening.[62] The first, executed by Holmes, represented the same cliff houses he had recorded earlier in pencil, watercolor, and oil.

Having surveyed up to the Utah border, the party concluded its Colorado field work in 1876. The following year Holmes remained in Washington to help with the preparation of Hayden's voluminous publication *Geological and Geographical Atlas of Colorado and Portions of Adjacent Territory*.[63] It was issued in 1877, just one year after Colorado achieved statehood, and was immediately valuable to Colorado citizens. The maps proved useful to

> such railroad builders as R. I. Berthoud of the Colorado Central, and General William J. Palmer, of the Denver and Rio Grande, and to such capitalists as Baron Rothschild and the well-known Colorado booster and first territorial governor, William Gilpin. . . . Even today . . . [the atlas] serves as an indispensable tool for geologists working in certain remote parts of the state where more modern methods of mapping have not yet been applied.[64]

During most of Hayden's extensive surveys his Washington, D.C., headquarters were a meeting place for eminent scientists and congressmen interested in expanding western territories. "Several of the rooms were equipped with drafting tables," and it was here that Gardner, Wilson, and Holmes worked over the materials for the atlas.[65] The general supervision of the publication was entrusted to

Pencil drawing in five parts, 7″ × 12″ each part. Courtesy National Archives, Washington, D.C.

Holmes. Gardner and his replacement, A. D. Wilson, contributed to the series of maps, including four devoted to the whole state of Colorado. These were enriched by Holmes's geologic sections and incredible panoramic views of mountains taken from high triangulation stations.

In 1878, Holmes returned to the field to serve as geologist for Hayden's final survey, which focused on Wyoming and Idaho with special concentration on the Yellowstone area.[66] The results of the expedition were reported in Hayden's twelfth and final summary. In the closing paragraph the explorer writes:

> During the season of 1878 and 1879, Congress passed a law, discontinuing the three surveys then in existence, on the 30th of June, 1879, and . . . establishing the United States Geological Survey. The members of the Geological Survey of the Territories were discharged, some remaining in Washington, having obtained positions in various departments of the government, others engaging in business in different parts of the country. These reports were, therefore, completed at such

leisure intervals as could be spared from other duties. . . .

> The editorial work has been under the supervision of W. H. Holmes who has also had charge of the business of the survey in Washington for the last two years. He has bestowed much time and labor upon the preparation and revision of illustrations as well as upon other details of work.

The report for 1878 was published in two volumes. In the second part of this voluminous work Holmes provides a summary of his geological observations of the Yellowstone National Park. After a few introductory sentences, in which Holmes recognizes the existence of several earlier reports, he writes:

> With regard to my own work, I wish to state that if I could have consumed years instead of months in the study of the 3,400 square miles, comprising the Park, I might justify myself in putting my observations on paper. Scarcely two months were passed within the Park, and during nearly one-half of this time storms of rain and snow prevailed to such an extent as to greatly interfere with the work. I have, consequently, gone just far enough to get glimpses of the splendid

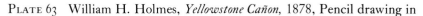

PLATE 63   William H. Holmes, *Yellowstone Cañon*, 1878, Pencil drawing in

problems of the rocks, and to enable me in the future to appreciate and understand the classic chapter that this district will some day add to the great volume of written geology.

The route of exploration, which Holmes describes in his report under the heading "The Narrative," is climaxed by the party's arrival at the Grand Cañon of the Yellowstone. Holmes describes the area's geological features in detail, including those seen while he was ascending the northern face of Washburn Peak to its summit. This high observation point was to provide him with the most comprehensive view obtainable of the Grand Cañon. Holmes spent all his available time sketching; his almost 180-degree view of the canyon and the surrounding countryside attests to his diligence and ability (plate 63). Running from northeast to southeast, the view is comprised of a series of continuous pictorial sections. On each section Holmes has noted key geological and geographical references, along with azimuth figures penciled in above certain peaks. In his narrative he comments on his endeavors:

All visitors to this region agree in pronouncing the view from this point unequaled, and I may, with the knowledge of experience, add that it is one which is unusually difficult to place upon paper. The broad expanses of the great plateau, with its lakes, cañons, and poorly defined forest-hidden drainage, is an almost unintelligible maze which has no strong lines to tempt the pencil. The distant ranges of the south and west, and the very complicated tangle of mountains to the north, consume hours in their analysis, and days ought to be allowed for their proper delineation. This is the point from which the great problems of the Park should be studied. No other point gives such a comprehensive view of the extraordinary formations of the volcanic Tertiary period.

Holmes made several other panoramic views during the season of 1878.[67] A few like this one were executed from high triangulation stations established by the party. Other sweeping vistas were achieved from lower areas, focusing on particular geologic wonders that were under examination, such as the lower geyser basin area.[68]

In mid-October, Holmes and his group left Yellowstone and at

three parts, 7″ × 12″ each part. Courtesy National Archives, Washington, D.C.

once headed back to Washington, D.C. He spent the remainder of the year preparing the voluminous report of 1878 and making drawings, sections, and maps for it.[69] In July, 1879, after the completion of this project, Holmes left for Europe to study in various art capitals. On returning home in late June, 1880, he was immediately assigned to Captain Clarence E. Dutton's Survey of the Grand Canyon of the Colorado, which culminated in his major artistic achievement: the combining of his scientific knowledge with his artistic skills to produce, in collaboration with Dutton, a classic masterpiece of geological history, *The Tertiary History of the Grand Cañon District.*[70] The collaboration of scientist and artist produced the perfect complement of artistic rendition and scientific prose on physical geology. The panoramas that grace the accompanying atlas are the culmination of many years devoted to the practice of describing in visual imagery hundreds of miles of varied topography with scientific accuracy, correct perspective, and subtly magnificent artistic skill.

In the realm of western topographical art Holmes's contribution is unique and seldom surpassed. He was unswervingly a realist, portraying the terrain with utmost truthfulness and precision, seldom giving full rein to his artistic imagination or poetic expression, ever mindful of his role in scientific mapmaking. It was only natural that, after forty-four years of exploring in the Rocky Mountain region, witnessing the development of the great surveys and the inception of the movement for establishing national parks, the artist-geologist should reminisce:

I have sketched perhaps every range and group of mountains from Montana to Mexico and have climbed nearly all of the great peaks of the ranges and explored the valleys and canyons. When I am homesick at all it is for these wilds and especially for the upland parks which nature has arranged with more than the skill of the landscape gardener. Everywhere there are subjects to inspire the painter's brush and at the same time to test his skill.[71]

7

THOMAS MORAN: "THE TURNER OF THE WEST"

Standing near the margin of the Lower Falls, and looking down the cañon, which looks like an immense chasm or cleft in the basalt, with its sides 1,200 to 1,500 feet high, and decorated with the most brilliant colors that the human eye ever saw, with the rocks weathered into an almost unlimited variety of forms, with here and there a pine sending its roots into the clefts on the sides as if struggling with a sort of uncertain success to maintain an existence—the whole presents a picture that it would be difficult to surpass in nature. Mr. Thomas Moran, a celebrated artist, and noted for his skill as a colorist, exclaimed with a kind of regretful enthusiasm that these beautiful tints were beyond the reach of human art. It is not the depth alone that gives such an impression of grandeur to the mind, but it is also the picturesque forms and coloring. Mr. Moran is now engaged in transferring this remarkable picture to canvas, and by means of a skillful use of colors something like a conception of its beauty may be conveyed.—F. D. Hayden[1]

Thomas Moran's intense interest in Yellowstone and the West began when he reworked some awkward field sketches for an article by N. P. Langford in *Scribner's Monthly* that recounted the Washburn-Doane expedition of 1870 (see chapter 6). Working with these sketches and drawing both on Langford's descriptions and on his own imagination, Moran created some "singular pictures. . . . Yellowstone was still so little known, and sounded so fantastic, that incredulity was the common reaction. One reviewer blasted Langford as the champion liar of the Northwest, and readers reminded the editors that the *Scribner's* prospectus had promised a moral tone, which presumably ought to exclude plain lies."[2]

A second article was proposed by *Scribner's*, for which Langford was to accompany Hayden's official survey of Yellowstone in the summer of 1871. Moran was again asked to provide illustrations. Naturally he wanted to see the wonders of the West for himself and sketch them on site, but, fresh from a study trip in Europe, he was financially strapped and hoped that *Scribner's* might finance the journey. When no such offer was forthcoming, he secured a loan from the publishers by offering his cherished *Children of the Mountains* as a guaranty. He also "borrowed five hundred dollars from Jay Cooke, who was eager to have the Northwest publicized in the interest of the Northern Pacific Railroad."[3]

Moran rode the Union Pacific to a point just north of the Great Salt Lake, "where he caught a stagecoach for a journey of four days and nights 'without stopping save for meals.'"[4] He finally joined Hayden's party in camp just outside Virginia City, equipped with only a small carpetbag stuffed with an inadequate supply of clothing. The lean young easterner was soon provided with a red-flannel shirt, rough trousers, and heavy boots. Riding a horse for the first time in his life, he suffered some tortures in his adjustment to the trail, but photographer William H. Jackson later recalled that "Moran made a picturesque appearance when mounted. The jaunty tilt of his sombrero, long yellowish beard and portfolio under his arm marked the artistic type, with something of local color imparted by a rifle hung from the saddle horn."[5] As has been mentioned, Moran's spontaneous watercolor sketches and Jackson's extraordinary photographs resulting from this trip of 1871 were persuasive enough to help Hayden persuade Congress to create Yellowstone National Park.

The celebrated landscape painter, whose work has often been compared with Turner's, was born in Bolton, Lancashire, England, on January 12, 1837. Bolton was a center of the British textile industry, a mecca for handloom weavers. Among them was the skilled Irish weaver Thomas Moran, Sr., and his English wife, Mary Higson. Three of their seven children, Edward, Thomas, and Peter, became painters; a fourth son, John, became a photographer. Life in the textile centers of Victorian England was hard, advancement was almost impossible, and educational opportunities for the children of the laboring class were negligible. In 1844, like so many other Britons during the "hungry forties," the Moran family sought relief—and promise—in America. They settled in Philadelphia, and Edward, the oldest of the children, soon joined his father working the looms in the bustling city. Thomas, who never served as an apprentice in the weaving industry, was enrolled in the Harrison Boy's Grammar School. He was a good student and won several prizes, many for his skillfully drawn maps—with sketches of Indians, Russians, Chinese, or Dutchmen (depending on the geographic location he was recording) in the margins.

Philadelphia, one of the outstanding cultural centers of the young nation, offered many opportunities for a boy like Tom. A focal point was the Pennsylvania Academy of Fine Arts, which he visited frequently despite the twenty-five-cent admission fee. There he could see Benjamin West's *Death on the Pale Horse,* works by the Peale family, and paintings by Thomas Sully and other early American masters. From 1830 to 1860 the academy sponsored special exhibitions of works by foreign artists that Moran undoubtedly explored as well, encountering the work of Andreas Achenbach, the Van De Veldes, Salvator Rosa, Nicolas Poussin, and Claude Lorrain. An especially interesting exhibition featuring the work of French, German, and Belgian painters was mounted at the academy in 1866;[6]

Moran, back in Philadelphia after two trips to Europe, probably attended. There he would have seen the alpine paintings of Swiss artist Alexandre Calame, whom even critics of Moran's day recognized as influencing his Rocky Mountain pictures in style and subject.[7]

In 1853, when Moran was sixteen, he was indentured to the wood-engraving firm of Scattergood and Telfer. Already spending every free moment working at his own pencil and watercolor sketches, he found the technique of wood engraving utterly boring. When reprimanded for his come-late, leave-early attitude, he threatened to quit—but Scattergood, aware of the youth's potential as an artist, kept him on Moran's own terms, even selling his watercolors to various clients. One of the buyers, C. J. Price, was the owner of a bookshop that featured imported English publications. Moran went to the shopkeeper and established a beneficial system of barter: he gave him watercolors in return for books. In this way the youth began building a creditable library that included English poetry, books on science, and volumes of engravings such as Turner's *Liber Studiorum* and *The Rivers of France.*[8] Moran remained with Scattergood and Telfer for three years, until 1856, when he suffered a severe attack of rheumatic fever. Once recovered, he refused to return to the engraver's shop and broke his seven-year indenture. Despite his dissatisfaction with the wood-engraving trade, the discipline he learned there—notably close attention to detail and exact definition of form by line—were to serve him well in the field.

Encouraged by the prices his watercolors were commanding (ten to fifteen dollars apiece), he decided to join his brother Edward, who had given up his job as a power-loom boss and established himself in a studio. Edward had taken this step on the advice of James Hamilton, a well-known marine painter who had seen his work, liked it, and suggested that the young novice make painting his career. The results of his full-time commitment to painting had been almost immediate: he had found buyers for his paintings and his work had been accepted for academy exhibitions. Established in the cramped quarters of his brother's first ill-equipped studio, an attic room over a barbershop, young Tom began working in oils under his brother's tutelage. Hamilton played an important role in the younger Moran's early development as well, introducing him to his own trademark of luminism and reinforcing his enthusiasm for the works of Turner, initiated when Moran had first seen the engraved views in his own copy of *Liber Studiorum.*

In the next four years Moran became recognized as one of the city's most promising young artists, but he was still in the process of establishing a personal style. He tried his hand at many different subjects. Under the influence of Hamilton and his brother, he produced romantic seascapes, such as *Storm on a Rocky Coast, The Coast of Newfoundland,* and *Spit Light, Boston Harbor, England,*[9] the last seeming to echo the muted tones of a Dutch marine. An indefatigable reader and a romantic at heart, Moran also painted imaginary scenes from literature of the day that were far removed from the usual cut-and-dried illustrations.

An undercurrent to all of Moran's experiments was his intense interest in and continuing study of Turner's engravings. Disenchanted with the eastern environment and yearning for more dramatic natural settings like those the English artist had captured, he painted *Winter in the Rockies* in 1867, four years before he actually traveled west.[10] Moran had a keen desire to see Turner's works in color, and, after saving money toward that end, he and his brother sailed for the British Isles in the summer of 1861. In October of that year the young artist spent day after day in London's National Gallery studying the works of his idol and copying his early paintings, for example, *Ulysses Deriding Polyphemus.*[11] Turner's changeable light effects, mist-filled atmosphere, and vivid coloring must have been a startling revelation to Moran after his long and assiduous study of the master's black-and-white engravings.

The collection assembled at the National Gallery included only works from Turner's earlier periods. Forms were still solid, not dissolved; the compositions followed a traditional layout; and the colors were lower-keyed in comparison with the explosive color orchestration of his later pictures. In studying Turner's early development, Moran discovered something about the imaginative synthesis of art and the way it can transform reality. In later years he would comment that it was the "character" of the scene he wished to capture, not a "literal transcription"—a concept that echoed his English mentor's work and philosophy. Later, when Moran had evolved a stable, uniquely personal style, his comments about the English artist reflected mature objectivity:

> Turner is a great artist, but he is not understood, because both painters and the public look upon his pictures as transcriptions of Nature. He certainly did not so regard them. All that he asked of a scene was simply how good a medium it was for making a picture; he cared nothing for the scene itself. Literally speaking, his landscapes are false; but they contain his impressions of Nature, and so many natural characteristics as were necessary adequately to convey that impression to others. The public does not estimate the quality of his work by his best paintings, but by his latest and crazier ones, in which realism is entirely thrown overboard.[12]

On his second trip to England and the Continent in 1866–67, Moran was accompanied by his wife, Mary Nimmo, who was to become a skilled graphic artist. The young couple shared many interests and looked forward to exploring the art centers of the Old World together. A focal point of the trip was Rome, where Moran was eager to see the works of Claude Lorrain and Nicolas Poussin, both of whom had exerted strong influence on Turner's early work. In studying these two master landscapists and others, Moran came to understand the construction of classic formal compositions—a structural strength that was to be incorporated into his own later work.

Despite Moran's arduous studies of the European masters, his concentrated studio efforts, and his continual search for material in the eastern United States, the real fountainhead of his success as a landscape artist was his encounter with the West. There Moran discovered subjects of the magnitude that his spirit demanded—scenes that could inspire the full realization of his artistry.

Moran's wanderings of 1860 in the wilderness along the south shore of Lake Superior[13] could hardly have prepared him for the expansive vistas and awesome beauty he was to encounter in Yellowstone Park during his journey with the Hayden expeditionary party in 1871 (see chapter 6). This first trip to the Far West marked the start of a long, close association between the artist and photographer William H. Jackson. In his reminiscences Jackson speaks of Moran's particular interest in the photographic operation of the survey. He was always willing to volunteer as an assistant, lingering behind or wandering far ahead to help select picturesque or unusual scenes; he shared the photographer's interest in "selecting the view points for each negative, having in mind, perhaps, the good use he could make of the photographs later in some of his own compositions."[14] Jackson's photographs often augmented Moran's simple watercolor washes and economical pencil field sketches, helping the artist recall essential textures and tonal values in developing his finished pictures. The demands of the rugged terrain and the limited time allotted for these western journeys restricted the artist to taking along only as much material as he could carry; consequently, his field sketches were rapid, precise contour lines with descriptive notes about objects and colors on the picture and along the margins. These accurate studies were the framework onto which he would apply his colors. Like his idol, Turner, Moran indelibly imprinted nature's colors on his memory—abetted by his careful color notes.

From his earliest days as an artist Moran was interested in the minutiae of nature,[15] carefully studying and sketching all its aspects. Despite the wildness and vastness of the western terrain—set on a much larger scale than the eastern landscapes of his early jaunts—Moran nevertheless approached it with this eye for detailed accuracy.

Shortly after the artist's return to the East he began producing a series of studio watercolors for American financier Jay Cooke, undoubtedly to repay him for the loan that made his trip possible. The series included a variety of subjects—hot springs, bubbling mud pools, active and extinct geysers and caldrons (Liberty Cap), and geological phenomena—drawn from Lower Falls and Upper Falls, Grand Canyon, Great Blue Spring, Geysers of Fire Hole Basin, Yellowstone Lake, and other sites. Several illustrations of the same geological wonders were provided for *Harper's Weekly* and *Aldine.*[16] In April, 1872, Hayden circulated Moran's Yellowstone watercolors in Washington to aid in promoting the park bill. They came to the attention of the wealthy British industrialist William Blackmore, sparking his interest in the young painter. Shortly thereafter Moran

journeyed to the nation's capital with his large oil *Grand Canyon of the Yellowstone* in the hope that Congress might be interested in acquiring it. Arrangements were made for an exhibition of the work in the old House of Representatives in late May and early June. According to William H. Truettner, "Hayden assisted . . . [Moran] in bringing a resolution to purchase the painting before Congress, and with steady pressure from other Washington friends, the bill was quickly passed. The $10,000 Moran received was equal to the highest price ever paid Frederic Church and was second only to Bierstadt's spectacular sales in the 1860's."[17] Blackmore was among the many who came to view the magnificent painting, and he decided to commission Moran to paint a series of aquarelles for his museum in Salisbury, England.[18]

In contrast to his finished studio productions, Moran's field sketches reflect the immediacy and spontaneity dictated by his minimal equipment. An excellent example of his work in the field is found in *The Yellowstone Range from near Fort Ellis* (plate 64). The sketch, taken from the mountains southeast of the expedition campsite, presents an aerial view of the distant Yellowstone Range. In this view and an earlier one, *Beaver Head Canon/Montana,* taken on July 4 (plate 65), the artist follows a familiar procedure, using the unpainted yellowish-tan-toned paper for his foreground and brushing in the bluish-gray bluffs and the nearby pool.

The artist also captured various views of Tower Falls, ranging in style and technique from a rapid pencil contour outline delineating a panoramic view of the pinnacles and surrounding country[19] to a delicate tonal calligraphic brush treatment in watercolor washes. As Jackson later recounted:

> The weird and fantastic towers and pinnacles along the turbulent creek above the falls contrast strangely with the chaste beauty of the Hot Springs and caught Moran's fancy. He had made some singular pictures, [merely] from description, of these rocks for Langford's article and naturally was greatly interested in getting his own interpretation of their picturesque and varied outlines.[20]

According to Moran's brief diary entry of July 26, the two men spent the greater part of the day sketching and photographing Tower Falls. In one watercolor wash[21] the artist portrays the white foam

Near Fort Ellis. Mo. 1871

PLATE 64

Thomas Moran, *The Yellowstone Range from near Fort Ellis,* 1871, Watercolor, 13¾″ × 10⅛″.
Courtesy National Park Service, Yellowstone National Park, Wyoming.

PLATE 65

Thomas Moran, *Beaver Head Canon/Montana*, 1871, Watercolor & chinese white, 10⅜″ × 14⅛″.
Courtesy M. and M. Karolik Collection, Museum of Fine Arts, Boston.

of the giant falls as it makes its vertical descent between what Hayden described as the "somber brecciated columns," standing like "gloomy sentinels."[22] His ultimate studio piece,[23] worked up from a pencil sketch and rough watercolor field sketches, is almost a replica of one of his small watercolor studies. Here, however, washes and opaque watercolor create strong, naturalistic, rainbow coloring; sharply contrasting tonal values; and atmospheric effects that contrast with the pale washes of his uncomplicated field study. In the finished watercolor he delineates the veining of the rocks and the stratification of the pinnacles with color patterns of incisive lines. This network of lines was to be used as abstract decorative patterning in many of his other elaborated drawings of Yellowstone; it is even more apparent in his views of the Great Blue Spring of Lower Geyser Basin (plates 66, 67, and color plate 24)—also worked up from a watercolor field study—in which the terraced, overflowing algae- and sulphur-tinted waters swirl into colorful patterned lines. In the third quarter of the nineteenth century line had been freed from the confines of literal application in topographical art. In these watercolors Moran was reflecting a trend that could also be seen in the work of a contemporary, the English topographical artist Edward Lear.[24] Because of his concern for retaining an object's structure, however, Moran's line was never to become as exaggerated as Lear's.

One of the stunning achievements of Moran's oeuvre is his first major painting, *The Grand Canyon of the Yellowstone* (color plate 25), a monumental oil he executed the year after his western journey. Between July 28 and 31, 1871, Moran had made sketches from points above and below the falls and along the rim of the immense, magically colored canyon. Here, Jackson noted, "Moran's enthusiasm was greater . . . than anywhere else among Yellowstone's wonderful features."[25] A number of these preparatory studies remain, revealing the impressive scale and steepness of the canyon walls, their textures, and the intensity and brilliance of their mineral hues. Unlike his large, symmetrically disposed oil composition, Moran's studies capture the canyon at dramatic angles where its overlapping forms build up asymmetrically. The drama is heightened by the use of alternating darks and lights. Save for one related sketch, no work from this vantage point (known on contemporary maps as "Artist

Point") remains among his series of canyon views. Truettner correctly suggests that Moran referred to Jackson's photographs of the Grand Canyon for a compositional memorandum, depending on his own sketches for color references.[26] While Jackson's photographic views zoom in close and at an angle, however, Moran arranges his composition in such a manner that the viewer looks directly out on the distant falls encircled by a wall of mountains. It is obvious that Moran enlarged this panoramic vista by widening the steep, narrow canyon walls; in what was to become his typical manner, Moran altered some of the literal aspects of the scene to produce an idealized version. In an interview of 1879 he described his approach to capturing the spectacular sights he garnered in the park:

> The motive or incentive of my "Grand Cañon of the Yellowstone" was the gorgeous display of color that impressed itself upon me. Probably no scenery in the world presents such a combination. The forms are extremely wonderful and pictorial, and, while I desired to tell truly of Nature, I did not wish to realize the scene literally, but to preserve and to convey its true impression. Every form introduced into the picture is within view from a given point, but the relations of the separate parts to one another are not always preserved. For instance, the precipitous rocks on the right were really at my back when I stood at that point, yet in their present position they are strictly true to pictorial Nature; and so correct is the whole representation that every member of the expedition with which I was connected declared, when he saw the painting, that he knew the exact spot which had been reproduced. My aim was to bring before the public the character of that region. The rocks in the foreground are so carefully drawn that a geologist could determine their precise nature. I treated them so in order to serve my purpose.[27]

Obviously Moran had assimilated Ruskin's teachings, believing that if an artist had an intimate working knowledge of "the rocks and trees, and the atmosphere, and the mountain torrents and the birds that fly in the blue ether above"[28] he could take any liberties necessary in creating his pictorial composition, as long as the result was true to nature. These same thoughts were set forth in Turner's writings: "Every look at nature is a refinement upon art. Each tree and blade of grass or flower is not to him the individual tree, grass or flower, but what it is in relation to the whole."[29]

PLATE 66

Thomas Moran, *Great Blue Spring of the Fire Hole*, 1871, Watercolor, 8⅛″ × 11⅛″.
Courtesy National Park Service, Yellowstone National Park.

PRANG'S AMERICAN CHROMO.

THE GREAT BLUE SPRING OF THE LOWER GEYSER BASIN YELLOWSTONE

PLATE 67

Thomas Moran, *The Great Blue Spring of the Lower Geyser Basin, Yellowstone*, 1876, Chromolithograph, 21″ × 24¾″.
Courtesy Buffalo Bill Historical Center, Cody.

COLOR PLATE 20

John H. Hill, *Shoshone Falls*, 1871, Watercolor, 12″ × 17½″.
Courtesy Arthur J. Phelan, Jr., Collection, Chevy Chase, Md.

187

COLOR PLATE 21

Gilbert Munger, *Wahsatch Range—from Salt Lake City—Utah*,
ca. 1869, Oil, 18″ × 36″. Courtesy Anschutz Collection,
Denver, Colo.

COLOR PLATE 22

Henry Wood Elliott, *Yellowstone Lake*, 1871, Watercolor,
10″ × 19¼″. Courtesy Phoenix Art Museum, Phoenix, Ariz.
Gift of Mr. and Mrs. Kemper Marley.

COLOR PLATE 23

William Henry Holmes, *Monument Park, Colorado*, 1874,
Watercolor, 17½″ × 11¾″. Courtesy Western History
Research Center, University of Wyoming, Laramie, Wyo.

COLOR PLATE 24

Thomas Moran, *The Great Blue Spring of the Lower Geyser Basin, Fire Hole River, Yellowstone*, 1872, Watercolor, 9¹⁄₁₆″ × 16³⁄₈″.
Courtesy Hirschl and Adler Galleries, New York City, N.Y.

COLOR PLATE 26

Thomas Moran, *Cliffs of Green River*, 1874, Oil, 25⅛″ × 45⅜″.
Courtesy Amon Carter Museum, Fort Worth.

Thomas Moran, *In the Teton Range, Idaho 1899*, Oil, 20″ × 30¼″.
Courtesy Kennedy Galleries, Inc., New York City, N.Y.

COLOR PLATE 28

Thomas Moran, *Pikes Peak through the Gateway to the Garden of the Gods*, 1880, Oil, 14½″ × 24½″.
Courtesy Garden of the Gods Club, Colorado Springs, Colo.

Many eminent critics have suggested that Moran's finely orchestrated coloring, seen through floating vapors, mist, and foam, was inspired by Turner's work. But the American artist's colors were never to explode into Turner's brilliant and often arbitrary hues—they remained subdued and naturalistic. Although Moran acknowledged taking certain artistic license, he was basically a realist with a romantic spirit. In many ways his work reflects the midnineteenth-century international mode. The emotional element, the theatrical qualities, and the pictorial content of his paintings suggest the influence of the late German Romantics and the Swiss artist Alexandre Calame, from whose alpine scenes Moran borrowed certain elements. For example, Moran, like many other American artists of this period, often uses Calame's tall sentinel fir tree in the foreground to establish scale and serve as a *repoussoir*, creating an illusion of depth and leading the eye back into space.[30] Moran's *Mount of the Holy Cross* (see plate 72) and his *Summit of the Sierras*[31] are remarkably close to the picturesque mountain scenes of the Swiss artist, though the American's brushwork is never as tight or his color as dark in tone.

When it was first unveiled, *The Grand Canyon of the Yellowstone* received critical acclaim and established Moran's reputation as one of America's leading young artists. Typical of the painting's wide acceptance was a thoughtful analysis published in *Scribner's Monthly:*

> [Moran] not only understands the methods of art but the processes and work of nature, so far as the faithful interpreter of natural scenery must know them. . . . It is noble to paint a glorious and inspiring poem; it is satisfying to render nature with firm mastery of technical detail. In "The Grand Cañon of the Yellowstone" . . . Moran has done both. He has produced a painting which has, we suppose, but a single rival in American landscape art; in certain elements of greatness it will be acknowledged to excel even this, and it is not likely soon to be surpassed by the work of any hand save, perhaps, that of Thomas Moran himself.[32]

Obviously the "single rival" to whom *Scribner's* critic refers is Albert Bierstadt; certainly Moran took his cue from the panoramic format of Bierstadt's highly successful Rocky Mountain scenes, and the two artists actually became competitors in the field. Despite these affinities in both subject and format, Moran himself was more impressed by the work of Frederic Church, whom he named "the greatest American painter," citing Church's *Niagara* and *Heart of the Andes* as "masterpieces" of landscape art.[33]

In the summer of 1892, Moran and Jackson revisited Yellowstone Park. On this second excursion the artist produced some of his boldest and most colorful and dramatic drawings, reflecting a change in technique and approach toward the familiar sites. His sketches of Golden Gate, "a narrow and winding defile flanked on the left . . . by Bunsen's Peak [pictured in his oil of this subject], and on the right by steep cliffs,"[34] exhibit his new orientation. These rapid pencil sketches, captured from different perspectives, though accurate in scale and description, provide only essential contours of the topography. The details were added later in his large oil *Golden Gate to Yellowstone* (plate 68). In constructing this studio picture, Moran "changed reality for the sake of heightened expressiveness . . . the ravine has been deepened, the cliffs heightened, distances lengthened, and the vista widened."[35]

On the same trip Moran also made dramatic sketches of Yellowstone Canyon from Inspiration Point on the east wall.[36] Positioning himself on an elevated shelflike eminence, he made some daring aerial views of the gorge that captured the canyon walls and river at extreme angles and gave the artist an opportunity to demonstrate his bold and dramatic hand. From the west side of Yellowstone River he sketched the sloping ridge of the canyon wall and its distinctive pinnacles—deftly adding tonal values and textures to illustrate the weathered landforms. In many of these sketches the decorative patterning of incisive lines seen in his earlier drawings of Yellowstone becomes even more abstract.

These sketches were incorporated into another large oil, *Grand Canyon of the Yellowstone*,[37] executed shortly after his return home. Here Moran's highly acclaimed panoramic showpiece of 1872 was, in a sense, re-created and expanded to include the nuances of the artist's emerging maturity. In general, the artist moves from a fairly literal treatment to a somewhat more generalized presentation. He also introduces a profusion of atmospheric effects like the mist and haze that envelop the peaks and the mountain canyon. A lighter palette is employed throughout, dictated in part by the painter's

PLATE 68

Thomas Moran, *Golden Gate to Yellowstone*, 1893, Oil, 36¼" × 50¼".
Courtesy Buffalo Bill Historical Center, Cody.

use of diffused light—a technique that helps unify the composition. In 1893, Moran sent his large oil, along with another picture, *Spectres from the North,* to the Chicago World's Fair. Neither work captured the coveted award.[38]

On his way to join Hayden's party in 1871, Moran sketched his first view of Wyoming's Green River from his train window.[39] In the years following his first western journey he crossed this wide expanse of green water bordered by huge, weathered, pink-tinged, castellated bluffs many times, and it became a favorite subject. His many interpretations of it varied only in perspective, direction, and height. In some views the usual foreground detail and lead-in are eliminated, providing a closer scrutiny of the huge cliffs; subtle nuances of color and changeable light effects also help vary the mood. Groupings of small figures are used in some of the Green River pictures as embellishment and to indicate scale. In his usual manner Moran took artistic license in exaggerating the height and prominence of the monolithic central form, which he dubbed "Castle Rock"; this is apparent in comparisons of his views with photographs of the actual site.[40] Perhaps the most striking of these views is his *Cliffs of Green River* (1874, color plate 26),[41] a shimmering composition that melds opalescent Turneresque color with veiled light and atmospheric effects.

As in much of his other fieldwork, Moran often employed a toned paper for his Green River scenes. Since most of his watercolor sketches capture Green River in the heat of the summer, its pinkish sandstone bluffs seen through the glaring desert sunlight, he usually selected yellow- or brown-toned paper for them to aid in capturing the warmth of the scene.

In the summer of 1879, Moran passed through Green River on his way home from a trip to the Grand Tetons.[42] Although he and his brother Peter, his companion on this journey, made several on-the-spot watercolor field sketches of the Tetons seen from the west, it was not until 1895 that Moran first captured them in oil. Several other views painted by the artist in 1899 portray the Grand Tetons covered in snow and swathed in floating mist against a bright-blue sky (color plate 27). The atmospheric effects of these oils and the small field studies conjure up a romantic vision of these imposing monarchs.

Moran made his first trip to Colorado in August, 1874, in quest of the snowy cross he had become aware of through Jackson's photographs, Holmes's field sketches, and Hayden's graphic descriptions (see chapter 6). In 1873 he had been commissioned by Appleton to provide thirteen illustrations for an article on the Rocky Mountains for *Picturesque America;* the celebrated *Mount of the Holy Cross* was included among them.[43] Using Jackson's photographs of the actual peak and the surrounding Holy Cross Creek Canyon (known in those days as Roche Moutonnée Cañon),[44] Moran composed a picture of a site he had never seen, adopting a hackneyed format and vertical composition for his *Mount of the Holy Cross.* The distinctive peak with the "sacred cross" etched in its creviced, snowy face rises in the background; a rushing waterfall cascades toward the boulder-strewn, lichen-covered foreground. Moran was undoubtedly familiar with this type of composition, which harked back to the alpine scenic paintings of the Late Romantic German and Swiss artists[45] and further to the early-nineteenth-century heroic landscapes of the Tyrolean artist Joseph Anton Koch.[46] By relocating and juxtaposing nearby Holy Cross Creek with the celebrated peak, Moran had adopted a simple format.

Two years later, after making a trip to the fabled peak, Moran painted a large oil that once again catapulted him into a fame that rivaled Bierstadt's as painter of the Rocky Mountains. The details of Moran's journey to the snowy cross are related in a series of letters the artist wrote to his wife while en route with a small group from Hayden's expeditionary party. At his request this group was assigned to escort Moran to the fabled peak.[47] The artist arrived at the survey headquarters on Clear Creek in early August.[48] On the eighth the party headed west on the first leg of the journey (plate 69).[49] While traveling along the north fork of the South Platte, the artist observed the "magnificent" Pikes Peak fifty miles distant but "did not make a sketch [of it] as we were on the march at the time." It made an indelible imprint on his mind, however, and was later to become a subject for his brush (color plate 28).[50] Several

PLATE 69

William H. Jackson, *On Trip to the Mount of the Holy Cross*, 1874, Photograph, 5" × 7". Courtesy Denver Public Library, Western History Department, Denver.

days later the party camped outside Fairplay, in South Park. By then Moran had already taken several rapid pencil sketches of scenery around their various campsites, more likely made as factual records than as memorandums for future paintings, since they lack the usual color and geological object references.[51]

Leaving Fairplay, the party followed the South Platte to its headwaters. The next day they crossed Mosquito Pass, one of the highest in the Park Range, which Moran described as "at an elevation of 11,000 feet [*sic*] . . . [and] an awfully steep road."[52] Moran left a visual testament of their arduous crossing of Mosquito Pass in an elaborate watercolor, dramatizing the fierceness of the ele-

ments and sublimity of the scenery (plate 70). In some ways this romanticized picture, whose forms Moran described as "very poor . . . Mt. Lincoln [at the right] like a big sand hill,"[53] recalls some of Turner's early watercolors of Swiss alpine scenery, for example, *Mer de Glace, Chamonix with Blair's Hut*,[54] though Moran's brush is never as fluid or his color as brilliant as the English master's. Like some of Moran's elaborate Yellowstone studio watercolors, this work was reproduced in Louis Prang's large portfolio of chromolithographs entitled *The Yellowstone National Park and the Mountain Regions of Portions of Idaho, Nevada, Colorado, and Utah*, published in 1876.[55] It would seem that *Mosquito Trail* was worked up from a field study,

198

PLATE 70

Thomas Moran, *Mosquito Trail, Rocky Mountains of Colorado*, 1875, Watercolor, 9¾″ × 14¼″.
Courtesy Hirschl and Adler Galleries, New York City.

suggested by a wash drawing of the Arkansas Divide,[56] in which the mountainous terrain is summarily indicated with washes over faint pencil lines, with gray paper showing through for the light areas. In the late 1870s, Moran produced two oils of the same subject.[57]

The artist made several pencil sketches of their next campsite near the Continental Divide before they crossed it at Tennessee Pass and descended the Eagle River toward the valley of the Holy Cross. On Thursday, the nineteenth, the small party began the ascent of the mountain that lay between them and the Roche Moutonnée Valley. Moran called this climb the most difficult that he had experienced: "Almost perpendicular, . . . [and] covered with burnt & fallen timber, lying 3 or 4 deep." When they finally reached the top, ". . . the view was perfectly magnificent. 2,000 feet below [us] lay the *Moutonnée Valley* with the Holy Cross Creek rushing through it & at the head of the valley the splendid peak of the Holy Cross, with the range continuing to the left of [us]." Here Moran sketched a panoramic view. While working their way up the valley, they encountered further difficulties: "A swamp, covered with the worst of fallen logs & projecting through which were the *Roche Moutonnée* or Sheep Rocks." Continuing their climb, they finally gained a clear view of the cross from 800 feet away. Moran captured this oblique view of the Holy Cross in pencil, taking care to show their small campsite below (plate 71). In the valley, the artist later recounted, was "one of the most picturesque waterfalls" he had ever seen: "I shall use it in the foreground of the picture."[58]

On September 1, after they retraced their steps to Denver, Moran left for the East. The *Rocky Mountain News* announced that the painter would immediately "commence work on a painting of the Holy Cross, and hopes to have it completed by January 1, 1875."[59] It was not until shortly after March 5, however, that Moran finished the picture.[60]

Although his visit to the actual site of the famous landmark had helped Moran gain a better picture of the terrain, it is doubtful that he actually obtained a frontal view of the cross. In his striking oil painting *Mount of the Holy Cross* (plate 72), Jackson's head-on photographic view of the upper portion of the "sacred" mountain has once more been lifted, and Moran has again combined and re-located the cascading creek and the picturesque waterfall he admired, so that they flow directly from the mountain. Some noticeable differences between Moran's illustration and his painting exist, however, despite similar artistic liberties taken in both. In contrast to the illustration's shallow or compressed format, the painting's compositional arrangement carries the eye back into space over a middle ground to the distant mountains. Although Moran has been truthful in his specifics, he has taken considerable artistic license in combining two topographically unrelated scenes. In contrast to the simplistic foreground of the illustration, the details in the lower two-thirds of the painting are extraordinarily complex, incorporating the scene Moran caught while looking up Cross Creek Canyon.

Although *Mount of the Holy Cross* was praised for its "moderate and graceful tone," it was criticized as being "very different from the extraordinary color in [his] previous works [of] this region."[61] At the same time critics remarked that the picture recalled the studies of Calame, "that almost unrivaled painter of wild mountain scenery," though it still carried Moran's "unmistakable stamp of originality."[62] The artist's foreground and middle distances in particular reminded his contemporaries of Calame "in a certain crispness of touch, with, at the same time, a monotonous attention to detail."[63] In defense of his intensely realistic foregrounds and overly elaborated rocks, Moran rebutted: "My purpose was to convey a true impression of the region; and as for the elaborated rocks, I elaborated them out of pure love for rocks. I have studied rocks carefully, and I like to represent them."[64]

From the time of its unveiling in March, 1875, the picture was an immediate success with the public. Shortly thereafter it was shown in New York, Washington, D.C., and Boston in a successive series of exhibitions. The following year Moran sent the picture to the United States Centennial Exhibition of 1876, for which he received a medal and a diploma.[65] While it was on exhibit at the Royal Academy, in London, in 1879, Mrs. William A. Bell, whose husband was vice-president of the Denver and Rio Grande Railroad, saw it and persuaded her husband to purchase it. The transaction was completed at the artist's studio in 1880. The picture was sent to the Bells' Manitou residence, where it hung until 1903, when it

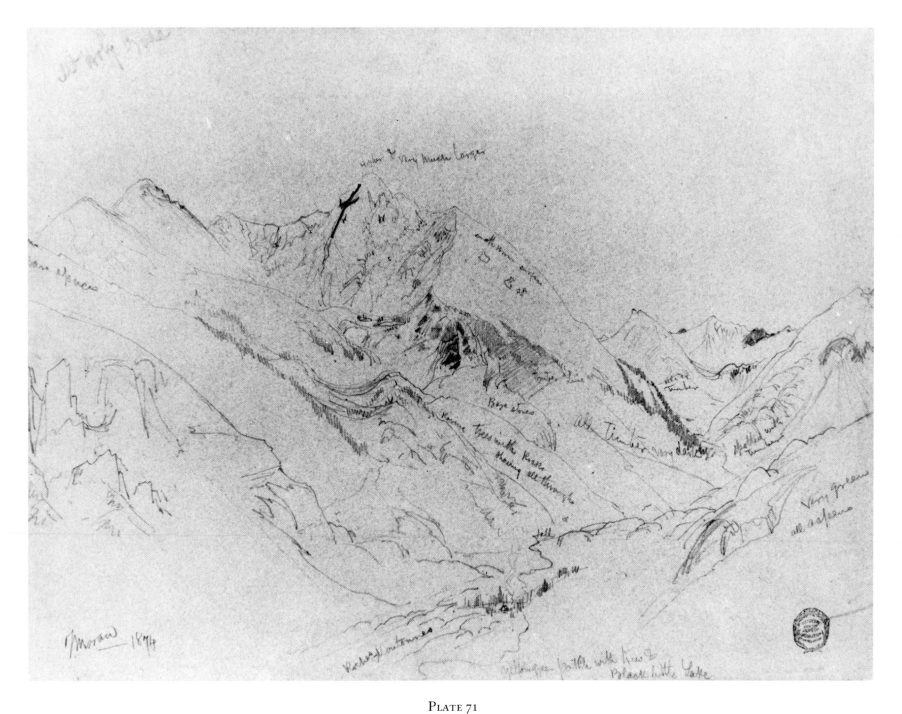

P<small>LATE</small> 71

Thomas Moran, *Mt. Holy Cross*, 1874, Pencil, 10½″ × 15″.
Courtesy Cooper-Hewitt Museum of Design, Smithsonian Institution, New York City, N.Y.

PLATE 72

Thomas Moran, *Mount of the Holy Cross*,
1875, Oil, 83½″ × 64½″. Courtesy National
Cowboy Hall of Fame and Western Heritage
Center, Oklahoma City, Okla.

was removed to Pendell Court, in England, where the Bells later resided.[66] After several changes in ownership, the large oil is now in the collection of the National Cowboy Hall of Fame, in Oklahoma City.

Although Moran made several watercolors of the same subject with slight variations, he painted only two oils of it—the original version of 1875 and one in 1892 for that year's Denver Art League exhibition.[67] According to the critics, it was one of the main attractions, exhibiting Moran's "superb technique of coloring and his faithfulness to nature." This version, smaller in format and with variations, exemplifies a later phenomenon in the development of landscape painting: the use of associative color derived from the art of photography—a concern for tonal values that paralleled photographic aims. The work's soft green and mauvish-gray tones indicate that the photograph, rather than reality, was Moran's model. In contrast to the earlier version, the artist's brush is more fluid than descriptive here. Although more modern in its interpretation, the later painting lacks the dramatic and romantic impact of Moran's initial impression.

In later years Moran made repeated trips to Colorado. In August, 1881, he and "Apple Jack" Karst, a wood engraver, made a trip to Denver, where they joined writer Ernest Ingersoll, his wife, and photographer Jackson for an extended trip over the Denver and Rio Grande Railroad and its branches.[68] Moran was engaged to provide a series of illustrations for the *Colorado Tourist,* a monthly magazine sponsored by railroad interests. Ingersoll, who had joined Hayden in the field in 1874 (an experience resulting in a book called *Knocking Round the Rockies,* with illustrations by Moran), was armed with a commission from *Harper's Magazine* for a firsthand account of the San Juan mining region's current silver boom. On August 20, the two men's groups combined forces and chartered a "train"—two boxcars and a parlor coach converted to a sleeper, a dining room, and a kitchen—heading south toward Colorado Springs, the first stop on their journey.[69] The details and itinerary of their travels through southern Colorado and northern New Mexico are chronicled in Ingersoll's book *Crest of the Continent,*[70] which was published in 1885 with illustrations by Moran and a local artist, Charles Craig,

engraved by Karst. Once again Moran used Jackson's photographs in working up his illustrations of scenic views that he was later to paint as well. One such view, *Toltec Gorge,* described by Ingersoll as the "king of cañons," was taken before Moran and Jackson left the party at Durango, Colorado, to sketch and photograph the mountainous scenery in the Arkansas Valley and Mosquito Pass, Tennessee Pass, and other noted passes on their way back to Denver. Ingersoll recounts the means by which Moran obtained his views of this glorious and wild grandeur:

> Our train having halted, the Artist sought a favorable position for obtaining the sketch of Toltec Gorge which adorns these pages, the Photographer became similarly absorbed, and the remaining members of the expedition zealously examined a spot whose counterpart in rugged and inspiring sublimity probably does not exist elsewhere in America. A few rods up the cañon a thin and ragged pinnacle rises abruptly from the very bottom to a level with the railroad track. This point has been christened Eva Cliff, and when we had gained its crest by dint of much laborious and hazardous climbing over a narrow gangway of rocks, by which it is barely connected with the neighboring bank, our exertions were well repaid by the splendid view of the gorge it afforded.[71]

By using ink wash, pencil, and watercolor with accents of opaque white, Moran elaborated *Toltec Gorge* into a finished drawing that was subsequently engraved by Karst and reproduced in Ingersoll's book.[72] In this drawing the artist has sharply defined his light and dark areas to create something of the drama the scene held for the group. Like much of Moran's other work, it was obviously based on a rough pencil field sketch, a rapid wash study, or perhaps both. Moran has once again produced a series of linear patternings by overlapping the folds of the massive rock-bedded cliff walls—elevating the standard topographical view into a lively pictorial rendering.

During the journey Moran also produced a rough oil study of an extended view, *Sultan's Mountain from Baker's Park,*[73] somewhat similar to Jackson's photographic view of the same sight. The theme, elaborated and enlarged into a finished work, was reproduced as an illustration in *Harper's* issue of April, 1882.

On December 4, 1892, the *Colorado Springs Gazette* announced with great fanfare the Denver Art League's forthcoming exhibition

of Moran's work, scheduled to open Christmas week. The show proved to be a tour de force, heralded by the press as "one of the finest exhibitions," being "valuable both as an object lesson and an educator in the line of aesthetic tastes." The collection of 275 objects, including oils, watercolors, etchings, and photogravures, was valued at $100,000[74] and embraced twenty-five years' work. Scenes of Venice, New Mexico, Mexico, Colorado, Yellowstone, and East Hampton, ranging from large, spectacular oils to small, rapid watercolor studies were shown; many of them were made during the artist's three-month summer tour of 1892. Two of his Denver views caught the eye of the reporter for the *Rocky Mountain News:*

> There are two little sketches here of Denver, made during the artist's last visit. They are faithful and true to the aspect of the scene at the moment they were made. It was during the artist's last visit here of a cold, cloudy day. These scenes are familiar to all Denverites, true as they are of that particular day and hour that the artist saw them.[75]

One of these two watercolors undoubtedly was Moran's *Smelting Works at Denver/June 12th 1892* (plate 73). Like Turner, Moran seemingly welcomed the pictorial possibilities of an industrial landscape, intrigued by its special qualities of light and atmosphere.[76] He had recorded this kind of theme and realism earlier in his series of paintings and drawings of the industrial complexes at Communipaw, New Jersey, in his own backyard. In this respect Moran's painterly interests were a far cry from the earlier didactic paintings of romantic spirits like Cole and his English counterpart Martin, who "saw Man as a puny being, living at the mercy of vast elemental forces that could become destructive in the twinkling of an eye."[77]

Moran lived a long and prolific life, producing a staggering number of pictures during his career. Although the Rocky Mountain region was only one of the areas he captured, it was undoubtedly the inspiration for his greatest works—symphonies of color that prompted some critics to dub him the "Turner of the West." Because his interests ranged over a wide spectrum of American art, however, it is extremely difficult to assign his work to any one school or individual. He had, as one critic remarked, his own "unmistakable stamp of originality."

Like many other international artists of the 1870s, Moran drew on a number of sources for inspiration, though he never shifted from traditional means of portraying them. Moran was basically a romantic realist and a traditionalist whose early predilection for the grand and sublime in nature continued throughout his long career. Although his brush became more fluid and his color palette lightened over the years, he was never as adventuresome as Turner in exploring new approaches; his forms never dissolved and his colors never exploded. Turner provided him with the technical means, but the pictorial content and emotional element in his work owed a debt to the Late Romantic German painters. Despite his eclectic means, Moran's emotionally charged, romantic, grand mountainscapes find few competitors; in the end they even outshine their German models.

8

THE INDEPENDENT VOYAGER:
"WESTWARD THE COURSE OF EMPIRE"

Even when the tide of emigration set out to the "Pike's Peak gold region" hundreds of the multitude believed that a long, waterless, nearly barren, dangerous stretch of country lay before them. As they proceeded along the way they were in daily anticipation of reaching before nightfall the region that the school-book pictures of their youthful days would make as familiar to them as the faces of their oldest friends. While the journey was tiresome, trying, and attended by hardships for many, and disastrous to some, the desert devotees could hardly believe their eyes when they saw the whitened peaks of the great mountains shining in the distant horizon, before they had yet traversed the stony, lonely, sandy, cactus-grown waste they had been taught to believe was one of the imperishable institutions of their country.

They had crossed the desert without knowing it or seeing it; the rolling plains swarmed with wild animals flourishing on the herbage there; their own cattle had subsisted on the wayside grasses through the length of their journey; they had not personally suffered anything much more serious than they would have endured in a similar trip; . . . and here they were, this soft, balmy June day, at the base of the mountains in a region of surpassing grandeur, beauty and fertility. Yet, when they started, in common with the friends they left behind them, many of this host believed they had entered upon an undertaking about as dangerous, as uncertain in its outcome, as we of these days are taught to regard an expedition to the North Pole. —Jerome Smiley[1]

AMONG the flood of immigrants—future settlers, spectators, and promoters—who ventured across the plains after the Civil War were a number of artists, assiduously filling their portfolios with sketches of nature's creations and scenes of the new frontier. Those adventuresome pioneer artists, who willingly submitted themselves to the arduous and dangerous trek through the wilderness by stagecoach and wagon, fit many descriptions: part-time prospectors, lured by recurrent gold and silver strikes; illustrator-journalists, sent west to provide firsthand pictorial records for illustrated newspapers and magazines; and independent voyagers, both painters and illustrators, in pursuit of strange and picturesque primeval scenery. They were forced to follow prescribed routes over the plains and mountains under the cloak of government protection, but thanks to the inauguration of the transcontinental railroad in 1869 and the diminishing threat of Indian hostilities, their successors in the 1870s and 1880s were free to crisscross the western half of the continent, discovering new sites for themselves.

For many midnineteenth-century Americans and Europeans the American West had become a popular subject. Both imaginary and factual reportage drawn from such varied sources as government exploratory reports, travelers' journals, and illustrated publications undoubtedly contributed to the enlightenment of the public's view of the West and its future as "the last, the greatest, the most glorious, wealthy and powerful empire in the world."[2] The earlier "desert myth"—that a vast tract of uninhabitable and uncultivable land lay between the 98th meridian and the Rocky Mountains—had gradually been dispelled after further explorations and the scientific observations of the many expedition parties that followed Long's journey to the Rockies: "Writers such as Josiah Gregg, chronicler of the Santa Fe trade, and John C. Frémont argued that the abundance of natural grasses made the area not an American desert but the Great Western Prairie." In 1850, William Gilpin, Colorado's first territorial governor, who journeyed west with Frémont in 1843, publicly shared and supported their views that "lands beyond the 98th meridian were in fact the 'Pastoral Garden of the world.'"[3] At a later date author-confreres like Bayard Taylor and Samuel Bowles joined these voices in paying tribute to "the future Switzerland of America." Their travel journals described the splendors of America's wilderness in efflorescent terms while praising the therapeutic nature of its climate: ". . . an air more delicious to breathe can scarcely be found anywhere. . . . [it] seems to support all one's happiest and healthiest moods."[4] Remarks like these unquestionably tempted many prospective travelers westward "to uplift their spirits through the sublime and the curious [and] to cure their bodies by exposure to [the salutary] climate."[5]

Just as "boosterism, promotion, and entrepreneurship" were responsible for encouraging and accelerating future settlements and industrial development in the West, artists' pictures, along with photographs, were equally effective in publicizing the West—particularly as a scenic mecca. Paintings of majestic and towering mountain peaks, cascades, pools, and verdant meadows stirred the emotions of Americans and Europeans alike and enticed many to join the movement westward—either in pursuit of beauty or purely as a recreational venture. Such awe-inspiring scenes of natural grandeur undoubtedly persuaded many artists to forgo the grand tour of Europe with its hackneyed views of antiquity for the fresh creations of the West.

Many artists were lured there solely by the sensational popularity and financial success of Bierstadt's large-scale, dramatic renditions of the Rockies and other western scenes. Accustomed to the smaller-scaled and less dramatic scenery of their eastern haunts, many were ill-prepared to meet the challenges of the majestic peaks. Although some artists did succeed in adapting their modes to the novel landscape, many found it difficult to crowd this vast western panorama onto their small canvases.

For many who made the journey west, the experience proved less than inspiring. Some tourists and artists, expecting Bierstadt's exaggerated peaks, peculiar light, and atmosphere, were disenchanted when they found

> no upper world of unbroken snow, as in the Bernese Oberland; no glaciers, thrusting far down between the forests their ever-moving fronts of ice; no contrasts of rich and splendid vegetation in the valleys; no flashing waterfalls; no slopes of bright green pasturage; no moss; and but rarely the gleam of lakes and rivers, seen from above.[6]

Nevertheless, by the eighties the trails across the Rockies had been well traveled by a continuous stream of artists and other itinerants. These independent travelers conformed for the most part to an earlier pattern established by their predecessors in the eastern wilds: they returned to their studios to transform their sketches or studies into finished works of art. A great number of these paintings, mostly by artists of recognized merit, were reproduced and published as embellishments to the varied travel literature of the day. Many were not even firsthand pictorial records; some were redrawn from artists' sketches or engravings, and others were merely mythical views drawn from the imagination. Of varying quality and types, the pictures produced after the Civil War reflect the diverse backgrounds, orientations, and painterly techniques of the artists, while demonstrating that they were discovering the beauty of the West and arousing the public's interest in its natural wonders.

Paradoxically, while the Union was locked in an intense and bloody struggle to decide its very existence, its government was pondering the question of decorations for the Capitol's new extension. For some time the celebrated German-American artist Emanuel Leutze had been working out a design for a mural illustrative of American expansion in the West—a subject that embodied in visual images the artist's own democratic ideals and "personal vision of the destiny that the New World–Promised Land was to fulfill."[7] Having submitted a sketch of this idea, he was awarded the coveted national commission on July 9, 1861.[8] Shortly thereafter, Leutze departed for the Colorado Rockies to gather additional material and information before beginning work on his mural, *Westward the Course of Empire Takes Its Way.*[9]

Why the artist decided to travel west at this point is somewhat baffling, since, except for some minor changes and the inclusion of additional figures and details, the design of the finished mural is essentially the same as that of the preliminary oil sketch (color plate 29).[10] Even the treatment of the terrain (the Rockies) and of the suggested limitless space fading into the distant waters of the Pacific is similarly idealized in both works. Perhaps, as Virgil Barker has suggested, Leutze traveled to the Rocky Mountains to reassure himself that the scenery had "the literal kind of accuracy then necessary to every history picture." Yet, according to Barker, the composite finished work "must be judged in terms of the theater": overly infused with the artist's visual excitement, mountains gesticulate along with human beings.[11] For Leutze the scenery undoubtedly served chiefly as a stage for the heroic actions of his pioneers, who were carrying out "the providential mission of the American people to extend their system across the hallowed land" to provide "asylum and opportunity for the oppressed of Europe."[12]

Leutze's arrival in Denver was announced by the *Rocky Mountain News* on August 24, 1861. Apparently he left immediately for Central City, where he spent about two weeks making sketches of the gold region, its mountain scenery, and frontier life.[13] It is highly probable that this well-publicized gold-mining region represented to him the excitement, speculation, and promise of wealth that the prospectors experienced while staking out their claims in the wilderness. Although the Denver press reported that a number of sketches resulted from the artist's sojourn in the mountains, only two watercolor drawings of mining in Central City have come to light. Coming from an artist who was better known for his great pictures of dramatic episodes from history and his political radicalism, these drawings offer a refreshing contrast. Unlike his labored works in oil, the two watercolors demonstrate Leutze's spontaneous and effective handling of the lighter medium. Even though there are a well-controlled buildup of light and dark areas and a precise handling of details in both, their sparkling and lively quality indicates that they were probably worked up on the spot. As was typical of his other watercolor studies, they illustrate recognizable places of topographical interest. *Gregory Extension/Central City/Colorado Territory/August 28th 1861* is easily identifiable from photographs taken in the gold fields during the summer of 1859 and later reproduced as woodcuts in *Leslies.*[14] The other drawing, the more finished of the two, shows a typical placer-mining operation with the prospector's log cabin nearby (plate 74). Surprisingly, neither scene was incorporated into the final mural.

Sometime after his return to Washington, Leutze produced another picture inspired by his Colorado sojourn, this time in oil. *Prairie Bluffs at Julesburg, South Platte, Storm at Sunset,* reflects familiar Düsseldorfian trappings.[15] Its lurid colors, idealized forms, and dramatic action come from the realm of narrative painting. Although Leutze traveled along the South Platte to Denver, it is doubtful that he constructed this view from firsthand experience. As his biographer, Barbara Groseclose, has aptly stated, the paintings of Indians he created late in his career were inspired less by the knowledge acquired during his trip west "than by his contemporaries and former Düsseldorf associates, Albert Bierstadt and Charles Wimar."[16] Perhaps Leutze was recalling the pictures of wild horses by the early Amerind painters who, like Catlin, actually witnessed such scenes.

As Leutze demonstrated in his small topographical watercolors of

PLATE 74
Emanuel Leutze, *Gulch Mine, Central City, Colorado*, 1861, Watercolor, 15″ × 20″.
Courtesy Denver Public Library, Western History Department, Denver. Whereabouts of original unknown.

Colorado's gold country, he could also be a competent painter of landscapes. Although the land figures prominently in many of the artist's paintings, his work reflects a greater concern with life itself and with episodes from history related to the cause of freedom. Nevertheless, Leutze's concern for the accuracy of his western terrain gave him the distinction of being the first professional artist to discover Colorado's scenic beauties, antedating Bierstadt's arrival by two years.

Among the several artists who had crossed the plains to the Rocky Mountains in the summer of 1866 was the portrait and animal painter William Holbrook Beard,[17] traveling companion of the writer-lecturer Bayard Taylor. In his book *Colorado: A Summer Trip*,[18] Taylor describes their journey of four hundred miles on horseback through the wild mountain country beyond Denver, which led them through several mining camps, across Middle Park and South Park, and thrice over the divide of the great range. During their travels they were introduced to the distinctive scenic and climatic features of the region and became convinced that Colorado was destined to become "the future Switzerland of America." They did little or no sketching, however; the discomfitures of western travel left them too "fatigued and demoralized" to capture the views Taylor described so eloquently.[19]

Unlike artists who dealt with human or animal activity in preference to the landscape, Beard found that the western scene was, in his own words, wanting in real "Western characters." Unlike his former Düsseldorf associates Bierstadt and Leutze, who had led the way westward, Beard was probably more interested in the acquisition of material for his limited repertoire (satirical humanizations of animals) so that he missed the opportunity to discover fresh subjects or formulate new ideas. His disenchantment is summed up in a letter to his wife from Denver:

> I think I shall go back to the States and make some sketches of different things much more useful to me than any thing I can get here. The fact is I am disappointed in the Rocky Mountains somewhat. Still I am very glad I came I have seen some grand things and I would not take anything for my experience, but I would not *like to go through with it again.*[20]

This is also borne out by the fact that no studies or paintings resulting from this trip have yet been discovered.[21] Beard's negative attitude toward the West, so uncharacteristic of the many western voyagers, once again is reaffirmed in his own words upon returning to the States:

> Thank God here I am again in a land of civilization! I have had more than enough of wild life and its hardships. I suppose its [*sic*] all well enough for those who are used to it, and like it but I have been too long accustomed to the comforts of civilization to enjoy wild life and Indian Society.[22]

Worthington Whittredge, who also visited the Rocky Mountains in the summer of 1866,[23] viewed the plains-mountain country somewhat differently. His fond memories of boyhood rambles in the thickets of the Ohio forests lured him in his later life to the primitive wilds of the West, and he seized upon the opportunity to join Major General John Pope on a tour of inspection through present-day Colorado and New Mexico. This trip and two subsequent trips west, one in 1870 with artists John F. Kensett and Sanford Gifford, and the other in the following year,[24] provided Whittredge with many vivid impressions and a rich legacy of material for his art.

As a self-proclaimed member of the Hudson River School and a lover of the simple and unpretentious in nature, Whittredge was, unlike his fellow artist Bierstadt, deeply impressed with the plains, caring "more for them than for the mountains." "Whoever crossed the plains at that period," he noted, "notwithstanding its herds of buffalo and flocks of antelope, its wild horses, deer and fleet rabbits, could hardly fail to be impressed with its vastness and silence and the appearance everywhere of an innocent, primitive existence." The studies and finished paintings that resulted from his three western trips seem to reflect his ardent love of the gentler and quieter aspects of nature, despite the several large mountainscapes that he produced during the 1850s while studying abroad in Düsseldorf and Rome. In most of his western pictures the plains figure prominently, with the distant snowcapped mountains providing a suitable backdrop—verifying the artist's statement that very few of his pictures were "produced from sketches made in the mountains."[25]

It is questionable whether Whittredge's study and sketching tours in Germany, Switzerland, and Italy actually prepared him for representing the western-plains scenery; it is certain, however, that they helped expand his vision beyond that of his early Cole-inspired landscapes, drawn from the scenery of his native Ohio.[26] Although he had been exposed to many artistic modes and techniques throughout his travels in Europe from 1849 to 1859, his work of that period reflects the influence of the Düsseldorf School. The artist's extant German and Swiss mountainscapes of the 1850s with their historic and legendary associations reveal Whittredge's debt to his Düsseldorfian mentor Karl Friedrich Lessing.[27] The sober tone, the ponderous handling, and the tight insistence on details that characterize these landscapes seem to suggest a conscious emulation of Lessing's style and treatment of similar subject matter, particularly his painting *Fight Below the Battlements*.[28] On the other hand, Whittredge's *Landscape near Minden* (1855) mirrors the early idealized Italianate forest compositions of the German landscapist Johann Schirmer.[29] Throughout his artistic career groves of trees provided a challenge to Whittredge's brush, obviously appealing to his poetic sensibilities and pastoral vision.

Although the artist painted several pictures of Swiss alpine scenery, he nonetheless found the subject unsuitable to his temperament. As he remarked nearly forty years later in his *Autobiography*, "My thoughts ran more upon simple scenes and simple subjects, or it may be I never got into the way of measuring all grandeur in a perpendicular line." It was on the western plains, he recalled later, that he discovered that grandeur might be measured horizontally.[30] As Anthony Janson has pointed out, most of the artist's oil sketches of 1866 "were painted on easily portable half-sheets of paper roughly 10 x 23 inches in size," an ideal format for sketches that "deal almost exclusively with the plains and similar terrain rather than the mountains." Several extant western sketches from this trip, however, illustrate other subjects, mountains among them—for example, *Santa Fé, Pecos Church* (New Mexico), and *Spanish Peaks from Raton Pass* [*in the Sangre de Cristo Mountains*].[31]

Shortly after his return home Whittredge hinted at a possible motive for his western trips, undertaken at the height of his involvement with the Hudson River School and the New York art scene:

I soon found myself in working traces but it was the most crucial period of my life. It was impossible for me to shut out from my eyes the works of the great landscape painters which I had so recently seen in Europe, while I knew well enough that if I was to succeed I must produce something new and which might claim to be inspired by my home surroundings.[32]

Initially he turned to the Catskills but found it difficult to adjust to their "mass of decaying logs and tangled brush wood" after the "well-ordered forests" of Europe. No doubt aware of the success and fame that Bierstadt had achieved with his western paintings, Whittredge was persuaded to assay his luck in the West. The number of extant sketches produced during his first trip west evince his interest in the changing panorama that he observed while touring with Pope and his entourage. These small gems of nature show the true character of the country, demonstrating the artist's careful attention to detail and his close observation of color, light, and atmosphere. In spite of their small scale, Whittredge has achieved in them a sense of painterly breadth by broadly and rapidly brushing in his forms. Both his early field studies and those of the 1870s, which show an even greater sense of freedom of brushwork as well as a lighter palette, have a freshness and vitality that is missing from most of his larger, more finished western paintings, which are marred by the tighter handling and hard coloring of the Düsseldorf School.

From his early extant sketches we are able to chart roughly the artist's itinerary, since several of them are inscribed with place-names and dates: *Spanish Peaks from Raton Pass* (1866, color plate 30); *Junction of the Platte Rivers/June 1866;* and *Santa Fe/July 20th 1866* (plate 75).[33] They also illustrate the variety of subject matter the artist recorded along the way: scenes of encampment, grazing animals on the plains, views of Long's Peak (from near present-day Fort Morgan), Pikes Peak, and the mountains from the Platte River near Denver, among others.[34] The last was probably the original model for Whittredge's famous painting *Crossing the Ford—Platte River, Colorado* (1868 and 1870, originally titled *Plains at the Base of the Rocky Mountains*, see color plate 31). Of greater topographical interest is the artist's sketch of Santa Fe, which depicts the old town accurately and in detail.[35] The small sketch served later as a model for a larger and more elaborate version of the same subject, painted

211

PLATE 75

Thomas Worthington Whittredge, *Santa Fe/July 20th 1866*, Oil, 8″ × 23⅛″.
Courtesy Yale University Art Gallery, New Haven, Conn. Lent by Peabody Museum.

in 1868.[36] Several of Whittredge's sketches of 1866 found their way into the collection of Othniel Charles Marsh, professor of paleontology in the Yale Scientific School and director of the Peabody Museum. It is possible that Marsh made the arrangements for Whittredge to accompany Pope since the military had supported several of Yale's scientific expeditions under his leadership.[37]

Shortly after his return to New York, Whittredge began translating his small field sketches into more finished pieces on canvas. During that time a New York reporter observed the artist at work on his epic western scene *Plains at the Base of the Rocky Mountains* (later entitled *Crossing the Ford*), providing us with our first knowledge of the picture through the eyes of a contemporary critic:

Entering the studio of Mr. Whittredge our first admiration is given to the patriarchal beard of the artist. . . .The prominent picture this afternoon soars mighty in proportions above the modest little study for it standing below. The scene represents the plains near Denver City, with the mountains rising into snowy heights. Indians are encamping in picturesque tents under the trees, before which slowly glides, over sandy bottom, a quiet river. The sand and the grass harmoniously alternate in giving the artist soft patches of color. The study would be to some more interesting as being a defiant little bit of form and color, not softened by the warm atmosphere of the great picture above, nor brightened by the light and color in the wigwams and figures, nor made more tender and graceful in form by art.[38]

Although his preparatory study for the large picture is still missing (sketched from near their camping grounds at Fort Lupton, just north of Denver), a slightly larger and more finished version titled *Indians Crossing the Platte* (1867)[39] does exist for comparison; it departs from the larger picture only in that the scene is captured here at twilight. In this small painting Whittredge has successfully manipulated light and heightened its effects to evoke a sense of mystery and an elegiac mood—perhaps hoping to rouse a responsive chord for the "Vanishing American," though he shared Pope's distrust of the Indian.[40] In achieving the visual impact of this small-scaled but spacious panorama, the artist has essentially adopted the luminist format of parallel planes of sky, land, and water dominated by light and executed in a smooth finish without traces of the artist's hand. Here the glowing evening sky and ominously dark trees are reflected in the translucent waters, evoking a feeling of calm and solitude. Even the presence of the Indian fails to disturb the tranquility, perhaps reinforcing the idea of the red man's personal and harmonious relationship with nature before the advent of the white man. Although the artist has explored a number of pictorial possibilities for idealizing his composition, he has preserved the specificity of place in his enlarged version: both paintings view Long's Peak from across the South Platte River near Denver.

By choosing to represent his large picture in full sunlight with softer atmospheric effects, Whittredge has failed to achieve the visual impact and drama of the smaller scene. Although the artist has employed the same academic formula in laying out his composition, he has lightened his palette and applied a freer and fuller brush, evincing the change in direction—basically toward a more realistic approach to nature—that characterizes his western scenes of the 1870s. Throughout most of the 1870s, Whittredge continued to paint variations, small and large, of this same subject, using increasingly freer brushwork and subtle nuances of color to capture the fugitive effects of nature so typical of the plains-mountain country.

Crossing the Ford, which bears two signatures and dates, was completed in 1868 and revised by the artist in 1870. Apparently Whittredge considered the picture finished in 1868, for he exhibited it that year at the National Academy of Design and the Brooklyn Art Association.[41] Despite enthusiastic reviews the painting failed to attract a purchaser; it was probably then that Whittredge became displeased with his rendering of a clump of cottonwood trees bordering the river and arranged to undertake a second trip to the Rocky Mountains to sketch a group of trees he remembered observing on the Cache la Poudre River, believing that they would improve his picture.[42] In July, 1870, the artist, accompanied by his friends Kensett and Gifford, left for Denver by train. From there the trio traveled by coach through the adjacent mountains as far west as Loveland Pass, sketching along the way.[43] On August 2, Gifford left them to join Hayden on his geological survey of the territory of Wyoming.[44] Because of several of Whittredge's and Kensett's extant sketches,[45] inscribed with place-names and dates, we can surmise that the pair continued traveling north along the base of the mountains, then headed northeast to Greeley, where Whittredge sketched the cottonwoods he remembered.[46] At the end of September they packed up their sketch boxes and headed back to New York.

To judge by the number of plein-air oil studies made by Kensett and Whittredge, the summer's sketching trip in Colorado proved to be a productive and rewarding one for both artists. Although Whittredge produced many studies on the plains as well as in the mountains, these appear to have engaged his total attention. Instead of presenting a panorama of the plains-mountain country, they focus closely on the foreground area, showing Indians engaged in various activities along a river bordered by large cottonwoods whose spreading foliage screens out most of the vista beyond. Interestingly enough, *Crossing the Ford* was engraved before the repainting was done, allowing us to pinpoint minor alterations in the later version.[47] They consist mainly of the repainting of the clumps of cottonwoods bordering the river bank, which are now more fully and convincingly modeled as powerful natural forms compared with the flabbily rendered trunks in the first version. The new treatment is also seen in the small revised studies, indicating that the artist now had a better understanding of structure and a greater knowledge of the subtleties and complexities of light, color, and atmosphere. These stylistic changes provide the key for distinguishing between Whittredge's early landscapes and those of the 1870s.

In June, 1871, Whittredge revisited Colorado, this time traveling alone. His third and final trip to the West led him to Denver and adjacent areas and then north to Greeley, where once again he sketched along the Platte, Thompson, Saint Vrain, and Cache la Poudre rivers. His wanderings did not go unobserved by a reporter of the *Greeley Tribune:*

> Whittredge, a New York artist of no little celebrity . . . has been stopping several weeks in our town, making sketches of mountain and river scenery. Unfortunately, the view of the mountains has been obstructed most of the time by a smoky atmosphere. A few sunsets, however, have been gorgeous, and these he has seized with marked success. The sketches made have been from various points along the river, and several in the neighbor hood [*sic*] of the island. A large cotton wood has been sketched and partly painted, and it now looks as though it would become a remarkably fine picture.
>
> . . . Whittredge was in Colorado last year, and as a result of his investigations he decided that there were no more beautiful mountain views, than from the valley of the Cache la Poudre and the Platte. Probably no locality is more striking than on the Platte, near the mouth of the St. Vrain, as here, Long's Peak is seen to the greatest advantage. His several pictures of this mountain are remarkably exact, while the breadth and grandeur of the scene are preserved. . . . Some of his views of the Cache la Poudre are charming, for there can be no more picturesque stream in the world; these, however, have been painted this summer, and are not wholly completed.
>
> This is a field almost wholly new to artists, for those who visit Colorado seem to think no studies worthy their attention below the mountains. With rare and good judgment, . . . Whittredge has lingered lovingly along the Cache la Poudre, the Thompson, St. Vrain and Platte, and he has reproduced some of their loveliest aspects. Still, there are many rare nooks, vales and points which he has been unable to visit, and they are left to others, who have been shown the way; and for all time, this valley region, between Greeley and Platte Canyon, and the mountains, must furnish favorable points where artists shall delight to take their stand.[48]

Certainly no observer was more enthusiastic about Whittredge's visit to Colorado and its results. Like other Colorado boosters of his day, however, the reporter was probably using this occasion to advertise that the area's wealth of scenery was worthy of a visit. The article is also helpful to some degree in dating some of Whittredge's western pictures, and, more important, it reaffirms the time of the artist's

third visit, a date merely hinted at in his single remaining pencil sketch of a cottonwood tree with the inscription "Platte River June 23/1871."[49]

Of Whittredge's many views of Long's Peak, three might be singled out as resulting from his second trip: two obviously plein-air studies and another large Indian encampment scene beside a river.[50] In these pictures, unlike most of his other views, the lofty peak faces the observer, towering above the surrounding mountains and occupying a prominent position in the composition, with traces of snow visible only in its storm-riven clefts. In the small studies (which the reporter may have seen) the artist has moved in more closely to capture his view. Both are similar except for minor embellishments—in one, mounted Indians at the river's edge with tipis in the distance; in the other, wild ducks visible in the gray water and on the brown, sandy banks. The large oil, also called *Crossing the Ford,* is a more distant view of Long's Peak, probably taken from farther out on the South Platte, near Platteville. It is a variation on the Indian encampment theme but shows obvious similarities to the first large *Crossing the Ford* (1868 and 1870) in both composition and technique, suggesting that it dates from the same time period. Although the small studies show a bit more pleinairism, they are stylistically close to the second large Indian encampment painting and therefore belong to its time period.

Although quite a few of Whittredge's recorded oil studies have not yet come to light,[51] many exist to reveal the variety and richness of his expression. One small scene, *On the Platte,* taken near Greeley, markedly shows the influence of the Barbizon School, particularly in the simplified, broadly brushed handling of the trees and thick grasses fringing the river.[52] Flecks of opaque color in the fields and in the clothing of the small Indian figures highlight the cool, grayed color scheme, another feature that reflects the inspiration of Barbizon painters such as Jean Corot and Charles Daubigny.[53] Like the older European painters, Whittredge had a consuming interest in translating his intimate pastoral scene—or the poetry of it—into a harmony of tone and color, though he never totally removed the distinguishing features of his view. Proto-impressionistic tendencies are also noticeable in his study *The Foothills . . . from Valmont*

Valley,[54] but the small canvas, like all his other western pictures, exhibits a structural firmness and a clear natural light that calls to mind his strong leaning toward objective realism. Another view, *Valmont Valley*,[55] probably executed at a later date, demonstrates a more airy naturalism. Here he captures his subject in full sunlight with spontaneous brushwork that conveys immediacy and directness. In addition to these studies focusing chiefly on the plains, Whittredge produced several small oil sketches in the mountains (plates 76 and 77). All are similarly characterized by well-modulated tonalities of pink, brown, green, and yellow; broad brushwork; and subtle effects of light and atmosphere.[56]

The immediacy and spontaneity of the artist's vision can also be observed in a small oil sketch of a large cottonwood tree taken on the plains near the Platte (plate 78). Of particular interest is the textural suggestion of bark rendered in short strokes of broken color and light, in direct contrast to the flat, controlled brushwork treatment of the tree trunks in his earlier work. It is obvious that this picture relates stylistically to his small pencil sketch of the cottonwood with its textural references and probably also dates from his third trip, evidencing his increasing knowledge of color, light, and texture.

Whittredge's culminating achievement as a landscapist of western subjects is fully realized in his large, masterful painting *Cottonwoods on the St. Vrain Creek [Cache la Poudre River]*. Here towering woodland patriarchs arch over the stream, which winds its way through fields of flowering grasses. Beyond are snowcapped mountains, veiled in hazy light. In the midst of this sacred grove deer lazily graze and rest, adding to the feeling of tranquillity and repose. In a lovingly tender manner the artist has impressionistically brushed in the plush earth carpet and the massive tree foliage with opaque color and light, breaking them up somewhat to let the eye penetrate their depths. In his overall handling of color, light, and atmosphere, Whittredge never loses sight of the peculiar character of the land or allows his local colors to recede into generalized tones; he is first and foremost a realist whose love for the woods is passionately expressed here.

A smaller version of this subject has recently been discovered in a private collection (color plate 32), promptly raising the question which is the original. Although there is no history on either picture, it is logical to assume that the smaller version was one of the "unfinished" Cache la Poudre views observed by the Greeley reporter in 1871 and therefore the model for the large painting. The two pictures are almost identical compositions except for a few minor details. The small picture, unquestionably finished in the artist's studio, exhibits the same freedom of brushwork and effective overall treatment of the subject.

Six years after his third trip to the Rocky Mountains, Whittredge painted his last known western scene, *On the Plains*.[57] The picture, marking the twilight of his western career, lacks the definition and vitality of his former work. At this point the artist was evidently too far removed from the actual subject; marriage had "checked his wanderings,"[58] and he had turned his attention to painting the "wide stretches of forest land" and the "rich meadow lands along the Passaic" near his home in Summit, New Jersey.

Whittredge's fondness for the plains-mountain country is, however, reflected in a letter he wrote to the *Greeley Tribune* on May 22, 1871:

> Dear Sir:—I received your bright little paper, for which I wish to return my thanks. It contains information both useful to me, and quite inspiring. Being an artist, I take a particular interest in whatever relates to the appearance of the landscape round about you, having never seen the Rocky Mountains at this season, although I am well acquainted with them and with your particular locality. I have spent two or three [*sic*] summers in making sketches near Greeley, and I have obtained several pictures from them which I have found produced considerable interest from the public. Your position in regard to the distance from the snowy range is an admirable one, being, according to my judgement, just far enough away from them to get sufficient intervening plain, and yet, to see the mountains in that mysterious detail which, to me, is so captivating. I distinctly remember the spot, and the many gorgeous sunsets that I have seen there, more gorgeous and beautiful I think, than anything ever witnessed on the world renowned Campagna of Rome. Those who have claimed so much for the atmosphere of Italy, never saw the atmosphere of our plains near the mountains, and it is pretty evident that they never dreamed of it, for they spent all their energies in glorifying what was around them, and declaring that there

PLATE 76

Thomas Worthington Whittredge, *In the Rockies* [*Bergen Park, Colorado*], 1870, Oil, 14½″ × 20″.
Courtesy Harmsen's Western Americana Collection, Denver, Colo.

PLATE 77

Thomas Worthington Whittredge, *Table Mountain near Golden, Colorado*, ca. 1870, Oil, 15″ × 23″.
Courtesy Kennedy Galleries, Inc., New York City.

PLATE 78

Thomas Worthington Whittredge, *On the Platte River, Col.*, ca. 1871, Oil, 9¼″ × 18″.
Photograph courtesy of Victor Spark, New York City, New York. Collection of Hirsch & Adler Galleries, New York City.

was nothing else in this world like it. . . . We need age, historical associations, and great poets and painters to make our land as renowned as the ash heaps of the Old World; but we need nothing of this kind to enjoy its beautiful scenery when it is before our eyes, if we will but strip ourselves of old prejudices, and use our common senses.

I expect to see you soon. I am glad there is a "west window" in Barnum's hotel, where I can look at the sunsets. I suppose I can shoot antelope out of the window, but if they have become shy in the town limits, I will try and content myself with shooting at the sunsets with my brushes. Truly yours,

W. W. WHITTREDGE.[59]

Time, distance, events, and even fate had removed Whittredge far from the West he loved, but his pictures of the plains were to provide indelible impressions on the American mind, transforming the rugged, primitive country into an "Arcadian landscape" when seen through his eyes.

John F. Kensett, the second member of the Hudson River School triumvirate, journeyed to the Rocky Mountains in 1870.[60] He brought with him his own inimitable style of working, seeking out the less sensational and dramatic subjects as the focus for his simple, gentle art. Like Whittredge, Kensett measured grandeur "horizontally" and saw nature through the eyes of a poet, painting his subjects accordingly—though with less vitality or vigor than that of his fellow artist. Both men were careful observers of the specifics of nature, capturing local character with verisimilitude; indeed, Kensett at times became too involved with minutiae, losing sight of the larger objective—the broad compositional powers of his picture. This trait is reflected to some extent in his western studies. It has often been said that his work reveals the "sweet serenity" and gentleness of his nature.[61] That is certainly true of his Colorado studies, which are charming and full of sentiment but lack the breadth of touch that characterizes his mature work. In mood and vision these pictorial recordings remind one more of the homely subjects painted by the Hudson River School artists. It is evident that Kensett's attitude and treatment of the plains-and-mountain country was largely unaffected by the unique character and spirit of the western terrain.

Although Kensett produced a few large paintings of Colorado scenery, most of the work that remains from this sojourn is in the form of small oil studies and pencil sketches.[62] Typically, the artist has freely and sketchily brushed in his forms to record quickly the local character, color, and light. Apart from the proto-impressionistic scumble notating light and texture surfaces, his pigment is applied rather thinly and is drab in tone. Most of the views emphasize the gentler aspects of nature, playing down the dramatic effects of warring elements. The unfinished state of these oil studies indicates that the artist considered them not as "works of art in themselves" but as ideas to jog his memory. This assumption is supported by the preserved preliminary pencil sketch and oil study for his large painting *Snowy Range and Foot Hills from the Valley of Valmount* [sic], *Colorado*,[63] now lost but photographed and recorded in the sale of 1873 of his previous summer's work. In transferring his delicate and precise pencil sketch onto canvas, he has faithfully followed its design without manipulating elements for added pictorial effects. The two oil versions exhibit a rather dry, unimaginative treatment of the subject, lacking the subtle nuances of color and light evidenced in his mature work, whereas the small linear drawing conveys an immediate impression of the area's vastness and solitude. With sensitivity and economy of means Kensett has successfully organized his composition to show breadth and space, while capturing the fleeting mood of the scene, the "sweet serenity" and the warm sunlight reflected on the translucent water.

The dense groves of evergreens in and around Bergen Park also offered picturesque prospects for Kensett's brush (plate 79).[64] From an elevated position the artist captured sweeping views of these dense patches of green in the high-meadow country with the snowy peaks beyond. These small, unfinished oil sketches in drab color tones are not particularly interesting; there is none of the marvelous light-filled atmosphere and subtle nuances of color found in his small paintings of the eastern lake country, and one does not sense the true spirit of the rugged mountain country—a spirit that Whittredge successfully captured in his small studies. Although these comments generally apply to most of the small studies Kensett made in Colorado, an exception exists: his small, appealing picture, poetically retitled by the former owner *In the Heart of the Rockies [Bergen Park]*

(color plate 33), which calls forth the immediacy of the moment through closeness of view, casualness of arrangement, and sketchy daubing of pigment. Through painterly effects and contrasts of light and shadow Kensett gives pleasing and animated life to this forest landscape.

As has been noted, Kensett's small field sketches also served as models for his large western compositional arrangements. In all probability his large painting *Scene near Greeley, Colorado* (plate 80)[65] was also based on such preliminary studies, which were either destroyed or lost. Of all Kensett's large mature works only this scene—of the cottonwoods near Greeley—fails to live up to the artist's high standards of technique and compositional arrangement. The work seems to lack clarity of organization, selectivity of details, and subtle handling of aerial perspective.

Kensett seems to have been overwhelmed by the vast scale of the western country and could not quite accommodate his quiet, narrow art to the unique, bold shapes and colors of the Colorado landscape. His subtle touch somehow did not seem to match the mood and poetry of this rugged land. Since Kensett's death occurred only two years after his trip to the Rockies, one hesitates to make qualitative judgments about his western work. Given an additional few years, he might have grown to understand the spirit of this land and created western pictures with a greater breadth of vision, like those of his colleague Whittredge.

In 1873, Kensett's studio effects were auctioned off for the extraordinary sum of $136,312. The record sale was a public testimony to the popularity of both the artist and his work. Before the sale the pictures had been on exhibit at the National Academy of Design. According to one newspaper reviewer, the collection ran "upward of a thousand in all," filling the walls of all the rooms and drawing crowds of admirers.[66] A great number of the pictures in the collection were unfinished sketches, approximately forty-five of which were of Colorado scenery.[67] All the latter sold as well, indicating the popular demand for western illustration that had been stimulated by the proliferation of travel literature. It is reasonable to assume that this successful sale was not lost on Kensett's close friend

and colleague John W. Casilear,[68] and that it probably provided the impetus for his excursion to Colorado in June of that year.

Apart from Casilear's several pencil field sketches (at first attributed to Kensett) and his single finished painting, *The Rockies from near Greeley, Colorado* (plate 81), no information is available about this artist's western journey. We do know, however, that he was in and around Denver on June 23, 1873, according to an inscription on one of his small, delicate linear drawings, taken on gray-tinted paper and heightened with white. The sketch shows a panoramic view of the illimitable expanse of plains with grazing animals and a horseman bounded by the profiled front range and snow-crowned Long's Peak beyond.[69] With a light but clear hand the artist has quickly sketched in his view, suggesting details with a few carefully placed strokes of the pencil within a series of receding planes. Like Kensett's small pencil drawings, this sketch evinces the dry, crisp touch characteristic of an engraver's technique, betraying the artist's early experiences.

Another drawing, titled *Cottonwoods near Denver* (plate 82), shows the same technical treatment and should probably also be considered a memory notation rather than a finished work;[70] it may have served as one of the models for Casilear's large painting of a similar scene. The large picture is static and tightly composed, lacking the subtle nuances of light and shade seen in the smaller work. Although Casilear took careful notations of the local colors (inscribed on his single dated drawing), his palette is muddy and fails to convey the delicate tonal values and evanescent effects he observed while sketching on the plains: "Sky clear blue and subdued/Mountains of a delicate purplish gray/Foothills slightly more purplish but tan/Prairie brownish green. Decidedly reddish and grayish green lights."

It is apparent that Casilear, like Kensett, was at his best when his canvases were small and his subjects the picturesque and homely landscapes of his native eastern haunts. The unusually large proportions of his western picture seem to support this idea; the work fails to express the characteristic "sweetness of tone" and "serenity" that the public admired in his cabinet-size paintings. Perhaps Casilear had in mind the "great displays" of magnificent scenery painted

PLATE 80

John Kensett, *Scene near Greeley, Colorado,* ca. 1871, Oil, 36″ × 60″.
Courtesy Kennedy Galleries, Inc., New York City.

PLATE 81

John Casilear, *The Rockies from near Greeley, Colorado*, 1881, Oil, 24″ × 46″.
Courtesy Harmsen's Western Americana Collection, Denver.

PLATE 82

John Casilear, *Cottonwoods near Denver*, 1873, Pencil and chinese white, 10½″ × 17⅜″.
Courtesy Museum of Fine Arts, Boston.

by Church and Bierstadt when he created his scene near Greeley. Even as late as 1881, when the painting was on exhibit at the National Academy of Design, it had still failed to attract a buyer, which may have discouraged the artist from making another foray into the western field.[71]

For an artist like Sanford Robinson Gifford,[72] whose specialty lay in painting pictures with colored atmosphere of glowing mellow light or hot pinks, the monotonous, drab coloring of the plains-and-mountain country was apparently uninspiring, its vistas wanting in picturesque subjects. The small number of plein-air oil studies that resulted from his summer sketching tour in 1870 seem to reflect Gifford's disenchantment with the barren, rugged Colorado-Wyoming landscape. As Whittredge remarked:

> [Gifford] started fully equipped for work, but when he arrived there, where distances were deceptive, he became an easy prey to Col. Hayden, who offered him a horse. He left us and his sketch box in cold blood in the midst of inspiring scenery. We neither saw nor heard from him for several months, until one rainy day on the plains we met him travelling alone in the fog towards our ranch by the aid of his compass. He had done literally nothing in the way of work during a whole summer spent in a picturesque region. Yet we dare not say that he did not study.[73]

Like so many of the other travelers who went to the Rockies expecting to see "those delicious turfy glades [and] enameled banks, which beautify the mountains of our Atlantic slope," Gifford must have been disappointed to find the landscape "without a single patch of bright green" and "mountains ris[ing] up in rugged, brawny masses, without the apology of color for a nakedness."[74]

Gifford's suddenly leaving his fellow artists to join Hayden and his survey party on a tour through Wyoming seems to have been more to satisfy his scientific curiosity about the physical geology of the western terrain than to obtain material for his art. That he never elaborated his small studies of "geological landmarks" into finished paintings further suggests that the Rocky Mountain region failed to appeal to his artistic sensibilities and poetic sentiment.[75] To judge from his sketches, which, along with William Henry Jack-

son's photographs (plate 83), recorded the remarkable land formations along their route,[76] the geological character of this exotic country held more fascination and interest for him than did the artistic nature of its creations.

In his autobiography Jackson gives a broad picture of the party's activities, remarking that each member performed an important and vital role in the quest for scientific knowledge:

> It was those independent excursions, or, rather, the spirit beneath them, that made this expedition and all the ensuing ones under Dr. Hayden so engrossing and satisfying. Every day we had an informal conference around the campfire and then we would set about our work individually, or in groups of two or three. One little division might be assigned to calculate the flow volume of a stream; another would be given the task of sounding a lake; several other men might investigate the geology of the region or hunt fossils; Gifford, Elliot[t] [the staff artist], and I would go off to record our respective impressions of a striking landmark, like Independence Rock or the Red Buttes.[77]

Through Jackson's journal it is also possible to retrace the trio's steps and to discover the various "impressions" both men recorded on their daily excursions off the beaten track. The party proceeded northward from Cheyenne to Fort Laramie, then westward along the line of the Union Pacific Railroad to Fort Bridger, where Gifford left the group on September 15 to return home.[78]

Gifford is said to have made many fine studies, imbued with "much poetic feeling," during his journey on the plains and in the mountains; however, no contemporary evidence of them exists.[79] Thus far only three small oil studies from his Wyoming venture have been discovered, two of them among the seven recorded in a "memorial" exhibition catalog of his paintings.[80] Gifford's small study *Valley of the Chugwater, Wyoming Terr.* (color plate 34) reflects the interaction of science and art and might be considered a close visual equivalent of Jackson's photograph of a similar view (plate 84). Both men have selected the same "singular" sandstone-capped mass for their subject, but Gifford has cropped his foreground in an effort to capture the extensive tableland and plains beyond. His broad compositional powers, freely brushed-in forms, and rich earth-

Color Plate 29

Emanuel Leutze, *Westward the Course of Empire Takes its Way*, 1861, Oil, 33¼″ × 43⅜″.
Courtesy National Museum of American Art, Smithsonian Institution, Washington, D.C. Bequest of Sara Carr Upton.

COLOR PLATE 30

Thomas Worthington Whittredge, *Spanish Peaks from Raton Pass*,
1866, Oil, 7½″ × 23¼″. Courtesy Yale University Art Gallery,
New Haven, Conn. Gift of the estate of William W. Farnam.

COLOR PLATE 31

Thomas Worthington Whittredge, *Crossing the Ford—Platte
River, Colorado*, 1868 and 1870, Oil, 40¼″ × 69⅛″.
Courtesy Century Association, New York City.

COLOR PLATE 32

Thomas Worthington Whittredge, *On the Cache La Poudre*, ca. 1871, Oil, 15⅛″ × 22¾″.
Courtesy Jeffrey R. Brown Fine Arts, North Amherst, Mass.

COLOR PLATE 33

John F. Kensett, *In the Heart of the Rockies* [*Bergen Park*], 1870, Oil on paper, 10″ × 14″.
Courtesy Kennedy Galleries, Inc., New York City.

230

COLOR PLATE 34

Sanford Robinson Gifford, *Valley of the Chugwater, Wyoming Terr.*, 1870, Oil, 8¼″ × 13⅜″.
Courtesy Amon Carter Museum, Fort Worth.

231

Color Plate 35

Ralph Blakelock, *Rocky Mountains*, ca. 1870, Oil, 34¾″ × 55½″.
Courtesy Collection of the Berkshire Museum, Pittsfield, Mass.

Color Plate 36

Samuel Colman, *Emigrant Train Attacked by Indians*, ca. 1870, Gouache over pencil, 9½″ × 13″.
Courtesy Bancroft Library Collection, University of California, Berkeley, Calif.

COLOR PLATE 37

George Caleb Bingham, *View of Pike's Peak*, 1872, Oil, 28⅛″ × 42¼″.
Courtesy Amon Carter Museum, Fort Worth.

tone palette reveal a more aesthetic treatment of the subject. Jackson, on the other hand, was more interested in presenting a "truthful representation" of his subject as a tool for geologists.[81] Gifford's small, painterly version evokes a mood and atmosphere absent from Jackson's straightforward documentary record.

In 1869 the romantic visionary Ralph Albert Blakelock crossed the plains on a journey through the western section of America, traveling alone by train, stagecoach, and horse.[82] The extant small pencil-and-pen drawings that resulted from this tour, inscribed with place-names and a few dates, along with his autographed itinerary and map, disclose that the artist traveled across Kansas, Colorado, Wyoming, Utah, Nevada, and northern California.[83] Two separate groups of California drawings exist, dated 1869 and 1872—raising a question whether the artist remained in the West for the entire three years or made two separate trips there. Blakelock's small drawing *Central Park* is dated 1871,[84] implying that he made two trips, returning to New York that year. Additionally, his large finished painting *Indian Encampment along the Snake River [Idaho?]*, also dated 1871,[85] must certainly have been worked up in his New York studio—a piece of evidence that further supports this assumption. Whether or not he actually made a short detour into southern Idaho from the Bear River in Corinne, Utah,[86] is still a mystery; no other evidence exists to support this trip.

From his western experience Blakelock brought back themes that he was to treat subjectively throughout his career, even though the symbolic Indian, the remote plains and shadowy forests, and the luminous skies of his strange, romantic pictures are generally not traceable to specific geographic locations. One art historian has remarked, "[They are] discoverable only in the reaches of the mind. Objects materialize out of the dark scumbled paint, but threaten at any moment to return again into the shadows."[87] This is particularly true of his better-known works; however, a few of his early western paintings, based on small preliminary drawings and closely related in compositional arrangement and details, evince a somewhat more objective approach to the landscape, suggesting that he was still working within the linear tradition of the Hudson River School at this early stage. In these paintings, as in his small abbreviated and agitated pencil-and-pen sketches, Blakelock has captured the general configuration of the distinct landforms he encountered on his journeys. The continual struggle between linear and painterly traditions that marked his career is particularly evident in these early paintings of the Rocky Mountain landscape; they also exhibit a certain physical sense of the expressive and tactile quality of paint, a characteristic feature of his later, more mature work.

Several of his many drawings of the West are views of Clear Creek Canyon, near Golden City, Colorado.[88] Although the topography is recognizable, the artist has summarily sketched in the massive mountains, wooded areas, and river in short, broken, agitated pen or pencil strokes (in some drawings pencil overlaid with pen), seemingly seized by wild excitement in a moment of wonderment. Using economical means, he has indicated water with wavy or broken parallel lines, the sun's rays with slanted lines, and shadows with closely placed parallel lines. His system varies according to his compositional needs. Oftentimes color notations are given, as in *Green River, Wyoming*,[89] a pen-and-ink sketch of the eroded, exposed sandstone cliffs bounding the river. One sketch, *Rocky Mountains, Colorado*,[90] a profile view of Lookout Mountain from Golden City, includes a specific color "recipe" for the artist's future use: "Very delicate distance, perfectly graduated—light red hills dotted with brilliant lights"—a description of a scene obviously viewed in full sunlight. Blakelock's large painting *Rocky Mountains* (color plate 35) seems to carry out the careful color observations notated on his small drawing of Lookout Mountain; here, however, he has chosen to represent a view looking up Clear Creek Canyon, a composition taken from another field sketch in the same locality (plate 85).[91] Although the contours of the mountains retain the sharp, jagged line seen in the drawing, their volume is indicated by whirling pigment and linear movement created by scratching. The water, echoing the same restless movement, is made up of daubs of paint and broken line within a linear framework. Soft atmosphere, subtle glazes, and scumbles of pigment—the unifying agents of his later work—are used hesitantly here. Typical of his early involvement

PLATE 84

William H. Jackson, *Castellated Rocks on the Chugwater, S. R. Gifford, Artist,* 1870, Photograph, 8″ × 10″.
Courtesy Amon Carter Museum, Fort Worth, Texas.

PLATE 85

Ralph Blakelock, *Rocky Mountains/Colorado*, 1869, Pen and ink, 6″ × 9½″.
Courtesy Collection of Mr. and Mrs. T. Scanlon, Catskill, N.Y.

with linearism, the small cottonwoods are drawn with paint rather than suggested by the tactile quality of the medium.

Several other early pictures drawn from his observations and dim recollections of the plains-mountain country are *Western Landscape, Indian Encampment, Colorado Plains,* and *Run of the Buffalo,* a small oil study.[92] The first landscape shares an affinity in style and composition with the painting *Rocky Mountains* and was probably also completed in the early 1870s, shortly after his second trip to the West. The recent discovery of the small study showing a herd of buffalo on the plains with the snowy range beyond is unusual in its descriptive handling of the landscape. Blakelock has captured the undulating plains along the Smoky Hill route to Denver with its isolated tablelands. Once again daubs of varicolored pigment make up the terrain, while the small buffalo are summarily recorded in black. Stylistically, this picture belongs to the same time period as *Rocky Mountains.* On the other hand, his two Indian encampment scenes, built up with heavy application of impasto and full of ominous, forbidding atmospheric effects, seem to be lonely, nostalgic works of a later date. Typically, they are imbued with a melancholy spirit drawn from a visionary's mind rather than from direct observation.

Indian Encampment along the Snake River [*Idaho?*] is a strange and puzzling picture, even though it does share some affinities with other paintings.[93] It is a large, finished composition that evinces artistic license combined with realistic detail, raising some doubt whether the picture represents an actual place—one not recorded in the artist's penciled itinerary. Large foliated barbizonesque trees in the foreground lend a poetic note to a pastoral landscape. A blasted tree trunk, towering, ominous cliffs, and scattered grayish clouds lend a romantic aura to this picturesque work. Small, summarily treated Indians and a distant tipi encampment are dwarfed by wooded green areas, partly cast in shadows. In some ways one is reminded of the forests in the works of Barbizon artists Narcisse Virgile Díaz de La Peña and Jules Dupré, paintings that Blakelock undoubtedly had observed in either private or public collections or in illustrated periodicals.[94] Since there is no documentation of Blakelock's sources of inspiration, it is possible only to draw inferences from stylistic features of his work. In fact, the brooding, shadowy, luminous forests that characterize Blakelock's mature work have often been compared to similar treatments and subject matter by Adolphe Monticelli. Both exhibit layers of subtle glazes and scumbling, chiaroscuro effects, and a limited palette.[95]

Unlike Gifford, Blakelock drew from his western wanderings memories of the Indian and the wilder aspects of nature upon which he continually drew for his imaginative and expressively haunting pictures. His was a world of dreams—woodlands with small, lonely Indian encampments, lit by moonlight or twilight—far removed from the cruelties of the actual world.

In contrast, the evanescent play of light and color had a magnetic attraction for Samuel Colman,[96] an indefatigable traveler in search of variety in nature. His picturesque views of Venice, North Africa, Spain, and the American West display the exquisitely harmonious tints and dazzling light he found there.

Colman's sunset scenes showing clouds ablaze with yellow or pink light, silhouetted oriental-medieval architecture, and opalescent mist shimmering over the water seem to reflect the inspiration of Turner, with whose engravings the artist undoubtedly became acquainted in his father's New York bookstore, for its day a unique depository of fine objects of art and foreign literature. His western pictures—the weathered, castellated reddish cliffs carved by the Green River, emigrant trains crossing Medicine Bow Creek and the plains, and the Spanish Peaks—also exhibit coloristic tendencies reminiscent of the English master. Colman's *Twilight on the Western Plains*[97] is perhaps the best illustration of this tendency toward a primarily picturesque treatment of his subjects. By selecting a low horizon for his painting, the artist has directed the observer's attention to the dramatic, colorful sky at sunset—a spectacle commonly visible in the West, particularly on the open plains. His careful, naturalistic rendering of the arid fields demonstrates a fidelity to nature instilled in him by his teacher, Asher B. Durand.

As the first president of the American Society of Painters in Water Color, an organization that he helped found in 1866, Colman spent considerable time working in watercolor and handled it with the utmost competency. His sketches have a sparkling quality that reflects the artist's immediate response to his subject. In his small studies of the bluffs of Green River (plate 86), the Colorado Canyon, Colorado Springs and Cheyenne Mountain (plate 87), the Garden of the Gods, and scenes of New Mexico, he has broadly brushed in forms built up with washes of vivid colors, then carefully added descriptive details to convey local character. Like Moran, his watercolors capture subtle gradations of atmosphere and luminous colors, but they also tend at times to approximate the effect of a heavier medium in their opacity and textural insistence. Later in the 1890s his watercolors became rapid notations of color with abstracted forms—a sharp contrast to his earlier insistence on topographical definition.

During his many trips to the plains-mountain country beginning in May, 1870, Colman employed various media to record his impressions of the landscape and made assorted studies for his larger oils.[98] The latter include views of yoked oxen, mounted Indians, desert flowers, and wagon trains (color plate 36),[99] a number of which figure in large paintings like *Ships of the Western Plains*[100] and *Covered Wagons Crossing Medicine Bow Creek* [*Wyoming*]. Sketches executed in Denver in May and June, 1871, document one of his return visits to the West;[101] a small watercolor sketch of a singularly bizarre sandstone landform, *Garden of the Gods*, dated May 11, 1886, informs us that he was once again in Colorado.[102] It was probably on this trip that he traveled to southern Colorado and then into New Mexico, making sketches along the way for his monumental painting of the Spanish Peaks (plate 88).

Colman's personal method of selectivity and his profound appreciation of the western landscape's picturesque qualities contributed to his highly identifiable style; the West was, however, only a small part of his total involvement with artistic beauty.[103]

Among the group of artists who came to Colorado for the salutary effects of its climate was the Missouri genre painter George Caleb Bingham, who arrived in Colorado Springs sometime in August, 1872. As early as July of that year Bingham had consulted his doctor about traveling to Denver and the vicinity or to northern New Mexico because of recurring troubles with consumption.[104] Just five miles west of Colorado Springs was Manitou Springs, which had recently been established as a "first-class Colorado watering place and spa" by the Denver and Rio Grande Railway interests: "This 'Saratoga of the West' boasted eight mineral springs with a number of large hotels and private villas to shelter thousands of fashionable tourists."[105] Bingham probably settled there during his stay of two and a half months in the Rocky Mountain territory; not only could he avail himself of the cure, but Colorado Springs was just a short distance from a number of scenic attractions that would appeal to an artist's romantic sensibilities. Bingham had largely concentrated on portraiture and genre painting with occasional spurts of interest in pure landscape art, but Colorado's sublime topography undoubtedly tempted him to try his hand at matching Bierstadt's and Church's grandiose scenic productions.

Many scenic spots were nearby to vie for the artist's attention—among them Ute Pass with its romantic scenery, the famous Garden of the Gods with its strange sandstone formations, and Cheyenne Canyon with its gushing waterfalls and sparkling brooks—but Bingham chose instead to capture on canvas the area's celebrated sentinel, Pikes Peak. From all available evidence he painted two different views of this lofty peak, a large southerly one, now lost, taken from near Woodland Park (about twenty-five miles from Colorado Springs up Ute Pass) and a smaller extant picture captured from the high plains slightly southeast of the monarch (color plate 37).[106] Both paintings were obviously worked up from oil studies and pencil sketches. It is likely that the several Colorado landscapes recorded for the artist were plein-air oil studies rather than finished works; unfortunately, since only one small study, *Colorado Mountain Landscape*, has been found,[107] it is impossible to substantiate this assumption. While it adheres more closely to the topography of the actual site, the study does share some compositional similarities with the large Pikes Peak picture, particularly the mountain profile and the small pool of water and cascade in the foreground. The latter feature suggests a southerly view from perhaps Woodland Park for both works, indicating that *Colorado Mountain Landscape* may actually have been the preliminary study for the large finished picture.

PLATE 86

Samuel Colman, *On the Green River, Wyoming*, 1871, Watercolor, 16″ × 21¾″.
Courtesy M. and M. Karolik Collection, Museum of Fine Arts, Boston.

PLATE 87

Samuel Colman, *Colorado Springs & Cheyenne Mountain*, n.d., Pencil, 9⅞″ × 12¼″.
Courtesy Mrs. Mitchell A. Wilder, Fort Worth, Texas.

The smaller Pikes Peak view was taken from the confluence of Monument and Fountain creeks, near a site on Colorado's high plains known as "Jimmy's Camp," a place where wagons stopped. Monument Creek can be seen through a slight opening in the trees bordering its banks. The peak, however, has been artistically altered to suit Bingham's interpretation. The summit has been dramatically heightened, an exaggeration that is understandable in that the exact altitude of Pikes Peak was still in doubt well into the twentieth century. It is equally probable, however, that Bingham simply wished to emulate Bierstadt's successful method of producing sublime effects. In spite of these alterations, the view corresponds closely to a later Jackson photograph of Pikes Peak taken from near the artist's viewpoint.[108] Bingham executed this view during his trip to Colorado in 1872. Local Colorado newspaper articles of October 15 and a later reprint in the *Missouri Republican* report the painting on exhibit at a Denver emporium.[109] The local reporter was careful to point out that the view was taken "about one mile north of Colorado Springs," a notation that corroborates the picture's viewpoint

241

PLATE 88

Samuel Colman, *Spanish Peaks, Southern Colorado*, 1887, Oil, 31⅛″ × 72¼″.
Courtesy Metropolitan Museum of Art, New York City. Gift of H. O. Havemeyer, 1893.

and verifies its date of execution. The reporter's descriptive account gives additional information about Bingham's first visual record of Pikes Peak:

> Mr. Bingham has been at work upon this sketch for several weeks, and has succeeded in a manner commensurate with his large genius, and produced a picture which will meet all criticisms of the art centres and bear the most rigid comparison with the efforts of the other great masters of the land. . . . Those who have stood beneath the towering height of that grand mountain, and under the bright sky watched the drifting clouds and the succeeding shadows, drunk in the grandeur of the scene, and felt its overpowering effect, will feel as they stand before this work of art that they are in the presence of the reality of towering crags and snow-capped peak. . . . We advise all to examine the picture soon, as it will be taken east for sale in a few days. The only point to which we object, and upon which we must pass censure is, that the moneyed men and art lovers of our territory will permit it to leave this section. Mr. Bingham's pictures are noted throughout the land, and there should be some pride felt in retaining this one near the scene of which it is the counterpart.[110]

It is clear that the reporter was commenting on the small version,

since the reflective pool and rivulet, integral parts of the large Pikes Peak composition, are missing from his description.

In the summer of 1878, Bingham, newly married, returned to Colorado with his wife to spend the honeymoon camping in the mountains.[111] The one visual record that may date from this second trip is a painting referred to in the artist's letter to Major J. S. Rollins of October 4, 1878: "I have sold a Mountain landscape which I painted since our return from Colorado for 160 acres land in Linn county near Brooklin and near the Hannibal [*sic*] and St. Joe Rail Road. It cost the gentleman from [whom] I obtained it $2000.00."[112] To judge from the value of the land for which he traded the painting (if the amount is accurate), the work must have been a large panoramic scene; it has, unfortunately, disappeared.

Although Bingham commented to a Denver correspondent that he intended "to devote a large portion of his time, in the future to landscape art, and to make [Colorado] the field of his studies," his ambitions were quickly forgotten; he never returned to the "future Switzerland of America."[113]

With the expansion of the western railroad network to outlying scenic attractions after the mid-1870s a greater number of professional artists from other regional centers were lured to the Rocky Mountains. From important railroad centers like Denver they made side excursions to well-advertised scenic spots and watering holes. The illustrated travel books, magazines, and guidebooks that flooded the market prepared them well for what to see and sketch. Joining increasing numbers of tourists, these artists crisscrossed the continent to and from the Pacific Coast. Some lingered briefly in the Rockies; those tempted to try their luck as resident artists were quickly discouraged and soon headed toward California—for some, the final leg of the journey.[114]

New York artist Lemuel Wiles made oil studies of Colorado, Wyoming, and Utah scenery on his journeys to and from California, where he painted a series of mission pictures.[115] Saint Louis artist Joseph Rusling Meeker, noted for his Louisiana landscapes, found Colorado's mountainscapes a marked change from the southern swamps and bayou scenery he usually depicted.[116] Andrew Melrose gave his pictures of Wyoming's mountains and lakes a Tyrolean flavor; it was evidently difficult for him to switch from his lyrical and picturesque style of painting to the more vigorous treatment needed to portray this rugged mountain terrain. The picturesque quality of his *Wind River Mountains* belies the true nature of the area.[117] John Williamson followed the tracks of emigrant trains along the overland routes to gather material for his romanticized plains-mountain pictures (plate 89),[118] while Cassily Adams, the painter of *Custer's Last Stand*, traveled north from Denver along Colorado's front range in 1888 to capture a northwesterly view of Long's Peak with the distinctive flatirons nearby.[119] As late as 1899 the one-time Hudson River School artist William Stanley Haseltine stopped briefly in Colorado Springs to sketch Pikes Peak during a trip to California.[120]

While some who sought out the Rocky Mountain region were disappointed and never returned, others were overjoyed with its scenic prospects and returned repeatedly. These visits were just the beginning; scores of professional artists with new modes would continue to rediscover the Rocky Mountains into the twentieth century.

ARTIST-CORRESPONDENTS: AMERICAN AND EUROPEAN

The artist-correspondent became an important figure during the Civil War, providing visual documentation of the American tragedy enacted on the battlefields in sketches that, transmitted by way of lithograph or engraving, were in a sense antecedents of modern news photographers' eyewitness views. The expansion of the railroads and improvements in telegraphic communication accelerated the development of speedy, accurate pictorial reporting. The postwar period was filled with exciting events in the western territories, and the public wanted explicit and accurate illustrations of them. To meet this demand, editors often financed western expeditions themselves—and eagerly sought work by free-lance artists, who set out on far-reaching journeys—recording the events of their travels, depicting the most unusual sites, preparing elaborate guidebooks for would-be travelers. These artist-correspondents were both native-born and European—most of them serious illustrators, some interested only in producing anecdotal descriptions of unusual frontier events.[121]

Frenchmen Jules Tavernier and Paul Frenzeny joined forces in the fall of 1873, when they were commissioned by *Harper's Weekly* to produce a series of sketches documenting an extensive journey across the continent from New York to San Francisco. Several months after their departure on November 8 the *Weekly* announced their western expedition:

> . . . our artists . . . will tell the story of an extensive tour, commencing at New York and intended to include the most interesting and picturesque regions of the Western and Southwestern portions of this country. These gentlemen will not restrict themselves to the ordinary routes of travel. They will make long excursions on horseback into regions where railroads have not yet penetrated, where even the hardy squatter, the pioneer of civilization, has not yet erected his rude log-cabin; and the pictorial record of their journeyings will be a most valuable and entertaining series of sketches.[122]

In his *Artists and Illustrators of the Old West*, Robert Taft reconstructs their itinerary from newspaper accounts and their published illustrations, which deal primarily with incidents and conditions of frontier life. The few that capture city views and topographical landmarks are most pertinent for this study.

Both artists had been involved in graphic arts before their collaboration for *Harper's*. Tavernier had had formal training in the Paris atelier of Felix Barrias,[123] where he studied from 1861 to 1865. From those years through 1870 he was a regular contributor to the Paris Salon, exhibiting a variety of subjects but never receiving the recognition—the coveted medal—he long sought.[124] Despite his academic background Tavernier's interest and talents led him toward the more easily accessible commercial route; before coming to America late in 1871, he contributed illustrations to the *London Graphic*, as documented by his two published drawings in the magazine's issue of March 4, 1871.[125]

Frenzeny had reportedly served in the French cavalry under Marshal François Bazaine in Mexico before his arrival in America sometime in 1868; beyond this scant information his early life and career are unknown. His first published sketches of Mexico in *Harper's Weekly* in 1868 document his arrival in the United States and substantiate the report that he had previously been in Mexico.[126] Like his fellow traveler-artist, Frenzeny had been a regular contributor to a number of popular illustrated magazines for several years before the trip of 1873. Robert Ewing, Tavernier's biographer, believes that he and Tavernier met in New York, "possibly through their mutual employers, the *Weekly* or the *Aldine*." He notes that they had already worked together on two other assignments for *Harper's* and might have found "a certain camaraderie or [discovered] mutual interests."[127] In any case, their partnership was to take them on a trip of nearly two years through America's western frontiers, eventually terminating in San Francisco, where both resided and practiced for a time while traveling and sketching elsewhere on the continent and abroad. Sometime in the late 1870s, Frenzeny returned to New York, where he continued to contribute illustrations to *Harper's* and *Leslie's* until 1889, the last date recorded for his activity.[128] A photograph showing Frenzeny with a group of men associated with Buffalo Bill's Wild West Show seems to indicate that he was traveling in 1877.[129] Tavernier also was imbued with wanderlust, traveling and changing residences frequently over a fifteen-year period. He eventually moved to Hawaii, where he died in Honolulu on May 18, 1889.

Tavernier and Frenzeny probably left for the West in late July, since a surviving signed-and-dated sketch indicates they had already arrived in Parsons, Kansas, by August 4.[130] After a circuitous route across the plains and a side excursion southward into Oklahoma, Arkansas, Texas, and back to Kansas, they finally boarded a Santa Fe Railroad train to Granada in southeastern Colorado and from there headed for Denver. Their arrival was announced by the *Rocky Mountain News* on November 6:

> Messrs. Frenzeni [*sic*] and Tavernier, artists for Harper's Weekly, arrived in Denver yesterday, and are registered at Charpiot's. These gentlemen have made an extensive tour of Texas, Indian territory and

southern Colorado, where they have made a large number of interesting sketches of frontier life. They will spend several weeks hereabouts, making sketches for the illustrated paper they represent.

Tavernier's watercolor sketch *Habitations Mexicaines, Las Animas, Col.*,[131] never reproduced, might well be one of the sketches made on their trip through southern Colorado. Tavernier has certainly captured the flat, sunbaked quality of the region, and even in this minimal rendering records with a surprising degree of accuracy the adobe structures with their projecting vigas, so characteristic of the regional architecture.

The artist-illustrators spent the winter of 1873-74 in Denver, making a number of side excursions westward into the mountains and southward to Colorado Springs and vicinity. A variety of scenes illustrating miners at work, long mule trains on the bend of a road leading toward a new digging, and details of Colorado's smelting process were reproduced in the *Weekly*, all obviously resulting from their visits to the area's mining communities. Other published sketches and reports indicate that they were also in Estes Park and Boulder.[132]

The pair's stay in Denver created quite a stir in the local press, which frequently commented on their activities. Their watercolor drawing *Denver from the Highlands* (color plate 38) prompted rave notices.[133] One such report effused:

> The blue of the mountains is most artistically rendered, while Denver is given the air of a metropolis. This picture will win for *Harper's Weekly* a host of friends, and for the artists themselves an envious reputation. We understand the water color is for sale at $250, sketches having been taken from it for the paper. The picture is to be placed on exhibition at Richards & Co.'s.[134]

A less-than-flattering remark was made by another reporter, who found the picture far from accurate in its representation of Denver's topography:

> Everybody who examines that painting of Denver, in Richards & Co.'s windows, comes at once to the conclusion that the artist must have been cross-eyed to have located the city between the Platte river and the mountains, and near sighted to have the foothills appear to be immediately joining the suburbs, when they are fully ten miles distant.[135]

This criticism was valid. Although Pikes Peak is prominent in the picture, it is really seventy miles south of Denver and even on the clearest day could have been seen only as a faint outline on the horizon from the artists' vantage point north of Denver. The panoramic view, however, has the picturesque charm of the foreground figures, costumed in fashions of the period; it also includes some historically interesting features: the horsecar of the Old North Denver Horse Car Company, the vanished Platte River bridge, and the familiar waterworks, long since replaced.

This same picture, taken from a slightly closer viewpoint and somewhat reduced in size, was published with three other Colorado scenes by the Tavernier-Frenzeny pair in a *Harper's Bazar* article on July 10, 1875. A Denver newspaper report indicates that the artists not only executed the sketches but transferred them onto wood blocks before sending them on for reproduction.[136] The *Harper's Bazar* article, titled "View of Colorado," reflects the enthusiasm for the West shared by Americans across the nation. The article begins: "The picturesque sketches by our own artists on page 448 will serve to illustrate the sublime scenery of one of the grandest regions of our country." The full-page spread of four illustrations features a typical Victorian layout with the panoramic scene *Denver*. In a circular inset at the upper left is *Larimer Street, Denver*. On the right in the upper section is a sketch of two rugged cliffs flanking a great opening in the center with a small tipi at its foot; it is labeled *Gateway Garden of the Gods*. At the far right, sweeping partly under the central Denver scene, is *Clear Creek Canon*, with a locomotive steaming on its way toward the canyon entrance.[137] The accompanying article concludes, "We need not go abroad, indeed, in search of fine scenery while our own territories are brought so near us by the Pacific Railroad."

Tavernier and Frenzeny were last recorded in Denver by the *Times* on March 20, 1874, when they were mentioned as being among "invited guests" at "Alderman James M. Broadwell's artificial trout ponds, situated some ten miles down the Platte." Taft believes that an unsigned illustration entitled *Trout-Hatching in Colorado*, published in the *Weekly*, was inspired by this visit and should be assigned to the pair.[138]

After remaining in Denver a little over five months, Tavernier and Frenzeny headed northward toward Wyoming and later Utah, where both produced more western illustrations. During the remaining years of their careers, the two artists continued to record western views of a reportorial and anecdotal nature based on their experiences in the Far West.

Painter, illustrator, and art critic James Farrington Gookins, who crossed the plains with Chicago artists Ford and Elkins in 1866, had served as a "special artist" for *Harper's Weekly* at various times from 1861 to 1865. Several of his Civil War illustrations were published in *Harper's* in 1861 and 1862. After the war Gookins and two other artists traveled through Tennessee and Virginia on a special assignment for *Harper's*, sketching postwar scenes for the magazine.[139]

Having thus launched his career as an illustrator, Gookins set out west, probably with the idea of gathering anecdotal material and sketches for another magazine article. As he later reported, the trip across the plains in a wagon proved an adventuresome one, providing a number of colorful incidents to capture the public's attention. He details one of them in a letter published in *Harper's Weekly* in the fall of 1866:

> One of our mishaps I have sketched . . . is entitled "Storm on the Plains," [when] a hurricane took down our tents and blew over heavy loaded wagons, on the night of the 9th June, near Cottonwood, Nebraska. Fortunately no serious damage resulted to any one, though many in the train were badly frightened.

Surprised by Denver's growth and industry, Gookins made a special point of providing a view of the city and elaborating on the reasons for its progress:

> The tide of emigration and enterprise is setting hitherward at an astonishing rate, yet it is not to be wondered at when one sees the immense wealth of this region. Denver, a city of seven thousand inhabitants, is well built, and is the commercial centre of a mining region where already over twenty millions of capital are invested in quartz mills and the like. It hardly needs the eye of a prophet to discern that as the prospective terminus of the Eastern Branch of the grandest national highway of the world—the railroad to the Pacific—and as the great outfitting place for trains for Montana, Idaho, and Utah, its growth must be rapid and its destiny that of a great city.[140]

The simple street scene in downtown Denver that appeared in the article was severely criticized by a *Rocky Mountain News* correspondent:

> Gookins, the artist, recently here from Chicago, has furnished *Harper's Weekly* with some sketches of this country. Some of the smaller views are correct enough, but his picture of Denver is a most miserable caricature, and were it not for the name of the city printed at the bottom of the engraving, there is no one here who would ever suppose the picture referred to this city. Either the artist or the engraver were sadly at fault in their work.[141]

Refuting such caustic remarks, Taft comments: "One always must take such criticism with a grain of salt. If city views did not present a most pleasing aspect, the booster spirit was sure to find fault."[142] In this instance Taft's remarks do not apply. Gookins's Denver street scene seems composed partly from memory and partly from his imagination. The mountains beyond and west of the city supposedly represent the front range, but their profile, scale, and distance in relation to the city is purely imaginative. The narrow street lined with a row of simple and unpretentious clapboard buildings, however, is what one would expect to see in any frontier town of that period. Although he was executing a topographical rendering, Gookins exaggerated the height of the mountains to dramatize his simple and somewhat picturesque view.

Among the eight woodcut illustrations based on Gookins's original sketches that appeared in *Harper's Weekly* in the fall of 1866 is *Pike's Peak*.[143] In 1870 the artist painted an oil of the same monarch at twilight; it is possible that the picture could have resulted from his second trip to Colorado in the summer of 1869 with his friend the Chicago artist Walter Shirlaw.[144] Gookins captured this view of the snow-crowned peak from a rocky outcropping near the confluence of Monument and Fountain creeks. It is obvious that at this point in his career he had only a limited knowledge of how to construct a composition. The grouping of tall, scraggly trees on the right is out of scale with the rest of the picture. The artist has attempted to structure his composition according to a simple classical formula, laying it out on symmetrical lines with a progression of planes and groupings of pyramidal forms. The result, however, is clumsy and unsuccessful. A short time later he followed Shirlaw to Europe, where he spent three years studying art at the Royal Academy in Munich under masters Raab Wagner and Carl von Piloty.

Before his departure for Europe, Gookins had established a studio in Chicago, where he became a leading figure in the art scene as one of the charter members and directors of the Chicago Academy of Design. Although his artworks have been referred to as "comedies in paint of fairies and flowers, lovely creatures which won him success at the start, and with a landscape gift in addition,"[145] he was more distinguished for an incredibly diverse and widespread variety of pursuits that ranged from writer, critic, teacher, artist, and illustrator to civic leader and civil engineer.

In the introduction to a guidebook of 1858 on Niagara Falls and the vicinity, the editor takes special care to point out that the engravings that embellished the work were "minutely correct, . . . most of them having been copied from photographs, and others taken from drawings made on the spot by Washington Friend, Esq., whose beautiful and cleverly executed panorama of American scenery is so well known to the public, and which is now exhibiting in England."[146]

Born in Washington, D.C., of English parentage, Friend was a practicing musician and teacher who established a music academy in Boston in 1846. After a disastrous fire in which he lost a fortune in props and equipment, he attempted to recoup his losses by creating a "floating museum" on the Wabash River. That venture failed, and Friend decided to try producing a panorama, a popular form of entertainment that guaranteed its author a source of revenue from admission charges and sales of original material such as engravings and sketches. In 1849, Friend had set out on a 5,000-mile sketching tour through North America and Canada that lasted three years and resulted in the production of a large scenic panorama of his travels. The premiere of the work was held in Quebec, attracting scores of curious people; it was followed by a triumphant exhibition tour that included Montreal, New York, Boston, Philadelphia, and London. Friend had a thirty-two-page pamphlet made up to accompany his panorama. Among the testimonials in it was one resulting from a showing before Queen Victoria at Buckingham Palace on August 20, 1864: "Major-General Grey presents his compliments to Mr. Friend, and is commanded by Her Majesty to express her great pleasure and interest at having witnessed his splendid views of Canada and the United States, and has been further pleased to make selections from his original sketches." A songfest and dialogue were also part of the panorama show, whose purpose, according to Friend, was to acquaint fully the prospective traveler with the major cities, lakes, and rivers of the North American continent.

Evidently his first panorama production proved highly successful, prompting him to attempt a second venture focusing on America's western lands. Although several paintings from this work remain, no documentation proves conclusively that Friend actually constructed this second panorama. Pictorial evidence shows that the artist-illustrator traveled to Colorado, Wyoming, Utah, and California. His watercolor paintings of Colorado and Wyoming exhibit a somewhat naïve approach to picturemaking. His watercolor of the Quakers, freak sandstone formations in Monument Park, Colorado,[147] seems to reflect an unsure hand; in the painting they are not very convincing geological structures. Friend does, however, successfully convey the barrenness and erosive character of the steppe terrain near Colorado Springs.

Another watercolor of a Colorado site is *King Solomon Mountain* (plate 90).[148] The artist probably chose this site because, as he notes in an inscription on the back, "the highest silver mine in the world" was near its almost 14,000 foot summit. He was focusing on a timely subject, for Colorado was experiencing a silver boom in the rugged San Juan Mountains at the time Friend made this view.

While Friend's western pictures were naïve, they enlarged his repertory and vision from the early simple scenic illustrations of Niagara and seaside resorts engraved in the small guide of 1858 to the immensities of Colorado's and Wyoming's mountain country.[149]

Of the four American artists discussed in this section Charles Graham was by far the most able. Not only was his work above the standard of the other three artist-illustrators, but, as Taft notes, almost "every

PLATE 90

Washington F. Friend, *King Solomon Mountain*,
1878–1880, Watercolor, 21¾″ × 15″. Courtesy
Denver Public Library, Western History
Department, Denver.

issue of *Harper's Weekly* from 1880 until 1893 contained a full page or a double-page spread by Graham." So skilled was he as a pictorial reporter, Taft continues, that he was assigned to cover "Presidential inaugurations, political conventions and other events of national interest."[150] Despite his popularity in the last two decades of the nineteenth century, Graham has been virtually overlooked until recent times.

Graham was born in Rock Island, Illinois, in 1852.[151] He revealed a propensity toward art at a very young age. Self-taught, he began his professional career as a scenic painter for Hooley's Theater in Chicago. In 1874, according to his daughter, he joined Henry Villard's surveying expedition for the western extension of the Northern Pacific Railroad, making his first contact with the frontier country of Idaho and Montana.[152] A few years after this undocumented expedition Graham moved from Chicago to New York City, where he continued to paint stage props and drop curtains until 1877, when he was hired by Harper Brothers as a staff artist. He remained on their staff until 1892, when he left to serve as an official artist for the World's Columbian Exposition of 1893. As a well-published free-lance illustrator, freed of journalistic deadlines, Graham began painting watercolors full time and exhibiting frequently in the American Water Color Society's annual shows.[153] During that time the artist made several trips to Europe. In 1900 he took up oil painting, making pictures of English and Dutch scenes probably reminiscent of his European travels.

As Taft has remarked, Graham was a prolific recorder who illustrated not only the western scene but many other subjects. His illustrations recording events in the West—for example, *In Pursuit of Colorow* (a Ute chief on the warpath), a historic event that Graham undoubtedly did not witness—were often more romantic than factual. The scenic backdrops for these works were frequently culled from his field sketches; he often appropriated the same scenery for two illustrations. As a former professional scenic painter he was repeatedly called on to provide landscape backgrounds for the illustrations of figure painters W. A. Rogers and T. de Thulstrup, also staff artists for *Harper's*.[154] Unlike these two illustrators and others of his day, Graham's major contributions to the field were his city and town views, which provide a permanent visual and social document of America's frontier settlements before their rapid transformation by the advance of civilization.

After his initial western journey Graham made frequent trips to the West in pursuit of illustrative material for *Harper's*. In the fall of 1883 he traveled to Helena, Montana, to witness and record for his readers the historic connecting of the eastern and western links of the Northern Pacific Railroad. A side excursion to Colorado Springs is corroborated both by a view of the *Antler's Hotel*, published in *Harper's* on November 20, 1886, and also by a rather effusive article in the local press:

> Words like these, spoken of a Colorado city by a journal of such great influence as *Harper's Weekly*, are very cheering to Colorado hearts. The people of Colorado are proud of Colorado Springs and of Manitou, its child, and they like to hear them well spoken of in the East. . . . The illustrations to which we have referred in the last number of the *Weekly* are from drawings made by Mr. Charles Graham, an artist of exceptional ability.

It is possible, however, that Graham worked up this illustration from a photograph, since he was known to have relied on this medium for some of his other views.

It has been suggested that the artist-illustrator may have made another visit to Colorado either before or after his trip to Yellowstone Park with photographer Haynes in January, 1887.[155] This assignment offered an unusual challenge: the January date was selected in the hope of securing something unique in pictorial journalism—novel winter scenes instead of the familiar summer views. The results of their expedition appeared in the April issue of *Harper's*: Graham's illustration *The Yellowstone in Winter—A Surprise*, photographic views by Haynes, and Haynes's verbal description. Referring to one of his photos, Haynes wrote, "Here we see our artist, snow shoes on back, standing on the ice . . . endeavoring to place upon paper the stirring scene spread before him." Graham's views of Denver and other Colorado scenes appeared in the same issue.[156]

On September 10, 1887, the *Weekly* announced that Graham "was leaving on an extended tour of 'the great West and Northwest.'" The possibility of a stop in Colorado is substantiated by an extant gouache drawing, *Eastern Slope, Marshall Pass—the Great Loop on the D. & R. G. R. R.* (1887, plate 91).[157] The geographic locale and the scene itself indicate that Graham was in Colorado in late fall or early winter, the right timing for the documented trip. It is possible that his field sketches were the inspiration for this view, but a photograph undoubtedly served as the model; his drawing of *Taos Pueblo*, for example, was based on Jackson's photograph of the same subject.[158]

Graham's marvelous handling of subtle nuances of black and white demonstrates that he was a skilled artist with a deft hand and an understanding of the full possibilities of his medium. These qualities fail to come across in the simple line woodcut engravings but are highly noticeable in the later halftone illustrations of his work that began appearing in the *Weekly*'s issues of 1891. Unfortunately, only a few of his original drawings have been discovered. Graham reportedly had a habit of giving his field sketches and drawings to his friends; none of his western views remains with the family today.[159]

Frederick Piercy, an English artist, may have been the first foreign artist-journalist to sketch the Rocky Mountain scenery when he followed the Overland Trail from Council Bluffs to Salt Lake City in 1853. The journey resulted in an elaborate travel book entitled *Route from Liverpool to Great Salt Lake Valley*. Piercy's sketches and drawings (some of the latter produced with the aid of a camera lucida), combined with careful notes concerning his experiences along the route, comprised the final publication. This work, published under the auspices of the Church of Jesus Christ of Latter-Day Saints, included a geographical and historical description of Utah, a map of the overland route, and a history of Mormon emigration from Europe between 1840 and 1855.[160]

Piercy's narrative includes informative observations about travel conditions on America's western frontier as a guide for the Mormon traveler. His drawings and sketches are also reportorial in nature and reveal that the artist had been trained in the manner of nineteenth-century English topographical landscape art and had a keen eye and skilled hand. They include rapid and spontaneous pencil sketches of trees, river bluffs, wagon camps, and other interesting topographical features, as well as finished pencil and sepia-wash drawings, heightened with chinese white, of towns, cities, and mountain vistas. Using a subtle modulation of tones in his washes, he captures on paper the illimitable stretches of frontier land and the marvelous atmospheric effects of the West.

Two drawings typical of Piercy's finished work are *Laramie from North Side of Platte, Wyoming* (plate 92) and *View of Great Salt Lake City.* Although the former view did not appear in his book, Piercy mentions there that he tried to sketch a view of Laramie from the Platte but could see little of it because of the intervening distance.[161] With the assistance of a camera lucida Piercy captured a topographical view of Salt Lake City (plate 93)[162] from the "'Bench,' north of it, and just above President H. C. Kimball's house, which is seen in the foreground, a little to the left of East Temple St." He explained his reasons for taking such a view:

> The site of the city is large, and at that early period the buildings were very much scattered, rendering it almost impossible to convey any idea of the place unless a large area was embraced in the view. Consequently a favourable point was chosen, commanding the principal buildings, and the chief portion of the city which was then built upon. This, on the other hand very much reduced the size of the objects, but not to indistinctness. On the whole I think it may be presented as a faithful portrait of Great Salt Lake City in 1853.[163]

Keeping the documentary purpose of his mission in mind, Piercy provided his readers with a viable visual record of America's Mormon capital.

Piercy was at best a social and scenic recorder, and his art was what one would expect from a midnineteenth-century English topographical artist—accurate in detail, with little verve or imagination. Nevertheless, his drawings provide a permanent record of America's early frontier.

French artist Albert Charles Tissandier, impressed by the energetic industry of the young nation, felt compelled to make an ocean voyage to America in 1885 to record important sites and monuments in the New World. During his six-month tour he managed to traverse the Rockies twice while traveling by train and coach from one end of

PLATE 91

Charles Graham, *Eastern Slope, Marshall Pass—the Great Loop on the D. & R. G. R. R.*, 1887, Wash and gouache, 12½″ × 18″.
Courtesy Denver Public Library, Western History Department, Denver.

PLATE 92

Frederick Piercy, *Laramie from North Side of Platte, Wyoming*, 1853, Pencil and gouache, 7¹⁄₁₆″ × 10¾″.
Courtesy Frank A. Kemp, Denver, Colo.

PLATE 93

Frederick Piercy, *View of Great Salt Lake City*, 1853, Pencil, 6⅞″ × 10⅜″.
Courtesy M. and M. Karolik Collection, Museum of Fine Arts, Boston.

the continent to the other. *Six mois aux États Unis,* published in 1886, resulted from this journey.[164] Tissandier's interesting and informative narrative is illustrated with a number of engravings based on some of the more than two hundred original drawings and sketches of both topical and scenic views he made on his trip.[165]

Tissandier had previously illustrated a two-volume French work about the science of ballooning, an experience that undoubtedly paved the way for his elaborate travel book. Trained as an architect at the École des Beaux-Arts, Tissandier was a skilled draftsman with a practical orientation. His deft hand, acute eye, and honest approach to subjects prepared him well for his task in the New World.

During his travels in America through a dozen or more states, Tissandier kept a careful log, including descriptive notes about monuments and geographical areas as well as travel conditions. His precise, straightforward drawings and sketches are what one might expect from a trained architect. Several of them are perspective renderings of architectural monuments and the interiors and exteriors of Pullman cars, which seem to have held a fascination for him. Most, however, capture America's well-touted scenic wonders. A literate cosmopolitan like Tissandier would have been familiar with America's main attractions and would have set his itinerary well in advance. In some ways his narrative recalls the popular commercial guidebooks of the day, such as Appletons', which he had undoubtedly read.

After the journey over the flat, monotonous stretch of land through Kansas, the sight of the splendid Rocky Mountain panorama, with Pikes Peak looming in the distance and the snowy summits of the Spanish Peaks on the south, must have been a pleasant relief. Arriving in Pueblo, Colorado, on May 3, Tissandier captured his first views of Indians and the town's adobe buildings. From there he traveled to Colorado Springs, where he made many pencil sketches and drawings of Colorado's bizarre sandstone formations; the red rocks near the Garden of the Gods and the Quakers in Monument Park intrigued him. He also made a view of the entrance to the Cave of the Winds, not yet a well-advertised tourist attraction. He stopped briefly in Denver and then proceeded into the mountains west of the city toward Leadville, a rich mining community. There Tissandier made a detailed topographical panoramic drawing showing the silver mines on Mount Fryer in the mountains behind the town (plate 94), which he inscribed *Mines de Chrysolithes et Argent sur le Mont Fryer pris de Leadville, Colorado.* Despite its precise rendering, the drawing was not reproduced in his book. From Colorado he proceeded on his journey to Salt Lake City and then westward to the Pacific Coast.

Not until Tissandier headed eastward did he make a side excursion into Yellowstone Park, where he made a series of sketches of the steaming, boiling geysers. With Hayden's official report in hand, the artist was well apprised of what to see in the park, but it was Old Faithful that most held his attention; it was, he said, by far the most "impressive and interesting" of all the geysers. *Vue d'ensemble du geyser le Old Faithful (le vieux Fidèle)* . . . ,[166] reproduced in the book, shows a bird's-eye panorama of the valley with Old Faithful erupting amid scattered small, steaming geysers nearby. Another sweeping vista of the same site taken from a slightly different vantage point features Castle Geyser, with Giantess Geyser and others nearby (plate 95). Like the Leadville drawing, this is a descriptive graphite rendering, probably intended to be reproduced in the book. Before leaving America's famous wonderland, Tissandier remarked that he was surprised to find so few visitors in the park, a situation so unlike that in Europe's celebrated scenic places.

Tissandier's grand, embellished travel book falls within a well-established tradition introduced in the eighteenth century with the popular Grand Tour. Coming from a virtually unknown part-time journalist-artist, these marvelous views of America were a real discovery.

The vision of German illustrator Rudolf Cronau, who came to America on a special assignment in 1881, is totally different from that of the other two foreign artist-correspondents discussed in this section. His visual description of America's scenic wonders is romantic and fantastic, far removed from the topographical and architectural precision of Piercy and Tissandier. Reflecting his training at the Düsseldorf Academy (influenced by the Late Romantic German painters), Cronau saw the splendors of the American landscape through a rosy haze. In his two-year stay he accumulated many sketches and draw-

PLATE 94

Albert Tissandier, *Silver Mines on Mt. Fryer, Leadville, Colorado,* 1885, Pencil and wash, 10¼″ × 13¾″.
Courtesy Utah Museum of Fine Arts, University of Utah, Salt Lake City, Utah.

PLATE 95

Albert Tissandier, *Castle Geyser*, 1885, Pencil and wash, 10⅜″ × 13½″.
Courtesy Utah Museum of Fine Arts, University of Utah, Salt Lake City.

ings, that were published in an elaborate two-volume edition under the title *Von Wunderland zu Wunderland* in 1885–86.[167]

According to Cronau's autobiography, in the family's possession,[168] the illustrator was born in Solingen, Germany, on January 21, 1855. Details of his youth are sketchy, but it is known that very early in life he showed an interest in and propensity for sketching and was an intermittent student, in and out of art school. He first enrolled in Andreas Müller's elementary class at the Düsseldorf Academy on June 25, 1870.[169] Less than a month later Napoleon III sent troops into Germany, launching the brief Franco-Prussian War. The lure of battle was too much for the adventurous young Rudolf, and he ran away from school, hoping to enlist in the German forces. He was turned down because of his youth. Undaunted, he attached himself to the ambulance corps. His service there somewhat dampened his patriotic inclinations, and he reenrolled in the elementary art class in October, 1870, continuing his instruction until Easter, 1871, when he set out on a sketching tour through the Rhineland. Afterward Cronau again returned to Müller's class but left permanently on August 15, 1872, to enter a private studio. It is reported in contemporary newspapers that the illustrator studied with Andreas Achenbach, Benjamin Vautier, and Carl Hübner between the years 1872 and 1875. School records on file in the Düsseldorf Hauptstaatsarchiv reveal that Cronau's "attitude was sufficient, his behavior good, but his industry negative." This rebellion, which was shared by many art students of the period, was capsulated by Cronau in his comment to his family that "he was bored stiff drawing the same plaster cast over and over again."[170] Despite Cronau's complaints about this typical academy approach, such instruction, along with his training in wood engraving, served him well during his career as an illustrator.

After his academic studies Cronau traveled to Leipzig, the leading publishing and cultural center of Germany and home of two important newspapers, *Das Illustrirte Zeitung* and *Die Gartenlaube.* He contributed to both papers, which published many articles on the United States, for the country and its style of life had long interested the German people. Cronau shared this fascination. He was obviously familiar with illustrations in large travel journals by Bodmer, Catlin,

and his fellow German Heinrich Möllhausen, and he was eager to try his hand at a similar project. His interest was further inflamed when he read James Fenimore Cooper's *The Last of the Mohicans.* He finally realized his ambition when he persuaded the editor of *Die Gartenlaube* to send him to America as a special foreign correspondent. His assignment was to "describe and depict all of those natural wonders which had been discovered in the Far West of the United States during the first part of the Nineteenth Century."[171]

During his first three months in the States, early in 1881, he visited eastern cities—New York, Baltimore, and Washington, D.C. In Washingon, D.C., he met Secretary of the Interior Carl Schurz, who provided him with a pass to enter the Indian reservations in the West. In May and June he made a twelve-hundred-mile grand tour of the Mississippi. During much of the summer and fall Cronau spent his time in the Indian country, taking portraits of Sioux Indians on the Sand Rock Reservation, along the upper Missouri River.

After returning to the East for the winter of 1881–82, he made a trip to the Far West the following summer and fall, traveling to California, Arizona, Oregon, Idaho, Utah, Wyoming, Colorado, and New Mexico with sketch pad and palette. Many of his elaborate drawings in pen and ink and wash were worked up on the spot. The artist also made small oil sketches,[172] but they lack the unique personal character so important in his skillful and dramatic drawings. During his trip Cronau contributed a series of twelve articles augmented with drawings to *Die Gartenlaube* under the title "Um Die Erde." Following his return to Germany in 1882 (he had originally planned a longer stay, but was forced to cut short his trip owing to illness), Cronau devoted the next several years to writing about his American adventures. His drawings illustrated several of his travel books: *Fahrten im Lande der Sioux, Im Wilden West,* and *Von Wunderland zu Wunderland,* a two-volume edition containing good collotype reproductions of Cronau's most interesting drawings, each accompanied by a descriptive page written either in prose or poetry.

Although Gerold Wunderlich states that his great-grandfather's extant drawings deal primarily with Indian subjects, several pen-and-ink drawings of western landscapes are to be found in the family's collection, among them views of Rocky Mountain scenery. To judge

PLATE 96

Rudolf Cronau, *Mammoth Hot Springs, Yellowstone,* 1882, Pencil and ink, 11¼″ × 16¾″.
Courtesy Wunderlich & Co., Inc., New York City.

PLATE 97

Rudolf Cronau, *Canon and Great Falls of the Yellowstone River in Wy.*, 1882, Pencil and ink, 11⅞″ × 16¾″.
Courtesy Wunderlich & Co., Inc., New York City.

from his existing western works, Cronau's most important effort was couched in an illustrator's technique and style, and the masterful strokes of his pen and brush reflect his rigorous instruction at the academy. Like his fellow German artists of the midnineteenth century, his spirit is romantic and his work strongly Germanic. Many of his landscape drawings exhibit a surreal quality—an exaggeration of fact combined with Cronau's own imagination to create an eerie world. His masterful pen works with incredible precision, producing quicksilver lines that whirl into convoluted shapes or shoot up into sharp peaks that resemble rockets ready for ignition. The artist's use of juxtaposed light and dark areas adds to the mystery of his imaginative "other world." The rhythmic lines that create such unusual decorative patterns become more important—for both the artist and the viewer—than the realization of the object's true form or its place in space.

Cronau's unusual style is especially effective in his drawing *Mammoth Hot Springs, Yellowstone* (plate 96),[173] known to early explorers as Sulphur Mountain. All the strong and intriguing hydrothermal features of the site—the spouting geysers, terraced springs, steaming fumaroles, boiling-hot pools, and bubbling mud pots—are included. Portrayed by Cronau, the scene is filled with surrealistic fantasy and might well have served as a pictorial reference for the fantastic tales of Jules Verne. The mystery of the scene is heightened by the lurid white light, and the entirely logical presence of a diminutive group of surveyors only adds to the uncanny quality of the picture—removing the scene even further from reality.

In his drawing *Canon and Great Falls of the Yellowstone River in Wy.* (plate 97),[174] Cronau creates the same fantastic surrealism. The spectacular falls in the canyon had been the main attraction in the park ever since its discovery by white explorers, surveyors, and

tourists. It had been subjected literally a thousand times to interpretations in various media. Unlike Moran's magnificent and sublime interpretation, filled with the chromatic splendors of the scene, Cronau's drawing in crisp black and white is filled with a bizarre and mysterious feeling of desolation. Both of these Yellowstone drawings were reproduced in *Von Wunderland zu Wunderland.*

Among the other western drawings reproduced in his two-volume edition is a view of Salt Lake City,[175] in which the artist is represented in front of his easel looking out at the city with its famous tabernacle and its neat rows of houses and buildings. In another view, reproduced in the same work, of Colorado's famous Garden of the Gods,[176] the artist has again pictured himself at his easel in front of the monumental gateway. On the ground at his side are his rifle and opened paint box. A small inexpertly handled oil of the same subject in the Thomas Gilcrease Institute of American History and Art[177] documents that Cronau worked in the field with oils as well as pencil and gouache. Unlike his drawings, however, his oils are handled awkwardly, and his palette is muddy, supporting the assumption that Cronau, a skilled draftsman, was much more comfortable with the lighter medium. Although his Colorado drawing has many of the familiar characteristics of his work, it is less bizarre and exaggerated than his Yellowstone Park interpretations.

The works of Cronau, Piercy, and Tissandier represent varied approaches and inspirations. Piercy and Tissandier produced truthful and direct records of their journeys in the New World, while Cronau created fantasies out of America's truly spectacular scenes for his German audience, reflecting the grotesque, mysterious, and bizarre aspects of early German Gothic literature.

THE CALIFORNIA CONTINGENT IN THE ROCKIES

A number of California-based artists periodically made excursions into the Rocky Mountains, eagerly seeking out the novel scenic possibilities that had won Bierstadt and Moran such popular acclaim. The most noted of these Californians were Thomas Hill and William

Keith, both of whom arrived in the Rockies in the early 1870s. Just how much the work of Bierstadt influenced many artists of the period is documented in some quotes from the book *Keith: Old Master of California*, by Brother Fidelis Cornelius, published in 1942.[178] The author of this curious and fascinating publication draws much of his material from the "Little old scrap-book of Keith Miscellany," which includes conversations reconstructed by Keith's first wife, Lizzie. In September, 1869, when the couple was traveling the overland route by rail from California on a journey headed for Düsseldorf, she quoted Keith as saying:

> And just think, Lizzie, of Bierstadt's splendid successes. He got $5,000 for that big canvas "Looking up the Merced River" which he painted for W. C. Ralston. As Mr. Avery says, he has stirred up the ambition of all the artists in California to a high point. Do you remember his "Crossing the Plains" two years ago at Snow & Roos': and what a sensation it created! But when I look at these prairies I think his picture is not true. His work is sensational and that's why it sells. But I think it is also because of the grand subjects he paints and the imposing size of his canvases.

This conversation is reinforced by a second quotation from the same book—Keith again speaking to Lizzie:

> [Bierstadt] is able to do what he wants with his brush. Much of that power comes from study in Europe. He was born in Duesseldorf and studied under Achenbach and his pupils Whittredge and Leutze. But I'm sure his ability comes also from much direct sketching face to face with nature roaming far in Europe and America. Direct to nature; that's the way, Lizzie; but also true to nature. Yet Duesseldorf is the place for us to study. Its royal academy, they say, is over a hundred years old.[179]

After a period of study in Düsseldorf, Keith returned to his California studio, later joining California's well-known photographer Carleton E. Watkins for a scenic trip into the mountains of Utah in November, 1873. "They chartered two railroad cars, . . . one of which contained horses, wagons, hay, and feed, while the other was supplied with all the appointments requisite for domestic life."[180] The *Overland Monthly*, February, 1874, reported that the two had returned from their trip along the Pacific Railroad as far as Echo Canyon, where the artist made studies in color.[181] In April the cor-respondent of the same journal reported that Keith was engaged "on a couple of large views of Cottonwood and Weber Cañons, Utah." After taking many sketches along the route and in the canyon, Keith painted several pictures of Weber Canyon.

Keith's extant oil painting *Devil's Slide, Weber Canon, Utah* (color plate 39)[182] shows much niggling detail and hard coloring, indicating that he was still under the influence of the Düsseldorfian mode, although the artist had stated that he was attempting to break away from it. Later his brush would free itself, creating broad, simplified forms, and his palette would lighten as a result of his interest in the Barbizon style. This romantic landscape was undoubtedly inspired by his trip to Utah in 1873 and based on his field sketches there. Keith's "full-length landscape" (an oversized canvas) demonstrates his ambitions to compete for the public's favor and equal the fame of the American master Bierstadt.

Thomas Hill,[183] whose reputation depends largely on his panoramic and monumental paintings of the natural splendors of Yosemite National Park, made only a few sporadic visits to the Rocky Mountain region. In fact, his painting *Colorado*, which was exhibited in San Francisco in 1872, is believed to be an imaginary scene, possibly based on a photograph or an illustration in one of the popular magazines or travel guides.[184] Hill's first documented trip to the Rockies was in the summer of 1873, when he and two other California artists, Hiram Bloomer and William Marple, made a hasty trip to Utah.[185] The following summer Hill made another trip to the area "around Salt Lake," where he apparently wished to visit the Promontory for a painting he was then preparing on the celebrated union of the Central Pacific and Union Pacific railroads. The enormous (8'2'' × 11'6'') finished oil painting, *The Last Spike*, was first exhibited in San Francisco in 1881. It was four years in the making and includes four hundred figures. The view stretches eastward along the track of the Union Pacific toward the horizon bounded by the Wasatch Mountains, which provide the scenic backdrop for the multitude of figures that dominate the foreground.[186] Hill's landscape painting *Wahsatch Mountains*, which was exhibited in 1876 at Roos and Company and again at the Mechanics Institute Fair,[187] may have been a preliminary study for this large panoramic scene of such notable Californians as Leland Stanford, Charles Crocker, Collis Huntington, and Mark Hopkins.

In August, 1884, Hill made still another trip to the Rocky Mountain region for a stay in Yellowstone Park. One of the broadly and rapidly painted oil studies from his month's visit, a closeup view of Old Faithful, *Giant Geyser* (plate 98),[188] lacks the inspired artistry evident in his paintings of Yosemite. Obviously for him Yellowstone could not equal the California park.

Several other California artists spent some time in the Rocky Mountain region. Edwin Deakin was one of the few Californians who actually settled in Denver and established a studio in the city, remaining from June, 1882, to June, 1883.[189] Originally from England,[190] Deakin was recognized as a professional and welcomed into local art circles. Several months after his arrival the press praised him as "really a wonderful artist" and noted that "a strong effort should be made to keep . . . [him] in . . . [the] city": "He is an artist of whom artists and art loving people could be justly proud. Mr. Deakin has established himself in a pleasant studio in the Cheesman block. The walls are lined with most excellent studies and the artist is at work upon several interesting canvasses."[191]

Deakin quickly found a market for his picturesque European landscape scenes, Dutch-inspired still-life studies, and romantic pictures of English abbeys. Despite his social and financial success, the actual number of his works inspired by the Colorado environment was somewhat limited and its content rather uninspired, not to be compared with his series of paintings of California missions, executed after he returned to his former home. For example, a small oil study, *On the Platte,*[192] reveals his ability to capture an image in a facile manner, though it is a sketchy representation of the river on a bleak, wintry day. A picket fence stretching partway across the middle distance helps contain the composition—one might say as a period ends a sentence. A larger version of the same theme, entitled *Outdoor Study near Denver, Colorado,* taken "December 26, 1882,"[193] is a far more effective and finished composition, focusing on the intertwining network of bare cottonwood branches—a device that draws the eye

back into space. The mood and atmosphere of a wintry day are effectively captured by the picture's stark simplicity and strong contrasts of light and dark. It might have been this work that caught a reporter's eye when he singled out Deakin's Colorado plein-air studies:

> While we admire . . . Deakin's natural handling of fruit, we consider his landscape essays to be his finest work, eclipsing everything he has yet exhibited. . . . We were also very much interested in his studies on the Platte. He certainly has an eye for the picturesque as well as the impressively grand. One particularly, taken during the thunderstorm of last Saturday, will make a powerful picture. We know we speak for the mass of the art loving public of Denver when we say we shall miss him; his studio is always a treat . . . [and] always interesting.[194]

Howard Streight,[195] also of California, spent almost a decade in Colorado, maintaining a studio in his North Denver home. His work was rather primitive, and his Colorado views followed a traditional, almost hackneyed format, as seen in his composition *Gray's Peak.*[196] The snowcapped peak dominates the picture, looming in the background; a rushing stream winds its way down toward the foreground, skirted by boulders and tall, scraggly evergreens. Streight's studio seems to have been filled more often with visitors interested in the mysteries of a séance than with either patrons or critics of art. The artist, noted the *Rocky Mountain News,* used his paintbrush as other psychics employed a crystal ball or a Ouija board:

> By invitation, a reporter . . . visited . . . Streight at his studio in North Denver, and while there saw him work on a landscape, while under so-called spirit control, which, taken altogether, was a very marvelous performance commencing and finishing a picture 20 by 24 inches in three sittings. The first effort lasted exactly seven minutes, the second thirteen, and the third fifteen minutes. He used tube colors, and the rapid manner in which he spread and mixed them on his palette was truly wonderful. His eyes at times were entirely closed and at others very nearly so; and when under full control, he became entirely unconscious. His hand was controlled to move with the rapidity of lightning, and one would suppose that the rapid flights of his brush from one color to another could result in nothing but a wretched daub. Having secured his canvas upon his easel, he set a large music box to playing, and the work of painting began. The scene which followed beggars all description. His brush at times moved in perfect accord with the

music; meanwhile, his left foot beat a lively tattoo upon the floor. His arm made all manner of gyrations, dashing from one end of the canvas with lightning strokes, with such force as to send his canvas bounding over the floor, and hitting the beholder with utter amazement. . . . In the brief space of *thirty-six minutes,* in three sittings, he produced clouds, a beautiful sky, mountain, valleys, a lake, trees, rocks, etc., all blended into a harmonious and beautiful picture, worthy a place beside the finest specimens of art.[197]

Despite his obvious charlatanism and promotional schemes, Streight's illustration *Gray's Peak* was accepted for use in the highly successful publication of 1888 *Picturesque California,*[198] a two-volume edition patterned directly on the format of *Picturesque America,* edited by William Cullen Bryant and published in 1872–74.[199] Such publications were a continuation of the early-nineteenth-century travel books that received such popular acclaim. This large picture album, edited by John Muir, contained reproductions of scenic paintings by contemporary artists, each accompanied by a descriptive essay. Despite the California designation in the title, volume two of Muir's compilation did include illustrations and descriptions of Colorado scenes—which may well have led other California artists into the Rocky Mountain region in search of material suitable for the publication. One of them was Thaddeus Welch, represented in the publication by his panoramic view of Pikes Peak (incorrectly labeled *Sierra Meadow*), taken from Manitou rather than the usual vantage point of Colorado Springs,[200] and another view, *In the Garden of the Gods,* executed in 1885.[201] The original for *Sierra Meadow* [*sic*] was shown in a loan exhibition held under the auspices of Colorado Commandery Knights Templar No. 1, in Denver, in August, 1892. The painting recently turned up in the same city and is now in the collection of the Crocker Art Gallery in Sacramento.[202] After spending the summer and fall of 1888 in Denver and Colorado Springs,

PLATE 98

Thomas Hill, *Giant Geyser,* 1884, Oil on panel, 20″ × 13½″. Courtesy Collection of Arthur J. Phelan, Chevy Chase, Md.

PLATE 99

James E. Stuart, *Old Park Lodge at Yellowstone Park*, 1885, Oil, 18″ × 30″.
Courtesy Kennedy Galleries, Inc., New York City.

Welch left for Santa Fe, New Mexico, where he sketched and painted until around April, 1889.[203]

While he was in Colorado in the summer of 1885 (perhaps with Welch?), Julian Rix, another Californian, produced a rather handsome small oil painting *Spanish Peaks,* a Barbizonesque treatment with atmospheric effects in cool grays and blues. It served as the model for a black-and-white illustration, labeled incorrectly *Sierra Blanca* [*sic*], that appears in the same publication.[204]

A plethora of other California artists can be documented as having sought out subject matter in the Rockies. Among them were Meyer Straus[205] and Henry Cleenewerck,[206] who spent a season in Colorado. Jules Mersfelder[207] visited the Rockies as a "special-artist correspondent" for *Scribner's* and spent the summer of 1888 in Manitou, sketching and painting scenic views. Artist James Everett Stuart,[208] also a part-time resident of California, painted in the Rocky Mountains in 1885; his painting *Old Park Lodge at Yellowstone Park* (plate 99) captures an aerial view of the valley and the large, luxurious hotel. William Marple[209] was a leading figure in San Francisco art circles in the 1870s—a founder of the San Francisco Art Association and a frequent visitor to European art centers while making buying trips for the well-known firm of Gumps. He first visited the Rocky Mountains with Thomas Hill in 1873,[210] and his return trip in 1880 with former California artist Harvey Young was to change his life. During that visit he became involved in Aspen mining ventures, which engaged his interest for the rest of his life; he never returned to California. Most of the California artists, however, did return to their homes—many of them lured by their fascination with the familiar grandeur of Yosemite.

AMATEUR ARTISTS

Ministers, missionaries, prospectors, itinerant artisans, military men, teachers, painters of stage scenery, lady hobbyists: all these and more are listed in the rolls of the amateurs who painted the Rockies for amusement and sometimes as a partial living. They came in droves, fascinated by the majestic vistas and the rustic frontier cities. The ways in which they captured these subjects were usually awkward. The results were two-dimensional, lacked perspective and scale, and generally exhibited what has been described as a "homely adequacy of expressiveness for homely expressions." Yet their value is unquestionable—not only as social documents recording events, migrations, and a passing era but also for their fresh naïveté, a quality that today's eye finds thoroughly enchanting.

When the first minister of the Congregational Church of Empire, Colorado, died seven months after the church was established, a fellow Andover-trained pioneer of Colorado's Congregational church, William Hamilton Phipps, took over his duties.[211] He was reportedly "as competent an artist as a preacher."

Phipps took his post in Empire on October 28, 1866, remaining with his congregation until July 11, 1869. He also served part time in Georgetown, a thriving mountain mining community below Empire. Because Phipps was one of the more active ministers, his name appears from time to time in the local newspapers, telling us that he moved to Denver sometime in the fall of 1869; he is mentioned again on January 11, 1877, at the time of the Denver conference of Congregational ministers. After that Phipps disappears altogether from the Denver scene.[212]

Phipps was born in Paxton, Massachusetts, on July 3, 1841. He graduated from Amherst College in 1862 and Andover Theological Seminary in 1866, and was ordained in the Congregational ministry in Paxton on August 29, 1866.[213] Nothing is known of his early artistic activities or schooling, but his existing watercolors of Colorado scenery reflect a long-term fondness for his avocation. The number of scenic sites inscribed on his drawings indicates that he took frequent sketching jaunts during the years of his Empire-Georgetown pastorate. The large collection of his watercolors in the Denver Public Library's Western History Department includes *Brown Mountain*

District—3 miles above Georgetown, Chicago Lakes, Daily District-Red Mountain-taken from Ruby Mountain, Grand Lake by Moonlight, and *The Twin Lakes.*[214] In another collection a drawing by Phipps, *Foothills near Boulder, Colorado,* captures the flatirons. Perhaps the liveliest and most decorative of all this amateur artist's existing works is an aerial view, *Looking toward Range up Georgetown Creek* (plate 100), inscribed in the artist's own hand.[215]

Phipps's enchanting and naïve visual record indicates that he, like the well-known primitive artist Edward Hicks, a Society of Friends minister, had "an excessive fondness for painting." Unlike Hicks, who believed that it was blasphemous to indulge oneself in artistic pursuits and felt compelled to unite "borrowed form with elevating themes" in his pictures,[216] Phipps was comfortable in the separation of his true vocation, the ministry, from his avocation, painting.

Like other unschooled provincial artists, Phipps found it difficult to perceive naturalistically. As is typical of many amateur artists, he conceptualized a literal scene into decorative two-dimensional patterns, which he outlined and filled in with pale washes of color. Phipps's watercolor *Chicago Lakes* (plate 101), for example, is typical of his work, exemplifying his personal mode.

Two decades before Phipps answered his summons to venture out into the wilderness, another artist-clergyman Nicolas Point, a Jesuit chronicler, had preceded him, traveling along the Oregon Trail in the early 1840s.[217] He and his superior, Pierre Jean De Smet, were responsible for establishing the first Jesuit mission "among the Flatheads in the Bitter Root Valley just west of the main chain of the Rockies in 1841 [and] the first mission among the Coeur d'Alenes of northern Idaho in 1842."[218] From 1840 to 1847 Father Point lived and worked among the Indians of the Rocky Mountain area. The incredible details of his zealous mission are recorded with unusual accuracy and uniqueness in his illustrated diary, the first fully documented record of Indian life in the Rocky Mountains.

In 1859, twelve years after Point left the Idaho-Montana area, he began assembling and rewriting his field journals. The miniature paintings he made to augment the text were placed opposite the related passages. Like his writings, Father Point's paintings graphically record his insightful observations of Indian life, traditional religious beliefs, and tribal customs, with some portrayals of places, people, and incidents that are remarkably free of his subjective religiosity.

Like other self-tutored artists, Point worked in a quaint, simple fashion, laying one color over another to obtain his desired effects. His muddy palette and unskilled draftsman's hand betray a lack of technical knowledge. The works exhibit an amateur's tilted perspective, lack of aerial perspective (near and far objects are painted in the same primary colors), and awkward handling of animal and human anatomy. Despite their rude handling, Father Point's miniature pictures, incorporated into his six-volume manuscript "Souvenirs des Montagnes Rocheuses," have become relevant pictorial documents for the student of history and anthropology, graphically bringing to life stories that have hitherto been available only through the written word.

Beckoned by the call of California's golden wealth was Joseph Goldsborough Bruff, a draftsman with West Point training. On April 2, 1849, Bruff, captain of the Washington City and California Mining Association, and his company of men joined the forty-niners on the huge westward migration along the Overland Trail.[219] As a trained military man, experienced seafarer, and professional draftsman to the United States Bureau of Topographical Engineers, Bruff ostensibly had all the essential qualities needed to lead a company of sixty-six men. During his travels over the long route Captain Bruff made daily descriptive notes and sketches of sites and incidents along the way. This detailed chronicle of events was originally intended to serve as a guidebook for future travelers on the Overland Trail.

J. Goldsborough Bruff, as he called himself, was born in Washington, D.C., on October 2, 1804, one of the eighteen children of Thomas Bruff, a physician and dentist, and his wife, Mary Oliver Bruff. At sixteen Bruff entered West Point Military Academy. He attended only two years and then was dismissed on charges of misconduct. "Smarting under his disgrace, his blighted career, [he]

William Hamilton Phipps, *Looking toward Range Up Georgetown Creek*, ca. 1867–1869, Watercolor, 6″ × 10⁵⁄₁₆″.
Courtesy M. and M. Karolik Collection, Museum of Fine Arts, Boston.

PLATE 101

William Hamilton Phipps, *Chicago Lakes*, ca. 1867–1869, Watercolor, 10½″ × 18″.
Courtesy Denver Public Library, Western History Department, Denver.

embarked upon a merchant vessel sailing from Georgetown, as a cabin boy." On June 2, 1827, shortly after his return, he went to work in the Gosport Navy Yard as a draftsman. At the time of his departure in 1849 he was serving as a draftsman to the Bureau of Topographical Engineers.

As a government draftsman Bruff had chiefly been involved in working up maps and ornamental designs for insignias and medals. On those special occasions, however, when he was asked to duplicate drawings and maps in Frémont's reports for the two houses of Congress, he said, "'it revived the Spirit of adventure So long dorment [sic], and I was anxious to travel over, and see what my friend had so graphically and scientifically realized.'"[220] Knowing that in addition a "golden reward" awaited him at the end of the route, Bruff resolved to form a company for western travel. Unfortunately, he was plagued with difficulties and miseries along the trail, returning home after two and a half years unrewarded. He could not have known, however, that something valuable resulted from his trip: a unique day-to-day pictorial account of the Great Migration.

Bruff apparently took his field notes and rough sketches in pocket-size notebooks, later elaborating and transferring them into larger notebooks. The initial recordings, although "almost illegible in places, . . . give a far sharper and more truthful picture than the florid verbiage of his later versions."[221] Many of the pencil sketches from the initial field notebooks were later used as prototypes for Bruff's large chalk drawings executed on brown paper. His *American Falls, Snake River* (color plate 40), for example, was initially recorded as a small outlined pencil sketch with the usual geological object and color notations.[222] In his journal Bruff describes this "'scene of great natural beauty'": "'The "American Falls" of the Columbia are very pretty cascades, but with more rapids and froth than fall of water, at this season. . . . A short distance below, sitting on my horse, I sketched the Falls & scenery.'"[223] While gazing far north, Bruff observed a familiar site that he had read about and seen in Frémont's illustrated *Report*, "'the three isolated rugged-looking little mountains commonly known as the *Three Buttes*.'"[224] One of these celebrated buttes was to stand out prominently in Bruff's elab-

orate pastel-colored drawing (see color plate 40). In spite of the artist's obvious lack of perspective, the work is naïvely enchanting and essentially correct in topographical detail.

Although Bruff intended his journal to serve as a "reliable guide to future travelers," his intentions were never realized. Today, however, this pioneer's experience of the dramatic migration on the Overland Trail is an invaluable aid for the social historian.

Harry Learned, an itinerant scenic artist whose life is little known,[225] was born in Boston, Massachusetts, in 1844. He and his family went to Kansas with one of the New England emigrant-aid parties in May, 1855.[226] As a member of the noble band of free-state men, Learned's father had forsaken a comfortable profession as carriage maker and "left the 'Old Cradle of Liberty' to establish a new 'alter' [sic] on the beautiful plains of Kansas."

Learned first ventured into Colorado at the height of the Pikes Peak gold rush. In the winter of 1860 he and his father joined a party of prospectors on an exploring expedition in the San Juans. The hardships of their journey into the wild and remote regions of southern Colorado are recounted by Henry Learned, Sr., in his "Reminiscences," written at Frisco, Colorado, on January 31, 1882:

> . . . twas a wild country then and many tribes of wild indians to contend with. On the Mexican plains were the Comanches, there was only fourteen of us, then the Apaches, and Kiowas bothered us some, then the warlike Navajoes harrassed [sic] us. Large numbers of the Ute Indians were on the Rio-de-los-Animas. We got along much better with them than with the Border Ruffians.

For them, as for many others, "the golden rewards proved small and the isolation and dangers great"; the Learned party left the San Juans for the headwaters of the Rio Grande, then headed for Fort Garland. From there they traveled to "California Gulch, Blue River, . . . and over to Gregory and Central City." In the winter of 1862, Henry Learned, Sr., left for Lawrence, Kansas, to be reunited with his wife and family. It is assumed that his son Harry remained in the territory as a prospector until he enrolled in Colorado's First Cavalry on August 19, 1863. After serving as a private for a little over two years, he was discharged on November 18, 1865.[227]

Learned's father had established himself in Kansas as a manufacturer of carriages; from 1866 until the early 1870s his business is listed in the city directory as "Learned & Son, carriage makers." Evidently Learned joined his father's firm as a bookkeeper when he returned to Kansas from Colorado.[228] In 1869 he decided to become a full-time artist and went to Chicago to study under Henry C. Ford.[229] Following a year's stay in Chicago, where he was admitted to the prestigious Academy of Design as an associate artist, Learned returned to Lawrence and established a studio there. His paintings were quickly noticed by the local press:

> Mr. Learned has two pieces of Kansas scenery—one, a view just below Perryville, on the Kansas Pacific Railway, and another on the Wakarusa, which impart a deep interest to them as sketches of Kansas scenery. They are suggestive of many works which may be expected from him of homesteads and rural scenery of prairies, rivers and woodlands which may impart as much interest to our Kansas country as the poetry of Burns gives to "The Banks and Braes o' Bonny Doon," and other places which we seem to see in reading his works.

On December 1, 1870, the press again reviewed Learned's work. At that time he was reportedly sharing a studio with a Mr. Reed from Chicago. Learned's Kansas pictures were once again singled out, along with his *Cordilleras of the Sierra Madre at a point near Baker's Park, New Mexico,* which elicited a favorable comment.[230] This work indicates that Learned had returned to Colorado to sketch, though it is possible that this view was taken when the artist was prospecting in the San Juan region in 1860-61. Two years later, on November 11, 1873, the *Rocky Mountain News* reported that "Learned, . . . who has been sketching Colorado scenery for some time, left for home [Lawrence] this morning with a full portfolio." His dozen or more sketches of "Boulder Canyon scenery" also caught the attention of the *Boulder County News,*[231] which incorrectly identified Learned's residence as "Providence, R.I.," a factual error that was later to cause confusion about his background.

Despite the encouragement he received from the Kansas press, Learned finally decided to make Denver his home. The *Rocky Mountain News* announced his arrival and called attention to his most recent work:

A not more than average effort of his may now be seen in "Sporis'" window on Fifteenth Street, and from it connoisseurs may judge what his more elaborate studies are like. It is a view of *Lily Lake in Estes Park,* in which the water is well managed, and the mountains in the distance are very true to nature.[232]

The meticulously detailed painting (now in a private collection) has all the typical limner characteristics and Learned trademarks.[233] The lack of modeling and aerial perspective only emphasize the bright gaiety of his colors, most of them beyond the realm of nature.

Learned, like many other artists of his kind, made his living largely in utilitarian work, as indicated by the advertisement in the *Boulder County News* announcing that a partnership had been formed between Learned, "an artist in landscape and portrait painting and a master of skill in lettering on glass and signs," and C. S. Faurot, "known by citizens as the best house painter and paper hanger."[234] The pair also offered their services for "fresco & scenery theatrical and decorative work." Learned exhibited landscape paintings at local fairs on at least two occasions. At the Second Annual Fair of the Boulder County Industrial Association he was awarded a diploma and three dollars for the "best painting of Colorado scenery."[235] In November, 1876, he dissolved his partnership with Faurot and advertised himself as a producer of "sign and ornamental work done in the best style."[236] In April of the following year Learned joined forces with Soward, a local sign painter; they were reported "painting two large signs for the First National Bank of Boulder."[237]

Learned resided in Boulder until 1881, when he was recorded as a scenic artist living in Longmont, Colorado.[238] It is likely that his sudden move to a new community was brought about by his appointment as scenic artist for the new Fort Collins Opera House.[239] Learned had been engaged by the opera association to finish the work begun by the Italian artist Signor Hurle, whose employment had been terminated after the company rejected his conventional scene of the Bay of Naples for a drop curtain. They chose instead to patronize a bit of "home industry so to speak" in Learned, who "took his idea from [his] own beloved Colorado scenery, and transferred to his canvas a charming likeness of a part of the San Juan valley." The design was actually adapted from one of his own paint-ings, *Head Waters of the South Fork of the San Juan river,* previously exhibited in Denver.[240] The finished curtain was unveiled at a private showing for a small, select company including the local press, which described the work as "not only comprehensive but elaborate." The detailed description that followed makes it possible to identify the presently missing scenic curtain as the one visible in a photographic view of the interior of the Fort Collins Opera House taken in the 1880s (plate 102). Hanging in the center of a drop curtain and sur-rounded by advertising "cards" is Learned's scenic panel. As the correspondent noted:

> Half way 'twixt fore ground, and back ground, from out a deep ravine, suggestive of a world beyond, wind the blue waters of the San Juan, and, growing broader and broader flow down across the fore ground. To the left, springing from the very water's edge, is a dark precipitous cliff, wooded with evergreens, with here and there a jagged boulder projecting from amid the trees. On the right bank of the river . . . is a narrow park, following the course of the river, the dead level of the grassy surface being relieved by monument-like boulders so char-acteristic of Rocky mountain scenery. One of these boulders brown and seamed springs up from the very front of the foreground, giving an air of ruggedness even to the park. Overhanging the park is another cliff fully as steep and rugged as the one on the opposite side of the San Juan. High up from a mass of rocks that stand in wild weird picturesqueness, springs a cascade, that tumbles down the mountain side, filling the air with sparkling spray, and a cloud of mist.
>
> Through the vista formed by the cliffs can be seen lofty mountain peaks ribbed with rocks and snow.[241]

The public was also informed that Learned had painted all the scenic props, which revealed the artist's "imaginative and poetic" expression.

Learned was well prepared for this assignment, having previously produced scenery for the theater production *Trip of the Nancy Lee,* performed at Denver's Academy of Music in May, 1880.[242] After his Fort Collins assignment, the press noted, Learned left "to paint scenery for the Greeley Opera House."[243] It appears that he later returned to Denver and became associated once again with the Palace Theater as scenic artist.[244] His tenure there seemingly lasted

PLATE 102

Harry Learned, *"Drop Curtain": Interior View of the Fort Collins Opera House, Colorado,* ca. 1881, Photograph, 5″ × 7″. Courtesy Denver Public Library, Western History Department, Denver.

until sometime before February 8, 1884, when he was married in Golden, Colorado.[245] From there the artist's tracks seem to lead to the mining districts of Summit County, particularly the vicinity of Robinson and Kokomo.[246] The area was only a stone's throw from Frisco, where his father had relocated in the late 1870s, having staked his claims in mining interests in the surrounding commu-nities.[247]

It is possible to assume that Learned began prospecting again and devoted himself to artistic ventures only during his spare time. With the arrival of his two children,[248] he turned more and more to his pastime, making a series of souvenir oil paintings of the min-ing town of Robinson (plate 103) captured in both winter and sum-mer.[249] His views of this small frontier community were taken from various directions, showing the Ten Mile Range and the creek of the

PLATE 103
Harry Learned, *Robinson, Colorado*, 1887, Oil, 18⅛″ × 30¼″.
Courtesy Amon Carter Museum, Forth Worth.

PLATE 104

Harry Learned, *Iron Mask Mine*, 1886, Oil, 29″ × 41″.
Courtesy Denver Art Museum, Denver, Colo.

same name. It was probably the winter scenes that attracted the greatest interest and number of patrons, earning him in the twentieth century the epitaph "Grandma Moses of Colorado."

In 1886, while he was busily engaged in painting homely views of Robinson, Learned ventured off the beaten track and made a large view of the celebrated Iron Mask Mine and the nearby mining community of Gilman, situated on Battle Mountain, 1,200 feet above Eagle River Canyon (plate 104).[250] Like his other works, he captured this site with his sharp-edged linear perspective.

Learned lived in Robinson during its boom period from 1884 to 1888 and then moved his family to Aspen. In 1891, however, he is recorded in the Denver city directory as living in North Denver and working as an artist.[251] It can only be assumed that Learned had a difficult time securing a job in Aspen and went to Denver to seek work as a scenic artist, while maintaining his family home in Aspen. The several surviving paintings executed during the last few years of his life were copied after prints or photographs. Among them are *Train in the Royal Gorge* and *Mount of the Holy Cross* ("after Moran"), both painted in 1894.[252] Neither has the freshness and vitality of the artist's former works; both lack inspiration and a certain inventiveness. On April 11, 1895, Harry Learned died in Denver.[253]

Another artist for whom the Rockies were to combine the promise of material wealth and the inspiration of new scenic material was Peter Petersen Tofft. Born in Kolding, Denmark, on May 2, 1825, Tofft demonstrated a love for travel as a teenager, shipping out on a whaler at age seventeen and eventually arriving in San Francisco as a crew member of the United States gunboat *Ohio*. He arrived just in time to join the gold rush. His reasonable success as a miner earned him enough money to finance a return trip to Denmark in 1859.[254]

In the early 1860s he returned to California, perhaps hoping to develop additional mining interests. He is also known to have exhibited works in San Francisco and to have met Albert Bierstadt during this period. When introduced to the American master as a fellow painter, Tofft could only utter, "No, no, not a painter, but a daub."[255]

In the autumn of 1865, Tofft was off again, beckoned by Montana's gold fields. He first traveled "across present-day Washington and Idaho" and "rode down the Clark Fork River" into the wild, virgin country celebrated for its recent gold strikes. He then went overland to the Flathead Reservation, where he made a number of scenes of the agency and nearby Fort Connah before heading south to the Bitterroot Valley and Fort Owen. One such view, a pencil sketch (plate 105), depicts the Flathead agency; the scene was obviously captured before winter set in, for Tofft hastily notates scattered vegetation with pencil scribblings. A watercolor executed at this time is a view of Fort Connah entitled *Hudson Bay Trading Post — On Flathead Indian Reservation/Montana Terr.* (plate 106). The artist had sketched this tiny outpost in winter; the pale washes of his brush convey the charm of the snow-covered valley and the small fort. Although the composition is not overly accomplished, the artist does capture the quiet majesty of the Mission Range and the inviting warmth of the frontier community, where log cabins and skin lodges share the protection of the valley floor.

Shortly after Christmas, 1865,[256] Tofft arrived in Bitterroot Valley, laboring under the usual burden of prospector's paraphernalia. John Owen, the proprietor of Fort Owen and Tofft's host for more than two months that winter, recalls his early impression of this itinerant prospector-artist: "He has taken Some Very pretty Sketches of different parts of the [Bitterroot] Valley — He does Well for an 'Amateur' — He Seems to have good taste & is Without doubt a Natural Artist."[257] On February 15, Major Owen noted in his journal that Tofft had departed from the fort on snowshoes "headed northwest to the Elk Creek mining district in present Deer Lodge County" to try his luck at placer mining there.[258]

During his wanderings in Montana, Tofft made a number of watercolor scenes of interesting sites and scenic vistas. A legendary area known as Hellgate captured his attention and brush; one result was *Hell Gate Pass — The Old Battleground of the Eastern and Western Indians* (color plate 41).[259]

PLATE 105

Peter Tofft, *Flathead Agency—Indian Reservation . . . M. T. Dec 1st 1865*. Pencil, 5¾″ × 9″.
Courtesy Carl S. and Elisabeth Waldo Dentzel Collection, Northridge.

PLATE 106

Peter Tofft, *Hudson Bay Trading Post—On Flathead Indian Reservation/Montana Terr[itory]*, 1865, Watercolor, 6″ × 9⅟₁₆″.
Courtesy M. and M. Karolik Collection, Museum of Fine Arts, Boston.

PLATE 107

Edmond Green, *Shoshone Falls of Snake River*, ca. 1879, Colored lithograph, 18⅜″ × 23¾″.
Courtesy Amon Carter Museum, Forth Worth.

A fall from his horse in the autumn of 1866 ended Tofft's activities in the placers, though he continued to travel throughout the mining communities, earning a considerable reputation as an artist. In fact, when Tofft announced his intended departure on May 28, 1867, the *Helena Herald* beseeched the artist to abandon his plan to return to California, proclaiming his work "decidedly exquisite and very worthy specimens of art." When Tofft finally left Montana, he headed instead for Rochester, New York, to seek medical treatment; he sailed for England in June, 1868.

Although he was not to return to the Rockies, Tofft's scenes were long remembered in the region and even internationally. A selection of his views was used to illustrate an article in *Harper's Magazine* entitled "Rides Through Montana." One of his drawings was even reproduced in the *London Illustrated News* in 1870.[260] Despite his unsophisticated technique, Tofft is recognized for his delightful portrayals of early Montana, its scenes, its towns, and its people.

An English draftsman named Edmond Greene, an itinerant artist who roamed Idaho's mountains, mines, and small towns between 1879 and 1884, left one of the most extensive pictorial records of Idaho scenery and mining operations in lithographic form (plate 107). The several surviving lithographs after Greene's sketches from nature were published by the San Francisco firm Britton & Rey and redrawn by their lithographer H. Steinegger.[261] Greene's presence in Idaho was first noted by the *Tri-Weekly Statesman* on September 2, 1879:

> While we were at Quartzburg a few weeks ago, Mr. Wm. Coughanour, the gentlemanly superintendent of the Gold Hill mine, presented the STATESMAN office with a beautiful lithographed view of the Gold Hill mill and works, taken from a crayon sketch made by an Idaho artist, Mr. Green [*sic*]. . . . The picture shows the mill and other buildings with the hoisting works and the surrounding mountains, all so true to nature that the smallest permanent object will be at once recognized.

At the end of the month the *Statesman* reported that Greene had returned

> from a tour through Alturas county, where he has been taking sketches of Idaho scenery. He has recently visited and sketched in crayon the Great Shoshone falls and the Twin falls on Snake river. Mount Graylock at Atlanta [Idaho mining community], and other interesting localities. When lithographed, these views will form splendid pictures. . . . His sketches of Snake river scenery cannot be surpassed in beauty of execution and fidelity to nature.[262]

His activities went unnoticed by the same press until mid-September of the following year, when a correspondent noted that Greene had recently arrived "from Bonanza City, coming by the way of Sawtooth City and Atlanta. Mr. Greene passed the summer months among the mines in Temhi county, where he was kept busy sketching the various improvements and surrounding scenery. He expects to return to Atlanta in a few days.[263] The last account of this artist appeared in April, 1884, when the *Statesman* described Greene's efforts to secure advance subscriptions to have his view of Boise City published.[264] After this report the artist's trail disappears.

Greene's lithographs reveal that his knowledge of perspective was somewhat limited, his small cubical buildings were drawn with a ruler, and his approach was typically naïve. Like the works of many other amateurs, his pictures of Idaho towns, mining operations, and scenery include a wealth of minute factual details, making them valuable historical records of early Idaho.

THE OBSERVERS OF THE SCENIC WEST: PAINTERS OF INDIANS AND WILDLIFE

Conscious of the havoc wrought by the advances of civilization, the painters of Indians and wildlife, like the scenic artists, were equally intent on capturing characteristic and lasting images of their subjects. During their treks they too discovered the beauty of the rugged primeval scenery. In some of their sketches, studies, and formal paintings, landscapes become important as realistic backdrops for dramatic pictures of Indians or of animals in their natural habitat. These painters occasionally even went beyond their immediate mission and sketched or painted pure landscapes for their own delight or as memory aids. These latecomers, possessed of diverse talents, came to the Rockies at various times but always with the same object—to capture the vanishing scene.

Although George Catlin was one of the first painters to venture into the frontier regions, he did not reach the Rockies until the mid-1850s, despite the earlier date he gave to the event. As early as 1832, Catlin trekked two thousand miles up the Missouri River from Saint Louis on his way to the mountains, but at his farthest point west he was still over a month's journey short of seeing their grand silhouette on the horizon. For many years it was believed, on the basis of Catlin's own writings about his journeys, that he had actually traveled to the Rocky Mountains in 1833:

> In the summer of 1833 I ascended the Platte to Fort Laramie, visiting the two principal villages of the Pawnees, and also the Omahas and Ottoes, and at the fort saw a great number of Arapahos and Cheyennes, and rode to the shores of the Great Salt Lake, when the Mormons were yet building their temple at Nauvoo, on the Mississippi thirty-eight years ago.[265]

Recent studies have disproved Catlin's account by uncovering contradictions in the statement itself. For instance, Fort Laramie, which the artist claimed to have visited in 1833, was not established until 1834; no application to enter Indian country was registered by Catlin in 1833; and no corpus of work exists from this asserted trip.[266] The artist, in fact, passed that summer in Cincinnati. Why Catlin fabricated this early journey in his "Itinerary" is a mystery.

The following year, however, he did journey into the West again, traveling onto the southwestern plains in the company of Colonel Henry Dodge and his dragoons to observe the Comanches. As in 1832, the western landscape (though not including Rocky Mountain views) was an important subject for Catlin. In a letter from Fort Gibson, dated June 13, 1834, he describes his impressions: ". . . the landscape scenes of these wild and beautiful regions, are of them-

selves a rich reward for the traveller who can place them in his port-folio."[267]

Catlin was reputedly recognized as a portrait painter. Although he was essentially self-taught, he acknowledged the influence of Thomas Sully and Charles Willson Peale. During his lifetime Catlin made a concerted effort to capture the distinctive facial expressions of his sitters. "Man, in the simplicity and loftiness of his nature," said Catlin, was "the most beautiful model for the painter." He was quick to point out, however, that "the country from which [man] hails is unquestionably the best study or school of the arts in the world: such I am sure, from the models I have seen, is the wilderness of North America."[268] It is obvious that the landscape as well as the faces and customs of its natives commanded Catlin's attention; of the 507 paintings that comprised "Catlin's Indian Gallery" in the 1840s, nearly 100 were devoted to pure landscape.[269]

Before his western travels Catlin had in fact been engaged in painting landscapes. In the 1820s, after abandoning a law career and deciding to become a full-time artist, he moved to Philadelphia, where he undoubtedly saw the landscape paintings of Cole, Doughty, and perhaps Seymour. In these early years as an itinerant painter Catlin produced a number of scenic views of such sites as the Erie Canal, West Point, and the Hudson River. His series of paintings of Niagara Falls, executed in 1827, was published as a set of colored lithographs four years later.[270] These views reveal Catlin's personal involvement with nature and his romantic attitude toward its sublime aspects—a characteristic that can also be observed in his western landscapes. One such painting, showing the exaggerated arch of the towering falls from a low viewpoint, rivals even the sublime effects in Cole's romantic views of the wild Catskill scenery.[271]

During his western travels the artist continued to be caught up in the romance and reality of the landscape, attempting to imbue his paintings with a sense of the drama he discovered in these remote regions. Despite his dramatizations he remained faithful to his objective: to portray the true physical features of the land. William Clark attested to Catlin's accuracy when he commented about the artist's landscapes: ". . . a considerable number of them I recognize as faithful representations, and the remainder of them are so much in the peculiar character of that country as to seem entirely familiar to me."[272]

Catlin's method of constructing his compositions—whether landscape views or portraits—was simple and direct. He was basically a realist who sought to capture the specifics, the character, and the spirit of his subject. As an artist-explorer, he was forced by the exigencies of time and place to record his impressions rapidly. Despite his lack of technical sophistication he accomplished this task with remarkable directness and spontaneity. In their freshness Catlin's on-the-spot scenic studies reveal the artist's personal communication with nature. Their rudeness was overlooked by contemporaries like Charles Baudelaire, who contradicted a criticism of work by Catlin exhibited in the Paris Salon of 1846:

> When M. Catlin came to Paris, . . . the word went around that he was a good fellow who could neither paint nor draw, and that if he had produced some tolerable studies, it was thanks only to his courage and his patience. Was this an innocent trick of M. Catlin or a blunder on the part of the journalists? For M. Catlin can paint and draw very well indeed.[273]

Like others of Catlin's day, Baudelaire was struck by the accuracy of the artist's colorations and impressed by his ability to render the clear, almost transparent, skies of the West.

In 1855, almost ten years after Baudelaire made his comments, Catlin set off on a series of adventures that finally took him into the Rockies. Accompanied by an escaped slave from Havana, Caesar Bolla, he sailed from South America up the Pacific Coast to the Aleutian Islands and beyond, then to Victoria and the Dalles, on the Columbia River. From there they proceeded on horseback, approaching the Rockies by way of the Columbia and Snake rivers.[274] In the company of an Indian guide they ascended the Snake River to the Salmon River valley. There, among the Crow Indians, Catlin stopped to paint *A Crow Village and The Salmon River Mountains* (color plate 42). Thirteen years later, in his book *Last Rambles Amongst the Indians of the Rocky Mountains and the Andes*, the artist recounted his impressions of the scene he had depicted on canvas:

> Our ride (or rather walk, for we had to walk and climb most of the way, leading our horses) was one which I deeply regretted from day to day, but which I never have regretted since it was finished. The eighth day opened to our view one of the most verdant and beautiful valleys in the world; and on the tenth a distant smoke was observed, and under it the skin tents, which I at once recognized as of a Crow village.[275]

Ten days after this first encounter with the Crow Indians the artist and his retinue departed hastily on a warning by a passing Hudson's Bay Company trapper that a Blackfeet attack was imminent. The trio proceeded south across the "Salmon River Mountain[s] into the Snake River Valley—[according to Catlin] a pass difficult to traverse, and requiring the most desperate resolution. Ravine after ravine [were passed], amidst the most frowning and defiant rocks of all sizes, which had tumbled down from the snow-capped summits on either side."[276]

Catlin seemed as impressed by the geology of the mountains they were crossing as by their scenic splendor. For many hours he made field notes of the rocks and formations. "What a field for geologists," he exclaimed, "and why are they not here?"[277] His studies in the present Lost River Range and the White Knob Mountains of southern Idaho constituted a portion of his treatise *The Lifted and Subsided Rocks of America*, which he published in London fifteen years later. There he noted that "no other portion of the globe presents so vast and sublime a spectacle of uplifted rocks as the American continent." He also assured his readers that when the geological marvels of the Rockies became known the "pecuniary interest of the commercial world" would be rewarded for men's "pockets will for ever be lined with their shining treasure."[278]

Passing southeast through the Rockies, Catlin and Bolla, whose Indian guide had abandoned them at the beginning of the mountain crossing, eventually reached the Snake River in the vicinity of Fort Hall. There they joined a troop of New Hampshire emigrants and journeyed west again toward the Pacific Coast on the Oregon Trail.

Between Fort Hall and Fort Boise, Catlin, Bolla, and a newly employed Indian guide made a side excursion to the "great, or 'smoking,' falls of the Snake River," which, according to Catlin, could be classified "amongst the greatest natural curiosities of the world."[279] Known today as Mesa Falls, this impressive series of cascades excited Catlin as much as Niagara had more than twenty-five years earlier:

> In the midst of this vast plain of desolation we discovered, at many miles distance—not a pyramid of spray rising, forming and piling away a mass of clouds in the heavens, as we see above the fall of Niagara—but a chain, of several miles in length, of jets of spray, rising apparently out of the level ground, not unlike the smoke of the camp fires of an army of men; and, approaching it, we scarcely realize its origins until we are quite upon the brink, and the awful abyss, with all its grandeur, is beneath us; and, even then, it is but here and there that we can approach near enough on the sand-covered brink, with no tree or rock to cling to, to catch more than a partial view of the scene before us.
>
> Instead of looking upwards, as we usually do, to see a waterfall, or of seeing it leaping off from the rock on which we are standing, all is here below us, at the bottom of an awful chasm, and the very surface of each successive fall is several hundred feet below us.[280]

Catlin recorded his wonderment on viewing this sight in an oil, *Mesa Falls of the Snake River* (plate 108).[281] This painting and others resulting from the artist's peregrinations in the 1850s are treated in a sketchy, rapid manner similar to that of his early works. Their somewhat contrived and pretentious compositions lack the natural force and artistry of Catlin's western-prairie scenes of 1832–34. It is obvious that he was technically ill-equipped to construct an elaborate composition like his painting *A Crow Village and The Salmon River Mountains* (see color plate 42). In this landscape and in that of Mesa Falls, trees and mountains are generalized, the former, with no consideration of generic type, notated by a repetitive patterning that becomes increasingly more desultory and unrelated to other forms in the composition. In spite of unsophisticated handling, Catlin's picture of Mesa Falls corresponds rather closely to his written description of the spectacular site. The artist has even portrayed himself sketching the awesome scene spread before his eyes.

Catlin is recognized today not only for his pictorial documents of the early western land and its native peoples but for the insightful views of the world around him that he recorded in his chronicles. Considered an advanced thinker for his time, he was one of the first to advocate setting aside land for "a nation's park" in which the natural habitat and its native peoples could be protected and preserved from the advances of civilization "in all the wild and freshness of their nature's beauty."[282]

Peter Moran, an animal painter and the youngest of the four Moran artists, accompanied his brother Thomas on a twelve-day journey to the Grand Tetons in August, 1879.[283] Although Peter was already a veteran of western travel, having visited the West several years before his brother arrived, he had never penetrated the heart of the Rockies.

Moran, like his older brother, had served as an apprentice to a printing firm, but his apprenticeship, like Thomas's, "was terminated abruptly by a quarrel with his employer." He later joined his brother in Edward's studio, specializing in animal painting. Attracted to the pictures of the popular English animal painter Sir Edwin Landseer, he made a trip to England in 1863 to study the master's work,[284] which he probably knew through engravings. He quickly became disillusioned by the artificiality of the pictures, however, and returned to Philadelphia, where he established a studio and began painting animal and rural scenic subjects. The following year he made his first trip to the Southwest, followed by two subsequent trips that are known only through pictorial evidence.[285] During the year preceding his Teton journey, the two brothers are thought to have been together in New Mexico; a small painting of a Hopi village by Thomas Moran suggests this possibility.[286]

Their trip to the western side of the Tetons is well documented by both brothers' sketches and by Thomas's daily entries in a vest-pocket diary.[287] Following a brief sketching trip in the Sierras, the brothers turned eastward and arrived at Fort Hall, Idaho, in mid-August. There Thomas presented his presidential communique:

> This will introduce to the Commanding Officer at Fort Hall, Idaho Territory, Mr. Thomas Moran a distinguished American artist for whom I bespeak such attentions and courtesies as he would extend to myself—
>
> Sincerely,
>
> R. B. Hayes[288]

On the twenty-first the Morans left the post escorted by twenty soldiers with two wagonloads of provisions. Thomas's journal notes

COLOR PLATE 38

Paul Frenzeny and Jules Tavernier, *Denver from the Highlands*, 1874, Watercolor and gouache, 15″ × 23″.
Courtesy Denver Public Library, Western History Department, Denver, Colo.

COLOR PLATE 39

William Keith, *Devil's Slide, Weber Canon, Utah*, 1874, Oil, 40″ × 72″.
Courtesy Lane Publishing Co., Menlo Park, Colo.

COLOR PLATE 40

J. Goldsborough Bruff, *American Falls, Snake River,* Pastel and chalk, 16½″ × 21½″.
Courtesy Collection Huntington Library, San Marino, Calif.

COLOR PLATE 41

Peter Tofft, *Hell Gate Pass—The Old Battleground of the Eastern and Western Indians,* 1865, Watercolor, 5⅞″ × 8⅜″.
Courtesy M. and M. Karolik Collection, Museum of Fine Arts, Boston.

Color Plate 42

George Catlin, *A Crow Village and The Salmon River Mountains*, 1855, Oil, 18½″ × 24½″.
Courtesy Mellon Collection, National Gallery of Art, Washington, D.C.

Color Plate 43

Peter Moran, *The Tetons*, 1879, Watercolor, 12″ × 18″.
Courtesy Roswell Museum, Roswell, N.Mex. Gift of Senator Clinton P. Anderson.

COLOR PLATE 44

Harvey Otis Young, *Picturesque Shanties, Near Pueblo, Colorado,* ca. 1900, Oil, 11″ × 19″.
Courtesy private collection.

COLOR PLATE 45

Harvey Otis Young, *The Heart of the Rockies*, 1899, Mixed media, 45″ × 52″.
Courtesy Penrose Public Library, Colorado Springs, Colo.

PLATE 108

George Catlin, *Mesa Falls of the Snake River*, 1855, Oil, 15⅜″ × 21⅞″.
Courtesy National Gallery of Art, Washington, D.C. Collection of Mr. and Mrs. Paul Mellon.

that they were plagued by furious winds and that the smoke from forest fires spread a gray cast over the sky, obscuring their view of the spectacular scenery that unfolded as they proceeded north. On the third day Thomas wrote that the "Tetons are now plainly visible but not well defined owing to the mistiness of the atmosphere."[289] Two days later, on August 25, the brothers climbed the Snake River Range to gain a full view of their objective. Having passed the divide, Moran noted, ". . . we found a gently (rolling) country (descending) to the Basin. The Tetons here loomed up grandly against the sky & from this point it is perhaps the finest pictorial range in the United States or even in N. America."[290] Before moving down across the Teton River the next day, Thomas and Peter took time, despite the smoky atmosphere and distance, to make watercolor sketches of the grand profile of the granite spires on the east. Thomas's *The Three Tetons, Idaho, 18 Miles Distant, August 26, 1879* shows their distinctive profile through hazy atmospheric effects (plate 109). In contrast to his brother's impression, Peter's watercolor of a similar view reveals their bold forms silhouetted against the sky without smoky effects (color plate 43).[291] Under the conditions, it was remarkable that the brothers could obtain sketches at all.

After his trip to the Tetons, Peter made several forays into New Mexico and Arizona, motivated by his ethnological interests. Watercolor washes of Taos and Santa Fe taken between 1880 and 1883 (plate 110) reveal the artist's new focus. In August and September, 1890, with four other artists he "traveled as a special agent for the Bureau of Indian Affairs in conducting the Eleventh Census among the Northern Arapahoe and the eastern Shoshone on the Wind River Reservation, Wyoming."[292] Several detailed wash drawings of Arapaho camps at Fort Washakie taken in August date from this trip.[293] Peter's sketches are as straightforward as his report about the miserable state of the Shoshoni, revealing him to be an insightful and observant recorder. Unlike his famous brother, he had no interest in presenting the impression, character, or poetry of a subject; he belongs to the long line of reportorial recorders whom he followed late in the century.

Among the latecomers to the Rockies was the German-born artist Carl Rungius, known as the "Big Game Painter,"[294] whose ambition was to study and paint big-game animals of North America. Reared in a rural atmosphere in Germany, he developed a fondness for outdoor life, becoming a student in natural history at an early age. Like other artists who had a youthful bent for sketching, he had little interest in school and cared only for his art. His parents insisted that he first learn a trade, and he was apprenticed to a Berlin decorating firm during the summers—undoubtedly to learn the trade of house painting. Later he attended the School of Applied Arts for three winters, studying basic drawing with Max Koch. He continued to pursue his study of the animal form by observing and painting horses at the royal stables; several of these animal paintings were shown at the International Exhibition, in Berlin, in 1890. After a brief military service, an event in the spring of 1894 altered the course of his life. An uncle in Brooklyn invited him on a hunting trip in America—a visit that was to turn into a permanent stay. The next winter Rungius met Ira Dodge, a picturesque Wyoming guide, at a New York sportsman's show; the meeting led to adventures in Wyoming and the Yukon that were to continue throughout the artist's lifetime.

In the summer of 1895, Rungius sketched and painted in Wyoming. In October he and his party decided to take a side excursion into Yellowstone National Park. He later told the story of this journey:

> It was really a remarkable trip. We started too late in the season, the middle of October, but luck was with us.
> In the divide between the Green River on Gros Ventre we ran into a blizzard; it got bitter cold, even our sleeping bags weren't warm enough. . . .
> There was one silver lining to the cloud. When it cleared we were in camp near a little lake, which for some reason wasn't frozen over. It was rough going for a wagon; there was no road, only a trail. . . .
> But we got to the Park. There weren't any bridges in those days. The hotels were closed at that time of the year. . . .
> I painted the Canyon, a breath-taking sight, but the rest of the Park hasn't much to offer for an artist. Of course, the geysers and paint-holes are interesting.[295]

Although disenchanted with the scenic prospects during his first

The Three Tetons, Idaho & Millions ... Aug 26th 1879

PLATE 109

Thomas Moran, *The Three Tetons, Idaho . . .* , 1879, Watercolor, 20¾″ × 30⅞″.
Courtesy National Park Service, Teton National Park.

PLATE 110

Peter Moran, *Pueblo, Taos,* 1880, Pencil and chinese white, 12¾″ × 19¾″.
Courtesy Roswell Museum, Roswell, N.Mex. Gift of Senator Clinton P. Anderson.

PLATE 111

Carl Rungius, *Lower Falls of Yellowstone*, n.d., Oil, 15¼″ × 23½″.
Courtesy Glenbow-Alberta Institute, Calgary, Canada.

trip into the heart of the West, Rungius did capture some views of the spectacular canyon. The vigorous, spontaneous oil study *Lower Falls of Yellowstone* reveals the essentially rugged character of this country (plate 111).[296] As in his other studies, intended mainly as background for his animal pictures, he painted boldly and directly with broad, fluent brushwork, using brilliant colors.

Whether his studies were of landscapes or animals, Rungius always combined fidelity to nature with a feeling for the overall impression he wished to convey. Although animals were his primary interest, his landscape backdrops are superbly painted. The Wyoming trip was just the beginning; Rungius was to return repeatedly to the West in search of material and ideas.

9

THE REGIONAL SCENE

Though Colorado lies below the line of our first Pacific Railroad, and above the second, which I take it will be the southern, she cannot be refused a first place among their revelations. Because of her mountains, which turn the tracks north and south, she allures the lovers of the grand and picturesque in scenery; because of her mines of gold and silver, she seduces the greedy for gain; because of the agricultural resources of her plains and her valleys, she will have steady growth, permanent prosperity, and moral rectitude, for these are the gifts of a recompensing soil; because of her many and various mineral springs, soda, sulphur, and iron, and of her wonderfully clear, dry, and pure atmosphere, she will be the resort of the health-seeking. Within her borders the great continental mountains display their most magnificent proportions, the great continental rivers spring from melting snows, the plains most warmly invite the farmer and the husbandman, and the best population, between the Missouri River and California, has organized itself into a State. —Samuel Bowles[1]

ALTHOUGH Bowles's message was part of the barrage of publicity to promote tourism and encourage settlement within Colorado's borders, his and other publicists' predictions that the state offered vast potential for growth were later realized: Colorado became synonymous with the "Rockies" in the minds of a great portion of the nation's populace.

In all of the Rocky Mountain region during the nineteenth century, Colorado and Utah were the only states that were able to support local art communities. The "land of Zion on earth," however, could boast of an earlier growth and development. Brigham Young led his flock to the area of present-day Salt Lake City, in July, 1847. From the very beginning Utah grew in an orderly fashion under the church's iron authority. Farmers and craftsmen were encouraged to uproot their families and immigrate to Utah to begin new settlements in the land of the Deserets. Salt Lake City's pioneer resident artists were essentially utility men who had been called upon to decorate the Tabernacle and paint stage scenery for the new Salt Lake Theater. Most of them were artisans who classified themselves as sign and ornamental painters.

Utah, with its magnificent mountain scenery, varied topography, and unique historical development, was second only to Colorado in evolving a cosmopolitan society and active cultural center in the Rocky Mountain region, attracting artists from across the continent and abroad. Artistic services were constantly in demand in its burgeoning communities, and even more dramatically after the arrival of the transcontinental railroad in the spring of 1869. Several reasons have been suggested for Utah's vigorous artistic growth, apart from the didactic nature of Mormonism.[2] The population included a sizable number of foreign-born settlers, who had come from European centers that possessed an artistic awareness. Utah also had a more stable population than that of any other Rocky Mountain state, being mainly an agricultural and manufacturing center; consequently, the citizens of Zion could immediately begin building a permanent artistic base. Brigham Young noted: "The Majesty of the Rocky Mountains, the sunsets on Great Salt Lake, the beauty of the canyons and streams in the new land, every spot seemed to bring out the artistic in the natures of the Pioneers and their children."[3] In 1894 the *Salt Lake City Herald* could look back and comment:

"Ever since our population was twenty thousand, and that means thirty years or more ago, there has been a definite art aim in this city. Artists of merit have painted and clung together and produced works worthy of appreciation."[4]

Many of Utah's pioneer artists arrived before the railroad. Carl C. A. Christensen, a scenic painter from Denmark known for his panorama of dramatic episodes from early Mormon history, immigrated to the "land of Zion" with a handcart company in 1857.[5] George Ottinger, a landscape and history painter, followed closely on Christensen as a member of a similar outfit in 1861.[6] Like other early pioneer artists, the two were immediately employed to paint stage scenery for the Salt Lake Theater. Two years after his arrival Ottinger, E. L. T. Harrison, one of the theater's architects, and the photographer C. R. Savage joined forces with art-minded citizens to found Utah's first art school, the Deseret Academy of Fine Arts, in 1863. Ottinger, its president, sadly recalled: "We had a good class which survived ten months. At the end of that time we realized it was a little premature."[7] The school closed its doors, but Ottinger and his associates had initiated an interest among community leaders in raising art standards.

Ottinger, photographer Savage, and a portrait painter, E. W. Perry, later founded the Deseret Art Union.[8] Like other regional western art unions, it was undoubtedly modeled after the successful American Art-Union in New York.[9] In 1881, Ottinger was also instrumental in helping organize the Salt Lake Art Association, which was launched that winter with an inaugural exhibition of two hundred paintings by "native and foreign artists."[10] A year later he was appointed the first professor of drawing in the University of Deseret.

In 1893, concurrent with the founding of the Artists' Club of Denver, the Society of Utah Artists was formed. The local press noted that the society's inaugural exhibition the following year "went off with much eclat," convincing "the public that there existed in . . . [its] midst a well-developed school of art worthy to be fostered and encouraged."[11] Six years later, in 1899, the state legislature established the Utah Art Institute, the first state-funded organization; it was mandated to assemble a state collection of art, present a series

of public lectures on art, and hold an annual art exhibition.[12] Thus by the end of the nineteenth century Utah was recognized as one of the most culturally developed states in the Rocky Mountain region (plate 112).

In the early years of Utah's cultural development a number of difficulties impeded artistic growth. Artist's supplies were often difficult to obtain because of the great distances from Utah to the eastern supply centers.[13] Patronage was hard to come by because, as Ottinger perceptively noted in his journals, people "as a general thing like pictures and admire them but they have no money to spend for them."[14] Artists were often forced to take employment in other fields to sustain themselves, practicing their art only as a pastime. Christensen's biographer recounted that the artist's "passion for the art life was never satisfied. Cast apart from art influence, his life was one of self suppression and toil."[15]

The Utah artists also received excessive criticism from eastern critics who doubted the truthfulness of their pictorial forms. In rebuttal one local art critic stated:

> Pictures that we paint of our mountain scenery . . . are said to lack atmosphere. Yet in nearly every case the effect of aerial prospective [*sic*] has been exaggerated by the artist. It is beyond the belief of eastern or European critics that air can be so keen and clear as that of these valleys and mountains, and our painters add air that they do not usually see in order to make them more acceptable. It is as easy to do as falling off a log, far easier than to render the clear ringing tones that we see around us. There is no color anywhere more palpitating and thrilling than those we see almost daily on every side, but because the painters and the critics of the lowlands never met with such effects they complain that they are false and overdrawn.[16]

Since many of Utah's artists were engaged in other services or employed by the church, few could indulge themselves in painting pure landscapes. One of the serious students of Rocky Mountain scenery was Henry L. A. Culmer, born in Darington, Kent, England, on March 25, 1854.[17] In 1867 he and his family embarked for America, where they settled in Brooklyn for a year and then moved west to Utah. At age fourteen young Culmer went to work digging wells. He subsequently tried his hand at carpentry and other odd jobs before settling into a business career, first as a bookkeeper, then

PLATE 112

Brigham Young Academy Art Class, ca. 1890, Photograph, 8″ × 10″.
Courtesy Utah Arts Council, Salt Lake City, Utah.

a publisher, and eventually a developer of mineral resources. Apart from his business pursuits Culmer was fond of writing and helped organize several early Utah publications, including the *Utah Miner,* the *Salt Lake Times,* and the *Salt Lake Journal of Commerce.*

Although untutored, Culmer spent his spare time painting Utah's mountain scenery. It is rumored that he studied briefly under Alfred Lambourne, a scenery painter for the Salt Lake Theater.[18] He was probably also influenced by the dramatic mountainscapes of Thomas Moran, whom he met in 1873 when the American master stopped briefly in Salt Lake City on his way to the Grand Canyon with Major John Wesley Powell. Culmer's ten-foot-wide magnum opus of Shoshone Falls,[19] completed four years after Moran's spectacular showpiece of the same site, seems to indicate this influence, but the technical differences between the works are vast. Culmer's technical skills were obviously limited; he lacked the ability to convey atmospheric effects and model in paint. His watercolors are basically washes of color applied over a linear structure.

In his celebrated writings on "Mountain Art" published in the *Western Monthly* in 1894, Culmer commented on his landscape subject:

> My own appreciation of mountain beauty and its pictorial allurements has grown out of my wanderings in Utah, particularly amidst the wild and picturesque scenery of the Wasatch and Uinta ranges. . . . Some of our mountains, with their splendid bold fronts rising from the grassy valley, are as fine in form and color as any in the world.[20]

His detailed topographical description of the western front of the Wasatch Range could easily stand in place of his scenic view of Salt Lake City (plate 113), executed ten years later:

> It is a marked characteristic of the Salt Lake Valley, that the western front of the Wasatch presents its massive wall sheer and precipitous above the level vale, without foot-hills [*sic*], and absolutely without the lateral ranges which are rarely absent from the neighborhood of high peaks in other countries. It is this feature which makes the Wasatch mountains so magnificently beautiful, challenging the admiration of artists particularly, who rejoice in the splendid lines carved in the mountain side, sometimes sweeping from the highest peak to mountain-foot.

It is obvious that Culmer had done his homework; as a student of geology he was a close observer of fact, which he attempted to bring to his pictures of mountain scenery. His wash drawings are lovely but lack the dramatic impact of his writings.

Alfred Lambourne, an English-born immigrant, became one of Utah's most favored artists.[21] A solitary man and a poet, Lambourne imbued his work with surreal clarity while working within the Romantic-Realist tradition. In the mid-1870s he combined forces with Reuben Kirkham, of Logan, Utah, to paint a scenic panorama depicting stories from the *Book of Mormon* and sent it on a traveling exhibition throughout Utah. Lambourne believed that pictures should "have a depth of purpose, . . . that they [should] tell a tale and have a moral, . . . enlighten the mind and interpret human emotions."[22] His religiosity was very much a part of his attitude toward his own art. It can be said that Mormonism was the chief factor that contributed to Utah's high standard of culture during the nineteenth century, achieving for it a unique status for a land so far removed from the influences of a cosmopolitan center.

Utah's history of settlement is comparatively recent when contrasted with that of New Mexico. This southernmost state of the Rocky Mountain region—characterized by high plateaus cut by deep canyons, intense light, and brilliant coloring—had been colonized by the Spanish in the late sixteenth century. Passing into the control of Mexico in 1821, then becoming United States territory after the war between Mexico and the United States in 1846–48, New Mexico remained comparatively isolated and remote, with only pockets of civilization until late in the nineteenth century. With the advent of the railroads and the cessation of Indian troubles, New Mexico's population and livestock industry grew. Although since the mid-nineteenth century a stream of artists had been traveling across the land to capture pictures of the scenery and likenesses of the native inhabitants, New Mexico had no resident artist colony until after the turn of the twentieth century.[23] The remoteness of this settlement and the lack of exhibition facilities and, in particular, patronage probably discouraged many. Joseph Sharp, for example, sketched briefly in Santa Fe and Taos in 1883 and was captivated by its color-

PLATE 113

Henry L. A. Culmer, *Salt Lake City,* ca. 1905, Ink wash and chinese white, 9″ × 17″.
Courtesy Utah State Historical Society, Salt Lake City, Utah.

PLATE 114

Bert Phillips, *Camp at Red Rocks, Colorado,* 1898, Watercolor, 6″ × 17″.
Courtesy Denver Art Museum, Denver. Gift of Ralph J. Phillips.

ful, picturesque subjects. His stories about New Mexico reached artists Ernest Blumenschein and Bert Phillips, in Paris, in 1895. Sharp's enthusiasm set the two younger artists on a westward course that culminated in their own dramatic discovery of Taos in 1898 (see plate 114). Shortly after the turn of the century, other eastern artists discovered its pictorial possibilities. Concurrently Santa Fe began attracting artists, eventually becoming another active New Mexico art center.

Although prominent American artists like Worthington Whittredge, Thomas Moran, and Frederic Remington had captured scenes of New Mexico before the turn of the century, the impact of the unique environment—with its myriad of fantastic forms and colors, ethereal light, mystique, and picturesque natives—was too

strong a force for the nineteenth-century artist's brush and his restricted palette of somber colors. In the late nineteenth century only a small group of venturesome American artists of eastern repute had discovered the blond tonalities and brush technique of the French Impressionists, a trend that was later to play a vital role in picturing New Mexico's exotic scenery.

Like Montana and Wyoming, Idaho remained generally unpopulated during the first half of the nineteenth century. Until the discovery of gold in the region, which prompted the organization of an enormous new territory on March 4, 1863, Idaho was a wild, virtually unsettled region of varied terrain with formidable mountain barriers. After the gold excitement of 1862, Idaho's population sud-

302

denly swelled, and hundreds of mining camps sprang up around the region's various mining districts, attracting eastern capital. Before this time only a small number of artist-explorers had traveled through this country and pictorially recorded its spectacular scenery,[24] usually to illustrate government reports. Those pioneer artists who settled in Idaho found it difficult to support themselves through their artistic endeavors alone; they "had to be both versatile and resourceful to maintain a steady income, and few succeeded."[25] Consequently, there is a dearth of nineteenth-century Idaho art; however, there were "plenty of amateurs who pursued the visual arts for pleasure, and art exhibits of their works were assembled from time to time, often to raise funds for worthy causes." Early fairs offered another forum for the amateurs' work, but strictly speaking, Idaho had no real art communities or societies like those of Colorado and Utah.

Several reasons exist for Idaho's delayed cultural development before the turn of the century.[26] Scenic areas were virtually inaccessible, and transportation was not as extensive in Idaho as in Colorado and Utah. Also, unlike Colorado, Idaho did not have flamboyant mining kings in residence; most lived out of state, inaccessible as a key source of patronage. Moreover, Idaho was (and still is to some extent) "off the beaten track," offering few compelling reasons for people to remain there. Their goals lay elsewhere—in Oregon and on the Pacific Coast.

Despite these drawbacks, some artistic encouragement was offered to Idaho pioneers. Local agricultural and livestock fairs often included a division for sculpture, painting, and drawing, enticing artists (mostly amateurs) with small cash awards; the category for painting included "best fancy painting in oil, best animal painting in oil, best fruit painting in oil and best flower painting." Prizes were also given for the "best Idaho landscape" and for architectural drawings and photography, the latter being considered at the bottom of the "artistic totem pole." One of the most talented women amateurs to take advantage of such opportunities was Mrs. Jonas Brown, of Idaho City,[27] whose painting *Deer Hunting in the Badlands of Missouri* was exhibited at the fair of 1876 and received special recognition from the press. Her painting of hydraulic miners (plate 115) is naïve, meticulously detailed, and enchanting. Other Idaho pioneer artists include Arm Hincelin, a talented Jack of all trades who painted "the earliest known view of the capital city in 1864," and Charles Ostner, one of the better-known Idaho painters, who is especially celebrated for his "gilt George Washington on horseback in the Statehouse." Like other Rocky Mountain states, Idaho had its share of amateurs—but no real colony of talented professional painters.

Like Idaho and Montana, Wyoming was sparsely settled in the nineteenth century. Even though its Platte River Road had been well traveled by a stream of immigrants, few stayed behind to populate the state until late in the century. "That Wyoming appeared to offer few rich agricultural areas only partly explained" the reason why the land remained unpopulated for such a long time.[28] Wyoming's transportation facilities were limited to one east–west route. In the beginning the state was mainly populated by tradespeople who serviced immigrants on the overland route. Although a number of explorer-artists, as well as independents, had wandered over Wyoming and sketched its spectacular scenic wonders, few if any resident artists settled there until late in the century. Like other Rocky Mountain states, Wyoming had a number of settlers who painted and drew for their own amusement, but no organized groups of artists practiced in the state before the twentieth century.[29]

Probably the most rugged of all the Rocky Mountain states in the nineteenth century was Montana, whose settlement also began with a series of gold strikes that caused a stampede across its borders in the 1860s. As in Idaho, camps and eventually cities sprang up around the state's mining districts. "By their very nature, the quickly exploitable placer camps of the West attracted an unstable population, men whose chief motto was 'Cash in and get out.'" Montana was no exception—lawlessness and disorder prevailed, and towns were often deserted as men rushed to other, more profitable gold strikes. As in Idaho and Wyoming, "another plague to the mining towns of Montana was inadequate transportation"—food sources were as far away as Utah.[30] The eastern three-fifths of the state remained unsettled until the 1880s, when the agriculture and livestock industries spread eastward. A graphic picture of Montana's early history can be

PLATE 115

Mrs. Jonas W. Brown, *Mining in Boise Basin in the Early Seventies*, 1870s, Oil, 27¼″ × 21¼″. Courtesy Idaho Historical Society, Boise, Idaho.

gleaned from the "reminiscences" of one of the state's earliest pioneers—Granville Stuart, miner, trader, merchant, rancher, politician, and amateur artist:

> I came to what is now our magnificent state of Montana when it was a trackless wilderness, the only white inhabitants being Jesuit fathers, and a few Indian traders and trappers at the missions and trading posts; when the mountains and valleys were the homes of countless herds of buffalo, elk, deer, moose, antelope, bear, and mountain sheep; when the streams swarmed with fish and beaver and the Indians were rich and respectable. I have watched the frontier push from the Mississippi river to the Rocky mountains.[31]

Stuart, a friend of Charles Russell, was born in Clarksburg, Virginia, on August 27, 1834. At an early age he moved with his family to Princeton, Illinois, and then settled in Iowa in 1838. In 1852, Granville, his father, and his brother James went to California to prospect. In 1858, while making their way back to Iowa, their curiosity about a rumor of gold in Montana paid off: the prospect hole they dug "was the first prospecting [for] gold done in what is now Montana." From this early beginning they followed the strikes from gulch to gulch, setting up small businesses in the towns that sprang up near each strike—moving back and forth across Montana's western gold fields. Granville even tried his hand at ranching, a business that brought him first wealth and later financial ruin. The Stuart brothers' experiences were recorded by Granville in small day-by-day "memoranda books, . . . in account books, and . . . in large sized blank books." These notes were later condensed into "a narrative about his most outstanding experiences of his life."[32]

Granville also sketched in pencil and pen many of the meaningful scenes of his wanderings. He often made small sketches "in a little leather-bound notebook of various memoranda, business accounts, itineraries, and lists."[33] When the occasion dictated, he selected a larger book (approximately 7 × 10¼ inches) to make a more elaborate drawing, sometimes in watercolor. A supply list in one of his account books includes crayons, pencils, watercolors, brushes, sketchbooks, drawing portfolios, and drawing paper. Many of these sketches were intended to augment his narrative, which he began preparing before his death on October 2, 1918.

To judge by his simple, naïve pencil-and-pen outline sketches and watercolor wash drawings, Granville had little if any art training. Despite his rough-and-ready pioneering background, he was evidently "a student of books and of nature, [and] a lover of music and art," who by his own account had enjoyed sketching and coloring as a youngster. His pencil-and-pen sketches also show that Granville was a close observer of factual detail; consequently they provide the social historian an invaluable pictorial record of an early Montana that quickly vanished. On July 5, 1865, for example, Stuart drew on the back of a calendar a semidiagrammatic pen sketch of a small town called Ophir, near the Marias River (plate 116). The following year, returning to Montana after a journey to Chicago, the pioneer-artist was saddened to discover that the town had "disappeared" and "left no trace behind," save for one solitary chimney and the foundation of an adobe house. Even the wood from the two log cabins had been taken. Stuart described the town's violent end:

> Thus passed away like a dream of the night the brilliant expectations of N. W. Burris and many others, who founded this city in the spring of 1865; and who to the number of ten now rest in their bloody graves on the river's brink, having been murdered in May of that year by an overwhelming force of the Blood band of Blackfeet.

The parallel lines Stuart uses to form his mountains or designate the slope of the valley terrain suggest that he knew something about how to prepare a topographic map, though his limited technique indicates that he had not had formal training in the art.

Stuart also captured an enchanting view of his hometown, Deer Lodge, in watercolor (plate 117), picturing his small general store in the foreground with the Gold Creek Mountains in the background. Pale washes fill in this outline drawing, with areas of white paper revealed to indicate snow and clouds.

Stuart published other writings during his lifetime, among them the text of Charles Russell's first illustrated book, *Studies of Western Life*, published in 1890.[34] Although Stuart's writings and sketches provide a historical and pictorial record of Montana's colorful early days, the arrival of Russell on the scene gave the state its first nationally recognized artist.

PLATE 116

Granville Stuart, *Ye Gaye and Festive Towne Yclepit "Ophir" at Ye Mouth of Ye Marias River, M. T., 12 Miles below Fort Benton/Looking East July 5th 1865*,
Pen and ink, 10″ × 13½″. Courtesy Carl S. and Elisabeth Waldo Dentzel Collection, Northridge.

View in Deer Lodge, showing the Gold Creek Mountains (13,800 feet high) taken in Nov. 1867

PLATE 117

Granville Stuart, *View in Deer Lodge, showing the Gold Creek Mountains (13,800 feet high) taken in Nov. 1867*, Watercolor, 6½″ × 9¼″.
Courtesy Carl S. and Elisabeth Waldo Dentzel Collection, Northridge.

Many artists were lured to Colorado by its magnificent primeval scenery, but few remained behind to become residents of the small, rude settlements spawned by the discovery of gold on the eastern slopes of the Rocky Mountains in 1858. By the 1870s, however, "Denver was transformed from a village into one of the . . . most progressive cities of the Union," an art colony appeared.[35] Formed by J. Harrison Mills, a transplanted eastern artist of some repute, the new colony struggled constantly against local indifference to the fine arts.[36]

Before Mills's immigration to Colorado in 1872, a move prompted by his wife's ill health, isolated attempts had been made by self-tutored local artists to reproduce scenic views. Alfred E. Mathews's drawings of Rocky Mountain scenery and Colorado townscapes, reminiscent of topographical views known in the East, were lithographed and published in book form.[37] Although picturesque, the views were questionable in their accuracy of detail and perspective. Amateur artists Esther Yates Frazier and Mary E. Achey provided early, awkward views of Colorado mining settlements and encampment scenes.[38] The few early records of Colorado scenery by the resident artists of the 1860s appear to be of little help in tracing the early history of Colorado's art colony. Unquestionably, Mills's arrival on the Denver scene seems to have been the dominant force in initiating art activities of any consequence. Aware of the role that the eastern art organizations played in stimulating the arts and encouraging patronage, Mills had a sense of professionalism and the ability to direct Colorado's artistic future.

In 1876, intent on raising art standards, Mills organized the Academy of Fine Arts Association of Colorado, an informal organization composed of artists, architects, and leading professionals. To supplement the work of this informal group, Mills established the Denver Sketch Club in 1880 to encourage exhibitions of the members' work. The club was reorganized in 1881 as the Colorado Art Association, often referred to as the "Kit Kat Club."[39] On February 12, 1882, the *Denver Tribune* reported the incorporation of the Academy of Fine Arts Association of Colorado, an organization formed by the union of the Kit Kat Club and the Art Reading Society with the pur-

pose of founding in the immediate future an art school to be known as the Colorado Academy of Design. The association's distinguished list of directors included Governor F. W. Pitkin, William G. Evans, and Mills, who was elected its first president.[40] Shortly after its formation the School of Design was opened in the association's quarters. In only three months of operation enrollment grew from "naught to a healthy 27 in number,"[41] and the association was forced to seek larger accommodations in the Tabor Grand Opera House, built by mining tycoon Horace Tabor. The liberal arrangements of Tabor and his agents enabled the artists to secure rooms for their studios at low rentals and to inaugurate a "Studio Flat." The initiation of the Artists' Reception on Saturday afternoons appeared to stimulate an interest in the artists' work and, according to a review in *Denver Inter-Ocean* on "Denver Artists," was responsible for an increase in art sales.

Further encouragement of the arts and the progressive cultivation of taste in Denver could be attributed to several well-publicized exhibitions in the 1880s—held under the notable auspices of the Denver Mining and Industrial Exposition in 1882 and 1883. Housed in a mammoth structure five hundred feet long, these great fairs provided ample exposure for Colorado's local artists and the few easterners whose work was exhibited.[42] These exhibitions seem semiprofessional when compared to earlier art displays at the territorial fairs.

Owing to a lack of support, the academy closed its doors sometime before 1885. In 1886 a small, courageous group of local artists formed the Denver Art Club;[43] John D. Howland, pioneer Colorado artist, was elected president.[44] Unfortunately, a schism in the society prompted its early demise in 1887.[45]

Sensing the discouragement of Denver's artists, the critics hastened to laud home talent:

The artists of Denver are worthy of encouragement and patronage. Many a brilliant young man and woman have been obliged to resign a flattering future in Eastern cities for considerations of health. Others have been attracted to Colorado by the peculiar beauty of its scenery. . . . As a consequence the people of means are gradually beautifying their homes with other than the stereotyped ornamentations of the paper hanger and the makers of good pictures are allowed to live.[46]

The critics recognized Colorado's growing wealth and the influx of a large number of cultured families from eastern cities. They attributed Denver's ambivalence about art to the acknowledged fact that new cities were slow to produce art centers, responding first to the immediate pressures of expansion and development of natural resources. They admonished their readers, however, against permitting Denver to take a back seat to cities like Omaha and Kansas City, whose artwork they considered inferior: ". . . in years past [artists] have been located [in Denver], until driven away by neglect and pecuniary embarrassment, men of the highest talent whose pictures to-day command respect and admiration in the great art centers."[47] The brief period of efflorescence in the arts during the 1880s suggests the inconstancy of Denver's citizenry in support of artistic activities.

The shifting art scene and the ensuing struggles of the small art colony were evident in the early 1890s. Replacing those artists who had failed to capture recognition and wealth in Colorado and had left for greener pastures was an ever-changing stream of artists drawn to the shifting mood and face of the land. One was Harvey Young, an eastern artist of some reputation who moved to Colorado in 1879, settling temporarily in Manitou Springs. His arrival in Colorado was heralded as providing "a new impulse to the growth of a standard of taste" in the community.[48] His paintings, reflecting the subtleties of plein-air sketching, stirred considerable interest among the local artists. His presence in the area was thought to lend prestige to the Denver colony, and he was eventually to step in where J. Harrison Mills had left off.

Apparently, Young came west both to gather sketches for commissioned paintings and to strike it rich by actively engaging in Colorado's mining ventures. In the 1880s his total preoccupation with mining matters virtually precluded his active participation in art activities. In an occasional review during these years the local critic mentioned that Harvey Young was sketching in Colorado and New Mexico, but the reports were infrequent, and the number of extant paintings from this period is small. Not until the founding of Denver's Paint and Clay Club and the notice of its first exhibition in 1889 does Harvey Young's name figure in the activities of a local organization. Having acquired money and leisure time, Young apparently realized the need to draw the public's attention to artists who endeavored to interpret nature in "a truthful and intelligent manner."[49] Once he had been initiated into Denver's art scene, Young's name was repeatedly mentioned in connection with local art affairs, and his work was lauded for its fidelity to nature and for its spiritual content. Appointed to the executive committee of the Artists' Club of Denver, founded in 1893,[50] he was named a jury member for the first two annual exhibitions of the Artists' Club, held in 1894 and 1895.[51]

Although lack of patronage continued into the 1890s, the small but spirited "colony" engendered enough support to continue to promote art in the community. On December 4, 1893, fourteen local artists gathered in the studio of Emma Richardson Cherry to form a new art society, "the Artists' Club of Denver, which in turn became the Denver Art Association and then the Denver Art Museum."[52] On December 16, 1893, a constitution was adopted. The eleven charter members included Harvey Young, Charles Partridge Adams, Marion J. Johnson, Alice H. Howes, Elisabeth Spalding, Helen Munson, Curtis Chamberlin, John R. Henderson, Charles M. Carter, Mrs. Cherry, and Henrietta Bromwell.[53] The club minutes describe at length the preparations for the annual exhibition, held in April (plate 118). Although its opening night preview was reserved for Denver's glamorous society, the show was open to the public and attracted large crowds. Throughout the Panic of 1893, the club continued to function and hold regular exhibits because of the active support of its associate membership.

As the years progressed, the club's prestige grew. On February 15, 1917, it incorporated as the Denver Art Association;[54] in 1922 the association moved to its first permanent home, Chappell House, and the following year incorporated as the Denver Art Museum.[55]

The perseverance of its small art community finally transformed Colorado into a major center of culture. From bleak beginnings

PLATE 118

The Artists' Club of Denver, *Second Annual Exhibition*, 1895, Photograph, 5″ × 7″.
Courtesy Denver Public Library, Western History Department, Denver.

caused by the desert myth, Colorado became a mecca for scenic artists. As leaders in the Artists' Club, Harvey Otis Young and Charles Partridge Adams were important figures in these early years. Their stories have been told elsewhere and will be discussed only briefly here.

Throughout his romantic career Harvey Young exhibited a passion for accomplishment, particularly in his interpretations of the varying moods of nature evident in his many scenes of Colorado. While standing in nature's presence, reverent, enthusiastic, watching for the delicate, evanescent effects and changes of light, he came to understand her gentler moods, her enchanting mysteries, and her serene grandeur.

From the limited documentary evidence available, we know that the artist was born in Lynden, Vermont, on November 23, 1840, and received an academic education.[56] In 1859 he traveled to California, "catching the gold fever," prospecting and sketching along the coast. His early, largely self-tutored artistic endeavors were followed by academic study in Paris at the Académie Julien. With recognition in the Paris Salon Exhibition of 1878 he returned home to establish a reputation as an artist in the East.[57] Once again, beckoned by the "lust for gold," he traveled westward to Colorado to make his fortune by prospecting. For several years he followed this course until financial reverses following the Panic of 1893 forced him to devote full time to painting.

Shortly before this time Young had suddenly shifted from oils to a mixed-media technique (wash and opaque watercolor). "It has been said that Harvey Young was a painter who dealt with effects rather than with subject and that light and air were materials with which he secured them."[58] Perhaps oil was "too heavy and slow to carry the faint, soft effects of sky and cloud and shadow that distinguished his pictures."[59] In the same period that Harvey Young shifted to the lighter medium, artists on the eastern seabord were also discovering the effects achieved by "a freer use of water-color and a more liberal employment of all those various agencies by which color is modified through manipulation."[60] Young's visits to the New England coast in the summers of 1888 through 1892 suggest that he was aware of these developments in the East.[61]

Young's interest in this new technique and his financial exigencies probably caused him to direct his energies toward advancing his artistic career. As he continued to experiment with a mixed-media technique, his pictures began to show a freer manipulation of body color, resulting in a depth and a brilliance approaching those of oils.[62] At this late stage in his career he also returned to oil painting, producing some remarkably effective works reminiscent of his French Barbizon inspiration (color plate 44).

The period from 1897 to his death on May 13, 1901, marks the culmination of Young's style and technique as a landscapist. His mature works achieve the subtle tonal qualities and atmospheric effects that were to become his trademarks. In Young's depictions of Colorado scenery the foreground is always prominent—either carpeted with soft, green shadow and splotches of tinted blooms or clothed in somber brown and yellow foliage. These dominant foregrounds provide the proper distance to the mountains, their shining silver peaks veiled in diaphanous blue-and-white atmosphere. Harvey Young's technique contributes greatly to the success of these effects, most fully realized in his major work, *The Heart of the Rockies* (1899, color plate 45).

Like Corot, Harvey Young had an intuitive feeling for composition, for the beautiful in nature, and for delicate color harmonies. Viewed in the proper historical perspective, despite his limited production, Young's talent for conveying these transient atmospheric effects in the mixed-media technique earns him a respected place in the history of American art.

Charles Partridge Adams, another artist highly acclaimed by local critics during his lifetime, was born in Franklin, Massachusetts, on January 12, 1858.[63] After his father's death, Charles's family moved to Vermont. After the death of his older sister in 1876, Charles's mother moved to Denver, believing, as Charles noted later, that the invigorating climate would be healthful for her frail son and daughter. Adams, then eighteen, took jobs to help augment the family's small savings. One, in the Chain and Hardy Book Store, influenced his whole life:

Books, pictures, paintings, artists, new ideas and ideals were brought to me. The junior member of the firm [Helen Chain, a local artist], by whom I was employed, was a beautiful character and became my lifelong friend. The work and surroundings were pleasant, but the salary was small. . . . Since early boyhood I had been interested in drawing, and gradually the charm, the romance and grandeur of an artist's life dawned upon me. . . . At last came the choice: "I am going to be a landscape painter."

Adams's life was now divided between frequent sketching trips to draw from nature and his work in the store, where he found books on art instruction, artists' engravings, and occasionally original works. He later attributed his growth as an artist to the invaluable criticism he received from the proprietor's wife, Helen Chain, a local artist and art teacher who had reportedly been a pupil of George Inness.[64] Sometime in the early 1880s, Adams and another aspiring local artist, A. Phimister Proctor, decided to open a Denver studio together and begin painting full time. The partnership was short-lived, for Proctor opted to move to New York, where his career had a "fighting chance." In 1882, after seeking Helen Chain's advice, Adams went to work for a local wood engraver, J. M. Bagley.[65] Poor health made him abandon this work for a career in drawing and painting.

Although he began by producing crayon portraits after photographs, he made a lasting reputation for himself in landscape painting. Sometime in the late 1880s or early 1890s, Adams traveled to New York and California, where he visited various artists in their studios. On his California trip, said Adams, "I met some artists, saw many fine paintings, and visited the studios of William Keith and Thomas Hill." To judge by his oils and watercolors of Colorado scenic vistas, Adams appears to have been most inspired by George Inness, under whom he may have studied briefly.

Adams's career was launched when he received a gold medal for his landscape *The Last of the Leaves* at the National Mining and Industrial Exposition of Denver in 1883.[66] From that time on his work was constantly in demand—from large oil landscapes to small watercolors ordered as wedding gifts. Although he later referred to these as "pot boilers," they are refreshingly lovely—often more appealing than his studio oils. Adams was often spoken of as "the painter of mountains and sunsets." His coloring and his broad, vigorous brush treatment were particularly admired. Adams described

one scene, a broadly painted watercolor of a fiery Colorado sunset (color plate 46): ". . . the sunsets; where can one see more brilliant displays of the pomp and pageantry of the skies? Sunsets which impress themselves upon the memory and gleam and glow like a vision of the heavenly city."[67]

Like other artists, Adams made many sketches both for his own enjoyment and as memory aids for future paintings. Many of these handsome pencil sketches still remain, revealing the artist's deft hand and careful eye in capturing the poetic moods of nature. Adams uses his pencil like a brush, easily producing painterly and atmospheric effects with light shadings heightened by chinese white. In capturing his views, Adams often hiked into the wilderness to find the exact mood, sight, and moment. One small, vigorous pencil drawing, for example, shows the rugged, windswept mountains, winter snow piled in their crevices (plate 119). After the turn of the century Adams and his wife left Denver and Estes Park, where they had their homes, and moved to Pasadena, California, where the artist died in 1942.

Although Denver's art community was the most active, other Colorado cities contributed to the flourishing growth of art in the state during the nineteenth century. Colorado Springs, a bustling city nestled in the shadows of Pikes Peak, attracted an affluent cosmopolitan citizenry. The therapeutic nature of its climate played a vital role in its development—artists joined the throngs to the city. Not all came for health reasons or for financial remuneration; some were lured by the magnificent scenery. Colorado Springs' roster of artists included English-born Walter Paris, Philadelphians Anne and Thomas Parrish, architect-painter Frank T. Lent, English-landscapist William Bancroft, Indian painter Charles Craig, landscapist and teacher Leslie Skelton, and many others.[68] Late in his career Harvey Young moved to the Springs and became an active and renowned member of the community. On November 27, 1882, the town's first "Art Loan Exhibition" was held under the auspices of the women of the Presbyterian Church; it was followed by similar shows in the 1880s.[69] In 1885 an exhibition of artworks by Charles Craig, Lent, Parrish, and several women amateurs was held in Nims & Company's photographic parlors, which, the local press reported,

PLATE 119

Charles P. Adams, *In the Rocky Mountains,* ca. 1900, Pencil, 6¾″ × 8¾″.
Courtesy Dines Collection, Denver, Colo.

were "crowded to their fullest capacity" at the opening reception.[70] Two years later, paintings from the easel of Craig, Charles Adams, Pueblo artist Joseph Hitchins, and others were exhibited at the Pikes Peak Avenue store.[71] The fame and fortune of Colorado Springs' fledgling art colony was, however, truly launched with the Art Loan Exhibition held for the benefit of the Bellevue Sanitarium under the auspices of the Colorado Springs Board of Trade. The show was described as "superior to any art exhibition ever held in the west."[72] The outgrowth was Colorado Springs' first art school, formed and run by Frank Lent and Thomas and Anne Parrish. Classes in drawing from casts and nature, painting, and other subjects were offered, all patterned after those of foreign and eastern schools.[73] Both of the Parrishes had been students at the Academy of Fine Arts in Philadelphia—Anne as a portrait painter and her husband as a landscapist and etcher. Thomas probably learned the latter profession from his brother Stephen Parrish, a well-known eastern etcher.[74] With the arrival of Canadian-born landscapist Leslie Skelton in Colorado Springs, the colony's efforts were established. Its first exhibition in Perkins Hall at Colorado College in February, 1900, was probably the most elaborate of its kind in the community; all the work shown was by local artists. Skelton, who supervised the exhibition, was responsible for initiating the idea. The press reported:

> The amount of material that has been offered will tax the energies of the hanging committee and it is expected that a selection will be made that will at once be both interesting and instructive. Amongst the exhibitors will be Mrs. Parrish, Messrs. Chas. Craig, Louis Soutter, Leslie J. Skelton, C. G. Lotave, . . . and several others whose work will for the first time claim the attention of the people of Colorado Springs.[75]

Although Eliza Greatorex, a New York author-etcher, was reportedly the first artist to sketch in Colorado Springs, her visit was brief, made chiefly to gather pen-and-ink sketches of surrounding natural wonders for her book *Summer Etchings in Colorado.*[76] Englishman Walter Paris was Colorado Springs' first resident artist.[77] Born in London, England, on February 28, 1842, Paris studied architecture under the English architect Benjamin Ferry from 1857 to 1858. While a practicing architect, he attended the Royal Academy of Art, reportedly as a student of T. L. Rowbotham, Paul Naftel, and

Joseph Nash.[78] According to the biographical sketch Paris gave to a Denver reporter in 1893, he was appointed by the India Office as an assistant architect to the government of Bombay in 1863. "In 1865 he was appointed architect to the government of Bombay in place of Mr. Trubshaw, and in that capacity continued to act until 1870, when he returned to England." It was at this point that Paris decided to become a painter and attended the Royal Academy in London. On the advice of his doctors he moved to Colorado in 1872, settling in Colorado Springs, where he purchased a small piece of property. He remained there until late in 1877, when he left for New York City. He returned briefly to his native country in the 1880s.[79] From 1887 to 1890 he was employed at the Royal Military Academy at Woolwich, where he had succeeded one W. Clifton, teaching landscape drawing, a skill that was then "taught mainly so that officers could sketch terrain for the purpose of surveillance."[80] Paris's training was more than adequate for this assignment, which followed closely the instruction provided in the United States at West Point Academy and emphasized topographical features. In 1891 he returned to Colorado Springs, but for the next two years he lived in Denver, where he had established a studio.[81] His last visit was short-lived; sometime in late 1893 or early 1894 he moved to Washington, D.C., where he remained until his death on November 26, 1906.[82]

Paris's small watercolors of Colorado scenes, together with his views of English abbeys and countryside and his decorative still-life studies, are similar in treatment. His precise drawings with their pale washes of color and minute details are typical of English topographical work. Paris attributed his careful attention to details to his architectural training. The only change that can be observed in the evolution of his style from his earliest recorded Colorado scenes in 1873 is to a looser and more impressionistic brush in his work of the 1890s. His subdued, pale washes of color never changed or took on a brilliant tone. In his lifetime Paris's drawings were recognized as faithful representations of scenery rather than fanciful works that stretched the imagination of the viewer. "Purity of tone, delicacy of touch, and immense fidelity to nature's marvelous detail" were the qualities that critics believed distinguished his work from that of others. His watercolor scenes of the Garden of the Gods, Monument Park, Manitou Park, Pueblo, Cheyenne Canyon, and Mount Ouray in the San Juan country were singled out by the Denver press as admirable studies of nature.

Paris was a long-term friend of geologist-artist William Holmes. They first met in October, 1874, when the English artist joined Ferdinand Vandeveer Hayden outside Colorado Springs as a guest of his survey.[83] Newspaper accounts often erroneously described Paris as an official member of this survey. A photograph by Jackson shows Paris sketching the scenery in Monument Park while the famous explorer stands at his shoulder, intently watching the artist at work (plate 120). In a letter to Holmes written in 1875, the artist remarks on his sketching tour in the Platte River canyon (present Roxborough Park) after leaving the troops, expressing his hopes of rejoining them in the field the following year.[84] The letter includes three marvelous pen sketches of the canyon's fantastic sandstone formations. One, a view similar to one captured by Seymour in 1820, was elaborated into a watercolor by Paris in 1874 (plate 121). Throughout his lifetime Paris continued his friendship and correspondence with Holmes. These letters help to fill in the gaps in the artist's life, providing an itinerary of his travels back and forth to England and even his sketching jaunts up and down the New England coast.[85]

After his return to Colorado in 1891, Paris produced a series of watercolors intended for a pictorial album augmented with geographical descriptions that he hoped to publish.[86] One of the more historically important and interesting scenes is *Glenwood Springs, Colorado* (1891, color plate 47); the watercolor is untitled, but the site has been identified by railroad historian Jackson Thode:

> The town can be none other than Glenwood Springs . . . c. 1892. The view is slightly north of directly west. The two timber Howe truss spans, and long curved trestle approach from the left, are the D&RG bridge across the Grand [now the Colorado] River on the line west to New Castle, Rifle and Grand Junction. The hill on the left is Red Mountain, while the long, straight, slightly inclined line from the left to the center of the picture, across the foot of Red Mtn., is the Colorado Midland's main line to the west.[87]

The works of regional artists like Paris, Young, Adams, and

PLATE 120

William H. Jackson, *Dr. Hayden and Walter Paris (sketching)*, 1874, Photograph, 5″ × 7″. Courtesy Denver Public Library, Western History Department, Denver.

Culmer, as well as those of other latecomers to the Rocky Mountain states, indicate that an array of talent existed in regional art centers. Although these artists were recognized in their lifetimes, they have fallen into obscurity and are largely forgotten today. It is hoped that this book has stated the case for including these artists in the mainstream of American landscape art, an inclusion that would give us a fuller picture of the development of the genre in this country.

PLATE 121

Walter Paris, *Platte River Cañon*, 1874, Watercolor, 6¾″ × 10″.
Courtesy William Bell Collection, England.

THE VANISHING SCENE: CHARLES M. RUSSELL, HENRY FARNY, FREDERIC REMINGTON, AND JOHN TWACHTMAN

The Americans have gashed this country up so horribly with their axes, hammers, scrapers and plows that I always like to see a place which they have overlooked; some place before they arrive with their heavy-handed God of Progress.

Leaving the Rio Grande Railroad at Tres-Piedras, in New Mexico, recently the driver and I trotted all day over the dry table-land, and yet the great blue wall of the Sangre de Cristo range seemed as near and as far as it had in the morning. It was as though we could not get near it. This vast table-land west of the mountains is itself eight thousand feet in the air, yet viewed from there, the mountains scallop skyward, range after range—snow-capped—beautiful—overpowering.—Frederic Remington[1]

IN the last decades of the nineteenth century the magic of the West continued to lure artists, even though many aspects of frontier life had already succumbed to the advance of civilization. Three important narrative artists—Charles M. Russell, Henry Farny, and Frederic Remington—were haunted by this transformation, and in these closing decades they devoted much of their time to the documentation of a fast-disappearing social and physical environment. They not only captured the spirit of an historic time but provided a record of the geological wonders of the vast territories in the backdrops of their storytelling pictures. During the same period, in 1894, John Twachtman came west, commissioned to produce a series of paintings of Yellowstone Park. Unlike Russell, Farny, and Remington, Twachtman was primarily a landscapist, yet in his own unique style he added importantly to the pictorial vision of the Rocky Mountains.

Charles Marion Russell,[2] born of well-to-do parents in Saint Louis in 1864, had from his earliest childhood an infatuation with Indians, the frontier, and the West. Throughout his boyhood he dreamed of the day when he could go west and become a cowboy. Finally, when he was sixteen, his parents, hoping that his romantic yearning might be cured through the experience of reality, allowed him to accompany a family friend to Montana Territory. The cure did not work. Russell stayed in the West for the rest of his life, supporting himself by working as a sheepherder, a cowhand, and a wrangler, rarely without his sketch pad and watercolors.

Unlike his contemporaries, Russell never felt a need to study in Europe's art academies, nor did he seek guidance in the lessons of accepted artists or styles of the day. His studio was the western scene; his inspiration, the men and actions of its history. Self-trained and self-confident, he denied all but nature's influence, considering Impressionism and other alien persuasions so much crazy-quilt madness. To Russell such approaches were too analytical and, therefore, irrelevant. He was interested in the romance and reality of the West, not in the exploration of painting theory.

With this vision of the West an important part of his temperament, it was natural that Russell followed the pattern of the narrative painters, creating action-filled pictures with scenes of the Old

PLATE 122

Charles M. Russell, *Hunting Party*, 1896, Watercolor on paper, 12⅜" × 23".
Courtesy Buffalo Bill Historical Center, Cody.

West, which he created out of the tales of old-timers and Indian friends. Several years ago the late K. Ross Toole, then director of the Historical Society of Montana, summarized Russell's art:

> The *real* power of Russell's work . . . resides in the fact that he felt, to the very depths of his being, that an era was dying—and that it meant *something*. For Charles M. Russell the extermination of the buffalo, the confinement of Indians to reservations, the fencing of the open range, the plowing under of the grasslands, and the pollution of the fresh air with smoke from copper smelters did not spell progress. He sincerely believed that these things desecrated the enchanting West that he loved, and that . . . [the] West was God's country.[3]

Although Russell possessed a profound appreciation for the beauty and mood of the Montana Rockies, it was the human element—the Indians, the trappers, cowboys, outfitters, and prospectors—which dominated his canvases and brought Russell his fullest realization as a painter (see plate 122). Nevertheless, his many sketchbooks indicate that he was a serious student of the natural environment that served as a dramatic background for his narrative paintings. These scenic backdrops are clearly views that Russell recorded in the mile after mile of high country he explored during his forty-six years in Montana. Naturally enough, they include many notations from Judith Basin, where he first settled and where he saw the distant Little Belt and Highwood mountains for the first time. Another inexhaustible source of material was Glacier National Park, where he had a summer cottage for many years. Whether in oil or in watercolor, Russell's sketches of these areas are fresh, spontaneous vignettes of nature, loosely executed, yet filled with precise attention to the details of rock formations, the lighting and coloration of distant mountains, and the multicolored highlights of foliage. Many of them include accurate depictions of the wild creatures of the region (plate 123).

Despite its small scale, a sample of his many oil sketches of mountain scenery conveys the immensity of the rocky promontories so characteristic of the Montana landscape (plate 124). Sketches similar to this one served as pattern for the background treatment in Russell's magnum opus, *Lewis and Clark Meeting the Flatheads at Ross' Hole* (color plate 48). The distant mountain range serves as a dramatic foil for the action in the foreground; Russell's introduction of a horned sheep skull and three dogs in the immediate foreground shows how valuable his innumerable, anatomically detailed sketches of native wild creatures had been. Although a serious student of history might find fault with anachronistic details, such as the costumes worn by the Indians,[4] the painting is undeniably the most dynamic re-creation of this historic event in existence. In it Russell achieved his true aspiration as an artist: he captured the life and spirit of the frontier West.

Henry Farny, another devotee of the frontier West, first came to the Rocky Mountain region in 1883. Although he achieved an enviable position in the art world during his lifetime, his reputation in subsequent decades was overshadowed by his contemporaries Russell and Remington. Only recently has his work been rediscovered and his brilliant interpretation of the West received the acclaim it so richly deserves.[5]

Farny was born in Ribeauville, France, on July 15, 1847. His father, Charles Farny, a man of substantial means, was a Protestant who fled to the United States with his family to escape religious and political oppression following the revolution of 1848. The senior Farny acquired a large acreage in western Pennsylvania. It was in this backwoods wilderness that the young Farny first encountered Indians, members of the Onondaga tribe, whose camp was only a few miles from the homestead. Fascinated by these intriguing figures, Farny developed a consuming interest in the native peoples of North America that continued throughout his career and became a dominant feature in his art.

In 1859, weary of the isolated existence, the family moved to Cincinnati. Henry attended school there until his father's death in 1863, when he left school to help support the family. Presumably he did illustrative work, for a group of Cincinnati views by him were published in a two-page spread in *Harper's Weekly* on September 30, 1865. That was the beginning of an association with Harper and Brothers that continued intermittently for nearly thirty years. In fact, the following year the firm sent him to New York, where he was employed as an engraver and cartoonist. Farny's heart

PLATE 123

Charles M. Russell, *C. M. Russell Sketch Book*, n.d., Watercolor, 5″ × 7″.
Courtesy Amon Carter Museum, Fort Worth.

PLATE 124

Charles M. Russell, *Mountain Landscape*, n.d., Oil, 5½″ × 9″.
Courtesy Amon Carter Museum, Fort Worth.

was set on a painter's career, however, not an illustrator's—and on September 7, 1867, he sailed for Europe, where he studied under the guidance of Thomas Buchanan Read in Rome. From there, at Read's suggestion, he went to Düsseldorf to study with the landscapist Hermann Herzog. A letter addressed to his mother indicated that he rebelled against this instruction:

> I wish to become a painter of figures and specially to study portraits (as a very profitable thing) and here this caprice [of] Mr. Read to put me with a landscapist. It is as if one put a young man who wished to become a priest with a lawyer. None the less, I work hard, for to know how to paint a landscape is at least something.

As his biographer Denny Carter points out, "His lack of interest in landscape painting was ironic, since perhaps Farny's greatest achievement as an artist, was his depiction of the western country."[6]

After almost three and a half years of study in Europe, where he probably became acquainted with such diverse trends as the compositions of Japanese printmakers and the lightened palettes of the Impressionists, he returned to Cincinnati in the fall of 1870. Despite his excellent training, Farny had difficulty finding commissions and resorted to odd jobs, including illustrations for *Harper's Weekly*. In 1873 his fortunes turned for the better: he began steadily receiving assignments from the various publications of the day, including innovative illustrations for the *McGuffey Readers*. Thanks to them, he was eventually able to establish a studio of his own. A commission for the Cincinnati Chamber of Commerce gave him the money necessary for a second trip abroad. In 1875, Farny joined three other young artists from Cincinnati—Frank Duveneck, Frank Dengler, and John Twachtman—for a year's study in Europe.

Five years later Farny made his first trip west. His journey took him to Standing Rock (Fort Yates), on the upper Missouri, where he had hoped to paint the great Sioux Chief Sitting Bull, who had been incarcerated there. By the time of Farny's arrival, however, Sitting Bull had been moved, but the artist spent several rewarding months sketching and photographing Indians in and around the fort. He also began collecting all kinds of artifacts, costumes, implements of war, and other tribal accoutrements. The

sketches, photographs, and objects were to provide him with a continuing source of reference throughout his painting career.

Farny's first contact with the Rocky Mountain region came in 1883, when, as a prominent citizen, he was invited to join the Henry Villard excursion traveling by rail to Missoula, Montana, to witness the ceremonial joining of the eastern and western divisions of the transcontinental railroad line. The very next year Farny returned to Montana in the company of the journalist Eugene V. Smalley. The two had been commissioned by *Century Magazine* to produce an illustrated article—an arduous assignment, as Smalley wrote:

> It was a *Century* expedition in its plan, and its object was, to descend the Missouri River in a skiff from some point near Helena, Montana, to the Great Falls, to make a portage around the falls and follow the river down to Fort Benton, and thence, by some sort of land transportation, to cross the country to the Yellowstone through the cattle and sheep ranges.[7]

Smalley's account of the journey is filled with descriptions, anecdotes, and interesting comments about the invasion of civilization observed along the way. Farny noted sites and events in his sketch pad or with his camera. The published article included seven of Farny's illustrations, five landscapes plus *The Ruins of Fort Benton* and *The Piegan Camp on Teton River*. As in all of Farny's other western travels, many of these sketches and photographs were incorporated in the background of his later Indian paintings.

After his trip with Smalley, Farny devoted more and more time to his painting. His years of study and his voluminous notes and sketches were about to bear fruit in the form of an unmistakable style that united precision of detail, sharp contrast, shifting angle of perspective, and cropped foregrounds—combining photographic technique with a Japanese printmaker's asymmetrical composition. Farny's many sketches of mountain peaks, canyons, and cliff-bound rivers are reflected again and again in his canvases. An excellent example of his mature work is his oil painting *Indian Marauding Party Fording the Stream* (color plate 49). The artist envisions the scene from a low point in the foreground; in typical Farny fashion the bodies of the two horses in the immediate right foreground are

COLOR PLATE 46

Charles P. Adams, *Sunset, Colorado*, ca. 1895–1900, Watercolor, 8″ × 12″. Courtesy Dines Collection, Denver, Colo.

COLOR PLATE 47

Walter Paris, *Glenwood Springs, Colorado*, 1891, Watercolor, 11½″ × 17½″. Courtesy Arthur J. Phalen, Jr., Collection, Chevy Chase, Md.

Charles M. Russell, *Lewis and Clark Meeting the Flatheads at Ross' Hole,* 1912, Oil, 11′ 5¼″ × 24′ 9″.
Courtesy Montana Historical Society, Helena, Mont.

324

COLOR PLATE 49

Henry Farny, *Indian Marauding Party Fording the Stream*, ca. 1900, Oil, 27″ × 36″.
Courtesy Kennedy Galleries, Inc., New York City.

COLOR PLATE 50

Henry Farny, *On the Trail in Winter*, 1894,
Gouache/watercolor, 16″ × 11″. Courtesy
Rockwell-Corning Museum, Corning, N.Y.

Color Plate 51

Henry Farny, *In the Foothills of the Rockies,* 1898, Oil, 22″ × 40″.
Courtesy Coe Kerr Gallery, Inc., New York City, N.Y.

COLOR PLATE 52

Frederic Remington, *Untitled*, ca. 1900, Oil, 27″ × 40⅛″.
Courtesy Buffalo Bill Historical Center, Cody.

COLOR PLATE 53

Frederic Remington, *Fight for the Stolen Herd*, ca. 1902, Oil, 50″ × 30″.
Courtesy private collection, on loan to Buffalo Bill Historical Center, Cody.

329

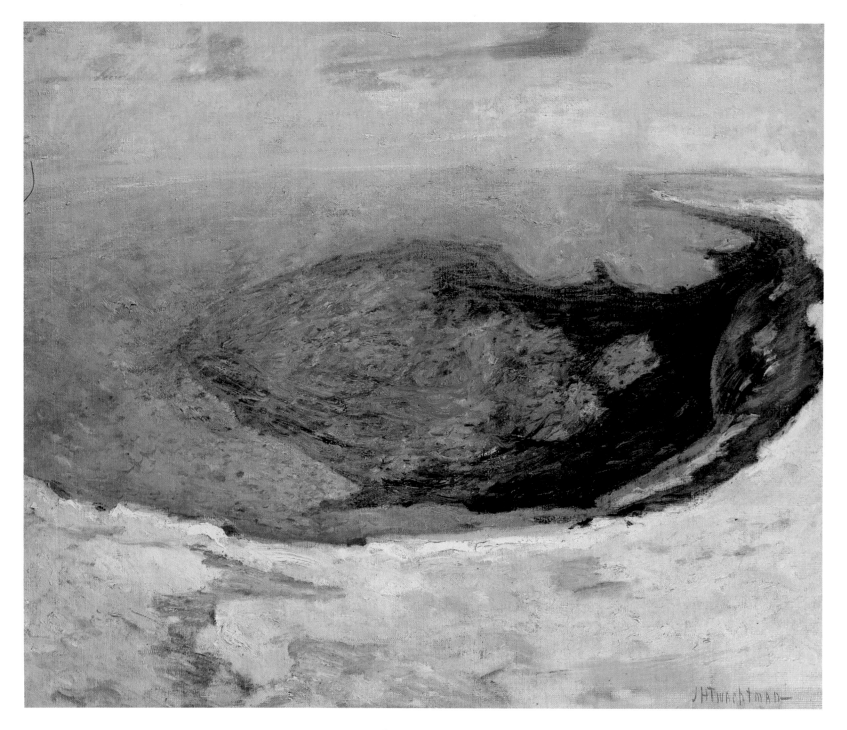

COLOR PLATE 54

John Twachtman, *The Emerald Pool, Yellowstone*, 1895, Oil, 25″ × 30″.
Courtesy Vose Galleries, Boston, Mass.

cropped. From this low viewpoint the composition leads the eye from the level riverbank along the curve of the stream and upward to three encircling mountains that seem to form a triangular intersection. Farny crops again here, eliminating parts of the mountain forms on the left and right to give full strength to the center peak. He models the stony formations with geological precision, and his exquisite coloring rivals the accuracy of a modern color photograph. A section in the Smalley article suggests that the artist was recalling a fording site described by the journalist:

> The surface of the country dipped suddenly into a narrow valley through which ran Sun River, . . . a clear, shallow stream. . . . At the place where we forded it the bottom was paved from side to side with large square rocks as smooth as flagstones. Far to the northward could be seen the snowy peaks of the main chain of the Rockies, where the river has its sources.[8]

Farny had not only favorite physical settings but favorite subjects that reappeared in his work. One was Indians on the move. *On the Trail in Winter* (color plate 50), executed on a fairly small scale in gouache, the medium of some of his most delightful work, is an example. Once again the artist selects a point of perspective below the foreground figures—a device that is even more effective in this vertical composition, since it provides a sense of movement for figures that diminish in size as the eye travels up the trail. Farny's cropping technique is an excellent ploy in this composition, allowing the artist to render the intricate pattern of beadwork and leather fringe on the colorful regalia of the two horsemen in the immediate foreground. Background landscape elements frame the group. In his treatment of the trees Farny's brushwork is fluid and fast, almost impressionistic, making for an entirely satisfying combination of atmospheric mood and definitive figure painting.

Equally masterful though perhaps less dramatic are Farny's many broad panoramic vistas, established on a horizontal format and frequently depicting Indian campsites. In these paintings the sense of space becomes enormous. The fairly large oil *In the Foothills of the Rockies* (color plate 51) is one such example. Here the figures are subordinate to the scenic view. A hint of luminous atmosphere

envelops the painting—an element that was to become more and more important in his later work.

Farny was a complex personality. He moved among eminent citizens as easily as he fraternized with the rugged characters of the frontier. He was definitely a narrative painter, totally fascinated with the lives and customs of the native American, yet he brought to his studies of Indians a sophisticated knowledge of both traditional academic art and the painterly modes introduced by the French. In the final analysis, however, his scenic backgrounds are probably his most notable contribution to American art of the nineteenth century.

Frederic Remington,[9] perhaps the most renowned of the western narrative painters, came west for the first time late in the summer of 1881. He was a strapping, sandy-haired easterner of nineteen, imbued like most others of his generation with tales of adventure enacted on the frontier of the young nation. One evening, traveling across the plains of Montana, he shared a campfire with a veteran wagon freighter, who recounted stories of his early days on the trail—of encounters with Indians, trappers, and mounted cavalry, of huge herds of buffalo and racing wild horses. Recalling this encounter sometime later, Remington wrote: "I knew wild riders and the vacant land were about to vanish forever. And the more I considered the subject, the bigger the Forever loomed. Without knowing how to do it, I began to record some facts around me, and the more I looked the more the panorama unfolded."

His life's ambition, formulated beside that Montana campfire, was to record the saga of the western frontier. During the remaining twenty-seven years of his life he produced several thousand paintings and drawings, cast twenty-two bronzes, and wrote more than ninety magazine articles and eight books on the subject. So popular was Remington's work that his name became synonymous with the West.

Remington was born in upstate New York on October 4, 1861. At the onset of the Civil War his father, Seth Pierre Remington, a journalist, received a commission in the Eleventh New York Cavalry Regiment, and young Fred grew up doting on the stories of his father's adventures in far-off Virginia and Tennessee. In his very early years Remington often made sketches of scenes from his father's army life, a valuable exercise for later paintings focused on martial subjects. At fifteen he attended the Highland Military Academy, in Worcester, Massachusetts, where his youthful imagination swirled with battle scenes, Indian wars, and western adventures; he began filling sketchbooks with rough sketches of such fancies. From that time forward his artistic endeavors held sway, and in the fall of 1878 he enrolled in the School of Fine Arts at Yale.

Several events in quick succession led to Remington's decision to take that first memorable trip to the Montana territory in the summer of 1881. Shortly after Christmas his father died. Remington left Yale for a succession of clerical jobs that he found boring. His request for his sweetheart Eva Caten's hand in marriage was refused by her father. Bitterly disappointed and disenchanted with the business world, Remington headed west—perhaps with some thoughts of returning with a fortune to impress his prospective father-in-law.

In the next five years Remington applied himself both to gaining a firsthand knowledge of the frontier and to establishing himself as an artist. He ran a small sheep ranch near Peabody, Kansas, and was so genuinely attracted to the region and its people that after his marriage to Eva, whom he finally won in the fall of 1884, he set up house and studio in Kansas City. There he invested in part ownership of a saloon and began painting pictures, which he sold through William Findlay, the proprietor of a local art-supply store and gallery. When the saloon investment failed, Findlay suggested that the young artist seek his livelihood in the booming illustration business. Remington moved back east in 1886 and began the search for publishers. He returned to school briefly, attending the Art Students League in New York, and within two years was well on his way to success.

Throughout his career Remington traveled widely in the West, Canada, and Mexico in search of material for his pictures. He relied heavily on a camera to record the scenes, events, and characters that captured his fancy, but he did a good deal of field sketching as well.

The figure was always Remington's primary focus, as it was for Russell and Farny. By his own admission, however, Remington was somewhat intimidated by the grandeur of the western panorama. In 1894 he made his first trip to Yellowstone Park. Its awesome impact on him is readily evident in his story "Policing the Yellowstone," published in *Harper's Weekly* on January 12, 1895:

> Posed on the trestled road, I looked back at the Golden Gate Pass. It is one of those marvellous vistas of mountain scenery utterly beyond the pen or brush of any man. Paint cannot touch it, and words are wasted. War, storms at sea, and mountain scenery are bigger than any expression little man has ever developed.

Even before Remington encountered this impressive vista, he had visited the spring exhibition of 1894 at the National Academy of Design, where he saw Thomas Moran's *Golden Gate to Yellowstone* (see plate 68). He was impressed not so much with the celebrated landscape artist's accomplishment as with his audacity: "Mr. Thomas Moran made a famous stagger at this pass in his painting; and great as is the painting, when I contemplated the pass itself I marvelled at the courage of the man who dared the deed."[10]

Despite his awe, Remington's drawings of the park (all executed in grisaille, a medium suited to the reproduction methods of that period) are his usual matter-of-fact records of human activity. Although Remington wrote about "marvellous vistas of mountain scenery," he continued to paint almost exclusively the hearty men he met in his wanderings. The most scenic of the illustrations from this series, *On the Headwaters—Burgess Finding a Ford* (plate 125), follows Remington's formula. Although the landscape elements are more specific than usual, the real focus of the scene is the Sixth Cavalry, precisely rendered with accurate anatomical details.

As more and more of his contemporaries scored successes with landscape paintings of the magnificent Rocky Mountain region, Remington, secure in the popularity of his own figurative and narrative work, adopted a defensive attitude. Why should he follow this route when, since "the stages of the Park Company run over this road, every tourist sees its grandeur, and bangs away with his Kodak"?

The more Remington's reputation as an illustrator grew, the more he wished to free himself of it and be considered a painter capable of dealing with many themes. As one critic wrote: "Mr.

PLATE 125

Frederic Remington, *On the Headwaters—Burgess Finding a Ford*, 1894, Watercolor, 20½″ × 30½″.
Courtesy Metropolitan Museum of Art, New York City.

PLATE 126

Frederic Remington, *Indian Camp on Cheyenne River*, n.d., Oil, 12″ × 16″.
Courtesy Buffalo Bill Historical Center, Cody.

PLATE 127

Frederic Remington, *Untitled*, n.d., Oil, 12¼″ × 18⅜″.
Courtesy Buffalo Bill Historical Center, Cody.

Remington recites what he has seen, but his splendid reputation as an illustrator for the magazines has failed to satisfy the ambition of an artist who bids to become equally established as a professional painter."[11] Remington's desire was not fully realized until the turn of the century, but as early as 1889 he was painting for private commissions as well as for illustration. Through these years, as he traveled in the West, Remington witnessed the transformation of the land and the people that he had predicted during his first trip to Montana. In the autumn of 1900 he wrote to his wife from Española, New Mexico, lamenting the bewildering metamorphosis: "Shall never come west again. It is all brick buildings—derby hats and blue overalls—it spoils my early illusions—and they are *my* capital."[12]

This element of disenchantment may have led Remington to an increasing interest in pure landscape; his untitled mountainscape (color plate 52), possibly of the Sangre de Cristos, could have been inspired by his visit to northern New Mexico. This scene and many similar landscape views of the Colorado and Wyoming Rockies taken in the last seven years of Remington's life exemplify the artist's changing viewpoint and a new willingness to seek mountain scenery as subject for his art. The painting is startling in its simplicity; devoid of figures, it shows greatly reduced tonal values and an increased sense of light.

Other examples of the artist's purely scenic work may be seen in the Remington Studio Collection at the Whitney Gallery of Western Art, Cody, Wyoming. The collection includes more than sixty landscape studies in oil—many of which, though small, are complete pictures in themselves, all captured by Remington's facile brush, lightened palette, and newly acquired impressionistic technique (plates 126 and 127). The awesome mountains that had previously challenged, even threatened, his brush now inspire some of his most satisfying works (color plate 53).

In the summer of 1902, Remington granted an interview to Edwin Wildman, of *Outing* magazine. Expanding on the mission of art and artists, he articulated the change in his outlook:

> Big art is a process of elimination . . . cut down and out. . . . What you want to do is just create the thought—materialize the spirit of

a thing, and the small bronze—or the impressionist's picture—does that: then your audience discovers the thing you held back, and that's skill.[13]

In this same interview Remington first noted his pleasure at painting various times of the day to capture the changing quality of light.

In the following years Remington continued to produce more and more landscape art. His close friendship with certain members of "The Ten"—Childe Hassam, J. Alden Weir, Robert Reid, and John Twachtman (see below)—continued to encourage Remington toward Impressionism. In 1907 he acknowledged that "lately some of our American landscape artists—who are the best in the world—have worked their spell over me and have to some extent influenced me, in so far as a figure painter can follow in their footsteps."[14]

By 1909, the last year of his life, Remington was even saying that Claude Monet's powerful canvases were having a favorable effect on his palette and vision. Like a disciple of the French master, Remington professed that all an artist "needs to see, study, and bring to his canvas is light."[15]

John H. Twachtman, one of America's most lyrical Impressionist painters, joined the procession of artists on the western trails in 1895, when he was commissioned by Major W. A. Wadsworth, of Buffalo, New York, to paint the geological wonders of Yellowstone Park. Earlier in the decade Twachtman had been persuaded by another Buffalo patron to paint the splendors of Niagara Falls, and Wadsworth had seen the paintings in an exhibition.

At this point in his career Twachtman had established a long-sought personal style rooted in the familiar, intimate country scenes of New England—a mode of expression far removed from the grandiose scenery of Niagara and Yellowstone. Nevertheless, he accepted the challenge. Although the details of his visit to Wyoming are not annotated, it is evident from the works that resulted from the trip that the artist traveled west during the summer season of 1895.

Twachtman, like so many other nineteenth-century American artists, had sought his formal training in European academies.[16] In 1875, at twenty-two, he went to Munich, where he developed a facile brushstroke and executed works in the somber tones so popular then. Still seeking a mode of expression more akin to his personal vision, he went on to the Académie Julien, in Paris, which offered no answers for him. The turning point came when Twachtman encountered the work of Jules Bastien-Lepage, whose plein-air paintings, combining diffused light with precise draftsmanship, were acclaimed as an exciting new departure. It was this influence that led Twachtman to abandon the bravura brushwork and somber brown tones of the Munich School for experiments with an even application of paint and the skillful introduction of diffused light; through them he began to find his own sensitive mode of expression. His development was further affected by his interest in the monochrome color of James Whistler's work and the elegant placement of form in Japanese prints. With each experiment Twachtman distilled these elements into a growing personal idiom, leaning more and more toward abstraction.

In the winter of 1885–86, Twachtman returned to the United States and a particularly lean period: his European paintings were lost at sea. Although a few oils were salvaged, the more fragile works were a total loss. In those difficult times he took any kind of art-related job that he could find. In the summer of 1886, for example, he was one of a crew of artists engaged to paint a huge cyclorama of a battle scene in Chicago, a job that paid well and allowed him time to pursue his own painting.

At about this time he began working in pastel, a medium well suited to his temperament and never-ending search for personal expression. He joined the Society of Painters in Pastel and in 1888 showed with the group in an exhibition, where he received favorable critical reviews. In his work on Twachtman, Richard Boyle points out the importance of pastel in the artist's development: "The matte surfaces of many of his canvases and the delicacy with which the paint is applied, as well as his finely balanced use of open areas, might well derive from his long familiarity with the pastel medium for which he was praised in his day."[17]

During his lifetime Twachtman never achieved popular acclaim or developed the buying public of Bierstadt or Remington. He was definitely a painter's painter. In the 1880s and 1890s, however, he gained the recognition of art critics, receiving several awards, including a Temple Gold Medal from the Pennsylvania Academy of Fine Arts and a silver medal at the World's Columbian Exposition, in Chicago. He also supplemented his painting income by teaching at the Art Students League and later at Cooper Union. Although Twachtman was a private man, a contemplative philosopher who enjoyed solitude and country living, he did not divorce himself from the more advanced art activities of his time. He and his good friend and colleague J. Alden Weir were among the leaders who formed the separatist group known as "The Ten," artists who, primarily interested in the Impressionist movement, had withdrawn from the more conservative Society of American Painters to hold exhibitions on their own.

In 1888, Twachtman was able to purchase a farm on Round Hill, near Greenwich, Connecticut, where he came into his own, painting the familiar, intimate scenes that he cherished. He employed many of the Impressionist techniques, painting the same scene again and again in different lightings and seasons. Twachtman's impressionism was a more subdued light painting than that of the French School—couched in colors that seem almost pastel when compared with the more robust bright light and color of his European counterparts. By the time he embarked on his Yellowstone trip in 1895, he was faced with an enormous challenge—that of adapting a style purposely suited for intimate scenes to subjects of grandeur, scale, and power.

Given Twachtman's complexity and his unfamiliarity with the western mountain terrain, it is not surprising that he arrived at a number of different solutions to the problem of capturing the park's wonders, especially Yellowstone Falls.[18] *Waterfall, Yellowstone* (plate 128), for example, exhibits a nonliteral, definitely formalized approach. The artist does not follow the usual method of creating a panoramic or romantic vista; instead, he employs the Impressionist technique of obscuring the depth of the painting in an atmospheric mist of light and spray. An echo of his experiments in pastel appears in the chalky haze that envelops the entire scene in diffused light,

Plate 128

John H. Twachtman, *Waterfall, Yellowstone,* ca. 1895,
Oil, 25⅜″ × 16½″. Courtesy Buffalo Bill Historical
Center, Cody.

PLATE 129

John H. Twachtman, *Lower Falls, Yellowstone*, ca. 1895, Oil, 30″ × 30″.
Courtesy Amon Carter Museum, Fort Worth.

decreasing the realistic imagery demanded by western enthusiasts of the day. In *Lower Falls, Yellowstone* (plate 129), Twachtman takes a slightly more orthodox approach. Pictorial elements are more emphasized, details are more clearly described, and a sense of depth is revealed. In short, as one student observed, Twachtman had made "a slight concession to popular taste." In both of these paintings, as Boyle points out, Twachtman was uncomfortable with the immensity of the subject: "As a painter of the quiet and more intimate aspects of nature, Twachtman could not handle the sheer size and power of the Falls, nor could he convey the sense of scale necessary to make the image convincing."[19]

The series of paintings in which Twachtman focused on the Emerald Pool are far more successful. In *The Emerald Pool, Yellowstone* (color plate 54), for example, the setting was less vast; the exquisite green and blue produced in the hot pool as algae merged with the crystal water evidently fascinated the artist. Freed of the immensity of space, he could create within the formalized mode of abstraction that had become an important part of his own personal idiom. The hazy, less intense green of the mist rising at the edge of the pool was perfectly suited to Twachtman's consuming interest in the light of color, and the surrounding yellow of the craterlike earth offered him an opportunity for abstract color orchestration, another important element of his mature development.

Twachtman returned to his beloved Connecticut countryside, his work with "The Ten," and his quiet impressionistic visions of cherished haunts—a single tree, a sailboat in the mist, the hemlock pool on his farm. For him the Yellowstone experience was an interlude not to be repeated. Yet his western trek was the beginning of a new form of expression in the Rocky Mountain region: a contemporary formula in place of Romantic-Realism. His interpretations of the West were to be followed by those of another generation of artists who expressed themselves in the modes of the twentieth century.[20]

Farny, Russell, Remington, and Twachtman were, in a sense, the last guardians of the western frontier. They not only inherited the wonder and sense of poetic beauty first expressed by Miller and Moran but set the stage for the future, while painting the finale of a great epoch.

NOTES

Preface

1. See reference to "Stoney Mountains" in Jedidiah Morse, *The American Gazetteer* (Boston: Thomas & Andrews, 1797), unpaged.

2. The so-called Soulard Map (1795), published in both English and French, refers to the range as "The Rocky Mountains" in the English edition and, in the French edition, separates the ranges into the "Pays des M. du Serpon" on the north and "M. de Roche douteuse" on the south. See Carl I. Wheat, *Mapping the Trans-Mississippi West* (San Francisco: Institute of Historical Cartography, 1957), 1:157–58. Ernest Ingersoll, in *Knocking Round the Rockies*, p. 144, discusses the origins of the name Rocky Mountains: "The first approach to the term Rocky Mountains is said to be found in Bellin's Map of North America, published in Charlevoix's 'History of New France,' in 1743, where they are called *Montagnes des Pierres Brillants.* The word *Rocky Mountains* first appears on a map in 'Morse's American Geography,' dated 1794." Alan N. Degutis, of the American Antiquarian Society, was kind enough to check out both sources mentioned by Ingersoll and found that the author was in error. In neither of the society's copies of Charlevoix's *Histoire et description de la Nouvelle France* (1744) do any of the various appellations for the Rocky Mountains appear on Bellin's map of North America. Degutis also pointed out that there was no *Morse's American Geography* of 1794. *The American Geography*, by Morse, appeared in 1789 and was followed by *The Universal American Geography*, which ran successive editions in 1793, 1796, 1801, 1802, 1805, 1812, and 1819. In these editions the only use of the term

Rocky Mountains appears in the fourth edition (Boston, 1802). Since Morse used the name Stoney Mountains far more consistently than he did Rocky Mountains, perhaps more credit for the current appellation should be given to the map's engraver, E. G. Gridley (see plate 1), than to the geographer.

3. John Wesley Powell, "Physiographic Regions of the United States," *The Physiography of the United States,* pp. 87–88.

4. Fitz Hugh Ludlow, *The Heart of the Continent,* p. 219.

5. Quoted in Roland Rees, "The Taste for Mountain Scenery," *History Today* 25 (May, 1975): 306.

6. Quoted from Albert Bierstadt's letter, "Rocky Mountains, July 10, 1859," printed in *Crayon,* September, 1859, p. 287.

7. Sadakichi Hartmann, *A History of American Art,* 1:78–79.

8. James Jackson Jarves, *The Art-Idea . . . ,* 2:231–32. In commenting about the "defects and merits of a distinct school" of landscape painting in America, Jarves concludes that Bierstadt's western scenes did not exhibit "the prominent defects of the school in general" nor "the conventional lifelessness of the mechanical Dusseldorf school" (ibid.). It would appear that Jarves considered Bierstadt a member of the Hudson River School. But art critic Henry T. Tuckerman, in his *Book of the Artists: American Artist Life, Comprising Biographical and Critical Sketches: Preceded by an Historical Account of the Rise and Progress of Art in America,* p. 392, calls Bierstadt "a true representative of the Dusseldorf school in landscape." Neither man refers to the "Rocky Mountain school" in his writings on artists in America.

9. James Thomas Flexner, *Nineteenth-Century American Painting,* p. 135. As this book demonstrates, as many American-born as foreign-born artists pictured the Rocky Mountain region on their canvases.

10. James Thomas Flexner, *That Wilder Image,* p. 299.

11. Ibid., pp. 272–73.

12. Ibid., p. 298.

13. See Nevin M. Fenneman's U.S. Geological Survey map, *Physical Divisions of The United States* (1945), prepared in cooperation with the Physiographic Committee of the Geological Survey. This definition of the Rockies also concurs with the one set forth in 1953 by the U.S. Board on Geographic Names, which distinguishes the Rocky Mountains as the eastern belt of the North American cordillera extending northwestward from central New Mexico to the Liard River valley in Canada. Although this U.S. Geological Survey definition is standard for all federal agencies, it is not, of course, the only interpretation available. See also Wallace W. Atwood, *The Physiographic Provinces of North America* (Boston: Ginn and Co., 1940), p. 281; and Clarence King's four geological-geographical field divisions west of the 101st meridian listed in the *First Annual Report of the United States Geological Survey* (Washington, D.C.: U.S. Government Printing Office, 1880), p. 6. We are grateful to Clifford M. Nelson, associate historian of the Geological Survey, U.S. Department of the Interior, for his assistance in researching the definitions and boundaries of the Rockies. We also extend our thanks to Donald J. Orth, executive secretary, Domestic Geographic Names, U.S. Board of Geographic Names.

Introduction

1. Oliver W. Larkin, *Art and Life in America*, pp. 153–54. It was natural that America would turn to England and the Continent for the basic ideology of Romanticism. Yet, as one historian has pointed out, "in America Romanticism turned out to be a much more constructive, individualistic, and democratically based movement than in Britain or Europe, a trend reinforced by the frontier tradition." Russell Blaine Nye, *Society and Culture in America, 1830–1860*, p. 23.

2. Ibid., p. 176. The early members of the Hudson River School (ca. 1825–1850) and their generation shared similar attitudes toward God, man, and nature that were inherent in the aesthetics of Romanticism. They believed, as did most Romantics of their time, that "it was the highest function of literature and art to portray man and his world in such a way that the presence of the infinite within the finite, of the ideal within the actual, would be revealed in all its beauty." Ernest Bernbaum, "The Romantic Movement," in *Romanticism: Points of View*, ed. Robert F. Gleckner and Gerald E. Enscoe, p. 91.

3. Asher B. Durand's "Letters on Landscape Painting," published serially in the *Crayon* in 1855, not only offer clues about general art practices of the time but also illustrate the philosophical preoccupations of the artist, which probably reflected the spirit of his generation. In one passage Durand reminds us that nature, "apart from its wondrous structure and functions that minister to our well-being, is fraught with lessons of high and holy meaning, only surpassed by the light of Revelation." *Crayon* 1 (January 17, 1855):34. It would appear that the portrayal of nature in words and pictures was intended not to supplant organized religion but to testify to the existence and glory of God in nature.

4. James T. Callow, *Kindred Spirits: Knickerbocker Writers and American Artists, 1807–1855*, p. 117. As Callow states, Bryant and Cooper were certainly the most consistent celebrators of American landscape before 1825 but were not the first writers to employ landscape in their writings. According to Callow, *Salmagundi* (1807) and *A History of New York* (1809) contained rhapsodies to nature, and in *The Backwoodsman* (1818), "Paulding used panoramic settings for dramatic effects, and by so doing paid tribute to the vastness of American scenery" (ibid.).

5. Archibald Alison, *Esssays on the Nature and Principles of Taste;* Edmund Burke, *Philosophical Enquiry into the Origin of Our Ideas of the Sublime and the Beautiful;* Uvedale Price, *Essays on the Picturesque, as Compared with the Sublime and Beautiful; and, on the Use of Studying Pictures, for the Purpose of Improving Real Landscape;* William Gilpin, *Three Essays; on Picturesque Beauty; on Picturesque Travel; and on Sketching Landscape; To Which Is Added a Poem, on Landscape Painting;* and others. Briefly, these aesthetic doctrines interpreted and described the various natural phenomena as being sublime, beautiful, or picturesque. Besides the classification of natural phenomena, these doctrines also included principles of taste and of man's relationship to the arts. The sublime was considered the most popular of the three classifications, and summed up what Burke described as "the strongest emotion which the mind . . . [was] capable of feeling." The second category, beauty, aroused the more lively and attractive emotions in contrast to the awe and horror evoked by the sublime. The third classification, the picturesque, referred to a scene which, like a pictorial composition, could be admired for the sake of its inherent beauty or charm instead of evoking the emotions of the beholder; this term gained significance after William Gilpin published his essays on his travels to the various parts of Great Britain and the art of sketching landscapes, written between 1770 and 1780. From the evidence that is available to us, it is apparent that American writers and later painters adopted this aesthetic jargon to celebrate and describe the virtues and glories of American scenery. We can observe how dependent these artists were on the aesthetic canons of their day from the following passage in Thomas Cole's journal: "The perfect repose of these waters, and the unbroken *silence* reigning through the whole region, made the scene peculiarly *impressive* and *sublime:* indeed, there was an *awfulness* in the *deep solitude*, pent up within the *great precipices*, that was *painful"* (Louis Legrand Noble, *The Life and Works of Thomas Cole*, ed. Elliot S. Vesell, p. 67; italics are added to indicate specific characteristics conjuring up the sublime). Cole consciously employed these same aesthetic values, conducive to natural sublimity or beauty, in his pictures. His wild, disorderly mountain scenes have all the cardinal ingredients for producing sublime effects. Similarly, the influence of Alison's associationist psychology on the nineteenth-century mind is well documented in the writing of the period. In essence, Alison believed that "when any object [paintings or other objects of taste], either of sublimity or beauty, is presented to the mind . . . every man is conscious of a train of thought being immediately awakened in his imagination, analogous to the character or expression of the original object." Thus to Alison it was the series of associations in the mind of the beholder rather than the object perceived which caused the delight (Alison, *Essays*, 1:4–5). That Cole was familiar with this theory is suggested by his allusion to "Alison's work on taste" in his journal (see Noble, *Thomas Cole*, pp. 81–82), as well as by his defense of American scenery for "want of associations" delivered before the American Lyceum in 1835 (see Thomas Cole, "Essay on American Scenery," *American Monthly Magazine* 1 [January, 1836]: 11). Sharing similar ideas with Cole and William Cullen Bryant, the artist Durand also borrowed from Alison, as indicated by his paintings and writings. (In his four-volume study of Durand "Asher Brown Durand: His Art and Art Theory in Relation to His Times" [Ph.D. diss., Princeton University, 1966], David Lawall shows how the artist developed his "recreational landscapes" from the associationist aesthetics of Alison "to effect a reintegration of the ego of the spectator.") The following quotation from one of Durand's letters also demonstrates the artist's appropriation of Alison's theory about man's relationship to the arts: "Suppose . . . [i.e., the rich merchant and the capitalist] disposed of in his favorite armchair, with one or more faithful landscapes before him, and making no greater effort than to look into the picture instead of on it, so as to perceive what it represents; in proportion as it is true and faithful, many a fair vision of forgotten days will animate the canvas, and lead him through the scene: pleasant reminiscences and grateful emotions will spring up at every step, and care and anxiety will retire far behind him" (Durand, "Letters," 1:98). Agreeing with Alison, the "kindred spirits" adopted his idea that all nature was a cathedral for the "Living God," which, according to Bryant,

was probably the most suitable "shrine for humble worshipper to hold Communion with his Maker" (Alison, *Essays*, 2:447; William Cullen Bryant, "A Forest Hymn," *Poetical Works*, 1:130–31, quoted in Callow, *Kindred Spirits*, p. 119). From the examples illustrated here, it is apparent that nineteenth-century Americans were aware of European ideas and appropriated them—with certain modifications to accommodate their tastes and philosophies.

6. Robert C. Bredeson, "Landscape Description in Nineteenth-Century American Travel Literature," *American Quarterly* 20 (Spring, 1968):89.

7. That American artists were becoming more concerned with capturing transient effects in nature is acknowledged by E. P. Richardson, who, in his discussion of the late phase of Romanticism and "the Generation of 1850," establishes "two main roads" of aesthetic development in the artists' exploration of nature: (1) luminism, "an intuitive search by American painters for a style of light, growing out of the tonal painting of the thirties and forties," and (2) naturalism, "a passionate faith in nature as the key to art." Church is his prime example of the naturalist style, while Kensett and Whittredge are key members of the luminist group of artists. The author says of this "prolific" period of landscape development that "variety is its keynote" and maintains that many artists drew their inspiration from both poles of painting, "luminism and objective naturalism." In commenting on the artists' exploration of light, Richardson singles out the camera as one of the three sources of change that affected the direction of artistic development during this period; however, he fails to expand on this subject (see *A Short History of Painting in America: The Story of 450 Years*, pp. 156–70, and elsewhere). It is reasonable to assume that the daguerreotype, with its silvery reflecting surface, inspired artists to emulate "the simulated realism of the camera," not necessarily for philosophical reasons, as Van Deren Coke suggests ("the age-old magic associated with the mirror") but for its visual elements, important because of their interest in the picturesque in nature (see Coke, *The Painter and the Photographer*; this book is an innovative and invaluable source in documenting the interplay between the artist and the photographer). This point is illustrated in Fontayne & Porter's daguerreotype views of Cincinnati's waterfront (1848); the silvery, mir-rorlike water in the foreground and precise linear design of the boats projected against a hazy, atmospheric background immediately remind us of the picturesque, "stagy," surreal scenery of a painting by John Frederick Kensett or Fitz Hugh Lane. As Aaron Scharf has noted, the daguerreotype as a model for the artist could equally have "served to heighten . . . [his] perception of both nature and art" and "demonstrated . . . correct aerial perspective by showing that the brightest parts of a view were in the foreground and not in the clouds or other parts of the sky as was thought to be the case by some artists" (for reproductions of Fontayne & Porter's daguerreotypes see Beaumont Newhall, *The History of Photography*, p. 29; Scharf's discussion of the symbiosis of art and photography is found in his *Art and Photography*, p. 57). Even the Knickerbocker writers explored ocular phenomena for pictorial effects and, like James Fenimore Cooper in *The Deerslayer* (1841), occasionally for specific symbolic meaning. Cooper's use of the chiaroscuro, or strong patterns of light and dark, in his landscapes—in particular the jewellike brightness of the water ("the Glimmerglass")—can be likened to a luminist painting. These calm, orderly scenes with their special light effects could suggest a prosperous, peaceful garden symbolizing "the eventual passing from American life of the values implicit in the untouched landscape, values that will ultimately be ignored as men invade and destroy the wilderness." It appears that the luminists and the writers were concerned with the loss of American values, which might be the motive for their particular expression; it seems more likely, however, that these artists were presenting an idealistic rendering of light and atmosphere, more unreal than real, for its picturesque effects and not necessarily for its spiritual import under the influence of Ralph Waldo Emerson and the transcendental philosophy, as some scholars would have us believe. For a discussion of Cooper's use of light and shadow see Donald A. Ringe, *The Pictorial Mode*, pp. 110ff.; Kay House, of San Francisco State University, an authority on Cooper, brought this article to our attention to illustrate that once again it was the writers who preempted the artists as explorers.

8. Barbara Novak believes that Cole was the first landscape painter to have a "fuller grasp" of the implications of civilization—in her words, "the dis-parity between natural time and man's time, which, in its extraordinary accelerations, can consume eons of growth" (Barbara Novak, "The Double-Edged Axe," *Art in America*, January–February, 1976, p. 46).

9. Cole, "Essay," p. 12.

10. Yet Perry Miller says that "for most Americans, no doubt, the course of empire meant no such cycle of rise and fall, but the steady advance of American farmers and artisans across the continent. Thus the nineteenth century was completing the seventeenth's errand into the wilderness: the meaning was at last emerging, the meaning hidden from . . . the Puritan pioneers. . . . [It] now appeared, they had been dispatched into the forests not to set up a holy city on some Old World model but to commence the gigantic industrial expansion which, launched upon a limitless prospect, would demonstrate the folly of anxieties about, or even lust for, the end of this physical universe" (Perry Miller, *Nature's Nation*, p. 236).

11. "The Journal of Madam Knight" (1704), quoted in Perry Miller and Thomas H. Johnson, *The Puritans*, p. 428.

12. See Hans Huth, *Nature and the American*, pp. 10–11.

13. Ibid., p. 31.

14. Mary E. Woolley, "The Development of the Love of Romantic Scenery in America," *American Historical Review* 3 (October, 1897):65.

15. Roland Van Zandt, *The Catskill Mountain House*, p. 190.

16. Gilpin, *Three Essays*, p. 46.

17. See Cole, "Essay," p. 4.

18. Ibid., p. 5.

19. Such popular and elaborate picture albums initiated a trend toward this kind of illustrated publication, which had its roots in eighteenth-century English travel books. For an example see N. P. Willis, *American Scenery; or Land, Lake, and River, Illustrations of Transatlantic Nature. From Drawings by W. H. Bartlett* . . . .

20. For reproductions of these early reportorial drawings see Hugh Honour, *The European Vision of America*, chaps. 4, 5, and 10. For a survey of panel decoration see Edward B. Allen, *Early American Wall Paintings, 1710–1850*. Examples of portrait art can be found in R. Peter Mooz, "Colonial Art," in

The Genius of American Painting, ed. John Wilmerding, p. 50, opp. p. 74, and opp. p. 78.

21. See Alfred Coxe Prime, *The Arts and Crafts in Philadelphia, Maryland and South Carolina, 1721–1785;* George Francis Dow, comp., *The Arts and Crafts in New England.*

22. *View of Boston, 1738,* oil on canvas, 30 × 50 inches (collection of Childs Gallery, Boston, Mass.), is illustrated on the back cover of *American Art Review* 3 (May–June, 1976); it is also recorded in 1738 as no. 159 in *The Notebook of John Smibert: with Essays by Sir David Evans [and Others] and with Notes Relating to Smibert's Am. Por. by Andrew Oliver.*

23. *The Notebook of John Smibert.* The whereabouts of the "landskips" recorded for Nathanael Emmons, Justus Engelhardt Kühn, Alexander Stewart, and others are presently unknown; we can only speculate that some of the views were imaginative and others topographical, just as Smibert's were.

24. Dow, *Arts and Crafts,* opp. p. 16. Oskar Hagen, in *The Birth of the American Tradition in Art,* p. 61, states that "Smibert ordered two different kinds [of landscape prints] from his agent in London: imaginative picturesque compositions, such as the *Antiquities* of Panini . . . and topographical landscapes, such as *Views from Greenwich.*"

25. J. Hall Pleasants, *Four Late Eighteenth Century Anglo-American Landscape Painters,* p. 6. Pleasants provides biographical information on these four artists with some art-history discussion. Although they were provincials, their work obviously affected younger artists, particularly those working around Philadelphia.

26. Both paintings are illustrated in ibid.

27. Frank H. Goodyear, Jr., "American Landscape Painting, 1795–1875," *In This Academy: The Pennsylvania Academy of the Fine Arts, 1805–1976,* p. 125. Groombridge's *View on the Schuylkill River* (1800) could be classified as an American version of a Richard Wilson (ibid., p. 124, illus.).

28. Noble, *Thomas Cole,* pp. 24–32.

29. In William Birch's "Memoirs" (Manuscript Division, Pennsylvania Historical Society, Philadelphia), he mentions receiving assistance from "[his] friend Seymour." Both Thomas Birch and Seymour assisted in the readying and engraving of William Birch's views of Philadelphia (a set of 28 plates,

printed in 1800). Samuel Seymour, who accompanied Major Stephen H. Long on his expedition to the Rockies in 1819–20, will be discussed in chap. 1.

30. See Charles Coleman Sellers, *Charles Willson Peale,* plates 8, 9. Other well-known American painters who might be included in this category are John Trumbull, Samuel F. B. Morse, and John Vanderlyn. Landscape was for all four a secondary pursuit; when they did engage in that field of endeavor, they expressed themselves in the lofty formulas and ideals of Classicism.

31. This was a recipe that most of the drawing books recommended to the beginner. Drawing was considered the "grammar" of art practices and was the first step discussed in such books. After the artist became proficient in the art of drawing, he proceeded to learn how to apply shadows in pencil, ink, or sepia wash and then to apply color to his outline, which was usually the last stage of his instruction. For a complete bibliography of American drawing books see Carl W. Drepperd, *American Drawing Books.* It is a well-known fact that English drawing books were imported into this country at an early date (the Free Library of Philadelphia collection of rare books includes several of the instruction manuals, which were accessioned in the first decade of the nineteenth century). In fact, many of the books were reprinted in America with the same engraved plates, which indicates the popularity of this form of instruction among American artists. American drawing books were often modeled after English versions and occasionally included the same engraved plates.

32. Goodyear, "American Landscape Painting," pp. 122, 265, n. 1.

33. Quoted from Luke Herrmann, *British Landscape Painting of the Eighteenth Century,* p. 59; see plates 51–53, 56 for illustrations of Wilson's topographical landscapes. See also Frank H. Goodyear, Jr., *Thomas Doughty, 1793–1856: An American Pioneer in Landscape Painting,* plate 1.

34. Information on Alvan Fisher is limited; a brief account of Fisher's life can be found in Frederick W. Sweet, *The Hudson River School and the Early American Landscape Tradition,* pp. 41–42. For illustrations of his paintings see Charlotte Buel Johnson, "The European Tradition and Alvan Fisher," *Art in America* 41 (Spring, 1953):79–87.

35. Jane Dillenberger and Joshua C. Taylor, *The Hand and the Spirit: Religious Art in America, 1700–1900,* p. 16.

36. Noble, *Thomas Cole,* p. 63.

37. Ibid., p. 83.

38. Ibid., p. 27; the Rosa oil was in the academy's collection as early as 1812.

39. For further discussion of Durand's religious attitudes toward God and nature as revealed in his landscape imagery, see Lawall, "Asher Brown Durand," 2:503–53 and elsewhere.

40. For example, see ibid., 2:467–68; and Henry T. Tuckerman, *Book of the Artists: American Artist Life, Comprising Biographical and Critical Sketches: Preceded by an Historical Account of the Rise and Progress of Art in America,* p. 194.

41. A number of these intimate oil studies from nature can be found in the collections of the New-York Historical Society.

42. It is interesting to reflect on the change in attitude of this second generation of Hudson River School artists toward the sublime features of nature from that of their leader, Thomas Cole. The discovery of the "magical powers" of light and atmosphere was obviously the key factor in this transformation. In a letter to his father during his travels in Europe, Gifford describes such a transformation caused by colored atmosphere: "From the opposite shore, and from around the upper end of the lake at the left where the Rhone enters, rise the grand mountains of Savoy. Their wild and savage outlines bristle with bare cliffs; and their sides, the lower slopes dark with pines, are gashed and scarred, rent and seamed by the storms of centuries. But distance and the tender blue atmosphere soften all their terrors into beauty. The different colors of patches of snow, rock and soil, with their light and shadow, of Alps (high pastures) and forests, glimmer and shine through the filmy air like the delicate and varying tints of the opal. I often compare the color of mountains seen through such an atmosphere to those of the opal" (S. R. Gifford to father, letter, Baden Baden [Germany], June 29, 1856 [microfilm of typescript copy], Archives of American Art, Smithsonian Institution).

43. See n. 7.

44. See Novak, "Double-Edged Axe," p. 302, n. 10.

45. John I. H. Baur, *American Painting in the Nineteenth Century: Main Trends and Movements*, p. 10.

46. David C. Huntington, *The Landscapes of Frederic Edwin Church: Vision of an American Era*, fig. 28.

47. Albert Ten Eyck Gardner, "Scientific Sources of the Full-Length Landscapes: 1850," *Metropolitan Museum of Art Bulletin* 4 (Summer, 1945):64.

48. See R. L. Stehle, "The Düsseldorf Gallery of New York," *New-York Historical Society Quarterly* 58 (October, 1974):2.

49. Karl Friedrich Lessing (b. February 15, 1808; d. June 5, 1880), history painter and landscapist; Andreas Achenbach (b. September 29, 1815; d. April 1, 1910), landscapist; and Johann Wilhelm Schirmer (b. September 7, 1807; d. September 11, 1863), landscapist, engraver, and lithographer. For a monograph on Leutze's life and career see Barbara S. Groseclose, *Emanuel Leutze, 1816–1868: Freedom Is the Only King*. Leutze is discussed in chap. 8.

50. Tuckerman, *Book of the Artists*.

51. This painting was on exhibit at the Sanitary Fair in New York in 1864, with Church's *Heart of the Andes*. Both drew record crowds and were the key attractions of the art show.

52. Joseph Mallord William Turner (b. April 23, 1775; d. December 19, 1851), English landscapist.

53. Moran quoted in George W. Sheldon, *American Painters*, p. 125.

54. See chap. 7.

55. For a discussion of the Barbizon influence in American art see Peter Bermingham, *American Art in the Barbizon Mood*.

56. According to Richardson, *Short History of Painting*, p. 206, "The most conspicuous reaction of American painters to Impressionism was, however, something quite different. They turned the new color harmonies and the atmospheric touch of French into a muted, decorative, luminist style."

57. See ibid., p. 209.

58. *New York Times*, November 9, 1878, quoted in Patricia Trenton, *Harvey Otis Young: The Lost Genius, 1840–1901*, p. 85, n. 62.

59. Many of the ideas presented here were first introduced in Trenton's graduate-seminar paper for the University of California at Los Angeles. Later, in the course of additional research, several of these ideas were expanded. We are indebted to the scholars who paved the way for the establishment of this viable relationship between literature and art.

Chapter 1

1. Baron Friedrich Alexander von Humboldt, *Cosmos: A Sketch of a Physical Description of the Universe . . .*, trans. E. C. Otté, 2:452.

2. For mention of Hennepin and his illustrated books about his explorations with La Salle to the Great Lakes and the upper Mississippi in 1679–80, see Theodore E. Stebbins, Jr., *American Master Drawings and Watercolors*, pp. 4–5. For reproductions of Davies's work see Hugh Honour, *The European Vision of America*, pp. 189f., figs. 163 and 164. For Webber's work see James Cook, *The Journals of Captain James Cook on his Voyages of Discovery: The Voyage of the Resolution and Discovery, 1776–1780*.

3. For example, Vancouver's instructions from the lord high admiral of Great Britain and Ireland specifically state that he was to turn over to the office his accounts of the proceedings and any copies of plans, charts, and drawings "constructed" by his men during this expedition to the Pacific Ocean (George Vancouver, *A Voyage of Discovery to the North Pacific Ocean, and Round the World . . .*, ed. John Vancouver, 1:viii).

4. Ibid., 1:xiv.

5. For reproductions of Sykes's original drawings see Marguerite Wilbur, ed., *Vancouver in California, 1792–1794: The Original Account of George Vancouver*, vol. 3.

6. See Jeanne Van Nostrand and Edith Coulter, *California Pictorial: A History in Contemporary Pictures*, p. 23, plate 9. The English naval schools may have offered a basic course in draftsmanship as part of their curriculum, as did Woolwich, the West Point of England; this would explain why the professional sailor as well as the army man was capable of rendering simple topographical sketches for descriptive or scientific purposes.

7. See J. G. Links, *Townscape Painting and Drawing*, p. 82; and R. V. Tooley, *Maps and Map-Makers*.

8. See Ellen Shaffer, *The Nuremberg Chronicle*.

9. Giuliano Briganti, *The View Painters of Europe*, trans. Pamela Waley, p. 2.

10. John Ruskin, *The Works of John Ruskin*, ed. E. T. Cook and Alexander Wedderburn, 6:31.

11. "The Louisiana Purchase added some 850,000 square miles, including eastern Colorado, nearly doubling the nation's size" (*Nothing Is Long Ago: A Documentary History of Colorado, 1776/1976*, p. 6).

12. William H. Goetzmann, *Exploration and Empire*, p. 3. As this historian mentions, the American West, despite the Lewis and Clark exploration, was to remain for some time afterward a "geographical mystery" whose limits "were gradually . . . [to be] define[d] by the explorers sent out into it by the governments and fur-trading companies along its margins" (ibid., p. 8).

13. Reuben Gold Thwaites, ed., *Original Journals of the Lewis and Clark Expedition, 1804–1806*.

14. See section on Samuel Seymour below.

15. William H. Goetzmann, *Army Exploration in the American West, 1803–1863*, p. 5.

16. Goetzmann, *Exploration and Empire*, pp. 240–41.

17. See section on Seymour below.

18. See Michael E. Moss, "Robert Weir as Teacher," *Robert W. Weir of West Point: Illustrator, Teacher, and Poet*, p. 38.

19. See Robert Taft, *Artists and Illustrators of the Old West, 1850–1900*, p. 251.

20. George W. Sheldon, *American Painters*, p. 251.

21. Edwin James, comp., *Account of an Expedition from Pittsburgh to the Rocky Mountains, Performed in the Years 1819 and '20, by Order of the Hon. J. C. Calhoun, Sec'y of War: Under the Command of Major Stephen H. Long . . .* (English ed.), 2:173. The American edition includes with the two-volume narrative an atlas with illustrations and maps.

22. The site of the June 30 encampment was slightly west of present-day Fort Morgan, Colorado. The Long party mistook the "three distinct conic summits" for the "highest peak" (Pikes Peak) discovered by Lieutenant Zebulon Pike during his exploration of the Southwest in 1806. This distinc-

tive peak, which now bears Major Long's name, was formerly known as *Les deux Oreilles* (Two Ears), a name assigned by early fur trappers. From near Fort Morgan the peak does appear as three distinct conic summits, as observed by the group. Actually, however, they were viewing Long's Peak and Mount Lady Washington. Thus Seymour's portrayal of the front range from this particular vantage point is a factually accurate pictorial record (confirmed by Michael Sanderson, of Doniphan, Nebraska). This description of Seymour's *Distant View of the Rocky Mountains* is from Patricia Trenton, *Harvey Otis Young: The Lost Genius, 1840–1901*, p. 2. Seymour's sketch of the *Distant View of the Rocky Mountains* (color frontispiece, English ed., vol. 1) is presently unlocated. In a note at the end of his narrative James says that Seymour made "one hundred and fifty landscape views" during the expedition but had finished only "sixty" at the time of publication (James, comp., *Account of an Expedition* [American ed.], 2:330).

23. See Trenton, *Harvey Otis Young*, p. 73, n. 1. For further discussion of Long's thesis see Richard H. Dillon, "Stephen Long's Great American Desert," *Proceedings of the American Philosophical Society* 3 (April, 1967):93–108. According to Dillon, "Edwin James had no inkling that, in only sixty-odd years, dry-farming techniques, irrigation, and hardy Turkey Red strains of wheat . . . would mock his prophecy" (ibid., p. 102). In his article on Seymour the historian John Francis McDermott provides a list of Seymour's illustrations both in preserved drawings and in reproductions (John Francis McDermott, "Samuel Seymour: Pioneer Artist of the Plains and the Rockies," *Annual Report of the Smithsonian Institution, 1950*, p. 499). McDermott includes the six views in the American edition; the seven in the English edition; the nine preserved drawings in the Coe Collection, Bienecke Rare Book and Manuscript Library, Yale University; and the original drawing in the Academy of Natural Sciences, Philadelphia. In the years since McDermott's publication, four original drawings have been sold from private collections: *Indian at the Upper Missouri* (which we have retitled *View of the Chasm through which the Platte Issues from the Rocky Mountains*), reproduced in the English ed., vol. 2, color frontispiece, formerly in the T. R. Peale Collection, sold

to Eberstadt Galleries, Inc., New York, by Peale's descendant, presently in the Paul Mellon Collection, Upperville, Va.; [*Indian Council Scene*], Peale descendant sold to Eberstadt, sold to Kennedy Galleries, Inc., New York; *Fort Smith, Arkansas*, Paul Mellon Collection, Upperville, Va.; and *View of James Peak [Pikes Peak] in the Rain—dist[ance] 25 Miles*, formerly in the Robert Carlen Collection, Museum of Fine Arts, Boston, misattributed to artist William B. McMurtrie (see *M. & M. Karolik Collection of American Water Colors and Drawings, 1800–1875* [Boston: Museum of Fine Arts, 1962], 1:233–34, accession no. 15.139). Correct identification of the artist was accomplished by Trenton on the basis of style, documentation, and an inscription, "S. S. delin.," discovered by Trenton on the face of the drawing. This change in attribution is discussed below, with an elaboration on the drawing.

24. According to Alfred Barnaby Thomas, the earliest date recorded for Spanish penetration into Colorado is the middle of the seventeenth century, when the governor of New Mexico "despatched to the northeast Juan de Archuleta . . . to bring back some Taos Indians who had fled to a spot afterwards known as El Quartelejo" (Alfred Barnaby Thomas, "Spanish Expeditions into Colorado," *Colorado Magazine* 1 [November, 1924]:292). Glenn R. Scott, in his *Historic Trail Maps of the Pueblo 1° × 2° Quadrangle, Colorado* (Washington, D.C.: U.S. Geological Survey, 1975), pp. 1–930, records Pierre and Paul Mallet and seven or eight French Canadian fur traders in the southeast corner of the Pueblo quadrangle en route from the Missouri River to Santa Fe on July 5 (?), 1739.

25. See Zebulon Montgomery Pike, *The Expeditions of Zebulon Montgomery Pike*, ed. Elliott Coues.

26. Reuben G. Thwaites, ed., "S. H. Long's Expedition," in *Early Western Travels, 1748–1846 . . .*, 14:9.

27. See Jessie Poesch, *Titian Ramsay Peale, 1799–1885: And His Journals of the Wilkes Expedition*, p. 18.

28. James, comp., *Account of an Expedition* (English ed.), 1:30.

29. Ibid.

30. U.S. Department of the Treasury, National Archives and Records Service, Records of the Office of the Second Auditor of the Treasury Department,

Accounts of Stephen H. Long, #1020/1823. On March 8 and 9, 1819, more drawing paper and artist's pencils were requisitioned from the same emporium (ibid.). On March 17, 1820, the following items were ordered: "1 cake of Vermillion & Lake, 2 cakes of Prussian Blue, 1 cake of Gamboge, 1 Burnt Sienna, 2 Sable hair Pencils [brushes], and 1 Camels hair Pencil [brush—fine point]" (ibid.).

31. For his services as a landscape painter for the expedition to the Rockies from October 1, 1819, to July 20, 1820, Samuel Seymour received $441 ($1.50 a day) and $58.80 subsistence (20 cents a day; see ibid.). It can be assumed that Titian Peale received about the same amount for his services and subsistence, since, in a way, both artists served as illustrators for the expedition.

32. Charles Willson Peale was responsible for his son's appointment to the Long Expedition. He also made arrangements for the articles collected to be deposited in his museum. Poesch, *Titian Ramsay Peale*, p. 23.

33. From available records and extant prints it appears that Seymour devoted his professional activities exclusively to engraving (see n. 36 below). His sketching tours along the Schuylkill River were evidently for his own amusement. As an associate member of the Society of Artists of the United States, founded by a group of artists in 1810 and incorporated in 1813 as the Columbian Society of Artists, Seymour entered several landscapes in the society's annual exhibitions: in the *First Annual Exhibition of the Society of Artists of the United States, 1811* he entered no. 14, *Landscape, view of the sea*, and no. 18, *The Traveller*, and in the *Fourth Annual Exhibition of the Columbian Society of Artists and the Pennsylvania Academy, 1814* he entered no. 294, *Landscape*. See "Charter and By-Laws of Columbian Society of Artists, Instituted 1810, 1813," *Catalogues of the Academy of Fine Arts: 1810–1826 (184)*, p. 7, Archives, Pennsylvania Academy of the Fine Arts.

34. In the issues of *Philadelphia City Directory* of 1808 through 1818 Seymour is listed as residing at Tenth and Pine. From 1808 to 1811 he is recorded only as an engraver. From 1819 through 1822, however, there is a notation to inquire for him with Joseph Seymour at 135 Moyamensing Road, Philadelphia. His name does not appear in directories after 1822. Samuel Seymour seemingly disappears

after Long's second western expedition. He is last recorded as having been seen in New York City on October 27, 1823 (Robert Taft, Papers, Kansas State Historical Society, Topeka; Taft refers to a letter by a member [?] of the Long expedition of 1823 for which no source is given). The artist does not appear in the *Trow's New York City Directory* or in the Boston or Worcester, Mass., city directories. In all probability he returned to his native country (England?) and changed professions (see n. 35). Joseph Seymour, who was also a professional engraver and a native of England (?), began his career in 1791 in Worcester in the employment of the printmaker Isaiah Thomas. According to an "advertisement" for a Bible published by Thomas in that year, Joseph served his apprenticeship in America (see David McNeely Stauffer, *American Engravers upon Copper and Steel*, 1:244). A letter addressed to Thomas from Seymour, dated September 28, 1792, indicates that Joseph had moved from Worcester to Boston, where he was a practicing engraver (J. Seymour to I. Thomas, letter, Boston, Mass. [Manuscript Department, American Antiquarian Society, Worcester, Mass.]). Stauffer also records Joseph as having moved to Philadelphia in 1796, but the engraver's name first appears in the Philadelphia city directories in 1803. On June 18, 1823, Joseph Seymour, a widower, died at fifty-four in Philadelphia (*Collections of the Genealogical Society of Pennsylvania: Vol. Old Swedes Gloria Dei Burial Records, 1750–1831* [Philadelphia, Pa., 1924], p. 692). Since Joseph was fifteen years older than Samuel, it is probable that he was a brother or a relative. That Samuel designated Joseph's address for any inquiries while he was away with Long's expeditions indicates some relationship between the two men. In the spring of 1823, Samuel Seymour was again serving in the same capacity under Long; this time they were "exploring the river St. Peter's and the country situated on the northern boundary of the United States, between the Red River of Hudson's Bay and Lake Superior" (see William H. Keating, comp., *Narrative of an Expedition to the Source of St. Peter's River, Lake Winnepeek, Lake of the Woods, &c. Performed in the Year 1823 . . .* , 2 vols. [London: Printed for Geo. B. Whittaker, 1825]).

35. William Dunlap, *A History of the Rise and Progress of the Arts of Design in the United States*,

ed. Rita Weiss, vol. 2, pt. 1, p. 259; ibid., vol. 2, pt. 2, p. 447; henceforth cited as *History of Design*. It is more than likely that Samuel Seymour was born in England, since Thomas Sully, who was an acquaintance and a member of the same artist society, was the informant for Dunlap. Without a designated parish, however, it is impossible to verify Seymour's birthplace in England. No record of his birth was found in Worcester, Boston, or New York City. Births were not recorded in Philadelphia until 1860, and the Pennsylvania baptismal records fail to record the artist's birth.

36. Stauffer, *American Engravers*, pp. 475–78, provides a checklist of Samuel Seymour's engravings. Nos. 2873 and 2876 are portraits, published in 1796 and 1797, signed only "Seymour Sc." The rest of the engraved portraits listed are signed in the same manner without the given name of the engraver or the date printed. It seems likely that Stauffer has inadvertently assigned these plates to the wrong Seymour. According to the Philadelphia census of 1810, Samuel's age was listed as between sixteen and twenty-six, which would have made him four to fourteen years old in 1796. Taking into consideration his tender years in 1796 and 1797, it would seem impossible that he engraved the plates assigned to him. It is natural to assume that Joseph was the engraver, since his work experience can be dated back to 1791 in Worcester. Since Samuel is first mentioned by William Birch in his "Memoirs," 1:47, in relationship to the engraved views of Philadelphia, published as an album in 1800, it is possible that the artist arrived in the city shortly before 1800 and secured employment with Birch and his son.

37. Dunlap, *History of Design*.

38. The book was accessioned into the collection of the Library Company of Philadelphia by 1815 (Anne P. Hennessey, letter to Trenton, Library Company of Philadelphia, June 9, 1977). We are indebted to Robert Wark, curator of art at the Huntington Art Gallery, San Marino, Calif., for his scholarly advice and guidance in the field of English topographical art.

39. U.S. Department of the Treasury, National Archives and Records Service, Records of the Office of the Second Auditor of the Treasury Department, Accounts of Stephen H. Long, #1020/1823.

40. Poesch, *Titian Ramsay Peale*, p. 42.

41. Seymour furnished several drawings of the area now known as Roxborough Park, which is approximately fifteen miles south of downtown Denver on the way to Colorado Springs. The red outcroppings can be observed in certain areas near the base of the Rockies from Boulder to Pikes Peak. Similar outcroppings can be found in the Red Rock area near Golden and the Garden of the Gods, near Colorado Springs. These are undoubtedly the "singular" rocks that James mentions as being sketched by both Peale and Seymour (*Account of an Expedition*, English ed., 2:201).

42. Watercolor, 5 × 8 inches, Coe Collection, Collections of the Bienecke Rare Book and Manuscript Library, Yale University.

43. James, comp., *Account of an Expedition* (American ed.), atlas.

44. It has been argued that Peale, as well as Seymour, was among the "initial delineators of the American Landscape west of the Mississippi" (Poesch, *Titian Ramsay Peale*, p. 24). Yet this painting, which was formerly attributed to Seymour, and the landscape settings in Peale's animal studies are mostly copies after the older artist's drawings; for example, compare the scenery in Peale's *Blacktail Deer* (collections of the American Philosophical Society) with Seymour's *View on the Arkansa[s] near the Rocky Mountains* (watercolor, 5 × 8 inches, Coe Collection, Collections of the Bienecke Rare Book and Manuscript Library, Yale University). As far as we can ascertain, there is no mention in the report of Titian sketching landscapes, and since it has been documented that several of Seymour's drawings were in Peale's possession at one time, it is natural to assume that he used these scenic views as models for his background settings. M. Knoedler & Co. attributes the painting to Seymour because the background in this work is identical to Seymour's *View of the Rocky Mountains on the Platte 50 miles from their Base* (the gallery seems to have first consulted Harold McCracken, who pointed out the similarities between the two works; see M. Knoedler & Co., letter to Mildred Goosman, former associate curator, Joslyn Art Museum, Omaha, Nebr., December, 1964). Evidently the museum had certain reservations about this attribution and consulted John Ewers, senior ethnologist of the Smithsonian Insti-

tution. In a letter to Goosman dated June 30, 1963, Ewers concludes that the painting is by Titian Peale and not by Seymour because of the prominent group of antelopes in the foreground, a direct copy after Peale's watercolor of the same subject. He further states that, as far as he knows, Seymour's work never included large groupings of wildlife. Several extant landscape oils by Peale are largely backgrounds for activity taking place in the foreground or for wildlife. Many of these oils, executed in the 1870s, are based on earlier sketches by Peale (Poesch, *Titian Ramsay Peale*, p. 110). It is our opinion that this painting is by Titian Peale and not by Seymour. This view not only concurs with John Ewers's but also is based on the nature of the inscription on the back of the picture (known through a photograph before relining): "Rocky Mountains . . . from a Sketch by S[eymour]." The painting came to Knoedler directly from one of Peale's descendants, a fact that, alone, does not support a change in attribution but adds to the case for reassigning the picture to Peale. We have taken the liberty of making this change of attribution here.

45. It has been documented that other drawings by Seymour were once in Titian's possession.

46. James, comp., *Account of an Expedition* (English ed.), 2:187.

47. Reuben G. Thwaites, ed., *Early Western Travels*, 15:287.

48. The engraving is reproduced in the English edition of the report as the frontispiece to vol. 2. The full title of the work is *View of the Chasm through which the Platte Issues from the Rocky Mountains* (color aquatint). The Mellon Collection still lists the incorrect title for this work (see n. 23).

49. See Thwaites, ed., *Early Western Travels*, 15: 290–91 for details of this side trip to gain entrance to the valley of the Platte beyond the headwaters. Thwaites believes that Pike may have entered South Park in 1806 but adds that "Long's failure to penetrate the mountains at this point left the famous park unknown, save to wandering hunters, until Frémont's time, more than twenty years later" (ibid., p. 292, n. 141).

50. A letter to Trenton from Beverly Carter, secretary, Paul Mellon Collection, March 9, 1978, provides the provenance for their painting.

51. Ten years later this engraving was reused to illustrate "The Indian Bride" in the May, 1832, issue of the *Lady's Book*.

52. Watercolor, approximately 5 × 8 inches, Coe Collection, Collections of the Bienecke Rare Book and Manuscript Library, Yale University.

53. See Weston J. Naef and James N. Wood, *Era of Exploration: The Rise of Landscape Photography in the American West, 1860–1885*, plate 105.

54. Thwaites, ed., *Early Western Travels*, 15:298.

55. Watercolor, approximately 5 × 8 inches, Coe Collection, Collections of the Bienecke Rare Book and Manuscript Library, Yale University.

56. James, comp., *Account of an Expedition* (English ed.), 2:204.

57. Long gave this "singular hill" the name Castle Rock and the rivulet nearby Castle Rock Creek (John R. Bell, *The Journal of Captain John R. Bell . . .*, ed. Harlin M. Fuller and LeRoy Hafen, pp. 159–60). Seymour's *View of the Castle Rock on a Branch of the Arkansa[s] at the Base of the Rocky Mountains* is reproduced in the American edition of the report (atlas). His delineation corresponds closely to Louis C. McClure's photograph of the same object taken from Pine Crest (Collections of the Denver Public Library, Western History Department; henceforth cited as DPL). Seymour's drawing is unlocated.

58. Bell, *Journal of Captain John R. Bell*, p. 160, n. 63.

59. Thwaites, ed., *Early Western Travels*, 15:314, n. 156.

60. James, comp., *Account of an Expedition* (English ed.), 2:210.

61. See n. 23. From the first, the attribution of the work to the artist William McMurtrie seemed questionable. An examination of several of McMurtrie's drawings indicated that *James Peak* was unlike his other work; it seemed instead to bear a striking resemblance to Seymour's preserved drawings. The small figure, the horizontal format, and the watercolor technique indicated that this drawing might be an undiscovered Seymour. The geographic location was another clue indicating an attribution to Seymour: the distinctive configuration of Pikes Peak, as well as the use of the appellation of "James Peak," which fell out of favor after 1843. McMurtrie, who visited Colorado in 1854 (?), would have titled his drawing *Pikes Peak* and not *James Peak*, as inscribed on the verso of the picture. On March 14, 1978, Trenton received a reply to her letter to Sue W. Reed, Prints and Drawings, Museum of Fine Arts, Boston, confirming her opinion about the questionable McMurtrie attribution: "I find it difficult to accept *James Peak* as by McMurtrie, but it took your attention to point it out." In the same letter Reed noted that this drawing is dissimilar to the other McMurtries received from Robert Carlen because "all the watercolors—except *James Peak*—are on wove paper; *James Peak* is on laid paper"; and it is the only one "completely worked over with pen." On March 31, Reed wrote that none of the drawings are signed by McMurtrie; she did confirm, however, that there is an inscription on the face of the drawing in the spot indicated by Trenton, lower left: "S. S. delin." The same type of inscription appears on several of Seymour's drawings. Taking all the facts into consideration, we believe that this drawing, *James Peak*, is by Samuel Seymour rather than by McMurtrie. As the first view of Pikes Peak, the famous Colorado landmark, it is an important historical document as well.

62. For a discussion of Sandby's style, see Iolo A. Williams, *Early English Watercolours*, pp. 29–35.

63. See n. 34. Since he was an apprentice under the engraver William Birch, he could have learned the technique of stippling from the master, who employed it for the plates in his book *Delices de la Grande Bretagne*.

64. Wilbur Fisk Stone, ed., *History of Colorado*, 1:55.

65. John Charles Frémont, *Memoirs of My Life*, p. 180; henceforth cited as Frémont, *Memoirs*.

66. *Kiowa Encampment* and *Kaskaia, Shienne Chief, Arrappaho* are illustrated in the English edition of James's report. See n. 44 for *View on the Arkansa[s] . . . .*

67. See Taft, *Artist and Illustrators*, pp. 249–52.

68. The drawings that the authors have handled are on buff-colored paper, measure approximately 5 × 8 inches, and are squared off. The same color range and application are uniform among them.

69. Quoted in Thwaites, ed., *Early Western Travels*, 22:70 ("Maximilian's Travels").

70. We are indebted to Charles Sellers for bringing to our attention his article listing C. W. Peale's copies after Seymour's three drawings (Charles Cole-

man Sellers, "Charles Willson Peale with Patron and Populus," *Transactions of the American Philosophical Society*, n.s. 59, pt. 3 [May, 1969]:45). The Peale Museum Records, deposited at the Historical Society of Pennsylvania, do not list Seymour's drawings as either acquisition or loan; also, the drawings fail to appear in the catalog of the 1854 sale of paintings from the Philadelphia Peale Museum (Wilbur H. Hunter to Trenton, letter, Peale Museum, Baltimore, Md., April 5, 1977).

71. Seymour's descendants have not yet been located. The National Archives has no knowledge of the present whereabouts of Seymour's original field sketches or other drawings; their records have been examined for this information.

72. Maximilian Alexander Philip, Prinz von Wied-Neuwied, *Travels in the Interior of North America*, trans. H. Evans Lloyd, p. vi.

73. We are grateful to William H. Goetzmann for advice on the Bodmer portion of this chapter. His recent research on the artist has brought to light much information that he has graciously shared with us. Standard sources, for example, suggest that Bodmer was discovered for Maximilian by the Swiss zoologist Heinrich Rudolf Schinz. Goetzmann's research indicates that Schinz did not know the artist and that very likely it was Jacob Holscher, a local Koblenz printer and publisher, who suggested that Maximilian consider Bodmer. Holscher had published some of Bodmer's views of the Mosel River Valley in 1831 and knew of the artist's skill. The most complete biography on Bodmer is found in Hans Lang, *Indianer Waren Meine Freunde: Leben Und Werk Karl Bodmers, 1809–1893*. The best current account in English of Bodmer's life appears in Mildred Goosman's introduction to Davis Thomas and Karin Ronnefeldt, eds., *People of the First Man*, edited version of Lloyd's English translation of Maximilian's *Reise in das Innere Nord-America* . . . (see n. 72) with additional material from his field journal, illustrated with Bodmer's original watercolors. There is a suggestion that Bodmer may have kept a diary of his travels with Maximilian, which is today lost (see Jean Bodmer Lange, "The Missing Bodmer Diary," *American Book Collector* 7 [November, 1956]: 24–26).

74. Maximilian, *Travels in the Interior of North America*, p. 111: "We found at his [O'Fallon's] house an interesting collection of Indian artifacts, and a great number of Indian scenes by Catlin, a painter from New York, who had travelled in 1831 [*sic*] to Fort Union." Catlin's first trip up the Missouri had actually taken place in 1832 (see chap. 8).

75. Ibid., pp. 109–11.

76. Ibid., p. 284.

77. Ibid., p. 268.

78. We are grateful to Philip G. Schlamp, forest staff officer of the Helena National Forest, for researching and establishing the subject of this Bodmer landscape study as the Highwood Mountains. Some confusion has existed about this view over the years. John Ewers, in *Artists of the Old West*, p. 87, suggests that the Highwoods may not be part of the Rocky Mountains, though the U.S. Geological Survey includes them in the chain. More recently Thomas and Ronnefeldt, *People of the First Man*, p. 128, suggest that the view is of the Little Belt Range, a spur of the Rockies about twenty miles south of the Highwood Mountains.

79. Maximilian, *Travels in the Interior of North America*, p. 284.

80. See Benjamin P. Draper, "American Indians —Barbizon Style—The Collaborative Paintings of Millet and Bodmer," *Antiques* 44 (September, 1943): 108–10.

81. Washington Irving, *The Rocky Mountains; or Scenes, Incidents, and Adventures in the Far West, Digested from the Journal of Captain B. L. E. Bonneville, U.S.A., and Illustrated from Various Other Sources*, 1:61.

82. Alfred Jacob Miller, "Notebook," unpaged (Macgill James File, Bernard De Voto Papers, Stanford University Research Library, Palo Alto, Calif.).

83. For an analysis of the notion that he studied with Sully, see Ron Tyler, ed., *Alfred Jacob Miller: Artist on the Oregon Trail*, p. 9. The most prominent benefactor in this early support of Miller was Robert Gilmor, a Baltimore patron of the arts. He is credited with being in major part responsible for Miller's foreign study. See Robert C. Warner, *The Fort Laramie of Alfred Jacob Miller*, who cites a contemporary reference from the journal of Miller's fellow European traveler Brantz Mayer.

84. Quoted from Miller, "Notebook." The records of the École Nationale Superieure des Beaux Arts, the Bibliothèque Nationale, and the Archives Nationales do not document Miller's enrollment. Miller's "Notebook" indicates, however, that he was admitted free of charge through the influence of the American consul; it may be that he simply audited classes during his stay and was not formally registered.

85. A contemporary reference to these copies appears in Mrs. John D. Early, *Alfred J. Miller* (Baltimore, ca. 1894), pp. [1–2], which quotes the *Baltimore Bulletin* for July, 1874. Early also makes reference to "a short sojourn in England" before he reached Paris. If that is true, it could have provided Miller an opportunity to observe Turner's works.

86. Miller, "Notebook."

87. Early, *Alfred J. Miller*, p. [2].

88. Miller, "Notebook."

89. Ibid.

90. Ibid.

91. For example, see Tyler, ed., *Alfred Jacob Miller*, pp. 19–45; Wilbur H. Hunter, Jr., "Alfred Jacob Miller: Artist of Baltimore and the West," in *The Paintings of Alfred Jacob Miller: Artist of Baltimore and the West;* and Richard H. Randall, Jr., "A Gallery for Alfred Jacob Miller," *Antiques* 106 (November, 1974):836–43.

92. Quoted in Marvin C. Ross, ed., *The West of Alfred Jacob Miller*, opp. p. 59.

93. See R. W. G. Vail, "The First Artist of the Oregon Trail," *New-York Historical Society Quarterly* 34 (January, 1950):27. See also Ross, ed., *The West of Alfred Jacob Miller*, p. xxi.

94. It is evident that the oil was painted several years after the watercolor. *Trappers Saluting the Rocky Mountains* is probably the painting referred to as "Trappers saluting Wind R Mt" in an 1864 entry in the "Account Book of A. J. Miller," a manuscript in the collection of the Walters Art Gallery Library, Baltimore, Md. *Wind River Chain* was commissioned between 1859 and 1860 by William T. Walters, of Baltimore.

95. Oil on cardboard, 6⅝ ×9⅜ inches, n.d., Collection of Carl S. and Elisabeth Waldo Dentzel, Northridge, Calif.; Vail, "First Artist," and Ross, ed., *The West of Alfred Jacob Miller*, p. xxi.

96. See Wilbur H. Hunter, Jr., "A 'New' Painting by Alfred Jacob Miller," *Antiques* 101 (January, 1972):221–25.

97. Quoted in Ross, ed., *The West of Alfred Jacob*

Miller, opp. p. 130.

98. *Baltimore American,* July 17, 1838.

99. *New York Weekly Herald,* May 18, 1839.

100. Miller to Decatur H. Miller, letter, London, February 10, 1842, in the Macgill James File, De Voto Papers.

101. Miller was troubled much of his adult life with inflammatory rheumatism. The illness was probably the cause of his decision not to accompany Stewart to the West in 1843. Another artist, P. Pietierre, was appointed in Miller's place. It was perhaps a modest consolation to Miller to learn that Pietierre, because of ill health or feeble courage, traveled no farther than Fort Laramie. See Warner, *Fort Laramie,* pp. 28–29. See also Charles H. Carey, ed., *The Journals of Theodore Talbot,* p. 34.

102. The "Account Book of A. J. Miller" records paintings completed between 1846 and 1874. Excerpts from this book related to his western work are reprinted in Ross, ed., *The West of Alfred Jacob Miller,* pp. lv–lix. For the idea of reproducing his western works Miller may owe a debt to Catlin, who was busy duplicating his western paintings in London when Miller visited him in the early 1840s.

103. See Marvin C. Ross, ed., *Artists' Letters to Alfred Jacob Miller* (typescript), p. 1; and "Account Book of A. J. Miller," which notes specific lessons that Miller offered to individual students. We are indebted to Wilbur H. Hunter, Jr., director of the Peale Museum, for pointing out Johnston's debt to Miller. Mayer to Miller, letter, Paris, August 22, 1865, quoted in Ross, ibid., p. 10. See also Frank Blackwell Mayer, *With Pen and Pencil on the Frontier in 1851,* ed. Bertha L. Heilbron (St. Paul: Minnesota Historical Society, 1932), p. 68.

Chapter 2

1. John Charles Frémont, *Memoirs of My Life,* p. 140; henceforth cited as Frémont, *Memoirs.*

2. Information and quotations are from William H. Goetzmann, *Army Exploration in the American West, 1803–1863;* henceforth cited as Goetzmann, *Army Exploration.* This work gives a historical account of the development of the Corps of Topographical Engineers and the principals involved.

3. Quoted from Charles Preuss, *Exploring with Frémont: The Private Diaries of Charles Preuss, Cartographer for John C. Frémont on His First, Second, and Fourth Expeditions to the Far West,* trans. and ed. Erwin G. Gudde and Elisabeth K. Gudde, p. 33; henceforth cited as Preuss, *Exploring with Frémont.* The Guddes provide a detailed biographical sketch of this artist; all biographical information on Preuss is taken from this source (for Preuss's death date, see ibid., p. xxix).

4. Ibid., p. xix.

5. Frémont, *Memoirs,* p. 70.

6. Ibid., p. 71.

7. See J[ohn] C[harles] Frémont, *Report of the Exploring Expedition to the Rocky Mountains in the Year 1842, and to Oregon and North California in the Years 1843–'44;* henceforth cited as Frémont, *Report.* The *Report* includes 13 illustrations by Preuss, several of which were also used in the earlier report of 1842. Set patterns and limitations of colors employed by a commercial printing house like Edward Weber & Company of Baltimore probably governed the translation of a drawing into a print. The black-and-white lithographs after Preuss's sketches exhibit this kind of uniformity. The two profile sketches, each measuring $4 \times 6\frac{1}{2}$ inches, were not reproduced in the Guddes' book (the diaries are in the Manuscript Division of the Library of Congress). They are effective sketches from a topographical point of view and display a more skilled hand than the lithographs indicate.

8. Quoted from Frémont, *Memoirs,* p. 151. On August 15, 1842, Preuss sketched the "Cirque of the Towers," a group of towering, jagged peaks encircling a small interior lake in the Wind River Range.

9. *View of the Wind River Mountains* is reproduced in Frémont, *Report.* The actual approach to South Pass is close to the illustration.

10. On September 24, 1843, Preuss sketched *The American Falls.* See Preuss, *Exploring with Frémont,* pp. 91–92.

11. Quoted from Frémont, *Memoirs,* pp. 244–45.

12. See Preuss, *Exploring with Frémont,* p. 16 and n. 15. The various vouchers reproduced in Donald Jackson and Mary Lee Spence, eds., *The Expeditions of John Charles Frémont,* vol. 1, *Travels from 1838 to 1844,* list only artist's pencils and sheets of paper. Henceforth cited as Jackson and Spence, *Expeditions.*

13. Quoted in Preuss, *Exploring with Frémont,* p. 32.

14. According to Robert Taft, in *Photography and the American Scene,* pp. 250–51 (henceforth cited as Taft, *Photography*), no daguerreotype views were taken of the West before 1850.

15. On July 10, Preuss sketched the "glittering" snowcapped peak from their encampment along the West Bijou Creek on their way to Manitou Springs, reproduced in Frémont, *Report.*

16. See Frémont, *Memoirs,* p. 180.

17. See chap. 3.

18. See Frémont, *Memoirs,* p. 413.

19. Allan Nevins, *Frémont: Pathmaker of the West,* pp. 196–97; henceforth cited as Nevins, *Frémont.*

20. Charles Preuss, *Topographical Map of the Road from Missouri to Oregon Commencing at the Mouth of the Kansas in the Missouri River Ending at the Mouth of the Wallah-Wallah in the Columbia in VII Sections . . . from the Field Notes and Journal of Captain J. C. Frémont . . . by Order of the Senate of the United States,* Baltimore, Md., 1846. In 1848, Preuss executed another map for Frémont which covered a larger portion of the West, with many of the details drawn from other maps.

21. Frémont, *Memoirs,* p. 426.

22. Ibid.

23. Ibid., p. 428; see chap. 2, section on Edward Kern.

24. The following sources were useful for biographical information on the artist: H. Bailey Carroll, ed., *Gúadal P'a: The Journal of Lieutenant J. W. Abert from Bent's Fort to St. Louis in 1845,* pp. 4–5; John Galvin, ed., *Western America in 1846–1847: The Original Travel Diary of Lieutenant J. W. Abert, Who Mapped New Mexico for the United States Army,* p. 3; henceforth cited as Galvin, *Western America;* George C. Groce and David H. Wallace, *The New York Historical Society's Dictionary of Artists in America, 1564–1860,* p. 1; henceforth cited as Groce and Wallace, *Dictionary of Artists;* Robert Taft Papers, Kansas State Historical Society, Topeka.

25. [James W. Abert], *Journal of Lieutenant James W. Abert, from Bent's Fort to St. Louis, in*

1845, 29th Cong., 1st sess., S. Ex. Doc. 438, p. 27; henceforth cited as [Abert], *Journal*. The copy of the journal in the Western History Department, Denver Public Library, contains 11 plates, most uncolored, of scenery; a map; and lithographs by Edward Weber & Company (hand-colored in this edition).

26. The original watercolor sketch is in the collection of Sir John Galvin, Dublin, Ireland, and is reproduced in his book *Western America*. It is also reproduced as a lithograph in [James W. Abert], *Report of the Secretary of War, Communicating, in Answer to a Resolution of the Senate, a Report and Map of the Examination of New Mexico, Made by Lieutenant J. W. Abert, of the Topographical Corps*, February 10, 1848, 30th Cong., 1st sess., S. Ex. Doc. 23, plate 15 (C. B. Graham Printers, Washington, D.C.); henceforth cited as [Abert], *Report*. This report contains 21 plates of scenery and portraits and three of fossils, a map, and plates lithographed by C. B. Graham (uncolored). Abert's views were reengraved in William Hemsley Emory, *Notes on a Military Reconnoissance from Fort Leavenworth in Missouri to San Diego in California, Including Parts of the Arkansas, Del Norte, and Gila Rivers*, 30th Cong., 1st sess., S. Ex. Doc. 7; henceforth cited as Emory, *Notes*.

27. S[eth] Eastman, *Treatise on Topographical Drawing*, p. 22.

28. See Charles W. Larned, "Historical Sketch of [the] Department of Drawing," *The Centennial of the United States Military Academy at West Point, New York, 1802-1902*, 1:294.

29. See [Abert], *Journal* and his *Report*.

30. Goetzmann, *Army Exploration*, p. 127.

31. Emory, *Notes*, p. 7.

32. Ibid., p. 43.

33. [Abert], *Report*. Ten of twenty-one illustrations in the *Report* are pueblos and ruins visited by Abert and Peck on their journey through New Mexico.

34. The original watercolor sketch is in Galvin's collection and is reproduced in his second book on the artist, *Through the Country of the Comanche Indians in the Fall of the Year 1845: The Journal of a U.S. Army Expedition led by Lieutenant James W. Abert of the Topographical Engineers . . .;* henceforth cited as Galvin, *Through the Country of the Coman-*

che Indians. *Bent's Fort* is viewed from across the Arkansas River.

35. Most of Abert's sketches from his 1845 and 1846-47 expeditions to the Southwest are held by Galvin. A series of Indian portraits is in the collection of the Bienecke Rare Book and Manuscript Library, Yale University. According to Galvin's account, "His sketches of 1846-47 measure 6⅝ × 8⅛ inches and are contained in a sketchbook of 136 leaves: Almost every leaf has on its recto side a watercolor sketch. There are also a few pen or pencil drawings. Some two dozen of the sketches are of landscapes or buildings, or details thereof. Most of the others are of plants, with or without flowers, and some of these are accompanied by drawings of insects. A handful are of birds or animals or reptiles. A few are of human beings." Galvin, *Western America*, preface. The sketchbook of the expedition of 1845, formerly held by Mrs. Hamilton Abert, includes 40 watercolors and pencil sketches. A bound copy of Abert's *Report* includes 12 watercolor sketches in addition to the hand-colored lithographs. The artist evidently inserted these sketches for his parents. These items are also in the Galvin collection, and several are introduced in Galvin's second book on the artist, ibid.

36. [Abert], *Journal*, 1845, quoted in Carroll, *Gúadal P'a*, p. 28; reproduced as a colored lithograph by Edward Weber & Company, along with other views of Colorado: *Valley of the Purgatory, A Cañoned Creek*, and *Scene near Camp N⁰ 10 Aug. 23rd [Fisher's Peak]*.

37. Quoted from [Abert], *Report*, p. 437; the sketch is reproduced in the *Report*.

38. Frémont, *Memoirs*, pp. 424-25.

39. Goetzmann, *Army Exploration*, p. 116.

40. Ibid., p. 117.

41. Frémont to [Edward Kern], letter, Washington City, March 20, 1845, quoted in Jackson and Spence, eds., *Expeditions*, 2:401. Drayton worked in Philadelphia before joining Wilkes's expedition in 1838; his sketches illustrate Wilkes's report (61 woodcuts). See Groce and Wallace, *Dictionary of Artists*, pp. 188-89 for a biographical sketch of the artist.

42. Jackson and Spence, eds., *Expeditions*.

43. For the number of artists who applied for this position, see Richard Kern's letter to John R.

Bartlett, Santa [Fe], March 14, 1851, Fort Sutter Papers, vol. 32, MS 138, Huntington Library, San Marino, Calif. See also Robert V. Hine, *Edward Kern and American Expansion*, p. 6. Hine's book provides the most current and detailed account of Edward and his brothers. The discussion here attempts to delve more deeply into the relationship of the Kerns with other artists of the period who were engaged in similar activities; however, all artistic judgments will be limited to the Kerns' scenic art in the Rockies—an attempt made possible by the recent discovery of an unpublished cache of drawings and sketches by the two brothers in a private collection.

44. See Anna Wells Rutledge, "Cumulative Record of Exhibition Catalogues, the Pennsylvania Academy of the Fine Arts, 1807-1870, the Society of Artists, 1800-1814, the Artists' Fund Society, 1835-1945," *American Philosophical Society Memoirs* 38 (1955).

45. These large watercolors are mostly unfinished. They and a number of other drawings by the Kerns in watercolor, wash, pencil, and pen and ink are in a private collection.

46. Hine, *Edward Kern*, p. 5.

47. The artist's sketchbook with scenes in and around Abiquiú, N.Mex., dated "Feby 1. 1850," includes the sheet with Weber's suggestions for painting landscapes—in particular, hints on how to achieve aerial perspective. In 1850-51, Edward was serving as "a forage master for the Quartermaster Corps" in Abiquiú. Hine, *Edward Kern*, p. 84. The sketchbook is in a private collection. For a biographical sketch of Paul Weber, see Groce and Wallace, *Dictionary of Artists*, p. 668. According to this account, Weber arrived in Philadelphia in 1848; that the artist was "chosen from among the Associates on July 15, 1847" to serve as an academician of the Pennsylvania Academy of the Fine Arts indicates that Weber must have been in the city several years before his reported arrival. It seems highly probable that Edward knew Weber before his departure with Frémont in 1845. See [Pennsylvania Academy of the Fine Arts], *Pennsylvania Academicians, March 10-April 8, 1973*. There is no conclusive proof, however, to rule out their having met after Edward's return from California in 1847.

48. The drawing is unsigned, but in our opin-

ion it should be assigned to Edward; it is far too skillful to be Richard's work. Both the figures and the trees are characteristic of the younger brother's hand (for example, *Babes in the Woods,* in Edward Kern, "Journal of a Trip to California, 1845–46–47," private collection; henceforth cited as Kern, "Journal"). For a discussion of winter landscapes and the German influence, see Martha Young Hutson, *George Henry Durrie (1820–1863), American Winter Landscapist: Renowned Through Currier and Ives.*

49. Richard's letter to Edward, Philadelphia, February 10, 1847, mentions that he is "making illustrations for a medical Botany by Dr. Carson . . . [and] a set of drawings in Microscopic Anatomy for Dr. Goddard." Fort Sutter Papers, vol. 29, FS 117.

50. Edward Kern to Joseph Drayton, letter, Philadelphia, Pa., March 20, 1845, Fort Sutter Papers, vol. 1, FS 2.

51. Joseph Drayton to Edward Kern, letter, Washington, D.C., March 22, 1845, Huntington Library Manuscript Collection, HR 122.

52. Frémont, *Memoirs,* p. 423.

53. The frontispiece of Kern, "Journal"; Frémont, *Memoirs,* p. 426.

54. See chap. 2, section on Abert.

55. Hine, *Edward Kern,* p. 20.

56. Frémont and Edward are generally in agreement on their itinerary, except for the date they left Bent's Fort. Edward's journal, however, is far more detailed than Frémont's recollections, which were written many years later. Kern even includes a small detailed topographical map to show the terrain they crossed while ascending the Arkansas to its headwaters.

57. Kern, "Journal." The same view was captured by the Kern brothers on their trip with Frémont's expedition to the Rockies in 1848–49.

58. Kern, "Journal."

59. Frémont, *Memoirs,* p. 429.

60. For the illustration see ibid., opp. p. 186.

61. Kern, "Journal," September 9, 1845.

62. Again, there is no mention by Edward or Frémont of a sketch made here.

63. Edward's journal at this juncture is rather sketchy. The other rivers are spoken of as branches or forks of the White. Frémont's route is fully discussed and pinpointed by William Joseph Heffernan in *Edward M. Kern: The Travels of an Artist-Explorer.*

64. This sketch, from Kern, "Journal," was executed on October 2, 1845 (see n. 48).

65. The sketches made along Smoky Hill Trail were executed in this manner (private collection).

66. Richard to Edward Kern, letter, Philadelphia, Pa., February 10, 1847, Fort Sutter Papers, vol. 29, MS HR 117.

67. Richard was born in Philadelphia on April 11, 1821. Both Richard and Edward were listed in the Philadelphia Artists' Fund Society's exhibition catalogs for 1840 and 1841 (see Rutledge, "Cumulative Record").

68. Hine, *Edward Kern,* p. 157.

69. Large watercolors by Richard and Edward are in the same private collection.

70. Richard to Edward Kern, letter, Philadelphia, Pa., February 10, 1847, Fort Sutter Papers, vol. 29, MS HR 117.

71. Hine, *Edward Kern,* p. 158.

72. This "recipe" is included in Edward Kern, "Abiquiu Sketchbook" (private collection) and Richard Kern, "Diary of Frémont's 1848–1849 Expedition" (Huntington Library Manuscript Collection, HM 4273).

73. Several of the Kerns' sketchbooks, along with Edward's journal of his expedition with Frémont in 1845 (the Colorado and Utah portions of which are unpublished) are in the same private collection. For a list (incomplete) of Edward's works and reproductions see Hine, *Edward Kern,* pp. 171–74.

74. Hine, *Edward Kern,* p. 50, n. 3. According to Hine's note, "Richard was elected May 25, 1847; Benjamin, September, 1847; and Edward, October 26, 1847." Many of the Kerns' drawings are included in the academy's collection, particularly subjects from their New Mexico assignments.

75. Hine, *Edward Kern,* p. 52. Most of the biographical information comes from Frémont, *Memoirs;* and from Hine, *Edward Kern.*

76. Allan Nevins, *Frémont: The West's Greatest Adventurer,* 2:390.

77. Benjamin Kern, "Diary," Huntington Library Manuscript Collection, HM 4272. Their camp was at Boone's Creek, about three miles west of Westport.

78. Nevins, *Frémont,* p. 397.

79. Benjamin Kern recorded this event in his "Diary," Huntington Library Manuscript Collection, HM 4272.

80. This sketch, on cream-colored paper, is one of a number of miscellaneous sketches by both brothers pasted into a scrapbook.

81. A group of watercolors contained in a sketchbook in the Amon Carter Museum Collection, Fort Worth, Texas, which have not been reproduced.

82. Recorded on November 17 in Richard Kern, "Diary," Huntington Library Manuscript Collection, HM 4273.

83. For a bibliographic listing, see LeRoy R. Hafen and Ann W. Hafen, eds., *Frémont's Fourth Expedition: A Documentary Account of the Disaster of 1848–1849* . . . .

84. Sketchbook, Amon Carter Museum Collection.

85. Ibid. The watercolor sketch measures 4 × 6¼ inches and is signed "R. H. Kern 1853"; however, the date appears not to be in Kern's hand and was probably added later. Its context with the other watercolors and its position at the beginning of the sketchbook indicate that the date should be 1848 and not 1853 as inscribed.

86. Benjamin Kern, "Diary," Huntington Library Manuscript Collection, HM 4272.

87. The sketch, which measures 5¾ × 4¼ inches, was probably made on December 3, when both Richard and Benjamin mention in their diaries that the party was on "Road Robidou."

88. The watercolor (in Sketchbook, Amon Carter Museum Collection) measures 4⁵⁄₁₆ × 5¹³⁄₁₆ inches and is inscribed with this date.

89. The sketchbook (ibid.) contains twenty-four watercolors and one untitled, unsigned pencil sketch. Several watercolors were taken during the Simpson and Sitgreaves expeditions through New Mexico in 1849 and 1851.

90. Ibid. This sketch measures 4⁵⁄₁₆ × 5¾ inches. There is a smaller version of the same subject in a private collection.

91. *Natural Obelisks,* opp. p. xvi; *In a Canyon of the San Juan Mountains,* opp. p. 28; and *Christmas Camp 1848, San Juan Mountains,* following p. 585. Cataloged by the Huntington Library as a prospectus, this volume contains material that did not appear in the *Memoirs,* of which only vol. 1 was pub-

lished.

92. Carvalho's daguerreotypes, which served as models for many of these illustrations, were made into photographic prints by Mathew B. Brady. In her introduction to Frémont, *Memoirs*, p. xvi, Jessie Frémont elaborates on the artists and engravers who were employed to work on the illustrations.

93. William Brandon, *The Men and the Mountains: Frémont's Fourth Expedition*, p. 272.

94. See Randolph B. Marcy, *Report of a Route from Fort Smith to Santa Fe*, 31st Cong., 1st sess., S. Exec. Doc. 64.

95. James H. Simpson, *Report and Map of the Route from Fort Smith, Arkansas, to Santa Fe, New Mexico . . .*, 31st Cong., 1st sess., S. Exec. Doc. 12. The report includes one plate, *View of Santa Fe and Vicinity from the East*, a lithograph made after a sketch by Richard Kern. See Hine, *Edward Kern*, fig. 15.

96. James H. Simpson, *Journal of a Military Reconnaissance, from Santa Fé, New Mexico, to the Navajo Country, Made with the Troops Under the Command of Brevet Lieutenant Colonel John M. Washington . . . in 1849.*

97. Ibid., p. 4.

98. See Hine, *Edward Kern*, p. 86.

99. The Sitgreaves expedition, searching for a southwestern railroad route to the Pacific, skirted the southern fringe of the Rockies, returned to Zuñi, crossed Arizona to Fort Yuma, and eventually moved on to San Diego. Today the Santa Fe Railroad follows this route. See Lorenzo Sitgreaves, *Report of an Expedition down to the Zuñi and Colorado Rivers*, 32d Cong., 2d sess., S. Exec. Doc. 59, chap. 3.

100. Of particular importance are the Kerns' ethnological and archaeological subjects, which have been reproduced in various publications. It appears that Edward and Richard sketched mainly landscapes while traveling through Colorado. None of these preserved sketches has been reproduced, however.

Chapter 3

1. Rev. Samuel Parker, *Journal of an Exploring Tour Beyond the Rocky Mountains . . .*, p. 73.

2. Ibid., p. 72.

3. *Message of the President of the United States. December 4, 1849* [Washington, D.C.: Globe, 1849], pp. 5-6.

4. Howard Stansbury, *An Expedition to the Valley of the Great Salt Lake of Utah . . .*, p. 5. Material about the expedition is drawn from this source unless otherwise noted.

5. 32d Cong., spec. sess., S. Ex. Doc. 3 (Philadelphia, Pa.: Lippincott, Grambo & Co., 1852).

6. Stansbury was scheduled to ride west with Colonel W. W. Loring, who was assigned to traverse the Oregon Trail with his regiment of mounted riflemen, establishing and outfitting posts along the way (see chap. 4).

7. Stansbury, *Expedition*, p. 15.

8. See George C. Groce and David H. Wallace, *The New-York Historical Society's Dictionary of Artists in America, 1564-1860*, p. 276; henceforth cited as Groce and Wallace, *Dictionary of Artists*.

9. See Dale L. Morgan, *The Great Salt Lake*, p. 233, and Henry R. Wagner, *The Plains and the Rockies: A Bibliography of Original Narratives of Travel and Adventure 1800-1865*, rev. ed., ed. Charles L. Camp, p. 285. A letter was written to the National Archives requesting information on these artists. Their reply to our inquiry was the following: "We have located among the records of the Office of the Chief of Engineers approximately 28 field books of the Stansbury Expedition. These include narrative journals, topographical notes, barometric and astronomical observations, and odometer readings. Some of the volumes are identified as to author, others are not. Among the field books is one journal kept by J. Hudson, April–June, 1850, 48 pages. Although some of the volumes contain miniature drawings and sketches, we could not locate the original drawings of Hudson or Grist.

"We have been unable to locate any biographical information about Hudson or Grist. The Letters Received by the Topographical Engineers may contain some references to Hudson and other members of the party, however, we do not have sufficient staff available to conduct such an extensive search." Brenda A. Beasley, Navy and Old Army Branch, Military Archives Division, National Archives to authors, letter, Washington, D.C., January 29, 1980.

10. Gunnison to his wife, Martha, letter, Camp Grist, October 7, 1849, Huntington Library Manuscript Collection, San Marino, Calif., HM 17062.

11. Gunnison to his wife, letter, Camp Grist, October 9, 1849, Huntington Library Manuscript Collection, HM 17063. For Gunnison's summary, see p. 121. The fold-out is opp. p. 100.

12. Morgan, *Great Salt Lake*.

13. Ibid.

14. Groce and Wallace, *Dictionary of Artists*, p. 333.

15. Reproduced in the *M. & M. Karolik Collection of American Paintings, 1815-1865*, pp. 367-68, fig. 68.

16. British spelling is used throughout, but this is not conclusive, for many Americans continued to use it until as late a date as this. Under April 11, 1850, Hudson speaks of a bird name "in my country." That the country was England is suggested by the close of the entry for April 29, where he says that he "turned in & was soon transported to old England by . . . Morpheus" (Hudson's journal, typescript copy, p. 7 in the Dale L. Morgan Collection, Bancroft Library, University of California, Berkeley [original journal in the National Archives; see n. 9]).

17. See below.

18. Edwin Griffin Beckwith, "Report of Explorations for a Route for the Pacific Railroad, by Capt. J. W. Gunnison, Topographical Engineers, near the 38th and 39th Parallels of North Latitude from the Mouth of the Kansas River, Mo., to the Sevier Lake, in the Great Basin," in *Reports of Explorations and Surveys, to Ascertain the Most Practicable and Economical Route for a Railroad from the Mississippi River to the Pacific Ocean . . . in 1853-4 . . .*, 33d Cong., 3d sess., H. Exec. Doc. 91, 2:10; henceforth cited as Beckwith, *Report*.

19. Robert V. Hine, *Edward Kern*, p. 95.

20. George Leslie Albright, *Official Explorations for Pacific Railroads, 1853-1855*, 11:38-39.

21. "Richard Kern's Report to Gwin on an Overland Railroad Route," Fort Sutter Papers, vol. 37, FS 153-158, Huntington Library Manuscript Collection.

22. These volumes were published by the federal government from 1855 to 1861. According to Taft, "Copies were published for the use of both Senate and House, and in several cases in more than one

printing. As a result there are variations, especially in illustrations." The author elaborates further on the complicated bibliographic record of the *Reports* (see Robert Taft, *Artists and Illustrators of the Old West, 1850–1900*, pp. 254–56).

23. Quoted from ibid., p. 5. The *Reports* constitute the results of six surveys carried out from 1853 to 1854 during the exploration of several alternate routes for the railroad.

24. Beckwith, *Report*, p. 11.

25. The view was taken near the Cuchara on August 6; see ibid., plate 1.

26. "In some copies, as many as three of the plates are credited to Kern alone; in others all are credited 'J. M. Stanley from sketch by R. H. Kern.' In addition to the twelve Kern sketches there is a thirteenth plate, 'View showing the formation of the Canon of the Grand River.' In some copies this is credited to F. W. Egloffstein; in others to 'J. M. Stanley from sketch by F. W. Egloffstein'" (Taft, *Artists and Illustrators*, pp. 261–62). The set that we examined at the Huntington Library includes three plates credited to Kern alone: *Coo-Che-To-Pa Pass* (plate 7); *Head of the First Cañon of Grand River* (plate 8); and *View of Ordinary Lateral Ravines of Grand River* (plate 9). These three views show more of the general character of the country, which might indicate that the lithographer was referring directly to Kern's field sketches rather than to Stanley's redrawn versions. For details of Kern's death and the Gunnison massacre, see below.

27. See Beckwith, *Report*, plates 2, 3, and 4. These views were executed between August 11 and August 13.

28. See *Fort Massachusetts: At the Foot of the Sierra Blanca; Valley of San Luis* (plate 5) and *Peaks of the Sierra Blanca: From near Fort Massachusetts* (plate 6). Both views were taken between August 15 and August 23.

29. See Beckwith, *Report*, plate 7.

30. See *Head of the First Cañon of Grand River: below the Mouth of Coo-che-to-pa Creek, Sept. 7* (plate 8) and *View of Ordinary Lateral Ravines of Grand River: from Camp Sept. 3rd* (plate 9).

31. This sketch is unsigned, but the location indicates that it must be Richard's.

32. Beckwith, *Report*, p. 50.

33. According to the explorer (ibid., p. 126), the scenes were "to exhibit on a small scale the character of its mountains and cañones, and of its plains and valleys, in their respective positions and extents, as seen in nature." He further states that they were taken from elevated positions in an effort to represent the panoramic character of the country; therefore "little attention . . . [was] paid to the beautiful execution of foregrounds."

34. See ibid., pp. 80ff.

35. Nolie Mumey, "John Williams Gunnison—Centenary of his Survey and Tragic Death (1853–1953)," *Colorado Magazine* 31 (January, 1954):30–31.

36. Albright, *Official Explorations*, p. 94. Beckwith continued where Gunnison left off. Accompanied by the Prussian artist F. W. Egloffstein, he examined the Wasatch Mountains, the Uinta Mountains, and the Great Basin for practical railroad routes.

37. Reprinted in Nolie Mumey, *John Williams Gunnison (1812–1853): The Last of the Western Explorers . . .*, pp. 129–30.

38. Unidentified newspaper clipping titled "Art Gossip," probably from the *Detroit Free Press* about 1865, in the John Mix Stanley Papers, Archives of American Art, Smithsonian Institution.

39. Several general biographical accounts exist for Stanley. Probably the most nearly complete appears in W. Vernon Kinietz, *John Mix Stanley, and His Indian Paintings*, much of which is taken from a manuscript account attributed to Stanley's son, Louis Crandall Stanley, furnished for the *Detroit News* and appearing there in July, 1924. The unpaged manuscript is now in the Burton Historical Collection, Detroit Public Library. Other general treatments can be found in David I. Bushnell, "John Mix Stanley, Artist-Explorer," *Annual Report of the Smithsonian Institution for the Year Ending June 30, 1924*, pp. 507–12; Charles Richard Tuttle, *General History of the State of Michigan . . .*, pp. 235–40; and Nellie B. Pipes, "John Mix Stanley, Indian Painter," *Oregon Historical Society Quarterly* 33 (September, 1932):250–58.

40. We are particularly grateful to Julie Schimmel, whose research on Stanley for a doctoral dissertation has brought to light many biographical elements heretofore unknown. We have found no record of Bowman in the Detroit directories; however, a clipping from the *Detroit Free Press* dated September 28, 1885, provides the following account: "The Daily Free Press was first issued September 28, 1833. The office was in the Sheldon block, north side of Jefferson avenue, between Griswold and Shelby streets. Over the door was the sign of the establishment upon which was a portrait of Benjamin Franklin. This sign was the means of bringing out the undeveloped artistic talent of a young man who in later years became one of the noted painters of this country. Mr. Bowman, a celebrated Italian artist [*sic*] here, employed in painting the portrait of some of the leading citizens of Detroit, seeing the head of Franklin on the sign, stepped into the office and asked who painted it. He was informed it was painted by John M. Stanley, a young house and sign painter on Atwater street. Mr. Bowman sought him out and invited him to his studio, offering to teach him gratuitously the art of mixing colors and give him lessons in portrait painting, saying to him that the painter of that head of Franklin should quit house and sign painting and devote himself to studying the higher art of portrait painting. Mr. Stanley availed himself of the kind offer and was a frequent visitor at the studio of Mr. Bowman, receiving instructions in the fine art. Shortly after Mr. Coolidge, Mr. Stanley's partner in the house and sign painting business, died. Mr. Stanley then joined with Mr. Bowman and they went to Chicago and opened a studio and a hall of fine art in which he invested and sunk his capital. Subsequently he conceived the project of getting up a gallery of Indian paintings and went West among the Indians for that purpose." Another reference to Bowman appeared in the *Detroit News-Tribune* in September, 1894. Both clippings are in the Burton Historical Collection, Detroit Public Library. James Bowman is listed in Groce and Wallace, *Dictionary of Artists*.

41. Louis C. Stanley, manuscript, Burton Historical Collection, Detroit Public Library.

42. George Catlin, *Letters and Notes on the Manners, Customs, and Condition of the North American Indians*, 1:3.

43. "The Fine Arts," *Arkansas Intelligencer*, July 15, 1843, p. 2.

44. Louis C. Stanley, manuscript, Burton Historical Collection, Detroit Public Library. The only reference we have found to suggest a visit to the northern plains appeared in the *Arkansas Intelli-*

gencer, May 3, 1845, p. 2, which mentions that "Messrs. Stanley & Dickerman have started to the Mo. of Yellow Stone, on the Upper Missouri, where they design to continue their paintings of Indian portraits and scenes." The only two paintings in "Stanley's Indian Gallery" that were dated from 1845, however, carried titles suggesting southern-plains origins—*An Osage Scalp Dance* and *A Buffalo Hunt* (subtitled *On the South-western Prairies*). See John Mix Stanley, *Portraits of North American Indians, with Sketches of Scenery, Etc.*, pp. 45 and 52, respectively. Robert Taft in *Artists and Illustrators*, pp. 9–10 and 269–71, discusses Stanley's experiences in the Southwest between 1842 and 1845.

45. John M. Stanley, *Catalogue of Pictures in Stanley and Dickerman's North American Indian Portrait Gallery.*

46. William H. Emory, *Notes on a Military Reconnoissance, From Fort Leavenworth, in Missouri, to San Diego, in California, Including Parts of the Arkansas, Del Norte, and Gila Rivers*, 30th Cong., 1st sess., S. Exec. Doc. 7, p. 10; henceforth cited as Emory, *Notes.*

47. Eight of the oil paintings, including Stanley's *San Felipe, New Mexico*, are in the collection of the Stark Museum of Art, Orange, Texas. See Julie Schimmel, *Stark Museum of Art: The Western Collection, 1978*, pp. 59, 225–26. Besides Stanley's *Butte on the Del Norte*, the remaining four extant oils are owned by Stanley's grandchildren, Alice Stanley Acheson (Mrs. Dean Acheson) and Peter Frantz. One final oil, *View of the Casa Grande, Nov. 10, 1846*, is unlocated.

48. Emory, *Notes*, p. 38.

49. The artist must have felt some dissatisfaction with the crows. Their scale within the composition is awkward; perhaps it was felt that they detracted from the human element. At any rate, they were removed from the picture when it was illustrated in the Emory account. Ibid., opp. p. 38.

50. Ibid., p. 45.

51. Ibid., p. 79. Some recent criticisms have been made of Stanley's ability to portray accurately the southwestern landscape. Reviewing the artist's depictions of the territory encountered by the Emory forces, historian Ross Calvin has commented that "some of the illustrations included in the body of the text itself, although they might have added anti-quarian charm, are so inaccurate as to make it clear that the draughtsman never beheld the scenes he was attempting to depict." Ross Calvin, ed., *Lieutenant Emory Reports: A Reprint of Lieutenant W. H. Emory's Notes on a Military Reconnoissance* (Albuquerque: University of New Mexico Press, 1951), pp. 3–4. Since Emory makes clear reference to the fidelity of many of Stanley's works and those of his views that can be compared with the depictions of other artists that are similar, like Heinrich Möllhausen's *San Felipe, Rio Grande, New Mexico* (1853; a photograph of this lost watercolor can be found in the Robert Taft Papers, Kansas State Historical Society, Topeka), the evaluation seems rather harsh. A comparison of Stanley's and Abert's views of the ruins of Pecos, New Mexico, reveals that Stanley was, in fact, the more diligent of the two in recording details.

52. Emory, *Notes*, p. 108.

53. Dwight L. Clarke, "Soldiers Under Stephen Watts Kearny," *California Historical Society Quarterly* 45 (June, 1966):140.

54. Emory, *Notes*, p. 114.

55. Unidentified clipping entitled "Interesting from California. Letters from John M. Stanley" (printing a letter to S. Dickerman from Stanley, San Diego Bay, January 24, 1847), in a scrapbook of Stanley clippings, Oakland Museum, Art Division, Archives, Oakland, Calif.

56. Edwin Bryant, *What I Saw in California*, ed. Richard H. Dillon, pp. 435–36.

57. Kinietz, *John Mix Stanley*, p. 7.

58. "Indians," *New York Tribune*, November 28, 1850, p. 1.

59. "Indian Gallery of Paintings," *National Intelligencer*, February 23, 1852, p. 4.

60. Published in *Smithsonian Miscellaneous Collections*, 2:[3].

61. *Oregonian*, June 25, 1853, p. 2.

62. "Puget's Sound Railroad Survey," *New York Tribune*, June 3, 1853, p. 5.

63. "The Puget Sound Expedition," *New York Tribune*, August 3, 1853, p. 5. This account lists Strobel as "assistant artist to Mr. Stanley." Strobel is acknowledged as a "very accomplished artist" who "on his return has rendered valuable service to Minnesota by his sketches of the Minnesota river from Lac qui Parle to Traverse des Sioux."

64. "Pacific Railroad. Northern Route," *Oregonian*, January 21, 1854, p. 1, quoting a letter from Stevens dated September 17, 1853.

65. The painting's title is recorded in the Gilcrease Institute's records as *Scouts in the Tetons*, an apparent mislabeling, since Stanley never saw the Teton Mountains. We are again grateful to Julie Schimmel for her insights. She has advised us that in the M. Knoedler & Co. correspondence for 1947 the painting is listed as *Encampment in the Teton Country* (1860). This is, of course, a more reasonable title, for it suggests the Teton River area of northern Montana, which Stanley crossed during the Stevens Expedition.

66. Several such watercolors are in the collections of Dr. and Mrs. Franz Stenzel, Portland, Oreg., and Mr. Paul Mellon, Upperville, Va. For illustrations of selections from the two collections, see William H. Goetzmann, "The Grand Reconnaissance," *American Heritage* 23 (October, 1972): 50–59; and Larry Curry, *The American West*, pp. 105–106.

67. Isaac I. Stevens, "Narrative and Final Report of Explorations for a Route for a Pacific Railroad, near the Forty-seventh and Forty-ninth Parallels of North Latitude, from St. Paul to Puget Sound," *Reports of Explorations and Surveys . . . for a Railroad from the Mississippi River to the Pacific Ocean . . .*, vol. 12, bk. 1, opp. p. 117; henceforth cited as Stevens, "Narrative."

68. Isaac I. Stevens, "Report of Explorations for a Route for the Pacific Railroad, near the Forty-seventh and Forty-ninth Parallels of North Latitude, from St. Paul to Puget Sound," ibid., 1:67.

69. "Oregon," *New York Tribune*, January 9, 1845, p. 5, notes that "Mr. J. M. Stanley, the Artist of the Expedition, came into Vancouver with Gov. Stevens, and was dispatched to Washington with the news of their arrival. Mr. Stanley arrived in the *Star of the West.*"

70. A letter from Stevens to Captain A. A. Humphreys of the War Department, September 26, 1854, emphasizes that "it is important that Mr. Stanley should at once commence preparing his sketches for publication. We have already made the selection in part. The compensation which I have agreed to pay him is $125 per month, a small compensation . . . in view of his ability and experience."

71. *Washington Daily Evening Star*, December 6, 1854, p. 2, provides a typical advertisement. Such ads appear as early as August 9 of that year. In midcentury the moving panorama, initiated a century earlier in Europe, became a popular form of entertainment and education in the United States. There were many forms but for Stanley's great scenic production the canvas was wound on two poles and manipulated from behind, accompanied by a lecture explaining the succession of painted scenes.

72. "Stanley's Panorama," *Washington Daily Evening Star*, December 7, 1854, p. 3.

73. *Washington Daily Evening Star*, December 11, 1854, p. 3.

74. Thomas S. Donaho, *Scenes and Incidents of Stanley's Western Wilds*. The only copy that we are aware of is in the Library of Congress. See Taft, *Artists and Illustrators*, p. 21.

75. Louis C. Stanley, manuscript, Burton Historical Collection, Detroit Public Library.

76. Smithsonian Institution, *Annual Report, 1865* (Washington, D.C.: 1872), p. 119. This report acknowledges the loss of 200 paintings. Louis C. Stanley, manuscript, Burton Historical Collection, Detroit Public Library, maintains that 300 were lost. Another account, "The Western Art Gallery," *Detroit Free Press*, November 11, 1870, p. 1, mentions the loss of "some 160 paintings."

77. J. A. B., "Mr. J. M. Stanley's Paintings . . . ," *Michigan Exchange*, September 12, 1864.

78. *Report on the Construction of a Military Road from Fort Walla-Walla to Fort Benton*, p. 11.

79. The following biographical information is taken from material contained in John C. Ewers, "Gustavus Sohon's Portraits of Flathead and Pend d'Oreille Indians, 1854," *Smithsonian Miscellaneous Collections*, 110:1-13.

80. Hazard Stevens, *The Life of Isaac Ingalls Stevens*, 2:68.

81. Mullan, *Report*, p. 2.

82. Hazard Stevens, *Isaac Ingalls Stevens*, 2:68.

83. The drawings are in the collection of Paul Mellon, Upperville, Va. The scene is reproduced in Stevens, "Narrative," plate 52. All the Sohon plates appear in the same publication following p. 184.

84. See Taft, *Artists and Illustrators*, p. 275.

85. Comparisons of other railroad-survey field-work by Stanley and Sohon can be readily seen in the watercolors illustrated in Goetzmann, "The Grand Reconnaissance," pp. 50-59. Sixty works by Stanley and ten by Sohon are also contained in the Paul Mellon Collection. We are grateful to Mary Ann Thompson, secretary of the collection, for making available a list of these drawings.

86. Ten of Sohon's watercolors were used to illustrate Mullan, *Report. Cantonment Stevens*, an illustrated view of Mullan's winter quarters during the 1853-54 expedition, is based on the same sketch as a similar scene illustrated in the Stevens report. A comparison of the two illustrations, produced by different firms, underlines the role of the lithographer in conveying the true appearance and spirit of the original.

87. Gwinn Harris Heap, *Central Route to the Pacific, from the Valley of the Mississippi to California: Journal of the Expedition of E. F. Beale . . . and Gwinn Harris Heap, from Missouri to California, in 1853*, p. 9; henceforth cited as Heap, *Journal*.

88. Quoted from Goetzmann, *Army Exploration*, p. 284. For Frémont's fifth expedition, with Solomon N. Carvalho, see below.

89. Ibid., p. 10. In the introduction to their edition of Heap's account (*Central Route to the Pacific, by Gwinn Harris Heap*, pp. 20-21; henceforth cited as Hafen and Hafen, *Heap*), LeRoy R. Hafen and Ann W. Hafen note: "If speed had been the only consideration, Beale would have voyaged to California by steamboat and across Panama, taking but thirty days to reach San Francisco. But he justified the land journey—which was to take three months—on the grounds that the law ordered him to examine possible reservation sites in Utah and New Mexico, and this could be most effectively done by land travel through these Territories.

"Beale's party would be small. Traveling with pack animals, it would be unencumbered with wagons. Thus spared the burden of making roads or detailed surveys, Beale should have a speedy and successful journey. His descriptive travel reports to be sent back to Benton, would be utilized by the Senator to publicize his favorite line."

90. Ibid., pp. 10-11.

91. Some pertinent facts on Heap's life are given in ibid.

92. The following biographical data on Heap have been obtained from ibid., pp. 23f., and from *Appletons' Cyclopedia of American Biography*, 3:153.

93. Quoted in Hafen and Hafen, *Heap*, p. 22.

94. In *Appletons' Cyclopedia*, Heap's death date is recorded as March 6, 1887.

95. See sections on Richard Kern and Carvalho.

96. Heap, *Journal*, p. 27, pl. 2.

97. Ibid., p. 37, pl. 8.

98. Ibid., p. 39, pl. 9.

99. In their investigations Hafen and Hafen failed to find any of Heap's original artwork or any other publication by him comparable to his *Journal* (Hafen and Hafen, *Heap*, p. 23).

100. S[olomon] N. Carvalho, *Incidents of Travel and Adventure in the Far West, with Col. Fremont's Last Expedition Across the Rocky Mountains: Including Three Months' Residence in Utah, and a Perilous Trip Across the Great American Desert, to the Pacific*, pp. 220-21; henceforth cited as Carvalho, *Incidents of Travel*.

101. For a biographical sketch of the artist, see Korn's preface to Solomon N. Carvalho, *Incidents of Travel and Adventure in the Far West, by Solomon Nunes Carvalho*, ed. Bertram Korn; Joan Sturhahn, *Carvalho, Artist—Photographer—Adventurer—Patriot: Portrait of a Forgotten American*, henceforth cited as Sturhahn, *Carvalho*; Robert Taft, *Photography and the American Scene*, p. 490, n. 485, henceforth cited as Taft, *Photography;* and Groce and Wallace, *Dictionary of Artists*, pp. 113-14. The information on Carvalho was drawn from a number of sources, but primarily from those cited above.

102. Korn, ed., *Carvalho*, p. 22.

103. According to the "Minutes" of the Beth Elohim Synagogue of October 21, 1838, Carvalho, then a resident of Philadelphia, wrote to the Board of the Congregation offering to do a painting of the synagogue as it was before its destruction "'for such Compensation as the Board . . . deem[ed] proper to allow.'" It is further stated that the board "judged the painting to be 'neat & accurate' and gave him fifty dollars for it" (quoted in Charles Reznikoff, *The Jews of Charleston*, p. 281, n. 68). Korn believes that Carvalho constructed his view from "memory" (*Incidents of Travel*, p. 23). In our opinion the detailed, "primitive" interior scene suggests strongly that Carvalho had worked from sketches (or perhaps a lost print) made before the

synagogue's destruction. The artist was known to have visited Charleston frequently after the family's removal to Philadelphia (Solomon Breibart to authors, letter, Charleston, S.C., November 11, 1978). The painting, an oil on canvas measuring 30 × 26½ inches, is in the collection of Beth Elohim. A lithograph by A. Hoffy after Carvalho's painting is reproduced in ibid.

104. Ibid.; for an inventory of paintings by Carvalho, see pp. 327–28.

105. Anna W. Rutledge, "Artists in the Life of Charleston: Through Colony and State from Restoration to Reconstruction," *Transactions of the American Philosophical Society*, n.s. 39, pt. 2 (November, 1949), p. 164 (reprint of the advertisement).

106. Korn, ed., *Carvalho*.

107. Carvalho, *Incidents of Travel*, p. 17.

108. Ibid., pp. 20–21.

109. Ibid., p. 58.

110. Ibid., p. 72.

111. Ibid., pp. 82–83.

112. Taft, *Photography*, p. 264.

113. From Carvalho's letter to H. H. Snelling (editor), *Photographic and Fine Art Journal* 8 (1855): 124; reprinted in Taft, *Photography*, p. 265. "A letter of Frémont's to the German scientist in St. Louis, George Engelmann, dated 12 Jan. 1856 speaks of Frémont's putting materials in order for a 3 volume work on his expeditions and that he will have about 200 illustrations 'nearly all from daguerreotype views'" (Mary Lee Spence to Trenton, letter, Urbana, Ill., July 15, 1969).

114. John Charles Frémont, *Memoirs of My Life*, p. xvi.

115. For example, *Uncompagre River, West Slope Rocky Mountains* appears to have been taken from a photograph; see illustration, opp. p. 200.

116. *Paintings, Engravings, / etc. / at the / Picture Gallery / of the / Artists' Association, / and of the Maryland Historical Society / Baltimore / 1856*, collection of Maryland Historical Society.

117. Collection of Kathe Jacoby, Fort Washington, Pa. This oil study measures 14½ × 18½ inches and is signed and dated on the boulder in the foreground. Apparently Joan Sturhahn, Carvalho's biographer and great-great-granddaughter, did not examine this study, for she would not have assigned the date 1854 to it (see Sturhahn, *Carvalho*, p. 120).

118. At the lower left the painting is signed and dated "S. N. Carvalho '75." The date was discovered by Trenton during a visit to the museum. Black light revealed that some inpainting had been done above the date and signature, smearing the top part of the "5" so that it is barely legible; however, the date and signature are in the artist's hand. In a letter to us dated August 16, 1977, Beverly J. Goodrich, director of the Historical Museum and Institute of Western Colorado, Grand Junction, pinpoints the approximate location of the painting.

119. See Sturhahn, *Carvalho*, p. 193.

120. *The National Academy of Design Exhibition Record, 1861–1900*, comp. and ed. Marie Naylor, vol. 1, no. 163. The full title of this painting is *Moonlight on Rio Virgin*.

121. A copy of the original letter is in the American Jewish Archives, Cincinnati, Ohio. Fannie Zelcer, archivist, furnished the date of this letter, which is not legible on our copy.

122. Since Carvalho never visited the Grand Canyon, it seems plausible that he referred to Powell's official report for his model. Moran joined the major on his trip of 1873 down the Grand Canyon of the Colorado, the inspiration for his spectacular painting *The Chasm of the Colorado*, an oil on canvas measuring 84 × 114 inches, executed in 1873, now in the collection of U.S. Dept. of the Interior.

Chapter 4

1. Reuben Cole Shaw, *Across the Plains in Forty-Nine*, pp. 74–75.

2. Quoted in Martin Ridge and Ray Allen Billington, eds., *America's Frontier Story: A Documentary History of Westward Expansion*, p. 533.

3. Osborn Cross, *A Report in the Form of a Journal, to the Quartermaster-General, of the March of the Regiment of Mounted Riflemen to Oregon, from May 10 to October 5, 1849*, p. 161; henceforth cited as Cross, *Report*.

4. Ibid., pp. 120–240.

5. Gibbs, a noted author and scholar as well as an amateur artist, was born in 1815 near Astoria, New York. With the discovery of gold in 1848, Gibbs abandoned legal work and joined the march of the mounted rifles in Saint Louis. Along the way he sketched and maintained a journal, initial installments of which appeared in the *New York Journal of Commerce* on July 25 and September 1, 1849. He was later appointed collector of the port of Astoria and settled for several years on a farm near Fort Steilacoom, Washington Territory. He became a respected student of northwest Indians and their languages and published widely on the subject. In 1858 he and artist James Madison Alden joined the Northwest Boundary Survey, Gibbs serving as geologist and interpreter. Returning to the east coast in 1860, he continued his Indian studies; several were published under the auspices of the Smithsonian Institution. He died in New Haven, Connecticut, in 1873. For bibliographic sources see "George Gibbs," *Dictionary of American Biography*, 7:245–46; John Austin Stevens, Jr., "A Memorial of George Gibbs," *The Annual Report of the Smithsonian Institution, 1873*, pp. 219–25; and David I. Bushnell, "Drawings of George Gibbs in the Far Northwest," *Smithsonian Miscellaneous Collections*, 97:1–28.

6. David McNeely Stauffer, *American Engravers Upon Copper and Steel*, 1:265.

7. Raymond W. Settle, ed., *The March of the Mounted Riflemen*, p. 27.

8. Edward Lurie, *Louis Agassiz: A Life in Science*, p. 151.

9. William H. Tappan is not to be confused with Henry Tappan, a relative of the artist from New York State. Henry traveled about a week ahead of William, reaching Fort Laramie on June 13, while William arrived on June 22. Henry's diary is published in Everett Walters and George B. Strother, eds., "The Gold Rush Diary of Henry Tappan," *Annals of Wyoming* 25 (July, 1953):113–39.

10. Cross, *Report*, p. 129.

11. Katherine Karpenstein, *Illustrations of the West in Congressional Documents 1843–1863*, pp. 96–99.

12. Cross, *Report*, p. 85.

13. At least five if not more of the fifty pencil sketches by Gibbs in the Bushnell Collection were taken during this trip west in 1849. One of these is illustrated here; two others made at this time are *Shoshonee [sic] Falls—from the South side, Aug. 15* and *Cañon on Snake River, below the Cataract, Aug. 15, 1849*.

14. See Cross, *Report,* p. 196.

15. Reproduced in ibid.; original in collection of the Oregon Historical Society.

16. Daniel L. Tappan, *Tappan-Toppan Genealogy: Ancestors and Descendants of Abraham Toppan of Newbury, Massachusetts, 1602–1672,* p. 49.

17. Ibid.

18. For an account of the discovery see Joseph Schafer, "Trailing a Trail Artist of 1849," *Wisconsin Magazine of History* 12 (September, 1928):97–108. The collection is in the State Historical Society of Wisconsin.

19. John Francis McDermott, ed., *An Artist on the Overland Trail: The 1849 Diary and Sketches of James F. Wilkins,* pp. 20–24; henceforth cited as McDermott, ed., *Wilkins.*

20. Ibid. Wilkins was not alone in his enterprising notion that the trail to the gold fields would make a popular panoramic theme. In fact, such works attracted attention not only in America but also abroad. For example, an article entitled "Panoramas in London" (*Bulletin of the American Art-Union* [New York: George F. Nesbitt & Co., 1850]) gave notice of the exhibition of an American production depicting "the route to California over the Rocky Mountains." The study of this panorama is told in Joseph Earl Arrington, "Skirving's Moving Panorama; Colonel Fremont's Western Expeditions —Pictorialized," *Oregon Historical Quarterly* 65 (June, 1964):133–72. Others, including Wilkins's resulting production, are discussed in John Francis McDermott, "Gold Rush Movies," *California Historical Society Quarterly* 33 (March, 1954):29–38. Skirving's panorama is of particular interest to this book, since the four artists involved are thought to have adopted sketches by Charles Preuss and Edward and Richard Kern as models for their finished work (see Arrington, "Skirving's Moving Panorama," pp. 136, 145).

21. The following account of Wilkins's travels is taken from Wilkins's diary (McDermott, ed., *Wilkins*).

22. Wilkins's panorama is discussed in McDermott, "Gold Rush Movies."

23. We are grateful to Gail R. Guidry and Judith Ciampoli, of the Missouri Historical Society, for bringing to our attention the existence of twelve Wilkins oils in their collections. Three of these, *Covered Wagons in the Rockies* (oil on canvas, 22 ×

30⅛ inches), *Immigrant's Night Camp* (oil on canvas, 26¾ × 36¼ inches), and the painting illustrated here depict scenes appropriate to this book.

24. James H. Simpson, "To California Emigrants and the Citizens of Utah Territory," *Deseret News,* August 7, 1859.

25. Simpson had already played a part in this story: as a lieutenant he had led the topographical unit under Colonel John Macrae Washington on a punitive expedition against the Navahos in 1849. Edward and Richard Kern had accompanied him as artists on this expedition (see chap. 2).

26. [James Hervey Simpson], *Report of the Secretary of War Communicating . . . Captain Simpson's Report and Map of Wagon Road Routes in Utah Territory,* 35th Cong., 2d sess., S. Doc. 40, p. 21.

27. Only eight of Young's original watercolors after Von Beckh's sketches are extant; all of them are in the National Archives. J. J. Young is assumed to be John J. Young, who was staff topographical artist on Lieutenant Robert S. Williamson's railroad survey in California and Oregon between the Sacramento Valley and the Columbia River (see R. S. Williamson, "Report of the Reconnoissance of a Route through the Sierra Nevada by the Upper Sacramento," in *Report of the Secretary of War Communicating Information in Relation to the Geology and Topography of California,* 31st Cong., 1st sess., S. Exec. Doc. 47, pt. 2 [Washington, D.C., 1850]). Young had also redrawn the sketches of expeditionary artists Albert H. Campbell, F. W. Egloffstein, Heinrich B. Möllhausen, and John Strong Newberry (see Robert Taft, *Artists and Illustrators of the Old West, 1850–1900,* pp. 265 and 268).

28. Reproduced in William H. Goetzmann, *Exploration and Empire,* p. 223; henceforth cited as Goetzmann, *Exploration and Empire.*

29. See Captain J. H. Simpson, *Report of Explorations Across the Great Basin of the Territory of Utah for a direct Wagon-Route from Camp Floyd to Genoa, in Carson Valley, in 1859 . . . .*

30. U.S. Army, Corps of Engineers, *Report of the Exploring Expedition from Santa Fe, New Mexico, to the Junction of the Grand and Green Rivers . . . in 1859, Under the Command of Capt. J. N. Macomb . . . with Geological Report by Prof. J. S. Newberry . . . ,* Washington, D.C.: U.S. Government Printing Office, 1876.

31. In a letter to Lieutenant Colonel H. Bache dated November 27, 1861, Macomb mentions that he is waiting for Newberry to finish his report, indicating that it was nearly completed at that time (15 years before the actual publication date).

32. Newberry's prefatory notes in Macomb, *Report.*

33. Goetzmann, *Exploration and Empire,* pp. 308, 355–57 (for preceding quotes).

34. Most of the biographical information on Newberry is drawn from *Dictionary of American Biography,* 13:445–46. His birth and death dates are recorded as follows: b. December 22, 1822; d. December 7, 1892.

35. For a detailed itinerary of the journey, see Macomb, *Report,* p. 5.

36. Ibid., pp. 75–76.

37. Ibid., p. 74.

38. Ibid. Newberry's black-and-white illustration *The Pagosa* varies somewhat from the color plate. In this view the steaming cauldron, much enlarged, is the central focus. Nearby stand miniscule figures to emphasize the immensity of this hot spring, which, said Newberry, was "40 by 50 feet in diameter . . . [and] of unfathomable depth" and gave off a column of vapor that in damp weather was visible for miles (ibid., p. 74). The formula for the arrangement of this composition is similar to that of most of the other illustrations except for its tighter construction and the diminutive scale of the figures beside the cauldron.

39. The color lithography was provided by T. Sinclair & Son, of Philadelphia. The limited color scheme employed for the illustrations is typical of that period.

40. *Rio Delores and Sierra de la Plata. From near Camp 21,* pl. 5; see pp. 86–87.

41. Newberry's name is usually missing from the roster of western illustrators, and his views are seldom reproduced. We are grateful to Charles Peterson, of Brigham Young University, Provo, Utah, for drawing our attention to Newberry's illustrated report.

42. John van Deusen Du Bois, *Campaigns in the West 1856–1861: The Journal and Letters of Colonel John van Deusen Du Bois,* ed. George P. Hammond, p. 84; henceforth cited as Hammond, ed., *Campaigns in the West.* All information on Du Bois and Heger's

army experiences comes from this source.

43. Quoted from Goetzmann, *Exploration and Empire*, p. 306. Information about Captain Randolph B. Marcy's trip comes from his own account, *Thirty Years of Army Life on the Border*, pp. 224–50.

44. Biographical information on Heger comes from Hammond's introduction to *Campaigns in the West*. This soldier-artist was born in Hesse, Germany, on January 11, 1835. On October 9, 1855, at age twenty, he enlisted in the army. Hammond believes that the family arrived in the United States sometime after the revolutions of 1848 in Europe.

45. Hammond suggests the collaboration (ibid). No records are available to substantiate this assumption.

46. These drawings are in the W. R. Coe Collection in the Beinecke Rare Book and Manuscript Library, Yale University, New Haven, Conn. Included among the Utah and Colorado scenes, for instance, are *Grand River, San Luis Valley, Camp Floyd, Epathrim, Monti,* and *Cedar Valley, Utah.*

47. See James K. Ballinger, *Beyond the Endless River*, p. 30.

48. Hammond, ed., *Campaigns in the West*, p. 82.

49. Du Bois and Heger took part in a punitive expedition against the Apaches of the upper Gila River the year before their trip to Utah. A portfolio of drawings of this expedition and later southwestern work is in the W. J. Holliday Collection of the Arizona Pioneers Historical Society, Tucson. Twelve of these drawings, including a later work appropriate to this book, *Pueblo of Taos* (1859), are illustrated in the Hammond edition, along with four of the Utah expedition drawings. Other illustrations of Heger's works may be found in Gary L. Roberts, "Conditions of the Tribes—1865," *Montana: Magazine of Western History* 24 (Winter, 1974):21.

50. Humphreys's letter is printed in Brevet Brigadier General W. F. Raynolds, *Report on the Exploration of the Yellowstone River . . . ,* 40th Cong., 1st sess., S. Exec. Doc. 77; henceforth cited as Raynolds, *Report.*

51. See also Dr. Franz Stenzel, *Anton Schonborn: Western Forts;* henceforth cited as Stenzel, *Anton Schonborn.*

52. Raynolds, *Report.*

53. Ibid., p. 18.

54. Ibid., p. 66.

55. A set of six drawings and watercolors by Schonborn in the W. R. Coe Collection in the Beinecke Rare Book and Manuscript Library, Yale University Library, is all that remains. The works result from the 1859 portion of the expedition, but all are taken from locations east of the Rockies. We are grateful to Archibald Hanna, former Curator of the Beinecke Library, for providing us with a list of these works (see Mary C. Withington, *A Catalogue of Manuscripts in the Collection of Western Americana Founded by William Robertson Coe, Yale University Library* [New Haven, Conn.: Yale University Press, 1952], p. 215).

56. Raynolds, *Report*, p. 92.

57. Pencil on paper, 1860, measuring 12½ × 17 inches, in the collection of Beinecke Rare Book and Manuscript Library, Yale University.

58. Stenzel, *Anton Schonborn*, p. [2].

59. Reproduced in *The Kennedy Quarterly* 11 (June, 1971).

60. Stenzel, *Anton Schonborn.*

61. These watercolor drawings are reproduced in *Amon Carter Museum of Western Art: Catalogue of the Collection, 1972*, pp. 160–65, figs. 457–67.

62. "Joseph Horace Eaton graduated from West Point in 1835. After serving as an aide to Zachary Taylor in the Mexican War, he spent eight years in the Southwest, stationed at Fort Defiance, New Mexico Territory, from 1848 to 1856" (*Kennedy Quarterly* 16 [June, 1979]:249). The *Quarterly* reproduces a watercolor drawing, *Fort Thorn, Santa Barbara, Looking South East towards San Diego Mountains, and the Organos Mountains, 1855,* fig. 168, along with scenes of Santa Fe, Albuquerque, and Taos by the soldier-artist. Charles Frederick Moellman was born in Prussia in 1844. He emigrated to the United States, and in 1863 he enlisted in the Eleventh Ohio Volunteer Cavalry and served as a bugler of Company G until 1866. During the time he was stationed in Wyoming, he "produced as many as sixty pencil, crayon, and watercolor drawings of Indian dances, western posts and telegraph stations such as Fort Laramie, Platte Bridge Station and Sweetwater Station—all located on the Oregon Trail. . . . After he left the army, Moellman lived in Cincinnati, Ohio, and worked as a zinc etcher" (see Maurice Grant Barr, "Art Trails of Wyoming," in the exhibition catalog *One Hundred Years of Artist Activity in Wyo-*

ming, 1837–1937, p. 66). Caspar Wever Collins was born in Hillsboro, Ohio, in 1844. He served, first as a civilian and later as an officer, in the Eleventh Ohio Volunteer Cavalry, on the Oregon and Overland Trails from 1862 to 1865, when he was killed by Sioux Indians at the battle of Platte Bridge Station. Collins is known for his naïve and charming pencil, pen, crayon, and watercolor drawings of Indians, wildlife, and forts, which serve as invaluable pictorial records of Wyoming during the Civil War period (ibid., p. 47).

63. See Aubrey L. Haines, *The Yellowstone Story,* 1:84–89.

64. Hayden, *Report,* 1871, p. 5 (see chap. 6 for a discussion and complete reference).

65. John G. Parke, "Report of John G. Parke," in Marcus Baker, "Survey of the Northwestern Boundary of the United States 1857–1861," *Bulletin of the United States Geological Survey,* no. 174, p. 71; henceforth cited as Baker, "Survey."

66. Quoted in Henry Steele Commager, ed., *Documents of American History,* p. 311.

67. For a list of these and other initial appointments to the commission in 1857, see U.S. Department of State, *Northwest Boundary Commission . . . ,* pp. 2–3.

68. Baker, "Survey," p. 9. This reference is the best general source on the history of the boundary survey. See also Goetzmann, *Army Exploration,* pp. 427–29.

69. See section on artists on the Oregon Trail.

70. Baker, "Survey," p. 58.

71. U.S. Department of State, *Northwest Boundary Commission,* pp. 1, 14, 17, 19.

72. For information on these two expeditions see Charles Wilkes, *Narrative of the United States Exploring Expedition During the Years 1838, 1839, 1840, 1841, 1842* (Philadelphia, Pa.: Lea and Blanchard, 1845), and *Annual Report to the Superintendent of the United States Coast Survey* (Washington, D.C.: U.S. Government Printing Office, 1850–1861).

73. This and subsequent biographical information is extracted from Franz Stenzel's definitive volume *James Madison Alden: Yankee Artist of the Pacific Coast, 1854–1860.*

74. U.S. Department of State, *Northwest Boundary Commission,* p. 2.

75. Robert D. Monroe, "William Birch McMur-

trie: A Painter Partially Restored," *Oregon Historical Quarterly* 60 (September, 1959):371.

76. Parke, "Report," in Baker, "Survey," p. 71.

77. George F. G. Stanley, ed., *Mapping the Frontier: Charles Wilson's Diary of the Survey of the 49th Parallel, 1858-1862, While Secretary of the British Boundary Commission*, pp. 156-57.

78. George Gibbs, reporting to the American Geographical Society over a decade later, acknowledged the significance of Alden's geological observations: "Mr. Alden, who ascended one of the peaks, describes the alternations as follows: The base was covered with débris to the estimated height of 1,500 feet above the level of the creek, where the rock was red sandstone. Over this was a belt of the same rock, metamorphic, and in waved or contorted strata, 150 feet thick, succeeded by 500 feet of green slates and red sandstones interstratified; then again by red sandstones 500 feet, the summit, to a thickness of 1,500 feet, consisting of an ochre-yellow earthy shale." See George Gibbs, "Physical Geography of the North-Western Boundary of the United States," *Journal of the American Geographical Society of New York* 4 (1874):384.

79. This watercolor and 66 others by Alden from the expedition are in the collection of the National Archives and Records Service, Washington, D.C.

80. Quoted in [William H. Truettner and Robin Bolton-Smith], *National Parks and the American Landscape* (Washington, D.C.: National Collection of Fine Arts, 1972), p. 46.

81. Parke, "Report," in Baker, "Survey," p. 17.

82. Stenzel, *James Madison Alden*, p. 147. The record of the Northwest Boundary Commission's disbursements for 1861 lists Alden as artist and notes that the following art supplies were bought: 2 sketchbooks, $7.25; 3½ cakes of cobalt, $0.88; 2 camel's-hair brushes, $0.67; 1 box of watercolors, $5.75; ½ quire of drawing paper, $3.00; 2 drawing boards, $4.25. See U.S. Department of State, *Northwest Boundary Commission*, p. 86.

83. Ibid., pp. 19, 86.

84. Baker, "Survey," pp. 11-12.

85. Archibald Campbell, *Reports upon the Survey of the Boundary Between the Territory of the United States and the Possessions of Great Britain from the Lake of the Woods to the Summit of the Rocky Mountains . . . .* Two lithographic views of Chief Moun-

tain on the northeastern edge of today's Glacier Park are reproduced in this book, both apparently taken from photographs.

86. Baker, "Survey," p. 63.

87. See Stenzel, *James Madison Alden;* Alden's known western works are listed in the appendix, p. 203.

88. Because of a *View of James Peak in the Rain* that has long been misattributed to McMurtrie, many sources credit him with a trip to Colorado. See, for example, Monroe, "William Birch McMurtrie," p. 374.

Chapter 5

1. Bayard Taylor, *Colorado: A Summer Trip*, pp. 39, 74.

2. *London Saturday Review*, quoted in *California Art Gallery* (San Francisco), April, 1873, news clipping in a scrapbook of Bierstadt memorabilia assembled and collated by Rosalie Osborne Mayer, courtesy of Mrs. Orville DeForest Edwards, Dobbs Ferry, N.Y.; henceforth cited as "Scrapbook."

3. Samuel Bowles, *Our New West: Record of Travel Between the Mississippi River and the Pacific Ocean*, p. vi.

4. For examples of such criticism see James Jackson Jarves, *The Art-Idea . . . ,* 2:232-33; and Samuel Isham, *The History of American Painting*, pp. 251-52.

5. George W. Sheldon, *American Painters*, p. 148.

6. Merle Curti, *The Growth of American Thought*, p. 498.

7. Donald Strong, "Bierstadt and California" (seminar paper, University of California, Los Angeles, March 14, 1962), introduction, p. v.

8. See the following publications: Richard Shafer Trump, "Life and Works of Albert Bierstadt," (Ph.D. diss., Ohio State University, 1963), henceforth cited as Trump, "Life of Bierstadt"; California Art Research Project, *California Art Research*, 2 vols. of First Series, December, 1937, pp. 98ff.; Gordon Hendricks, "The First Three Western Journeys of Albert Bierstadt," *Art Bulletin* 46 (September, 1964):333-65; and Gordon Hendricks, *Albert Bierstadt: Painter*

of the American West, the most current and comprehensive biography on the artist; henceforth cited as Hendricks, *Albert Bierstadt*. Donald Strong, in a critical review of Hendricks's book, raises some interesting questions about the artist's work. See Donald Strong, "Albert Bierstadt, Painter of the American West," *American Art Review* 2 (November–December, 1975):132-44; henceforth cited as Strong, "Albert Bierstadt." In addition, Mathew Baigell, in his book *Albert Bierstadt*, has recently brought some perceptive aesthetic insights to bear in discussing the artist's work.

9. It seems likely that Bierstadt would have kept sales ledgers and miscellaneous information, being obviously a businessman. Perhaps much of this material was lost in the fire that destroyed Malkasten, his Irvington home on the Hudson, in November, 1882. Various accounts place the damage of his property between $160,000 and $200,000. The current family holdings of Bierstadt memorabilia include only a notebook of anecdotes, an autograph album (sold by Parke Bernet in 1973), and the "Scrapbook" (see n. 2), Mrs. Orville Edwards to Trenton, letter, Dobbs Ferry, N.Y., (1969).

10. In his monograph on Bierstadt, Hendricks, who bases his information on family tradition, states that the artist and his family arrived in the United States "sometime in February of 1832." After checking the passenger arrival lists at the National Archives and Records Service, we found the family recorded on the "Brig. Hope," arriving in New Bedford the last quarter of that year. See Hendricks, *Albert Bierstadt*, p. 13.

11. Both Hendricks (ibid., p. 15) and Trump ("Life of Bierstadt," p. 22) rely on family tradition for their information.

12. A month later Bierstadt issued a flyer announcing an additional class offering this kind of instruction. (Flyer in collection of New Bedford Library, New Bedford, Mass.)

13. For a biographical sketch of Wall see George C. Groce and David H. Wallace, *The New-York Historical Society's Dictionary of Artists in America 1564-1860*, p. 65; henceforth cited as Groce and Wallace, *Dictionary of Artists*.

14. A technique of painting executed in different tints of one color, with representation of light and shade. Well suited for rendering drawings for illus-

trative purposes, it was a popular midnineteenth-century pictorial art form.

15. Strong, "Albert Bierstadt," p. 141.

16. Works cited in Hendricks, *Albert Bierstadt*, pp. 16–17, 20, n. 8.

17. Ibid., pp. 189, 193.

18. Ibid., p. 17; for biographical data on George Harvey see Groce and Wallace, *Dictionary of Artists*, p. 298. In his discussion of Bierstadt's involvement with light shows Hendricks fails to point out the possible connection with the artist's later development of light effects. The author has made it clear, however, that he is merely presenting the facts of Bierstadt's life, leaving art criticism of his work to others.

19. Bierstadt could easily have seen the Saint Louis artist Leon Pomarede's "Panorama of the Mississippi River and Indian Life," which circulated in the East until its destruction by fire in 1850 (see Groce and Wallace, *Dictionary of Artists*, p. 510). It is also possible that he was aware of the moving panoramas of Benjamin Russell and Benjamin Champney exhibited in Boston in 1848–49 (ibid., pp. 118, 552). For a discussion of the panorama see Wolfgang Born, *American Landscape Painting: An Interpretation*.

20. See Joseph W. Snell, "Some Photographs by Albert Bierstadt Now in the Historical Society Collection," *Kansas Historical Quarterly* 24 (Spring, 1958):1–5.

21. For a biographical sketch of Hasenclever, see Irene Markowitz, *Die Düsseldorfer Malerschule*, pp. 57–60.

22. Henry T. Tuckerman, *Book of the Artists: American Artist Life, Comprising Biographical and Critical Sketches: Preceded by an Historical Account of the Rise and Progress of Art in America*, p. 392.

23. For the history of the New York Düsseldorf Gallery, see R. L. Stehle, "The Düsseldorf Gallery of New York," *New-York Historical Society Quarterly* 58 (October, 1974):305–10. For a sampling of a selection of German works shown in America, see *The Düsseldorf Gallery Catalogue of Paintings, by Artists of the Düsseldorf Academy of Art, Now on Exhibition at 548 Broadway, New-York*, June 22, 1859, and the publication *Gems of Düsseldorf* (a bound volume which includes reproductions) in the collection of the New York Public Library.

24. Tuckerman, *Book of the Artists*, p. 387. In some sources Hasenclever's death date is recorded as September 16, 1853; in others, as December 16, 1853.

25. Information about the artist's travels abroad can also be found in S. R. Gifford, "European Letters to His Father," vol. 2, March 10, 1856–August 10, 1857 [typescript copy]; and *William Stanley Haseltine*, Helen Haseltine Plowden's account of her father, an American artist who was also in Düsseldorf and joined Whittredge and Bierstadt in Rome in 1856–57.

26. John I. H. Baur (ed.), *The Autobiography of Worthington Whittredge, 1820–1910*, pp. 26–27; henceforth cited Whittredge, *Autobiography*.

27. Ibid. Various sales exhibitions of his German pictures were announced by the local newspapers. One reporter commented that the artist's work showed evidence of improvement. He was quick to point out that these paintings were "in the style of the modern German artists, minute and elaborate, but . . . very free from mannerism," and advised the public to attend the exhibit to view the attractive works for themselves. *New Bedford Daily Mercury*, August 4, 1855.

28. A rather obvious example by Bierstadt is illustrated in Sotheby Parke Bernet's sales catalog, *American 18th, 19th & 20th Century Paintings, Drawings, Watercolors & Sculpture*, April 17, 1975, no. 16, titled *House in the Woods*, dated 1856, oil on canvas measuring 37¾ × 43½ inches. For an example by Achenbach see Markowitz, *Düsseldorfer*, no. 30, titled *Erftmühle*.

29. In a letter from Düsseldorf, dated June 1, 1856, Gifford describes the evening gatherings at the local artists' club called the Malkasten (Paint Box): "This club, or guild, includes about all the artists here. It has a fund, from which any member who becomes reduced by misfortune or sickness may borrow without interest. There is a permanent, yet always changing, exhibition of pictures by the members of the society. . . . Artists of all grades of merit meet here on terms of the most perfect and genial social equality. I was introduced to many of them—Achenbach, Hübner, Weimar &c. . . . The manners of the artists are very kindly, simple and unaffected. A true brotherhood seems to reign among them." Gifford, "European Letters," vol. 2.

30. Examples of Hobbema's rusticated scenes are illustrated in *The National Gallery Illustrated General Catalogue*, pp. 314–16, nos. 685, 995, 2570.

31. Reproduced in Wolfgang Hütt, *Die Düsseldorfer Malerschule, 1819–1869*, p. 51, no. 21. The author discusses Lessing's role in the direction of realism in the Düsseldorf School of painting, pointing out that the German painter made studies from nature that exhibited his close observation of geological forms: "It is said that he took a textbook on mineralogy and geology with him on one of his first study trips to the Eifel." Several of his plein-air pencil sketches of realistic bits of nature are illustrated in the Cincinnati Art Museum's 1972 catalog of its collection of Lessing's drawings, donated by collector Joseph Longworth in 1882.

32. Whittredge, *Autobiography*, p. 27.

33. Donelson F. Hoopes, *The Düsseldorf Academy and the American*, p. 31.

34. We are indebted to the archivist of the Hauptstaatsarchiv in Düsseldorf who searched for but failed to find Bierstadt's name recorded in "Die Schülerlisten der Königlichen Kunst-Academie zu Düsseldorf." Letter to Trenton, February 25, 1976.

35. Whittredge, *Autobiography*, pp. 30ff. In his letter from Bellinzona, Italy, dated August 10, 1856, Gifford mentions meeting "Whittredge, Bierstadt, and Haseltine at Lucerne on Sunday 27th of July." Gifford, "European Letters."

36. This picture and a larger version are reproduced in Hendricks, *Albert Bierstadt*, pp. 40, 41, figs. 22, 23.

37. Examples of Claude's work are found in *The National Gallery Illustrated General Catalogue*, pp. 125–30.

38. Bierstadt's arrival in the States was first announced in the *New Bedford Evening Standard*, September 3, 1857: "We understand . . . Bierstadt, who has been pursuing his studies in Europe, has returned to this city, and has already been engaged to paint a picture for a gentleman in Boston."

39. *Catalogue of the New-Bedford Art Exhibition, Commencing July 1st, and Closing August 7, 1858*, collection of the New Bedford Free Public Library (pamphlet box 87). Many of the 150 works on exhibit were borrowed from local collectors; others were offered for sale. A twenty-five-cent admission was charged; evidently the event did not turn out to

be a money-maker (see Hendricks, *Albert Bierstadt,* p. 57).

40. Francis S. Frost (1825?–1902) was a landscape artist and co-owner of an art emporium (Frost & Adams) in Boston from 1869 to 1902. He is listed as an artist in the Boston city directories of 1864 and 1865. In 1859 he traveled with Bierstadt to the Wind River country. His *View Among the Rocky Mts.,* probably based on studies taken during the trip of 1859, was exhibited at the Boston Athenaeum in 1861 (currently in the collection of Kennedy Galleries, Inc., New York City). He also exhibited work there in 1855–59 and 1864. From 1870 until his death he was a member of the Boston Art Club, though his work is not listed in the exhibition records. Frost died at his home in Arlington, Mass., on December 26, 1902. Information provided by Janice R. Hynes, Fine Arts Reference Librarian, Boston Public Library. Frost is not listed in any biographical dictionary of American artists.

41. Tuckerman, *Book of the Artists,* pp. 388–89.

42. Whittredge, *Autobiography,* p. 42.

43. Ibid., p. 31.

44. Hendricks, *Albert Bierstadt,* p. 58.

45. Quoted in Hendricks, *Albert Bierstadt,* p. 63. According to the author, the announcement was released on January 17, 1859; however, there seems to be some confusion over the publication date, for Mary Cabral, librarian of the New Bedford Free Public Library, has been unable to find any mention of the proposed trip in either the *New Bedford Daily Mercury* or the *Evening Standard* for that date. Letter to Trenton, August 1, 1979.

46. "Reports of F. W. Lander . . . for 1859 and 1860, made under the direction of the honorable Jacob Thompson, Secretary of the Interior" in *Maps and Reports of the Fort Kearny, South Pass, and Honey Lake Wagon Road,* 36th Cong., 2d sess., H. Exec. Doc. 64, pp. 2–3; henceforth cited as *Maps and Reports.*

47. Reported in *Crayon* 6 (May, 1859):161 (reprint from a Boston newspaper, April 15, 1859).

48. Frost is mentioned by name in Bierstadt's letter of July 10, 1859, to the *Crayon,* published in September, 1859; in Lander's official report in *Maps and Reports;* and in newspaper accounts.

49. Frost's *View Among the Rocky Mts.,* oil on canvas, 12 × 18 inches and Hitchings's watercolor

drawings are in the collection of the Kennedy Galleries, Inc., New York City. Strangely enough, Hitchings's drawings seem to document Lander's travels along the Oregon Trail, continuing beyond the point where Bierstadt left the party (that is, *On Ross Fork of Snake River/Near Fort Hall Oregon* [1859], located on Lander's cutoff; see Lander's official report in *Maps and Reports*). Unfortunately, the accounts dated 1850–1878 of the Third Auditor of the Treasury Department, which would include vouchers for payment, were destroyed with congressional authority, so it is impossible to verify whether Hitchings was an official party member of Lander's expedition (James L. Harwood, Judicial and Fiscal Branch, Civil Archives Division, to Trenton, letter, Washington, D.C., March 15, 1979). Henry A. Hitchings (?–1902) was a landscape artist and teacher of drawing in the Boston Public Schools from 1872 to 1880. Curiously, in 1869 he is listed in the Boston city directories as being a clerk at 35 Cornhill Street, the address of Frost & Adams. In 1881 he is listed as director of drawing of the Boston Public Schools; then he disappears from the city directories until 1886, when he reappears as a teacher of drawing at the Boston Latin School. The following year, 1887, he was reappointed director of drawing of the Boston Public Schools, a title he held until 1897. From 1898 until his death in January, 1902, he was a teacher of drawing at his home in Dedham, Mass. He exhibited at the American Art-Union in 1849, at the Boston Athenaeum in 1856–57, at the National Academy in 1868–69, and at the Boston Art Club from 1874 to 1891 (the latter an organization of which he was a member from the late 1870s until his death). Information provided by Janice R. Hynes, Fine Arts Reference Librarian, Boston Public Library. See also Groce and Wallace, *Dictionary of Artists,* p. 320; and *Kennedy Quarterly* 6 (June, 1967): 124–25.

50. Hitchings captured this view from the Sweetwater River about six miles due south of Old South Pass. Here South Pass is shown off to the right, indicating that the artist was looking northwest at the most southern peaks in the Wind River Range. He has correctly identified the view as *Near Rock Creek;* at this location the stream empties into the Sweetwater. We are grateful to the celebrated photographer-mountaineer Finis Mitchell, of Rock Springs,

Wyoming, who expertly identified the geographical location of this view. Mitchell also generously offered his expertise in documenting the geographical locations of Bierstadt's paintings (for information on Mitchell see *Wall Street Journal,* September 20, 1970). This watercolor, measuring 12 × 16½ inches, is in the collection of the Kennedy Galleries, Inc., New York City. The date of Lander's crossing of South Pass is verified in his official report in *Maps and Reports.*

51. Quoted from Lander's official report in *Maps and Reports.*

52. Hendricks, *Albert Bierstadt,* pp. 68–69 and Lander's official report in *Maps and Reports.*

53. Quoted from Bierstadt's letter, Rocky Mountains, July 10, 1859, published in the *Crayon,* September, 1859, p. 287.

54. Ibid.

55. Bierstadt's letter, Wolf River, September 3, 1859, published in *New Bedford Daily Mercury,* September 14, 1859.

56. The stereograph and painting are reproduced in Hendricks, *Albert Bierstadt,* p. 66, fig. 41, and p. 82, fig. 63.

57. Quoted from Bierstadt's letter, Wolf River, September 3, 1859, published in *New Bedford Daily Mercury,* September 14, 1859.

58. According to Finis Mitchell, who has climbed virtually all the mountain speaks in the Wind River Range, Bierstadt's dramatic mountain paintings of this area were fabrications of the artist's imagination, executed "by someone merely observing the mountain ranges while crossing the plains some 15 to 20 miles at the closest and 40 to 60 miles [at the farthest]." For two examples, see *The Rocky Mountains, "Lander's Peak"* (Fogg Art Museum, Harvard University, Cambridge, Mass.) and *Storm in the Mountains* (M. and M. Karolik Collection, Museum of Fine Arts, Boston); reproduced in Hendricks, *Albert Bierstadt,* figs. 108, 138. The latter, formerly considered a scene in the Wind River Mountains, has recently been called "a scene of the Grosser Wachtman, near Berchtesgaden" (ibid., CL 110, following p. 323). It can be said that the first example is a poor facsimile of Lander's Peak and does not resemble any other peak in the 2.25-million-acre Wind River Range. In fact, the terrain represented is foreign to the area: the square-topped mountain on the

right and the exaggerated height of the waterfall seem more typical of the scenery found in California's Yosemite National Park. Since Bierstadt first visited California in 1863 and the painting was executed that year, it is very possible that this is a fanciful view of Yosemite. We are again grateful to Finis Mitchell for his geographical expertise.

59. For example, his *On the Sweetwater River near the Devil's Gate* [*sic*], *Nebraska* [*Wyoming*] (in the collection of the National Academy of Design, New York City) is erroneously titled. The view is on the Sweetwater River, but not at Devil's Gate, which has perpendicular cliffs on either side and lies between Muddy Gap and Names Rock (Independence Rock). The stacked formation depicted here along the river is fifty-two to fifty-five miles upstream from Devil's Gate, just below the Narrows, southwest of South Pass City. This kind of formation begins in the vicinity of Antelope Hills and is depicted in several of his other pictures. Information provided by Finis Mitchell.

60. Some of his sketches of Shoshone Indians engaged in various activities were later incorporated into several large landscapes executed shortly after his return home. Three of them are reproduced in Hendricks, *Albert Bierstadt* (figs. 59, 67, 68). On the other hand, animals are employed frequently in his landscapes as a picturesque motif. Several of his animal studies were adapted as illustrations in Arthur Pendarves Vivian, *Wanderings in the Western Land;* for example, see *Rams in Dunraven,* 1876, oil on board, 7¼ × 9⁵⁄₁₆ inches, collection of the National Cowboy Hall of Fame and Western Heritage Center, Oklahoma City, reproduced as *Scene in Estes Park,* opp. p. 137.

61. Bierstadt's letter, Rocky Mountains, July 10, 1859, published in *Crayon,* September, 1859, p. 287.

62. It is said that his interest in the American Indian developed in his early teens after he read "with avidity the works of the then portrayers of the early settlement of the continent. Irving, Cooper, Prescott, and other fathers of American prose, inspired him with an idea to rescue the aboriginal life of the continent from oblivion, and perpetuate it in natural and historical studies in color." Untitled, newspaper article, "Scrapbook," p. 33.

63. Bierstadt's arrival back in the States was reported by the *Crayon,* which also informed its readers

that the artist had "some intention of taking a studio in New York." At the same time the reporter announced Whittredge's occupancy in the Studio Building (*Crayon* 4 [November, 1859]:349). According to Hendricks: "Bierstadt lived at the Tenth Street Studio until 1866, when his house in Irvington [Malkasten] was finished. He kept it as a New York pied-á-terre until 1881, when he moved his studio into the magnificent Rensselaer Building at 1271 Broadway. Meanwhile, befitting his wealth and position, the studio was only his studio and not his living quarters: these were at the Brevoort Hotel, two-and-a-half blocks away." Hendricks, *Albert Bierstadt,* p. 94.

64. See *Crayon* 4 (November, 1859):349; *New York Tribune,* January 20, 1860; March 27, 1861. Trump writes that it was Bierstadt's practice to place his sketches in boxes classified by subject matter or to place them around the studio walls so that they were readily available. Trump, "Life of Bierstadt."

65. Hendricks, *Albert Bierstadt,* pp. 94–96; Marie Naylor, comp., *The National Academy of Design Exhibition Record, 1861–1900,* vol. 1, no. 547. While retracing their steps homeward, Bierstadt and his companion Frost stopped for several days at Fort Laramie to stock up on provisions. There the artist made a number of sketches of the spectacular scenery, particularly of Laramie Peak, which left a vivid impression on his mind. See Bierstadt's letter, Wolf River, September 3, 1859, published in *New Bedford Daily Mercury,* September 14, 1859. His first large western picture was undoubtedly the result of his enthusiastic reaction to this scenery.

66. Quoted from Finis Mitchell.

67. Some extant field sketches show that he also worked in pencil, charcoal, and watercolor. Bierstadt was merely following academic procedures in taking working notes. Although his impressionistic studies are popularly received today, they were never meant as aesthetic works in their own right.

68. For the first example see note above on his *On the Sweetwater River near the Devil's Gate, Nebraska* [*sic*] [*Wyoming*]. The second work, an oil on canvas, 19 × 29 inches (1859), is in the collection of the Museum of Fine Arts, Boston. The artist's vantage point appears to be from the Old Lander Trail along Lander Creek "just before it empties

into the Sweetwater River, because the jagged outline of the peak in the center resembles Independence Peak with the big Wind River Peak barely distinguishable in the clouds at the right." The stacked rock slabs are typical of the terrain found only near Lander and Blucher Creeks. Quoted from Finis Mitchell. The third example is in a private collection. See Hendricks, *Albert Bierstadt,* fig. 52.

69. Untitled and undated news clipping in "Scrapbook," p. 19; picture reproduced in Hendricks, *Albert Bierstadt,* p. 99, fig. 76.

70. The Wasatch Range was about 160 miles south of them, in Utah. Even on a clear day in 1859 he could have seen the range only from the summit of Fremont Peak at 13,745 feet.

71. Hendricks acknowledges Bierstadt's error but mistakenly identifies the mountains as the Salt River Range, which is in fact behind the Wyoming (Hendricks, *Albert Bierstadt,* p. 80). Quoted from Bierstadt's letter, Rocky Mountains, July 10, 1859, published in *Crayon,* September, 1859, p. 287.

72. *View from the Wind River Mountains, Wyoming,* 1860, oil on canvas, 30¼ × 48½ inches, M. and M. Karolik Collection, Museum of Fine Arts, Boston. On the reverse in the artist's hand is "View looking Northwest from the Wind River Mountains, the Wahsatch Mountains seen in the distance. Sketched from nature July 1st 1859." The latter suggests that there was a preliminary field sketch for this painting that has been lost.

73. Reproduced in Hendricks, *Albert Bierstadt,* fig. 75 (the caption is incorrect; it should read *Morning in the Rocky Mountains* [1861], oil on paper, mounted on canvas, 8½ × 11½ inches, collection of the R. W. Norton Art Gallery, Shreveport, La.). Geographical information provided by Finis Mitchell.

74. Many critics have associated Bierstadt's technical manner of execution with the Düsseldorf School; however, they generally agree that he had largely freed himself from its obvious defect—conventional mechanical lifelessness—and had evolved his own personal style and expression.

75. Critic George W. Sheldon amplifies this expression: "Bierstadt is a believer in Wagner's principle of the value of mere quantity in a work of art. He has painted more large canvases than any other American artist. His style is demonstrative and

infused with emotion; he is the Gustave Doré of landscape-painting." *American Painters*, p. 149.

76. The title appears only on a plaque attached to the frame; its origin is unknown. Thelma Paine, reference librarian, to Trenton, February 2, 1979.

77. Hendricks, *Albert Bierstadt*, reproduces two preliminary oil sketches for Bierstadt's large work *The Rocky Mountains*, figs. 106, 107.

78. We are again indebted to Finis Mitchell for his geographic expertise of the Wind River chain.

79. For the history of ownership and exhibition record, see Hendricks, *Albert Bierstadt*, pp. 140–41, 154. In August, 1979, Trenton had an opportunity to view this work in the basement of the Metropolitan Museum. While inspecting the painting, she discovered a pencil inscription in block letters along the bottom edge, just above the frame: "EVENING [blank or obscured] MOUNTAINS 7. 59." The inscription could be the original title of the painting (?). By filling in the missing words, it could read: "EVENING [IN THE ROCKY] MOUNTAINS."

80. Untitled newspaper clipping [March, 1864] from "Scrapbook."

81. Untitled newspaper clipping, New York, November 11, 1865, "Scrapbook," p. 29.

82. McHenry, with his friend and associate T. W. Kennard, was responsible for establishing the first continuous broad-gauge railroad line from New York to Saint Louis, the Atlantic and Great Western Railway. In 1868, Kennard acquired Bierstadt's second major work, *Storm in the Rocky Mountains —Mt. Rosalie;* see Hendricks, *Albert Bierstadt*, p. 154.

83. Quoted from Bierstadt's flyer "The Rocky Mountains," "Scrapbook."

84. Ibid. It would have been impossible to see Lander's Peak from the Green River Lake region (Upper Green River), and it is doubtful that the artist even reached the area because of the distance and the direction they had to travel: "100 miles from the Sweetwater to the N. W. and then 30 miles back into the valley, only to retrace their tracks back out" (information provided by Finis Mitchell). Bierstadt named the peak purely out of friendship for the explorer.

85. Tuckerman, *Book of the Artists*, pp. 395–96.

86. Quoted from George Bancroft, "Nature and Life," *Spirit of the Fair* (New York), April 22, 1864, p. 186.

87. Untitled newspaper clipping [March, 1864], "Scrapbook."

88. Jarves, *The Art-Idea*, 2:233.

89. Ludlow's remarks seem to support this idea: "We were going into the vale whose giant domes and battlements had months before thrown their photographic shadow through Watkins's camera across the mysterious wide Continent, causing exclamations of awe at Goupil's window, and ecstasy in Dr. Holmes's study. At Goupil's counter and in Starr King's drawing-room we had gazed on them by the hour already,—I, let me confess it, half a Thomas-a Didymus to Nature, unwilling to believe the utmost true of her till I could put my finger in her very prints. Now we were going to test her reported largess for ourselves." Quoted from Fitz Hugh Ludlow, *The Heart of the Continent*, p. 412; henceforth cited as *Heart*.

90. Sumner to [Lincoln's Secretary of War] Edwin M. Stanton [?], March 31, 1862; Bierstadt's letter to Alpheus Hyatt, April 27, 1862, quoted in Hendricks, *Albert Bierstadt*, p. 108.

91. See *New York Evening Post*, May 12, 1863, "Scrapbook."

92. Four sections from Ludlow's narrative were published earlier in *Atlantic Monthly*, in April, June, July, and December, 1864.

93. Most of the information for Bierstadt's western trip of 1863 comes from this author's account; however, the artist's excursion to the Chicago Lakes district just west of Denver in the Colorado Rockies is drawn from William Newton Byers's journal, which was published in the *Rocky Mountain News* upon their return to Denver. See issues for June 23–25, 1863.

94. Ludlow, *Heart*, p. 130.

95. Ibid., p. 138. The trip from Atchison to Denver by overland stagecoach was advertised as taking six days. *Rocky Mountain News*, 1863. According to Ludlow, they left Atchison on May 29; thus they should have arrived on June 4.

96. *Rocky Mountain News*, June 10, 1863.

97. Ludlow, *Heart*, p. 139.

98. Ibid., p. 180. To judge from most of his monumental showpieces, Bierstadt preferred the dramatic and grand effects of nature to its geological curiosities.

99. Announcement in the *Rocky Mountain News*, June 17, 1863.

100. Byers's journal printed in *Rocky Mountain News*, June 23, 1863. Unless otherwise specified, the chronicling of Bierstadt's excursion to Chicago Lakes comes from this journal.

101. The present Bergen Park "was a favorite wintering spot for elk." See C. M. Hamilton, *Our Memories of Bergen Park* (pamphlet), Denver Public Library, Western History Department (1951), p. 9.

102. "Mt. Evans is the highest peak of a group including Mt. Bierstadt (also 14,000 feet) and Mt. Rosalie, Mt. Epaulet, Mt. Warren, Mt. Rogers, and Mt. Goliath (all under 14,000 feet).

"This group was originally called the Chicago Mountains. The highest peak was named Rosalie by Albert Bierstadt, the painter. This name became corrupted into Rosa and Rosalia. Finally [in 1870] the name was changed to Mt. Evans [for the second territorial governor of Colorado]. The name Rosalie became used for the next most prominent peak as seen from Denver, and the name Bierstadt was given to the peak, over 14,000 feet, directly west of Mt. Evans." John L. J. Hart, *Fourteen Thousand Feet*, p. 12.

103. This monumental work was considered by art historians lost or "destroyed" for about a century until its rediscovery in a London warehouse in 1974. The confusion was caused by the *Rocky Mountain News*, which, on September 13, 1869, incorrectly identified it as the painting "destroyed" in a fire at Earle's Gallery in Philadelphia. Yet in the very year of the report by the *Rocky Mountain News* the painting was on exhibit at Munich's International Exposition.

104. Both Strong and Hendricks discuss this possible lovers' triangle. See Strong, "Bierstadt and California," p. 75, n. 32; and Hendricks, *Albert Bierstadt*, pp. 113, 165. On December 12, 1866, the *Rocky Mountain News Weekly* reprinted an announcement of Bierstadt's marriage from the *New York Tribune*: "Albert Bierstadt was married in Waterville, on the twenty-first instant, to Rosalie Osborne, of this city. Mr. Bierstadt has just erected at Irvington a residence costing $50,000, and commanding one of the finest views of the Hudson. It is really a studio with house attached. The studio is eighty

feet in length, with walls thirty-four feet high, galleries for art studies, and lovely views from its windows. Mr. Bierstadt's 'Storm in the Rocky Mountains' goes to the Exposition."

105. Probably from Bierstadt's sketchbook of 1863. The rough sketch, executed in pencil, measures 5 × 8 inches; reproduced in Hendricks, *Albert Bierstadt*, p. 159, fig. 116, cited as in John P. Kelly's collection (the author gives Kelly's address only as Connecticut and does not offer any other information related to this singular Colorado field sketch). The sketch was probably executed just as they were "turning" the mountain before dropping into the amphitheater of Lower Chicago Lake, or "Trout Lake," named by Byers and Bierstadt after their successful fishing venture there (see Byers, "Bierstadt's Visit to Colorado," *Magazine of Western History* 11 [January, 1890]:238-40). Bierstadt would have been standing approximately 200 feet above the lower, or first, lake on the western slope, the same vantage point suggested by the English journalist in the *London Saturday Review* (see Tuckerman, *Book of the Artists*, p. 394 for a reprint). Trenton's husband and son, with the assistance of a forest ranger, made the same journey in August, 1970, establishing the position from which Bierstadt captured his overall view of the two small lakes in the horseshoe valley and the lofty mountain (Evans) off in the distant west: *A Storm in the Rocky Mountains — Mt. Rosalie.*

106. Hendricks takes the opposite position, saying that "neither Byers . . . nor anyone else, then or now, would or could identify the locale with anything in Colorado, the Rocky Mountains, or, indeed, anywhere on earth." Hendricks, *Albert Bierstadt*, p. 160. Photographs taken on the spot with the aid of a topographical map (by Trenton's son Jim) conclusively document the site of this picture as the Chicago Lakes district. The exaggerated height of the peaks is considered later in this chapter.

107. Ludlow, *Heart*, p. 194; *Rocky Mountain News*, June 24, 1863.

108. Two of Bierstadt's small, undated oil studies of Utah scenery have come to light: *Wasatch Mountains* (see Fenn Galleries, Santa Fe, N.M., sales catalog, June 19, 1977) and *The Great Salt Lake* (reproduced in Hendricks, *Albert Bierstadt*, p. 128, fig.

96; collection of Charles and Emma Frye, Art Museum, Seattle, Wash.). Stylistic similarities to his oil studies of Yellowstone Park, made during his sketching tour of 1881, indicate that these pictures date from the same trip, during which Bierstadt and his friends also visited Utah.

109. Hendricks, *Albert Bierstadt*, p. 134.

110. *Watson's Weekly Art Journal* (New York), n.s. 4 (November 25, 1865):82 (reprint of *New Bedford Daily Mercury*) reports that "the great painting, 'The Storm in the Mountains,' upon which [Bierstadt] has been for more than six months engaged, will be finished in about two months." The same news item is repeated in *Rocky Mountain News*, November 27, 1865, except that the painting is titled *Storm in the Colorado Valley*. Perhaps Bierstadt had not decided on the picture's title at the time of these news releases.

111. Storm clouds become the central focus in a number of the artist's landscapes developed after his journey of 1863 to the West, for example, his *Storm in the Mountains* and *The Storm*, both illustrated in Hendricks, *Albert Bierstadt*, figs. 138, 143. Bierstadt's literary contemporaries were employing the same dramatic and coloristic imagery found in the artist's work, heightening effects just as he did to evoke emotional responses. Take for instance, Ludlow's colorful description of an electric storm on the plains: "Into the blackness there rose out of the ground, apparently from a high divide, not a mile beyond our leaders, a column of lightning, sized and shaped like the trunk of a tall pine. Straight and swift, but with a more measurely motion than that of the higher discharges, it shot up, shedding its glare for many rods around, and making a sharply cut band of fire against the black background of the clouds, until it struck the nearest mass of vapor. Then, with the most tremendous flash and peal of the whole storm, its blazing capital broke into splinters, and went shivering across the area, right over our heads. If it were only possible to paint such things! But on canvas they would seem even more theatrical than they do in these inadequate words." Ludlow, *Heart*, pp. 20-21.

112. Achenbach painted a number of Dutch seascapes under cloudy skies in the 1830s and 1840s, but never with the same dramatic impact or on such a grand scale as Bierstadt's.

113. Quoted from Thomas B. Hess, "Art/Brooklyn Heights," *New York*, August 30, 1976, pp. 59-60; the critic bases his information on curator Linda Ferber's theory. The story is rather obvious, and the anecdotal passage merely reinforces the picture's central theme. In Bierstadt's day contemporary critics never mentioned the small figures; they were obviously considered subordinate to the landscape.

114. See note above on sketch.

115. In Bierstadt's first production, *The Rocky Mountains*, the two different viewpoints were faulted by art critic Jarves in *The Art-Idea*.

116. Quoted from Hess, "Art/Brooklyn Heights," p. 60.

117. See notes above on site of work.

118. Quoted from Hess, "Art/Brooklyn Heights."

119. Quoted in Tuckerman, *Book of the Artists*, pp. 394-95.

120. *New York Times*, February 5, 1866, announcement of the exhibition of Bierstadt's *Storm in the Rocky Mountains* at Somerville and Minor's Gallery. On March 3, 1866, *Watson's Weekly Art Journal* (n.s. 4:307) reported that Bierstadt's picture had, as they understood, "increased the funds of the charitable society . . . by $2,200."

121. February 27, 1866. A critical review of the picture was sent from New York to the paper on February 14.

122. Quoted in Hendricks, *Albert Bierstadt*, p. 160.

123. Untitled newspaper clipping [1865-66], "Scrapbook," p. 12.

124. The following information on Sir Samuel Morton Peto (1809-89) was assembled by dealer James Maroney: Peto is listed as a contractor, member of Parliament, civil engineer, and partner in the firm of Grissell and Peto (1830-47). In 1846 he entered into partnership with Edward L. Betts; the firm was responsible for the construction of South Eastern, Great Northern, and Great Eastern Railway Lines in England and Minor's, on the Continent, and in America. He received his baronetcy on February 22, 1855. Peto's visit to the United States in the fall of 1865 resulted in the publication of *The Resources and Prospects of America*. If the sales transaction actually took place then, the picture would have been Peto's property at the time of the Paris exposition in April of 1867; however, there are con-

flicting reports that announce its sale in Paris for varying sums of money. Perhaps the transfer of ownership from Peto to Kennard in 1868 (?) might account in part for the discrepancies in sales figures and ownership names in the literature.

125. We are grateful to James Maroney for the history of the painting's provenance and the biographical data on the owners. Thomas William Kennard (1825–93) was celebrated as "an Engineer of great merit." He came to the United States as engineer-in-chief of the Atlantic and Great Western Railway. As an associate of Peto's, he designed the Great Western Railway lines west. Kennard and McHenry were responsible for the first continuous broad-gauge line from New York to Saint Louis, the Atlantic and Great Western Railway. According to various reports, Kennard presumably purchased *A Storm in the Rocky Mountains* from Peto in 1868. How long the painting remained in Kennard's possession is unknown. It is certain, however, that the picture was still owned by Kennard at the time of the Munich International Exposition in 1869 (see Friedrich von Boetticher, *Malerwerke des Neunzehnten Jahrhunderts . . .* , 1:93, n. 12). Apparently, Kennard sold the painting to Peto's son, Herbert Peto, sometime before 1872, when Townley cited the work as being in the latter's possession (the artist's niece, quoted in D. O. C. Townley, "Living American Artists," *Scribner's Monthly* 3 [March, 1872]:605). Herbert Peto was among the group of friends who joined Bierstadt on a visit to Niagara Falls in 1869. James Maroney adds this bit of information about the painting's whereabouts after Kennard's death, which further complicates the history of ownership: "No record has been found which accounts with certainty for ownership of the picture between Kennard's death in 1893 and Armand Blackley's possession of it in the 1930s. Bourlet & Sons's [*sic*] records substantiate that the painting was the property of Armand D. Blackley. It can probably be assumed that Blackley's father, David, owned the picture before it passed on to his son in the 1930s." Currently, large gaps still exist in the painting's provenance.

126. For a critical review of the painting see *Illustrated London News*, June 15, 1867, p. 599.

127. Quoted in Tuckerman, *Book of the Artists*, pp. 394–95.

128. See Naylor, *Record*, vol. 1, no. 291. The painting was listed for sale and priced at $3,000, indicating it was not overly large.

129. See Jackson's catalog index, no. Z10571, collection of the State Historical Society of Colorado.

130. *Rocky Mountain News*, October 17, 1873.

131. *Rocky Mountains, Colorado* (inscribed on back of paper before mounting) was formerly assigned the date 1873; M. and M. Karolik Collection, Museum of Fine Arts, Boston.

132. *Rocky Mountain News*, December 23, 1876. On January 9, 1877, the same newspaper reported their return from Estes Park.

133. One example is *Rocky Mountains, Colorado.* For other examples see *Indian Encampment: Evening* (Long's Peak, Estes Park), reproduced in Hendricks, *Albert Bierstadt*, CL-264; and *Winter—Estes Park, Col.* (Twin Sisters, Estes Park, Colo.) reproduced in *Kennedy Quarterly* 3 (October, 1962):52.

134. Quoted from *Rocky Mountain News*, August 31, 1877.

135. The painting was acquired by the Denver Public Library in 1956 from the widow of Dunraven's grandson, Desmond Fitzgerald, who had inherited it from his aunt, Aileen, countess of Meath, Dunraven's daughter. The transaction was made possible by a gift of $5,000 from Roger Mead. Several fairly large oils with dubious Estes Park titles have been recorded for the artist. Most seem to have been drawn from the artist's imagination and do not exhibit any distinguishable topographical features of the area. These paintings are *Dream Lake, Estes Park, Colorado* (the name of an actual lake), collection of the National Museum of American Art, Smithsonian Institution, Washington, D.C.; *Whyte's Lake, Estes Park*, formerly in the collection of John Herron Art Institute, Indianapolis, Ind.; *Estes Park, Colorado*, collection of Buffalo Bill Historical Center, Cody, Wyo.; and *Estes Park*, collection of Mrs. Libbie Moddy Thompson, Washington, D.C.

136. *Colorado Springs Gazette Weekly*, September 19, 1895.

137. Quoted from Hendricks, *Albert Bierstadt*, p. 253.

138. *Rocky Mountain News*, August 31, 1877 (reprint from a special correspondent, Estes Park, Au-

gust 23).

139. Hendricks, *Albert Bierstadt*, p. 254. On November 20, 1877, the *Rocky Mountain News* correspondent reported that the artist had canceled his trip to Nassau to continue working on his commissioned painting.

140. *Denver Times*, May 28, 1878.

141. F. duPont Cornelius (conservator) to Trenton, letter, Cincinnati, Ohio, August 30, 1976. The painting was turned over to duPont Cornelius after it had been "inexpertly treated by a Denver restorer."

142. *Rocky Mountains, Colorado* is a typical example; for others (undated and not inscribed), see Hendricks, *Albert Bierstadt*, figs. 177, 178.

143. Oil on paper, mounted on masonite, 13⅞ × 19⅜ inches, collection of Hirschl & Adler Galleries, New York City.

144. Information on the artist's trip comes from John Sherman, *Recollections of Forty Years in the House, Senate and Cabinet*, 2:823ff.; newspaper accounts; and the artist's remaining works of Yellowstone.

145. *New York Express*, October 28, 1881, "Scrapbook," p. 62.

146. For examples see *Geyser, Yellowstone Park* (1881), oil on paper mounted on cardboard, 14 × 19½ inches, M. and M. Karolik Collection, Museum of Fine Arts, Boston; and *Fountain Geyser, Yellowstone*, oil on paper, 14 × 19 inches, collection of the Kennedy Galleries, Inc., New York City. Bierstadt's oil study *Yellowstone Lake* is reproduced in *Kennedy Quarterly* 1 (October, 1960):110. The small study *Yellowstone Falls* is in the Georgia Museum of Art, University of Georgia. The enlarged version is in the Buffalo Bill Historical Center, Cody, Wyo.; it is an oil on canvas measuring 43½ × 29¾ inches.

147. See Eberstadt & Sons' catalog *Americana*, no. 167, p. 21: "40 double page panoramic views . . . and smaller sketches, studies of buffalo." The present location of these sketchbooks is unknown. Most of Bierstadt's small oil studies on paper appear to measure 14 × 19 inches, which indicates that they were sized to fit into his color box. Photograph of Bierstadt in his New York City studio (ca. 1900) with his small oil study *Geyser, Yellowstone Park* (1881), collection of M. and M. Karolik,

Museum of Fine Arts, Boston, hanging on the wall (lower right side), Denver Public Library, Western History Department.

148. Several of Bierstadt's major paintings were reproduced as chromolithographs, among them *The Rocky Mountains* and *A Storm in the Rocky Mountains—Mt. Rosalie.* It is likely that Bierstadt's work was better known through this medium than through the paintings themselves. Bierstadt's canvases were frequently exhibited in major cities like Chicago, which had an active art colony in the 1860s and 1870s, but artists outside the mainstream, working in regional centers, could more readily have referred to reproductions for their models and inspiration. Bierstadt's brief residency in San Francisco, which attracted considerable attention, probably contributed to his widespread fame among artists isolated from the eastern seaboard. For instance, two paintings by itinerant artists were lifted from Bierstadt's chromolithographs: one, titled *Western Landscape,* by W. C. Sharon, is after *A Storm in the Rocky Mountains;* the other, an unsigned pastiche, draws heavily on *The Rocky Mountains.* Sharon's picture, an oil on canvas measuring 20 × 33 inches, is in the M. H. de Young Memorial Museum, San Francisco; the other, is in the collection of the California Institute of Technology, Pasadena.

149. We are deeply grateful to Bernice George and Ruth Blom, Elkins's granddaughter and grandniece, for making accessible all the artist's memorabilia—sketches, letters, and newspaper clippings—in their possession. For a discussion of Gookins, see chap. 8. Henry Chapman Ford (1828–1894), landscape painter, was born in Livonia, N.Y. He went to Europe in 1857, studying in Paris and Florence during his three years abroad. In December, 1861, at the onset of the Civil War, he enlisted in the army and served for three years, during which time he is said to have furnished various illustrated presses with sketches of war scenes. Following his discharge because of a physical disability, he moved to Chicago to recuperate, later opening a studio there. He was one of the charter members of the Chicago Academy of Design and served as its president in 1873. He made two sketching tours in Colorado, in 1866 and 1869, the second trip with fellow Chicago artists George S. Collis (another founder of the academy) and G. F. Rams-

dell (see *Rocky Mountain News Weekly,* July 21, 1869; September 20, 1869). His *Rocky Mountain Scene* (?) was listed as one of his principal works (see artist biographical card filled out by his widow, Helen Ford Sloan, in 1910, on deposit at the California Section, California State Library, Sacramento). Other paintings, *The Garden of the Gods* (1867) and *Arkansas Valley,* resulted from his Colorado journeys (see *Rocky Mountain News,* April 8, 1867; and *Chicago Academy of Design "Permanent Exhibition"* [1871], no. 103). His studio in the academy was burned in the great fire of 1871, along with his accumulated studies of many years. In January, 1875, he moved to Santa Barbara, Calif., because of poor health. In 1883 he published his *Etchings of the Franciscan Missions of California,* his principal achievement. He died in Santa Barbara on February 27, 1894. Ford's biography can be found in Taft, *Artists and Illustrators of the Old West, 1850-1900,* p. 294; and Groce and Wallace, *Dictionary of Artists,* p. 234.

150. September 3, 8, 22, 27, 1866.

151. Quoted from Bayard Taylor, *Colorado: A Summer Trip,* pp. 145–46. For Beard and Taylor's trip see the section on "The Professional Artists."

152. Pencil sketch of "1866 camp," 2¼ × 4¼ inches, inscribed on back: "#113 This is the camp where Mr. Elkins, Mr. [Ford], Mr. Cogerville and Mr. James G[ookins] camped in 1866. Mr. Elkins' first sketching trip out of Chicago. He was 18 [*sic*] years old." There are other sketches from the same trip; all are in the family's collection.

153. *Rocky Mountain News,* September 3, 8, 1866.

154. Elkins's birthplace and date of birth are verified by the family and recorded in his obituary (see *Chicago Tribune,* July 26, 1884). All biographical data on the artist are drawn from these sources.

155. Reported in various newspaper accounts: see, for example, *Trinidad Daily News,* June 28, 1881; *Chicago Tribune,* July 25, 1884; *Chicago Telegram,* August 3, 1884; *Elkhorn Independent,* [1870]. The current whereabouts of this large oil (30 × 50 inches) is unknown.

156. Letter from the United States Consulate in Vienna to E. A. Otis, No. 22 LaSalle Street, Chicago, Ill., November 19, 1873 (family's collection). Emulating his mentor, Bierstadt, Elkins had

a similar leaflet printed with geographical information to accompany his large showpiece *Mt. Shasta* (leaflet in family's collection). The information in this leaflet, however, was extracted from Clarence King, *Mountaineering in the Sierra Nevada.*

157. Information about *Crown* comes from *Rocky Mountain News,* December 19, 1874, March 16, 1875, and October 7, 1875. The painting, an oil, measured 9 × 12 feet. The present location of this monumental work is unknown.

158. *Rocky Mountain News,* September 2, 1873. Besides these studies Elkins painted a small scene, *Virginia Cañon* (*Rocky Mountain News,* December 19, 1874). A similar version with a slightly different vantage point is in the Kennedy Galleries, Inc., New York City. Also called *Crown of the Continent,* it is an oil on canvas measuring 22 × 36 inches.

159. *Chicago Times,* March 9, 1875.

160. The souvenir postcard is in the family's collection; it appears that the painting is cropped in the faded photograph. Through this image, however, it is possible to verify the title on the Kennedy Galleries' study.

161. The unlocated painting *The Thirty-Eighth Star,* measuring 6 × 10 feet, commemorated Colorado's statehood. See *Rocky Mountain News,* January 4, 1877, and *Chicago Telegram,* August 3, 1884. The sketch is in the family's collection; the present whereabouts of *The Valley of Tomichi* is unknown. *Elk Park . . .* was offered for sale in Eberstadt's Catalog 146 [69], 1958, under the title *Indian Camp in the Rocky Mountains* (the title *Elk Park, Colorado* was inscribed on the back of the canvas; the picture has been relined). At the time of the fire the painting had been purchased by F. F. Wilson for $1,500. *Kansas City Times,* April 14, 1884.

162. In a letter to his father from Düsseldorf dated June 1, 1856, Gifford remarked about this German practice, saying that he believed that it caused the Germans' pictures to darken after a while. As an example he singled out the work of the Düsseldorfian artist Carl Hübner.

163. Several members of the Elkins family have sketches by the artist; for example, one has a sketchbook of 1883 comprised of sketches taken along the Platte. All have a few medium-sized oil paintings as well; none of them is titled or dated.

164. Information assembled by the Chicago His-

torical Society from city directories lists Elkins's various studios in Chicago. For the artist's studios outside the city see *Chicago Tribune*, July 25, 1884; *Kansas City Times*, June 2, 1884.

165. To judge from his sketches and newspaper reports, Elkins toured Colorado in 1866, 1868, 1869, 1873, 1881, 1883, and 1884. His sudden death occurred in Georgetown, Colo., on July 25, 1884.

166. According to several unidentified and undated newspaper clippings (ca. 1875) in the family's collection, Elkins had put together a large collection of American and European paintings. One newspaper announcement suggests that the artist may have been dealing in art on the side: "Elkins, by way of relief to the visitor's eye from the numerous landscapes on the walls, has added to his gallery at Almini's, State Street, four choice works from his private collection by masters of 50 to 100 years ago."

167. Information provided by unidentified, undated newspaper clippings (ca. 1877) in the family's collection. One newspaper account suggested that Elkins's success appeared to have turned his head and forced the liquidation of his personal collection of paintings. According to the report, at age 30 in 1877 "he became a habitual drunkard," and his "income of $10,000 to $20,000 a year soon dropped to the price of the one or two pictures a year he might paint in his soberer moments." Quoted from *Trinidad Daily News*, June 28, 1881.

168. Other California artists who traveled to the Rocky Mountains will be treated in a special section; see chap. 8. The source for Holdredge's birthdate and place of birth is the *San Francisco Chronicle*, April 16, 1899; a few newspaper reports mistakenly give his birthplace as England. The artist is listed in the San Francisco city directories from 1864 to 1868 as a "draughtsman." Although his pictures are mentioned in the local papers as early as 1867, it is not until 1869 that he is listed in the city directories as a "landscape painter." From 1872 to 1880 he is not listed in the city directories; it is possible that he was making frequent scenic jaunts and missed the compiler, for his work is mentioned in the local papers now and then during those years. There are, however, two documented trips for the artist between 1872 and 1880, one to the East in late 1872–73 and the other to Europe from late

1877 to 1879, when he was studying in Paris and Munich. In 1881 his name reappeared in the San Francisco directories. He remained in the city until 1896, then moved to Alameda, where he died penniless on April 15, 1899, at the age of 63. According to his obituary, he was a charter member of the San Francisco Art Association and an early member of the Bohemian Club. *San Francisco Chronicle*, April 16, 1899. Biographical information compiled by Eleanor Bancroft, Bancroft Library, Berkeley, Calif., contained in a letter to Robert Taft, March 1, 1944, in the Robert Taft Papers, Kansas State Historical Society, Topeka. For additional information on the artist and his work see Dwight Miller's exhibition catalog, *California Landscape Painting, 1860–1885: Artists around Keith and Hill*, Stanford University Art Gallery, December 9, 1975.

169. *San Francisco News Letter and California Advertiser*, December 12, 1868.

170. Holdredge left for Europe in late 1877 and returned to San Francisco in September, 1879; see *San Francisco Chronicle*, December 8, 1879. Several of his large landscapes with Indian encampments were developed after this overland trip; they are listed for sale in Lamson's and Spear's auction sales catalogs of 1882 (in the collection of the Bancroft Library, University of California, Berkeley). The sale at Lamson Hall listed the artist's large *Sioux Camp in Colorado*. The same painting was later sold by the auctioneer Troy in 1884 for $75 (William Dick to Trenton, letter, San Francisco, 1973). A large painting, *Indian Encampment* (30 × 50 inches), in the Harmsen's Western Americana Collection is thought to represent the high sierra country; however, this picture closely resembles another large encampment scene whose title is inscribed on the back of the canvas: *A Sioux Encampment in the Rocky Mountains* (see color plate 19).

171. Biographical information on Schafer was provided by William Dick, who obtained the artist's biographical data from his death certificate (Schafer died in Oakland, Calif., on July 18, 1927). We are deeply indebted to Dick for his generosity in turning over to us this research material.

172. See *San Francisco Bulletin*, October 3, 1876.

173. Presumably the artist and his family traveled along the overland route by Union Pacific Railway. On the artist's death certificate, Dick says, is

the statement that the artist was in "the U.S. 50 years" and in "California 50 years."

174. Information about this recorded sale was provided by Elliot Evans, former curator, Society of California Pioneers, San Francisco, Calif.

175. The painting hangs in the dining room of the Craigdarroch Castle, Victoria, B.C.; it was supposedly auctioned off in 1909, when it was listed in an "Executors' Sale" after the death of Mrs. Dunsmuir, the original owner of the castle (Craigdarroch Castle brochure).

176. Oil on canvas, 51 × 69 inches, collection of Harmsen's Western Americana, Denver, Colo. The only information about William R. Eaton that we have been able to find is taken from the Chicago city directory and from exhibition catalogs. It appears that Eaton arrived in Chicago in 1878, for he is listed in the *Inter-State Exposition Chicago Art Catalogue, 1878* with *View of New Hampshire* and his address recorded at "170 State Street, Chicago." His *Laguna Valley, Cal.* is listed in *Chicago Academy of Design Catalogue Exhibition*, December 1878, where he is recorded at the same address. The following year, 1879, he is listed in the Chicago city directory as "Artist" with his home address. Thereafter he disappears from the city directories. He submitted a New Hampshire view to the Inter-State Industrial Exposition, Chicago, in 1884, the same year he painted the Harmsen's Colorado picture. The two New Hampshire views and his disappearance from the Chicago art scene may suggest that he returned home somewhere in the East.

Chapter 6

1. Clarence King, quoted in Richard A. Bartlett, *Great Surveys of the American West*, p. 141; henceforth cited as Bartlett, *Great Surveys*. Bartlett provides the first comprehensive literary study of the four "Great Surveys" and their contributions to the history of the American West. Most of the introductory information here has been drawn from this excellent source.

2. Wheeler's surveys, carried out from 1869 to 1881, were primarily concerned with filling in the geographic knowledge of California, Utah, Nevada,

Arizona, Idaho, and Colorado. John E. Weyss served as topographer and draftsman for most of those surveys. Although he produced some elaborate drawings for Wheeler's final report, they are essentially topographical renderings and, though not lacking artistic merit, are more concerned with mapmaking than with artistic production. See George M. Wheeler, *Report upon U.S. Geographic Surveys West of the One Hundredth Meridian*, vol. 1. We wish to express our gratitude to historian Clifford Nelson, U.S. Geological Survey, Reston, Virginia, for bringing this topographer to our attention.

3. The dates of this publication, *Report of United States Geological Exploration of the Fortieth Parallel*, run from 1870, when James D. Hague's monograph "Mining Industry" first appeared, until 1880, when Othniel Marsh published his work "Odontornithes." King's own contribution, "Systematic Geology," vol. 1, did not appear until 1878. "In the 800-page monograph, King traced the geologic history of the 'Middle Cordilleras'—104° 30′W. to 102°, a distance of 800 miles—from the ancient deposits of the Archean era on through the Paleozoic, the Mesozoic, and the most recent, the Cenozoic, with breakdowns into the various geologic periods including the recent Quarternary." Bartlett, *Great Surveys*.

4. William H. Goetzmann, *Exploration and Empire*, p. 439.

5. Clarence King, "The Falls of the Shoshone," *Overland Monthly* 5 (October, 1870):379–85. John Henry Hill (1839–1922) was a landscape painter, aquatintist, and etcher and the son of John William Hill and grandson of John Hill, engravers and topographical artists. He was born in West Nyack, N.Y., in 1839, and began his art career under the tutelage of his well-known father. In the late 1850s he began exhibiting in New York City and Philadelphia. He was a member of the American Society of Painters in Water Colors (the American Water Color Society) and submitted ten entries to its first exhibition. In London he became acquainted with Ruskin, who undoubtedly advised him to study the works of Turner and the Pre-Raphaelites. In 1888 he produced *An Artist's Memorial* in honor of his father, illustrating it with his own etchings after his father's paintings. During his lifetime he traveled to Europe and to the West, sketching in the Rockies and California. He died in 1922. George C. Groce and David

H. Wallace, *The New-York Historical Society's Dictionary of Artists in America, 1564–1860*, p. 460.

6. *New Path*, May, 1863, quoted in Joshua C. Taylor, *America as Art*, p. 121.

7. Hill's sketchbook and watercolors from his trip with King are in the collection of Laurance Rockefeller, Jr., New York City. We wish to express our gratitude to Joan Washburn, of Washburn Gallery, New York City, for bringing this collection to our attention. O'Sullivan's photograph, 1868, is reproduced in the exhibition catalog of Jonathan L. Fairbanks et al., *Frontier America: The Far West*, p. 67, no. 79.

8. For a discussion about changes taking place in the use of watercolor, see Patricia Trenton, *Harvey Otis Young: The Lost Genius, 1840–1901*, pp. 54–55.

9. Gilbert Davis Munger (1837–1903) was born in Madison, Conn., on April 14, 1837. In the 1850s he was employed by the United States government as an engraver in Washington, D.C. While engraving plates for scientific reports, Munger studied painting on his own, sketching from nature. During the Civil War he served as an engineer in the Union army. After the war he opened a studio in New York City and began exhibiting his paintings. His travels took him to the Rockies, California, and Canada. In 1873 he made a trip to England, sketching there and in Scotland and France. During his twenty years in Europe he became influenced by the French Barbizon painters and eventually altered his style of painting. He died in Washington, D.C., on January 27, 1903. See Groce and Wallace, *Dictionary of Artists*, p. 460; *Kennedy Quarterly* 6 (June, 1966):79–81.

10. See King, "Systematic Geology."

11. The painting is presently called *Glacier Lake* but should be retitled *Lake Lal and Mt. Agassiz—Uinta Range—Utah* to correspond with the caption under plate 8, opp. p. 153.

12. For an example of O'Sullivan's photographic views, see King, "Systematic Geology," opp. p. 153, plate 9.

13. The original oil on which the Wasatch Range chromolithograph was based is incorrectly titled *View of Grand Lake and Long's Peak, Colo.*, and should be retitled to correspond with the caption under color plate 21. An oil of the Wasatch Range

by Munger, painted from a slightly different vantage point from the painting reproduced in King's report, is published in *Kennedy Quarterly* 6 (June, 1966):79–81 as *Indian Camp in the Tetons* [*sic*]; the small oil study on which this large painting was based is also reproduced in the same issue of the *Quarterly*.

14. King, "Systematic Geology," p. 388.

15. See chaps. 7, 8.

16. Quoted from *Kennedy Quarterly* 6 (June, 1966):79–81.

17. Biographical information drawn from Bartlett, *Great Surveys*, and Goetzmann, *Exploration and Empire*. See also F. V. Hayden, "Letter from the Secretary of the Interior . . . Transmitting Report of Professor Hayden upon Geological and Geographical Surveys," in *U.S. Geological and Geographical Survey of the Territories*. 45th Cong. 2d sess. H. Exec. Doc. 81. Washington, D.C.: U.S. Government Printing Office, 1878; henceforth cited as Hayden, Summary Report, 1878.

18. F. V. Hayden, *Geological and Geographical Atlas of Colorado and Portions of Adjacent Territory*.

19. The following information comes from F. V. Hayden, *Preliminary Field Report of the United States Geological Survey of Colorado and New Mexico;* henceforth cited as Hayden, *Report*, 1869.

20. [U.S. Geological and Geographical Survey of the Territories], *Profiles, Sections and Other Illustrations, . . . Sketched . . . by Henry W. Elliott;* henceforth cited as Elliott, *Profiles*, 1872.

21. *Who Was Who in America*, 4:284.

22. *New York Herald*, reprinted in *Rocky Mountain News*.

23. "Part I, Sketches Made by the Artist of the U.S. Geological Survey of Colorado & New Mexico, 1869," deposited in the U.S. Geological Survey Library, Reston, Va., access. no. Historic 321 a–k. We are grateful to Bonnie Skell Hardwick, librarian, Denver Public Library, for directing our attention to Elliott's field sketchbooks. No. 11, *Camp Scene in Rocky Mountain foothills near Cache la Poudre, July 2, 1869;* a similar view is reproduced in Elliott, *Profiles*, 1872: *'Hog Backs' at Cache a la Poudre. Looking North*, plate 8.

24. Reproduced in Elliott, *Profiles*, 1872, plate 11.

25. Stated in F. V. Hayden, *Preliminary Report*

of the United States Geological Survey of Wyoming, and Portions of Contiguous Territories [1870].

26. Hayden, Summary Report, 1878.

27. See chap. 8, section on Gifford.

28. Reproduced in Elliott, *Profiles,* 1872, plate 17 (bottom).

29. Quoted from William Henry Jackson's autobiography, *Time Exposure,* p. 189.

30. See chap. 8, section on Gifford, color plate 34 and plate 84.

31. F. V. Hayden, *Preliminary Report of the United States Geological Survey of Montana and Portions of Adjacent Territories; being a Fifth Annual Report of Progress* [1871]; henceforth cited as Hayden, *Report* [1871].

32. See chap. 7.

33. Nathaniel P. Langford, "The Wonders of the Yellowstone," *Scribner's Monthly* 2 (May–June, 1871):1–17, 113–28. See also Hayden's account of his expedition to Yellowstone: "The Wonders of the West—II," *Scribner's Monthly* 3 (February, 1872): 388–96; most of the illustrations are by Moran.

34. Moore's and Trumbull's sketches from the Yellowstone expedition of 1870 are in the collection of the National Park Service, Yellowstone National Park.

35. For Moran's view, see Hayden, *Report* [1871], p. 95, fig. 31.

36. Figures cited in Hayden, Summary Report, 1878. Information about the survey of 1872 from F. V. Hayden, *Sixth Annual Report of the United States Geological Survey of the Territories, embracing Portions of Montana, Idaho, Wyoming, and Utah; being a Report of Progress of the Explorations for the Year 1872.*

37. *William Henry Holmes: Artist, Geologist, Archeologist, and Art Gallery Director,* (reprinted from the *Ohio Archaeological and Historical Quarterly* 36 [October, 1927]:493–527); John R. Swanton, "Biographical Memoir of William Henry Holmes, 1846–1933," *National Academy of Sciences Biographical Memoirs* 17 (1936):223–52; and William Henry Holmes, "Random Records of a Lifetime Devoted to Science and Art," vol. 1 (henceforth cited as Holmes, "Random Records"). The sources listed contain biographical information on the artist-scientist.

38. The "Random Records" are made up of the artist's memoirs, letters, newspaper clippings, articles, photographs, and some sketches amassed by Holmes in preparation for his autobiography. Bonnie Skell Hardwick advises us that volumes 17–20 are in the artist's granddaughter's possession (information received in 1974).

39. F. V. Hayden, [*Seventh*] *Annual Report of the United States Geological and Geographical Survey of the Territories, embracing Colorado, being a Report of Progress of the Exploration for the Year 1873.*

40. Sketch by Holmes in his "Diary for the Field Season of 1873," "Random Records," vol. 4, pt. 1.

41. Information obtained from Holmes, "Diary for the Field Season of 1873," in "Random Records," vol. 4, pt. 1, pp. 1–5.

42. For the photographic reproduction, see Clarence S. Jackson and Lawrence W. Marshall, *Quest of the Snowy Cross,* following p. 128; the caption reads: "From a painting made in 1873 by W. H. Holmes, artist and scientist of the 1873 Survey." The watercolor is also initialed and dated by the artist on a boulder: "W.H.[?] 73." Despite this inscription and Jackson's publication, in more recent years the watercolor has been attributed to Moran. Returning the work to the Holmes canon was effected by Trenton.

43. See chap. 7.

44. One version is in the collection of the Kennedy Galleries, Inc., New York City.

45. The sketch is in the "Diary" of 1873, "Random Records," vol. 4, pt. 1. On Saturday, August 23, Jackson also records the same spectacle: "As I was going up with them [Coulter & Tom Cooper] this last time I saw a peculiar circular rainbow away down in the valley below us. It was a complete circle with all the rainbow's colors & was right in the midst of the driving mist or clouds that were in the valley." Quoted from William Jackson, *The Diaries of William Henry Jackson . . . ,* ed. LeRoy R. Hafen and Ann W. Hafen, p. 251.

46. Holmes, "Diary," 1873, "Random Records," vol. 4, pt. 1.

47. Ibid.

48. Sketchbooks, 1873–74, access. nos. 830–A, 830–B, Field Records File, U.S. Geological Survey, Geological Division, Denver, Colo. The granite dome stucture in Estes Park is reproduced in F. V. Hayden, [*Eighth*] *Annual Report of the United States Geological and Geographical Survey of the Terri-tories, embracing Colorado and Parts of Adjacent Territories; being a Report of Progress of the Exploration for the Year 1874,* plate 10; henceforth cited as Hayden, *Report,* 1874. The engraver, however, has elaborated the foreground with trees and water.

49. *Washington Star,* September 29, 1919, from Holmes, "Random Records," vol. 4, pt. 1. Although this quotation is applied to his watercolors, it is equally appropriate for his topographical field sketches.

50. Bartlett, *Great Surveys,* p. 79.

51. We wish to give special thanks to Richard F. Logan, professor of geography, University of California, Los Angeles, for his scholarly counseling. The azimuth figures can be observed on a number of Holmes's panoramic sketches; for an example, see plate 63.

52. Hayden, *Report,* 1874.

53. For some examples, see sketchbooks, Field Records File, 1873–74, U.S. Geological Survey, Geological Division, Denver, Colo.

54. *Pike's Peak Range, Colorado,* watercolor, 1874, in Holmes, "Random Records," vol. 20, no. 21; we are again grateful to Bonnie Skell Hardwick, who brought this drawing to our attention.

55. Both watercolors are in the National Museum of American Art, Smithsonian Institution.

56. These same singular formations are illustrated in Hayden, *Report,* 1874, plate 3. Hayden devotes several pages of his narrative to them: "This group was named by me in 1869 the Monument Creek Group, from the fact that the atmospheric agents have carved out of some of the beds a very peculiar kind of monument, or columns, which long ago attracted the special attention of the traveler."

57. Included in F. V. Hayden, *Tenth Annual Report of the United States Geological and Geographical Survey of the Territories, embracing Colorado and Parts of Adjacent Territories; being a Report of Progress of the Exploration for the Year 1876;* henceforth cited as Hayden, *Report,* 1876.

58. *Cave Houses of the Rio Mancos, Colorado. 10 miles from its mouth,* 1875, watercolor, 13⅞ × 9¼ inches, National Museum of American Art, Smithsonian Institution; the same view was reproduced in Hayden's *Report,* 1876, plate 32.

59. William H. Goetzmann, "Limner of Grandeur: William H. Holmes and the Grand Canyon,"

American West 15 (May–June, 1978):63.

60. *Cliff-Houses of the Rio Mancos, Colorado*, 1875, oil on canvas, 21⅛ × 15¼ inches, National Museum of American Art, Smithsonian Institution; reproduced in Hayden, *Report*, 1876, plate 35.

61. For Jackson's account of his visit of 1874 to the Mesa Verde ruins, see Hayden, *Report*, 1874, pp. 369–81.

62. Information from F. V. Hayden, *Eleventh Annual Report of the United States Geological and Geographical Survey of the Territories, embracing Idaho and Wyoming, being a Report of Progress of the Exploration for the Year 1877*.

63. A copy of the atlas is in the Huntington Library, Rare Book Department, San Marino, Calif.

64. Bartlett, *Great Surveys*, p. 103.

65. Ibid., p. 100.

66. Hayden, *Twelfth Annual Report of the United States Geological and Geographical Survey of the Territories: A Report of Progress of the Exploration in Wyoming and Idaho for the Year 1878*, pt. 1 of 2 vols.

67. National Archives and Records Service, RG 57, Geologists' Field Notebook No. 3882, pp. 7–25.

68. Contained in the same Field Notebook No. 3882.

69. "Exploration of the Yellowstone National Park by the U.S. Geological and Geographical Survey of the Territories, 1878. Diary of W. H. Holmes, Geologist," "Random Records," vol. 3, pt. 2.

70. Published by Peregrine Smith, Inc., Layton, Utah, 1977; facsimile edition, including folio-size color atlas, of Dutton's work of 1882.

71. Holmes, *The Painter and the National Parks* (Washington, D.C.: Government Printing Office, 1917), in "Various Articles on Art and the Art Gallery," "Random Records," vol. 16.

Chapter 7

1. Quoted from F. V. Hayden, *Preliminary Report of the United States Geological Survey of Montana and Portions of Adjacent Territories; being a Fifth Annual Report of Progress* [1871], p. 84; see also chapter 6 on the Great Surveys.

2. Quoted from Thurman Wilkins, *Thomas Moran: Artist of the Mountains*, p. 58. Most of the biographical information in this essay comes from this excellent source; the art-related discussions, however, represent the authors' own views and interpretations.

3. Ibid., p. 59.

4. Ibid.

5. William H. Jackson, ". . . With Moran in the Yellowstone: A Story of Exploration, Photography and Art," *Appalachia* 21 (December, 1936): 152 (henceforth cited as Jackson, *Appalachia*).

6. Alexandre Calame's *Ober-Ofen, Switzerland* (study from nature) is listed in "Exhibition of Pictures; the Contribution of French, German, and Belgian Artists . . . at the Pennsylvania Academy of Fine Arts," 1866 (see p. 11, no. 11; catalog in Philadelphia Academy of Fine Arts archives).

7. For example, see *Rocky Mountain News*, April 16, 1875.

8. In his letter to Trenton dated May 21, 1976, Wilkins gives his reasons for believing that Moran owned both Turner publications: "A25, Gilcrease, mentions only one of Turner's books by name: 'He [Price] was a dealer in fine editions of books & we made an arrangement by which I was to take books in trade for water colors. . . . I got a number of fine books in this way, some which I have yet in 1903— Cowper's "Task" & Turner's Rivers of France, being two of them.' Ruth Moran went further, however, in 'The Real Life of Thomas Moran, as Known to His Daughter,' in *American Magazine of Art*, Dec. 1926, p. 646: 'My father traded his pictures to an old bookseller for "The Rivers of France" and the "Liber Studiorum," and everything that contained the work of Turner, so that when he went to England, about 1860 [*sic*] he knew his master perfectly in black and white.' . . . My other notes confirm Ruth's printed statement, and Fryxell mentions the two books by title on page 7 of his little book about Moran [see Fritiof Fryxell, *Thomas Moran: Explorer in Search of Beauty*]." Moran undoubtedly became aware of Turner's engravings in Hamilton's studio, since the older artist was equally inspired by the English landscapist.

9. Wilkins, *Thomas Moran*, p. 28; *Spit Light, Boston Harbor, England* (1857) appears opp. p. 16. Photographs of some of Moran's early work can be found in his papers on deposit in the Gilcrease Institute of American History and Art, Tulsa, Okla.

This extensive collection of Moran memorabilia includes his correspondence, personal documents, partial diary entries, account books, articles, clippings, photographs, lists of works, and miscellaneous materials. The other large collection of Moran material is held at East Hampton Free Library, East Hampton, N.Y.

10. A photograph of this painting is in the Moran Papers in the Thomas Gilcrease Institute of American History and Art. Like Moran's *Haunted House* (collection of Period West Gallery, Scottsdale, Ariz., 1976), *Winter in the Rockies* shares a stylistic affinity with Andreas Achenbach's *Forest Deep in Snow* (Donelson F. Hoopes, *The Düsseldorf Academy and the Americans*, no. 3). It is evident that Moran had enlarged his art vocabulary, adding Continental sources after his second trip to Europe in 1866–67.

11. A photograph of Moran's painting after Turner is in the Moran Papers on microfilm, Archives of American Art, Smithsonian Institution; Moran's copy is quite close to its model. See Luke Herrmann, *British Landscape Painting of the Eighteenth Century*, figs. 106–107.

12. George W. Sheldon, *American Painters*, p. 123.

13. For a reproduction of Moran's *Wilds of Lake Superior* see Wilkins, *Thomas Moran*, following p. 16.

14. Jackson, *Appalachia*, p. 154.

15. For illustrations of these drawings see Thomas S. Fern, *The Drawings and Watercolors of Thomas Moran . . .* , figs. 3, 4. Aside from Wilkins's excellent biography, Fern presents the most thorough study to date of Moran's watercolors and drawings. The material is chronologically and geographically organized; a critical analysis by the author accompanies each work illustrated.

16. See Wilkins's extensive bibliography in *Thomas Moran* for some of these listings.

17. William H. Truettner, "'Scenes of Majesty and Enduring Interest': Thomas Moran Goes West," *Art Bulletin* 58 (June, 1976):246.

18. Wilkins, *Thomas Moran*, p. 70.

19. *Tower Falls*, 1871, measuring 4¾ × 7¾ inches, is in the collection of Jefferson National Expansion Memorial, Saint Louis, Mo.; this pencil sketch is reproduced in Colorado State University's exhibition catalog *Thomas Moran in Yellowstone— 1871*, Fort Collins, 1972.

20. Jackson, *Appalachia*, p. 155.

21. Moran's diary, July–August, 1871 (typescript copy) Al, July 26, Moran Papers, Thomas Gilcrease Institute of American History and Art. This watercolor study, measuring 7¾ × 5 inches is in the collection of the National Park Service, Yellowstone National Park; it is also reproduced in Colorado State University's exhibition catalog *Thomas Moran in Yellowstone—1871.*

22. Quoted from F. V. Hayden, "The Wonders of the West—II," *Scribner's Monthly* 3 (February, 1872):392.

23. *Tower Falls*, dated 1872 and measuring 11 × 8 inches, is in the collection of the Thomas Gilcrease Institute of American History and Art.

24. Edward Lear (1812–88) is better known for his children's stories. The Huntington Library Art Gallery, San Marino, Calif., has several fine watercolor drawings by this artist.

25. Jackson, *Appalachia*, p. 155.

26. Illustrated in Truettner, "Thomas Moran," p. 245, fig. 9; pp. 244–45, figs. 10 and 11.

27. Sheldon, *American Painters*, pp. 125–26.

28. Moran Papers, env. no. 57, p. 3, Thomas Gilcrease Institute of American History and Art.

29. Quoted from Lawrence Gowing, *Turner: Imagination and Reality*, p. 13.

30. For a biography and some illustrations of Calame's work, see Maurice Pianzola, *Paysages Romantiques Genevois*, catalog nos. 1, 16; see also Liselotte Fromer-Im Obersteg, *Die Entwicklung der Schweizerischen Landschaftsmalerei im 18. und Frühen 19. Jahrhundert*, pp. 127–57. For reproductions of Calame's lithographs, see A. Schreiber-Favre, *La lithographie artistique en Suisse au XIXᵉ siècle, Alexandre Calame le paysage.*

31. *Summit of the Sierras* is reproduced in Wilkins, *Thomas Moran*, following p. 128.

32. Quoted from *Scribner's Monthly* 4 (June, 1872):252.

33. Moran Papers, env. 57, p. 4, Thomas Gilcrease Institute of American History and Art.

34. Moran's three-month summer tour that year took him from Denver to the Grand Canyon in Arizona and a few other localities in the Southwest, then back to Denver before he set out for Yellowstone. On June 18, 1892, the *Rocky Mountain News* announced Moran's presence in Denver and his in-

tended plans to visit Yellowstone Park: "Thomas Moran, one of the greatest of American artists, is a guest of the St. James. Mr. Moran is on his way to the Yellowstone national park. He will be accompanied on his trip by W. H. Jackson of this city and the world's fair commissioners of Wyoming, the object of the trip being to secure materials for a large picture to be exhibited at the world's fair." On the way to Yellowstone, Moran and Jackson made a side excursion to Devil's Tower, where they made pictorial images of the "grand and imposing sights." Moran's narrative, augmented by his pictures, published in the *Century Magazine* 47 (January, 1894): 450–55, details this scenic jaunt. For examples of his Yellowstone work of 1892, see Fern, *Thomas Moran*, figures 100ff.; quoted in ibid., p. 122.

35. Fern, *Thomas Moran*.

36. For example, see ibid., fig. 105.

37. *Grand Canyon of the Yellowstone* (1893–1901), oil on canvas, measuring 8 × 14 feet, is in the collection of the National Museum of American Art, Washington, D.C.

38. Wilkins, *Thomas Moran*, p. 207. Before sending them off to the World's Fair in Chicago in 1893, Moran exhibited the two paintings in the Denver Art League's show in the winter of 1892–93 (discussed below).

39. *First Sketch made in the West at Green River, Wyoming, 1871*, watercolor, in the collection of the Thomas Gilcrease Institute of American History and Art.

40. See William Jackson's photographic views *Green River Bluffs-Utah/UPRR*, in the collection of the State Historical Society of Colorado (negs. 7256, 7257).

41. It is possible that this is the work painted for Major John W. Powell (Thurman Wilkins to Hassrick, letter, New York, November 17, 1974).

42. Moran's vest-pocket-size diary of his trip of 1879 was discovered by his daughter Ruth Moran after the artist's death. See Fritiof Fryxell, *Thomas Moran's Journey to the Tetons in 1879.*

43. Wilkins, *Thomas Moran*, p. 95. Hayden had asked Moran to join him on the expedition of 1873 to the Holy Cross, but the artist had already made a commitment to Major John W. Powell to accompany him to the Grand Canyon that year. For the history surrounding this celebrated peak, see Fritiof

Fryxell, "The Mount of the Holy Cross," *Trail and Timberline*, no. 183 (January, 1934):5.

44. Jackson's photograph *"Roches Moutonnies"/ Near the Mountain of the Holy Cross* is in the Denver Public Library, Western History Department Collection. Since the view was taken on the expedition of 1873 to the cross, it is obvious that Moran also referred to this photograph in composing his picture.

45. Examples could include emotionally charged alpine scenes of German Romanticists Eduard Schleich and A. Zimmerman. See Von Eberhard Ruhmer et al., *Schack-Galerie: München Gemaldekätaloge*, vol. 2, figures 74, 115. For references to Alexandre Calame's work, see n. 30.

46. For an illustration of Koch's heroic alpine landscapes, see Neue Pinakothek und Staatsgalerie München's catalog *Meisterwerke der Deutschen Malerei des 19. Jahrhunderts*, vol. 2, opp. p. 17. J. W. Schirmer's *Das Wetterhorn* (ca. 1837) is reminiscent of Koch's alpine pictures. See Irene Markowitz, *Die Düsseldorfer Malerschule*, fig. 11.

47. See [Thomas Moran], *Home-Thoughts, from Afar . . .*, ed. Amy O. Bassford, intro. and notes by Fritiof Fryxell; henceforth cited as [Moran], *Home-Thoughts.*

48. Wilkins, *Thomas Moran*, p. 96.

49. [Moran], *Home-Thoughts*, p. 45.

50. Ibid., p. 47. The painting is listed in Moran's ledger of his work as owned by [J. H.] Johnston [New York jeweler] with the comment "not paid." Moran's ledger was compiled by the artist late in his career; it is mostly drawn from memory, indicating that it could be inaccurate.

51. Most of these sketches are reproduced in Fern, *Thomas Moran*.

52. [Moran], *Home-Thoughts*, p. 51.

53. Hayden, quoting Moran in Louis Prang's large portfolio of chromolithographs.

54. The small Turner watercolor, dated 1802, is in the Courtald Collection, London.

55. Both *Mount of the Holy Cross* and *Mosquito Trail* are reproduced in this portfolio; Hayden's descriptive text augments the illustrations.

56. This pencil-and-black-wash drawing, dated "Aug. 1874" and measuring 14 × 18 inches, is in the collection of the Cooper-Hewitt Museum of Design, Smithsonian Institution, New York City.

57. One version was exhibited at the National

Academy of Design in 1877. Marie Naylor [comp.], *The National Academy of Design Exhibition Record, 1861–1900*, vol. 2, no. 366.

58. [Moran], *Home-Thoughts*, pp. 53, 55.

59. *Rocky Mountain News*, September 3, 1874.

60. T. Moran to [?] Richards, letter, Newark, New Jersey, March 5, 1875 (typescript copy in Western History Research Center, University of Wyoming, Laramie).

61. *Boston Evening Transcript*, November 16, 1875.

62. *New York Herald*, May 14, 1875.

63. *Boston Daily Advertiser*, November 11, 1875.

64. Moran, quoted in *Art Journal*, 1879, p. 43.

65. Diploma in Moran Papers, Thomas Gilcrease Institute of American History and Art.

66. Information on the history of ownership is drawn from Colonel Henry Dudley Teetor, "Mountain of the Holy Cross," *Great Divide*, February, 1980, p. 193. See also *Colorado Springs Weekly Gazette*, June 26, 1880.

67. This fact is confirmed by Fritiof Fryxell in a letter to Trenton, Rock Island, Ill., June 4, 1969: "As regards the Mount of the Holy Cross I know only about the two oils you mention, and feel quite sure that Ruth Moran never mentioned any other since I would have made note of that fact." This second version of the *Mount of the Holy Cross*, an oil on canvas dated ca. 1892, measuring 39½ × 29½ inches, is in the collection of the Denver Public Library, Western History Department; it was on exhibit at the Denver Art League show. *Denver Republican*, December 22, 1892.

68. *Colorado Springs Gazette*, August 23, 1881.

69. "Tour of Artists and Author," *Denver Times*, September 21, 1881.

70. Ernest Ingersoll, *The Crest of the Continent* . . . .

71. Ibid., pp. 117–18.

72. This drawing, measuring 12½ × 9½ inches, is in the Cooper-Hewitt Museum of Design, Smithsonian Institution, New York City; reproduced in ibid., opp. p. 124. The date 1892 assigned to the drawing by Cooper-Hewitt is based on an inscription "upon the lower margin of the mounting cardboard: D[enver] & R[io] G[rande] . . . R[ailroad] 1892 [*sic*]." The unknown hand obviously made a mistake in dating this trip, which is recorded as having occurred in 1881. Moran could have taken the same train back to Denver in 1892 and sketched the gorge again; however, the reproduction and drawing in Ingersoll's book published in 1885 are almost identical, indicating that the drawing must have been made before the date of publication.

73. This oil study, measuring 12 × 16 inches, is in the collection of the Northern Natural Gas, Joslyn Museum of Art, Omaha, Nebr.

74. *Events* 3 (January 7, 1893):2.

75. See January 8, 1893.

76. For example, see Turner's *Keelman Heaving in Coals by Night*, in *Turner*, Tate Gallery Exhibition Catalogue, 1974, opp. p. 136, plate 513.

77. Raymond Lister, *British Romantic Art*, p. 133.

Chapter 8

1. *History of Denver, with Outlines of the Earlier History of the Rocky Mountain Country*, p. 165.

2. Caleb Atwater, *A History of the State of Ohio*, p. 283, quoted in Carl Abbott, *Colorado: A History of the Centennial State*, p. 82.

3. Ibid., p. 152 for this and preceding quote.

4. Bayard Taylor, *Colorado: A Summer Trip*, p. 162; Samuel Bowles, *Our New West: Record of Travel Between the Mississippi River and the Pacific Ocean*.

5. Abbott, *Colorado*, p. 178. In a letter to his wife the explorer John Gunnison had remarked on the invigorating and healthy western climate during an expeditionary journey through the Wind River country (HM 17062, Manuscript Collection, Huntington Library, San Marino, Calif.).

6. B. Taylor, *Colorado*, pp. 161–62.

7. Quoted from Barbara S. Groseclose, *Emanuel Leutze, 1816–1868: Freedom Is the Only King*, p. 61. Emanuel Gottlieb Leutze, N.A., historical and portrait painter, was born in Schwäbisch-Gmund (Württemberg), Germany, and reared in Philadelphia. In 1840 he departed for Europe with the objective of studying under Lessing at the Düsseldorf Academy and remained for almost twenty years before returning to the United States in 1859 to paint *Westward the Course of Empire* . . . , an allegorical-historical mural for the Capitol extension. He died in Washington, D.C. on July 18, 1868. As early as April 5, 1852, Leutze had been in contact with the United States government about a commission. In a letter to the artist dated January 12, 1854, the newly appointed superintendent of the Capitol extension, Captain M. C. Meigs, introduced the subject anew by encouraging him to submit a design for a mural decoration. In his response Leutze suggested "Emigration to the West" as an appropriate subject. Although the correspondence between the two continued over the next few years, Meigs failed to make a concrete offer. In the spring of 1861, Meigs once again asked Leutze to submit a design for decorating the western staircase wall of the Capitol; the resulting design finally received the official approval by the secretary of war on July 2, 1861. For further discussion of this matter, see Charles E. Fairman, *Art and Artists of the Capitol of the United States of America*, pp. 135–38, 201–202; Groseclose, *Emanuel Leutze*, pp. 40, 57, 60; Raymond L. Stehle, "The Life and Works of Emanuel Leutze" (typescript copy) [Washington, D.C.], 1972, pp. 69, 87, 94–95, 101.

8. The contract agreement is reprinted in Fairman, *Art and Artists*, p. 202.

9. *Westward Ho!* (alternate title) "is stereochromed upon the wall of the great stairway in the House of Representatives, a modern technique in which brilliance of color is achieved by applying pigment directly to plaster and sealing it with waterglass" (Groseclose, *Emanuel Leutze*, p. 60).

10. The second, a more finished sketch and perhaps the working model, was produced later that year (Collection of the National Museum of American Art, Smithsonian Institution, Washington, D.C.). The two models are very similar in composition and size.

11. Virgil Barker, *American Painting: History and Interpretation*, pp. 466, 469.

12. Richard Hofstadter, William Miller, and Daniel Aaron, *The United States: The History of a Republic*, pp. 313–14.

13. *Rocky Mountain News*, September 5, 1861.

14. An alternate title for the watercolor is *Gold Mining, Central City*, 13¹⁵/₁₆ × 10⅜ inches, M. and M. Karolik Collection, Museum of Fine Arts, Boston. For photographic examples of "Gregory Diggings," see Terry Wm. Mangan, *Colorado on Glass: Colorado's First Half Century as Seen by the Camera*,

pp. 20–21, illus.

15. The painting, an oil on canvas measuring 18 × 48 inches, in the Diplomatic Receptions Rooms, Department of State, Washington, D.C., was included in a sale of Leutze's work held before he departed for Europe in 1863. See Edward Sintzenich, auctioneer, *Catalogue of a Valuable Collection of Oil Paintings comprising the most recent and Important Works of E. Leutze, Esq.*, May 7, 1863, no. 18.

16. Groseclose, *Emanuel Leutze*, p. 98. Charles Wimar, a German-American artist who specialized in Indian subjects, studied in Düsseldorf under the history painter Joseph Fay and then with Leutze.

17. William Holbrook Beard (1824–1900), N.A. Born on April 13, 1824, at Painesville, Ohio, he practiced as an itinerant portrait painter during the 1840s and then moved to Buffalo in 1850 and established a studio. From 1856 to 1858 he lived in Europe, painting in Rome, Switzerland, and Düsseldorf. In 1858 he returned to Buffalo and remained there two years before relocating in New York City, where he died on February 20, 1900. George C. Groce and David H. Wallace, *The New-York Historical Society's Dictionary of Artists in America, 1564–1860*, p. 38; Henry T. Tuckerman, *Book of the Artists: American Artist Life, Comprising Biographical and Critical Sketches: Preceded by an Historical Account of the Rise and Progress of Art in America*, pp. 498–501; Groseclose, *Emanuel Leutze*, p. 148. The following artists can be included in this group: Alfred E. Mathews, Henry C. Ford, James F. Gookins, Henry A. Elkins, and Worthington Whittredge. Interestingly enough, Whittredge had originally planned to join Taylor and Beard but instead, for some reason or another, joined Major General John A. Pope on a tour through Colorado and New Mexico that summer (Taylor to Beard, letter, May, 1866, Taft Papers, Kansas State Historical Society, Topeka; also see Whittredge section). According to Taylor, they missed seeing Whittredge, who at the time was in the neighborhood of Pikes Peak, but they did encounter the Chicago contingent (Gookins, Ford, and Elkins) in South Park (B. Taylor, *Colorado*, p. 146).

18. Ibid., p. 161. Beard arrived in Denver on June 22 and joined Taylor several days later in Central City. Together they also visited Colorado Gulch, Empire, Breckenridge, Buckskin Joe, Mid-

dle Park, and South Park, returning to Denver on July 9. Itinerary ascertained from Taylor's book (a collection of his letters) and Beard's letters to his wife on his western trip of 1866 (typescript copies), Taft Papers, Kansas State Historical Society, Topeka.

19. For example, in a letter to his wife dated July, 1866, Beard comments: "We have ridden very hard today and stopped early to camp. I have tried to make a sketch but was too tired, so gave it up to write you." See also B. Taylor, *Colorado*, p. 128: "'Fatigue,' as Mr. Beard truly remarks, when laying aside a half-finished sketch, 'demoralizes.'" In addition to his writing, Taylor apparently enjoyed dabbling in art. In his published letter to the artist Jervis McEntee, Kennett Square, Pa., September 17, 1866, Taylor remarks that he and Beard had the "roughest, wildest, grandest, jolliest time among the great mountains" and "didn't make a great many sketches, being too much demoralized by fatigue." In the same letter he also mentions discovering oil painting and finding it more effective than watercolors for making pictures. The few sketches that Taylor did make, which also have not come to light, were undoubtedly in the lighter medium. Bayard Taylor, *Life and Letters of Bayard Taylor*, ed. Marie Hansen-Taylor and Horace E. Scudder, 2:461.

20. Denver, July 9, 1866.

21. Written records, however, indicate that Beard did produce some paintings of western subjects. For example, the *Rocky Mountain News*, December 11, 1866, refers to the artist's summer visit to Colorado and reports that he had "painted so vividly most of . . . [their] exquisite mountain scenery." Beard's recorded paintings of scenes on the prairie were executed before his trip west with Taylor. In a letter to his wife from Denver dated June 22, 1866, he inquires about the sale of his two versions of *Deer on the Prairie*. Additionally, *On the Prairie* (a later version?) was exhibited in the *Chicago Academy of Design Fifth Annual Exhibition, for 1871* (no. 29) and listed for sale. On the other hand, his painting entitled *Grizzly in Western Landscape*, in the Collection of the Kennedy Galleries, Inc., New York City, is a purely imaginary scene, bearing no resemblance to western topography; the title was probably assigned by the former owner.

22. Beard to his wife, letter, Omaha, July 20,

1866. Sanford Gifford's comments in a letter to his father seem to shed some light on the artist's personality: "Beard is an eccentric in dress and manners, but [one] of the best hearted fellows I know." ("European Letters," Vienna [Austria], August 10, 1857, typescript copy, Archives of American Art, Smithsonian Institution.)

23. Thomas Worthington Whittredge (1820–1910), N.A., landscape painter, was born on May 22, 1820, in Springfield, Ohio. He began his art career as a portrait painter in Cincinnati around 1840, also working as a daguerreotypist for a few years. In 1849 he went abroad to study, spending five years at Düsseldorf, followed by a sketching tour of Switzerland and Italy. He eventually settled in Rome, where he lived for five years. On his return to America in 1859, the artist opened a studio in New York City. In 1866 he accompanied Major General John Pope on a tour of inspection through Colorado and New Mexico, making many sketches of the scenery in preparation for his major work *Crossing the Ford—Platte River, Colorado* (1868 and 1870, Collection of the Century Association, New York City). In 1870 he returned to Colorado with two fellow artists, J. F. Kensett and S. Gifford (*Rocky Mountain News*, August 2, 1870), and toured it again alone in the summer of 1871, sketching primarily in the vicinity of Greeley (*Greeley Tribune*, June 7, 1871). For biographical information on the artist, see Whittredge Papers, microfilm copy, Archives of American Art, Smithsonian Institution, and *The Autobiography of Worthington Whittredge, 1820–1910*, edited by John I. Baur. Recent findings have conclusively confirmed that Whittredge accompanied Pope on a tour of inspection through Colorado and New Mexico in the summer of 1866, not in 1865, as previously recorded. For a discussion of the confusion over the date of his first trip, see Robert Taft, *Artists and Illustrators of the Old West, 1850–1900*, p. 294. See also Major General John A. Pope's official report for 1866 (U.S. War Department, *Annual Report of Secy of War, 1866* [39th Cong. 2d sess. H. Exec. Doc. 1], pp. 29–30) for a confirmation of the tour dates, though no mention is made of Whittredge. Additional documentation for Whittredge's presence can be found in the *Rocky Mountain News*, June 26, 1866, reporting that Pope and his staff had arrived at their campsite three

miles east of Denver on the Platte: "We had the pleasure of meeting this morning, Mr. Whittredge, a distinguished landscape painter of the east, who accompanies General Pope on his tour through Colorado and New Mexico. He is in ecstacies [*sic*] over our mountains, and hopes to have a nearer view of them before he leaves." The party is also mentioned by the *Santa Fé Weekly Gazette* on July 26 and 28 and August 2 and 8, 1866; however, Pope's letter to General Sherman dated August 11 from Fort Union, N.Mex., negates the early departure date cited by the *Santa Fe Weekly Gazette*.

24. Both trips will be discussed in this text. The date of Kensett and Gifford's journey with Whittredge has often been misquoted as 1866; sketches by both artists inscribed with place-names and dates confirm the date 1870 (see also Ellen H. Johnson, "Kensett-Revisited," *Art Quarterly* 20 [1957]:91, n. 32, who first recognized the error and provided the proper documentation of the correct date of their trip with Whittredge).

25. Whittredge, *Autobiography*, p. 45.

26. For an example of Whittredge's Cole-inspired landscapes, see Hirschl & Adler's exhibition catalog, *Quality an Experience in Collecting*, November 12–December 7, 1974, no. 46, illus., *View of Hawks Nest*, 1847.

27. Whittredge had first tried to take lessons from the German landscape painter Andreas Achenbach, whose works he felt "were always sprightly and full of grace," but he was soon rebuffed by the older artist because of his antipathy toward formal instruction. Whittredge then developed a close friendship with the landscape and history painter Karl Lessing, with whom he made a number of sketching trips to the countryside near Düsseldorf. It was undoubtedly the latter who counseled Whittredge and criticized his work. As Groseclose has stated, "Whittredge soon learned to take advantage of the casual interrelationship among the artists in the community, the easy atmosphere so conducive to working on one's own" (*Emanuel Leutze*, p. 138). Like a number of other young American artists who were attracted to Düsseldorf, Whittredge was not enrolled in the academy's landscape classes (see "Die Schülerlisten der Königlichen Kunst-Akademie zu Düsseldorf," information contained in a letter to Trenton from the archivist of the Haupt-staatsarchiv, Düsseldorf, dated February 25, 1976). For a discussion of the role of the Düsseldorf Academy in American painting between the 1840s and the 1860s, see Donelson F. Hoopes, *The Düsseldorf Academy and the Americans*.

28. This painting is recorded in Whittredge's "Journal Accountbook" for the year 1850, on p. 126; it is illustrated in the Vose Galleries sales catalog, Fall, 1976, p. 14. For comparative study, see Lessing's painting *Die Belagerung* illustrated in Wolfgang Hütt, *Die Düsseldorfer Malerschule, 1819–1869*, p. 53, plate 23.

29. Whittredge's painting is illustrated in Anthony F. Janson, "The Western Landscapes of Worthington Whittredge," *American Art Review* 3 (November–December, 1976): 64, henceforth cited as Janson, "Worthington Whittredge." It is an oil on canvas, measuring 52½ × 66¼ inches, dated 1855. For an illustration of one of Schirmer's forest compositions, see Friedrich Schaarschmidt, *Zur Geschichte der Düsseldorfer Kunst*, p. 200.

30. See Whittredge, *Autobiography*, pp. 31, 32.

31. Quoted from Janson, "Worthington Whittredge," p. 60. The author lists only four field sketches in oil on paper from the trip of 1866. He suggests that two small oils on canvas, one in the M. and M. Karolik collection, Museum of Fine Arts, Boston, and the other in Edgar Richardson's collection, might also date from the first journey. In addition, he states that *Graves of Travellers, Fort Kearney* (1866, Cleveland Museum of Art) is the "only securely dated sketch" of that trip. Making a rough count, we find that there are approximately twelve small sketches (some extant and others recorded) known from the journey of 1866. Most of them seem to have been executed on paper and measure around 8 × 22 inches. Several that are designated oil on canvas might also be on paper but mounted on canvas; the medium and support are often incorrectly identified and mislabeled. According to William Katzenbach, "When his grandfather [Whittredge] died in 1910 he left a lot of unsigned paintings which his daughter Olive signed" [and supposedly "put her name underneath"] (quoted in a letter to Trenton from Frances Whitney, a close friend of Katzenbach, New York City, dated May 2, 1970). It is also possible that Olive might have inscribed the titles with the confusing date "1865"

on the backs of several small oil paintings that belong stylistically to the group of studies executed during his second trip west in 1870. Frances Whitney's small oil on canvas inscribed with the title *On the Platte—1865* falls within this category; the signature and the inscription are not in the artist's hand. Janson is mistaken about the single "securely dated 1866 sketch." Several others have the date as well as the place inscribed on the obverse side. A few are listed in this essay.

32. Whittredge, *Autobiography*, p. 42.

33. All three are listed as being on canvas (perhaps paper mounted on canvas?), and measure approximately 8 × 22 inches. Currently they are in the Yale Art Gallery, on loan from the Peabody Museum, Yale University, New Haven, Conn.; they were originally in O. C. Marsh's collection and were recorded for sale at the American Art Galleries, New York City, on February 26–March 3, 1900.

34. *An Encampment on the Plains*, oil on paper, mounted on canvas, 7½ × 23¼ inches, Joslyn Art Museum, Northern Natural Gas Company Collection, Omaha, Nebr., was formerly in O. C. Marsh's collection too. *On the Platte River*, oil on canvas [?], 6¼ × 20 inches, M. and M. Karolik Collection, Museum of Fine Arts, Boston; probably the painting *On the Platt* [sic] *River, Our Animals Grazing*, exhibited at the Century Association, New York, in 1904. *Long's Peak Colorado/June 18, 1866/Long's Peak /80 miles below/June 18* (inscribed on reverse side of sketch). Written in lower right on obverse side: "Long's Peak . . . ," oil on paper, mounted on canvas, 8 × 21½ inches, Joslyn Art Museum, Northern Natural Gas Company Collection, Omaha, Nebr. *Pikes Peak* (small field sketch sold by Whittredge's daughter [Katzenbach's mother] in the 1940s; information provided by William Katzenbach to our letter, New York City, September 19, 1969); mentioned also by Whittredge in his *Autobiography*, p. 46. *Mountains from the Platte River near Denver*, oil, 8½ × 23 inches, recorded in the O. C. Marsh sale of 1900, no. 91.

35. The small sketch was taken from the bluffs northwest of the present town near Fort Marcy, where their campsite was most likely located.

36. "Mr. Whittredge, from these Western sketches, has also painted an elaborate picture of Santa Fe for the Union League Club [New York

City]. It hangs in their fine-exhibition room, and has never been publicly exhibited" (*Leslie's Weekly* 27 [January 9, 1869]:267). In response to our query about the present whereabouts of this large painting, the Union League Club's Fine Arts Representative, Guy St. Clair, in a letter dated April 9, 1979, states: "We did own the painting at one time, beginning in 1868 when it was accepted by the Committee on Admissions partly in payment for Whittredge's initiation fee and partly in payment of his first year's dues. Unfortunately, like so many of our early Hudson River School paintings, it was removed from the collection at some point and its' whereabouts are not known today. It was recorded in our inventory of 1909, so we know the painting was part of the collection at that time, but there is no later mention of it."

37. At one time Marsh owned eight small field sketches from the trip of 1866 and six larger oil studies from the journey of 1870; all were sold in 1900.

38. Quoted from *Harper's Bazar* 1 (January 25, 1868):202.

39. Illustrated in Janson, "Worthington Whittredge," p. 59. The stiff rendering of the cottonwoods supports the early date of this picture, painted before he began modeling his trees in a more realistic manner after his second trip west.

40. "At that time the Indians were none too civil; the tribe abounding in the region were the Utes. We seldom saw any of them, but an Indian can hide where a white man cannot, and we had met all along our route plenty of ghastly evidences of murders, burning of ranches, and stealings innumerable" (Whittredge, *Autobiography*, p. 46).

41. In the exhibition catalog (NAD 1868 no. 353) the painting is listed as "*The Plains at the Base of the Rocky Mountains* (owner: artist)," Marie Naylor, comp., *The National Academy of Design Exhibition Record, 1861–1900*, vol. 2; recorded in Tuckerman, *Book of the Artists*, p. 517: "Among his principal landscapes, since his return [is] a large picture, lately finished [1867], called 'The Plains . . .'"; Brooklyn Art Association November 1868 no. 224 "*The Plains* . . . (owner: artist)." The same painting with the title *Rocky Mountains, from the Platte River* (Century Association) is listed in the U.S. Centennial Commission, *Official Catalogue of the U.S. Inter-*

national Exhibition, 1876, p. 31, no. 491.

42. See Whittredge, *Autobiography*, p. 64.

43. Ibid., p. 60; *Rocky Mountain News*, August 2, 1870: "Announcement of Arrivals and Departures, Per John Hughes & Co.'s Lines, from Georgetown: J. F. Kennett [*sic*], W. Whittredge, S. R. Gifford."

44. Hayden met Gifford on August 2, in Denver. On the following day he returned with the artist to the campsite at Cheyenne, Wyoming, where his men had been awaiting his arrival before setting off on their expedition through Wyoming. Just how the two men made contact is clouded with mystery; it would not be too surprising if the publisher of *Rocky Mountain News*, William Byers, who had accompanied the explorer Hayden on several of his earlier surveys through Colorado, had arranged the introduction. The information about Hayden's whereabouts comes from William Henry Jackson, *Time Exposure*, p. 188 (henceforth cited as Jackson, *Time*); and William Henry Jackson, Diary, 1870–73, Manuscript Division, New York Public Library, August 7, 1870. The photographer's account of Hayden's trip to Denver was probably overlooked by Janson ("Worthington Whittredge," p. 66), who stated that Gifford left to join Hayden when "the trio entered Wyoming by early August." None of Kensett's or Whittredge's extant field sketches are inscribed with Wyoming place-names, which again supports the idea that Gifford joined the explorer in Denver while the latter was there on business.

45. Kensett's Colorado scenes are discussed in another section in this chapter.

46. *Greeley Tribune*, July 19, 1871.

47. A reproduction of the engraved picture can be found in *Leslie's Weekly* 27 (January 9, 1869): 268; the painting is reproduced as an engraving in William Cullen Bryant, ed., *Picturesque America*, vol. 2, opp. p. 488.

48. *Greeley Tribune*, July 19, 1871.

49. M. and M. Karolik Collection, Museum of Fine Arts, Boston; reproduced in Edward H. Dwight, *Worthington Whittredge (1820–1910): A Retrospective Exhibition of an American Artist*, p. 48, no. 25.

50. The two studies are *Western Scene with Indians*, oil on canvas, 18¼ × 27¾ inches, formerly in the Collection of Victor Sparks, New York City,

and *Long's Peak, Colorado*, oil on canvas, 14½ × 22 inches, M. and M. Karolik Collection, Museum of Fine Arts, Boston, reproduced in *M. & M. Karolik Collection of American Paintings, 1815–1865*, pp. 512–13, no. 226. The large painting is also entitled *Crossing the Platte River;* it is an oil on canvas, measuring 40¾ × 60¾ inches, and was given to the White House Permanent Collection by C. R. Smith.

51. Sales of Whittredge's oils at Ortgies Art Galleries, New York City, 1887; Fifth Ave. Art Galleries, New York City, 1890; and the Century Association, New York City, 1904 and 1909, list works that have not been located: for example, *The Rocky Mts. Ranchman in search of his Cattle, Bowlder* [*sic*] *Cañon Rocky Mts*, and *Emigrants on the Plains, Evening*.

52. *On the Platte* (inscribed and dated incorrectly by Olive Whittredge), oil on canvas, 15 × 22 inches, Collection of Frances Whitney, New York City. The same oil study was exhibited in National Academy of Design Exhibition of 1894 as *On the Plains* (see Naylor, comp., *Record*, vol. 2, 57, no. 229).

53. See Whittredge, *Autobiography*, p. 21; a few of his later paintings show a similar inspiration.

54. Oil on paper, mounted on canvas, 12¼ × 20½ inches, Denver Art Museum, formerly in O. C. Marsh's collection.

55. See Janson, "Worthington Whittredge," p. 65; the artist is viewing Boulder Creek and the Flatirons from Valmont Valley, just east of the present city of Boulder.

56. Other examples of scenes along Clear Creek and views taken in the mountains are *Indian Camp on the Platte* [*Indian Camp at the Mouth of Clear Creek, below Lookout Mountain, near Golden*], oil on canvas, 14½ × 22 inches, Collection of Mr. & Mrs. Bronson Trevor, N.Y.; *The Mesas/at Golden, Colorado* [*Clear Creek below Table Mt.*], oil on paper, mounted on canvas, 11½ × 15½ inches, formerly in Marsh's collection; and *Indian Camp at Lakeside*, retitled *Indian Encampment in the Rockies* [*A view of Lookout Mountain near Golden*], oil on canvas, 15 × 23 inches, Collection of Terry DeLapp Gallery, Los Angeles, and Coe Kerr Gallery, New York City, formerly in the Eberstadt Collection, no. 373.

57. *On the Plains, Colorado* (1877), oil on canvas, 30 × 50 inches, Saint Johnsbury Athenaeum, Saint

Johnsbury, Vt.; exhibited at the National Academy of Design in the years 1880, 1884, and 1894. The view of Longs Peak was captured near present-day Platteville. An untitled small oil study dated 1870, formerly in the Collection of Victor Sparks, New York City, and *Indian Encampment-Platte River*, oil on canvas, 14½ × 21½ inches, in the Joanne and Julian Ganz Collection, Los Angeles, may have served as preliminary studies for this large picture, which was worked up in his studio at a later date.

58. Whittredge, *Autobiography*, p. 64.

59. Printed June 7, 1871.

60. John Frederick Kensett (1816–1872), N.A., landscape painter and engraver was born on March 22, 1816, in Cheshire, Conn. Kensett worked first as an engraver in the New Haven shop of his father and uncle until around 1828 and then for a while with the banknote engraver Peter Maverick in New York City, where he met the painter-engraver John Casilear. In 1840 he and his artist friends Casilear, Asher B. Durand, and Thomas Rossiter sailed for England, where they made the rounds of picture galleries. Kensett remained in Europe for seven years, traveling, studying, and sketching in England, France, Germany, Switzerland, and Italy. On returning to New York City in November, 1847, he opened a studio and established his reputation as a landscape painter. In 1849 he was elected to the National Academy. In addition to his summer excursions to the eastern lake country and coastal areas, he also made trips abroad to Wales, Scotland, and Ireland to sketch the landscape. In 1870 he traveled to Colorado with fellow artists Sanford Gifford and Worthington Whittredge. A prominent artist of his time, Kensett was also one of the founders and a trustee of The Metropolitan Museum of Art. He died in New York City on December 14, 1872. For additional information on the artist and his work, see Ellen H. Johnson, "Kensett-Revisited"; the best and most thorough treatment to date on Kensett is John K. Howat's monograph *John Frederick Kensett, 1816–1872*, henceforth cited as Howat, *Kensett*, a catalog of an exhibition organized by the American Federation of Arts, New York, 1968.

61. On December, 1872, a meeting in his memory was held at the Century Association, at which time various friends and artists paid tribute to their beloved lost friend (see Daniel Huntington et al., *Proceedings at a Meeting of the Century Association, held in Memory of John F. Kensett*).

62. The three pencil sketches that can be identified positively as Colorado scenes are in the Collection of James Kellogg, Richmond Hill, N.Y.: *Bear Cannon* [sic] *nr. Boulder*, inscribed and dated "9/24/70"; *Valmount* [sic] *Col.*, n.d. (both sketches measure approximately 6½ × 9½ inches); *Rocky Mt.* [view of mountains and a conestoga wagon with two oxen in middle distance], n.d., 10 × 14 inches. Other sketches undoubtedly existed that were possibly destroyed or are lost. For a complete listing of his oil studies, see Robert Somerville, *The Collection of Over Five Hundred Paintings and Studies by the Late John F. Kensett*, exhibition and sale catalog of the Kensett estate art collection, henceforth cited as Somerville, *Collection*. See also Bartlett Cowdrey, "The Return of John F. Kensett, 1816–1872, Painter of Pure Landscape," *Old Print Shop Portfolio* 4 (February, 1945):122–36, henceforth cited as Cowdrey, "Kensett."

63. The painting is presently unlocated; it is reproduced in the photographic album of the National Academy of Design exhibition preview (album in the Collection of James Kellogg) and is recorded in the exhibition and sale catalog: no. 283, *Valley of Valmont, Colorado*, 30 × 44 inches, oil, purchased by Mr. Parker for $1,050 (Somerville, *Collection*). To judge by the photograph, which is rather faded, the painting appears to be a finished work, bearing a close resemblance to the preliminary oil study *Snowy Range, Colorado (Foothills from the Valley of Valmount* [sic]*)*, oil on canvas, 7⅜ × 19 inches, Collection of the Denver Art Museum, and pencil sketch, *Valmount* [sic] *Col.*, James Kellogg Collection.

64. Approximately ten small oil studies of Bergen Park are recorded in the sale of 1873. Several of the titles, such as *Idaho Springs* and *In the Mountains . . .*, may also be views of the same location.

65. The painting is reproduced in the photographic album of the National Academy of Design exhibition preview but is not recorded in the exhibition and sale catalog of 1873 (Somerville, *Collection*). The title of this picture was embossed on the original frame, now destroyed (Kennedy Galleries to Trenton, letter, New York City, October 16, 1974). The size of the painting seems to indicate that it was commissioned. Certain areas of the picture appear hazy and unfinished, suggesting that the artist may have died before its completion.

66. The exact amount received from the sale varies; the figures cited here come from Howat, *Kensett*, quoted from *Aldine* 6 (1873):107.

67. An oil painting by Kensett with the assigned title *Storm, Western Colorado* (oil on canvas, 18⅛ × 28⅛ inches, Collection of the Toledo Museum of Art, Ohio, gift of Florence Scott Libbey) was also included in the National Academy of Design exhibits in 1873. This picture, which remained in the family until 1945, when it was sold through the Old Print Shop, is thought to be of Colorado (see Cowdrey, "Kensett," frontispiece; Howat, *Kensett*, illus., no. 43; and the Toledo Museum of Art, *Heritage and Horizon: American Painting, 1776–1976* [Ohio, 1976], illus., no. 12). It is our belief that the scene represented is not Colorado but the northern Italian lake country, which the artist toured in 1866–67. According to Kensett's and Whittredge's preserved oil studies, inscribed with place names, the trio did not travel farther west than Loveland Pass while they were sketching in the mountains near Denver. As we recall, the only lakes in the area they traversed are man-made ones of recent date. Furthermore, the mountain configuration and the foliage depicted bear no resemblance to those of Colorado. Although the small painting represents Kensett at his best, we cannot in all honesty include it in a study of Rocky Mountain scenery. When Trenton conferred with Kensett's grandnephew James Kellogg in 1969, he was rather vague on some of the actual titles of paintings that had remained in the family; perhaps this was one of those titles they grabbed out of thin air.

68. John William Casilear (1811–1893), N.A., engraver and landscape painter, was born in New York City, on June 25, 1811. He was apprenticed under the master engraver Peter Maverick, and later worked under the engraver-landscape painter Asher B. Durand, later becoming a prominent banknote engraver. Most of his professional career was spent in New York City and sketching in upstate New York and Vermont, except for two excursions abroad—one in 1840–43 with artists Durand, Kensett, and Thomas Rossiter and the other in 1857–58. In 1873 he traveled to Colorado, sketching from late June to mid-September ("June 23, 1873" in-

scribed on a drawing; "letters advertised," *Rocky Mountain News*, July 4, August 9, September 12, 1873). In 1851 he was elected a full academician. He died on August 17, 1893. For additional biographical information, see Groce and Wallace, *Dictionary of Artists*, p. 114; John Howard Brown, ed., *Lamb's Biographical Dictionary of the U.S.* (Boston: James H. Lamb Co., 1900), 1:590.

69. [*Near*] *Denver, Colorado* (probably from Brighton), pencil on gray-tinted paper, heightened with white, 10¼ × 19⅜ inches, M. and M. Karolik Collection, Museum of Fine Arts, Boston; former Collection of Mrs. Chas. Burr (descendant), New York City. The drawing originally was attributed to Kensett; it came with the Kensett lot but was reassigned to Casilear by Ellen Johnson. The drawing is inscribed with color notations and dated "June 23 '73."

70. Other drawings in the M. and M. Karolik Collection, Museum of Fine Arts, Boston, are as follows: *Rocky Mountains from near Denver*, pencil on gray-tinted paper, heightened with white, 8¼ × 19⅜ inches; *Boulder Canyon, Colorado*, pencil on gray-tinted paper, heightened with white, 10¾ × 14 inches; scene from the plains looking toward the front range, south of Denver (panorama with tablelands at the base of the mountains), pencil on gray-tinted paper, 10⅝ × 19¼ inches; unfinished schematic drawing, probably taken from the divide on the way to Colorado Springs, looking toward Pikes Peak; *Clear Creek Canyon*, pencil on gray-tinted paper, heightened with white, 10 × 14 inches.

71. Naylor, comp., *Record*, vol. 2, no. 313; listed "NFS" by the artist. Casilear is considered a second-generation member of the Hudson River School and was noted for his bucolic-pastoral landscapes of cabinet size. His technique reflected his engraver's training in its delicate, elegant, firm line, but his landscapes were also full of soft light. This picture exhibits some of those qualities but does not seem to hold together, perhaps because of its unusually large size.

72. Sanford Robinson Gifford (1823–80), N.A., landscape painter, was born in Greenfield, Saratoga County, N.Y., on July 10, 1823. After attending Brown University for two years (1842–44), he left for New York City to study under the drawing master John Rubens Smith, learning the rudiments of drawing, perspective, and anatomy. In 1846 he made a sketching tour through the Catskill Mountains and the Bershire Hills that led to his interest in landscape painting. In 1855 he departed on his first trip to Europe, studying and sketching there for three years; he made a second trip in 1868–69. He served briefly in the Civil War. Apart from his sketching trips in the Northeast, he traveled several times to the West, visiting Colorado and Wyoming in 1870. He died in New York City on August 24, 1880. For additional information on the artist, see Groce and Wallace, *Dictionary of Artists*, pp. 257–58; Ila Weiss, "Sanford Robinson Gifford" (Ph.D. diss., Columbia University, 1968), henceforth cited as Weiss, "Gifford"; and [Nicolai Cikovsky, Jr.], *Sanford Robinson Gifford*.

73. Whittredge, *Autobiography*, p. 60. For a listing of Gifford's Wyoming oil studies, see John F. Weir, *A Memorial Catalogue of the Paintings of Sanford Robinson Gifford, N.A. . . .* (henceforth cited as Weir, *Memorial Catalogue*), nos. 553–58 and no. 616 (*Camp Gifford*, or *Sunset on the Sweetwater* is the largest work recorded [13 × 24 inches], which indicates that it may be a finished work rather than a study like the others). According to Jackson's journal, the studies were taken between August 9 and September 12, 1870 (see Jackson, Diary, 1870).

74. Fitz Hugh Ludlow, *The Heart of the Continent*, pp. 142–43.

75. Although Hayden stated in his report of 1870 that Gifford joined them "for the purpose of studying the grand scenery of the Rocky Mountains in an artistic sense," the artist's own statement in a letter to the Rev. O. B. Frothingham dated November 6, 1874, proves otherwise. As the artist remarked, the journey was taken chiefly to increase his knowledge of his country and its people (typescript copy, Collection of Sanford Gifford, M.D., Boston, Mass.). The small painting, *Camp Gifford* or *Sunset on the Sweetwater*, may have been based on a preliminary sketch, though there is no evidence to indicate that such was the case; however, the painting was on exhibit at the National Academy of Design in 1874 (see Naylor, Comp., *Record*, vol. 2). There was also no record or evidence of any pencil sketches of Colorado or Wyoming, which is surprising, since, according to Whittredge, "he would frequently stop in his tracks to make slight sketches in pencil in a small book which he always carried in his pocket" (Whittredge, *Autobiography*, p. 59).

76. For a listing of the various impressions they took of geological landforms, see Jackson, Diary, 1870. Descriptive catalogs of Jackson's photographs from the U.S. Geological Survey exist for the years 1869 to 1875 (see Beaumont Newhall and Diana E. Edkins, *William H. Jackson* [Fort Worth, Texas: Amon Carter Museum of Western Art, 1974], p. 152).

77. Quoted from Jackson, *Time*, p. 190; see also Jackson, Diary, 1870. While they were at Red Buttes from August 23 to 25, Gifford made two small studies of this badland and canyon country, recorded in Weir, *Memorial Catalogue*: no. 557, *Near the Red Buttes, Wyoming Territory*, dated August, 1870, 8½ × 6½ inches, owned by Mrs. S. R. Gifford, currently in the Collection of Jeffrey R. Brown, North Amherst, Mass.; and no. 556 [106], *Near the Red Buttes on the Platte River, Wyoming Territory,—a Sketch of the Artist Himself*, dated August, 1870, 7 × 6 inches, owned by Richard Butler.

78. For their route, see Jackson, Diary, 1870; Hayden, *Report*, 1870; and Elliott's profiles' sections in the volume of 1872 (see chap. 6).

79. *Art Journal* 2 (1876):203; and Samuel G. W. Benjamin, *Wide Awake*, p. 307, quoted in Ila Weiss, "Gifford," p. 331. Weiss takes the opposite view from ours, believing that Gifford's venture west was chiefly for aesthetic reasons and that this objective was fully realized.

80. *Near the Red Buttes, Wyoming Territory*, recently located in the Collection of Jeffrey R. Brown; *A Sketch at the Camp on the La Bonté, Wyoming Territory*, dated August 15, 1870, 5½ × 13 inches, owned by the estate. Recorded in Weir, *Memorial Catalogue*, no. 554; former Collection of Joanne and Julian Ganz, Los Angeles, Calif.; Carl S. and Elisabeth Waldo Dentzel Collection, Northridge, Calif. (now lost). His other small extant oil study is discussed in this section.

81. This was Jackson's first trip with the Hayden survey as an official photographer, and at this point he undoubtedly wanted to impress the explorer with his ability to contribute to the scientific objective. Hayden recognized his talents and immediately thereafter appointed him permanently to the survey team as official photographer. In later years,

especially under the influence of Thomas Moran, Jackson experimented with paste-ups and retouching to achieve different pictorial possibilities and painterly effects.

82. Ralph Albert Blakelock (1847–1919), N.A., landscape painter, was born in New York City, on October 15, 1847. The son of an English homeopathist, Blakelock was a nervous and imaginative child who showed an early propensity for drawing and painting. At the insistence of his parents, who wanted him to become a physician, he entered the Free Academy of the City of New York (City College of New York) in September, 1864, but he stayed for only two years, leaving to pursue his interest in art. Primarily a self-taught artist who experimented with techniques and materials and studied from nature, Blakelock first exhibited a landscape painting at the National Academy of Design in 1867. In 1869 he left for the West on a sketching tour across Kansas, Colorado, Wyoming, Utah, Idaho, Nevada, and northern and coastal California. Sketches in the family's collection, inscribed with dates and places, help document the artist's itinerary. See also David Gebhard and Phyllis Stuurman, *The Enigma of Ralph A. Blakelock, 1847–1919* (exhibition catalog, henceforth cited as Gebhard and Stuurman, *Blakelock*); [Warren J. Adelson, David D. Blakelock, and Susielies M. Blakelock], *Ralph Albert Blakelock, 1847–1919* (exhibition catalog), henceforth cited as Adelson, D. Blakelock, and S. Blakelock, *Blakelock;* Norman A. Geske, "Ralph Albert Blakelock in the West," *American Art Review* 3 (January–February, 1976):123–35, henceforth cited as Geske, "Blakelock."

83. A number of these small sketches are in the family's collection, along with the penciled itinerary and map (the latter probably jotted down by the artist at a later date; it is a rather loose kind of recollection).

84. Collection of Herbert F. Johnson Museum, Cornell University, Ithaca, N.Y.; see Geske, "Blakelock," p. 128.

85. Oil on canvas, 48 × 92 inches, Collection of Grace Phillips Johnson Art Gallery, Phillips University, Enid, Okla.

86. A drawing, *Bear River, Corinne, Utah,* pen over light pencil, 5⅞ × 7¾ inches, M. and M. Karolik Collection, Museum of Fine Arts, Boston, suggests that he could have made this side excursion.

87. Quoted from Joshua C. Taylor, *To See Is to Think: Looking at American Art,* p. 71.

88. For example, *Clear Creek Canyon, Rocky Mts., Colorado,* pen and ink, 8 × 11 inches, reproduced in *Catalog of the Works of R. A. Blakelock, N. A. and His Daughter Marian Blakelock Exhibited at Young's Art Galleries from April 27 to May 13, 1916, by J. W. Young . . .* (Chicago: 1916), p. 33, no. 49, property of J. W. Young.

89. Collection of Mrs. David D. Blakelock, Glendale, Calif. It measures 5½ × 8½ inches and is reproduced in Adelson, D. Blakelock, and S. Blakelock, *Blakelock,* p. 28.

90. Pen and ink, 5⅝ × 8¹³⁄₁₆ inches, signed and numbered "225,"; on verso "Sketch, Rocky Mts. Colo.," 6 × 9½ inches, also numbered. M. and M. Karolik Collection, Museum of Fine Arts, Boston; former Collection of Mrs. R. A. Blakelock; reproduced in Young catalog, 1916, p. 32, no. 44.

91. *Rocky Mountains, Colorado,* pen and ink, 6 × 9½ inches, Collection of Mr. and Mrs. T. Scanlon, Catskills, N.Y. The sketch is undoubtedly the model for the large painting, which shares a similar viewpoint and compositional arrangement.

92. The first work, an oil on canvas, 34 × 60 inches, is in the Collection of the Newark Museum, Newark, N.J. The second work, an oil on canvas, 16 × 24 inches, is in the Collection of Marshall and Jamie Field, Chicago. The third work, an oil on canvas, 16 × 24 inches, is in the Collection of the Corcoran Gallery of Art, Washington, D.C.; the painting is inscribed with his arrowhead signature. The fourth work, an oil on canvas, 15½ × 22 inches, is in the Collection of Arpad Antiques, Inc., Washington, D.C. This small study came to our attention in May, 1976; Robert Vose, Jr., of Vose Galleries, Boston, has been kind enough to authenticate the picture as painted by Blakelock: "It is not the kind of thing the fakers selected" (Robert Vose, Jr. letter to Trenton, Boston, May 5, 1977).

93. Regarding the possibility of an Idaho location, Jim Davis writes: "One of our staff members, with a good knowledge of Idaho terrain, thinks the Blakelock painting could depict the area north and east of Idaho Falls, but very probably is not in this state at all. The locale is more likely to be Wyoming, perhaps around Jackson Hole" (Jim Davis, letter to Trenton, Idaho State Historical Society, Boise, May

18, 1979).

94. Narcisse Virgile Díaz de la Peña (1808–76) and Jules Dupré (1811–89). Many suggestions have been made about the possible source or sources of Blakelock's pictorial mode. The most often repeated assumption has been that his work was derived from the French Barbizon tradition. Gebhard believes that "the influence was most likely an indirect one— through other American painters such as Charles Henry Miller" or through prints and reproductions (Gebhard and Stuurman, *Blakelock,* pp. 16–17, n. 31); however, it is reasonable to assume that the artist may also have seen the actual paintings, since a number of Barbizon artists' works were represented in eastern collections by the 1880s (see Peter Bermingham, *American Art in the Barbizon Mood).*

95. Adolphe Monticelli (1824–86); see Gebhard and Stuurman, *Blakelock,* pp. 16, 18, and n. 32.

96. Samuel Colman (1832–1920) N.A., landscape painter and etcher, was born in Portland, Maine, on March 4, 1832. He was the son of Samuel Colman, Sr., a bookseller and publisher of Portland and later New York City. The artist, who studied under Asher B. Durand, was elected to the National Academy of Design as an associate in 1855 and a full academician in 1862. He made his first trip to Europe to study works of art in 1860 and his second in 1872; he was sketching in Switzerland in 1874. Colman first exhibited at the National Academy of Design at eighteen; his *Emigrant Train Crossing Medicine Bow Creek* [*Wyoming*] was exhibited there in 1870. From 1867 to 1871 he served as president of the American Society of Painters in Water Color. He died in New York City on March 26, 1920. See the following references for additional information on this artist: "Data for American Art Directory, 1912" (Florence N. Levy, Editor), contributed by the artist, Robert Taft Papers, Kansas State Historical Society, Topeka; henceforth cited as Taft, Taft Papers; Groce and Wallace, *Dictionary of Artists,* p. 141; Tuckerman, *Book of the Artists,* pp. 559–61; *M. & M. Karolik Collection of American Water Colors and Drawings, 1800–1875,* 1:117.

97. Oil on canvas, 30 × 40 inches, 1870 (retitled by Eberstadt Galleries *Indian Encampment on the Plains*), former Collection of Virginia Scott Foundation, Pasadena, Calif.; former Collection of Kennedy Galleries, Inc., New York City; exhibited at National

Academy of Design in 1871 (Naylor, comp., *Record*, vol. 2, no. 152) and at the Philadelphia Centennial, 1876, no. 463, owner William A. Hamilton; mentioned in *Aldine* 4 (June, 1871):99.

98. This first trip is documented by a small watercolor-and-pencil sketch of Council Bluffs, May 10, 1870, from one of his sketchbooks, formerly in the Collection of his daughter, Helen Colman; it is on gray-tinted paper and is heightened with white. The drawing measures 2 × 8¼ inches, taking up a third of a sheet.

99. *Emigrant Train Attacked by Indians* probably served as one of the small studies for the painting *Covered Wagons Crossing Medicine Bow Creek* [*Wyoming*], oil on canvas, 19 × 33 inches, Collection of Hall Park McCullough, North Bennington, Vt.

100. *Ships of the Western Plains* (1872), oil on canvas, 49 × 47 inches, Collection of the Union League Club, New York City.

101. See n. 98 above.

102. Watercolor on paper, 10⅛ × 14½ inches, Collection of Kennedy Galleries, Inc., New York City; reproduced in James K. Ballinger, *Beyond the Endless River...*, p. 100, plate 40.

103. Colman was an avid collector of early Chinese porcelains, pottery, and Japanese prints; his home exhibited the finest interior decorations—most designed by him.

104. Bingham's life and career have been fully covered in E. Maurice Bloch, *George Caleb Bingham: The Evolution of an Artist;* for Bloch's discussion on Bingham's Colorado landscapes, see pp. 181–83; henceforth cited as Bloch, *George Caleb Bingham. A Catalogue Raisonné* accompanies this volume; for a listing of Bingham's Colorado pictures, see pp. 138–39 and 148–49, henceforth cited as Bloch, *Catalogue Raisonné*. See Bingham's letter to Major J. S. Rollins, Kansas City, Mo., July 4, 1872, *Missouri Historical Review* 33 (1938):215.

105. Quoted from Abbott, *Colorado*, p. 174.

106. The large *Pike's Peak*, an oil on canvas measuring approximately 48 × 60 inches, was included in Bingham's estate sale, held at Findlay's Art Store, Kansas City, Mo., on March 25, 1893, and purchased by R. Saunders for $61 (see Bloch, *Catalogue Raisonné*, pp. 137–38, CL no. 353). The painting was apparently "destroyed" in 1914 at the time Findlay's liquidated its stock. We are indebted to librarian-historian Nancy E. Low, Pikes Peak Regional Library, Colorado Springs, who identified the geographical locations for Bingham's two views of Pikes Peak.

107. Oil on canvas measuring 10½ × 14¼ inches, in the Collection of William Rockhill Nelson Gallery of Art, Kansas City, Mo. See Bloch, *Catalogue Raisonné*, pp. 148–49; Fern Helen Rusk, *George Caleb Bingham: The Missouri Artist*, pp. 125–26. Rusk lists "4 Colorado landscapes owned by Mrs. J. M. Piper in 1902": the present whereabouts of these pictures is unknown. Bingham's *Colorado Mountain Landscape* has the same red underpainting found in his mature finished work—a technique the artist used to unify his picture. Traces of red underpainting can be seen in the rock formations and in the sky. This monochromatic underpainting is responsible for the greenish cast of Bingham's skies, which appear almost a turquoise color. According to former conservator James Roth, of the William Rockhill Nelson Gallery of Art, Kansas City, Mo., "The use of this red in the final concept of his pictures is most individual, and is almost a trade-mark in his work. The idea of a warm underpainting (such as red) is not new, however in my experience the intense red he used is unique" (James Roth, letter to Trenton, August 8, 1969).

108. State Historical Society of Colorado Collection; Jackson's view is slightly north of the artist's viewpoint.

109. *Rocky Mountain News*, October 15, 26, 1872; *Missouri Republican*, November 3, 1872 (a reprint of *Rocky Mountain News*, October 26, 1872).

110. *Rocky Mountain News*, October 15, 1872.

111. Bloch, *George Caleb Bingham*, p. 174; his return from Denver is mentioned in his letter to Major J. S. Rollins, Kansas City, Mo., November 20, 1878, *Missouri Historical Review* 33 (1939):217.

112. Quoted from Bloch, *George Caleb Bingham*, p. 174.

113. *Missouri Republican*, November 3, 1872.

114. The artists discussed in the following paragraph are a random selection drawn from the scores of professional and semiprofessional artists who traveled to the Rocky Mountain region in the last decades of the nineteenth century. Others include, for example, artists Edward B. Gay and Charles H. Chapin; the latter produced the grand, awe-inspiring *Lower Falls, Grand Canyon of the Yellowstone River* (1886; see *The Art Collection of the First National Bank of Chicago* [Chicago, 1974], pp. 19, 46, no. 565).

115. For biographical information on Lemuel Wiles, see Groce and Wallace, *Dictionary of Artists*, p. 686. See *Historical Wyoming* 6 (April, 1953):68–71, where several of Wiles's western views are mentioned (p. 66); and an updated exhibition catalog, *The Stowell Art Gallery and Stowell-Wiles Collection of Oil Paintings* (Perry Public Library, Perry, N.Y.). According to these biographical sources and comments made by Wiles's son Irving in a letter to Robert Taft dated November 28, 1939 (Taft, Taft Papers), the artist made two early trips to the West, one in 1872–74 and another in 1876–77. During both trips the artist made a number of oil studies of the California missions; some were later donated to the Los Angeles Natural History Museum by his son Irving Wiles. On the second trip Wiles also made oil studies of sites in Colorado and in Yellowstone Park (*New York Tribune*, September 17, 1877); the whereabouts of the Yellowstone Park views are not known to the authors. His Colorado oil studies of 1876—*Manitou Springs, Garden of the Gods*, and *Clear Creek Canyon*—are in the Kennedy Galleries, Inc., New York City. Another view of Clear Creek Canyon in the same collection dated 1905 suggests that Wiles made another trip to the West.

116. Information on the artist can be obtained from Groce and Wallace, *Dictionary of Artists*, p. 437. From pictorial evidence it appears that Meeker visited Colorado in 1870 and 1871. Three extant oils of his Colorado subjects exist: *Pike's Peak* [*near Woodland Park*] (n.d.), 15 × 35 inches, Collection of the City Art Museum of St. Louis, Mo.; *Green Lake, Colorado* (1871), 10 × 20 inches, formerly in the collection of Kennedy Galleries, Inc., New York City (see *Kennedy Quarterly* 5 [October, 1964]:21, no. 19); and *Cañon of the P[latte] river, Col. Ter.* (1870), 10 × 19¾ inches, Denver Public Library, Western History Department (based on William Chamberlain's stereopticon view of the same terrain, *South Platte Cañon* [n. d., same collection]; the location of this scene appears to be the Platte River canyon in the South Platte Valley near Pike National Forest). The whereabouts of his *On the North Platte, Col.*, recorded in the catalog *Chicago Academy*

of Design Fifth Annual Exhibition, 1871, no. 99, is unknown.

117. For biographical information on Melrose, see Groce and Wallace, *Dictionary of Artists,* p. 438; Walter T. Eickmann, *History of West New York, New Jersey,* pp. 62–63; and a compilation of miscellaneous material contained in a scrapbook at the New York Public Library. The painting, an oil on canvas measuring 24 × 42 inches, was offered for sale by the Old Print Shop, Inc., New York City, in 1972 (Kenneth Newman to Trenton, letter, February 15, 1972). Another painting, *Elk River Valley, Colorado* [?], was recorded in Eberstadt's catalog no. 146, no. 12 (1958).

118. For the artist's biography, see Groce and Wallace, *Dictionary of Artists,* p. 691.

119. For Adams's biographical data, see Robert Taft, *Artists and Illustrators of the Old West,* pp. 142–43, 334–35, nn. 44–47; henceforth cited as Taft, *Artists and Illustrators.* The oil painting, listed as *Crossing Medicine Bow Creek* [*sic*], measures 15 × 26 inches and is in the Collection of the Kennedy Galleries, Inc., New York City.

120. Biographical information about this artist can be obtained in Groce and Wallace, *Dictionary of Artists,* p. 299; and in Helen Haseltine Plowden's work on her father, *William Stanley Haseltine* (London: Frederick Muller, 1947). In a letter to his wife from Salt Lake City dated June 8, 1899, Haseltine mentioned that they had just arrived in the city that "morning after a delightful journey from Colorado Springs" (ibid., p. 187). Researcher Sandi Feldman told Trenton about the small Pikes Peak watercolor sketch and mentioned that it was in a museum somewhere near Worcester, Mass.

121. For example, fine artist-illustrators like Valentine W. Bromley (see Paul Hogarth, *Artist on Horseback*) and Mary Hallock Foote (see Rodman W. Paul, ed., *A Victorian Gentlewoman in the Far West: The Reminiscences of Mary Hallock Foote)* also traveled and sketched in the Rocky Mountain region but were primarily concerned with anecdotal subjects.

122. Quoted from *Harper's Weekly* 17:961, 994. Taft provides a full account of the pair's western journey and lists their published illustrations (Taft, *Artists and Illustrators,* pp. 94–116). Jules Tavernier was born in Paris in 1844. When he was two, his family, French Huguenots of English origin, moved to England, where he resided for five years before returning to France to live with relatives. His life and career have been carefully delineated by Robert Nichols Ewing in "Jules Tavernier (1844–1889): Painter and Illustrator" (Ph.D. diss., University of California at Los Angeles, 1978), henceforth cited as Ewing, "Jules Tavernier". A brief biographical sketch of Paul Frenzeny is provided by Taft, *Artists and Illustrators,* p. 96.

123. Felix Barrias was a member of the French Academy and a teacher at the École des Beaux-Arts. Tavernier's study was confined to the master's studio; he is not listed on the school's enrollment register.

124. Madeleine Barbin, conservateur, Bibliothèque nationale, to authors, letter, Paris, August 19, 1977.

125. Biographical information was drawn from Ewing's dissertation except where noted.

126. Taft, *Artists and Illustrators,* p. 96.

127. Ewing, "Jules Tavernier," p. 45.

128. Taft bases his information on Frenzeny's published sketches.

129. The photograph, dated 1887, is in the Collection of the Denver Public Library, Western History Department. It is possible that the artist-illustrator was traveling with Buffalo Bill Cody that year, perhaps gathering material for his illustrations for Harrington O'Reilly's book *Fifty Years on the Trail: A True Story of Western Life,* published in 1889.

130. Ewing discovered this sketch, which refutes Taft's date of September for their departure (Ewing, "Jules Tavernier," p. 56).

131. The picture, inscribed by the artist, measures 4¾ × 10 inches; it is in the Collection of the Denver Public Library, Western History Department.

132. *Boulder County News,* November 21, 1873.

133. The picture was originally owned by lecturer-author Bayard Taylor. Both Taft and Ewing have attempted to separate the part each artist played in their collaborative efforts. We believe that it is almost impossible to determine each artist's hand because of the nondistinctive character of these somewhat naïve topographical outline drawings.

134. *Rocky Mountain News,* February 17, 1874.

135. *Rocky Mountain Herald,* February 28, 1874.

136. *Rocky Mountain News,* February 28, 1874.

137. Sometime in 1972 a watercolor entitled *Clear Creek Cañon—June 8 '75,* by a "J. T. T.," was offered for sale in London. Trenton learned about this picture later from Melvin Roberts, of Denver, a collector of western art. It is possible that the initials stand for Jules (?) Tavernier; however, Clear Creek Canyon was a popular subject for artists of the nineteenth century. The measurements of the drawing (no. 429 in a catalog [?]) were recorded as "9⅞ × 6⅞ inches," according to Roberts.

138. Taft, *Artists and Illustrators,* p. 109.

139. James Farrington Gookins (1840–1904), landscape and still-life painter, illustrator, writer, and engineer, was born in Terre Haute, Ind., on December 30, 1840. In April, 1861, he enlisted in Lew Wallace's Eleventh Indiana Infantry Regiment, serving for only three months owing to illness. After his discharge he served as a volunteer aide on Wallace's staff while acting as a part-time "special artist" for *Harper's Weekly* from 1861 to 1865. In 1865 at the suggestion of his friend Bayard Taylor he studied art under James and William Beard in Cincinnati while maintaining a studio in Chicago. Gookins made two overland trips to Colorado, one in 1866 and the other in 1869. His painting *Lost Cañon Mountain* created quite a stir in the Denver paper (see *Rocky Mountain News,* March 19, 1867). In 1870 he made a trip to Europe; after spending a year traveling to London, Paris, and Vienna, Gookins enrolled at the Royal Academy in Munich, where he studied art under masters Raab Wagner and Carl von Piloty from 1871 to 1874. In 1877 he returned to Indiana and became a charter member and teacher of the Indiana School of Art, in Indianapolis. He also enrolled at Wabash College, Crawfordsville, Ind., graduating with a Master of Arts degree. From 1893 to 1904 he was involved in the planning and financing of a subway system for downtown Chicago, distinguishing himself as a civil engineer. In the later decades of his life he composed a number of oils of Colorado scenes, probably based on his early sketches, memories, and imaginings; many of these are presently in the Collection of the Sheldon Swope Art Gallery, Terre Haute, Ind. Gookins died in New York on May 23, 1904. Biographical data on the artist is drawn from several sources, primarily Shirlaw Gookins's notes on his father compiled for the Local History Division in the Vigo County Pub-

lic Library, Terre Haute, Ind. We wish to express our gratitude to local librarian-historian Betsy R. Merrill for bringing our attention to the Gookins biographical sketch. See also Taft, *Artists and Illustrators,* p. 294, n. 8.

140. See vol. 10 (October 13, 1866):644.

141. October 19, 1866.

142. Taft, *Artists and Illustrators,* p. 294, n. 6.

143. These illustrations are listed in ibid. The *Pike's Peak* representation also appears to have been drawn from Gookins's imagination.

144. The painting is mistakenly attributed by the owner to James Francis Cropsey and should be reassigned to Gookins. The oil, measuring 27 × 42 inches and dated "1870," is in the Collection of F. duPont Cornelius, Cincinnati, Ohio. The three printed, backhand-slanted initials "J. F. G." on the back of the canvas correspond closely to those inscribed on several other paintings by Gookins in the Sheldon Swope Art Gallery, Terre Haute, Ind. According to the gallery's registrar, Beth A. Bitzegaio, "Gookins' signature is very distinctive and seems to match your initial drawing [*sic*] quite well, e. g., the ornamentation of the letters, the bottom flourish on the 'F,' etc." (Bitzegaio, letter to Trenton, March 21, 1977). Gookins's trip west with Shirlaw, a Chicago resident artist, is noted in a number of biographical sources on the artist.

145. Quoted from Mary Q. Burnet, *Art and Artists of Indiana,* p. 121. Burnet's book errs on dates and facts of the artist's life and career; in the copy Trenton used at the Museum of Art, Indianapolis, corrections had been inserted by Wilbur D. Peat, who had compiled information on Indiana artists for his book *Pioneer Painters of Indiana.*

146. Quoted from *The Falls of Niagara: Being a Complete Guide to All the Points of Interest Around and in the Immediate Neighborhood of the Great Cataract, with Views Taken from Sketches by Washington Friend, Esq. and from Photographs,* p. 9. Biographical information on Washington F. Friend's early life and career has been drawn from *M. & M. Karolik Collection of American Water Colors & Drawings: 1800–1875,* Addenda, vol. 2, p. 332; this rather sketchy account of the artist was supplied by the National Gallery, Ottawa, to the researcher for the Karolik publication. Our discussion of Friend's venture into the West is based solely on pictorial evidence. Since

the artist-illustrator's watercolors are undated, it can only be assumed that he traveled through the West sometime in the late 1870s or early 1880s during the silver boom in Colorado. An inscription, possibly the artist's, on his picture *King Solomon Mountain* makes a factual reference to "the highest silver mine in the world" (North Star, discovered in 1875), near the mountain's summit. This indicates that Friend's trip to Colorado's San Juan Mountains took place during or soon after the silver strike.

147. This watercolor, measuring 19¼ × 14 inches, is in the Collection of the Kennedy Galleries, Inc., New York City. Friend also portrayed the Garden of the Gods, including a whimsical feature—the crescent-shaped moon (M. and M. Karolik Collection, Museum of Fine Arts, Boston).

148. King Solomon Mountain is in the San Juan Mountains in San Juan County near Silverton, Colo. (see Henry Gannett's *Gazetteer of Colorado* [Washington, D.C.: Government Printing Office, 1906], p. 97).

149. It appears that Friend used a commercial paper glued to a gray-finished pasteboard backing, making his drawings a uniform size. Other watercolor views of western scenery by Friend can be found in *Kennedy Quarterly* 8 (June, 1968):63–64; these include *Upper Falls of the Yellowstone District, American Fork Canyon, Utah,* and *Bridal Veil Falls, Yosemite Valley.* His *Big Horn Mountains* is reproduced in *Sotheby's Belgravia Catalogue,* November 12, 1974, p. 5, fig. 7.

150. Quoted from Taft, *Artists and Illustrators,* p. 177.

151. Biographical data on the artist's life and career are based on Taft, *Artists and Illustrators,* pp. 177–78; and letters from Graham's daughter, Elizabeth Hurlbert, to Robert Taft (Taft, Taft Papers).

152. Mentioned in Hurlbert's letter to Taft, February 28, 1949 (Taft, Taft Papers); however, Taft disagrees with her date of 1874, believing that the artist journeyed west in 1873. No conclusive evidence exists for Taft's choice of date.

153. To our knowledge none of these watercolors has come to light.

154. From Hurlbert's letter to Taft, Taft Papers.

155. Taft, *Artists and Illustrators,* p. 180.

156. Quoted from *Harper's Weekly* 31 (April 9,

1887):259, (April 23, 1887):296–97.

157. The gouache-and-wash drawing is reproduced in *Harper's Weekly* 32 (February 4, 1888): 85.

158. *Taos Pueblo* is in the Collection of the Denver Art Museum, Denver, Colo.; Jackson's photographic view is in the Collection of the Denver Public Library, Western History Department.

159. From Hurlbert's letter to Taft, Taft Papers.

160. Published by Franklin D. Richards, of Liverpool, in 1855. A brief biography of the artist can be found in Groce and Wallace, *Dictionary of Artists,* p. 505.

161. Frederick Piercy, *Route from Liverpool to Great Salt Lake Valley,* pp. 91–92.

162. The published version is opposite p. 109 in ibid.

163. Ibid., pp. 114–16.

164. Further information on the Tissandier can be found in Ulrich Thieme and Felix Becker, eds., *Allgemeines Lexikon der Bildenden Künstler von der Antike bis zur Gegenwart,* 33:218; Ballinger's catalog, *Beyond the Endless River,* p. 173. Details of his journey are drawn from his book *Six Mois aus États Unis.*

165. His portfolio of sketches and drawings is in the Collection of the Utah Museum of Fine Arts, Salt Lake City. We are grateful to Frank Sanguinetti, director of the museum, who provided us with photographs of the artist's works.

166. Tissandier, *Six Mois aux États Unis,* reproduced opp. p. 176.

167. Published in Leipzig by T. O. Wiegel.

168. We are indebted to Gerold M. Wunderlich, who generously shared Cronau's biography with us. Wunderlich is presently writing his master's thesis on his great-grandfather, "The Western Paintings, Drawings and Illustrations of Rudolf Cronau (1855–1939)." Cronau died on October 27, 1939.

169. This information was obtained from the "Regierung Düsseldorf" (file in Haupstaatsarchiv, Düsseldorf); quoted in Gerold Wunderlich's letter to Trenton, New York City, August 21, 1978. His instruction included "elementary drawing in geometry and perspective; drawing from the 'antique' as well as from the live model with some painting permitted" (Hoopes, *Düsseldorf Academy,* p. 20).

170. Quoted in Wunderlich's letter to Trenton.

171. From Cronau's *By Gone Days,* quoted in Wunderlich's letter.

172. A number of his small, on-the-spot oil studies are in the Collection of the Gilcrease Institute of American History and Art, Tulsa, Okla.

173. The drawing, dated 1882, was reproduced in *Von Wunderland zu Wunderland,* vol. 1, plate 3.

174. The drawing is reproduced in ibid., vol. 1, plate 11.

175. See ibid., vol. 1, plate 16.

176. See ibid., vol. 2, plate 24.

177. The oil, measuring 10 × 14 inches, is in the Collection of the Gilcrease Institute of American History and Art, Tulsa, Okla. It is dated 1882, whereas the reproduction is dated 1883. The artist obviously worked up this drawing after he returned to Germany.

178. The best study of Keith is found in Brother Fidelis Cornelius, *Keith: Old Master of California.*

179. Quoted in ibid., pp. 34–35.

180. From the "Little old scrap-book," K. M. [Keith Miscellany], p. 44, cited in ibid.

181. Ibid.

182. The painting is dated 1874; two distinctive tower formations pinpoint the geographical area as Devil's Slide, Weber Canyon, Utah.

183. Hill was born in Birmingham, England, on September 11, 1829. He came to America with his family in 1844. His youth was spent in Taunton, Mass. He is reported to have begun his career as a decorative painter in Taunton in 1845. He briefly resided and practiced in Philadelphia and Baltimore before moving to California in 1861. He studied art in Paris in 1866, and on his return to the States he settled in Boston until the early 1870s, when he moved back to California. He died on June 30, 1908. Although he painted floral and genre scenes, Hill was primarily noted for his grandiose landscapes of Yosemite, several of which are in the Kahn Collection in the Oakland Museum, Art Division, Calif. Biographical information from Groce and Wallace, *Dictionary of Artists,* pp. 316–17. Hill's younger brother Edward spent several years in Denver, where he established a studio (1888–90, 1902, 1904–1905) and exhibited occasionally with local artists (see, for example, Patricia Trenton, *Harvey Otis Young: The Lost Genius, 1840–1901,* pp. 77, n. 38, 87, n. 31, 11, 52, 112; henceforth cited as

Trenton, *Harvey Otis Young).* He also had studios in Nashua, N.H., in the early 1870s and later in the 1890s; Orange, Mass., in 1873–75; Salt Lake City, Utah, in 1900–1901 and later, in 1910–11; and finally in Hood River, Oreg., where he died on August 27, 1923. Edward was born in England on December 9, 1843, and later became a naturalized citizen of the United States. A notation on one of the cards in the New Hampshire Historical Society says that "Thomas and Edward Hill worked for several years for Heyward-Wakefield Furniture Company in Gardiner, Massachusetts, as decorators of furniture" (Doris F. Purvis to Trenton, letter, Concord, N.H., November 6, 1969).

184. Most of the information about Thomas Hill's Rocky Mountain journeys comes from William Dick's sources. Again, we are grateful to him for sharing his source material with us. Dick's information is based on San Francisco newspaper articles.

185. A biography of Hiram Reynolds Bloomer can be found in Trenton, *Harvey Otis Young,* p. 80, n. 38. For Marple, see below and n. 209.

186. Information about Hill's celebrated work is drawn from Taft, *Artists and Illustrators,* p. 310, n. 2. The painting now hangs in the Railroad Museum, Sacramento.

187. William Dick to Trenton, letter, San Francisco, January 10, 1980.

188. The painting, an oil (on paper? mounted on panel) measuring 20 × 13½ inches, is in the Arthur J. Phelan, Jr., Collection, Chevy Chase, Md. Hill's trip to Yellowstone is confirmed by a news article in the San Francisco *Argonaut,* August 23, 1884. According to William Dick, who bases his information on newspaper reports, the artist left late in August, 1884, for Yellowstone, where he remained for several weeks, sketching many of its scenic spots, such as the geysers and the spectacular Grand Canyon.

189. Local newspaper reports substantiate the dates of Deakin's stay in Denver. We are indebted to former historian Marjorie Arkelian, of the Oakland Museum, Art Division, who forwarded copies of these news articles on her great-uncle.

190. Edwin Deakin, landscape and still-life painter, was born in Sheffield, England, on May 21, 1838. At age twelve he became an apprentice

of decorative japanning at Wolverhampton, where the family had taken up residence. After a few years the Deakin family moved to America. In 1856, Deakin settled in Chicago and became a photographic colorist. In 1867 he resolved to leave that branch of art and strike out on his own as a painter. Finding little acceptance for his work in Chicago, Deakin left for California, where he established a studio in 1870. Once he had accumulated enough funds from the sales of his paintings, Deakin and his wife left for Europe, spending three years traveling and studying in Paris, London, Switzerland, and other art centers. In 1879 two of his pictures were accepted at the Paris Salon. Deakin returned to San Francisco in 1881, then left for Cincinnati, and finally arrived in Denver in June, 1882. Sometime before coming to the mile-high city, he had sketched outside Salt Lake City and Ogden, producing several paintings of the Wasatch Mountains. One of them caught the attention of Harrison Mills, Denver's artist-critic-teacher: "At Closson's is a lovely painting by the artist Deakin, that is a revelation of grandeur and beauty on natural scenery to all those who know nothing of the atmosphere and extent of vision of the Far West. The picture is a view of the Wahsatch Mountains, that close in with their purple sides and shining roseate, snowy peaks the valley of Salt Lake. It is so rich in color and so unusual that many might consider it the dream of an artist; but it is not so. An artist's brush could not paint any combinations so gorgeous as are the sunset lights that play around the purple peaks, and that travelers across the stretch of plain between the Wahsatch Mountains and the summits of the Sierra Nevada chain, watch with wonderment and delight" (J. Harrison Mills, "Art in Denver," *Mercury* [Denver, Colorado], July 22, 1882, from Deakin's scrapbook, Oakland Museum, Art Division, Archives, courtesy of Marjorie Arkelian). After a year in Denver the artist returned to San Francisco and reestablished himself in the art community. In 1900 he published a book of reproductions of his California mission paintings. Deakin died in Berkeley, Calif., on May 11, 1923. Biographical information on the artist has been drawn from *Evening Wisconsin,* April 23, 1883, and miscellaneous newspaper clippings in Deakin's scrapbook.

191. *Rocky Mountain News,* August 6, 1882.

192. The picture, measuring 7 × 10 inches, is in the Harmsen's Western Americana Collection, Denver, Colo.

193. This oil study, measuring 17 × 25 inches, is in the Collection of the Oakland Museum, Art Division, California; gift of Mr. and Mrs. Howard Willoughby.

194. *Inter-Ocean* (Denver) 6 (May 5, 1883):15; the same paper announces Deakin's planned departure the following month (ibid., p. 16).

195. Howard Streight, landscape painter, was born in Brown County, Ohio, on May 24, 1836. During his childhood his family resided in Virginia, Ohio, and Iowa. In 1869 he married a young Englishwoman and moved to Fort Madison, Iowa, where his friends and patrons encouraged him to pursue art as a profession. The couple lived in Palmyra, Mo., and Chicago before moving to Denver in June, 1874, owing to his failing health. Streight lived and practiced there for over a decade before moving to California, where he remained until his death in San Jose, October 21, 1912. Biographical data from *History of the City of Denver, Arapahoe County, and Colorado,* p. 574; *Denver Times,* October 22, 1912.

196. This oil on canvas, measuring 30 × 60 inches, is in the collection of Mike Ernst, Denver, Colo.; formerly in the Collection of Adolph Coors, Denver, Colo. The view is slightly different from the one of Gray's Peak reproduced in John Muir, ed., *Picturesque California: The Rocky Mountains and the Pacific Slope . . . Illustrated . . . by Eminent American Artists,* vol. 2, opp. p. 292, henceforth cited as Muir, *Picturesque California.*

197. *Rocky Mountain News,* January 14, 1877.

198. Muir, *Picturesque California.*

199. Paintings by Thomas Moran, Whittredge, and other prominent artists were reproduced as engravings in this earlier publication.

200. Thaddeus Welch, landscape painter, was born in Indiana in 1844. He and his family crossed the plains in 1847, settling on a farm in Oregon. In 1863 he went to work for a printer in Portland, where he met watercolorist Peter Tofft, who had come to have his pictures bound into a book. Welch credited his brief encounter with Tofft as the inspiration that led him to change his career. In 1865 he moved to San Francisco, performing odd jobs to make a living while painting in his spare time. A wealthy San Francisco patron gave him money to study art in Munich, where he enrolled at the Royal Academy in 1874. After four years of study and travel in Europe, Welch returned to America in 1881, working in the East for several years. In 1888–89 he traveled through Colorado and New Mexico. His dated illustration *In the Garden of the Gods,* in the Muir publication, however, indicates that he traveled through Colorado in 1885. In the winter of 1889, Welch was in Australia painting cycloramas. In 1894 the Welches moved back to San Francisco; in 1905 they moved to Santa Barbara, where they remained until his death in 1919. Biographical data on this artist can be found in Helen V. Broekhoff, *Thad Welch: Pioneer and Painter;* Marjorie Arkelian, *The Kahn Collection of Nineteenth-Century Paintings by Artists in California,* pp. 47–49, henceforth cited as Arkelian, *Kahn Collection.* The illustration is reproduced opposite p. 296 in Muir, *Picturesque California.* The painting that served as its model is also labeled *Sierra Meadow;* it appears that the artist combined two compositions—a background with Pikes Peak and a foreground with a California meadow. In a letter to Trenton, Helen Broekhoff, a former pupil of Welch's, remarks that the artist often took artistic license in working up his compositions: "Occasionally in choosing a subject for a painting Thad would remark: 'The background is fine but not the foreground—I must alter that' which must have occurred in the Pike's Peak painting" (Broekhoff, letter, Los Altos, Calif., November 7, 1971). The painting, an oil on canvas measuring 36 × 48 inches, is in the Collection of Mr. & Mrs. William D. Bowser, Oakland, Calif.

201. Muir, *Picturesque California,* reproduced in vol. 2 on p. 299.

202. The painting, an oil on canvas measuring 40 × 60 inches, was executed in Colorado in 1888.

203. See *Denver Times,* September 14, 1889.

204. Julian Rix, landscape painter, was born in Peacham, Vt., in 1850. Four years later the family moved to California and settled in San Francisco. By 1872, Rix had established himself as a painter and was a member of the local art community. From 1880 he and Tavernier shared a studio for several years. Apart from a trip to the East and Europe, Rix remained in San Francisco; he died in New York City on November 19, 1903. Biographical data drawn from [Trenton], *Colorado Collects Historic Western Art: The Nostalgia of the Vanishing West* (Denver, Colo.: Denver Art Museum, 1973); Dwight Miller, *California Landscape Painting, 1860–1885: Artists Around Keith and Hill.* The oil, measuring 12 × 19 inches, is in the Collection of Mrs. Anthony R. White, Hillsborough, Calif.; it is reproduced in Muir, *Picturesque California,* vol. 2, p. 311.

205. Meyer Straus, landscape painter, was born in Germany in 1831. He came to America in 1848 and settled in Saint Louis. In 1872 he was in Chicago, where he was listed in the city directories as painter of signboards. Owing to his failing health, Straus moved to San Francisco and established a studio in 1874, becoming a member of the Bohemian Club there. In 1886–87 he traveled to various cities throughout the West, taking up residence in Denver for a brief period. Apart from those two years the artist remained in California until his death in 1905. We are grateful to Elliot Evans, former curator of the Society of California Pioneers, San Francisco, for providing a brief biography on Straus.

206. Henry Cleenewerck (1860–90?), landscape painter, was born in Watou, Belgium. He arrived in San Francisco in 1879 and remained there until the mid-1880s. His painting *Yosemite Trail* was exhibited at the National Academy of Design in 1882. In the summer of that year he sketched in Colorado (see *Inter-Ocean* (Denver) 5 [June 3, 1882]:380). The artist's biography was obtained from Elliot Evans and *Kennedy Quarterly* 5 (May, 1965):161.

207. Jules Mersfelder, landscape painter, was born in Stockton, Calif., on August 26, 1867. He studied art at the Mark Hopkins Institute and later in Antwerp, Belgium. In 1886–87 he traveled in Europe and the American Middle West. He exhibited at the National Academy of Design and with the Society of American Artists, New York City. He died in San Francisco in 1937. Information on the artist was compiled by Lewis Ferbrache, California Historical Society, San Francisco.

208. James Everett Stuart was born in Bangor, Maine, on March 24, 1852. In 1860 he went to California with his family by way of Panama and settled in Sacramento. From 1875 to 1878 he studied art at the California School of Design under Virgil

Williams. He established his first studio in Portland, Oreg., in 1881. In 1912 he moved to San Francisco, where he also established a studio. He died in 1941. Biography drawn from Arkelian, *Kahn Collection*, pp. 44–45.

209. William Lewis Marple, landscape painter, businessman, and art dealer, was born in Philadelphia, Pa., on February 16, 1827. He and his brother Charles arrived in San Francisco in April, 1849. From 1850 to 1866 he lived in Placerville, where he was a miner and owner of an emporium. His art career began when he moved to San Francisco around 1866. He was a founding member of the San Francisco Artists' Union in 1868 and the San Francisco Art Association in 1871. In 1870 and 1872 he traveled to Europe, returning with many art objects from Paris and Munich for Gumps Art Gallery in San Francisco, with which he was associated, in the 1870s—the heyday for his art. In 1878 he left for Saint Louis, where he lived until moving to Aspen in 1880. He died there on February 23, 1910. The artist's biography was compiled by his son Charles L. Marple (courtesy of William Dick). See also Trenton, *Harvey Otis Young*, p. 129, n. 57. Marple's dates of birth and death are confirmed in his death certificate. The artist is listed in the Saint Louis city directory for 1879. Newspaper accounts corroborate that he was in the city in 1878.

210. See section on Hill in this chapter.

211. Information about Phipps's professional activities has been taken from local newspaper citations (see *Rocky Mountain News*, July 16, 1867, August 4, 1869, January 11, 1877).

212. According to a necrological notice in the *Congregational Year-Book* [*1922*], p. 482, Phipps's pastorates included Empire-Georgetown, Colo. (1866–69); Southville and Cordaville, Mass. (1870–71); East Woodstock, Conn. (1871–73); Poquonock, Conn. (1873–77); and Prospect, Conn. (1878–1906). The biographical data included here and in the following note were provided by Harold F. Worthley, secretary and archivist of the Congregational Christian Historical Society, Boston, Mass.

213. Phipps was married to Mary Elizabeth Williams in Chaplin, Conn., on October 10, 1872. They had five children. He died of a cerebral hemorrhage at Waterbury, Conn., on March 29, 1922. The biographical information included in this book

is the first published account of this amateur artist. His work is listed and illustrated in the *M. & M. Karolik Collection of American Water Colors & Drawings: 1800–1875*, but no biography is included; in fact, the wrong middle initial is given for his name.

214. Phipps's drawings range from 6 × 9 inches to 10½ × 18 inches and are variously dated from September 17, 1867, to 1869.

215. These two drawings are in the M. and M. Karolik Collection, Museum of Fine Arts, Boston. The first watercolor measures 6 × 10⁵⁄₁₆ inches (illustrated in the *M. & M. Karolik Collection of American Water Colors & Drawings: 1800–1875*, p. 262, fig. 133 [cat. 612]); the second watercolor measures 10¼ × 16 inches (ibid., p. 261 [cat. 613]); "On verso at bottom in ink: *Hold at a distance for it is done roughly/One of my first attempts.* —; at left: *Douglass M't.;* center: *Union Pass over/this low 'divide';* upper right: *Colfax;* lower right: *Foot of Columbia or Giffth M't.*" Such an initial "attempt" must date from late 1866 to early 1867, soon after Phipps took over the Empire pastorate.

216. Quoted from Alice Ford, *Edward Hicks, 1780–1849*, exhibition catalog, Abby Aldrich Rockefeller Folk Art Collection, Williamsburg, Va., 1960, p. 4.

217. Information on Point's life comes from Nicolas Point, *Wilderness Kingdom: The Journals & Paintings of Father Nicolas Point: Indian Life in the Rocky Mountains, 1840–1847*, trans. Joseph P. Donnelly, S.J., appreciation by John C. Ewers (New York: Holt, Rinehart, and Winston, 1967), henceforth cited as Point, *Wilderness Kingdom*. Nicolas Point was born in Rocroy, France ("a small village located on the left bank of the Meuse River") on April 10, 1799. Little is known of his early life except that he had almost no education and a propensity for sketching. On June 28, 1819, he offered himself to the Society of Jesus to become a missionary. On March 9, 1827, he took his vows, binding himself to the society. Amid increasing European anticlericalism, Point was finally ordained to the priesthood on March 20, 1831. Because the Jesuits were unable to work in France, Father Point was sent to Freiburg, Switzerland. After a series of peregrinations made necessary by the expulsion of the Jesuits from various European countries, Point was welcomed into the American hierarchy on De-

cember 15, 1835, taking up his first post at Saint Mary's, in Kentucky, as a teacher. After several brief appointments and unfortunate experiences, Father Point was summoned to Saint Louis and selected to assist Father De Smet in launching his new mission. On November 1, 1840, he was sent ahead to Westport, a staging area for the wagon trains, to make all necessary arrangements. The six Jesuits, along with a large caravan of travelers led by John Bidwell, left Westport on April 30, 1841. Father Point was appointed chief diarist for the Jesuits, though notes were also taken by Father De Smet and several of the settlers. On August 15, 1841, an advance guard of Flatheads joined the caravan at Fort Hall on the Snake River and escorted the party into the Bitterroot basin. Biographical notes drawn from Donnelly's introduction (see pp. 1–9). See also Pierre Jean De Smet, *Oregon Missions and Travels over the Rocky Mountains in 1845–46*, with small pen-and-ink sketches by Father Point.

218. Quoted from Ewers's appreciation, viii, in Point, *Wilderness Kingdom*.

219. See J. Goldsborough Bruff, *Gold Rush: The Journals, Drawings, and Other Papers of J. Goldsborough Bruff . . . April 2, 1849–July 20, 1851*, ed. Georgia Willis Read and Ruth Gaines, foreword by F. W. Hodge.

220. Ibid., p. xviii.

221. Ibid., p. liv.

222. Ibid., p. 110.

223. Ibid., pp. 109, 111.

224. Ibid., p. 628, n. 303.

225. The only biographical sketch of this artist appears in a printed newsletter entitled *Sugar and Spice* (November–December, 1971), p. 3, published and distributed by the Jolly Rancher Candy Co. Information for the sketch was provided by Fred Mazzulla, of Denver, Colo. The account of the artist's life presented in the article is full of factual errors. Learned's biography, presented here for the first time, is drawn mainly from primary research. Trenton, quite by accident, ran across an announcement in the *Rocky Mountain News*, November 11, 1873, which provided the first clue that Learned resided in Lawrence, Kans. Following up this lead, she wrote to the Kansas State Historical Society at Topeka, requesting any information on a Henry Learned family who had resided in Kansas in the

1870s. In its archival holdings the society found Learned's father's "Reminiscences," written from Frisco, Summit County, Colo., on January 31, 1882, to F. G. Adams, then secretary of the Kansas State Historical Society. The forty-three-page work contained enough clues to begin assembling the pieces of a puzzle: the story of Learned's life and career. Following up a lead gleaned from this paper, Trenton wrote the National Archives and Records Service in Washington, D.C., for Learned's army pension records. This document proved to contain many of the vital statistics of Learned's life: physicians' certificates, marriage certificate, discharge records, etc. Newspaper articles helped fill in the rest of the information; pictorial evidence provided the means for analyzing his development and style. Unfortunately, the whereabouts of Learned's living descendants was never discovered in several years of research.

226. Learned, Sr., "Reminiscences." Learned devotes a considerable portion of his recollections of early Kansas to the struggles between the free-state men and the proslavery group.

227. Information recorded in Learned's army pension records.

228. Information provided in a letter to Trenton from librarian L. F. Aydelotte, Kenneth Spencer Research Library, University of Kansas, Lawrence, May 6, 1970.

229. *Kansas Weekly Tribune*, June 23, 1870.

230. Ibid., December 1, 1870. Learned evidently maintained a studio in Chicago in 1871, for he is listed in the following records: *Census Directory Chicago City 1871 . . . :* "artist, res. 127 W. Washington, b. Mass." and *Chicago Academy of Design Fifth Annual Exhibition 1871:* "Learned, A. H. [*sic*] studio 17 Academy of Design."

231. October 24, 1873.

232. August 14, 1874.

233. This oil on canvas, dated 1874 and measuring 26 × 45 inches, is in the Harmsen's Western Americana Collection, Denver.

234. November 5, 1875.

235. *Boulder County News*, October 8, 1875.

236. Ibid., November 24, 1876.

237. Ibid., April 13, 1877.

238. *Colorado State Business Directory*, 1876, 1877, 1878, 1879, 1881. See also Learned's father's letter to the editors of the *Boulder County News*, December 31, 1875.

239. The following information is drawn from the *Larimer County Express, Fort Collins*, March 31, 1881.

240. *Rocky Mountain News*, December 7, 1879.

241. Quoted from *Larimer County Express, Fort Collins*, March 31, 1881. Learned's scenic design for the theater's drop curtain met the demands of the times; he was simply expressing the current trend in theater decoration, which was "a mixture of realistic detail, gathered from observation of real-life . . . and stage exaggeration" (Richard Moody, *America Takes the Stage . . .* , p. 237).

242. *Rocky Mountain News*, May 25, 1880. Earlier, in January of that year, Learned had worked at Denver's Palace Theater (which featured musical and humorous sketches), and his scenery caught the eye of a reporter: "To-night the elegant new drop curtain will be lowered after the opening sketch. This beautiful work of art has been expressly painted to order by Harry Learned" (*Rocky Mountain News*, January 28, 1880).

243. *Rocky Mountain News*, May 28, 1881.

244. See *Corbett & Ballenger's Eleventh Annual Denver City Directory for 1883.*

245. Information from Learned's certificate of marriage in the army pension records. This was the artist's second marriage; his first wife died in 1883.

246. His extant paintings for the years 1884 to 1887 are chiefly views of Robinson. On the back of his painting *Iron Mask Mine* (1886), Learned inscribes his residence as Robinson.

247. Learned, Sr., "Reminiscences," *Breckenridge Daily Journal*, June 6, 1881; February 27, 1882; March 28, 1903 (obit.).

248. Birth certificates in Learned's army pension records.

249. Some of his other versions of this subject are as follows: *Robinson Looking South* (1884, present whereabouts unknown); *Robinson, Colorado* (1884, Collection of Mr. and Mrs. Fred Schwartzberg, Denver, Colo.); *Robinson, Colorado* (1885, Collection of the State Historical Society of Colorado); *Fremont Pass from Robinson, Colo.* (1885, Collection of M. F. Iserman, Denver, Colo.); *Robinson* (winter scene, 1886, Collection of Mrs. B. F. Kitchen, Loveland, Colo.); *Robinson* (winter scene, 1886, Collec-

tion of Denver Public Library, Western History Department); and [*Robinson, Colorado, winter scene*], (1887, Collection of Harmsen's Western Americana; painting incorrectly titled *Silverton, Colorado*). The summer scenes are mostly painted on canvases measuring approximately 15 × 26 inches, whereas the winter scenes are executed on smaller canvases measuring approximately 10 × 15 inches. The one exception is the Amon Carter Museum picture, which appears to be the largest view Learned made of Robinson: "Robinson was one of the important towns of the Ten Mile District and had sprung up in 1880 when the mines began to produce. . . . In 1878 George B. Robinson, a Leadville merchant, outfitted two men whom he sent to prospect in the Ten Mile District with the understanding that he be entitled to half their findings. By the following June they had located ten mines, which became known as the Robinson Group and which George Robinson hastened to acquire. Backed by New York capitalists, he organized a company with a capital stock of $10,000,000 and sold shares. . . . These mines produced such promising ore that the 1500 inhabitants of the district believed their camp might rival Leadville which also was in its infancy.

"A stampede to the diggings began, and even with the snow ten feet deep, the town of Carbonateville was laid out in December 1878. It was followed early in 1879 by Kokomo, which from the first challenged Carbonateville for supremacy. In the spring of 1880 Ten Mile City or Robinson's Camp materialized, becoming from the first the rival of Kokomo, two miles away. George Robinson took great pride in his town and was largely responsible for its growth and development . . . .

"Then in November 1880 two unexpected events brought the new camp to the attention of the whole state. In the election Robinson was chosen Lieutenant Governor of Colorado, but before the end of the month he was dead. The tragedy was the result of a dispute over the ownership of his Smuggler mine . . . .

"In 1880 the Rio Grande railroad extended its track to Robinson and Kokomo, under the most adverse circumstances, since 'much of the grading and most of the track laying was done under a heavy fall of snow'; but on New Year's day, 1881, the first train puffed into Robinson and thereafter trains ran 'with gratifying regularity.' . . . By 1890 the high grade ores were nearly exhausted, and since then mining in the region has been spasmodic" (Muriel Sibell Wolle, *Stampede to Timberline*, pp. 66–67). The Climax Molybdenum Company purchased the site of the former town and began dumping its wastes there; it had completely covered it up with tailings by 1968.

250. For the history of Iron Mask Mine and Gilman, see ibid., p. 254.

251. *Ballenger & Richards' Nineteenth Annual Denver City Directory for 1891;* in 1893, Learned was recorded in Leadville, Colo. (ibid., 1893). It seems that Learned was traveling to other cities in Colorado to seek work as a painter of theater scenery. Many of Colorado's major towns and cities in the late nineteenth century had opera houses and active theater programs; Leadville was one of the important centers of such cultural activity in the 1880s. The rash of cultural activities in Denver in the 1890s was probably responsible for the artist's presence there in 1891 (and possibly on other occasions as well).

252. The former, an oil on canvas measuring 29½ × 17½ inches, is in the Denver Public Library, Western History Department Collection. Two versions of *Mount of the Holy Cross* "after Moran" exist. The larger of the two measures 30 × 18 inches and is in the Collection of Howard Bachman, Denver; the smaller one, measuring 14 × 10 inches, is in the Collection of Richard Kitchen, Denver.

253. April 21, 1895; Learned was buried in Riverside Cemetery on April 22, 1895. He evidently became ill in Denver and died there, for his wife is reported as arriving for the funeral from Aspen, where the family still had their home. The army pension records confirm the date of death and burial, also reporting his children as being under sixteen years of age. A few years after the artist's death his widow married Levi Burnside, of Aspen. From there the Learned family's tracks disappear, save for the father's obituary notice in the *Breckenridge Journal* on March 28, 1903.

254. Peter Tofft to Mary Avery, October 12, 1876 (Asahel Johnson, "Peter Tofft," Biography Collection, California Historical Society, San Francisco, henceforth cited as Johnson, "Peter Tofft"). See also Robert Bigart and Clarence Woodcock,

"Peter Tofft: Painter in the Wilderness," *Montana: The Magazine of Western History* 25 (Autumn, 1975): 2–15, henceforth cited as Bigart and Woodcock, "Peter Tofft."

255. Johnson, "Peter Tofft."

256. See [John Owen], *The Journals and Letters of Major John Owen: Pioneer of the Northwest, 1850–1871 . . .* , ed. Seymour Dunbar, 2:15, 16, 18. According to Owen's account, Tofft arrived at Fort Owen on December 28, 1865 (ibid., p. 15).

257. Ibid., p. 18.

258. Bigart and Woodcock, "Peter Tofft," p. 5.

259. Tofft's watercolors can be found in the M. and M. Karolik Collection, Museum of Fine Arts, Boston, Mass., and the Montana Historical Society Collection, Helena, Mont. Several of them are illustrated in Bigart and Woodcock, "Peter Tofft."

260. See ibid., pp. 9–12.

261. We are indebted to Jim Davis, former librarian of the Idaho State Historical Society, Boise, who supplied us with newspaper articles about this artist. A selection of Greene's lithographs can be found in *Amon Carter Museum of Western Art: Catalogue of the Collection, 1972,* p. 358.

262. *Tri-Weekly Statesman,* September 30, 1879; this paper was published in Boise, Idaho.

263. Ibid., September 16, 1880.

264. *Idaho Statesman,* Boise, June 12, 1978, one of a series of articles on early Idaho artists by Arthur Hart.

265. Quoted in Thomas Donaldson, "The George Catlin Indian Gallery in the U.S. National Museum," *Annual Report of the Smithsonian Institution* (July, 1885), pt. 5, p. 475.

266. See Marjorie Catlin Roehm, *The Letters of George Catlin and His Family,* pp. 55–56; Harold McCracken, *George Catlin and the Old Frontier,* pp. 130–31.

267. Catlin's letter is printed in the *Arkansas Gazette,* September 23, 1834, under the heading "Catlin, the Painter of Indians."

268. Quoted from George Catlin, *Letters and Notes on the Manners, Customs, and Condition of the North American Indians* (1844), 1:2.

269. See George Catlin, *A Descriptive Catalogue of Catlin's Indian Gallery . . .* , pp. 31–37.

270. See William L. Stone, *Narrative of the Festivities in Honor of the Completion of the Grand Erie*

Canal (New York, 1825). The two other works, a view of the West Point parade ground and one of the Hudson River, were published by Catlin in 1828 and engraved and hand-colored by J. Hill. See Catlin's portfolio, *Views of Niagara, Drawn on Stone from Nature* (1831), New York Public Library, Rare Book Division.

271. See *Faces and Places: Changing Images of 19th Century America* (New York: Hirschl & Adler Galleries, Inc., 1973), pp. [10–14].

272. George Catlin, *Catalogue of Catlin's Indian Gallery . . .* , p. 55.

273. Charles Baudelaire, "The Salon of 1846: On Some Colonists," *The Mirror of Art,* trans. Jonathan Mayne, p. 73.

274. See George Catlin, *Last Rambles Amongst the Indians of the Rocky Mountains and the Andes;* henceforth cited as Catlin, *Last Rambles.* For illustrations of the paintings that resulted from his late adventures, see George Catlin, *George Catlin: Episodes from* Life Among the Indians *and* Last Rambles, ed. Marvin C. Ross.

275. Catlin, *Last Rambles,* p. 151.

276. Ibid., p. 160.

277. Ibid., p. 161.

278. George Catlin, *The Lifted and Subsided Rocks of America . . .* , p. [v].

279. Catlin, *Last Rambles,* p. 169.

280. Ibid., p. 170.

281. We are grateful to James Davis, former librarian of the Idaho Historical Society, Boise, for identifying the site of Catlin's view.

282. Quoted from George Catlin, *Letters and Notes,* (1841), 1:162. See also Alfred Runte, "Origins and Paradox of the American Experience," *Journal of Forest History,* April, 1977, p. 66; Hiram Martin Chittenden, *The Yellowstone National Park,* p. 87.

283. See Fritiof Fryxell, ed. "Thomas Moran's Journey to the Tetons in 1879," *Augustana Historical Society Publications,* no. 2, (1932), 3–12, henceforth cited as Fryxell, "Thomas Moran's Journey." The journal is in the Grand Teton National Park Collection.

284. See *Kennedy Quarterly* 5 (May, 1965):171.

285. For reproductions, see ibid., pp. 170, 188–89.

286. See Thurman Wilkins, *Thomas Moran: Art-*

ist of the Mountains, p. 121.

287. In the Collection of the Grand Teton National Park.

288. Fryxell, "Thomas Moran's Journey," p. 4.

289. Ibid., p. 7.

290. Ibid., p. 9.

291. Apart from this watercolor, the Roswell Museum owns a sizable collection of sketches and watercolors by Peter Moran, most of them of southwestern subject matter. For other watercolors and pencil sketches by Peter Moran, see *Amon Carter Museum of Western Art: Catalogue of the Collection, 1972*, pp. 58-66. There is a possibility that the Moran brothers were joined by a friend, the amateur artist Frederick William Billing, of Salt Lake City, whose dated and title-inscribed pencil sketch of the same view indicates that he may have joined this expedition (see Mackenzie Gordon, "The Gentlemanly Painter: A Rediscovery Showing of Late 19th Century Paintings by Frederick William Billing," *Palo Alto Medical Clinic* [September–October, 1966]). We wish to express our gratitude to Richard Love, of R. and H. Love Galleries, Inc., Chicago, who brought this artist and his work to our attention.

292. Quoted from *Kennedy Quarterly* 5 (May, 1965): 179. For Peter Moran's special report on the Shoshoni and Arapaho tribes accompanied by three illustrations, see *Report on Indians Taxed and Not Taxed in the United States . . . Eleventh Census, 1890*, 10:629-34. For a general account of the five artists—Julian Scott, Gilbert Gaul, Walter Shirlaw, Henry R. Poore, and Peter Moran—who were special agents for this census task, see Taft, *Artists and Illustrators*, pp. 215-16, 365-66.

293. See *Kennedy Quarterly* 5 (May, 1965):188-89.

294. All biographical information on this artist comes from William J. Schaldach, *Carl Rungius: Big Game Painter*.

295. Rungius, quoted in ibid., pp. 33-34.

296. Unfortunately for this book, most of Rungius's Rocky Mountain work dates from the twentieth century.

Chapter 9

1. Quoted from Bowles's guide for travel to and through western America, *The Pacific Railroad—Open, How to Go: What to See*, pp. 27-28.

2. See James L. Haseltine, *100 Years of Utah Painting*, p. 9; henceforth cited as Haseltine, *100 Years*.

3. Kate B. Carter, *Heart Throbs of the West*, 2:1; henceforth cited as Carter, *Heart Throbs of the West*.

4. December 9, 1894.

5. See LeRoy R. Hafen and Ann W. Hafen, *Handcarts to Zion: The Story of a Unique Western Migration, 1856-1860 . . .* , pp. 159, 304. Christensen was born in Copenhagen on November 28, 1831, and was orphaned at a young age. His schooling at the Royal Academy of the Arts was funded by several of his sponsors. At twenty-one he joined the Church of Jesus Christ of Latter-Day Saints and became a Mormon missionary. In 1857, a year after emigrating to America, he and his wife walked from Iowa to Utah with their pushcarts. In Utah, Christensen established himself as a farmer, indulging in his art as a pastime. During the winter months he hauled his panorama through Utah, Idaho, and Wyoming. This *Panorama of Mormon Art*, composed finally of twenty-two scenes from dramatic episodes of early Mormon history, was painted over a period of twenty-two years, from 1869 to 1890. Each piece of heavy linen measured 8 × 10 feet (probably vertical on the long dimension). Stitched together, the twenty-two pieces formed one long scroll of approximately 175 feet. Hauling his panorama by wagon, he stopped at towns along the way and set up shows accompanied by lectures. Whether this effort was commissioned by the church or was simply a money-maker for the artist is not known. In 1978 twenty-two of Christensen's scenes, separately mounted, were shown at the Pioneer Art Exhibit, held at the Mormon Visitors Center in Salt Lake City (some sources record that twenty-three scenes were shown). Information about this artist's life and career comes from the pamphlet published at the time of the exhibit; see "Paintings by C. C. A. Christensen," Mormon Visitor Center, Independence, Mo., 1978.

6. See Heber G. Richards, "George M. Ottinger, Pioneer Artist of Utah: A Brief of his Personal Journal," *Western Humanities Review* 3 (July, 1949), 209-18; henceforth cited as Richards, "George M. Ottinger."

7. Alice M. Horne, *Devotees and Their Shrines: A Handbook of Utah Art*, p. 22; henceforth cited as Horne, *Devotees and Their Shrines*.

8. Richards, "George M. Ottinger," p. 212.

9. The New York American Art-Union was a commercial venture that centered its program around drawing by lots: "For a moderate membership fee every subscriber got a chance to win one among a number of original oils purchased by the Art-Union for that purpose. . . . Not only did a few each year receive valuable prizes in this way but everybody received excellent engraved reproductions of paintings. . . . The American Art-Union drew its memberships from all over the country, but this did not prevent the establishment of other Unions, patterned after it and regionally successful" (Virgil Barker, *American Painting: History and Interpretation*, p. 460). It is not known for certain whether Utah's union functioned in a similar way.

10. Richards, "George M. Ottinger," p. 214.

11. "The Art Exhibition," *Salt Lake City Herald*, December 2, 1894.

12. Horne, *Devotees and their Shrines*, p. 64.

13. See Carter, *Heart Throbs of the West*, 2:6-7.

14. Richards, "George M. Ottinger."

15. Horne, *Devotees and Their Shrines*, p. 29.

16. "Art and Artists," *Salt Lake City Herald*, January 6, 1895.

17. Biographical information on Culmer comes from Leonard J. Arrington, "H. L. A. Culmer—First President of Salt Lake Rotary" (paper presented to the Salt Lake Rotary Club, July 22, 1975). A copy of this paper is in the Special Collections Department, Marriott Library, University of Utah.

18. For information on Lambourne, see below.

19. The present whereabouts of Culmer's *Shoshone Falls* is unknown to us. It was originally owned by Colonel and Mrs. E. F. Holmes, of Salt Lake City, Utah.

20. H. L. A. Culmer, "Mountain Art," *Western Monthly* 24 (1894).

21. Alfred Lambourne was born "in England on River Lambourne near Donnington Castle, Feb. 2, 1850. Encouraged by parents from age six to be painter. Came to America at early age, lived in St.

Louis, 1860–66. Migrated to Salt Lake City, 1866, driving father's oxteam, walking good part of way, sketching en route. Painted scenery for Salt Lake Theatre, receiving technical instructions from J. Guido Methua, George Tirrell, Henry D. Tryon, though essentially self-taught as artist. Traveled, sketched, painted in most Western States. With Reuben Kirkham in 1870s painted large panorama of American scenes, traveled with it from Cache Co. to St. George, lecturing. Lived as recluse on Gunnison Island, Great Salt Lake, 14 months, homesteading. Journal lists 610 works from 1869 to 1899. Painted five works for Salt Lake Temple, 1892–93. In midcareer, turned more and more to poetry and prose, writing 14 books, some of which he illustrated with black-and-white tempera drawings. Died in Salt Lake City, June 6, 1926" (Haseltine, *100 Years*, p. 42). Examples of Lambourne's work are illustrated in Horne, *Devotees and Their Shrines*, pp. 36–37. His pictures can also be found in the Utah Museum of Fine Arts, University of Utah, Salt Lake City.

22. "Art and Artists," *Salt Lake City Herald*, December 16, 1894.

23. Information about New Mexico's art communities can be found in [Patricia Trenton], *Picturesque Images from Taos and Santa Fe* (an exhibition catalog).

24. Although Lewis and Clark traveled across present-day Idaho, Preuss, with Frémont's 1843–44 survey, was probably the first to record its scenic wonders (see chap. 1).

25. Arthur Hart, "Idaho Yesterdays," *Idaho Statesman*, May 29, 1978. Hart, former director of the Idaho Historical Society, wrote a series of newspaper articles on pioneer artists in Idaho.

26. We are grateful to Jim Davis, former librarian, Idaho State Historical Society, Boise, for providing material on Idaho art. Information on art in Idaho in the nineteenth century comes from Davis and the research of Merle Well, director of the library and archives for the Idaho State Historical Society.

27. Arthur Hart, "Idaho Yesterdays," *Idaho Statesman*, June 5, 1978. A brief biographical sketch of Mrs. Jonas Brown is included in Hart's article.

28. T. A. Larson, *Wyoming*, p. 50; most of the historical background comes from this source.

29. See Maurice Grant Barr, "Art Trails of Wyoming," in *One Hundred Years of Artist Activity in Wyoming, 1837–1937*.

30. David Lavender, *The American Heritage History of the Great West*, ed. Alvin M. Josephy, Jr., p. 320.

31. Granville Stuart, *Forty Years on the Frontier*, ed. Paul C. Phillips, 1:19. This autobiographical narrative was published posthumously.

32. Ibid., 1:14, 36.

33. Granville Stuart, *Granville Stuart: Diary & Sketchbook of a Journey to "America" in 1866, & Return Trip up the Missouri River to Fort Benton, Montana* (reprinted from *Virginia City Montana Post*, January, 1867), introduction by Carl Shaefer Dentzel, biographical sketch by Glen Dawson (Los Angeles: Dawson's Book Shop, 1963). Examples of Stuart's work can be found in his published narrative *Forty Years on the Frontier* and in the *Diary and Sketchbook of a Journey to "America."* His comments about Ophir (see below) come from the *Diary and Sketchbook . . .* , p. 50.

34. Stuart provided descriptions for Russell's illustrations in the second edition; see Karl Yost and Frederic G. Renner, comps., *A Bibliography of the Published Works of Charles M. Russell*, p. 3, 1a.

35. Frank Hall, *History of the State of Colorado . . .* , 4:30. The history of the evolution of Colorado as a scenic mecca for nineteenth-century artists is drawn from Patricia Trenton, *Harvey Otis Young: The Lost Genius, 1840–1901*, pp. 6–15, nn. 17–47; henceforth cited as Trenton, *Harvey Otis Young*.

36. John Harrison Mills (1842–1916), painter, sculptor, engraver, illustrator, and writer, was born on a farm near Buffalo, N.Y. During the years of his Colorado residence he engaged in painting portraits, landscapes, and figure studies, as well as illustrating and writing for magazines. In 1881 he served as president for the Colorado Academy of Fine Arts, and in 1882 he managed the first art exhibition in Colorado held under the auspices of the Mining and Industrial Exposition. In 1885 after his wife's health improved, he returned to New York, where he was involved in art activities until his death in 1916 (Trenton, *Harvey Otis Young*, p. 75, n. 18).

37. Alfred E. Mathews (1831–74), topographical artist, landscape and panorama painter, and lithographer, was born in Bristol, England. He came to the United States with his family at the age of two and grew up in Rochester, Ohio. Before the Civil War he traveled in northern and southern states as a bookseller and artist. In 1861 he enlisted in the Union Army, producing many battle sketches during his service. Immediately after the war he went west, made his headquarters at Denver, and devoted himself for a number of years to producing lithographs of western topography. Many of these were issued separately, others in his now-scarce books: *Pencil Sketches of Colorado, Its Cities, Principal Towns and Mountain Scenery* (1866), *Pencil Sketches of Montana* (New York, 1868), and *Gems of Rocky Mountain Scenery, Containing Views Along and near the Union Pacific Railroad* (New York, 1869). After acquiring an extensive tract of land near Canon City, Colo., he published five lithographs of views around Canon City, one of which was a panorama of Pikes Peak, to promote colonization in that area. See *Canyon City, Colorado, and Its Surroundings* (Trenton, *Harvey Otis Young*, p. 75, n. 19).

38. Esther Yates Frazier (1830–1903), who was born in Mass. and died in Denver, was a self-taught artist. Her naïve interpretation, *Arapahoe Cheyenne Encampment/Denver/1861* (Collection of the State Historical Society of Colorado), is the only known extant example of her artistic activity. Little else is known of her life or career. Mary E. Achey (active in Colorado, 1860–80) was a self-taught artist who lived in Central City during her years in Colorado. Later she moved farther west when she was engaged to paint murals for the home of an early settler near Aberdeen, Wash. *Nevadaville/Colorado/1860* typifies Achey's untutored approach to her subject (Collection of the State Historical Society of Colorado). See *Central City Register*, October 23, 1868, November 28, 1868; see also *Rocky Mountain News*, November 17, 1869.

39. *Tabor Grand Opera House*, p. 34.

40. *Denver Tribune*, February 12, 1882.

41. *Tabor Grand Opera House*, p. 34.

42. *Rocky Mountain News*, August 1, 1882, mentions local and eastern artists represented in the Art Exposition of 1882; the issue of July 27, 1883, reviews the pictures exhibited in the Art Exposition of 1883.

43. Edgar C. McMechen ("Art, Drama and Music," *Colorado and Its People*, ed. LeRoy R. Hafen, 2:426) mentions that "the Kit Kat got lost some-

where in the jungle, so the Denver Artist's [*sic*] Club was organized in 1886." Henceforth cited as McMechen, "Art, Drama and Music."

44. Articles of Incorporation and Constitution of the Denver Art Club (Collection of the State Historical Society of Colorado). John Dare Howland (1843–1914), the son of a riverboat captain, was born in Ohio. He left home at age fourteen in search of Indian country. In Saint Louis, Howland met the veteran fur trader Robert Campbell, who arranged for the boy to go up the Missouri River with the American Fur Company. His knowledge of the different tribes brought him an appointment with the Indian Peace Commission, 1867–69. During the Civil War he earned money for study in Europe by serving as sketch artist and reporter for *Harper's Weekly* and other publications. Eventually, he settled in Denver, where he founded the Denver Art Club in 1886. His talent was devoted largely to telling the story of the West, as evidenced by his skillful delineations of wildlife of the region.

45. "The Club lasted only about a year, the room occupied being taken away because of very violent disagreements between some of the official members" (John R. Henderson to Kate Howland Charles, letter [Denver], n.d. [typewritten copy], Collection of the State Historical Society of Colorado). For a review of the Denver Art Club's Spring Exhibition, see *Rocky Mountain News*, June 1, 1887.

46. *Denver Times*, September 14, 1889.

47. *Denver Republican*, January 11, 1891.

48. Register, 1879, Cliff House, Manitou Springs, Colo. (Collection of Proctor Nichols, Colorado Springs), lists board and balance for Young on August 6.

49. *Catalogue of the First Annual Exhibition of Denver Paint and Clay Club*, December 21, 1889–January 2, 1890, in Bromwell Scrapbook (Collection of the State Historical Society of Colorado); *Denver Republican*, November 24, 1889, review of pictures to be exhibited.

50. See Artists' Club Minute Book [1893–95], December 16, 1893, p. 7 (Collection of the State Historical Society of Colorado).

51. Ibid., February 21, 1894, p. 15, February 13, 1895, p. 50.

52. McMechen, "Art, Drama, and Music," p. 430.

53. Artists' Club Minute Book, December 16, 1893, p. 3.

54. *The Denver Art Association: Its Past and Future* (Denver, 1919); see *Denver Times*, January 6, 1917.

55. Archival Records, Collection of the Denver Art Museum.

56. See Trenton, *Harvey Otis Young*, p. 77, n. 3; all information on this artist comes from this source.

57. For Young's exhibition record, see ibid., pp. 103–107.

58. *Colorado Springs Gazette*, May 19, 1901.

59. *Denver Post*, May 14, 1901.

60. Talcott Williams, "The Philadelphia Watercolor Exhibition," *International Studio 22* (June, 1904): ccxxx.

61. *Denver Times*, September 14, 1889; *Denver Republican*, January 11, 1891.

62. Body coloring is a painting method that "employs comparatively heavy layers of opaque paint or pigment, and obtains its white and pale shades by the admixture of white pigments" (Ralph Mayer, *The Artist's Handbook of Materials and Techniques*, pp. 32–33). Young's work in mixed media can be divided into three phases: early (1889–92), transitional (1893–96), and mature (1897–1901).

63. Information on Adams's life and career comes from his own reminiscences "Go West, Young Man" (typescript copy in Dines Collection, Denver, Colo.). We are grateful to the Dines Collection for sharing Adams's reminiscences with us.

64. Information on Helen Chain can be found in the Manuscript Department of the State Historical Society of Colorado and in local newspaper accounts; see "Death of Mr. and Mrs. J. A. Chain," *Coloradan* 1 (November 1, 1892):7–8. No documentation exists to substantiate Chain's visit to Inness's studio; to judge by her work, it seems unlikely that she studied under that American master of tonalism.

65. Bagley's etchings were reproduced in a number of promotional pamphlets (Collection of the Denver Public Library, Western History Department).

66. Recorded in a biographical sketch of the artist by Ruth Brill Adams, of the *Pasadena Star News* (typescript copy in Collection of the State Historical Society of Colorado); Adams's work was also exhibited at the National Academy of Design,

as well as at other shows.

67. Adams quoted in *The Western Club Woman/Denver, Colorado,* December, 1898 (Bromwell Scrapbook, the Collection of the State Historical Society of Colorado).

68. Biographical sketches and reproductions of the work of these artists can be found in Robert L. Shalkop, *A Show of Color: 100 Years of Painting in the Pike's Peak Region* (exhibition catalog in honor of the centennial of Colorado Springs); henceforth cited as Shalkop, *A Show of Color.*

69. See *Colorado Springs Gazette*, November 27, 1882.

70. Ibid., December 16, 1885.

71. Ibid., June 17, 1885.

72. Ibid., October 2, 6, 13, 14, 17, 1888.

73. Ibid., October 27, 1888.

74. For Anne Parrish, see George C. Groce and David H. Wallace, *The New-York Historical Society's Dictionary of Artists in America, 1564–1860,* p. 489. Thomas Parrish came to Colorado Springs with his first wife in 1872. At the beginning of his Colorado residence he was involved in mining matters with his first wife's family. After his wife died, he went back east and enrolled in the Philadelphia Academy of Fine Arts, where he met his second wife, who was also an art student at the time.

75. *Colorado Springs Gazette*, November 29, 1900.

76. See Shalkop, *A Show of Color*, p. 5.

77. Paris's biography is drawn from a number of sources, such as replies to Trenton's letters of queries; Paris's letters to William Holmes in the Collection of the National Museum of American Art Library, Smithsonian Institution; newspaper accounts; the artist's death certificate; and other, miscellaneous material. Pictorial evidence has aided in the reconstruction of the artist's itinerary. Cross referencing of sources verified some of the information previously reported in other accounts of the artist; Trenton found a number of generalizations that could not be proved.

78. Information provided by National Museum of American Art Library, Smithsonian Institution, and the *Dictionary of American Biography.*

79. "Biographical Sketch of Mr. Walter Paris," *Events* 3 (March 18, 1893):6. See also letters to Holmes written from England in 1881 and 1882 (National Museum of American Art Library, Smith-

sonian Institution).

80. Letter to Trenton from M. G. Wright, deputy librarian, Royal Military Academy, Sandhurst, England, October 13, 1976.

81. Denver city directory, 1891, 1893; Colorado Springs city directory, 1892.

82. This date is recorded on his death certificate.

83. William Henry Jackson, *The Diaries of . . . ,* ed. LeRoy R. Hafen and Ann W. Hafen, p. 332.

84. Letter in the National Museum of American Art Library, Smithsonian Institution.

85. Paris was in New York City in 1877-79; he was one of the founders of the Tile Club there. This information comes from his letters to Holmes (National Museum of American Art Library, Smithsonian Institution).

86. *Events* 3 (April 1, 1893):6; other newspaper accounts confirm this report. We have been unable to locate such an item.

87. Jackson Thode to Trenton, Denver, Colo., December 21, 1979.

Chapter 10

1. Van Deren Coke, *Taos and Santa Fe: The Artist's Environment, 1882-1942,* p. 10.

2. John C. Ewers, *Artists of the Old West,* pp. 220-34. The biographical data on Russell come from this source.

3. Toole quoted in ibid., p. 234.

4. Ewers discusses the various anachronisms in this picture (ibid., p. 233).

5. Biographical information on the artist has been obtained from Denny Carter, *Henry Farny;* Robert Taft, *Artists and Illustrators of the Old West, 1850-1900.*

6. Farny quoted in Carter, *Henry Farny,* p. 16.

7. Eugene V. Smalley, "The Upper Missouri and the Great Falls," *Century Magazine* 35 (January, 1888):408.

8. Ibid., p. 414.

9. The artist's biography and quotations from his writings are drawn from Peter Hassrick, *Frederic Remington.*

10. *Harper's Weekly,* January 12, 1895.

11. Hassrick, *Frederic Remington.*

12. Remington to his wife, Missie [Eva], letter, November 18, 1908, in Taft Papers, Kansas State Historical Society, Topeka.

13. Edwin Wildman, "Frederic Remington, the Man," *Outing* 41 (March, 1903):715-16.

14. Perriton Maxwell, "Frederic Remington—Most Typical of American Artists," *Pearson's Magazine* 18 (October, 1907):407.

15. Giles Edgerton, "Frederic Remington, Painter and Sculptor: A Pioneer in Distinctive American Art," *Craftsman* 15 (March, 1909):669.

16. The artist's biography is drawn from Richard J. Boyle, *John Twachtman.*

17. Ibid., p. 17.

18. For a listing of his Yellowstone works, see John Douglas Hale, "The Life and Creative Development of John H. Twachtman," (Ph.D. diss., Ohio State University, 1957) 2:514-16, 580-82. Of the twenty-two Yellowstone paintings listed here, only four studies, nos. 773-76, appear to have ended in Wadsworth's possession.

19. Boyle, *John Twachtman,* p. 60. Other students of Twachtman have discussed the import of such vistas on the artist's expression, not necessarily in agreement with Boyle's conclusions. The critic Duncan Phillips ("Twachtman—An Appreciation," *International Studio* 66, no. 264 [February, 1919]:cvi) believed that the grandeur of the Yellowstone Falls inspired him: "The man was thoroughly American and in his paintings we find at times a typical New England reserve, only to discover later that his brush was imbued with the candour and elemental directness of the Far West. When he painted the splendour of gorgeous canyons and mighty cataracts, the greatness of nature seemed to pass into him and speak through him."

20. One other American Impressionist, Willard Metcalf, visited the Rockies during this period, but his trip to the Southwest (New Mexico and Arizona) between 1881 and 1883 occurred before he had really absorbed any Impressionist lessons. A few illustrative sketches touch on subject matter within the Rockies, but no finished paintings seem to have resulted. We are grateful to Metcalf's biographer, Elizabeth G. de Veer, and her colleague Francis Murphy for searching their records in our behalf for references to any finished Rocky Mountain paintings.

BIBLIOGRAPHY

NOTE: Contemporary exhibition catalogs, newspaper references, state and city directories, public records, and correspondence from families, collectors, scholars, and institutions are cited only in the endnotes as appropriate.

MANUSCRIPTS

Adams, Charles P. "Go West, Young Man." (Autobiography, typescript copy. Dines Collection, Denver, Colo.

Arrington, Leonard J. "H. L. A. Culmer—First President of Salt Lake Rotary," Paper presented to the Salt Lake Rotary Club on July 22, 1975. Typescript copy. Special Collections Department, Marriott Library, University of Utah.

Artists' Club of Denver. Records and Correspondence, 1893-1917. State Historical Society of Colorado, Denver.

Beard, William H. Letters to his wife on his western trip of 1866. Typescript copy. Robert Taft Papers, Kansas State Historical Society, Topeka.

Bierstadt, Albert. Scrapbook of newspaper clippings. Mrs. Orville DeForest Edwards, Dobbs Ferry, N. Y.

Birch, William. "Memoirs." Manuscript Division, Pennsylvania Historical Society, Philadelphia, Pa.

Carvalho, Solomon N. Letters. American Jewish Archives, Cincinnati, Ohio.

Colman, Samuel. Sketchbooks. Helen Colman, New York City.

Columbian Society of Artists. Charter and By-Laws. In *Catalogues of the Academy of the Fine Arts, 1810-*

1826. Bound volume of catalogues, reviews, and miscellany. Archives, Pennsylvania Academy of the Fine Arts, Philadelphia, Pa.

Cronau, Rudolf. "Autobiography"; sketches and drawings. Rudolf Wunderlich Family Collection, New York City.

Deakin, Edwin. Scrapbook of newspaper clippings. Art Division, Archives, Oakland Museum, Oakland, Calif.

Denver Art Club. Records and Correspondence, 1886-87. State Historical Society of Colorado, Denver.

Elkins, Arthur H. Memorabilia: sketches, letters, newspaper clippings, and photographs. Family collection.

Elliott, Henry Wood. Sketchbooks: "Part I, Sketches Made by the Artist of the U.S. Geological Survey of Colorado & New Mexico, 1869." U.S. Geological Survey Library, Reston, Va. Access. no. Historic 321 a-k.

——. Sketches. National Archives and Records Service, Washington, D.C. Access. no. 57-HAC-5, 8, 36.

Gifford, Sanford Robinson. Papers. Correspondence 1855-69. Microfilm of typescript copy. Archives of American Art, Smithsonian Institution, Washington, D.C.

Gookins, James Farrington. Biographical notes compiled by Shirlaw Gookins. Local History Division, Vigo County Public Library, Terre Haute, Ind.

Graham, Charles. Letters from Graham's daughter, Elizabeth Hurlbert, to Taft. Robert Taft Papers, Kansas State Historical Society, Topeka.

Gunnison, John. Letters. Manuscript Department, Huntington Library, San Marino, Calif.

Holmes, William Henry. "Random Records of a Lifetime Devoted to Science and Art." Vols. 1-16 in National Museum of American Art Library, Smithsonian Institution, Washington, D.C.; vols. 17-20 in possession of granddaughter Mrs. Laughlin Campbell (as of 1974), microfilm copy in U.S. Geological Survey Library, Reston, Va.

——. "Reminiscences of Prof. W. H. Holmes (Colorado). Narrative of Explorations by W. H. Holmes, 1875." Manuscript Division, State Historical Society of Colorado, Denver.

——. Sketchbooks in U.S. Geological Survey Denver Center; U.S. Geological Survey Library, Reston, Va., and National Archives and Records Service, Washington, D.C.

Hudson, J. Journal, April-June, 1850. Dale L. Morgan Collection. Typescript copy. Bancroft Library, University of California, Berkeley.

Jackson, William Henry. Diary, 1870-73. Manuscript Division, New York Public Library, New York City.

Kensett, John F. Journal, 2 vols. June 1, 1840-May 31, 1841; England and France. Frick Art Reference Library, New York City.

——. Papers. Microfilm. Archives of American Art, Smithsonian Institution, Washington, D.C.

——. Sketches, diaries, notes, letters, passports, photographs, record of sales, etc. James Kellogg Collection, Richmond Hill, N.Y.

Kern, Benjamin. "Diary, 1848-1849." Huntington Library, Manuscript Department, San Marino, Calif.

Kern, Edward. "Journal of a Trip to California, 1845-46-47." Sketchbook (1850). Loose sketches, drawings, scrapbook of pasted drawings and sketches, and several sketchbooks, primarily southwestern material. Private collection.

———, and Richard Kern. Fort Sutter Papers, Manuscript Department, Huntington Library, San Marino, Calif.

Kern, Richard. "Diary of Fremont's 1848–1849 Expedition." Huntington Library, Manuscript Department, San Marino, Calif.

Königlichen Kunst-Academie zu Düsseldorf. "Die Schulerlisten." Haupstaatsarchiv, Düsseldorf, Germany.

Learned, Henry A. Army pension records. National Archives and Records Service, Washington, D.C.

Learned, Henry S. "Reminiscences." Manuscript Division, Kansas State Historical Society, Topeka.

Long, Stephen H. Accounts, 1823. Department of the Treasury, Records of the Office of the Second Auditor, no. 1020. National Archives and Records Service, Washington, D.C.

Miller, Alfred Jacob. "Account Book of A. J. Miller." Walters Art Gallery Library, Baltimore, Md.

———. "Artists' Letters to Alfred Jacob Miller." Typescript copy. Edited by Marvin C. Ross, 1951. Walters Art Gallery, Baltimore, Md.

———. "Notebook" and Macgill James File, Bernard DeVoto Papers, Stanford University Research Library, Palo Alto, Calif.

———. "Rough Draughts for Notes to Indian Sketches" [1857?]. Thomas Gilcrease Institute of American History and Art, Tulsa, Okla.

Miscellaneous Artist Papers. Prints and Drawings Department, Museum of Fine Arts, Boston, Mass.

Moran, Thomas. Drawings, sketches, and sketchbooks. National Park Service, Yellowstone National Park; Jefferson National Expansion Memorial, Saint Louis, Mo.; and Cooper-Hewitt Museum, Smithsonian Institution, New York City.

———. Papers. East Hampton Free Library, New York.

———. Papers. Thomas Gilcrease Institute of American History and Art, Tulsa, Okla.

———. Papers. Microfilm. Archives of American Art, Smithsonian Institution, Washington, D.C.

Paris, Walter. Letters to William Henry Holmes. National Museum of American Art Library, Washington, D.C.

Peale, Titian. Sketchbooks and drawings. American Philosophical Society, Philadelphia, Pa.

Peale Museum Records. Historical Society of Pennsylvania, Philadelphia, Pa.

Preuss, Charles. Diaries, 1842–44. Manuscript Division, Library of Congress, Washington, D.C.

Society of Artists. Minutes. Archives, Pennsylvania Academy of the Fine Arts, Philadelphia, Pa.

Stanley, John Mix. Biographical sketch (attributed to Stanley's son Louis Crandall Stanley). Burton Historical Collection, Detroit Public Library, Detroit, Mich.

Trenton, Patricia. Trenton Papers, 1969–73. Denver Public Library, Western History Department, Denver, Colo.

Weyss, John E. Sketchbook no. 221, "Colorado Mountains." U.S. Geological Survey Library, Reston, Va.

———. Sketchbooks, "Utah," "California," and "Colorado." National Archives and Records Service, Washington, D.C.

Whittredge, Worthington. Papers. Microfilm. Archives of American Art, Smithsonian Institution, Washington, D.C.

UNPUBLISHED MATERIALS

Ewing, Robert Nichols, "Jules Tavernier (1844–1889): Painter and Illustrator." Ph.D. dissertation, University of California at Los Angeles, 1978.

Hale, John Douglas. "The Life and Creative Development of John H. Twachtman." Ph.D. dissertation, Ohio State University, 1957.

Hassrick, Peter Heyl. "Artists Employed on United States Government Expeditions to the Trans-Mississippi West before 1850." Master's thesis, University of Denver, 1969.

Johnson, Asahel. "Peter Tofft." Biography Collection, California Historical Society, San Francisco.

Lawall, David B. "Asher Brown Durand: His Art and Art Theory in Relation to His Times." 4 vols. Ph.D. dissertation, Princeton University, 1966.

Marturano, Mary Lou. "Artists and Art Organizations in Colorado." Master's thesis, University of

Denver, 1962.

Smith, Henry Nash. "American Emotional and Imaginative Attitudes toward the Great Plains and the Rocky Mountains, 1803–1850." Ph.D. dissertation, Harvard University, 1940.

Stehle, Raymond L. "The Life and Works of Emanuel Leutze." Typescript copy. [Washington, D.C.], 1972.

Strong, Donald. "Bierstadt and California." Seminar paper, University of California at Los Angeles, March 14, 1962.

Trenton, Patricia. "Acceptance of American Landscape." Seminar paper, University of California at Los Angeles, August 6, 1968.

———. "Evolution of Landscape Painting in Colorado: 1820–1900." Ph.D. dissertation, University of California at Los Angeles, 1980.

Trump, Richard Shafer. "Life and Works of Albert Bierstadt." Ph.D. dissertation, Ohio State University, 1963.

Weiss, Ila. "Sanford Robinson Gifford." Ph.D. dissertation, Columbia University, 1968.

BOOKS

Abbott, Carl. *Colorado: A History of the Centennial State.* Boulder: Colorado Associated University Press, 1976.

[Abert, James W.] *Journal of Lieutenant James W. Abert, from Bent's Fort to St. Louis, in 1845.* 29th Cong. 1st sess. S. Exec. Doc. 438. Washington, D.C., 1846.

———. *Report of the Secretary of War, Communicating, in Answer to a Resolution of the Senate, a Report and Map of the Examination of New Mexico, Made by Lieutenant J. W. Abert, of the Topographical Corps,* February 10, 1848. 30th Cong. 1st sess. S. Exec. Doc. 23. Washington, D.C., 1848.

[Ackermann, Rudolph.] *A Treatise on Ackermann's Superfine Water Colours, with Directions How to Prepare and Use Them, Including Succinct Hints on Drawing and Painting.* London: Printed for R. Ackermann, [1801].

[Adelson, Warren J., David D. Blakelock, and Susielies M. Blakelock.] *Ralph Albert Blakelock, 1847–1919.* New York: M. Knoedler & Co., 1973.

Albright, George Leslie. *Official Explorations for Pacific Railroads, 1853–1855*. Vol. 11. Berkeley: University of California Press, 1921.

Alison, Archibald. *Essays on the Nature and Principles of Taste*. 2 vols. 1790. 2nd ed. Edinburgh: Bell & Bradfute, 1811.

Allen, Edward B. *Early American Wall Paintings, 1710–1850*. New Haven, Conn.: Yale University Press, 1926.

Amon Carter Museum of Western Art: Catalogue of the Collection, 1972. Fort Worth, Texas: Amon Carter Museum of Western Art, 1973.

Appleton, Jay. *The Experience of Landscape*. New York: John Wiley & Sons, 1975.

Arkelian, Marjorie. *The Kahn Collection of Nineteenth-Century Paintings by Artists in California*. Oakland, Calif.: Oakland Museum, Art Department, 1975.

Athearn, Robert G. *High Country Empire: The High Plains and Rockies*. New York, Toronto, London: McGraw-Hill Book Co., 1960.

Bachmann, Frederick W., and William Swilling Wallace, eds. *The Land Between: Dr. James Schiel's Account of the Gunnison-Beckwith Expedition into the West, 1853–1854*. Los Angeles: Westernlore Press, 1957.

Baigell, Matthew. *Albert Bierstadt*. New York: Watson-Guptill Publications, 1981.

Baird, Joseph A., Jr., comp. *Catalogue of Original Paintings, Drawings and Watercolors in the Robert B. Honeyman, Jr., Collection*. Berkeley: Bancroft Library, University of California, 1968.

Ballinger, James K. *Beyond the Endless River . . . .* Phoenix, Ariz.: Phoenix Art Museum, 1979.

Balston, Thomas. *John Martin, 1799–1854: His Life and Works*. London: G. Duckworth, 1947.

Barker, Virgil. *American Painting: History and Interpretation*. New York: Macmillan Co., 1950.

Barr, Maurice Grant. "Art Trails of Wyoming." In *One Hundred Years of Artist Activity in Wyoming, 1837–1937*. Laramie: University of Wyoming Art Museum, 1976.

Barrell, Joseph. "A Century of Geology—The Growth of Knowledge of Earth Structure." In *A Century of Science in America*. New Haven, Conn.: Yale University Press, 1918.

Bartlett, Richard A. *Great Surveys of the American West*. Norman: University of Oklahoma Press, 1962.

Baudelaire, Charles. "The Salon of 1846: On Some Colonists." In *The Mirror of Art*. Translated by Jonathan Mayne. New York: Doubleday & Co., 1956.

Baur, John I. H. *American Painting in the Nineteenth Century: Main Trends and Movements*. New York: Frederick A. Praeger, 1953.

———, ed. *The Autobiography of Worthington Whittredge, 1820–1910*. 1942. Reprint. New York: Arno Press, 1969.

Beckwith, Edwin Griffin. "Report of Explorations for a Route for the Pacific Railroad, by Capt. J. W. Gunnison, Topographical Engineers, near the 38th and 39th Parallels of North Latitude from the Mouth of the Kansas River, Mo., to the Sevier Lake, in the Great Basin." In *Reports of Explorations and Surveys, to Ascertain the Most Practicable and Economical Route for a Railroad from the Mississippi River to the Pacific Ocean . . . in 1853–54 . . . .* Vol. 2, 33d Cong., 3d sess. H. Exec. Doc. 91. Washington, D.C.: A. O. P. Nicholson, Printer, 1855.

Bell, John R. *The Journal of . . . .* Edited by Harlin M. Fuller and LeRoy R. Hafen. Glendale, Calif.: Arthur H. Clark Co., 1957.

Benjamin, S. G. W. *Art in America: A Critical and Historical Sketch*. Harper & Brothers, 1880.

Bermingham, Peter. *American Art in the Barbizon Mood*. Washington, D.C. National Collection of Fine Arts, Smithsonian Institution Press, 1975.

Bernbaum, Ernest. "The Romantic Movement." In *Romanticism: Points of View*. Edited by Robert F. Gleckner and Gerald E. Enscoe. Englewood Cliffs, N.J.: Prentice-Hall, 1962.

Billington, Ray Allen. *America's Frontier Heritage*. 1966. 3d ed. New York: Holt, Rinehart, and Winston, 1970.

———. *The Far Western Frontier, 1830–1860*. New York: Harper & Brothers, 1956.

Birch, William. *Delices de la Grande Bretagne*. [Engravings after painting masters.] London: Wm. Birch, 1791.

———, and Son. *The City of Philadelphia, in the State of Pennsylvania North America; as it Appeared in the Year 1800*. [Twenty-eight plates drawn and engraved by W. Birch & Son.] Philadelphia, Pa.: W. Birch, 1800.

Blackmore, William. *Colorado: Its Resources, Parks, and Prospects as a New Field for Emigration; with an Account of the Trenchara and Costilla Estates, in the San Luis Park*. London: Sampson Low, Son, and Marston, 1869.

Bloch, E. Maurice. *George Caleb Bingham: The Evolution of an Artist*. 2 vols. Berkeley and Los Angeles: University of California Press, 1967.

Boas, George. *Romanticism in America*. Baltimore, Md.: Johns Hopkins Press, 1940.

Boetticher, Friedrich von. *Malerwerke des Neunzehnten Jahrhunderts . . . ,* vol. 1. Dresden: Fr. Boetticher, 1891.

Bonsal, Stephen. *Edward Fitzgerald Beale: Pioneer in the Path of Empire, 1822–1903*. New York: G. P. Putnam's Sons, 1912.

Born, Wolfgang. *American Landscape Painting: An Interpretation*. New Haven, Conn.: Yale University Press, 1948.

Bowles, Samuel. *Our New West: Record of Travel Between the Mississippi River and the Pacific Ocean*. Hartford, Conn.: Hartford Publishing Co., 1869.

———. *The Pacific Railroad—Open. How to Go: What to See. Guide for Travel to and Through Western America*. Boston: Fields, Osgood & Co., 1869.

Boyle, Richard J. *John Twachtman*. New York: Watson-Guptill Publications, 1979.

Brandes, George. *Main Currents in Nineteenth-Century Literature*. New York: Macmillan Co., 1902.

Brandon, William. *The Men and the Mountains: Frémont's Fourth Expedition*. New York: William Morrow and Co., 1955.

Briganti, Giuliano. *The View Painters of Europe*. Translated by Pamela Waley. London: Phaidon, 1970.

Broekhoff, Helen V. *Thad Welch: Pioneer and Painter*. 1924. Reprint. Oakland, Calif.: Oakland Museum, 1966.

Bruff, J. Goldsborough. *Gold Rush: The Journals, Drawings, and Other Papers of J. Goldsborough Bruff . . . April 2, 1849–July 20, 1851*. Edited by Georgia Willis Read and Ruth Gaines. Foreword by F. W. Hodge. New York: Columbia University Press, 1949.

Bry, Théodor de. *Wunderbarliche, Doch Warhafftige Erklärung, von der Gelegenheit, und Sitten der Wilden in Virginia*. Pt. 1. Frankfurt on the Main: Iohann Wechel, 1590.

Bryant, Edwin. *What I Saw in California*. Edited by

Richard H. Dillon. Palo Alto, Calif.: Lewis Osborne, 1967.

Bryant, William Cullen, ed. *Picturesque America.* 2 vols. New York: D. Appleton & Co., 1872–74.

Burke, Edmund. *Philosophical Enquiry into the Origin of Our Ideas of the Sublime and the Beautiful.* Baltimore, Md.: Neal, 1833.

Burnet, Mary Q. *Art and Artists of Indiana.* New York: Century Co., 1921.

Caffin, Charles H. *The Story of American Painting: The Evolution of Painting in America from Colonial Times to the Present.* 1907. Reprint. New York and London: Johnson Reprint Corporation, 1970.

California Art Research Project. *California Art Research.* 2 vols. of First Series. San Francisco: December, 1936.

Callow, James T. *Kindred Spirits: Knickerbocker Writers and American Artists, 1807–1855.* Chapel Hill, N.C.: University of North Carolina Press, 1967.

Campbell, Archibald. *Reports upon the Survey of the Boundary Between the Territory of the United States and the Possessions of Great Britain from the Lake of the Woods to the Summit of the Rocky Mountains . . . .* Washington, D.C.: U.S. Government Printing Office, 1878.

Carey, Charles H., ed. *The Journals of Theodore Talbot.* Portland, Oreg.: Metropolitan Press, 1931.

Carroll, H. Bailey, ed. *Gúadal P'a: The Journal of Lieutenant J. W. Abert from Bent's Fort to St. Louis in 1845.* Canyon, Texas: Panhandle-Plains Historical Society, 1941.

Carter, Denny. *Henry Farny.* New York: Watson-Guptill Publications, 1978.

Carter, Kate B. *Heart Throbs of the West.* Vol. 2. Salt Lake City, Utah: Daughters of Utah Pioneers, 1940.

Carvalho, S[olomon] N. *Incidents of Travel and Adventure in the Far West, with Col. Fremont's Last Expedition Across the Rocky Mountains: Including Three Months' Residence in Utah, and a Perilous Trip Across the Great American Desert, to the Pacific.* New York: Derby & Jackson. London: Sampson Low, Son, & Co., 1856.

———. *Incidents of Travel in the Far West by Solomon Nuñes Carvalho.* Edited by Bertram Korn. Philadelphia, Pa.: Jewish Publication Society of America, 1954.

Catlin, George. *Catalogue of Catlin's Indian Gallery. . . .* New York: Piercy & Read, 1837.

———. *A Descriptive Catalogue of Catlin's Indian Gallery . . . .* London, [1842].

———. *George Catlin: Episodes from* Life Among the Indians *and* Last Rambles. Edited by Marvin C. Ross. Norman: University of Oklahoma Press, 1959.

———. *Last Rambles Amongst the Indians of the Rocky Mountains and the Andes.* London: Sampson Low, Son, and Marston, 1868.

———. *Letters and Notes on the Manners, Customs, and Condition of the North American Indians.* 2 vols. London: Published by the Author at Egyptian Hall, 1841.

———. *Letters and Notes on the Manners, Customs, and Condition of the North American Indians.* 2 vols. London: David Bogue, 1844.

———. *The Lifted and Subsided Rocks of America . . . .* London: Trübner & Co., 1870.

[Century Association.] *Clarence King Memoirs.* New York: G. P. Putnam's Sons, 1904.

Charvat, William. *The Origins of American Critical Thought: 1810–1835.* New York: A. S. Barnes and Company, 1961.

Chateaubriand, Viscount de. *Travels in America and Italy.* 2 vols. London: Henry Colburn, 1828.

Chittenden, Hiram Martin. *The Yellowstone National Park.* Cincinnati, Ohio: Robert Clarke Co., 1895.

[Cikovsky, Nicolai, Jr.] *Sanford Robinson Gifford [1823–1880].* Austin: University of Texas Art Museum, 1970.

Clark, Carol. *Thomas Moran: Watercolors of the American West.* Austin: University of Texas Press, 1980.

Clark, Eliot. *John Twachtman.* New York: American Artist Series, 1924.

Clark, Harry Hayden. *Transitions in American Literary History.* Durham, N.C.: Duke University Press, 1953.

Clark, John Heaviside. *A Practical Essay on the Art of Colouring and Painting Landscapes in Water Colours: Accompanied with Ten Engravings.* London: Printed for and sold by Edward Orme, 1807.

Clark, Kenneth. *Landscape Painting.* New York: Charles Scribner's Sons, 1950.

Coke, Van Deren. *The Painter and the Photographer.* Albuquerque: University of New Mexico Press, 1964.

———. *Taos and Santa Fe: The Artist's Environment, 1882–1942.* Albuquerque: University of New Mexico Press, 1963.

Commager, Henry Steele, ed. *Documents of American History.* New York: Appleton-Century-Crofts, 1958.

Cook, Clarence C. *Art and Artists of Our time.* 3 vols. New York: S. Hess, 1888.

Cook, James. *The Journals of Captain James Cook on His Voyages of Discovery: The Voyage of the Resolution and Discovery, 1776–1780.* 4 vols. in 5. Cambridge, Eng.: Published for the Hakluyt Society at the University Press, 1955–74.

Cooper, James Fenimore. "American and European Scenery Compared." In *The Home Book of the Picturesque; or, American Scenery, Art, and Literature.* New York: G. P. Putnam, 1852.

Cornelius Fidelis, Brother. *Keith; Old Master of California.* New York: G. P. Putnam's Sons, 1942.

Cox, David. *A Treatise on Landscape Painting and Effect in Water Colours: from the First Rudiments to the Finished Pictures: with Examples in Outline, Effect, and Colouring.* London: Printed by J. Tyler, Rathbone Place, for S. and J. Fuller, 1814.

Craig, W. M. *An Essay on the Study of Nature in Drawing Landscape, with Illustrative Prints, Engraved by the Author.* London: Printed by W. Bulmer and Co., 1793.

Cronau, Rudolf. *Von Wunderland zu Wunderland.* 2 vols. Leipzig: T. O. Weigel, 1885–86.

Crone, G. R. *Maps and Their Makers.* London: Hutchinson's University Library, 1953.

Cross, Osborne. *A Report in the Form of a Journal, to the Quartermaster-General, of the March of the Regiment of Mounted Riflemen to Oregon, from May 10 to October 5, 1849.* Washington, D.C., 1850.

Cummings, Thomas S. *Historic Annals of the National Academy of Design, New York Drawing Association, etc. with Occasional Dottings by the Way-Side, from 1825 to the Present Time.* Philadelphia, Pa.: George W. Childs, 1865.

Curry, Larry. *The American West.* New York: Viking Press, 1972.

Curti, Merle. *The Growth of American Thought.* 1943. 3d ed. New York: Harper & Row, 1964.

Daniell, Thomas, and William Daniell. *A Picturesque Voyage to India; by the Way of China.* London: Longman, Hurst, Rees, and Ormes; and William Daniell, 1810.

Dawson, Christopher M. *Romano-Campanian Landscape Painting.* Yale Classical Studies, vol. 9. Edited by Alfred R. Bellinger. New Haven, Conn.: Yale University Press, 1945.

De Voto, Bernard. *Across the Wide Missouri.* Boston: Houghton Mifflin Co., 1947.

Dillenberger, Jane, and Joshua C. Taylor. *The Hand and the Spirit: Religious Art in America, 1700–1900.* Berkeley, Calif.: University Art Museum, 1972.

Donaho, Thomas S. *Scenes and Incidents of Stanley's Western Wilds.* Washington, D.C.: Evening Star, 1854[?].

Dow, George Francis, comp. *The Arts and Crafts in New England.* Topsfield, Mass.: Wayside Press, 1927.

A Drawing Book of Landscapes. Philadelphia, Pa.: Johnson & Warner, 1810.

Drepperd, Carl W. *American Drawing Books.* New York: New York Public Library, 1946.

Drumm, Stella M., ed. *Down the Santa Fé Trail and into New Mexico: The Diary of Susan Shelby Magoffin, 1846–1847.* New Haven, Conn.: Yale University Press, 1926.

Du Bois, John van Deusen. *Campaigns in the West 1856–1861: The Journal and Letters of Colonel John van Deusen Du Bois.* Edited by George P. Hammond. Tucson: Arizona Pioneers Historical Society, 1949.

Dunlap, William. *A History of the Rise and Progress of the Arts of Design in the United States.* 2 vols. in 3. Edited by Rita Weiss. 1834. Reprint. New York: Dover Publications, 1969.

Dupree, A. Hunter. *Science in the Federal Government.* Cambridge, Mass.: Harvard University Press, Belknap Press, 1957.

Düsseldorf Gallery, New York. *Catalogue of a Private Collection of Paintings and Original Drawings by Artists of the Düsseldorf Academy of Fine Arts.* New York: Wm. C. Bryant & Co., 1851.

———. *Gems from the Düsseldorf Gallery, New York, Photographed from the Original Pictures . . . Under the Superintendence of B. Frodsham.* New York: D. Appleton, 1863.

Dwight, Edward H. *Worthington Whittredge (1820–1910): A Retrospective Exhibition of an American Artist.* Utica, N.Y.: Munson-Williams-Proctor Institute, 1969.

Eastman, S[eth]. *Treatise on Topographical Drawing.* New York: Wiley and Putnam, 1837.

Easy Lessons in Perspective Including Instructions for Sketching from Nature. Boston: Hilliard, Gray, Little and Wilkins, 1830.

Eickmann, Walter T. *History of West New York, New Jersey.* West New York, N.J.: Golden Jubilee Committee, 1948.

Emory, William Hemsley. *Notes on a Military Reconnoissance from Fort Leavenworth, in Missouri, to San Diego, in California, Including Parts of the Arkansas, Del Norte, and Gila Rivers.* 30th Cong. 1st sess. S. Exec. Doc. 7. Washington, D.C.: Wendell and Van Benthuysen, 1848.

Ewers, John C. *Artists of the Old West.* 1965. Rev. ed. Garden City, N.Y.: Doubleday & Co., 1973.

The Expeditions of John Charles Frémont. Edited by Donald Jackson and Mary Lee Spence. 4 vols. Urbana, Chicago, and London: University of Illinois Press, 1973.

Fairbanks, Jonathan L. et al. *Frontier America: The Far West.* Boston: Museum of Fine Arts, 1975.

Fairman, Charles E. *Art and Artists of the Capitol of the United States of America.* Washington, D.C.: U.S. Government Printing Office, 1927.

The Falls of Niagara: Being a Complete Guide to All the Points of Interest Around and in the Immediate Neighbourhood of the Great Cataract, with Views Taken from Sketches by Washington Friend, Esq. and from Photographs. Toronto: T. Nelson & Sons, 1858.

Fern, Thomas S. *The Drawings and Watercolors of Thomas Moran . . . .* South Bend, Ind.: University of Notre Dame Press, 1976.

Flexner, James Thomas. *Nineteenth-Century American Painting.* New York: G. P. Putnam's Sons, 1970.

———. *That Wilder Image.* Boston & Toronto: Little, Brown and Co., 1962.

Frémont, John Charles. *Memoirs of My Life.* Chicago and New York: Belford, Clarke & Co., 1887.

———. *A Report on an Exploration of the Country Lying between the Missouri River and the Rocky Mountains . . . .* Washington, D.C.: Printed by Order of the U.S. Senate, 1843.

———. *Report of the Exploring Expedition to the Rocky Mountains in the Year 1842, and to Oregon and North California in the Years 1843–'44.* Washington, D.C.: Gales and Seaton, 1845.

Fromer-Im Obersteg, Liselotte. *Die Entwicklung der Schweizerischen Landschaftsmalerei im 18. und Frühen 19. Jahrhundert.* Basel: Emil Birkhäuser & Cie, 1945.

Galvin, John, ed. *Through the Country of the Comanche Indians in the Fall of the Year 1845: The Journal of a U.S. Army Expedition Led by Lieutenant James W. Abert of the Topographical Engineers . . . .* San Francisco: John Howell—Books, 1970.

———. *Western America in 1846–1847: The Original Travel Diary of Lieutenant J. W. Abert, Who Mapped New Mexico for the United States Army.* San Francisco: John Howell—Books, 1966.

Gebhard, David, and Phyllis Stuurman. *The Enigma of Ralph A. Blakelock, 1847–1919.* Santa Barbara: University of California, 1969.

Gilpin, William. *Remarks on Forest Scenery, and Other Woodland Views . . . .* 2 vols. London: Printed for R. Blamire, Strand, 1771.

———. *Three Essays; on Picturesque Beauty; on Picturesque Travel; and on Sketching Landscape; To Which Is Added a Poem, on Landscape Painting.* London: Printed for R. Blamire, in the Strand, 1792.

Goetzmann, William H. *Army Exploration in the American West, 1803–1863.* 1959. 3d ed. New Haven, Conn.: Yale University Press, 1965.

———. *Exploration and Empire.* 1966. 3d ed. New York: Alfred A. Knopf, 1971.

Goldyne, Joseph R. *J. M. W. Turner: Works from American Collections.* Berkeley, Calif.: University Art Museum, 1975.

Goodyear, Frank H., Jr. "American Landscape Painting, 1795–1875." In *This Academy: The Pennsylvania Academy of the Fine Arts, 1805–1976.* Philadelphia, Pa.: Pennsylvania Academy of the Fine Arts, 1976.

———. *Thomas Doughty, 1793–1856: An American Pioneer in Landscape Painting.* Philadelphia, Pa.: Pennsylvania Academy of the Fine Arts, 1973.

Gowing, Lawrence. *Turner: Imagination and Reality.* Garden City, N.Y.: Doubleday & Co., 1966.

Greenshields, E. B. *Landscape Painting and Modern Dutch Artists.* New York: Baker & Taylor Co., 1906.

Groce, George C., and David H. Wallace. *The New-*

York Historical Society's Dictionary of Artists in America, 1564–1860. New Haven, Conn.: Yale University Press, 1957.

Groseclose, Barbara S. Emanuel Leutze, 1816–1868: Freedom Is the Only King. Washington, D.C.: National Collection of Fine Arts, 1975.

Hafen, LeRoy R., ed. Colorado and Its People: A Narrative and Topic History of the Centennial State. 4 vols. New York: Lewis Historical Publishing Co., 1948.

Hafen, LeRoy R., and Ann W. Hafen, eds. Fremont's Fourth Expedition: A Documentary Account of the Disaster of 1848–1849 . . . . Glendale, Calif.: Arthur H. Clark Co., 1960.

————. Handcarts to Zion: The Story of a Unique Western Migration, 1856–1860 . . . . Glendale, Calif.: Arthur H. Clark Co., 1960.

Hagen, Oskar. The Birth of the American Tradition in Art. New York: Charles Scribner's Sons, 1940.

Haines, Aubrey L. The Yellowstone Story. Boulder: Colorado Associated University Press, 1977.

Hall, Frank. History of the State of Colorado . . . . Vol. 4. Chicago: Blakely Printing Co., 1895.

Hardie, Martin. Water-Colour Painting in Britain . . . . Edited by Dudley Snelgrove et al. 3 vols. 1966. 2d ed. London: B. T. Batsford, 1967.

[Harrington, Charles]. Summering in Colorado. Denver, Colo.: Richards & Co., 1974.

Harris, Neil. The Artist in American Society. New York: George Braziller, 1966.

Hart, John L. J. Fourteen Thousand Feet. Denver: Colorado Mountain Club, 1931.

Hartmann, Sadakichi. A History of American Art. 2 vols. 1901. 2d ed. Boston: L. C. Page & Co., 1913.

Haseltine, James L. 100 Years of Utah Painting. Salt Lake City, Utah: Salt Lake City Art Center, 1965.

Hassrick, Peter. Frederic Remington. Fort Worth, Texas: Amon Carter Museum of Western Art, 1972.

————. The Way West: Art of Frontier America. New York: Harry N. Abrams, Inc., 1977.

Hayden, F. V. Preliminary Field Report of the United States Geological Survey of Colorado and New Mexico. Washington, D.C.: U.S. Government Printing Office, 1869.

————. Preliminary Report of the United States Geo-
logical Survey of Montana and Portions of Adjacent Territories; being a Fifth Annual Report of Progress. [1871] Washington, D.C.: U.S. Government Printing Office, 1872.

————. Preliminary Report of the United States Geological Survey of Wyoming, and Portions of Contiguous Territories . . . . [1870] Washington, D.C.: U.S. Government Printing Office, 1872.

————. Sixth Annual Report of the United States Geological Survey of the Territories, embracing Portions of Montana, Idaho, Wyoming, and Utah; being a Report of Progress of the Explorations for the Year 1872. Washington, D.C.: U.S. Government Printing Office, 1873.

————. [Seventh] Annual Report of the United States Geological and Geographical Survey of the Territories, embracing Colorado; being a Report of Progress of the Exploration for the Year 1873. Washington, D.C.: U.S. Government Printing Office, 1874.

————. [Eighth] Annual Report of the United States Geological and Geographical Survey of the Territories, embracing Colorado and Parts of Adjacent Territories; being a Report of Progress of the Exploration for the Year 1874. Washington, D.C.: U.S. Government Printing Office, 1877.

————. Ninth Annual Report of the United States Geological and Geographical Survey of the Territories, embracing Colorado and Parts of Adjacent Territories; being a Report of Progress of the Exploration for the Year 1875. Washington, D.C.: U.S. Government Printing Office, 1878.

————. Tenth Annual Report of the United States Geological and Geographical Survey of the Territories, embracing Colorado and Parts of Adjacent Territories; being a Report of Progress of the Exploration for the Year 1876. Washington, D.C.: U.S. Government Printing Office, 1878.

————. Eleventh Annual Report of the United States Geological and Geographical Survey of the Territories, embracing Idaho and Wyoming; being a Report of Progress of the Exploration for the Year 1877. Washington, D.C.: U.S. Government Printing Office, 1879.

————. Geological and Geographical Atlas of Colorado and Portions of Adjacent Territory. Washington, D.C.: U.S. Government Printing Office, 1877.

————. Twelfth Annual Report of the United States
Geological and Geographical Survey of the Territories: A Report of Progress of the Exploration in Wyoming and Idaho for the Year 1878. In Two Parts. Washington, D.C.: U.S. Government Printing Office, 1883.

————. Maps and Panoramas, Twelfth Annual Report of the United States Geological and Geographical Survey of the Territories, 1878. Washington, D.C.: U.S. Government Printing Office, 1883.

————. "Letter from the Secretary of the Interior . . . Transmitting Report of Professor Hayden upon Geological and Geographical Surveys." In U.S. Geological and Geographical Survey of the Territories. 45th Cong. 2d sess. H. Exec. Doc. 81. Washington, D.C.: U.S. Government Printing Office, 1878.

Heap, Gwinn Harris. Central Route to the Pacific by Gwinn Harris Heap . . . . Edited by LeRoy R. Hafen and Ann W. Hafen. Glendale, Calif.: Arthur H. Clark Co., 1957.

————. Central Route to the Pacific, from the Valley of the Mississippi to California: Journal of the Expedition of E. F. Beale . . . and Gwinn Harris Heap, from Missouri to California, in 1853. Philadelphia, Pa.: Lippincott, Grambo, and Co., 1854.

Heffernan, William Joseph. Edward M. Kern, the Travels of an Artist-Explorer. Bakersfield, Calif.: Kern County Historical Society, 1953.

Hendricks, Gordon. Albert Bierstadt: Painter of the American West. New York: Harry N. Abrams and Amon Carter Museum of Western Art, 1974.

Herrmann, Luke. British Landscape Painting of the Eighteenth Century. London: Faber & Faber, 1973.

Hindle, Brooke. The Pursuit of Science in Revolutionary America. Chapel Hill, N.C.: University of North Carolina Press, 1956.

Hine, Robert V. Edward Kern and American Expansion. New Haven, Conn.: Yale University Press, 1962.

————. In the Shadow of Frémont: Edward Kern and the Art of American Exploration, 1845–1860. 2d ed. Norman: University of Oklahoma Press, 1982.

Hipple, Walter John, Jr. The Beautiful, the Sublime and the Picturesque in Eighteenth-Century British

Aesthetic Theory. Carbondale, Ill.: Southern Illinois University Press, 1957.

History of the City of Denver, Arapahoe County, and Colorado. Chicago: O. L. Baskin & Co., 1880.

Hofstadter, Richard, William Miller, and Daniel Aaron. *The United States: The History of a Republic.* 1957. 2d ed. Englewood Cliffs, N.J.: Prentice-Hall, 1967.

Hogarth, Paul. *Artist on Horseback.* Fort Worth, Texas: Amon Carter Museum, 1972.

Honour, Hugh. *The European Vision of America.* Cleveland, Ohio: Cleveland Museum of Art, 1975.

Hoopes, Donelson F. *The Düsseldorf Academy and the Americans.* Atlanta, Ga.: High Museum of Art, 1972.

Hopkins, Walter S. et al. *The Bible and the Gold Rush.* Denver, Colo.: Big Mountain Press, 1962.

Horne, Alice M. *Devotees and Their Shrines: A Handbook of Utah Art.* Salt Lake City, Utah: Deseret News, 1914.

Howat, John K. *John Frederick Kensett, 1816–1872.* New York: American Federation of Arts, 1968.

Humboldt, Friedrich Alexander, Baron von. *Cosmos: A Sketch of a Physical Description of the Universe . . . .* Translated by E. C. Otté. 5 vols. London: George Bell and Sons, 1878.

————, and Aimé Bonpland. *Personal Narrative of Travels to the Equinoctial Regions of the Continent, During the Years 1799–1804.* Translated by Helen Maria Williams. Philadelphia, Pa.: M. Carey, 1815.

Hunter, Wilbur H., Jr. "Alfred Jacob Miller: Artist of Baltimore and the West." In *The Paintings of Alfred Jacob Miller: Artist of Baltimore and the West.* Baltimore, Md.: Peale Museum, 1950.

Huntington, Daniel. *Catalogue of Paintings, by Daniel Huntington N.A., Exhibiting at the Art Union Buildings,* New York: Snowden, 1850.

———— et al. *Proceedings at a Meeting of the Century Association, Held in Memory of John F. Kensett.* New York: Century Association, December, 1872.

Huntington, David C. *The Landscapes of Frederic Edwin Church: Vision of an American Era.* New York: George Braziller, 1966.

Huth, Hans. *Nature and the American.* Berkeley and Los Angeles: University of California Press, 1957.

Hutson, Martha Young. *George Henry Durrie (1820–1863), American Winter Landscapist: Renowned Through Currier and Ives.* Los Angeles: American Art Review Press, 1977.

Hütt, Wolfgang. *Die Düsseldorfer Malerschule, 1819–1869.* Leipzig: E. A. Seemann, 1964.

Ingersoll, Ernest. *The Crest of the Continent . . . .* Chicago: R. R. Donnelley & Sons, 1885.

————. *Knocking Round the Rockies.* New York: Harper & Brothers, 1882.

Irving, Washington. *The Rocky Mountains; or Scenes, Incidents and Adventures in the Far West, Digested from the Journal of Captain B. L. E. Bonneville, U.S.A., and Illustrated from Various Other Sources.* Philadelphia, Pa.: Carey, Lea, and Blanchard, 1837.

Isham, Samuel. *The History of American Painting.* 1905. New ed. New York: Macmillan Co., 1936.

Jackson, Clarence S. and Lawrence W. Marshall. *Quest of the Snowy Cross.* Denver, Colo.: University of Denver Press, 1952.

Jackson, Donald and Mary Lee Spence, eds. *The Expeditions of John Charles Frémont.* Vol. 1, *Travels from 1838 to 1844.* Urbana: University of Illinois Press, 1970.

Jackson, William Henry. *Descriptive Catalogue of the Photographs of the United States Geological Survey, . . . 1869–1873.* U.S. Geological and Geographical Survey of the Territories, Miscellaneous Publications, no. 5. Washington, D.C.: U.S. Government Printing Office, 1874.

————. *The Diaries of William Henry Jackson . . . .* Edited by LeRoy R. Hafen and Ann W. Hafen. Glendale, Calif.: Arthur H. Clark Co., 1959.

————. *Time Exposure.* New York: G. P. Putnam's Sons, 1940.

James, Edwin, comp. *Account of an Expedition from Pittsburgh to the Rocky Mountains, Performed in the Years 1819 and '20, by Order of the Hon. J. C. Calhoun, Sec'y of War: Under the Command of Major Stephen H. Long . . . .* 2 vols. and atlas. Philadelphia, Pa.: H. C. Carey and I. Lea, 1822–23.

————. *Account of an Expedition from Pittsburgh to the Rocky Mountains . . . .* 3 vols. London: Longman, Hurst, Rees, Orme & Brown, 1823.

Jarves, James Jackson. *The Art-Idea . . . .* 2 vols. 1864. 4th ed. New York: Hurd and Houghton, 1877.

Jones, Howard Mumford. *O Strange New World.* 1952. 2d ed. New York: Viking Press, 1964.

Karlstrom, Paul J. *An Exhibition of Views of Venice in the Graphic Arts from the Late 15th Through 18th Century.* Los Angeles: Grunwald Graphic Arts Foundation, Dickson Art Center, University of California, 1969.

Karpenstein, Katherine. *Illustrations of the West in Congressional Documents, 1843–1863.* Rochester, N.Y.: University of Rochester Press, 1953.

King, Clarence. "Systematic Geology." In *Report of United States Geological Exploration of the Fortieth Parallel,* vol. 1. 7 vols. Washington, D.C.: U.S. Government Printing Office, 1878.

Kinietz, W. Vernon. *John Mix Stanley, and His Indian Paintings.* Ann Arbor: University of Michigan Press, 1942.

[Lander, F. W.] "Reports of F. W. Lander . . . for 1859 and 1860, made under the direction of the honorable Jacob Thompson, Secretary of the Interior." In *Maps and Reports of the Fort Kearny, South Pass, and Honey Lake Wagon Road.* 36th Cong., 2d sess., H. Exec. Doc. 64. Washington, D.C., 1860.

Lang, Hans. *Indianer Waren Meine Freunde: Leben Und Werk Karl Bodmers, 1809–1893.* Bern: Hallway, 1976.

Lanman, Charles. *Letters from a Landscape Painter.* Boston: James Munroe and Co., 1845.

Larkin, Oliver W. *Art and Life in America.* 1949. Rev. ed. New York: Holt, Rinehart & Winston, 1960.

Larned, Charles W. "Historical Sketch of the Department of Drawing." In *The Centennial of the United States Military Academy at West Point, New York, 1802–1902,* vol. 1. Washington, D.C.: U.S. Government Printing Office, 1904.

Larson, T. A. *Wyoming.* New York: W. W. Norton & Co., 1977.

Lavender, David. *The American Heritage History of the Great West.* Edited by Alvin M. Josephy, Jr. New York: American Heritage Publishing Co., 1965.

Lawrence, Ellen. *1800–1874: European and American Landscape: To Look on Nature.* Providence, R.I.: Brown University, Department of Art, 1972.

Links, J. G. *Townscape Painting and Drawing.* New York and London: B. T. Batsford, 1972.

Lister, Raymond. *British Romantic Art.* London: G. Bell & Sons, 1973.

Lorant, Stefan. *The New World: The First Pictures of America.* New York: Duell, Sloan and Pearce, 1946.

[Lucas, Fielding, Jr.] *Lucas' Progressive Drawing Book in Three Parts . . . . : Original Views of American Scenery . . . .* Baltimore, Md.: Fielding Lucas, Jr. [1827].

Ludlow, Fitz Hugh. *The Heart of the Continent.* New York: Hurd and Houghton, 1870.

Lurie, Edward. *Louis Agassiz: A Life in Science.* Chicago: University of Chicago Press, 1960.

Lydenberg, H. M. *Archibald Robertson, Lieutenant-General Royal Engineers; His Diaries and Sketches in America, 1762–1780.* New York: New York Public Library, 1930.

M. & M. Karolik Collection of American Paintings, 1815–1865. Cambridge, Mass.: Harvard University Press, 1949.

M. & M. Karolik Collection of American Water Colors and Drawings, 1800–1875. 2 vols. Boston: Museum of Fine Arts, 1962.

McClinton, Katharine. *The Chromolithographs of Louis Prang.* New York: C. N. Potter, Crown Publisher, 1973.

McCracken, Harold. *George Catlin and the Old Frontier.* New York: Dial Press, 1959.

McDermott, John Francis, ed. *An Artist on the Overland Trail: The 1849 Diary and Sketches of James F. Wilkins.* San Marino, Calif.: Huntington Library, 1968.

————. *Seth Eastman: Pictorial Historian of the Indian.* Norman: University of Oklahoma Press, 1961.

McMechen, Edgar C. "Art, Drama and Music." In *Colorado and Its People.* Edited by LeRoy R. Hafen. New York: Lewis Historical Publishing Co., 1948.

McShine, Kynaston, ed. *The Natural Paradise: Painting in America, 1800–1950.* Essays by Barbara Novak, Robert Rosenblum, and John Wilmerding. New York: Museum of Modern Art, 1976.

Magoon, E. L. "Scenery and Mind." In *The Home Book of the Picturesque.* New York: George P. Putnam, 1852.

Mangan, Terry Wm. *Colorado on Glass: Colorado's First Half Century as Seen by the Camera.* Denver, Colo.: Sundance Limited, 1975.

Marcy, Randolph B. *Report of a Route from Fort Smith to Santa Fe.* 31st Cong., 1st sess., S. Exec. Doc. 64. Washington, D.C.: U.S. Government Printing Office, 1850.

————. *Thirty Years of Army Life on the Border.* New York: Harper & Brothers, 1866.

Markowitz, Irene. *Die Düsseldorfer Malerschule.* Düsseldorf: Kunstmuseum Düsseldorf, 1967.

Mathews, Alfred E. *Canyon City, Colorado, and Its Surroundings.* New York: Published by Authority of the Citizens of Fremont County, Colorado, 1870.

————. *Gems of Rocky Mountain Scenery, Containing Views Along and near the Union Pacific Railroad.* New York, 1869.

————. *Pencil Sketches of Colorado, Its Cities, Principal Towns and Mountain Scenery, 1866.* [New York, 1866].

————. *Pencil Sketches of Montana.* New York, 1868.

Mayer, Frank Blackwell. *With Pen and Pencil on the Frontier in 1851.* Edited by Bertha L. Heilbron. Saint Paul: Minnesota Historical Society, 1932.

Mayer, Ralph. *The Artist's Handbook of Materials and Techniques.* 3d rev. ed. New York: Viking Press, 1970.

Miller, Dwight. *California Landscape Painting, 1860–1885: Artists Around Keith and Hill.* Stanford University Art Gallery, December 9, 1975, n.p. (exhibition catalog, reproduced from typewritten copy).

Miller, Perry. *Nature's Nation.* Cambridge, Mass.: Harvard University Press, Belknap Press, 1967.

————, and Thomas H. Johnson. *The Puritans.* New York: American Book Co., 1938.

Monk, Samuel H. *The Sublime: A Study of Critical Theories in Eighteenth-Century England.* New York: Modern Language Association of America, 1935.

Moody, Richard. *America Takes the Stage . . . .* Bloomington: Indiana University Press, 1955.

Mooz, R. Peter. "Colonial Art." In *The Genius of American Painting.* Edited by John Wilmerding. New York: William Morrow & Co., 1973.

[Moran, Thomas.] *Home-Thoughts, from Afar . . . .* Edited by Amy O. Bassford, Introduction and Notes by Fritiof Fryxell. New York: East Hampton Free Library, 1967.

Morgan, Dale L. *The Great Salt Lake.* Indianapolis, Ind.: Bobbs-Merrill Co., 1947.

Moss, Michael E. "Robert Weir as Teacher." In *Robert W. Weir of West Point: Illustrator, Teacher and Poet.* West Point, N.Y.: U.S. Military Academy, 1976.

Muir, John, ed. *Picturesque California: The Rocky Mountains and the Pacific Slope . . . Illustrated . . . by Eminent American Artists.* 2 vols. New York and San Francisco: J. Dewing Publishing Co., 1888.

Mullan, Captain John. *Report on the Construction of a Military Road from Fort Walla-Walla to Fort Benton.* Washington, D.C.: U.S. Government Printing Office, 1863.

Mumey, Nolie. *John Williams Gunnison (1812–1853): The Last of the Western Explorers . . . .* Denver, Colo.: Artcraft Press, 1955.

Naef, Weston J., and James N. Wood. *Era of Exploration: The Rise of Landscape Photography in the American West, 1860–1885.* New York: Buffalo Fine Arts Academy, Albright-Knox Art Gallery, and Metropolitan Museum of Art, 1975.

Nasatir, A. P. *Before Lewis and Clark: Documents Illustrating the History of the Missouri, 1785–1804.* 2 vols. Saint Louis, Mo.: Saint Louis Historical Documents Foundation, 1952.

Nash, Roderick. *Wilderness and the American Mind.* New Haven, Conn.: Yale University Press, 1967.

The National Academy of Design Exhibition Record, 1861–1900. Compiled and edited by Marie Naylor. 2 vols. New York: Kennedy Galleries, 1973.

The National Gallery Illustrated General Catalogue. London: National Gallery, 1973.

Neue Pinakothek und Staatsgalerie München. Meisterwerke der Deutschen Malerei des 19. Jahrhunderts. Vol. 2. Munich: Hirmer, 1967.

Nevins, Allan. *Frémont: Pathmaker of the West.* New York: D. Appleton-Century Co., 1939.

————. *Frémont: The West's Greatest Adventurer.* 2 vols. New York: Harper & Brothers, 1928.

Newhall, Beaumont. *The History of Photography.* New York: Museum of Modern Art, 1964.

————, and Diana E. Edkins. *William H. Jackson.* Fort Worth, Texas: Amon Carter Museum of Western Art, 1974.

Nicholson, Francis. *The Practice of Drawing and Painting Landscape from Nature, in Water Colours: Exemplified in a Series of Instructions Calculated to Facilitate the Progress of the Learner; Including the Elements of Perspective, Their Application in Sketching from Nature, and the Explanation of Various Processes of Colouring, for Producing from the Outline a Finished Picture; with Observations on the Study of Nature, and Various Other Matters Relative to the Arts.* London: Printed for the Author; and Published by J. Booth and T. Clay, 1820.

Nicholson, Marjorie Hope. *Mountain Gloom and Mountain Glory: The Development of the Aesthetics of the Infinite.* Ithaca, N.Y.: Cornell University Press, 1959.

Noble, Louis Legrand. *The Life and Works of Thomas Cole.* Edited by Elliot S. Vesell. Cambridge, Mass.: Harvard University Press, Belknap Press, 1964.

The Notebook of John Smibert; with Essays by Sir David Evans [and Others] and with Notes Relating to Smibert's Am. Por. by Andrew Oliver. Boston: Massachusetts Historical Society, 1969.

Nothing Is Long Ago: A Documentary History of Colorado, 1776/1976. Denver, Colo.: Denver Public Library, 1976.

Novak, Barbara. *American Painting of the Nineteenth Century . . . .* New York: Praeger Publishers, 1969.

————. *Nature and Culture: American Landsacape and Painting, 1825–1875.* New York: Oxford University Press, 1980.

Nye, Russell Blaine. *The Cultural Life of the New Nation, 1776–1830.* 1960. Reprint. New York: Harper & Row, 1963.

————. *Society and Culture in America, 1830–1860.* New York: Harper & Row, 1974.

Ogden, Henry V. S., and Margaret S. Ogden. *English Taste in Landscape in the Seventeenth Century.* Ann Arbor: University of Michigan Press, 1955.

[Owen, John.] *The Journals and Letters of Major John Owen: Pioneer of the Northwest, 1850–1871 . . . .* Edited by Seymour Dunbar. 2 vols. New York: E. Eberstadt, 1927.

Parker, Rev. Samuel. *Journal of an Exploring Tour Beyond the Rocky Mountains . . . .* Ithaca, N.Y.: Published by the Author, 1838.

Paul, Rodman W., ed. *A Victorian Gentlewoman in the Far West: The Reminiscences of Mary Hallock Foote.* San Marino, Calif.: Huntington Library, 1972.

Peat, Wilbur D. *Pioneer Painters of Indiana.* Indianapolis, Ind.: Art Association of Indianapolis, 1954.

[Pennsylvania Academy of the Fine Arts.] *Pennsylvania Academicians, March 10–April 8, 1973.* Philadelphia, Pa.: 1973.

Peters, Harry T. *America on Stone.* New York: Doubleday, Doran, and Co., 1931.

Pianzola, Maurice. *Paysages Romantiques Genevois.* Geneva: Musée d'art et d'histoire, 1977.

Piercy, Frederick. *Route from Liverpool to Great Salt Lake Valley.* Liverpool: Franklin D. Richards, 1855.

Pike, Captain Zebulon Montgomery. *An Account of Expeditions to the Sources of the Mississippi, and Through the Western Parts of Louisiana, to the Sources of the Arkansaw, Kans, La Platte, and Pierre Jaun, Rivers; Performed by Order of the Government of the United States During the years 1805, 1806, and 1807 . . . .* Appendix to pt. 2. Philadelphia, Pa.: C. & A. Conrad & Co., 1810.

————. *The Expeditions of Zebulon Montgomery Pike.* Edited by Elliott Coues. 3 vols. New York: Francis P. Harper, 1895.

Pleasants, J. Hall. *Four Late Eighteenth Century Anglo-American Landscape Painters.* 1942. Reprint. Worcester, Mass.: Proceedings of the American Antiquarian Society, 1943.

Plowden, Helen Haseltine. *William Stanley Haseltine.* London: Frederick Muller, 1947.

Poesch, Jessie. *Titian Ramsay Peale, 1799–1885; And His Journals of the Wilkes Expedition.* Philadelphia, Pa.: American Philosophical Society, 1961.

Point, Nicolas. *Wilderness Kingdom: The Journals & Paintings of Father Nicolas Point: Indian Life in the Rocky Mountains, 1840–1847.* Translated by Joseph P. Donnelly, S.J., Appreciation by John C. Ewers. New York, Chicago, and San Francisco: Holt, Rinehart and Winston, 1967.

[Pope, John.] "General John Pope's Official Report to General Sherman, Fort Union, N.M., August 11, 1866." In U.S. War Department, *Annual Report of Secy of War, 1866.* 39th Cong. 2d sess.

H. Exec. Doc. 1. Washington, D.C., 1866.

Powell, John Wesley. "Physiographic Regions of the United States." In *The Physiography of the United States.* New York: American Book Company, 1896.

Preuss, Charles. *Exploring with Frémont: The Private Diaries of Charles Preuss, Cartographer for John C. Frémont on His First, Second, and Fourth Expeditions to the Far West.* Translated and edited by Erwin G. Gudde and Elisabeth K. Gudde. Norman: University of Oklahoma Press, 1958.

Price, Uvedale. *Essays on the Picturesque, as Compared with the Sublime and Beautiful; and, on the Use of Studying Pictures, for the Purpose of Improving Real Landscape.* 3 vols. London: Printed for J. Mawman, 1810.

Prime, Alfred Coxe. *The Arts and Crafts in Philadelphia, Maryland and South Carolina, 1721–1785.* Topsfield, Mass.: Walpole Society, 1929.

Prout, Samuel. *Hints on Light and Shadow, Composition, Etc. as Applicable to Landscape Painting. Illustrated by Examples [by the author].* London: Published by Ackermann and Co., 1828.

Raynolds, Brevet Brigadier General W. F. *Report on the Exploration of the Yellowstone River . . . .* 40th Cong., 1st sess., S. Exec. Doc. 77. Washington, D.C.: U.S. Government Printing Office, 1868.

Report on Indians Taxed and Not Taxed in the United States . . . Eleventh Census, 1890. Vol. 10. Washington, D.C.: U.S. Government Printing Office, 1894.

Reznikoff, Charles. *The Jews of Charleston.* Philadelphia, Pa.: Jewish Publication Society, 1950.

Richardson, E. P. *A Short History of Painting in America: The Story of 450 Years.* 1956. Abbrev. ed. New York: Thomas Y. Crowell Co., 1963.

Ridge, Martin, and Ray Allen Billington, eds. *America's Frontier Story: A Documentary History of Westward Expansion.* New York: Holt, Rinehart, and Winston, 1969.

Ringe, Donald A. *The Pictorial Mode.* Lexington: University Press of Kentucky, 1971.

Roberts, James. *Introductory Lessons, with Familiar Examples in Landscape, for the Use of Those Who Are Desirous of Gaining Some Knowledge of the Pleasing Art of Painting in Water Colours; to Which Are Added Some Clear and Simple Rules,*

Exemplified by Suitable Sketches and More Finished Paintings. London: Printed by W. Bulmer and Co., St. James's, for the Author, 1800.

Robertson, Archibald. *Elements of the Graphic Arts.* New York: David Longworth, 1802.

Roehm, Marjorie Catlin. *The Letters of George Catlin and His Family.* Berkeley: University of California Press, 1966.

The Romantic Vision in America. Dallas, Texas: Dallas Museum of Fine Arts, 1971.

Ross, Marvin C., ed. *The West of Alfred Jacob Miller.* Norman: University of Oklahoma Press, 1951.

Rusk, Fern Helen. *George Caleb Bingham: The Missouri Artist.* Jefferson City, Mo.: Hugh Stephens Co., 1917.

Ruskin, John. *Modern Painters.* Vol. 1, Preface to 2d ed. (1844). *The Works of John Ruskin.* Edited by E. T. Cook and Alexander Wedderburn. Library Edition, vol. 3. 39 vols. London: George Allen; New York: Longmans, Green and Co., 1903.

Rutledge, Anna Wells, comp. *Cumulative Records of Exhibition Catalogues: The Pennsylvania Academy of the Fine Arts, 1807–1870 . . . .* Philadelphia, Pa.: American Philosophical Society, 1955.

Sawitzky, William. *Connecticut Portraits by Ralph Earl, 1751–1801.* New Haven, Conn.: Gallery of Fine Arts, Yale University, 1935.

The Scenery of the United States. New York: D. Appleton & Co., 1855.

Schaarschmidt, Friedrich. *Zur Geschichte der Düsseldorfer Kunst.* Düsseldorf: Kayser, Christian, 1902.

Schaldach, William J. *Carl Rungius: Big Game Painter.* West Hartford, Vt.: Countryman Press, 1945.

Scharf, Aaron. *Art and Photography.* Baltimore, Md.: Penguin Press, 1969.

Schimmel, Julie. *Stark Museum of Art: The Western Collection, 1978.* Orange, Texas: Stark Museum of Art, 1978.

Schreiber-Favre, A. *La lithographie artistique en Suisse au XIXᵉ siècle, Alexandre Calame le paysage.* Neuchâtel: À la Baconnière (Suisse), 1937.

Sellers, Charles Coleman. *Charles Willson Peale.* New York: Charles Scribner's Sons, 1969.

A Series of Progressive Lessons Intended to Elucidate the Art of Landscape Painting in Water Colours; with Introductory Illustrations on Perspective and Drawing with Pencil. London: T. Clay, 1828.

A Series of Progressive Lessons Intended to Elucidate the Art of Painting in Water Colours. London: Published by T. Clay, 1811.

Settle, Raymond W., ed. *The March of the Mounted Riflemen.* Glendale, Calif.: Arthur H. Clark Co., 1940.

Shaffer, Ellen. *The Nuremberg Chronicle.* Los Angeles: Dawson's Book Shop, 1950.

Shalkop, Robert L. *A Show of Color: 100 Years of Painting in the Pike's Peak Region.* Colorado Springs Fine Arts Center, 1971.

Shaw, Reuben Cole. *Across the Plains in Forty-nine.* Farmland, Ind.: W. C. West, 1896.

Sheldon, George W. *American Painters.* New York: D. Appleton and Co., 1879.

Sherman, John. *Recollections of Forty Years in the House, Senate and Cabinet.* 2 vols. New York: Werner Co., 1895.

Simpson, James H. *Journal of a Military Reconnaissance, from Sante Fé, New Mexico, to the Navajo Country, Made with the Troops Under the Command of Brevet Lieutenant Colonel John M. Washington . . . in 1849.* Philadelphia, Pa.: Lippincott, Grambo, and Co., 1852.

————. *Report and Map of the Route from Fort Smith, Arkansas, to Santa Fe, New Mexico . . . .* 31st Cong., 1st sess., S. Exec. Doc. 12. Washington, D.C.: U.S. Government Printing Office, 1850.

————. *Report of Explorations Across the Great Basin of the Territory of Utah for a direct Wagon-Route from Camp Floyd to Genoa, in Carson Valley, in 1859 . . . .* Washington, D.C.: U.S. Government Printing Office, 1876.

————. *Report of the Secretary of War Communicating . . . Captain Simpson's Report and Map of Wagon Road Routes in Utah Territory.* 35th Cong., 2d sess., S. Doc. 40. Washington, D.C. 1859.

Sitgreaves, Lorenzo. *Report of an Expedition Down to the Zuñi and Colorado Rivers.* 32d Cong., 2d sess., S. Exec. Doc. 59. [Washington, D.C.: R. Armstrong, 1853.]

Smiley, Jerome C. *History of Denver with Outlines of the Earlier History of the Rocky Mountain Country.* Denver, Colo.: Denver Times, 1901.

Smith, George Otis. "A Century of Government Geological Surveys." In *A Century of Science in America.* New Haven, Conn.: Yale University Press, 1918.

Smith, Henry Nash. *Virgin Land: The American West as Symbol and Myth.* Cambridge, Mass.: Harvard University Press, 1950.

Somerville, Robert. *The Collection of Over Five Hundred Paintings and Studies by the Late John F. Kensett.* New York: 1873.

Spencer, Frank C. *Colorado's Story.* Denver, Colo. World Press, 1930.

Stanley, George F. G., ed. *Mapping the Frontier: Charles Wilson's Diary of the Survey of the 49th Parallel, 1858–1862, While Secretary of the British Boundary Commission.* Seattle: University of Washington Press, 1970.

Stanley, John M. *Catalogue of Pictures in Stanley and Dickerman's North American Indian Portrait Gallery.* Cincinnati, Ohio, 1846.

————. *Portraits of North American Indians, with Sketches of Scenery, Etc.* Washington, D.C.: Smithsonian Institution, 1852.

Stansbury, Howard. *An Expedition to the Valley of the Great Salt Lake of Utah, Including a Reconnaissance of a New Route Through the Rocky Mountains.* Philadelphia, Pa.: Lippincott, Grambo & Co., 1852.

Stauffer, David McNeely. *American Engravers upon Copper and Steel.* 2 vols. New York: Grolier Club, 1907.

Stebbins, Theodore E., Jr. *American Master Drawings and Watercolors.* New York: Harper & Row, 1976.

Stechow, Wolfgang. *Dutch Landscape Painting of the Seventeenth Century.* London: Phaedon Press, 1966.

Stein, Roger B. *John Ruskin and Aesthetic Thought in America, 1840–1900.* Cambridge, Mass.: Harvard University Press, 1967.

Stenzel, Franz. *Anton Schonborn: Western Forts.* Fort Worth, Texas: Amon Carter Museum, 1972.

————. *James Madison Alden: Yankee Artist of the Pacific Coast, 1854–1860.* Fort Worth, Texas: Amon Carter Museum, 1975.

Stevens, Hazard. *The Life of Isaac Ingalls Stevens.* 2 vols. Boston, Mass.: Houghton, Mifflin and Co., 1900.

Stevens, Isaac I. "Narrative and Final Report of Explorations for a Route for a Pacific Railroad, near the Forty-seventh and Forty-ninth Parallels of

North Latitude, from St. Paul to Puget Sound," In *Reports of Explorations and Surveys . . . for a Railroad from the Mississippi River to the Pacific Ocean . . . .* Vol. 12, Bks 1 and 2. Washington, D.C.: Thomas H. Ford, Printer, 1860.

———. "Report of Explorations for a Route for the Pacific Railroad, near the Forty-seventh and Forty-ninth Parallels of North Latitude, from St. Paul to Puget Sound." In *Reports of Explorations and Surveys . . . for a Railroad from the Mississippi River to the Pacific Ocean . . . in 1853-4 . . . .* Vol. 1. Washington, D.C.: Beverley Tucker, 1855.

[Stewart, Sir William Drummond]. *Altowan: or, Incidents of Life and Adventure in the Rocky Mountains by an American Traveler.* Edited by J. Watson Webb. 2 vols. New York: Harper & Bros., 1846.

Stokes, I. N. Phelps, and Daniel C. Haskell. *American Historical Prints: Early Views of American Cities, Etc. . . . .* New York: New York Public Library, 1932.

Stone, Wilbur Fisk, ed. *History of Colorado.* Vol. 1. Chicago: S. J. Clarke Publishing Co., 1918.

Stuart, Granville. *Granville Stuart: Diary & Sketchbook of a Journey to "America" in 1866, & Return Trip up the Missouri River to Fort Benton, Montana.* Reprint from *Virginia City Montana Post,* January, 1867. Introduction by Carl Shaefer Dentzel. Los Angeles: Dawson's Book Shop, 1963.

———. *Forty Years on the Frontier.* Edited by Paul C. Phillips. 2 vols. Cleveland, Ohio: Arthur H. Clark Co., 1925.

Sturhahn, Joan. *Carvalho, Artist—Photographer—Adventurer—Patriot: Portrait of a Forgotten American.* Merrick, N.Y.: Richwood Publishing Co., 1976.

Sweet, Frederick A. *The Hudson River School and the Early American Landscape Tradition.* Chicago: Art Institute of Chicago, 1945.

Tabor Grand Opera House. Denver, Colo.: Dove and Temple, 1883.

Taft, Robert. *Artists and Illustrators of the Old West, 1850-1900.* New York: Charles Scribner's Sons, 1953.

———. *Photography and the American Scene.* New York: Macmillan Co., 1938.

Tappan, Daniel L. *Tappan-Toppan Genealogy: Ancestors and Descendants of Abraham Toppan of Newbury, Massachusetts, 1602-1672.* Arlington, Mass.: Privately printed, 1915.

Taylor, Bayard. *Colorado: A Summer Trip.* New York: G. P. Putnam and Son, 1867.

———. *Life and Letters of Bayard Taylor.* Edited by Marie Hansen Taylor and Horace E. Scudder. Vol. 2. Boston: Houghton, Mifflin and Co., 1884.

Taylor, Joshua C. *America as Art.* Washington, D.C.: National Collection of Fine Arts, 1976.

———. *To See Is to Think: Looking at American Art.* Washington, D.C.: Smithsonian Institution Press, 1975.

Templeman, W. D. *The Life and Work of William Gilpin.* Urbana, Ill.: University of Illinois Press, 1939.

Thieme, Ulrich, and Felix Becker, eds. *Allgemeines Lexikon der Bildenden Künstler von der Antike bis zur Gegenwart.* Vols. 1-37. Leipzig: E. A. Seemann, 1940.

Thomas, Davis, and Karin Ronnefeldt, eds. *People of the First Man.* New York: E. P. Dutton & Co., 1976.

Thomas Moran in Yellowstone—1871. Fort Collins: Colorado State University, 1972.

Thwaites, Reuben Gold, ed. *Early Western Travels, 1748-1846: A Series of Annotated Reprints of Some of the Best and Rarest Contemporary Volumes of Travel, Descriptive of the Aborigines and Social and Economic Conditions in the Middle and Far West, During the Period of Early American Settlement . . . .* 32 vols. Cleveland, Ohio: A. H. Clark Co., 1904-1907.

———. *Original Journals of the Lewis and Clark Expedition, 1804-1806.* Vols. 1-7. Atlas. New York: Dodd, Mead & Co., 1904.

Tissandier, Albert. *Six Mois aux États Unis.* Paris: G. Masson, 1886.

Tooley, R. V. *Maps and Map-Makers.* 1949. 4th ed. New York: Bonanza Books, 1970.

Townsend, Francis G. *Ruskin and the Landscape Feeling: A Critical Analysis of His Thought During the Crucial Years of His Life, 1843-56.* Urbana, Ill.: University of Illinois Press, 1951.

[Trenton, Patricia.] *Colorado Collects Historic Western Art: The Nostalgia of the Vanishing West.* Denver, Colo.: Denver Art Museum, 1973.

———. *Harvey Otis Young: The Lost Genius, 1840-1901.* Denver, Colo.: Denver Art Museum, 1975.

———. *Picturesque Images from Taos and Santa Fe.* Denver, Colo.: Denver Art Museum, 1974.

[Truettner, William H., and Robin Bolton-Smith.] *National Parks and the American Landscape.* Washington, D.C.: National Collection of Fine Arts, 1972.

Tuckerman, Henry T. *Book of the Artists: American Artist Life, Comprising Biographical and Critical Sketches: Preceded by an Historical Account of the Rise and Progress of Art in America.* 1867. Reprint. New York: James F. Carr, 1967.

Tuttle, Charles Richard. *General History of the State of Michigan . . . .* Detroit, Mich.: R. D. S. Tyler & Co., 1873.

Tyler, Ron, ed. *Alfred Jacob Miller: Artist on the Oregon Trail.* Fort Worth: Amon Carter Museum, 1982.

Ubbeholde, Carl, Maxine Benson, and Duane A. Smith. *A Colorado History.* 1972. Rev. ed. Boulder, Colo.: Pruett Publishing, 1976.

U.S. Army, Corps of Engineers. *Report of the Exploring Expedition from Santa Fe, New Mexico, to the Junction of the Grand and Green Rivers of the Great Colorado of the West, in 1859, Under the Command of Capt. J. N. Macomb . . . with Geological Report by Prof. J. S. Newberry . . . .* Washington, D.C.: U.S. Government Printing Office, 1876.

U.S. Centennial Commission. *Official Catalogue of the U.S. International Exhibition, 1876.* Philadelphia, Pa.: John R. Nagle and Co., 1876.

U.S. Department of State. *Northwest Boundary Commission . . . .* 40th Cong., 3d sess., H. Exec. Doc. 86. Washington, D.C.: U.S. Government Printing Office, 1869.

U.S Geological and Geographical Survey of the Territories. *Profiles, Sections and Other Illustrations, . . . Sketched . . . by Henry W. Elliott.* New York: Julius Bien, 1872.

Vancouver, George. *A Voyage of Discovery to the North Pacific Ocean, and Round the World . . . .* Edited by John Vancouver. 3 vols. London: Printed for G. G. and J. Robinson [etc.], 1798.

Van Nostrand, Jeanne, and Edith Coulter. *California Pictorial: A History in Contemporary Pictures.* Berkeley: University of California Press, 1948.

Van Zandt, Roland. *The Catskill Mountain House.*

New Brunswick, N.J.: Rutgers University Press, 1966.

Vivian, Arthur Pendarves. *Wanderings in the Western Land.* London: Sampson Low, Marston, Searle, and Rivington, 1879.

Von Ruhmer, Eberhard et al. *Schack-Galerie: München Gemaldekatäloge.* Vol. 2. Munich: Bayerische Staatsgemäldesammlungen, 1969.

Wagner, Henry R. *The Plains and the Rockies: A Bibliography of Original Narratives of Travel and Adventure, 1800–1865.* Rev. ed. Edited by Charles L. Camp. Columbus, Ohio: Long's College Book Co., 1953.

Warner, Robert C. *The Fort Laramie of Alfred Jacob Miller.* Laramie: University of Wyoming, 1980.

Weir, John F. *A Memorial Catalogue of the Paintings of Sanford Robinson Gifford, N. A. . . . 1881.* Reprint. New York: Olana Gallery, 1974.

Wheeler, George M. *Report upon U.S. Geographic Surveys West of the One Hundredth Meridian.* Vol. 1. Washington, D.C., 1889.

White, John. *The Birth and Rebirth of Pictorial Space.* 1967. 2d ed. New York: Harper & Row, 1972.

Whitney, R. R. *The Young Draftsman's Companion, Consisting of Important Instructions in the First Rudiments of Drawing, the Nature and Method of Drawing in Perspective; Without Reference to the Rules: Together with Information in the Use of Water Colours, in Landscape and Flower Painting; to Which Are Added, the Requisite Lessons in the Beautiful and Expeditious Arts of Etching and Engraving in Aquatinta; the Whole with Upwards of Thirty Designs and Sketches of Different Parts of the Human Form, Landscapes, Trees, Flowers, &c.* New York: D. Mitchell, 1830.

Wied-Neuwied, Maximilian Alexander Phillip, Prinz von. *Travels in the Interior of North America.* Translated by H. Evans Lloyd from *Reise in das Innere Nord-America . . . .* 1 vol. and atlas. London: Ackermann & Co., 1843.

Wilbur, Marguerite, ed. *Vancouver in California, 1792–1794: The Original Account of George Vancouver.* 3 vols. Los Angeles: Dawson's Book Shop, 1953.

Wilkins, Thurman. *Clarence King.* New York: Macmillan Co., 1958.

———. *Thomas Moran: Artist of the Mountains.* 1966. 2d ed. Norman: University of Oklahoma Press, 1969.

William Henry Holmes: Artist, Geologist, Archeologist, and Art Gallery Director. Reprinted from the *Ohio Archaeological and Historical Quarterly,* for October, 1927. Columbus, Ohio: F. J. Heer Printing Co., 1929.

Williams, Iolo A. *Early English Watercolours.* 1952. Reprint. Bath: Kingsmead Reprints, 1970.

Willis, N. P. *American Scenery; or Land, Lake, and River, Illustrations of Transatlantic Nature, from Drawings by W. H. Bartlett . . . .* 2 vols. in 1. London: George Virtue, 1840.

Wilton, Andrew. *British Watercolors, 1750–1850.* London: E. P. Dutton-Phaidon Press, 1976.

Withington, Mary C. *A Catalogue of Western Manuscripts in the Collection of Western Americana Founded by William Robertson Coe, Yale University Library.* New Haven, Conn.: Yale University Press, 1952.

Wolle, Muriel Sibell. *Stampede to Timberline.* 1949. Rev. ed. Chicago: Sage Books, 1974.

Wood, Richard G. *Stephen Harriman Long, 1784–1864: Army Engineer Explorer Inventor.* Glendale, Calif.: Arthur H. Clark Co., 1966.

The Yellowstone National Park, and the Mountain Regions of Portions of Idaho, Nevada, Colorado and Utah, Described by Professor F. V. Hayden . . . Illustrated by Chromolithographic Reproductions of Water-color Sketches by Thomas Moran . . . . Boston: L. Prang & Co., 1876.

Yost, Karl and Frederic G. Renner, comps. *A Bibliography of the Published Works of Charles M. Russell.* Lincoln: University of Nebraska Press, 1971.

PERIODICALS

American Art Review 3 (May–June, 1976), cover illustration.

Arrington, Joseph Earl. "Skirving's Moving Panorama: Colonel Fremont's Western Expeditions —Pictorialized." *Oregon Historical Quarterly* 65 (June, 1964):133–72.

Baker, Marcus. "Survey of the Northwestern Boundary of the United States, 1857–1861," Bulletin of the United States Geological Survey, no. 174. Washington, D.C.: U.S. Government Printing Office, 1900.

Benjamin, S. G. W. "Pioneers of the Palette." *Magazine of Art* 5 (February, 1882):89–93.

Bierstadt, Albert. Letter, "Rocky Mountains, July 10, 1859." *Crayon,* September, 1859, p. 287.

Bigart, Robert, and Clarence Woodcock. "Peter Tofft: Painter in the Wilderness." *Montana: The Magazine of Western History* 25 (Autumn, 1975): 2–15.

Binyon, Lawrence. "The Drawings of John White, Governor of Raleigh's Virginia Colony." *Walpole Society* 13 (1925):2–24.

Blunt, Anthony. "The Heroic and the Ideal Landscape in the Work of Nicholas Poussin." *Journal of the Warburg and Courtald Institute* 13 (1950): 237–84.

Bredeson, Robert C. "Landscape Description in Nineteenth-Century American Travel Literature." *American Quarterly* 20 (Spring, 1968): 86–94.

Brockway, Jean Lambert. "Early Landscape Drawings by John Trumbull." *Magazine of Art* 26 (January, 1933):35–38.

Brownell, William C. "The Younger Painters of America." *Scribner's Monthly* 20 (May, 1880): 1–2; 20 (July, 1880):321–32.

Bushnell, David I. "Drawings of George Gibbs in the Far Northwest." In *Smithsonian Miscellaneous Collections,* Vol. 97. Washington, D.C.: Smithsonian Institution, 1938.

———. "John Mix Stanley, Artist-Explorer." In *Annual Report of the Smithsonian Institution for the Year Ending June 30, 1924.* Washington, D.C.: U.S. Government Printing Office, 1925.

Clarke, Dwight L. "Soldiers Under Stephen Watts Kearny." *California Historical Society Quarterly* 45 (June, 1966):133–48.

Cole, Thomas. "Essay on American Scenery." *American Monthly Magazine* 1 (January, 1836):1–12.

Cowdrey, Bartlett. "The Return of John F. Kensett, 1816–1872: Painter of Pure Landscape." *Old Print Shop Portfolio* 4 (February, 1945):122–36.

Dillon, Richard H. "Stephen Long's Great American Desert." *Proceedings of the American Philosophical Society* 3 (April, 1967):93–108.

Donaldson, Thomas. "The George Catlin Indian Gallery in the U.S. National Museum." In *The Annual Report of the Smithsonian Institution.* Pt.

5. Washington, D.C.: U.S. Government Printing Office, 1885.

Draper, Benjamin P. "American Indians—Barbizon Style—The Collaborative Paintings of Millet and Bodmer." *Antiques* 44 (September, 1943):108-10.

Drepperd, Carl W. "American Drawing Books: A Contribution Toward a Bibliography." *Bulletin of New York Public Library* 49 (November, 1945): 795-812.

Durand, Asher B. "Letters on Landscape Painting." *Crayon* 1 (January 17, 1855):34-35; 1 (February 14, 1855):97-98.

Edgerton, Giles. "Frederic Remington, Painter and Sculptor: A Pioneer in Distinctive American Art." *Craftsman* 15 (March, 1909):658-70.

Ellis, Havelock. "The Love of Wild Nature." *Contemporary Review* 63 (1898):538.

Everett, Edward. Review of Edwin James's (comp.) "Account of Long Expedition." *North American Review* 16 (1823):242.

Ewers, John C. "Gustavus Sohon's Portraits of Flathead and Pend d'Oreille Indians, 1854." *Smithsonian Miscellaneous Collections*, vol. 110. Washington, D.C.: Smithsonian Institution, 1948.

Fryxell, Fritiof. "The Mount of the Holy Cross." *Trail and Timberline*, no. 183 (January, 1934): 3-9.

———. "Thomas Moran's Journey to the Tetons in 1879." *Augustana Historical Society Publications*, no. 2 (1932):3-12.

Gardner, Albert Ten Eyck. "Scientific Sources of the Full-Length Landscapes: 1850." *Metropolitan Museum of Art Bulletin* 4 (Summer, 1945): 59-65.

Geske, Norman A. "Ralph Albert Blakelock in the West." *American Art Review* 3 (January-February, 1976):123-35.

Gibbs, George. "Physical Geography of the North-Western Boundary of the United States." *Journal of the American Geographical Society of New York* 4 (1874):298-392.

Goetzmann, William H. "The Grand Reconnaissance." *American Heritage* 23 (October, 1972): 44-59.

———. "Limner of Grandeur: William H. Holmes and the Grand Canyon." *American West* 15 (May-June, 1978):20-21, 61-63.

Goodrich, Lloyd. "Ralph Earl." *Magazine of Art* 39 (January, 1946):2-8.

Hayden, F. V. "The Wonders of the West-II." *Scribner's Monthly* 3 (February, 1872):388-96.

Hendricks, Gordon. "The First Three Western Journeys of Albert Bierstadt." *Art Bulletin* 46 (September, 1964):333-65.

Hess, Thomas B. "Art/Brooklyn Heights." *New York*, August 30, 1976, pp. 59-60.

Hunter, Wilbur H., Jr. "A 'New' Painting by Alfred Jacob Miller." *Antiques* 101 (January, 1972):221-25.

Jackson, William H. ". . . With Moran in the Yellowstone: A Story of Exploration, Photography and Art." *Appalachia* 21 (December, 1936):149-58.

Janson, Anthony F. "The Western Landscapes of Worthington Whittredge." *American Art Review* 3 (November-December, 1976):58-69.

Johnson, Charlotte Buel. "The European Tradition and Alvan Fisher." *Art in America* 41 (Spring, 1953):79-87.

Johnson, Ellen H. "Kensett-Revisited." *Art Quarterly* 20 (1957):71-92.

Jones, Howard M. "James Fenimore Cooper and the Hudson River School." *Magazine of Art* 45 (October, 1952):243-51.

Kellner, Sydney. "The Beginnings of Landscape Painting in America." *Art in America* 26 (October, 1938):158-68.

Kennedy Quarterly 5 (May, 1965):170-72, 188-89; 6 (June, 1966):79-81.

King, Clarence. "The Falls of the Shoshone." *Overland Monthly* 5 (October, 1870):379-85.

Lange, Jean Bodmer. "The Missing Bodmer Diary." *American Book Collector* 7 (November, 1956):24-26.

Langford, Nathaniel P. "The Wonders of the Yellowstone." *Scribner's Monthly* 2 (May-June, 1871):1-17, 113-28.

McDermott, John Francis. "Gold Rush Movies." *California Historical Society Quarterly* 33 (March, 1954):29-38.

———. "Samuel Seymour: Pioneer Artist of the Plains and the Rockies." In *Annual Report of the Smithsonian Institution, 1950*. Washington, D.C.: U.S. Government Printing Office, 1951.

Maxwell, Perriton. "Frederic Remington—Most Typical of American Artists." *Pearson's Magazine* 18 (October, 1907):396-412.

Monroe, Robert D. "William Birch McMurtrie: A Painter Partially Restored." *Oregon Historical Quarterly* 60 (September, 1959):352-74.

Moran, Thomas. "A Journey to the Devil's Tower in Wyoming." *Century Magazine* 47 (January, 1894):450-55.

Mumey, Nolie. "John Williams Gunnison—Centenary of His Survey and Tragic Death (1853-1953)." *Colorado Magazine* 31 (January, 1954): 30-31.

Novak, Barbara. "American Landscape: The Nationalist Garden and the Holy Book." *Art in America* 60 (January-February, 1972):46-57.

———. "The Double-Edged Axe." *Art in America* 64 (January-February, 1976):44-50.

Parry, Lee. "Landscape Theater in America." *Art in America* 59 (November-December, 1971):52-61.

Phillips, Duncan. "Twachtman—An Appreciation." *International Studio* 66 (February, 1919):cvi-cvii.

Pipes, Nellie B. "John Mix Stanley, Indian Painter." *Oregon Historical Society Quarterly* 33 (September, 1932):250-58.

Randall, Richard H., Jr. "A Gallery for Alfred Jacob Miller." *Antiques* 106 (November, 1974):836-43.

Rees, Roland. "The Taste for Mountain Scenery." *History Today* 25 (May, 1975):306.

Richards, Heber G. "George M. Ottinger, Pioneer Artist of Utah: A Brief of His Personal Journal." *Western Humanities Review* 3 (July, 1949):209-18.

Roberts, Gary L. "Conditions of the Tribes—1865." *Montana: The Magazine of Western History* 24 (Winter, 1974):14-25.

Rollins, C. B., ed. "Letters of George Caleb Bingham to James S. Rollins." *Missouri Historical Review* 33 (1938-1939):215, 217.

Rutledge, Anna W. "Artists in the Life of Charleston: Through Colony and State from Restoration to Reconstruction." *Transactions of the American Philosophical Society, n.s. 39, pt. 2* (November, 1949):164.

———. "Cumulative Record of Exhibition Catalogues, the Pennsylvania Academy of the Fine Arts, 1807-1870, the Society of Artists, 1800-1814, the Artists' Fund Society, 1835-1945." *American Philosophical Society Memoirs* 38 (1955).

Schafer, Joseph. "Trailing a Trail Artist of 1849." *Wisconsin Magazine of History* 12 (September, 1928):97–108.

Sellers, Charles Coleman. "Charles Willson Peale with Patron and Populace." *Transactions of the American Philosophical Society,* n.s. 59, pt. 3 (May, 1969):1–146.

Shulsinger, Stephanie. "Mightier than the Sword." *Terra* 15 (Winter, 1977):22–24.

Smalley, Eugene V. "The Upper Missouri and the Great Falls." *Century Magazine* 35 (January, 1888):408–18.

Smith, Robert C. "The Brazilian Landscapes of Frans Post." *Art Quarterly* 1 (1938):246–62.

Snell, Joseph W. "Some Photographs by Albert Bierstadt Now in the Historical Society Collection." *Kansas Historical Quarterly* 24 (Spring, 1958):1–5.

Snyder, Martin P. "William Birch: His Philadelphia Views." *Pennsylvania Magazine of History and Biography* 73 (July, 1949):271–315.

Stanley, John M. "Portraits of North American Indians, with Sketches of Scenery, Etc." *Smithsonian Miscellaneous Collections,* vol. 2. Washington, D.C.: Smithsonian Institution, 1862.

Stehle, Raymond L. "The Düsseldorf Gallery of New York." *New York-Historical Society Quarterly* 58 (October, 1974):305–10.

———. "Five Sketchbooks of Emanuel Leutze." *Quarterly Journal of the Library of Congress* 21 (April, 1964):81–93.

Stevens, John Austin, Jr. "A Memorial of George Gibbs." In *Annual Report of the Smithsonian Institution, 1873.* Washington, D.C.: U.S. Government Printing Office, 1874.

Strong, Donald. "Albert Bierstadt, Painter of the American West." *American Art Review* 2 (November–December, 1975):132–44.

Swanton, John R. "Biographical Memoir of William Henry Holmes, 1846–1933." *National Academy of Sciences Biographical Memoirs* 17 (1936):223–52.

Teetor, Henry Dudley. "Mountain of the Holy Cross." *Great Divide,* February, 1890, p. 193.

Thomas, Alfred Barnaby. "Spanish Expeditions into Colorado." *Colorado Magazine* 1 (November, 1924):289–300.

Townley, D. O. C. "Living American Artists." *Scribner's Monthly* 3 (March, 1872):605–608.

Truettner, William H. "'Scenes of Majesty and Enduring Interest': Thomas Moran Goes West." *Art Bulletin* 58 (June, 1976):241–59.

Vail, R. W. G. "The First Artist of the Oregon Trail." *New-York Historical Society Quarterly* 34 (January, 1950):25–30.

Walters, Everett, and George B. Strother, eds. "The Gold Rush Diary of Henry Tappan." *Annals of Wyoming* 25 (July, 1953):113–39.

Wildman, Edwin. "Frederic Remington, the Man." *Outing* 41 (March, 1903):712–16.

Williams, Talcott. "The Philadelphia Watercolor Exhibition." *International Studio* 22 (June, 1904):ccxxx.

Woolley, Mary E. "The Development of the Love of Romantic Scenery in America." *American Historical Review* 3 (October, 1897):56–66.

INDEX

Note: Plate page numbers are italicized.

Abert, James W.: life and career of, 44–45, 350n.24; with Frémont's 1845 expedition, 44, 46, 48, 49; trip of, to New Mexico (1846-47), 45–47, 79, 351nn.33–35
—Works of: *Acoma, N.M.*, 45, 46, 351n.26; *Bent's Fort*, 46, 351n.34; *A Cañoned Creek*, 351n.36; *Las Cumbres Españoles*, 46, 351n.37; *Scene near Camp N° 10 Aug. 23rd* [*Fisher's Peak*], 351n.36; *Valley of the Purgatory*, 351n.36; *"Wah-to-yah"* [*Spanish Peaks, Colo.*], 46, *47*
Abert, Col. John J.: 39, 44
Academy of Natural Sciences, Philadelphia: 22, 51, 352n.74
Achenbach, Andreas: influence of, on American artists, 13, 118–20, 179, 258, 262, 345n.49, 361n.29, 365n.-112; *Erftmühle* by, 361n.28; *Forest Deep in Snow* by, 371n.10
Achey, Mary E.: 308, 389n.38; *Nevadaville/Colorado/1860* by, *389n.38*
Acoma, N.Mex., representation of: 45, 46
Adams, Cassily: 244; *Crossing Medicine Bow Creek* by, 244, 381n.119; *Custer's Last Stand* by, 244
Adams, Charles Partridge: 309, 315; life and career of, 311–12, 390nn.63–67; "Go West, Young Man" (MS) by, 390n.63
—Works of: *In the Rocky Mountains*, 312, *313*; *The Last of the Leaves*, 312, 390n.66; *Sunset, Colorado*, 312, *323*
Aesthetics, nineteenth-century doctrines of: 3, 8, 10, 342-43n.5, 344n.42
Agassiz, Louis: 97
Agate, Arthur: 48
Alden, James, Jr.: 113, 359n.72
Alden, James Madison: with Northwest Boundary Survey (1857-60), 112-13, 357n.5, 360nn.78, 79, 82; life and career of, 115, 359n.73, 360n.87
—Works of: *Kintla Mountains from the Summit of Kishnehnehna*, 113, *133*, 360n.79; *A Rocky Mountain Reconnoissance*, *59*
Aldine: 245; Moran's Yellowstone illustrations for, 181
Alison, Archibald: 3, 4; *Essays on the Nature and Principles of Taste* by, 342-43n.5
American Falls, Snake River, Idaho: description of, 40, 270; representations of, *43*, 270, *285*, 350n.10

American Fur Company: 31, 33, 390n.44
American Philosophical Society: 22
Andrews, Joseph (engraver): 97
Appleton & Co., D.: *Picturesque America* of, 197, 264, 384n.199; western guidebooks of, 255
Archuleta, Juan de: 346n.24
Arkansas River: 48; Royal Gorge of, 28, 50, *63;* descriptions and representations of, 30, 149–50, 161, 347n.44, 367n.149
Art academies and schools: 8; Académie Julien, Paris, 311, 337; American Lyceum, 5, 342n.5; Brigham Young Academy, art class of, *299;* Chicago Academy of Design, 248, 271, 367n.149, 386n.230; Cooper Union, New York, 337; Düsseldorf Academy, 118, 255, 258, 262, 361n.34, 373n.7, 375n.27, 382n.169; École des Beaux-Arts, Paris, 32, 255, 349n.84, 381-n.123; English Life School, Rome, 32; National Academy of Design, New York, 144, 213, 221, 225, 332, 377nn.60, 65, 67, 378n.75, 379nn.82, 96, 384-nn.206, 207, 390n.66; Pennsylvania Academy of the Fine Arts, 23, 49, 179, 337, 351n.47, 371n.6; Royal Academy, London, 145, 200, 314; Royal Academy, Munich, 248, 381n.139, 384n.200; School of Fine Arts, Yale, 332; *see also* Academy of Natural Sciences, Philadelphia
Art colonies, western regional: xviii, 297–315; *see also* Denver, Colo.: art colony of; New Mexico: art colonies of; Salt Lake City, Utah: art colony of
Art exhibitions: Centennial Exhibition, Philadelphia, 174, 200; Industrial Exposition, Chicago, 150; International Exposition, Berlin (1890), 292; International Exposition, Munich (1869), 366n.125; International Exposition, Paris (1867), 144, 365n.124; International Exposition, Vienna (1873), 150; Mechanics Institute Fair, 262–63; National Gallery, London, 180; Paris Salon, 245, 311; Sanitary Fair, Chicago, 128; Sanitary Fair, New York (1864), 128, 345n.51; World's Columbian Exposition, Chicago (1893), 197, 250, 337, 372nn.34, 38
Art-instruction books: 8, 117, 344n.31
Art organizations: American Art-Union, 298, 388n.9; American Society of Painters in Water Color, 238, 379n.96; American Water Color Society, 250, 369-

n.5; Art Students League, New York, 332, 337; Art Union, San Francisco, 153; Columbian Society of Artists, 346n.33; Society for the Advancement of Truth in Art, 157; Society of American Painters, 337; Society of Artists of the United States, 346n.33; Society of Painters in Pastel, 337; *see also* Denver, Colo.: art clubs and expositions of; Salt Lake City, Utah: art organizations of
Audubon, John James: 46

Bagley, James M. (engraver): 312, 390n.65
Baker, Marcus: 113
Bancroft, William: 312, 390n.68
Barbizon School, influence of, on American artists: xvii, 10, 13, 153, 214, 262, 266, 311, 345n.55, 369n.9, 379n.94
Barret, George: 8
Barrias, Felix: 245, 381n.123
Bartram, John: 4
Bastien-Lepage, Jules: 337
Baudelaire, Charles: 281, 387n.273
Beale, Edward F.: 89–90, 356n.89
Beard, James: 381n.139
Beard, William Holbrook: 381n.139; 1866 western trip of, 149–50, 210, 367n.151, 374nn.18-22; life and career of, 374n.17
—Works of: *Deer on the Prairie*, 374n.21; *Grizzly in Western Landscape*, 374n.21; *On the Prairie*, 374n.21
Bear River, Utah: 98; representations of, 157, *163*, 235
Beaver Head Canyon, Mont.: representation of, 181, *183*
Beck, George: 6, 344n.25
Beckwith, Lieut. Edwin Griffin: 73, 75, 94, 353n.18, 354nn.26-30, 36
Beechey, Frederick William: 17
Bell, William A.: 200, 203
Bellin, Jacques Nicolas, map of North America by, in Charlevoix's *Histoire et description de la Nouvelle France:* 341n.2
Benton, Sen. Thomas Hart: 52, 88–89, 92, 356n.89
Bent's Fort, Colo.: 44, 45, 48, 74, 352n.56; representations of, *19*, 46, 49, 52
Bergen Park, Colo., representations of: *216*, 219, *220*,